SCAPEGOAT

The Lonesome Death of
Bruno Richard Hauptmann

SCAPEGOAT

The Lonesome Death of Bruno Richard Hauptmann

Anthony Scaduto

G. P. Putnam's Sons
New York

SBN: 399-11660-5

Library of Congress Cataloging in Publication Data:

Scaduto, Anthony.
  Scapegoat: the lonesome death of Bruno Richard Hauptmann.

  Includes index.
  1. Hauptmann, Bruno Richard, 1899–1936.
2. Kidnapping—New Jersey.   3. Lindbergh, Charles Augustus, 1930–1932. I. Title.
HV6603.L553   364.1'54'0924 [B]   76-15205

For Anna Hauptmann, who never doubted;

And for the memory of Richard Hauptmann

Preface

The letter arrived one day in April 1973. It was brief and went directly to the point:

"I have the true 'Lindbergh Story.' This will be a story the world has never heard. I was there. I worked on the case. I can prove Bruno Richard Hauptmann was innocent. Perhaps you can help me write my book. Please contact me by calling Assistant U.S. Attorney. . . ."

I recognized the signature at the bottom of the letter, as the writer knew I would. During the decade or so that I had been the so-called Mafia expert for the *New York Post*, investigating organized crime and writing feature articles about the men of the Mafia, this man's name was occasionally mentioned. He was not Mafia, but he'd been involved with New York *mafiosi* in a number of nonviolent criminal schemes and financial swindles, and he'd served several prison terms. I had never met him. I knew only that a year or so earlier he'd been caught in a fraudulent stock scheme and when he realized he'd been shortchanged by his associates, he became a witness against them, rather than go to prison while the Mafia men remained free with most of the profits from their swindle.

I'll call him Murray Bleefeld. That's not the name he signed to the letter or the name he has been using for more than forty years. But it is his actual name.

I tried to reach him right away. It was difficult because he was surrounded by layers of protection, to keep him from being harmed for cooperating with federal prosecutors who were establishing a case against some rather nasty men. I left my name and telephone number with several federal agents and with an attorney who I was told represented Murray. When I didn't hear anything for more than a week, I began to fear that Murray had contacted another writer and was already telling him his story. I didn't want that to happen because to me there seemed something inevitable about his letter, as if all my years as a crime writer and investigative reporter had been simply preparation for this moment. For I had never fully believed the accepted version of Hauptmann's guilt.

The known facts of the Lindbergh case are relatively simple and straightforward. On the night of March 1, 1932, the son of Charles A. Lindbergh, the most famous man in the world, was kidnaped from the nursery of the Lindbergh home in New Jersey. A $50,000 ransom was paid one month later, but the child was not returned. His body was found partially buried in a stand of woods a few miles from his home a little more than two months after he'd been kidnaped. For more than two years police investigated thousands of leads, without success. Then in September 1934 they arrested a thirty-five-year-old German carpenter, Bruno Richard Hauptmann, after a ransom bill he had passed was traced to him. In the garage behind Hauptmann's home in the Bronx, investigators found nearly $15,000 in Lindbergh ransom money secreted under his workbench. Hauptmann claimed he had been given the money by a friend, who had since died, but his story was believed by no one. He was placed on trial for murder. The state proved that he had built the ladder used to climb into the child's nursery and that he had written the ransom letters; a number of eyewitnesses identified Hauptmann as the man who had negotiated the payment of the ransom and had received the money. Hauptmann was convicted and on April 3, 1936, was electrocuted.

But I had remembered my doubts about this case against Hauptmann. They had begun in my childhood. I remember when I was about eight—which would have been eight years after the kidnaping—how sternly my parents warned me against accepting candy or automobile rides from strangers and how dramatically they punctuated those warnings with a lecture about the kidnaping of the "Lindbergh baby," as that child will always be called by those who were alive when he was abducted in 1932. I also remember my father discussing the verdict in the Lindbergh case with his brothers and their friends, all of them doubting Hauptmann's guilt almost as vehemently as they denied the guilt of two other immigrants, Sacco and Vanzetti. There, back in my childhood, was germinated my attitude toward the conviction of Hauptmann. Later, my experiences as a police reporter and then a feature writer further shaped my temperament and inclination, for I learned through direct involvement in several cases that innocent men are sometimes convicted.

The letter from Murray Bleefeld stirred doubts about Hauptmann's guilt that had long been dormant. It started me on a three-year investigation of the Lindbergh case, a search for the reality behind the surface case against Hauptmann. Eventually the search went far beyond Murray's personal and highly colored story of his own involvement in the case. In exploring this most famous of American crimes, I found that the truth would depend on the answers to these crucial questions:

Did Hauptmann kidnap the Lindbergh child?

Was Hauptmann convicted on evidence contrived by police, and by lies and distortions on the part of every witness against him, including Charles Lindbergh himself?

Did police and prosecutors know that Hauptmann did not kidnap the child, and that his explanation as to how he came into possession of some of the ransom money had the ring of truth? Did they know that the evidence against him was contrived and perjured? Did they suppress the evidence of their own investigations, which showed that Hauptmann was innocent?

Did police and federal investigators know who the actual kidnapers were, and then halt their investigation when Hauptmann came under suspicion?

My three-year search for the answers to these questions has convinced me that the trial and execution of Bruno Richard Hauptmann may be the most terrifying example in American history of the defects in our system of criminal justice and of the arrogance of police power.

Ridgefield, Connecticut
March 1976

If justice cannot be made to operate under the worst possible conditions of social hysteria, what does it matter how it operates at other times?

—E. L. Doctorow, *The Book of Daniel*

SCAPEGOAT

The Lonesome Death of
Bruno Richard Hauptmann

1

About ten days after I began trying to reach him, Murray Bleefeld finally called me. We talked briefly about his background—"I'm really straight now," he said, "I have to be to survive"—and then I asked him about his role in the Lindbergh kidnaping.

"It's really too complicated to go into over the phone," he said. "But basically, I was hired by Ellis Parker, the chief of detectives of Burlington County, New Jersey. Ever hear of him?"

"Of course. I've read old newspaper and magazines articles about him," I said. "They used to call him the Old Fox because he solved cases other detectives couldn't."

"That's the guy. Ellis Parker. He hired me to help catch the real kidnaper of the Lindbergh baby. I worked with Parker and with his good friend Harold Hoffman—you know, the governor—we were all trying to catch the real killer."

"Did you catch him?"

"We sure did. His name's Paul H. Wendel. A disbarred lawyer, very brilliant, but a psychopath. Paul H. Wendel. Remember that name. Paul Wendel was a man who believed everybody in the world had done him wrong and he was going to show the world he was smarter than everybody else by kidnaping the baby of the world's hero, the Lindbergh baby. Paul H. Wendel killed that baby, not Hauptmann. Hauptmann had nothing to do with it, he

15

was just a dumb carpenter who became the fall guy. I met Haupt-mann and I . . ."

"You what?" I asked.

"I met Hauptmann. He was in his cell in the Trenton Prison death house and I was taken there by Ellis Parker and Governor Hoffman. They went there to question him."

"Why?"

"Because Hoffman was trying to figure out how to save the poor guy's life and he wanted to question the man personally to be sure he could believe in his innocence. But I'll tell you all about that when we meet, it's too long to go into over the phone right now."

"Okay, but tell me why you're so certain Wendel did it. "

"Because he *confessed, "* Murray said, placing a dramatic stress on the word. "I got a confession from Wendel, me and my brother-in-law and Parker's son, Ellis, Jr. Parker always called him that, Ellis, Jr. Wendel confessed that he did it and my hair stood on end because he was telling us things about the kidnaping and how he got rid of the ransom money, things only the kidnaper could know."

"But Hauptmann was executed," I said. "Why did . . ."

"Because of David Wilentz, the prosecutor. He got to Wendel and before anybody knew what was happening Wendel twisted around everything in his confession—I tell you the man had a bril-liant mind—and he made it look like we beat the confession out of him. It was politics. David Wilentz wasn't going to permit the gov-ernor and Ellis Parker to cast doubt on his solution of the crime of the century—that's what they called it and that's what it was, the most incredible crime in history. David Wilentz was the man send-ing Hauptmann to the chair and he wasn't going to admit he made a mistake because he had a big political future to worry about. So Hauptmann did go to the chair and I went to prison for trying to get the truth—me and Parker and his son, everybody connected with the Wendel case. We all went to prison and the real killer became a hero, wrote a book and magazine articles and all that. Ellis Parker died in prison, he died of a broken heart—forty years a detective and he was sent to prison to die because of politics."

The conversation went along like that for half an hour, Murray leaping about in his reminiscences of that most famous of crimes, throwing out morsels about all the major players and about Paul Wendel, a name that was only vaguely familiar to me. I finally sug-

16

gested that we meet in a few weeks to conduct a more formal interview, on tape. In the meantime, I told Murray, I would read through some of the material in the Lindbergh case to refresh my memory.

From past readings about the Lindbergh case, I remembered some of the things that Murray had just told me. And although I had always believed there was something wrong about the conviction of Hauptmann, my impression had been that Ellis Parker, famous in the 1920s and 1930s as a country detective who was frequently called in to help the big-city sleuths when they had a particularly tough case to solve, had grown a little soft in the head with age and had manufactured evidence against someone in a futile attempt to save Hauptmann and to gain some glory for himself. In fact I recalled reading somewhere that Parker had a strong ambition to become director of the FBI, and that his good friend Governor Harold Hoffman was being boomed as the Republican choice to run against Franklin D. Roosevelt in the 1936 presidential election.

Sitting at my desk, making notes of my conversation with Murray, I was very skeptical of his claim of having been involved in the Lindbergh case. After all, Murray had been a swindler. Perhaps he was trying to use me as a lever to pry loose a large advance from a publisher for an exciting piece of fiction disguised as fact—as Clifford Irving had done in the Howard Hughes fiasco. Why, I wondered, had Murray waited forty years to tell his story? Was it because he'd been forced to retire from his illegal pursuits and now wanted to make a killing on a book? Most of all, could I really believe he had met Hauptmann, had worked for Ellis Parker and Governor Hoffman, and had played a role in a futile attempt to save Hauptmann's life?

I called Lenny Katz at the *New York Post*. We had been copyboys together in the early 1950s, had been promoted to reporter around the same time, had worked together on several major stories, and were close friends. I asked Lenny to pull from the *Post* library the clippings on Murray Bleefeld, reportedly connected to the Lindbergh case just before Hauptmann was executed—that would be in 1936—and sent to prison in an offshoot of the case.

Lenny called back in a little while. "This guy Bleefeld did exist," he said. "I'll read some of it to you. Murray Bleefeld, convicted in Newark Federal Court on kidnaping charges, in 1937, a

17

few months after being convicted on the same charge in Brooklyn along with a couple of other guys, Ellis Parker and his son and some others. They kidnaped a man named Paul H. Wendel, one *l* in Wendel, in midtown Manhattan on February 14, 1936, and forced him to confess that he kidnaped the Lindbergh baby. Wendel testified his confession was a lie. He said he confessed because he was tortured. Bleefeld and everybody else got prison terms.''

There could be no doubt that a Murray Bleefeld was involved with Ellis Parker and that the man who had confessed was Paul Wendel. Another quick phone call to a federal agent confirmed that the man I'd talked to, who had long been known on police records under another name, was actually Murray Bleefeld. "I have it on his pedigree," the agent said. "He served time in Lewisburg Federal Penitentiary for—get this—violation of the Lindbergh Law. Funny thing, our files show he was trying to solve the Lindbergh case in some way and instead he went to the pen for kidnaping.''

I now had verification that Murray Bleefeld was not lying about the role he'd played in the Lindbergh case. But could even these verifications make me believe him? I wanted to believe him very much. Ever since becoming a police reporter in 1954 I've been fascinated by the criminal law, crimes and criminals, and especially the cases of injustice that have been documented by numerous authorities—including a few cases I've personally witnessed.

I'd been a police reporter for the *Post* between 1954 and 1959, when I became a feature writer. Back then when a copyboy—as I had been for a couple of years—was sent "out on the street" to learn his craft as a reporter, the street was usually Brooklyn Police Headquarters, or rather a string of storefronts on Sixth Avenue across the street from the central police station. They were drafty abandoned stores, with antique linoleum on the floor and embossed sheet-metal ceilings, in which every newspaper in the city had leased space barely large enough for a desk, a filing cabinet, a telephone, and an ancient typewriter salvaged, I was sure, from the era when Teddy Roosevelt was police commissioner and Jacob Riis was peering into the slums of the city.

At first I threw myself completely into my assignment, speeding to the scenes of murders, rapes, robberies, teen-gang battles, and all the other obscenities and absurdities members of our society inflict upon each other, usually without much grace. The mystique

18

that surrounded policemen and their camp followers, the police re-porters, fascinated me. We, all of us, detectives and reporters, were working together to bring malefactors to book. Or so I at first believed. In those first months I didn't understand what police work actually entailed. I was simply a reporter reporting, and what I saw in the beginning was the glamour, the excitement, and the righteousness of the crime-catchers, in contrast to the sordidness of the criminals. I was too busy collecting facts, learning to speak the language of policemen, and learning who to call for special in-formation or news, to be able to see through what I was experienc-ing. But somewhere around my sixth month as a police reporter I suddenly had forced upon me a realization that the American sys-tem of justice which my high school and college textbooks so proudly hailed was, in the reality of the back rooms of police sta-tions and the Criminal Courts Building, quite another matter.

My first and therefore most traumatic awakening came several hours after the murders of two young black men, members of a teen-age gang in the black ghetto of Bedford Stuyvesant. They were stabbed to death in a school playground one morning, appar-ently by members of a rival gang. When I learned that a large group of suspects were being questioned by detectives and some were confessing, I drove to the Atlantic Avenue police station. I ran up to the second floor of the building and into the detective squad room, a facsimile of all the other detectives' quarters in New York: walls painted a pale green from the ceiling to a point roughly equal to the average man's shoulders and the lower part of the wall paint-ed darker green in a futile effort to disguise the smudges, coffee stains, and other refuse that accumulate in the standard ten years between paintings. In one corner stood a heavy wrought-iron cage, which held prisoners while detectives typed out their reports.

The squad room was filled when I arrived: twelve or fifteen black kids were in the cage, crowded into a space built to contain six at most; several of the kids were sitting on the floor, their backs to the wall, holding their heads and crying. Four detectives sat typing, each of them asking questions of a suspect and then pecking out a few more sentences. I stood outside the oak railing for several mo-ments, until the detective lieutenant in command came out of his office, giving me a glimpse through his door of several other detec-tives and black kids inside.

"You'll have to wait in the hall," he said. "We're getting some confessions and we'll have the whole story for you in twenty minutes."

I went out to the corridor and sat on a balcony railing overlooking the main floor. As I waited, I learned firsthand how an investigation sometimes is conducted. Every few moments a detective led a handcuffed young black man from the squad room directly in front of me and shoved him into a locker room a few feet down the corridor. The door closed, and the unmistakable sounds of a boy's head being smashed against the steel lockers and his screams filled the building.

At least five boys were questioned in this fashion while I was there. In less than an hour the senior detective officer stepped into the corridor and grandly announced that the investigation had resulted in seven confessions—seven young men charged with "juvenile delinquency, homicide." When I called the *Post* city desk to turn in the story to a rewrite man for the late editions I first described for my editor what I had witnessed. His response: "Forget it. The cops hate the *Post* enough as it is, so let's not stir things up. Just turn in the police version and forget the rest of it."

It wasn't only black men who were denied the full meaning of justice by the police and, in many cases in which I became involved as a reporter, by prosecutors and judges. For me, the most emotionally unsettling case involved an attempt by detectives and the district attorney's office in Staten Island to charge an eight-year-old boy with the murder of his parents.

The boy was Melvin Dean Nimer, Jr., called Deany by everyone who knew him. At a few minutes after 2 A.M. on September 2, 1958, a telephone operator answered a call and heard a woman gasp, "I've been stabbed." The operator got her address and within minutes two patrolmen arrived at the rented home of Dr. Melvin Nimer and his wife, Lou Jean, in the Clifton section of Staten Island. They were greeted at the front door by Deany, in pajamas.

On the kitchen floor lay his father, thirty-one, a physician at the U.S. Public Health Service hospital two blocks down the street. He was covered with blood from several deep stab wounds. Upstairs in the master bedroom the police found Mrs. Nimer, also thirty-one, slumped on the floor beside the bed she had sat on while phoning for help. She, too, was bleeding heavily from stab wounds.

20

Both were conscious and responded to questions while awaiting an ambulance. Deany's father died of his wounds only moments after arriving at the hospital. His mother died on the operating table a few hours later.

By the time I arrived, shortly before dawn, Deany was being questioned by police and prosecutors in the office of District Attorney John Braisted. The boy said he had been asleep in his bedroom, across the hall from his parents' room, when he was awakened by something that shook his bed. He saw a man standing before him, his head covered with a white mask that had slits cut into it for the eyes. Deany screamed. The man seized him by the throat and began to choke him. Mrs. Nimer was awakened by the screams and rushed into her son's room.

Deany told police: "Mommy came and the man hit her with something and she started bleeding. Then Daddy ran in and they started fighting and Daddy started bleeding." He said the intruder broke loose and ran down the stairs, with Dr. Nimer following him. Mrs. Nimer stumbled back to her bedroom and phoned for help, and later told Deany to go downstairs and let police in. Deany was questioned repeatedly and he told the same story, that a man who was "a little bigger than Daddy," and who wore a mask over his face, had stabbed his mother and father.

From the outset the police and the district attorney's office made it clear to reporters that they had some "reservations" about Deany's story. Privately, off the record, members of DA Braisted's staff told us that the evidence weighed heavily against the boy. "But don't print it," they cautioned us, "because we're not out to harm this child." Most damning of all, we were told, was that it seemed to be the classic puzzle of mystery writers, a "locked room" killing. Police had been unable to find any evidence that anyone had entered the Nimer home from outside, we were told. An open cellar window was ruled out because dust on the sill had not been disturbed. No window had been forced. When the first patrolmen arrived at the house the front door was partially open but the aluminum screen door was latched. Deany was questioned about the door but he could not remember whether he had latched it himself as a precaution against the return of the killer. "Thus we must assume it had never been unlatched and no intruder ever entered the house."

"Why make that assumption?" a few reporters asked.

"It's more than an assumption, it's in keeping with all the other evidence we have," we were told. But investigators would not tell us what the other evidence was, not even off the record.

Eight days after the Nimers were murdered, the *Journal-American* announced in banner headlines that Deany was the major suspect in the murder of his parents. We, who had been sitting on the story for almost a week and had refused to break the confidence by publishing it, were sickened. Most reporters were upset because they had been "scooped"—we still used that word back then—by a writer sitting in his office in Manhattan, getting his information over the telephone. Only a very small minority of us were deeply disturbed for another reason, one we had discussed from the outset: that the district attorney and his aides had presented us with a story (not for publication) that allowed for no other possibility but that eight-year-old Deany was a killer; and we were highly suspicious because such simplistic solutions happened only in movie scripts.

Our suspicions were further inflamed when, after much shouting, many demands and threats, District Attorney Braisted finally condescended to see us and answer questions about the *Journal*'s sensational disclosure. We all expected the prosecutor to deny the story or to refuse comment, because an eight-year-old cannot be charged with murder and to confirm the story would pillory the child. But Braisted surprised us all by conceding that the story was accurate. He even added, gratuitously, that Deany had been examined by psychologists several days before and was found to be suffering from "a paranoiac type of schizophrenia" and that his "illness and basic personality were compatible with the commission of the crime." I made a snap judgment while scribbling Braisted's comments into my notebook: the DA and the police, under enormous pressure from the public and the newspapers to solve the crime and solve it quickly, had chosen the simple way out and had accused this child. I knew that children have murdered their parents, children only a little older than Deany, but I could not accept it this time.

I still refused to accept it that evening, when reporters and photographers were summoned to the small Cape Cod house on Vanderbilt Avenue. I sat on the front lawn, picking at the tall blades of grass in a lawn neglected because the occupants of the house were dead, and watched as police led Deany up the steps and through the front door, with photographers snapping pictures of the detectives and their tiny prisoner. When everyone emerged about a half hour later, Deany was placed in a patrol car and driven off. And then we were formally told what we suspected had been taking place inside: Deany Nimer had "reenacted" the crime, he had "confessed" the murder of his parents and had actually picked out for police "the knife he used to kill them."

It was official now. Deany Nimer was a confessed killer. What little doubt may have existed was quickly disposed of the next day when DA Braisted, in a noisy press conference, was asked if there was any evidence to indicate that Deany could not have killed his parents. "The one important thing that would negate the confession," he replied, "is that it comes from the mouth of a child."

The press conference was noisy because some of us refused to accept Braisted's pronouncements. Was it possible that the psychologists who had said Deany was disturbed enough to have stabbed his parents may have suggested a confession to him? And perhaps played on a child's normal feelings of guilt over the death of his mother and father? Most certainly not, Braisted said; the psychologists were professionals and expert in the handling of children. If Deany had stabbed both of his parents, we demanded, then why did his pajamas have only two small spots of blood on them? Braisted: "I don't know if that's accurate, about his pajamas, but in any case I can't comment on the physical evidence." But, we insisted, this is not going to lead to a murder trial—and I remember shouting, "You're crucifying this boy and you're not being honest with us." Braisted grew terribly angry at that remark. And he was adamant: he would not comment on the physical evidence.

Yet during that conference he marshaled an impressive array of facts to convince us that Deany was guilty, including physical evidence. The most important of these facts was the autopsy report, which showed that both the Nimers had been stabbed in the soft, fleshy area of their chest, just under the rib cage. Even a four-foot-four, sixty-pound boy could have driven a knife deeply enough into that area of the body to cause death.

The case was solved, so far as police and prosecutor were concerned; all that remained was the formality of a court hearing to determine whether Deany should be sent to a psychiatric institution.

But I didn't feel it was solved. Neither did Vincent Sorge, a reporter for the *World Telegram*. We both had worked on the story from the first and we both felt strongly that the official version of the murders was, at the very least, incomplete. In the early morning hours of September 12, ten days after the Nimers were killed, Sorge and I met in front of the Staten Island police headquarters in St. George, a few blocks up the hill from the ferry. We went inside to see whether any detectives were available for a discussion of the case and were told that we had missed everyone; only an hour earlier every member of the prosecutor's staff and every detective who had worked on the case had gone home after an all-night meeting in the detective squad room upstairs. We went up anyway; "just in case there's somebody still around we can talk to," we told the desk officer.

Upstairs, the door to the detective district office was open and an elderly man was mopping the floor. "They've all gone home," he said. We told him we'd wait. He mopped from a far corner to the desk of the detective commander in the center of the room, pulled a wastepaper basket from under the desk, and placed it outside where we were standing. He then stepped back into the room and closed the door behind him. A glance passed between Sorge and me and we quickly searched through the basket, gently lifting out cups filled with remains of coffee so that we could get at a large number of papers underneath. When we had rifled everything that appeared to have writing on it, we ran down the back stairs and into our cars, Sorge leading me to his home at the other end of Staten Island.

Of the several documents we found, the most remarkable was a sheet of ruled yellow legal notepaper, written in a hand we recognized, that of Inspector Edward Byrnes, commander of detectives in Manhattan, who had been sent to the island to fill in for the regular commander during his vacation. Detectives had apparently been reviewing the evidence to bring Byrnes up to date and he had been making extensive notes. The document we had discovered was Byrnes' notes of the brief question-and-answer sequence between Mrs. Nimer and the detective who had interviewed her as she was being prepared for surgery. Braisted and other officials had always insisted that neither murder victim had said anything that would support Deany's story of a prowler who had stabbed his parents. Yet there on Vinnie Sorge's kitchen table we read in Mrs. Nimer's deathbed interview:

Q. Can you tell us anything?
A. A mask, a mask.
Q. Can you tell us anything else?
A. A hood, a hood.
Q. What kind?
A. White.
Q. Slits in the eyes?
A. Yes, covered full head.
Q. How tall?
A. Tall as my husband. Same build.
Q. Why did you get up?
A. Heard the boy scream.
Q. Where did you see the man? In the hallway?
A. Yes.

Mrs. Nimer, in this statement made a short time before she died, had confirmed much of what her son had told police. Yet Braisted and the police had withheld that statement as, it turned out, they had suppressed other information favorable to Deany.

We broke the story in our first editions the next day. Once more a mob of reporters descended on Staten Island and many more voices demanded that Braisted tell the full truth. He went into hiding, refusing to see reporters. One of his aides did concede that the statement we had stolen from police headquarters and published was absolutely accurate. Inspector Byrnes, a cop I knew well and respected enormously, was obviously disturbed by what Braisted had done to the boy and he revealed that Dr. Nimer had also told police as he lay dying that he had been stabbed by "a prowler with a mask"—the only words he spoke before he died.

Deany was released and taken out to Utah to live with his grandparents. Many months later two doctors at the hospital where Deany had been detained, feeling that the passage of time had relieved them of their promise to police not to discuss the case publicly, disclosed that when they had examined Deany shortly after the murders they were still able to see choke marks on his neck, conclusive evidence that someone had attempted to strangle him,

25

as he had told the police. "The marks are more than halfway back," the doctors read from their original report to detectives. "He could not have done it himself." But investigators chose to ignore the evidence.

Somewhere in the police department files, I am certain, is further evidence which would prove that the police knew, in the earliest days of their investigation, that Deany did not kill his parents. Such evidence is not needed to demonstrate that Deany was treated callously by police and by Braisted and his aides; it would simply show the full extent of that callousness. Were Deany old enough and were it not for a few reporters who did not trust police and prosecutor, he may very well have been executed for a crime he did not commit.

After talking to Murray I thought about these two cases, and especially the Nimer case, for a long time. I dwell on them at length because they are necessary to an understanding of my approach to the Lindbergh investigation. It had become clear to me, in my first couple of years as a police reporter, that police commonly forced confessions from suspects and then lied about it in court—and were always believed by judge and jury. That prosecutors, anxious to win headlines and guarantee their reelection, or even a chance to run for governor or the Senate, sometimes suppress evidence or knowingly accept manufactured evidence from police and send innocent men to prison. And that certain judges behave as prosecutors under their judicial robes and help persuade juries to convict on the flimsiest evidence. I have personally seen a number of examples of the perversion of justice by each actor in the legal process: police, prosecutor, and judge.

After the Nimer case, I must admit here, I developed a hostility toward the guardians of our peace and tranquility. I came to question the morality and integrity of many policemen and prosecutors with whom I came into contact, and developed a perpetual cynicism toward their pronouncements.

My experiences in the Nimer investigation also prompted me to study other cases in which there appeared to be some doubt as to the correctness of the verdict of the jury and of history. Including the Lindbergh case. As I read whatever I could find in print, and thought about that most famous of American crimes, I began to feel a strong conviction that Bruno Hauptmann should not have been executed. I could not be certain whether he was completely innocent of the kidnaping and death of Lindbergh's child, whether he had played a secondary role as part of a group that extorted the $50,000 ransom from Lindbergh, or whether he had actually killed the child. I knew, I felt it with growing certainty as I studied the case in the late 1950s, that Hauptmann could not have committed the crime alone and that there was something very strange about the passionate and obscene haste by New Jersey officials to kill Hauptmann legally, in the electric chair, and to close the case in spite of so many unanswered questions.

I lacked documentary evidence, of course; I had no evidence that would even tend to show that Hauptmann did not commit the crime for which he was executed. I had only my intuition, linked to my personal experiences. And there the matter rested over the years, no more than an academic interest, a nagging doubt about a case that would never, I felt, give up the truth. But when, in the spring of 1973, I received that letter from Murray Bleefeld, I knew I was being drawn into a search for Bruno Richard Hauptmann, who was either a killer or a victim.

My immediate problem wasn't whether I believed Murray. I decided to worry about that later, when I met him, sized him up, got him to answer questions into my tape recorder. The first thing I had to do was go back over the Lindbergh case, from the beginning. Although I had voraciously read, fifteen years earlier, everything I had been able to find about the kidnap-murder of Charles A. Lindbergh, Jr., and considered myself quite familiar with the crime and the trial of Hauptmann, I wanted to be certain I had an accurate account before I talked to Murray. I pulled down from my shelves a half-dozen books about the kidnaping, some written immediately after Hauptmann was convicted, and I also pulled from my files a fourteen-page FBI synopsis dated April 19, 1935, two months after Hauptmann was convicted, titled: "Bruno Richard Hauptmann, with alias—Kidnaping and Murder." And because all the written materials I spread out on the large old oak table I use as a desk were cops-and-robbers accounts of the brilliant manner in which police had captured Hauptmann and the prosecutor, David Wilentz, had convicted him, I turned to the only writer I knew of who had publicly expressed doubts about the verdict. He was Alan Hynd, whose articles were somewhat breathless, in the style required by *True* magazine, for which he did most of his writing, but whose cases appeared to be solidly researched. One of Hynd's arti-

27

cles was about the Lindbergh case. "Everybody Wanted to Get Into the Act," it was called, a recitation of how and why investigators from three state and federal agencies totally bungled the case, at first destroying evidence and then falling over one another to convince us all that Hauptmann was guilty. I settled down with all this material and wrote a synopsis of the case, a reference tool from which I could branch out into the hundreds of dark, complex ramifications that might develop should I decide to investigate this forty-year-old crime. I didn't want to admit it to myself then, but I damn well intended to dig into the Hauptmann case.

2

Tuesday, March first, 1932, was a scowling, bleak day on New Jersey's Sourland Mountain. A heavy rain had fallen all day, but soon after seven o'clock it lifted and the clouds sped off as if ashamed, leaving a pure, rain-washed sky. Almost as soon as the rain stopped, great winds leaped out of the east, tearing at the shrunken surface of the hills and rushing into the valley. In its flight the wind wrenched at the shutters and roof of a big twin-gabled house of whitewashed fieldstone that sat high on the mountain's south slope, in the center of an estate of five hundred acres that Colonel Charles A. Lindbergh had chosen as a retreat from his public.

Construction work on the house and on Lindbergh's private airfield had not been quite completed and the Lindberghs were using the "farm," as they called it, only on weekends. But their only child, young Charles, was just recovering from a heavy cold and they decided not to return to the Englewood estate of Anne Lindbergh's mother, Mrs. Dwight Morrow, as they usually did on Monday afternoon.

At about seven-thirty the boy was tucked into his maple crib by his mother and his nurse, Betty Gow. He was dressed in a flannel shirt that Betty had just made for him, with another woolen shirt over it, diapers, rubber pants, and a sleeping suit. A shiny metal cylinder had been slipped over each thumb and tied to the cuff of his sleeping suit, thumbguards to discourage sucking. His blankets and sheets were fastened to the mattress by three-inch safety pins. After getting the boy settled and secured, the two women made a round of the windows in the second-floor nursery. They closed the outside shutters of two windows but left one of them open slightly, for air. But the shutter on the southwest window had warped and could not be locked; Anne Lindbergh said she must remember to have that shutter repaired. The women left the room. About twenty minutes later Betty Gow slipped back into the nursery and found young Charles sleeping soundly.

At 10 P.M. Betty again returned to the boy's room, as she always did at that hour to take him on his final trip to the bathroom. She turned on an electric heater to drive the chill from the room, then went over to the crib to lift out the child. He was not in his crib. Betty walked down the hall into Anne Lindbergh's room; the child was not with his mother. The nurse then ran downstairs, to the library directly below the nursery, where Colonel Lindbergh was reading. He did not have his son.

Alarmed, Lindbergh raced up the stairs and snapped on the nursery light. At that moment his wife entered through a passage which led into her room. "Do you have the baby?" she asked.

Lindbergh didn't answer. He stared at the empty crib for a long moment. The bedclothes seemed untouched, still forming the outline of his son's body. The two large safety pins were still in place; it was obvious the boy hadn't crawled out of the crib by himself. Lindbergh turned to his wife.

"Anne," he said, "they have stolen our baby."

Those six words summed up five unbelievable years in Charles Lindbergh's life. To him, "they" were the faceless people who had plucked buttons off his clothes for souvenirs, had pushed into his hotel bedroom to advance crackpot schemes, had demanded he endorse breakfast cereals or become a candidate for the U.S. Senate. "They" were a vast amorphous body who had created a tragedy by making him their hero.

In 1927, Lindbergh had been an obscure airmail pilot who made the first solo, nonstop airplane flight from New York to Paris, in quest of a $25,000 prize. He won not only the money but a burst of adulation that no other American had ever received—and he was harmed not at all by the fact that he was young, only twenty-five, slim and photogenic, apparently modest and unaffected by the first wild burst of fame.

But the frenzy of the acclaim soon revolted him. He seemed to be fighting to remain himself, to limit the publicity, to avoid personal contacts with the press and the public. But the harder he fought the closer it enveloped him. Paradoxically, while he loathed the demands of the newspapers and the newsreel cameras for more interviews and photographs, he also showed one of the truest gifts ever seen for attracting publicity, sometimes appearing to go out of his way to get it when it might not have been pressed upon him.

Even his introduction to and courtship of Anne Morrow seemed to be a publicity man's dream. Eight months after his record-setting flight to Paris in the *Spirit of St. Louis,* he flew his plane to Mexico on a goodwill tour. At a reception in Mexico City he met Anne, the twenty-year-old daughter of the American ambassador, Dwight Morrow. His courtship was a public one, in Mexico and back in the United States, and the romance and marriage in 1929 were newspaper extravaganzas.

In the meantime Lindbergh went on doing what he knew best, which was to make spectacular airplane flights. They were well advertised, Lindbergh deliberately inviting reportage; then he would become furious at the men who met him to report the successful conclusion of his flights. He seemed unwilling to permit the legend of the heroic "Lone Eagle" to be erased from the public consciousness by other events, yet he detested the men and women who kept that legend alive in their newspapers.

After his marriage to Anne Morrow, Lindbergh became more brusquely insistent on personal privacy. Some of the adulation turned to malice. When his son was born new heights of adoration were reached, and new lows of viciousness. Few babies ever received more gifts from strangers or became the subject of more ugly rumors. Some of those rumors had it that Charles, Jr., was deformed, a physical monstrosity. To end this particularly embarrassing report, Lindbergh published photographs of the blond, curly-haired, and quite beautiful child. Perversely, they caused an enormous demand for more pictures—to Lindbergh a further intrusion.

He and his wife and child had been living in the Morrow mansion in Englewood, so close to New York City that reporters and photographers were constantly driving out to seek interviews and photographs. Lindbergh had to get away. He took to the air and flew over the mountains and farmlands of southern New Jersey and

31

finally chose a site on Sourland Mountain for his future home. It was the most remote and inaccessible spot he could find that would still be near enough for him to drive to New York, where he worked as a consultant to two airlines, one of which would later become TWA, "the Lindy Line." He wanted privacy and he bought 500 acres of it—although the very isolation of his home made it easier to steal his son.

After discovering that the boy had been kidnaped, Lindbergh rushed into his bedroom and pulled a rifle from the closet. He began loading it, at the same time shouting to the butler, Oliver Whately, to telephone the police. Whately alerted Harry Wolfe, police chief of Hopewell, the nearest town, and then Lindbergh made two quick calls. He phoned his friend and advisor, Colonel Henry Breckinridge, a Manhattan lawyer, asking him to rush out to Hopewell, then called the state police.

"Don't touch anything," Lindbergh ordered his wife and three servants, the nurse, the butler, and the butler's wife, Elsie Whately. He ran downstairs with his rifle, out the front door, and with long strides he dashed the hundred yards down the driveway to the road. About ten minutes later he returned, his search of the road unsuccessful. He went back into the nursery and for the first time noticed an envelope on an enclosed radiator which formed the sill of the southwest window, the one with the defective shutter. He also noticed several smudges of clay leading from that window to the crib.

For more than two hours Lindbergh would not permit anyone to touch the envelope. Chief Wolfe arrived with his constable but they had no idea how to proceed. Then the first of the state troopers burst upon the scene, and every few minutes thereafter more troopers wheeled up on motorcycles or in patrol cars. They were gorgeously dressed in light-blue uniforms with orange piping and as they drove around the property and tramped around in the dark they successfully obliterated every clue that might have been found in the March mud.

Some time after midnight Trooper Frank Kelly, the state police fingerprint expert, arrived at the house and dusted the envelope and the note inside it. The police later reported they found no fingerprints on the ransom note or anywhere in the nursery. The note was now read. It said:

        Dear Sir!
        Have 50.000$ redy 25.000$ in
20$ bills 15.000 in 10$ bills and
10.000$ in 5$ bills. After 2-4 days
we will inform you were to deliver
the Mony.
        We warn you for making anyding
public or for notify the Police
        the child is in gut care.
        Indication for all letters are
        singnature
        and 3 holes.

The "singnature" in the lower right-hand corner was a peculiar symbol: two interlocking circles drawn in blue ink, each about the size of a quarter; a solid red ball of color within the oval formed by the intersection of the circles; and three holes piercing the symbol.

By the time the nursery note was read it was too late to keep the news from police and public, as the kidnaper had demanded. Moments after Lindbergh called the state police an alarm was sent out over a six-state teletype wire, alerting the Northeast to the kidnaping and also alerting the press; by ten-thirty, less than a half hour after the child's crib was found empty, every radio station in the country was broadcasting news flashes and every newspaper was replating its front page with a one paragraph bulletin and a startling headline: "Little Lindy Kidnaped." Within hours of the kidnaping the beginnings of an army of hundreds of reporters and photographers were streaming into the little town of Hopewell, seeking directions to the Lindbergh house.

Lindbergh personally greeted the first reporters to arrive. He welcomed them warmly, thanking them for their interest and ordering Oliver Whately to make certain there was enough coffee and sandwiches for them, served in the living room. In those first hours Lindbergh saw the newspapermen as his allies: through the press, he could broadcast descriptions and publish the most recent photographs of his child so that he might be recognized and rescued; he could release to the kidnapers information about his son's diet and need for medication; through the newspapers he could also make

33

appeals to the kidnapers and hopefully facilitate his child's safe return.

But the press refused to accept so subordinate a role. To the newspaper proprietors, the Lindbergh tragedy was good for business. Hearst's International News Service (INS) dispatched its entire staff of photographers and technicians to Hopewell, chartering two ambulances outfitted with improvised darkrooms in which photographs could be developed as they raced back to New York with sirens wailing. INS also had five reporters with three cars at Hopewell; the Associated Press had six reporters and four cars; the United Press, six men with three cars. The *New York Daily News* had a dozen reporters on the scene within twelve hours of the kidnaping. The *New York American* sent ten men and women, the team personally directed by William Randolph Hearst, Jr., the paper's president. Ultimately, approximately four hundred reporters, photographers, newsreel cameramen, and radio commentators wandered all over the area, interviewing Lindbergh neighbors, tramping over the grounds, invading the Lindbergh garage in which the police had set up a battlefield command post, and turning Hopewell into the center of the world.

With the dawn Lindbergh began to realize the reporters were both a nuisance and a danger: with all the activity of the press the kidnapers might grow frightened and kill his child. Midmorning on March second he held an off-the-record press conference in which he discussed with reporters his fears, asked them to withdraw from the grounds, and requested they leave his family and servants alone until his child was safely returned. All further information about the crime and the investigation, he said, would have to come from the state police. The reporters, obviously sympathizing with Lindbergh, agreed to leave.

Their feverish activities, however, did not decline. Under enormous pressure from their editors, the reporters phoned and cabled hundreds of thousands of words to their offices every day. INS sent out over its wires 50,000 words within the first twenty-four hours, 30,000 words the following day, and it continued sending out at least 10,000 words daily over the next weeks. The United Press and Associated Press each sent out a similar amount of copy. Most newspapers devoted all of their front pages to the story for a week, filling many more pages of "news" on the inside. There was, however, no real news after the first day; most of what was then published was reporters' inventions and speculations. "Today's best clue" was diligently hunted by every reporter, and no matter how absurd or outrageous the "clue" it was developed into a long story, usually announcing that a solution was near.

Almost from the moment the news broke in the papers the morning after the kidnaping, the American public went into a long paroxysm of excitement and, occasionally, hysteria. Wild rumors, many of them based on the public's imaginative interpretation of the reporters' imaginative writing, flashed about. All over America people began reporting they'd seen Lindbergh's son. All over America men and women who were carrying, wheeling, or walking with an infant resembling the Lindbergh child, or driving with a child in their car, were stopped, arrested, and not released until they had satisfactorily proved the identity of the infant. Even the parents of dark-haired children were not spared arrest and questioning. After all, it was said, the kidnapers would probably have dyed young Lindbergh's hair to prevent recognition. One young couple with a blond toddler were arrested three times in as many days in an upstate New York city, and continued to be harassed even after the police commissioner gave them a note attesting to the fact that their child was not the Lindbergh boy.

The news from Hopewell pushed all other news to the back pages. Some commentators said that this was perhaps not inadvertent, for in an election year the Republican-dominated newspapers were helping a Republican administration by diverting public attention from the Depression. At the time, professional men and manual laborers alike were selling apples on street corners and lining up for thin soup ladled out by charitable organizations. The "Bonus Expeditionary Force," composed of war veterans demanding bonuses that had been voted by Congress in 1925 but never paid, was planning a protest march on Washington for the following June. But the nation's economic and social ills were ignored for months as even the jobless and the hungry became more concerned with the fate of Little Lindy than with their own problems. President Herbert Hoover issued statements that condemned the crime. Gangster Al Capone offered to help—provided he was released from the prison in which he was serving a long sentence for tax fraud. Clergymen of all denominations prayed over the radio for the child's safe deliverance. The *New York Times* reported it had received more than 3,000 phone calls in one day asking for the latest news. A New York psychiatrist told the press that among Americans there was "an intense feeling of individual and personal affront at this crime against the adored citizen of the world." He and other analysts speculated in print on the psychological motivation behind the kidnaping of the first son of a man who "was a god," as one popular historian wrote.

The wave of excitement and anger was worldwide. The President of Mexico, the premiers of Great Britain and France, political leaders in Europe, China, Japan, and South American countries, all expressed their horror at the crime and condemned the kidnapers. European and South American newspapers printed extra editions, with bold headlines, through the first days, and their switchboards were jammed with inquiries—"Has the baby been returned?" was a question asked around the world, and no one had to explain which baby was meant.

Such enormous publicity served the publishers' purposes. In Philadelphia, newspaper sales went up some 15 percent, according to a scholarly magazine survey. In New York, sales rose by 20 percent, a "tremendous increase," according to the article, when it was understood that the New York City papers already virtually blanketed the metropolitan area. In all areas of the country, the sale of radios rose dramatically as Americans sought more instantaneous reporting than was available from the newspapers.

The kidnaping stories also pried loose from the two rooms of their lives practically every crank and every emotionally disturbed person in the nation. Most of them sent letters, thousands of letters of advice, foreboding, prayer, and viciousness in the first day alone. A large number of such people living within driving distance of Hopewell descended on Lindbergh's house. Most of them were turned away by the police. Some, more skillful in generating belief in the urgency of their information, were ushered into Lindbergh's presence until it became clear they were mere curiosity-seekers, or just ghouls. One man who convinced police he had valuable information that he could convey only to Anne Lindbergh was taken to her. He shook her hand, stepped back a few paces, and began declaiming Hamlet's soliloquy. Doddering old men and half-witted women living out dreary lives in shacks throughout the Sourland Mountains sought their share of momentary fame. They suddenly remembered the strangest coincidences about their neighbors that proved they were involved in the crime; these "witnesses" were gravely interviewed by the police and the press. More than twenty-eight months later, with the arrest of Bruno Richard Hauptmann, other men and women with the same aberrant need to participate in history (and perhaps a $25,000 reward) would come forward to offer their "evidence" against the suspect.

But in those pre-dawn hours before the reporters arrived and the nation went on an emotional binge that has since been matched only by the public reaction to Pearl Harbor and the assassination of John F. Kennedy, the police were conducting a search of the grounds. Lying in the mud and clay about seventy feet from the nursery window, they found a homemade ladder. It was built in three sections, the second section slightly narrower than the first and the third even narrower still, so that they could be nestled within one another and easily carried. When fully extended, each section could be securely fastened to the next by wooden dowel pins. The ladder showed considerable mechanical skill and ingenuity but dreadful carpentry. The rungs were flat slats of wood and were placed several inches farther apart than a tall man could easily step. The top rung of the bottom section and the side rail into which it had been nailed were badly split, as if they had given way under the weight of the kidnaper.

The ladder was carried into the Lindbergh home—with no attempt to safeguard it for a fingerprint examination—and shown to Lindbergh. He gazed almost greedily at the broken rung and side rail and suddenly remembered something that had happened about forty-five minutes before Betty Gow raised the alarm that his son was missing. He and Mrs. Lindbergh had been sitting on a sofa in front of the living room fire after dinner, talking about the day's personal news. At about nine-fifteen, Lindbergh said, he had heard a sharp snapping of wood. "It sounded like the top slats of an orange crate falling off a chair," he said. He had asked his wife, "What was that?" She said she thought it might have been the sound of a tree branch cracking under the force of the wind. They quickly dismissed it from their minds.

State troopers reasoned that the sharp crack of wood had actually been the sound of the ladder rung snapping under the kidnaper's weight. That permitted police to set the approximate hour of the kidnaping. But after examining the ladder, police began to wonder whether it had been planted near the house to mislead them. It appeared to be almost useless as the instrument of access to the nursery, more like a stack of shelves than a proper ladder. A still graver suspicion was raised. The kidnapers seemed to have researched their victim so well that they knew in which room he was sleeping, which window had a warped shutter, and, even more incredibly, that the Lindberghs had stayed over at the house on Monday night and even on Tuesday night, which they had never done before. If the kidnapers were so knowledgeable, the police asked, why didn't they know that in an unlocked garage near the house was a strong, well-built ladder that could have served their purpose? Most suspect of all, police said after carrying the ladder outside again and raising it against the nursery window, was that it almost certainly could not have been used by the kidnaper to carry the Lindbergh child from the nursery. When all three sections of the ladder were joined and placed against the house, the top of the ladder rested so far above the window that a man would have to be an acrobat to climb inside and then climb out again. But when only two sections of the ladder were joined the top rung fell precisely thirty inches below the window ledge. An intruder could certainly have climbed onto the ledge and into the nursery, but it was doubtful that he could have climbed out again carrying a twenty-month-old boy—presumably awake, frightened, and possibly crying—stepped the thirty inches to the top rung, closed the window and the shutters, and climbed down to the ground.

The most logical reconstruction of the crime, investigators decided, was that a kidnap gang had had the cooperation of one or more members of the Lindbergh household staff and that the ladder was a false clue.

Armed with flashlights, the police conducted a further search of the grounds around the Lindbergh home. Under the nursery window, half-buried in the mud, they found a three-quarter-inch chisel, a Bucks Brothers brand that had been manufactured more than thirty years earlier. They told the press that it had apparently been used to pry open the window and had been dropped by the intruder. Investigators also said they had found two footprints in the mud under the nursery window. One was large and indistinct and was presumed to be that of a man who had wrapped a towel or some kind of rag around his shoes to blur his footprints. The other was tiny, appearing to be that of a woman. Police announced that a man and a woman, at the least, had taken part in the kidnaping.

Later, after interviewing Anne Lindbergh, police said the small footprint was hers. Mrs. Lindbergh told them, they said, that during a lull in the rainstorm earlier in the afternoon she had gone for a brief stroll, keeping to a temporary wooden walk that been placed around the house until a permanent concrete walk could be constructed in the spring. At one point in her stroll she had stood under the nursery window and called up to Betty Gow to bring her son to the window. As Charles, Jr., waved down to his mother she stepped away from the house, into the mud, to get a better view of him. Only the large footprint could be considered a real clue, police said. There were no other footprints anywhere on the property, they told reporters, and some writers attacked police for driving all over the place and destroying footprints.

It was troublesome to investigators: they had a portrait of the crime they could not accept. Shortly before dawn the state police chief, Colonel H. Norman Schwarzkopf, was briefed by his investigators and brought up to date on the evidence, theories, and deductions. All the evidence, Schwarzkopf was told, pointed to a gang of kidnapers working with at least one Lindbergh employee. They summed up their early suspicions and strengthened them with an additional piece of information and a further logical deduction.

The information was that the decision to stay over at the Hopewell house had been a last-minute one. Anne Lindbergh always left Betty Gow behind in Englewood when the Lindberghs spent the weekend at their Hopewell home, both to give the nurse a couple of days off and to permit mother and son to have some time together without his nurse. Mrs. Lindbergh had called Betty in Englewood on Tuesday morning to inform her they were remaining for still another day and had asked her to have the chauffeur drive her down to Hopewell. Betty had arrived at one-thirty on the afternoon of the kidnaping. Obviously, detectives said, Betty and the chauffeur and possibly all twenty-nine servants at Mrs. Morrow's home knew the Lindberghs would be in their new home on Tuesday night.

The deduction made by investigators seemed compelling. Assuming that outsiders had kidnaped the child, without assistance from employees, wouldn't they have waited until everyone went to sleep and the house was dark before taking the child? Of course they would have; they most certainly would not have risked discovery by any of the four adults awake in the house, nor would they have risked the barking of the Lindberghs' dog, which often yelped at minor disturbances but who had somehow slept peacefully through the kidnaping. Obviously, the kidnapers had had the help of employees, especially since no fingerprints were found, as if someone had wiped every surface clean.

Something was nagging at me. I read through what I had just written about the police inside-job theory, then read all the source material again. It occurred to me that all the writers I'd been consulting were firmly convinced Hauptmann was the kidnaper, and it appeared to me that every writer was attempting to make the same point: even with such a paucity of solid clues at hand, the police were leaving no stone unturned in their attempts to solve this crime; faced with a master criminal (Hauptmann) whose identity they did not know, they naturally chased after false clues (suspicion of employees), for they were doing their professional best.

The source of my discontent came to me after I had read the sources carefully for the third time. The fingerprints. The official version, that no prints were found, didn't make sense. As a crime detection tool, fingerprints are not all they're said to be by mystery writers. Few crimes are solved by fingerprints, because conditions must be ideal for a fingerprint man to detect even one clear print. Fingerprints usually can be raised only from hard surfaces and only if the person touching the surface didn't move his fingers laterally; the slightest movement and the prints will be smudged. Yet I couldn't believe that Trooper Kelly, the fingerprint expert, didn't find a single clear print in the nursery, as police officials insisted in their press briefings and in their later testimony at Hauptmann's trial.

It was clear that Anne Lindbergh, Betty Gow and the Lindbergh baby had spent considerable time in that nursery and must have touched many surfaces in the room. Colonel Lindbergh undoubtedly visited his son in the nursery also. On the night of the kidnaping the two women closed windows and shutters after putting the child in his crib; the boy himself must have touched the rails of his crib. Some prints must have been found. But police said they found none at all, not even of the Lindberghs or the staff.

If none were raised it could mean only one of three things. Either Trooper Kelly was a most inept fingerprint man. Or, if the kidnapers were outsiders, it meant an intruder had lifted the child from his crib, wiped clean every surface in the room, climbed out the window with the child in his arms, and then wiped the ladder clean. Or, finally, assuming that the kidnaping had been carried out with the assistance of an employee, there was a third, even more absurd possibility: after the child was taken away the employee inside the house had slipped into the nursery and removed every single fingerprint, risking premature discovery.

I felt almost certain there was something incorrect about the official version, and made a note to investigate the fingerprint question further when I began my inquiries.

Police next questioned Betty Gow. And their deductions seemed about to be confirmed when they heard her response to the question, did she have any friends who knew the Lindberghs were not returning to Englewood that evening? Betty told them about a phone call from her boyfriend, Henry Johnson, who was known as Red. He was a sailor on the yacht of banker Thomas Lamont, a partner of Lindbergh's father-in-law. She had been dating him regularly since being introduced to him when Lamont's yacht tied up near the house in Maine where the Lindberghs had been vacationing the summer before. In fact, she and Red had had a date for that evening, March first, but the unexpected summons to Hopewell had interfered. Before leaving for the Lindbergh home she had tried to reach Red at his apartment in Englewood, which he had rented to be near her, but he wasn't in and she had left a message for him to call her. She had also told the help at Englewood that if Red should call her there, he should be told their date was off because she had to go to Hopewell; everyone at Englewood was aware that the Lindberghs were not returning that night. Did Red call you? The police asked. Certainly, Betty responded. He phoned her at about eight-thirty, less than an hour before the presumed time of the kidnaping, and they chatted for a few moments.

Red Johnson was in jail in a matter of hours. He had been located, at Betty's suggestion, in the home of his brother in West Hartford, Connecticut. In the rumble seat of Red's car police discovered an empty milk bottle, which they were certain had been purchased to feed the kidnaped child. Red said he always drank a lot of milk, but police could not believe that of a sailor. He was questioned repeatedly over the next eighteen days, the primary suspect in the kidnaping. Finally, when the police could bring no

41

other charge against him than one of illegal entry into the United States, he was deported to his native Norway.

Detectives, under the direct command of State Police Captain John Lamb, now began to investigate the twenty-nine Morrow servants and three Lindbergh servants. It took several weeks to question them all because most of them were immigrants and their European backgrounds had to be carefully checked out.

The police belief in the inside-job theory of the kidnaping and the imprisonment of Red Johnson brought to a head a conflict between Lindbergh and police that frequently arises in kidnaping cases. The police were primarily interested in capturing the kidnapers; Lindbergh, in the return of his son. On March fourth, three days after his son was abducted, Lindbergh and his wife issued a joint statement:

Mrs. Lindbergh and I desire to make a personal contact with the kidnapers of our child. . . . We urge those who have the child to select any representative that they may desire to meet a representative of ours who will be suitable to them at any time and at any place that they may designate. If this is accepted, we promise that we will keep whatever arrangements that may be made by their representative and ours strictly confidential and we further pledge ourselves that we will not try to injure in any way those connected with the return of the child.

It was Lindbergh's dramatic way of saying that, at least until his son was returned, he was barring police from any role in the ransom negotiations. By now the police had been practically replaced by what appeared to be a high-level diplomatic-military tribunal. Led by Colonel Lindbergh, it included Colonel Breckinridge, Lindbergh's lawyer and advisor, Colonel William (Wild Bill) Donovan, then preparing to run for Governor of New York, and Colonel Schwarzkopf, who wasn't really a policeman at all, although he commanded the Jersey state police.

A graduate of West Point, Schwarzkopf had been a floorwalker in Bamberger's department store in Newark before his appointment to head the state police. Out of his depth in this investigation, he went along with any plan suggested by the other three colonels.

In actuality, Lindbergh was in command of the case, a chief executive with two colonels for advisors and a third colonel, Schwarzkopf, as his assistant, almost an errand boy transmitting Lindbergh's orders to the state cops.

Adela Rogers St. Johns later wrote: "Syd Boehm (a Hearst reporter) heard Lindbergh threaten coldly to shoot any policeman or agent who dared make a move. Over and over, enforcing it with his rifle, Lindbergh said, 'As far as I can I must obey the kidnaper and wait for his instructions.' "

One of these four colonels—it isn't clear which one from the materials at hand—came up with the brilliant idea of summoning from New York City a small, dark, and sharply dressed Broadway character named Mickey Rosner, who was a bootlegger, speakeasy operator, and was then under indictment in a stock market bucketshop operation. Lindbergh, reacting against the police theory of an inside job and angered at the arrest of Red Johnson and the persistent and far from gentlemanly questioning of all the servants, said he was certain his son had been kidnaped by underworld professionals. Logically, then, to effect the return of the boy he must turn to the underworld. Schwarzkopf's detectives did not agree; they insisted that professionals would have demanded at least $250,000 ransom and not the paltry $50,000 cited in the ransom note.

(During the several weeks that I spent reading all the material at hand and writing this summary of the case, I received further evidence that the four colonels had been told persuasively that no one in the professional criminal world had kidnaped Lindbergh's son. In trying to recapture the highlights of the case, I spoke with Lenny Katz of the *Post* several times. Lenny was then writing a book about Frank Costello, later published under the title *Uncle Frank*. One of the major figures of the Mafia, and a man of large influence with *mafiosi*, free-lance criminals, and the political powers of Tammany Hall, Costello had reminisced with friends about the Lindbergh case many years later. Those friends told Lenny that Costello said he'd been approached by one of Lindbergh's advisors, on Lindbergh's orders, and asked to help find the missing child. Costello investigated. He had a force of several thousand New York area *mafiosi* at his disposal and contacts with every criminal group in the country, Mafia or otherwise. And he determined to his satisfaction that no one in the underworld had kidnaped the child, that it

43

could only have been the work of nonprofessionals. He sent word of his findings to Lindbergh.)

Ignoring the police (and Costello), Lindbergh had Mickey Rosner brought out to Hopewell and asked for his help. Rosner laid down several demands. He needed $2,500 for expenses because he was a little short of cash; Lindbergh gave him the money. He was never to be followed by police while he attempted to make contact with the kidnap gang; the promise was given. And, Rosner said, Colonel Lindbergh must publicly appoint two very good men, Salvatore Spitale and Irving Bitz, as official intermediaries to deal with the kidnapers; that promise was also given, and Lindbergh issued a statement to the press announcing the appointment of Bitz and Spitale.

The newspapers immediately pointed out that Rosner, Bitz, and Spitale were bootleggers, narcotics dealers, and crooks in general, but the executive committee in Hopewell ignored those reports. None of the four colonels seemed to see anything improper about withholding information from federal agents and other investigators who offered assistance—and who complained so loud it reached the newspapers—and dealing instead with a pack of thieves and swindlers called in by Lindbergh.

Rosner began living in the Lindbergh home, answering the telephone, and identifying himself as Lindbergh's private secretary. He was present on the afternoon of March fifth when a second ransom letter was delivered in the many thousands of pieces of mail that were flooding into Hopewell every day. Detectives were certain this letter was authentic because it bore the same identifying symbol of the nursery note, the two interlocking circles traced in blue with the solid red oval in the center and the three square holes punched through. The envelope was postmarked Brooklyn, 9 P.M., March 4. It said, in part:

Dear Sir: We have warned you note to make anyding Public also notify the Police now you have to take the consequences. This means we will holt the baby until everyding is quiet. . . . We are interested to send him back in gut health. ouer ransom was made aus for 50.000$ but now we have to take another person to it and probable have to keep the baby for a longer time as we expected So the mount will be 70.000$. . . .

44

In my reading to this point, most of the books and magazine articles I consulted seemed to be in general agreement. But now I came across a passage in Alan Hynd's article in *True* that differed from the other accounts. Hynd had written:

When the first of a long series of follow-up ransom letters arrived for Lindbergh through the mails, Rosner . . . grabbed it and rushed to New York. His mission apparently was to show the letter to underworld authorities on penmanship. But somewhere in its travels the letter lay prostrate under a camera lens, for copies of it were soon being peddled by various enterprising characters. . . . Lindbergh was not aware that every confidence man, penman, swindler and forger east of the Rockies was in possession of the photograph of the ransom letter . . . and that an extortion plot, separate and distinct from the kidnaping, could conceivably be under way.

No other writer had said that the ransom note was in general circulation among criminals. If this were true, then it was possible that all the later ransom notes were written by an extortionist not connected with the original kidnaping—perhaps Hauptmann, I thought. I remembered that many authorities, including Clarence Darrow, had said Hauptmann was guilty of nothing more than extortion, at the most, and should not be executed. Were Darrow's and similar statements based on a knowledge that Rosner had taken the letter to New York, where it was copied? Hynd gave no source for his statement; it was undocumented.

I could see that if I ever hoped to upset the verdict in the Hauptmann case, I would have to find the documentation to verify Hynd's assertion. And as I thought about it, I realized I was hooked—there was no longer any doubt that I was going to investigate the Hauptmann case as thoroughly as I could, that I was going to try and peel off the layers of gloss that had been brushed over it through the years.

3

While Lindbergh and his consultants were dealing with criminal figures in an attempt to recover his son (I read in my source material), some state troopers did continue their investigations in the towns and farmhouses of the area. Every house for miles around was visited and the occupants questioned. Several people, police said, told them they had seen suspicious men near the Lindbergh home on the day of the kidnaping or in the weeks preceding.

One of them was Ben Lupica, a seventeen-year-old student at Princeton Prep who lived with his parents near the Lindbergh estate. On the morning after the kidnaping, Lupica came forward and told police that while driving home the previous afternoon he had stopped as usual at the family's mailbox, which was very near the gatehouse at the foot of Lindbergh's driveway. He was sitting in his car, reading the mail, when he heard another automobile coming toward him. He glanced up. The car was a black or dark-blue Dodge sedan, probably a 1928 or 1929 model, with New Jersey license plates. It was being driven fast and erratically. The driver was in his mid-thirties, with a thin, sharp-featured face.

(The description, brief as it was, did match Hauptmann. And Hauptmann did drive a Dodge sedan. But it was a 1930 model, painted green, with New York license plates, and it had on its rear a handmade wooden chest to supplement the tiny trunk on those cars; I was certain Lupica would have noticed that chest and com-

47

mented upon it to police. And I found it strange that none of the writers on the case, appearing so anxious to verify the "facts" as given them by Wilentz and police, mentioned that chest. I learned about it only because I stumbled across a picture of Hauptmann's car in an old magazine article.)

Lupica told police he had noticed two sections of a ladder resting on the top of the front seat beside the driver, stretching from the windshield to the rear window of the car. Shown the sections of the ladder found near the Lindbergh home, Lupica said he thought they could be the ladder he'd seen in the stranger's car. And he felt certain he could identify the man if he ever saw him again.

In the Bronx, three hours by car from the Sourland Mountains, Dr. John F. Condon, an eccentric, long-winded bore of seventy-two, sat in his living room on the afternoon of March sixth, reading the newspapers about the kidnaping and growing ever more enraged that gangsters had dared kidnap the Lone Eagle's son. Condon threw the newspapers aside and composed a letter to the Bronx *Home News,* a local paper.

In his letter, Condon offered to act as intermediary between Lindbergh and the kidnapers. He also offered $1,000 of his own funds as additional ransom money. The newspaper printed a front-page article about the offer, because Condon was well known to its editors and their readers. A Fordham University football player in 1883, later a teacher and public school principal, now lecturer in education at Fordham and a physical education enthusiast, Condon had for years written poems, essays, and letters on current topics for the *Home News.* He always signed his material with pseudonyms designed to emphasize his point, P.A. Triot for the patriotic letters, J.U. Stice, and so on. Whenever the editor wanted a local angle on a national story, he sent a reporter to interview the garrulous Condon, who was always good for columns of quotable material. Condon's appeal to the kidnapers was the perfect local angle on a crime that had become an international sensation.

Things began happening to Condon a few nights after the story was published. He returned home from a lecture late on the evening of March ninth and found an envelope addressed to him in a crude, uneven combination of script and printing. Inside was a note to him and another envelope, which was sealed. The note to Condon said:

Dear Sir: If you are willing to act as go-between in Lindbergh cace follow stricly instruction. Handel incloced letter personally to Mr. Lindbergh. . . . After you gets the money from Mr. Lindbergh put them words in New York American. Money is ready. After notise we will give you further instruction. don't be afrait we are not out for your 1.000$. Keep it only act stricly. Be at haus every night between 6-12 by this time you will hear from us.

Not having the faintest notion what to do next the doctor took a trolley to Maxie Rosenhein's restaurant, where he habitually had a midnight snack with his friend Al Reich, a retired heavyweight fighter. Reich wasn't there yet. Over several cups of coffee, the doctor read and reread the note. He finally laid the whole matter before Rosenhein and another friend, Milton Gaglio, who suggested that Condon should phone Hopewell immediately. They put the call through for him, and after some delay Condon got a noncommital voice which implied it was Lindbergh and asked him to read the letter. Condon read the one addressed to him, and the voice on the other end of the phone asked him to open the envelope and read the second letter. Condon did so.

Dear sire, Mr. Condon may act as go-between you may give him the 70.000$ make one packet. the size will be about . . . [and here the extortionist drew a box, six by seven by fourteen inches]. We have notify you allredy in what kind of bills. We warn you not to set a trapp in any way . . . after we have the mony in hand we will tell you where to find your boy. . . .

The voice at the Lindbergh home asked Condon: "Is there anything else on the letter?"

"There is no signature," Condon replied, "except for some circles and holes, secantal circles I would say . . ."

Another voice suddenly cut in. "This is Colonel Lindbergh," it snapped with authority. "I will get the car and come to you. Where are you?"

"In the Bronx," Condon said. "But you have other things to do. I will come to you."

Accompanied by Rosenhein in a car driven by Gaglio, Dr. Condon arrived at Hopewell about three hours later. When Lindbergh, Breckinridge, and others at the house read the notes they decided they were genuine. Not only did the note addressed to Lindbergh repeat the demand for an increased ransom of $70,000, which had been made in the letter of March fourth and which was still a secret so far as Lindbergh knew, but it also bore the strange symbol present on the earlier ransom notes. Lindbergh accepted Condon as an intermediary and signed a letter authorizing him to pay the kidnapers $70,000—a sum that Lindbergh promptly drew from the Morgan bank and deposited in Condon's bank in the Bronx.

Condon spent the night in the Lindbergh house, sleeping on a cot in the only available room, the nursery. He knelt beside the crib for a few moments before going to sleep and prayed for the boy's safe return. In the morning, when he awoke, he stared once more at the empty crib and an idea suddenly occurred to him: he would take the two safety pins which had fastened the blankets to the mattress and, when he finally met the kidnapers, he would show them the pins and ask what they were. If the answers were correct, Condon would know he was in contact with the actual kidnapers. Lindbergh agreed to the plan.

The doctor had also noticed something else in the nursery and pointed it out to Lindbergh: on a smudged handprint at the edge of the window frame, believed to have been left by the kidnaper when he climbed into the room, Condon saw a "prominent and well-defined mark left by the ball of the thumb . . . there is evidence of muscular development there . . . the print might have been left by a painter, a carpenter, a mechanic." Prophetic words, Condon later wrote.

Over breakfast, Condon, Lindbergh and Breckinridge discussed the need for a pseudonym for the doctor, to prevent the newspapers from learning the identity of the man placing ads in the classified columns that would undoubtedly be recognized as a contact with the kidnapers. And it suddenly occurred to Condon: "By putting my initials together I get J.F.C.—Jafsie." Lindbergh agreed and Condon became known as Jafsie, which would turn out to be one of the more famous names of the 1930s.

Colonel Breckinridge drove Condon back to the Bronx and moved into the neat two-story house on Decatur Avenue; since Condon's home would be the focal point of the case during the ransom negotiations, Breckinridge said, it would be wise for him, Lindbergh's lawyer and chief advisor, to live there during that time. Condon had agreed. He did not seem to suspect, as several writers did later, that Lindbergh and Breckinridge didn't trust him and wanted to keep a close watch on him.

State police meanwhile continued to question the servants. A little more than a week after the kidnaping and only hours after Condon returned to the Bronx from Lindbergh's home, investigators finally got around to Violet Sharpe, a serving maid on the Morrow staff in Englewood. Violet was English, twenty-eight, quite pretty, and slightly plump, considered a bit saucy and temperamental by other members of the staff. But in the two years she had worked for Mrs. Morrow, her employer had found not a fault with her.

On March tenth one team of detectives drove Violet to the Lindbergh home for routine questioning while another team, pursuing the usual police routine, searched her room without her permission. They found letters and books, addresses of several friends, and a half-dozen business cards of a cab service in White Plains called the Post Road Taxi Company. White Plains was in Westchester County, immediately north of the Bronx. The night before, Dr. Condon had received the first contact from the kidnaper, who probably lived or worked in the Bronx for he had responded to a story in the local newspaper. So the police immediately became suspicious of Violet. That suspicion was heightened by another discovery in her room, a New York City savings account bankbook which showed she had saved $1,600 in two years out of her $100 a month salary; further investigation disclosed she had managed to send money regularly to her parents.

When questioned, Violet struck a defiant attitude. She also seemed to be suffering from a loss of memory. Her personal affairs were no one's business but her own, she told the police. Besides, she couldn't properly remember what she did the afternoon and night of the kidnaping. But finally, after investigators insisted they must know her movements on that day—simply routine to eliminate her and go on to more urgent matters, they said—she told them.

Some time before eight o'clock on the evening of March first an acquaintance, a man she didn't know very well, had telephoned and asked her to a movie. She accepted. The man came at eight-thirty to fetch her. When he walked her back to his car she realized another couple was going along. Her escort introduced them to her. They had then driven to the Englewood Theater, seen the film, and her escort had driven her directly back to the Morrow mansion. It was a little before eleven and he did not come inside; they said good night at the servants' entrance in the rear. She had not seen the man since, Violet said, nor had she ever seen the other couple again.

Her escort's name? She couldn't remember that or the names of the other couple. The name of the movie also eluded her; the plot escaped her memory; the stars of the film made no impression on her. Detectives pushed a little harder for the identity of her young man friend. Where, they demanded, had she met him? She remembered that much: she had met him "on the Sunday"—two days before the kidnaping—while she was out walking. But she could remember nothing more, not the street she had met him on, not the conversation they'd had before she gave him the telephone number of the Morrow house, not the amount of time they'd spent together that Sunday. Violet promptly became a suspect in the case, as deeply under suspicion as the still imprisoned Red Johnson, and she was listed for a more intensive investigation and further questioning.

Two days later, on March twelfth, when Dr. Condon returned to his home after a day at school, his wife told him he had received a phone call from a man with a German accent who had said he would call back later. He did, at seven that evening. He asked Condon whether he had received the letter "with the signature." Condon said he had. The caller then instructed Condon to remain at home "every night this week from six to twelve" because an important message would be delivered to him.

"Dr. Condon," the man asked in his heavy accent, "do you write sometimes pieces for the papers?"

"Yes, I sometimes write articles for the papers," Condon said.

The man spoke again, but this time not to Dr. Condon. The caller had turned his head away from the phone and said to someone else in the room with him, "He say sometimes he writes pieces for the papers."

The man spoke to Condon again, repeating the orders to remain at home and warning, "Act accordingly or all will be off."

"I shall stay in," Condon said.

Suddenly Condon heard another voice in the background, obviously that of the person to whom the caller had spoken a moment before, shout quite clearly in Italian, which Condon understood, *"Statto citti!"* a colloquial expression meaning "Shut up." The caller then said he would hear from them again, and hung up.

Right there, I remembered, in that little bit of information that all writers agreed upon because Condon never wavered in his telling of that conversation, not even after Hauptmann was dead—right there was evidence that more than one man had been involved in the kidnaping and extortion. That was one reason why, in the back of my mind, I'd always felt all these years that Hauptmann should not have been executed; he could not have acted alone and to kill him meant to destroy any possibility of finding his associates— assuming he had actually played any role in the crime at all. I was being led, inevitably, to the belief that there was something implausible about the case against Hauptmann.

After receiving the call from a man who was obviously part of the kidnap gang, Condon and Breckinridge waited for another contact. At about eight-thirty that night a taxicab driver brought an envelope to Condon's door. The doctor tore it open as the cabbie and Breckinridge watched. The letter, bearing the ransom note symbols, ordered Condon to

take a car and drive to the last supway station from Jerome Ave. line. 100 feet from the last station on the left seide is a empty frank-further-stand with a big open Porch around, you will finde a notise in senter of the porch underneath a stone. . . . after ¾ of a houer be on the place. bring the mony with you.

The cab driver was questioned. He said his name was Joseph Perrone and he had been driving along Gun Hill Road, a short distance away, when a man came running toward him with his hand upraised. Perrone stopped and the man leaned into his cab through the window opposite the driver's seat.

"Do you know where Decatur Avenue is?" he asked.

"Yes, sure," Perrone said.

"Do you know where 2974 is?"

"Of course," Perrone said.

53

The man reached into his overcoat pocket and drew out an envelope. He put his hand into the same pocket and drew out a dollar bill. He gave the envelope and bill to Perrone, who noticed that a name, Dr. Condon, and the address were written on the envelope. Perrone said he took a good, close look at the man and he would never forget that face: long and narrow, with a pointed chin and prominent cheekbones and eyes that were a piercing blue. And he spoke with a very heavy German accent, Perrone said.

Condon dismissed the cab driver after getting his name and address, for he was anxious to follow the instructions in the note and get to the frankfurter stand. Persuading Breckinridge to remain behind in his home, the doctor called his friend Al Reich and asked him to drive him to the rendezvous with the kidnapers. When they arrived at the designated place, Condon found another note, bearing no symbols, which directed him to cross the street to the fence of Woodlawn Cemetery and walk in the direction of 233rd Street. Condon did so. After a short walk his attention was riveted by the flutter of a white handkerchief through the bars of the cemetery gates.

"I see you!" Condon shouted, breaking into a run toward the man.

"Not so fast!" yelled the kidnaper in alarm. He promptly scaled the eight-foot fence, leaped down to Condon's side, shouting "The police!" and began to run into nearby Van Cortlandt Park. A cemetery guard, attracted by their voices, approached Condon, who now understood what had frightened the kidnaper.

"It's all right," Condon told the guard, "that man's with me."

Condon ran after the fleeing man and finally caught up with him inside the park. They sat together on a bench. The night was extraordinarily cold and the kidnaper was shivering.

"Why your coat is too thin," Condon said. "Here, take mine."

The kidnaper refused, but he thanked Condon. His voice was the same as that of the man who had phoned, with a heavy guttural accent, undoubtedly German.

They had a long conversation there on the park bench. The kidnaper said his name was John and that he was a Scandinavian sailor, which Condon did not fully believe because of the accent. There were six members of the kidnap gang, John said, four men and two women. The baby was safe on a boat somewhere.

"Tell me how I am to know I am talking to the right person?" Condon demanded.

"You gottit my letter with the signature," John replied. "Same signature that was on my note in the crib."

Condon claimed that he talked to John for well over an hour, and he later wrote in his book about the case, *Jafsie Tells All!*, that "I wanted, as I studied him, to keep him talking and I plied him with questions." Yet he neglected to ask one vital question: how could John say the note had been left in the crib when everyone involved in the case, including the Lindberghs, said it had been found on the windowsill? Having failed to ask that question, Condon later constructed a strange explanation in order to deny the possibility that the man in the park wasn't the man who had been in the nursery. In his book the doctor wrote:

"My own opinion remains that the ransom note was left in the baby's crib—the logical place for it—but that in the confusion and excitement attending discovery of the child's theft, someone carried the note to the windowsill, where it later was found."

The doctor's "opinion" is so far beyond possibility that it becomes pure fantasy. To me, that illogical note in the doctor's scenario was further evidence that Condon may have been dealing with an extortionist who had not been involved in the abduction. Perhaps, then, Hynd's undocumented assertion that the original ransom note had been copied many times was accurate.

John and Condon continued to talk and the doctor attempted to gain further verification that he was dealing with the actual kidnaper. He pulled from his pocket the two safety pins he had taken from the child's crib and asked, "Have you ever seen these before?"

John looked at them and nodded. "Yes, those pins fastened the blankets to the mattress in the baby's crib," he said. "Near the top. Near the pillow."

"That is right," Condon said. And he later wrote: "I was jubilant. There could be no doubt, now, that I was dealing with the proper person."

Because Condon felt so certain John was actually a German, he decided to trap the man with a question in German: "*Bist du Deutsch?*" (Are you German?) Condon didn't get the answer he had hoped for. "That question," he later wrote, "inserted casually

55

and unexpectedly in the native language of a man, would have elicited instinctively a reply in the same language from nine men out of ten, would have thrown them immediately off guard. But not this fellow! Crafty, cunning, cool, his mind as furtively alert as his eyes, he made no reply whatever."

It must have occurred to Condon that perhaps the man was not a German, that he did not automatically respond in German because he didn't understand the language. The earliest stories about the case, and Condon himself, said the man was believed to be either Scandinavian or German. Condon later claimed he had told police John might possibly be Scandinavian solely because John had said he was. But perhaps Condon was not so certain of John's origins in the days following the cemetery conversation with him as he was years later.

(Was it not possible that Condon desperately wanted to believe he was dealing with the correct man? He had said again and again that one of his strongest interests in life was helping others, that his main ambition after learning of the kidnaping was to be the man who restored the child to its mother's arms, that he had idolized Lindbergh as a national hero, that the crime was a national disgrace, and the highest duty of all loyal citizens was to rout out the gangsters who had brought discredit to America. Condon was also a publicity-seeker according to even the friendliest of writers. I wondered, *could he have possibly accepted John as the genuine kidnaper because his mind could not admit he had been duped by the ransom notes? Would an overwhelming need to participate in and to help solve the crime that had shocked the entire world have prompted Condon to lie about the events he witnessed?* Men have lied, grossly so, with much less at stake. Had he indeed lied, the evidence might be found in his original statements to police—if I could locate them.)

After getting no response to his question in German, Condon continued speaking to John in English. They now began discussing the ransom payment. Condon insisted that Lindbergh was not as wealthy as everyone thought and that John should settle for the original $50,000 demand. John replied that was not possible because his boss, the commander of the kidnap gang, would refuse and would probably beat John should he even suggest the cut-rate ransom. It must be $70,000 and Condon must place an advertisement in the *Home News* immediately, informing the gang that "the money is ready." Then John volunteered to furnish proof that his gang actually had Lindbergh's son; he would mail to Condon the sleeping suit the child had been wearing when he was taken from his crib and with it instructions on how to conclude the negotiations.

"Now I go," John said.

Both men rose from the bench and Condon said he would place the ad in the *Home News* first thing in the morning. He held out his hand to shake on the agreement and, he said, to verify his hunch that the smudged handprint in the nursery he had pointed out to Lindbergh indicated the kidnaper's hand had a "muscular over-development at the ball of the thumb." And, on shaking John's hand, Condon later wrote, "the hard lump of muscle I had expected to find at the base of the thumb was there."

When Condon returned to his home he told Breckinridge there wasn't any doubt John was one of the kidnapers. All that now remained was to follow John's instructions. The baby's sleeping suit was delivered to Condon through the mails within a couple of days and Lindbergh positively identified it as the one his son had been wearing when put to bed, even though the garment was a very common Dr. Denton, sold by the millions. There then followed several other ransom notes and a number of ads placed in the newspapers by Condon.

In the meantime, the ransom money was being prepared. Lindbergh was given a fresh package of $70,000 in bills by the Morgan bank, at the urging of Breckinridge and of Elmer Irey of the Treasury Department, who had been ordered by President Herbert Hoover to assist Lindbergh; both men had insisted that the serial number on each bill be recorded, which was done. The ransom was divided into two packets, one containing the $50,000 in denominations originally specified in the nursery note, the other, $20,000 in fifty-dollar bills.

The $50,000 was placed in a wooden box built to the specifications in one of the early ransom notes. It was made of five different kinds of wood for possible later identification; that idea was Condon's, who seemed to be adding to his role as intermediary, one as detective. The other $20,000 was tied in a brown paper bundle. Two packets were needed to hold the ransom money because the wooden box, made to the size recommended by the kidnaper, would barely accept even $50,000; when he tried to close the box

57

with that smaller sum inside, Lindbergh had to lean on it with his knee with such force that the lid cracked.

About $15,000 of the ransom money placed in the wooden box was in gold notes, bills bearing gold seals, which would make them that more easily recognizable when the kidnapers began passing the money.

A week had passed since his first meeting with John, and Condon grew worried because there had been no definite response to his ads. Had the kidnaper been frightened off by wild rumors being printed in the papers? On Saturday, March 19, Condon went to work at a charity bazaar designed to raise money for the construction of a chapel on Harts Island, the site of a city prison. A lifelong collector of violins, he had decided to donate a few of his to the fund-raising effort and to sell them personally from a booth at the bazaar.

Late in the afternoon a plainly dressed middle-aged woman "with the oval face and olive skin of an Italian," Condon later wrote, paused near his booth. She appeared timid, so Condon asked whether he could help her. She said she was interested in violins and Condon gave her a lengthy discourse about the instrument. But the woman didn't seem to be listening. She leaned close to him and spoke quickly, in a whisper.

"Nothing can be done until the excitement is over," she said. "There is too much publicity. Meet me at the depot at Tuckahoe, Wednesday at five in the afternoon. I will have a message for you."

She walked swiftly away. Condon watched as she crossed Webster Avenue toward the Third Avenue elevated line and climbed the stairs to the station. He did not try to follow.

The following Wednesday he went to the Tuckahoe station in Westchester County. The woman never showed up. Condon was certain, he later wrote, that she had been "a direct agent of the kidnaper, sent to reassure me." Only the secretive Lindbergh circle and the kidnapers knew Condon was the Jafsie of the newspaper ads, so the woman must have been part of the kidnap gang.

On the night of April second Condon received another note delivered by taxi. Lindbergh was in Condon's home when the note arrived and he tore open the envelope. The instructions inside ordered them to drive to a florist shop opposite St. Raymond's Cemetery, where they would find still another note with further instructions under a rock on a bench. Lindbergh, with a revolver in a shoulder holster, drove to the shop with Condon, the $70,000 ransom on the seat beside them. Condon picked up the second note and he and Lindbergh read it in the car:

Cross the street to the next corner and follow Whittemore Ave to the soud. take the money with you. come alone and walk. I will meet you.

Condon started off, leaving the money behind. "I want to talk to John first," he explained to Lindbergh. After he had walked a short distance a voice shouted at him out of the darkness, "Hey, Doctor!" Both Lindbergh and Condon heard the shout. Condon turned and called out, "All right."

The voice cried again, "Hey, Doctor. Over here!"

Condon realized a man was standing behind a tombstone and he started into the cemetery. The man began walking between the tombstones. He climbed a low fence and jumped down behind a hedge on the other side. Condon came up and, peering through the leafless branches, recognized John.

"Did you gottit the money?" John asked.

"No, I didn't bring any money. It is up in the car."

"Who is up there?"

"Colonel Lindbergh."

"Is he armed?"

"No," Condon lied. "Where is the baby?"

"You could not get the baby for about six, eight hours," John said.

Condon pleaded with John to let him see the baby before the ransom was paid. "You must take me to the baby," he concluded.

"I have told you before," John said, his voice growing irritable. "It is impossible. It cannot be done. . . . Give me the money."

"Not until you give me a receipt," Condon demanded. "A note showing where the baby is."

"I haven't got it with me," John said.

"Then get it."

"All right. You will wait?"

Condon said he would, but he then began to harangue John about the Depression, the hard times everyone was going through, even a man as famous as Lindbergh. "Why don't you be decent to him?

59

He can't raise the extra money, but I can go up to the auto right now and get the fifty thousand.''

"Since it is so hard it will be all right, I guess,'' John said. "I suppose if we can't get seventy, we take fifty.''

John then said he would be gone about ten minutes, to get the note Condon had demanded. He turned and strode away. Condon looked at his watch—sixteen minutes past nine o'clock—and began to time John, hoping to later find the place where he obtained, or wrote, the "receipt.'' Hurrying back to Lindbergh, he described his conversation with John and said he'd agreed to accept only $50,000. Condon put the wooden box under his arm and hurried back to the hedge. In a few moments he saw John threading his way through the tombstones. He checked his watch again. John had taken exactly thirteen minutes to go wherever he had kept the note or written it.

"Have you gottit it?'' John asked as he returned to the hedge.

"Yes. Have you got the note?''

They exchanged the note and the box of money simultaneously. John knelt in the soil, placed the box in front of him, and said "Wait until I see if it is all right.''

"It is all right as far as I know,'' Condon said. "There is fifty thousand dollars in there.''

John opened the lid of the box. Using a flashlight, which he shaded with his hand, he examined the bills briefly. "I guess it is all right,'' he said. He rose, holding the box. "Don't open that note for six hours,'' he warned.

"I will not open it. You can trust me.''

"Thank you, Doctor,'' he replied. "We trust you. Everybody says your work has been perfect. . . . The baby is all right. You will find him on the boat *Nelly*, like the note says.''

They shook hands and parted.

A short time later Condon and Lindbergh read the note, which said:

The boy is on boad Nelly. It is a small boad 28 feet long. two persons are on boad. they are innosent. You will find the boad between Horsenecks Beach and Gay Head over Elizabeth Island.

The area indicated was in Buzzard's Bay, which separates Martha's Vineyard from Massachusetts' southern coast. After some

60

telephone preparations Lindbergh, Breckinridge, and Condon drove to Bridgeport, Connecticut, where at dawn they took off in a small amphibian. Flying from dawn to dusk, they searched the area for two days while a U.S. Coast Guard cutter hovered in the vicinity. Each fruitless hour made it more certain there was no boat named *Nelly*.

Feeling betrayed by John, Lindbergh now listened more closely to Commodore John Hughes Curtis, president of a boat-building firm in Norfolk, Virginia, who had claimed to be in touch with the kidnap gang. Back on March tenth, two days before Condon had his first meeting with John, at Woodlawn Cemetery, Curtis had gone to the Dean of Norfolk's Christ Episcopal Church, H. Dobson Peacock, and told him an awe-inspiring story. He had just been approached by a man he knew only as Sam, the Commodore said. He had once repaired a boat for Sam but they were not on social terms, because Sam was a rum-runner. Nonetheless, Curtis had felt compelled to listen to Sam's plea:

"Help get the Lindbergh baby back to its mother. The kidnapers approached me to ask you to act as intermediary. They want you to form a group of prominent Norfolk citizens to become go-betweens."

Curtis said he wasn't certain Sam was telling the truth and he'd been inclined to forget the incident. But after thinking about it during a sleepless night he decided that, for the sake of his own two children, he would ask the Dean's advice. He knew, he said, that the Dean was acquainted with Anne Lindbergh and her mother. He didn't say that everyone in Norfolk knew it because at every possible opportunity the Dean boasted that he had been friendly with the Morrow family.

Dean Peacock said he would be thrilled to help. The first step was to call Lindbergh; he promptly placed the call. When he finally got through he spoke to Mickey Rosner, who identified himself as "Colonel Lindbergh's secretary" and listened politely as both Peacock and Curtis alternately jabbered about this latest development. Rosner appeared absolutely indifferent to their story. He finally grew silent, too indifferent to ask the proper questions, and the men in Norfolk hung up.

Dean Peacock reflected on the rude treatment he had received from that ill-bred man who claimed to be Lindbergh's secretary. An idea suddenly occurred to Curtis: enlist the aid of another prominent Norfolk citizen, Admiral Guy Burrage, who had commanded the warship which had returned Lindbergh and his plane to America after the flight to Paris. Burrage was called, listened to Curtis's story, and promised to help. Eventually, after several phone calls and a letter, Lindbergh wrote to Burrage that he would be glad to receive him and his two friends at Hopewell on Tuesday, March twenty-second.

On that date, Curtis repeated for Lindbergh the story he had first told his fellow Virginians and added further details.

"Sam told me," Curtis said, "that you are negotiating with another member of the same gang up here. Sam says the man up here wants $50,000, maybe as much as a $100,000. Sam is willing to deliver the baby to me for $25,000."

Lindbergh and his aides were impressed; the Norfolk gang apparently knew about Condon's negotiations and the increased ransom demand, even though not a word had leaked to the press. He told the Virginians to proceed with the negotiations in Norfolk, but he refused Curtis's request that Lindbergh place $25,000 in a Norfolk bank account so that it could be paid over simultaneously with delivery of the baby.

But now, in the first week in April, after John had taken $50,000 and failed to return his son, Lindbergh started paying closer attention to Curtis. During Condon's negotiations with the kidnaper, Curtis had been keeping Lindbergh abreast of his own negotiations. He said he had been taken to Newark by Sam, his original contact, and introduced to four Scandinavian men who said they kidnaped the child. They drove Curtis down to Cape May, New Jersey, where he met the wife of one of the men. She told him the child was safe on a boat at sea, in charge of a nurse. The boat, named the *Mary B. Moss*, was cruising in the Atlantic off the Jersey coast, Curtis said. For several days after it became obvious John was not going to return his son, Lindbergh and Curtis flew over the area. They were unable to find the *Mary B. Moss*. Lindbergh then borrowed a yacht and began scouring the area once more.

He was still searching the Atlantic with Curtis when, on the afternoon of May twelfth, a truck driver named William Allen stopped on the road between Hopewell and Princeton and went into the woods to urinate. He had walked about seventy-five feet when he noticed a small, unclothed corpse only partially covered by leaves. The child's body was face downward, veiled in vermin, so badly decomposed that not much more than a skeleton remained. Some fragments of clothing lay with it.

The scraps of cloth were taken to Betty Gow. Matching the material and the strands of thread with remnants she had kept from the night she made a flannel shirt for Lindbergh's son, she and the police declared they were the same. The body was taken to an undertaker's establishment in Trenton. Betty Gow viewed the corpse briefly and identified it as Charles A. Lindbergh, Jr.

Police tried to wire Lindbergh on the yacht but were unable to reach him. Later that night, when the boat put into Atlantic City, every paper and radio station in the country was shouting the sickening news: *Lindbergh baby found dead!* Two Lindbergh aides met the yacht and realized the colonel was one of the few people in the world who had not heard about the corpse found less than four miles from his home. One of his aides told Lindbergh:

"Colonel, your son has been found. He is dead."

Midafternoon the next day, Lindbergh was driven to the mortuary, his face looking tired, his body sagging as if he had suddenly aged. He walked to the autopsy table, which was covered by a sheet. "Take that thing off," he said. The sheet was removed. Lindbergh stared at the remains of the body. A flush came into his face. He counted the teeth, looked at the corpse for a moment, then turned away. He had been inside the morgue for less than ninety seconds. Asked by the local prosecutor whether he was able to identify the body, Lindbergh said: "I am perfectly satisfied that is my child." The body was cremated within an hour, without being subjected to pathological or toxicological tests.

But a superficial autopsy was performed by Dr. Charles Mitchell, the county physician. He found, he wrote in his official report, that decomposition had been so severe it wasn't possible even to determine the sex of the child, that the "body shows evidence of prolonged exposure & usual decomposition that would occur in the course of approximately two to three months time depending on climatic and other conditions that might produce such results." And he noted that the left leg was missing from the knee down, the left hand and the right arm were missing, as were all the major organs except the heart and the liver.

"Diagnosis of the cause of death is a fractured skull due to external violence," Mitchell wrote. The autopsy disclosed a massive fracture from the top of the skull down the left side and to the left ear, where it broke into two other distinct fractures; and a small round hole on the right side of the skull, about a half-inch in diameter, that Mitchell later said looked like a bullet hole.

Some police officers were not convinced the body was that of young Lindbergh. The physical characteristics of the body itself led a few investigators to believe Lindbergh was mistaken in his identification. Dr. Mitchell's autopsy report noted that the skeleton was thirty-three and a half inches long. Young Lindbergh's height, just before he was kidnaped, was twenty-nine inches. Even making allowance for the normal stretching of muscle and cartilage during decomposition, the body, had it been Lindbergh's son, should not have been more than thirty-one inches long. Since Dr. Mitchell said the child he autopsied had probably died within forty-eight hours after the night of March first, the only logical conclusion was that the child had grown more than two inches after death; that wasn't logical at all.

The autopsy report also stated that the "fontanelle was not closed, the opening of the skull at this point being about one inch in diameter." Questioned later, at Commodore Curtis's trial for obstruction of justice, Dr. Mitchell testified: "It had an unclosed fontanelle. In other words, to make it clear to you, it is what is commonly known as the soft spot on the top of the child's head after birth, which usually closes within about the first year, but in this case the fontanelle was still open. I made a measurement of the fontanelle, which was larger than normally should be present in a twenty-month-old child."

Most of the writers I consulted at this time seemed to have skimmed over the autopsy report (when they mentioned it at all) and the police doubts about the identification of the corpse. They accepted without reservation the belief that the body uncovered in the shallow grave was that of the Lindbergh child. But Alan Hynd—again—had a contrary opinion. Hynd claimed in his article that "a major mystery" in the case was "how the identification could have been made so quickly and so positively . . ."

According to Hynd, Charles Lindbergh, Jr., had been examined by the family doctor, Philip Van Ingen of New York City, a couple of weeks before the kidnaping. Called to the morgue to help identify the corpse, Van Ingen took a long look at it and told the local coroner: "If someone were to come in here and offer me ten million dollars I simply wouldn't be able to identify these remains."

64

That from the last medical man to have examined the child before he was kidnaped.

Furthermore, Hynd wrote, Ellis Parker, sitting out the case because it was in an adjoining county and not within his jurisdiction, had been getting information from his friends in the state police. They told him it was rather curious that the body had not been discovered earlier because the very spot where it was found had been thoroughly searched at least two or three times by police, the Boy Scouts, and an army of local volunteers. The body had not been buried, had in fact been simply covered by leaves, and how it could have lain there avoiding discovery for more than two months was difficult to explain.

After considering these reports, Parker looked up weather records for the area because the thought occurred to him that the body had decomposed to a remarkable extent considering the cold weather which had prevailed in the seventy-two days between the kidnaping and discovery of the corpse. The official records showed the average temperature for March was only thirty-seven degrees, the average for April only forty-nine degrees, and the average for the twelve days in May that the corpse was presumed to have lain in the woods was fifty-five degrees. Moreover, the body was found on a site where the trees, even though bare of leaves in winter, shut off all sunlight; the temperature around the corpse would certainly have been several degrees lower than that shown in the weather records.

Parker brought his findings to several pathologists. They told him it would have been necessary for the temperature to have hovered around seventy degrees for many consecutive days to cause such extensive decomposition. Not one of the seventy-two days came close to that temperature; the average for the entire month of March was only five degrees above freezing, at which decomposition is completely arrested.

Parker deduced, according to Hynd, that Lindbergh and Betty Gow had been victims of a psychological trick. They had entered the morgue expecting to see the remains of the child and, even though they couldn't possibly recognize any features on the corpse, they positively identified the body. Parker was certain the body had been planted by bootleggers, who had dug it up somewhere and only partially buried it where it was found so that police, who had been disrupting the alcohol trade along the state's highways, would call off their search. And Parker refused to give much weight to Betty Gow's identification of the cloth found with the body.

Murray Bleefeld had been calling me every few days from his home in another state, to ask about the progress of my studies. About the time I was putting together all I could find on the strange circumstances surrounding the discovery of the body, Murray phoned once more. Had I, he asked, begun to investigate Paul Wendel? I hadn't yet gone that far into the Lindbergh story, I told him, but I did want to question him about something. Just give me a minute, I said, to hook my tape recorder into the phone.

"Did Ellis Parker ever talk to you about the body found in the woods?" I asked.

"Oh, sure, lots of times," Murray said. "Ellis told me it was a plant, it couldn't be the Lindbergh baby."

"Why not?"

"Because nothing matched up. The size was wrong, a lot of things were wrong, especially it was so far decomposed. Ellis said to me, 'You ever build a compost heap, Murray?' I told him I was a city boy, I didn't know about compost heaps. And he said, 'In a compost heap, even tiny leaves take more than three months to decompose and you're doing everything you can to make them decompose faster, you're adding manure and other stuff to make it break down as quickly as you can. And it still takes months. This body they want us to believe is the Lindbergh baby, it decomposed much too fast to have been out there for three months.' That's how he put it."

"You said he called it a plant; what was his theory?"

"It was no theory," Murray said. "Ellis Parker had a lot of friends in the bootlegging business, they were his contacts and sources of information to help him solve crimes. And those friends told him that a gang of bootleggers from New York that used to ship liquor from Philadelphia and Atlantic City along the back roads around there, those guys were always being stopped by cops looking for the Lindbergh baby. So they found a body that looked a little bit like the baby and dumped it in the woods where they were sure somebody was going to find it. That's what bootleggers told Parker."

"What else did Parker say about the body?" I asked.

66

"He said, during one of my talks with him, 'Planting a body was the only way they could get police to lay off their liquor trucks and get back to business as usual. Besides, Murray, would a kidnaper be so stupid as to return to Hopewell to drop off the body? Those woods were searched hundreds of times and no body was ever found. Now a body suddenly turns up where one didn't exist before.'

"And Parker also told me, he said, 'Murray, I'm willing to bet my last cent that Colonel Lindbergh and Betty Gow were told the baby's body was found and they went into the morgue *expecting* to see his body. They were fooled by a psychological trick. It's happened hundreds of times in identification of bodies and of living people accused of crimes; the eyes see what the mind wants it to see.'"

If Parker's opinions, as related by Murray and by Hynd, turned out to be correct, if the body in the woods wasn't that of the Lindbergh child, then technically Hauptmann should never have been convicted of murder because there was no proof the child was dead. No bloodstains in the nursery or on the ladder. None on the sleeping garment mailed to Condon. None on the chisel found under the nursery window. And if the child had not been murdered, he might possibly be still alive. I had read somewhere about a man in Connecticut who believed he was Lindbergh's kidnaped son, and I thought: *I really should try to find him. He may have information that could be helpful in my investigation.* But the more I thought about it the more fearful I became of being led into a maze from which there'd be no possible exit. It would be difficult enough to locate documents, after forty years had passed, that might prove a man was innocent of the crime for which he was convicted and executed. But to find the actual kidnaper, as Murray hoped to do? Or to find the victim, still alive? A line from Bob Dylan, and the feeling of despair in his voice as he sings it, kept floating through my mind: "Oh, Mama, can this really be the end . . ."

After the body was discovered and identified, Commodore Curtis stuck to his story about his contact with the kidnap gang until, according to some accounts, Captain John Lamb of the State Police led him to the basement of the Lindbergh home and beat the hell out of him. Curtis promptly confessed it had all been a hoax, dreamed up in an attempt to pull himself out of debt by eventually selling his story to the newspapers. In June, Curtis was brought to trial in the Flemington, New Jersey, courthouse, charged with obstructing justice in that "he was actually in contact with the kidnapers . . . and that he did not disclose their whereabouts," as the prosecutor expressed it.

After a trial of several days the county attorney successfully persuaded the jury that Curtis had been involved with the kidnapers, and he was convicted. It is perhaps the only kidnaping case in history in which the same victim was abducted by both a gang and a lone wolf (as Hauptmann would later be called) simultaneously, with neither party aware of the existence of the other. But that, as one writer put it, was part of the charm of the Lindbergh case. It was also another major flaw in what has been called the perfect criminal prosecution.

Investigators were still certain the kidnaping had been carried out with the help of one of the Lindbergh or Morrow servants. Their suspicions focused on Violet Sharpe, the maid in the Morrow home, when she changed her story about her activities on the day and evening of the kidnaping. She now remembered her date's name, she said: it was Ernie. He had taken her to a roadhouse, where they danced and had fun with the other couple, and her story about going to a movie had been a lie.

During a third round of questioning, Violet identified a police rogue's gallery photo as the man she had known as Ernie; investigators had traced him through the business cards they had found in her room, of the Post Road Taxi Company in White Plains, New York. The man was a petty thief, perhaps capable of kidnap and murder.

Wasn't it a fact, one investigator shouted at her, that Ernie had called her at one o'clock on the afternoon of the kidnaping? And wasn't it a fact she had talked to him less than two hours after learning the Lindbergh baby had a cold and would remain in Hopewell that night?

Violet admitted that was true and the investigators seemed pleased; she could have told Ernie about the baby in plenty of time for him to tell others in his kidnap gang. But Violet insisted she didn't know anything about Ernie and she grew hysterical. A doctor was called and he told police the questioning would have to end for the time being; Violet was near collapse.

The next morning, June tenth, a police official called the Morrow home and ordered Violet to get ready; a patrol car was on the way to take her to the state police barracks in Alpine for further questioning.

Violet slammed down the phone and cried to other members of the Morrow staff, "I won't go to Alpine. I won't! I won't!" She hurried to her room. A few minutes later she came down, tried to say something to a chambermaid she met on the stairs, and collapsed. The butler carried her to her room and put her on the bed. On her night table was a tin can labeled *"Poison. Cyanide Chloride, 73–76 percent."*

By the time a doctor arrived, Violet was dead. A suicide, the coroner declared. And State Police Chief Schwarzkopf announced to the press: "The suicide of Violet Sharpe strongly tends to confirm the suspicions of the investigating authorities concerning her guilty knowledge of the crime against Charles Lindbergh Junior."

Inspector Harry W. Walsh of the Jersey City police, who had been assisting the state police and who had conducted most of the questioning of Violet Sharpe, went even further. "The girl's suicide," he told reporters, "was an admission of guilt. An innocent girl would not kill herself."

There it is again, I thought as I read through the accounts of Violet's death. *Condon had heard the kidnaper speaking to a second man in the background, the man who had shouted "statto citti," and now police were saying that Violet had been involved in the crime. That certainly weakened the lone-wolf theory.*

4

I'd been reading and making notes about the Lindbergh crime for almost two weeks when I got another phone call from Murray.

"I'm in New York," he said. "Let's get together so I can tell you my story."

I told him I'd drive down from my home in Connecticut and meet him that evening. Murray seemed reluctant to have me come to his hotel room; he appeared to be afraid to reveal his whereabouts to anyone. After several phone calls we finally agreed to meet in an apartment on West Fifty-seventh Street. A friend had loaned the apartment to Stephanie Bennett, a young English literary agent who was visiting New York, and she persuaded him to let us use his place for the interview.

When Murray arrived I was surprised by his appearance. I had expected him to be one of those typically and melodramatically hard-looking Mafia types I'd met a number of times during my newspaper days, men like Joey Gallo and Johnny Dio, who modeled themselves after Richard Widmark. But Murray had more of the appearance of a show business accountant, or a garment center manufacturer wearing the next season's fashions.

He seemed diffident at first, and yet remarkably confident and youthfully excited about his story's commercial potential.

"This is going to be the biggest book to hit the public in years," he said after I introduced him to Stephanie. "And it's going to be a

71

great movie. I think Walter Matthau should play Ellis Parker. Great idea?"

"Let's not jump too far ahead," I said. "Let me hear your story about Wendel before we start talking Hollywood."

Stephanie was also surprised at Murray's appearance. (Because he has changed that appearance somewhat, at the urging of federal authorities, I won't describe him any further; Murray was obviously enjoying the games he could play with his new identity. "If I go on TV to promote this book I'll have to wear a mask, right?" he said.)

When Stephanie and I went into the kitchen to pour some of our friend's Scotch, she whispered: "He doesn't look like Mafia. He looks like a nice old man, like my grandfather did at his age. I'm disappointed. I expected Mafia. Murray looks too sweet to have been involved in anything illegal."

I agreed, but I felt something else about Murray's perfect haircut, careful tailoring, and gentle manners. "Maybe he's a con man. He looks perfect for the role," I said.

I was still skeptical about Murray's story as I set up my tape recorder on an end table next to the chair he was sitting in.

"Let's try to do this as chronologically as possible," I began, "because it'll help me understand your story. But first I have to jump to something out of time sequence. How did you meet Hauptmann?"

"Well, I've got to tell you this first," Murray said. "Ellis Parker swore me in as his deputy in the Wendel case—it wasn't the Hauptmann case to us, it was the Wendel case. The day after Ellis asked me to help him catch Wendel he took me to Trenton to meet Governor Hoffman. He'd told me about Hoffman, that Hoffman was his friend and Hoffman's father before him was his friend. And he watched the Governor grow up from a little pup, that's how he put it, and he said Hoffman is going to be the next President of the United States.

" 'Not because of this, Murray, this will help him,' he says, 'but this man is destined to become the next President.' As a matter of fact . . .''

"Wait a minute. Get to Hauptmann in the death house."

"I'm coming to that. But I've got to tell you first that Parker took me to the State House to meet the governor. I was introduced to Hoffman and Parker told him, 'This is the man I want to work with

Ellis, Jr., the man I want to be my deputy.' And he asked me to raise my right hand and I did and in front of the governor I was sworn in as Parker's deputy.

"Hoffman, Parker, and I talked, this is just a few months before Hauptmann is executed. We talk and Hoffman says he's going to visit Hauptmann and he wants Anna Bading there to take notes. She's Ellis Parker's secretary. They dressed her up like a man, you know, because only men are allowed into that prison. We went there with Mark Kimberling, the warden; he took all the guards off for secrecy. Kimberling was a trusted man of Hoffman and the Parkers, Hoffman had people in the administration he knew he could trust. Wilentz, on the other hand, had his own people. Wilentz, of course, wasn't as strong as Hoffman and Parker, but . . ."

"Wait," I interrupted again. "What was the governor's motive, visiting Hauptmann?"

"He said he's gonna tell Hauptmann that he's going to commute his sentence to life imprisonment if Hauptmann only tells him the part he plays in the kidnaping. Now, if you had a chance to save your life . . ."

"Were you there when he said this to Hauptmann?" I began to understand now that Murray was one of those interview subjects who have to be halted constantly, to make him stick to the main narrative. There's a danger in attempting to confine an interview within strict limits—the possible loss of that one unexpected comment or bit of information that causes everything to fall into place in your mind—but I had to risk it with Murray because his trip to New York was a brief one. I wanted the basic thread, for now; later, we could talk again and flesh it out.

"Yes, I was there," he replied. "First we talked about it in the governor's office, that he was going to make one last attempt to get Hauptmann to talk even though he knew Parker was absolutely certain of all the facts he had against Wendel and all the facts to show Hauptmann was innocent. The governor wanted to find out for himself, satisfy his own mind that Hauptmann had nothing to do with this thing.

"He said he was going to talk to Hauptmann, he was going to tell Hauptmann that as the governor of the state he would commute his sentence to life imprisonment if Hauptmann would tell him the part he played in this crime.

"Now if you were sitting in the death house waiting to be electrocuted and a guy came and said he could save your life—we're talking about the *governor* of the state—wouldn't you manufacture a story for him? Hauptmann didn't manufacture a story. He said, 'I told the truth,' in that heavy German guttural accent, and he dropped his head in his hands and cried like a baby . . ."

As Murray continued his narrative, my mind fastened on what he had just said. I had read many years before about Hauptmann's refusal to concoct any kind of story for Governor Hoffman, his refusal to invent a story about his role in the case even in return for $100,000 from the Hearst newspapers, although he knew his wife and child would have a hard time of it after he was executed. Hauptmann could have saved his life, could have received a near fortune, simply by creating a yarn for the governor and for the Hearst press. He could have named a friend of his—now dead—as the actual kidnaper and killer and assigned to himself a minor role; he could have, as Murray just said, manufactured a story. But he did not. If he was innocent, as he claimed right up to the moment of his execution, then in the last analysis he sacrificed himself for his private conception of dignity, right, and justice; he refused to save his life by demeaning the moral value of that life. That sacrifice, if indeed it was one, appeared to me rather heroic and I began to wonder at the kind of man Hauptmann had actually been.

". . . we went to his cell, he wasn't allowed out of his cell," Murray was saying. "The death house was locked, the cells were locked. Mark Kimberling has the keys, as the warden, he opens the cell and we go in. As a matter of fact Hauptmann was in a tier by himself, he was separated from the other death-house guys because he was called the baby-killer and the warden was afraid of what the other guys might do to Hauptmann.

"We went into the cell, a very small cell, about six by eight, with a cot, bowl, sink. Hauptmann wore just pants, shirt, and slippers. Hoffman went in with Parker. Bading and Kimberling and I stood at the entrance. Parker spoke to him, trying to get over to him, but the man didn't understand. You had to talk very slowly and point out everything you were saying. And he kept saying, '*Mein Gott, mein Gott*, I know nothing, nothing,' and then he'd rattle off into German.

"I understood him. He said he didn't know, *weis-nichts, weis-nichts* . . . this is the *samen*, the germ, seed, the truth—and he was telling the truth. This poor guy was. He knew nothing. Cried like a baby. Couldn't talk any more. Didn't want to talk.

"Hoffman said, 'There's nothing to say. This man is innocent. He knows nothing.' This Hoffman, he's going all the way to help, all the way."

"What I don't understand is why Hoffman didn't commute his sentence if he was so certain Hauptmann was innocent," I said.

"I didn't understand it either, back then," Murray replied. "But New Jersey had a crazy law on the books. In most states the governor has the right to pardon anybody he wants to pardon, or commute any death sentence to life. But not in New Jersey. Only the Court of Pardons could do that. Hoffman was a member of the court, but he was only one member out of maybe a dozen or so. That's why he couldn't act. And that's why he was moving so slow, being so careful—he had to get enough evidence that Hauptmann was innocent and Wendel guilty to convince most of the other members of the Pardons Court."

I asked Murray how he had met Parker and become involved in the Hauptmann case and he explained it had begun with the arrest of his elder brother, Jeff, who was convicted in Trenton on a "racketeering" charge in 1935, when Prohibition had been repealed but the rackets it had spawned had been put on a professional level by organized criminal groups that have always been lumped together carelessly as "the Mafia."

Jeff Bleefeld was secretary of a cleaners and dyers association in Trenton. With only about a dozen members, the relatively young organization was attempting to recruit new shopkeepers into its ranks. At the same time that Jeff was trying to persaude balky cleaners and dyers to join, a group of young hoodlums started offering "protection" to Trenton's dry cleaners.

"It was extortion," Murray said. "They damaged stores, wrecked trucks, put phosphorous compounds into clothes so the whole drum of clothes would turn to ashes and the dry cleaner would lose his customers—things like that. And my brother was arrested. For whatever reasons there were at the time, he was around to take the rap . . ."

"Just a minute," I said. "If we're going to work together you have to be absolutely straight with me. I don't want you to gloss over your brother's actions."

Murray looked hurt. "I'm not trying to whitewash him," he said.

75

"Jeff was really innocent. The plain truth is he had nothing to do with it. But they convicted him anyway because the newspapers just kept harping on rackets, rackets, rackets—you had Tom Dewey in New York, the rackets-buster, getting headlines, and every time somebody was arrested and called a racketeer he was dead because the newspapers convicted him. That's what happened to Jeff."

"What kind of evidence did they have against him?"

"Just the dry cleaners talking about Jeff's coming around trying to get them to join the association, and how it must have been his group because they were putting pressure on. The cops had a racketeer and they weren't going to be bothered with punk street kids when they had those kind of headlines."

Jeff's appeals from his conviction all failed, Murray went on, and he surrendered for imprisonment near the end of 1935. The morning after Jeff was locked into Trenton State Prison a friend of the Bleefelds, Jack Arbitell, a former bootlegger who was then New Jersey manager for the American Distilling Company and living in the Trenton area, called Murray at his home in Manhattan and asked him to come out to Trenton.

"I'm going to take you to see a friend of mine," Arbitell said. "He's got a lot of pull and I think he can do a whole lot to help Jeff."

That night, at around nine o'clock, Murray was sitting in the Elks Club in Mt. Holly with the chief of detectives of Burlington County, Ellis Parker.

"I told Parker the whole story about Jeff, from top to bottom," Murray said, "and Parker knew I was telling the truth. He knew there was a miscarriage of justice there. And he promised he'd help. He said he'd have Jeff transferred from Trenton State, the worst hole in the country, to the Bordentown Prison Farm. We talked for a long time about Jeff's case and then Parker told me I was to call him the next day.

"When I called him he says, 'Jeff will be at the Bordentown Farm this weekend, you can go and visit him.'

"I said, 'I don't know if I can make it until Friday but there's no visiting days on Friday.'

"He said, 'Don't worry about it, I'll arrange it.'

"And sure enough my brother was at Bordentown by Friday and I went there and was permitted to see him despite the fact there was no visiting on Fridays. Parker had given me the name of the superintendent and the man let me see Jeff."

"Did you ask Parker why he was doing this for you?"

"No," Murray said.

And Stephanie, who had been sitting quietly, appearing to be enthralled by Murray's story, said, "Perhaps he thought it was a miscarriage of justice."

"Right, yes," Murray said. "Now, I should tell you this to show you the kind of man Parker was. I didn't know it then, but Jack told me later how his own friendship with Parker had started. Jack was a bootlegger during Prohibition. One day he gets a call from some New York people who tell him that a truckload of their alcohol was hijacked in New Jersey. This was a common occurrence in those days. They asked Jack to start making inquiries to find out what happened or who did it. They told Jack the route the truck normally took, so Jack went along that road and he saw a truck parked on it and he went up to the truck. The driver was slumped over the wheel, dead; the hijackers had killed this guy and run and left the truck there.

"As soon as Jack looked into the truck, state troopers came out of the woods from everywhere and arrested Jack. They figured he was one of the hijackers, coming back to get the alcohol. Jack is out on bail and he goes to Ellis Parker, this is years before I met Parker, he tells Parker the story and Parker investigates. And he gets Jack cleared away of all charges and Jack becomes Parker's friend."

"This raises an obvious question," I said. "Was Parker a fixer?"

"No way. You couldn't buy him a cigarette. He was as straight as they come. To describe him, he wore a suit that looked like he wore it every day for a year. He was a roly-poly guy, fat and bald, and he swore like a trooper. I think he was about sixty-five when I met him. He smoked a corncob pipe that he never took out of his mouth except to eat.

"Ellis was quite a guy. Just as plain as day and just as straight as can be. He would use every kind of contact and influence he had if he believed in somebody or something. He had many friends. You couldn't buy him, not a cigarette, you couldn't put the fix in with Ellis. He would help you if he believed in you and he did help many people that I know. He even used to take them into his home in Mt. Holly and put them up.

77

"He died a poor man, he didn't have any money. He had a big family, maybe seven or eight kids that lived out of a dozen or so that were born. He lived in a big country farmhouse on Main Street, right across from his detective office. It might have been a mansion a hundred years before, maybe fifteen or sixteen rooms, but when I met him it was just an old house on the business street."

"Okay," I said. "Let's get back to the way you got into the Lindbergh investigation."

"Well, as I'm talking to Parker on the phone about visiting my brother, he says, 'When you get a chance I'd like you to come up here with Jack, I want to sit down and talk to you about something.' I told him I would and the following week Jack and I are in Parker's office.

"Parker tells me, 'Murray, in talking with you I recognize you're the kind of man that could be trusted. I'm on top of a situation that I want to bring to a close. I have very few people that I can trust. My son, Ellis, Jr., has been handling this with me. And of course Anna Bading, my secretary, knows all about this. And Clint Zeller, my chief deputy. Now I need help from you.'

"I asked, 'What kind of help?'

"He said, 'I want to make you my deputy.'

"I said, 'What does that mean?'

"He said, 'Well, I want you to meet Harold Hoffman.'

"I said, 'Governor Hoffman?'

"He said, 'That's right. Harold Hoffman knows everything that I'm doing on this case. I want to make you my deputy and I want you to work on this with my son. I want you, if you can, to get for me one or two people you can trust to work for you. Because this scene will take place in New York. There is a man that I've had under surveillance for some time now. He's living in New York and I'm going to apprehend him. I can't do it personally and I don't want my son to do it, because this man knows me and my son. I need someone else to apprehend him.'

"I said, 'Why does it have to be done that way?'

"And he said, 'That's the only way to do it because it's the only way this man is going to tell the truth to somebody. Not to us, not to me and my son. We've been watching him, we've been talking to him, we've been working with him or so he believes. But from the

78

little things he's told us from time to time we've pieced together the whole story. And we're certain this could be the only man that was involved in this crime.'

"I said, 'What's the crime?'

"He said, 'The Lindbergh case.' And then he tells me all about the Lindbergh case, how this man he wants to arrest was the real kidnaper and killer.''

"What was your reaction? And what did Parker tell you?''

"My hair was standing on end,'' Murray said. "Sitting in a man's office, just the second time I met him, and everybody in the world knew about the Lindbergh case—and he's telling me he wants me to be his deputy to help him arrest the killer of that baby. I thought it was the greatest thing that ever happened to me. I was a young man, twenty-seven, and I wanted to get involved in it. When I heard his story, the things he told me about his suspect, Paul Wendel, and the way he described them to me, I was just shocked dumb. A pleasant kind of shock, to think he was talking to me about helping him solve the crime that was considered the biggest thing in the world. When he told me that he knew the real kidnaper it became the biggest, *biggest* thing in the world, because a man goes to trial and gets convicted and that's supposed to be the end of it, but here somebody else comes along and says they have the wrong man. And it's Ellis Parker saying it, everybody knows Ellis Parker, the kids all knew of him. I wasn't a kid but I knew every case he ever worked on. And I'm sitting talking to *the* Ellis Parker, who's talking about the governor and talking about making me a deputy to apprehend the man who really committed this crime.''

"What did Parker tell you about Paul Wendel?'' I asked.

"That he, Parker, saw fit at one time right after the kidnaping to make a statement to the press that said that if the kidnaper would come forward and talk to him, then he would do all in his power to see that the kidnaper was not punished; all he wanted to accomplish was the safe return of that baby. Parker felt that this would draw out the kidnaper. And he got many letters, many calls, from all over the country. Anna Bading, his secretary, would take the calls and she'd push the buzzer and signal Parker to listen in on the more promising calls. And one of the calls they got was the voice of Paul H. Wendel, trying to disguise his voice.''

"How did he know it was Wendel?''

79

"Ellis told me that Paul H. Wendel in his opinion was one of the smartest men he ever encountered in all his detective career of forty years. He said, 'Murray, here's a man that I've known all his life. I knew his father before him, I've known Wendel since he was born.' Wendel at this time is maybe forty-three. And Parker tells me, 'This man, Murray, had a father who was a minister. As a young man Wendel studied for the ministry, but he never went into the ministry. He practiced pharmacy at one time. He also studied law and became a lawyer. But when he was in the pharmacy business this man perpetrated a holdup against himself to collect the insurance. Following that he became a lawyer. And as a young lawyer he embezzled clients' funds and was convicted for this and went to jail. I helped him get a parole and following his release I tried to get him reinstated with the Bar Association but I didn't succeed.'

"Wendel then was doing nothing, Parker said, he wasn't working at anything, but there came a time he was studying medicine. The man had a brilliant mind, Ellis told me, anything he studied he could absorb but he couldn't stick to anything without getting into trouble. But the things he had in his background were medicine, the law, the ministry, and pharmacy. This is Paul H. Wendel.

"Now there came a time just before the kidnaping when Paul Wendel began to issue worthless checks. They got warrants out for him and he ran to Parker and told Parker they were looking for him. Parker suggested that he go away someplace until this thing could be straightened out. So he went away, leaving his wife, daughter, and son behind in Trenton, and from time to time he would call Parker. And it was during this time that he called Parker in a disguised voice, replying to the story Parker put in the papers about getting the baby back.

"Wendel said he had friends who had the baby and he'd like to come in and talk to Parker and discuss what he knew. The conversation was that he wanted to talk to the man that put the story in the paper, he asked for Ellis Parker. Anna Bading said, 'Can he call you back?' and he said, 'Well, I want to talk to him and ask him about what he said in the newspaper about the baby . . .'

"And Anna flashed Parker and he picked up the extension and they both recognized Wendel's voice despite the disguise. The man said he would come in to talk to Parker. And there came a time that Wendel did come into the office. He didn't tell Parker and Bading that he was the man that made the call, he just came in and said that he knew people that had the baby . . ."

"Were the worthless checks cleared up by now?"

"No, they were never cleared up."

"Then Parker, in effect, was hiding a man wanted on worthless check charges?"

"Parker knew warrants were out for him because Wendel told him," Murray said. "And Parker knew that Wendel was being sought on those warrants. Parker wasn't hiding the man. He had no right to pick up the man and turn him over to authorities, his jurisdiction didn't permit that. Wendel was wanted in the next county and Parker could have called Mercer County authorities to come and get Wendel. But he didn't know when Wendel was coming into his office, to be able to alert anybody. And when Wendel comes in this time he's talking about knowing where the Lindbergh baby is, and that's more important to Parker and everybody else than bum checks."

"But Parker was also trying to help the son of an old friend," I said.

"Sure, yes. That was part of it. If he had a friend in trouble he'd go all the way to help the man.

"So Wendel came into the office and said, 'I have contact with people who have the baby and I'd like to go to work on this.' And he tells Parker he's staying at the Hotel Stanford in New York City, which is the first time that Parker knew where he could reach Wendel. All through the talk, Wendel is leading him on, about his friends who have the baby and how he, Wendel, wants to work for Parker to get the baby back. And Parker tells me that Wendel had the brains and the ability to do this job, that Wendel lived in Trenton on either Central or Clinton Avenue, I forget which, he lived there for many years. And Parker tells me that Wendel could get into his car at his house, start up the motor, and drive to Hopewell in seventeen minutes. When Wendel took the baby he was back in his home . . ."

"Hold it, you're running ahead again. Did Parker tell you why he suspected Wendel in the first place?"

"Sure, because when Wendel came into his office and said he knew the people that had the baby, he then indicated to Parker that he wanted to work with him on the case and Parker said to go ahead, Parker wanted to see where it would lead. And Wendel started to run and tried to show Parker that he was running on the case, investigating. But after a time it became clear he was doing nothing, just filling Parker with a lot of stories.

"But from time to time, as he was talking to Parker, he would say things that made Parker suspicious. He would tell Parker the baby was alive when it turned out later that maybe the baby was dead—Parker wasn't sure of the body, I told you that—but Wendel also told him that the kidnaper never came down the ladder but went out the front door of the house. He would tell him that the authorities are not smart because while they're all talking about the window being lifted with a chisel it was really lifted with a screwdriver. You see, Parker had friends on the state police and they told him the chisel wasn't used to open the window, the only marks on the window were made by a screwdriver. So Parker got all these bits of information—and a lot more—from Wendel during that time, and he got to suspecting him.

"But that wasn't all that made him suspicious. Wendel had told Parker, some time after his conviction as an embezzler, long before the kidnaping, what his attitude was on life and the world and people. He told Ellis that for all the things he had studied for in his lifetime, the things he had tried to do—becoming a lawyer, his father a minister, the pharmacy, and really wanting to go into medicine above all else—that nothing good ever happened to him because everybody was against him. This was his attitude always, when he talked about it to Parker.

"He said, 'The world has always mistreated me, Ellis, but one day I'll do something that will make the world sit up and take notice.' And he also said, 'I'd like to get my hands on fifty thousand dollars.' Remember, fifty thousand was a lot of money in those days. Parker was telling me all this the first day he asked me to work with him and he said Wendel was a hater. Parker said, 'Murray, this is a psychotic, a very brilliant man with a criminal twist to his mind.'

"And Wendel, with his sick mind, decided to kidnap the Lindbergh baby to get even with the world that was always against him. Because Lindbergh was an international hero and kidnaping his baby would make him more famous than Lindbergh without disclosing it was him that did it. Wendel selected this man Lindbergh and his baby as a way to get even with the world, that's what Parker figured after Wendel came to him with his story about knowing the kidnapers. Parker had the kind of mind that could put all the pieces together, from the things Wendel told him. All the things Wendel said and did led Parker to believe that there was nobody involved in the kidnaping except Paul H. Wendel. Nobody but him.''

"Did Parker say there was anything else that made him put these pieces together and come up with Wendel?" I asked. "Because it seems to me he didn't have that much to go on."

"Oh, he had a lot more than what I've told you. This is just the things about Wendel he was telling me that first night. And he also said, 'Murray, this is the type individual that I'm dealing with. Wendel wants to tell me the story in the worst way, he wants to tell it to somebody. That's the kind of man he is. He did something that he believes proves he is better than Lindbergh, the world's hero, and that makes Wendel a bigger hero. But he must tell somebody, he can't be a hero and not let somebody know, he can't be the man who planned the crime of the century and executed the plan and then remain silent about it. That's why he's let so many things slip, he wants me to know.'

"That's the reason Parker put it all together—Wendel gave him the clues. He wanted Ellis Parker to know about it."

"What did Parker say about Hauptmann's conviction?"

"He was telling me as much as he could about the case in a short evening, we sat there until two in the morning, but he kept saying, 'More important, Murray, is that time is getting short. A man is sitting in the death house about to be executed for a crime he's completely innocent of.' This is now late January or early February, 1936, it's just after the governor gave Hauptmann a thirty-day reprieve. Parker's telling me all he can to convince me he's got the right man, Wendel, but he's also telling me that we have to move fast and he doesn't have time to explain it all that night.

"He said, 'You'll meet Hauptmann so you can judge for yourself, but this man Hauptmann not only didn't know where Hopewell was, he couldn't spell it. He could no more do this thing . . . not only wasn't he capable of doing this thing but he didn't have the intelligence to do it.' "

"Parker thought Hauptmann wasn't very intelligent?"

"No, no," Murray said. "Intelligence is the wrong word. Illiterate is better. Parker was saying that on the one hand Wilentz contended only a criminal genius could have committed this crime, then on the other they take this illiterate, this man who is strictly illiterate in English, and he gets on the stand and tries to defend himself in his own dumb way and he doesn't even know what's taking place in an American courtroom and this man was convicted."

"What I'm most anxious to know is what Parker said very specifically about Hauptmann being innocent. Did he give you reasons based on evidence or on his logic?"

"Hundreds of reasons," Murray said, "I mean hundreds. The fact that his friends in the state police said a screwdriver was used to pry open the window and at the trial they lied and said a chisel was used and then they traced the chisel to Hauptmann's toolbox. Parker said the thing about the chisel was a complete fake, it wasn't Hauptmann's chisel and it had nothing to do with the crime.

"Another one was the ladder, with the piece of wood from Hauptmann's attic. Parker called that bullshit. He laughed at it, he said it was a farce and a frame-up."

"I haven't gotten that far in my research and my memory is hazy on the ladder," I said. "What wood from Hauptmann's attic?"

"At the trial the state police claimed they found that a floorboard from Hauptmann's attic had been cut in two and a piece taken away," Murray explained. "When the police matched the half that was still in the attic with one of the pieces of wood on the ladder, they claimed it fit perfectly—the ladder was traced right to Hauptmann's home. That's what Parker said was bullshit.

"Parker said, 'Now, Murray, you're the kidnaper of this baby. You're the master criminal of this century, you plan the crime of the century and you execute it. If you're such a genius do you take a piece of wood from your own attic to make a ladder and then leave it behind as a clue? Never. Especially not if you're Hauptmann, who has all kinds of lumber in his garage and his cellar. That wood from the attic is a fake. By no stretch of the imagination does it match any wood in the ladder. It was contrived evidence, I know that from my friends in the state police. It's bullshit.' "

"I hope I can find proof of that," I said. "As I remember it, the ladder was the crucial evidence against Hauptmann."

"You'll find it," Murray said. He glanced at his watch. "I'll get to the heart of the story next session," he said. "I have to stop now, my wife's waiting for me in the hotel room and she's probably worried by now. Tomorrow night okay?"

"Can you make it tomorrow afternoon? I can stay over with a friend."

Murray said he had a grand jury appearance, another Mafia case on which he had some information, and we agreed to meet the next evening. Riding down in the elevator I asked him about something that had been bothering me for some time: "Why are you telling this story now, after all these years?"

"My children," Murray said. "They're grown now and they're old enough to handle the fact that their father has been in prison and they'll be able to handle any sort of publicity this story could bring. I was waiting for them to grow up. Protecting them, I guess. But I'm sixty-five and if I'm ever going to tell it, I have to tell it now."

5

The next day I continued my readings in the Lindbergh materials and continued making notes toward my investigation. And it immediately became clear that most of the writers had omitted some pertinent information about the police attitude toward John Condon, the Jafsie of the newspaper ads—an omission, I suspected, that was part of a design to build such an overwhelming case against Hauptmann that the public would have no doubt he was as guilty as the police claimed.

Following the discovery of the body identified as Lindbergh's son, and the suicide of Violet Sharpe, the police investigation appeared to bog down. At the same time the newspapers severely criticized the police for their stupidity and for causing Violet's death. Condon, however, appeared to be above all criticism. He became quite active, giving interviews, posing for photographs, and racing around to several cities on the East Coast where various suspects were held on the vaguest suspicion. In all such cases, Condon said flatly that the suspect bore no resemblance at all to the man who had taken the ransom money.

What was not reported by any writer—not even later writers who must have read it in Condon's own book about the case—is that he was suspected of being part of the kidnap-extortion gang. A few days after Violet Sharpe's death, Condon was lured from his home in the Bronx to New Jersey, on the pretext that he was to look through rogue's gallery photos in still another attempt to identify John. But once the state troopers got him on the other side of the Hudson, they told him their orders were to take him to headquarters at Alpine—the threat of which had caused Violet to swallow poison.

On their arrival, Condon was placed in a room with a number of troopers, none of whom even smiled at him although most knew him, and he was made to stand for about fifteen minutes. Inspector Harry Walsh, who had questioned Violet Sharpe before her death, came into the room. He walked up to Condon, folded his arms in front of his chest, and shouted:

"All right, Condon, it's about time you confessed!"

Condon wrote that Walsh threatened to beat him, did attempt to trick him into statements that could be damaging, and asked him dozens of questions about his negotiations with John. And after every few questions Walsh would demand to know what Condon had done with his share of the ransom money.

After an hour of this, Walsh insisted that Condon accompany him on a little walk, to continue the questioning in the bright June sun. And Condon wondered, he wrote, whether Walsh would beat him as police beat a confession out of Curtis, or whether he had another inquisitorial technique in mind. The inspector led Condon to the edge of the Palisades, with its sheer drop of 700 feet to the Hudson. He forced Condon to walk at the very rim of the cliff. Rather than becoming frightened, Condon wrote, he stepped closer to the edge "that I might obtain a better view of the beautiful river beneath us." Walsh, quite upset, pulled Condon back and the questioning ended.

Over the following weeks, police dug up the grounds around Condon's summer cabin on City Island, searching for the ransom money. Not finding it there, they ransacked his house, tearing out new wallpaper in his study because they were certain Condon had redecorated in order to cover over hidden panels. They tapped his telephone, Condon was certain, and they intercepted all his outgoing mail; Condon said he had proof of that because he carried his mail to a drugstore substation near his home, but when it was finally delivered it bore the downtown Manhattan postmark of the City Hall station.

Police suspected Condon from the moment the ransom was paid until the trial of Hauptmann. Then, suddenly, Condon was transformed into a patriot and a hero who had done his best to recover the stolen child but had been thwarted by a cunning fiend. (Those words, or variations upon them, were repeatedly used by contemporary writers.)

While some investigators were attempting to find evidence against Condon, others were concentrating on the ransom bills in hopes that some bank teller or store clerk would spot the serial number of a kidnap bill quickly enough for the police to seize the passer; the Treasury Department had sent to banks, brokers, and other merchants dealing in large sums of money a list of every one of the bills that had made up the $50,000 ransom.

The first ransom bill to be spotted, on April 11, a little more than a week after the money was paid, had been briefly handled by a woman who owned a pastry shop in Greenwich, Connecticut. She told police that she was about to close up her shop when a green Packard town car, chauffeur-driven, pulled up outside. A smartly dressed woman, dark-complexioned and in her forties, stepped out of the car and came into the shop. She asked for a loaf of bread and a strawberry pie and offered a twenty-dollar bill. The owner glanced at a list of Lindbergh ransom bills pasted to the side of the register and realized she held one of them in her hand.

"This bill is part of the Lindbergh money," she said. The customer grabbed the bill and dashed from the shop. Her chauffeur drove her away quickly.

For police, that information came to a dead end, as did other reports of the discovery of ransom bills. Some detectives felt the bakery owner was a publicity seeker. But it became clear the extortionists were being very cautious, for bills that did turn up were passed one at a time by customers who were so unobtrusive that no bank teller or shopkeeper ever remembered the passer. As time went by, clerks handling money paid less and less attention to the ransom bill list. The result was that only a trickle of Lindbergh money was showing up here and there in the New York area and adjoining states, apparently long after it had originally been put into circulation by the extortionist.

On April 5, 1933, a year after the kidnaping, President Franklin D. Roosevelt exercised the emergency powers given him by the Banking Relief Act and ordered all persons possessing gold (including bills) valued at more than $100 to exchange it at banks for non-gold currency. The deadline was May 1; the penalty for hoarding gold was a $10,000 fine or ten years' imprisonment or both.

Lindbergh investigators were jubilant. They were certain that now, after so many disappointments, they would at last find John. It would be extremely dangerous for John to defy the gold ban and hold onto the Lindbergh gold notes, police reasoned, because if he tried to pass them after the deadline their very appearance would raise suspicion. Therefore, John most certainly would turn in his notes before the deadline, police believed. And, with luck, he'd be caught.

More than half the ransom money was in gold notes. Treasury agents working on the Lindbergh case quickly made up a new list of ransom bills—gold notes only—and delivered it to officials and cashiers of the Federal Reserve Bank of New York and affiliated banks in the city, with personal pleas to be alert for Lindbergh gold notes.

No ransom bills were spotted between the announcement of the gold ban and the deadline for converting gold to currency. And on May 1, the deadline date, there was such a last-minute rush of people exchanging gold bullion, coins, and bills at banks that tellers didn't have time to examine serial numbers. No one noticed a man who walked into the Federal Reserve Bank and exchanged $2,980 in gold certificates that was part of the ransom payment.

That exchange was discovered during an examination of the records the next day and police were called. On the exchange slip that was required to be filled out was written: J. J. Faulkner, 537 West 149th Street, New York City. The handwriting on the slip, while not a large enough sample to make an absolute judgment, bore a resemblance to that on the ransom notes, Justice Department handwriting experts said.

Police and federal agents went to the address on the slip, which was a small apartment house. No J. J. Faulkner lived there and none of the tenants remembered anyone by that name. Police records disclosed that an automobile stolen from Lakehurst, New Jersey, about forty miles from Lindbergh's home, only a few days before the kidnaping, had been discovered across the street from that apartment house.

Investigators were certain they were drawing close to the kidnapers and they began sifting through old telephone books and city directories in an attempt to locate any Faulkner who lived around West 149th Street at any time in the past. They found listed in a

1913 directory a Miss Jane Faulkner, whose address had been that given on the deposit slip.

Jane Faulkner was traced through marriage license records. They disclosed she had married a German immigrant, Carl O. Geissler, part owner of a Madison Avenue florist shop, in 1921. They were now living in Larchmont, a few miles north of the Bronx. Police and federal agents conducted a discreet inquiry in Larchmont and learned that Jane Faulkner Geissler was living in a house with her husband, her sister, and her sister's husband, Alvin Weigner.

The handwriting of all four was compared to the Faulkner bank slip by handwriting experts who, it was said, disagreed as to whether any of them had filled out the slip. The police continued to investigate. They learned that Geissler had two grown children from a previous marriage. The son, Carl D. Geissler, became a suspect along with his father because he customarily did business in a store in which one of the ransom bills had been passed. But that was as far as the police investigation went, according to published accounts; the police could find no evidence linking these four people to the kidnaping or the ransom money.

Could it have been as simple as that? I wondered. If the statements made by some writers were true, that police and Justice Department handwriting experts had disagreed about whether any of the four had signed the Faulkner name and address, it could only mean that at least one of those handwriting analysts had given a positive decision. And if that was so, then police must have kept the Geissler family under surveillance and investigated them much more thoroughly than appeared in my research materials.

I made a note to explore the Geissler connection to the case in greater depth than had been done by Alan Hynd in his magazine article and by the only other writer to discuss the Geisslers in depth, George Waller, author of *Kidnap*, a history of the case published in 1961 which became a best seller. While Hynd claimed that a relative of Geissler committed suicide after being questioned repeatedly by police, Waller never mentioned that fact. Instead, Waller completely cleared the Geissler family and their relatives and friends. Stressing that the elder Geissler was "unimpeachably respectable," Waller went on to say that Geissler "was able to prove that neither he nor Mrs. Geissler . . . had any connection

with the $2,980 exchange slip or the kidnap-murder of the Lind-
bergh baby.''

Waller's conclusion troubled me greatly. Although he claimed to
have spent twenty-five years on his book, which was thoroughly
researched and was almost a moment-by-moment account of the
case, I sensed that Waller had consulted only official sources and
had swallowed their accounts whole. He had made no attempt to
fully investigate the discrepancies he must have seen. His sources
appeared to have been primarily the book written by Condon,
newspaper articles of the day, and the trial transcript. None of
those sources is completely satisfactory. Condon was protecting
his reputation. The newspapers were, as is normal in police matters, publishing statements made by investigators, relying on police
and prosecutors for their information. The trial transcript is the
least reliable of all; rules of evidence are so restrictive (and police
and prosecutors so desirous of hiding evidence that might aid the
defense) that too often the most vital evidence is not produced at
trial.

In any case, I went back to my research in the books that I was
now certain represented no more than the official wisdom I had so
long suspected as a newspaper journalist. That wisdom had it that
police, after deciding the Geissler family had no connection with
the kidnaping or extortion, spent the following year attempting to
construct a portrait of the kidnaper by questioning all bank tellers
and shopkeepers who had received ransom notes.

In the office of New York City Police Lieutenant James J. Finn,
file cabinets of interviews with those who had accepted ransom
bills were beginning to get filled. Pins stuck in a map to show the
spot where each bill was cashed began to form a pattern: the passer
seemed to be operating on the perimeter of a circular area in the
Bronx where not a single bill had shown up. Police theorized that
the passer lived in the center of this circle and was taking the precaution of not passing any of the gold notes in his own neighborhood, where he might be recognized.

Slowly, a portrait of the passer began to emerge from descriptions given by everyone who had reported finding a ransom note.
Most tellers and store clerks who could remember the man described him as about forty years old, with a German accent. He
was six feet tall, had a long thin face and light hair and complexion.
To a large degree, the description matched that of John.

John seemed to have a strange idiosyncrasy. Every bill he passed was folded in half along its entire length, then doubled over twice; when unfolded, it showed a pattern of creases dividing it into eight rectangles. Those who had remembered John said that he always took one of the folded bills from a pocket and tossed it onto the counter so the clerk or cashier would have to unfold it to determine its denomination.

The bills were subjected to a chemical analysis, revealing some further information about the passer. Many of the bills bore a touch of emery dust in oil, suggesting that John was a carpenter or machinist who ground his own tools. A carpenter, of course, police reasoned; the man who built the kidnap ladder.

By the end of 1933 police were beginning to hope that John was growing careless, because he seemed to be calling more attention to himself than he had in the past with his weird folding of the ransom notes. On the night of November 26 of that year, a very cold night, Mrs. Cecile M. Barr was sitting inside her ticket booth at the Loew's Sheridan Square Theater in Greenwich Village, counting the night's receipts. It was nine-thirty and the last show had just begun.

Suddenly a tightly folded bill was thrown on the counter in front of her. Quite rudely, Mrs. Barr thought. She looked up, annoyed, and stared at her customer as she started to unfold the bill. She later told police he was in his middle thirties, medium height and weight, with blue eyes and the triangular face that was now so familiar in each detail: high cheekbones, flat cheeks, and a pointed chin. She would never forget that face, she told Lieutenant Finn when he interviewed her the next day; the man had seemed almost contemptuous of her. And oh, yes, there was one other thing—the man wore no topcoat even though it was very cold, just a dark suit.

In the first weeks of 1934 the flow of ransom bills slowed considerably and then almost stopped completely. John appeared to be growing cautious. More than four hundred bills, mostly five-dollar notes, had been recovered so far and police were hoping John would begin passing the more conspicuous ten- and twenty-dollar gold notes. Now, however, police began to fear John might have died or have decided to stop using the ransom bills until he felt safe once more.

The drought of bills continued for many months. Then, in early September, reports of Lindbergh ransom money began to come in again, even more frequently than before. On the fifth, Lieutenant Finn was notified by the National Bank of Yorkville that a ten-dollar gold note on the ransom list had been included in a deposit made by a Third Avenue grocery store. The store owner, questioned by Finn, remembered his customer very clearly because he had offered the ten-dollar bill in payment for a six-cent purchase. The owner had argued with the customer, practically cursed him out.

The description he gave matched John in every detail.

Over the next week the same man passed almost a dozen ten- and twenty-dollar gold certificates in Yorkville and in the Bronx. The pins on the ransom map began to grow.

On Tuesday, September 18, Lieutenant Finn received a call from the head teller of the Corn Exchange Bank branch at Park Avenue and 125th Street; a ten-dollar gold certificate with a ransom list serial number had just been discovered. Finn, accompanied by a federal agent and a New Jersey state police detective, went to the bank and examined the bill. It was indeed a ransom note. Finn turned it over. On a margin there was a penciled notation: "4U-13-41, N.Y."

Quite obviously, it was a license plate number. Finn reasoned that it had been written down by a filling station attendant, because all gas stations had been given the ransom list and had been asked to jot down the license plate number of all customers tendering a gold note. The nearest filling station, Finn was told, was a block away.

Investigators drove there and showed the bill to Walter Lyle, manager of the station. Lyle said he remembered jotting down the number the previous Saturday and he clearly remembered the customer who had given him the gold certificate. Lyle said he had objected to accepting the note and the customer said, "They're all right. Any bank will take them."

"You don't see many of them anymore," Lyle said.

"No," the customer agreed. "I have only about a hundred left."

Once more the ransom-passer was calling attention to himself. I was finding it difficult to believe that the man who had extorted $50,000 from Lindbergh, in what seemed to be a carefully planned and daringly executed crime, would be stupid enough to boast about his hoard of gold certificates.

Whether Finn and the other officers considered such subtleties is

94

not recorded. Perhaps they were too excited to do so, for they immediately telephoned the Motor Vehicle Bureau to trace the license plate number and were told it was registered to a Richard Hauptmann, of 1279 East 222nd Street, in the Bronx. Finn later said he knew, the moment he was told the address, that Hauptmann lived in the center of the small area on his map that was surrounded by pins. The other information on Hauptmann's license applications showed that he was thirty-four, had blue eyes and blond hair, and was in other physical details very close to the description of the bill-passer given by the grocery store owner and also matched Condon's description of John. And his license application revealed that Hauptmann was a carpenter—perhaps the man who built the kidnap ladder!

Late that afternoon, a dozen carloads of police and federal agents converged on the streets and in the woods around Hauptmann's home, maintaining a close watch on the small two-story structure and the garage at the rear, keeping it under surveillance from all sides. The police sat there through the night without seeing Hauptmann; they had decided not to question him at home because they hoped to catch him in the act of passing a ransom bill.

By dawn, six police officers in three cars were still at the house, waiting for Hauptmann to emerge. He did so at five minutes to nine. From a half block away, Finn watched the man through field glasses: long legs, medium height and weight, a triangular face that Finn later said made him know instantly that this was John. The man, Hauptmann, walked to the garage, unlocked the padlock, and opened the double doors. Moments later a dark-blue four-door Dodge sedan backed out. Finn searched for the license number: 4U-13-41. There could be no doubt now.

After relocking the garage doors, Hauptmann began to drive south, toward Manhattan. He drove slowly and cautiously and did not appear to suspect that three police cruisers were strung out behind him. The procession traveled for about fifty blocks. Then, as Hauptmann was forced to a near halt behind a city sprinkler truck, the lead police car shot forward and veered in front of the Dodge to cut it off; the police had begun to fear they would lose Hauptmann in the growing traffic and decided to arrest him immediately.

Drawing their guns, police leaped from their cars. One of them, Sergeant John Wallace of the New Jersey state police, slid into the Dodge's passenger seat and pressed his gun against Hauptmann's chest. Hauptmann glanced quickly, startled, toward the intruder, then turned away, a blankness over his face, and edged his car to the curb. Finn opened the driver's door. Assisted by other officers, he pulled Hauptmann out, led him to the sidewalk, and snapped handcuffs on his wrists.

"What is this?" Hauptmann said, speaking for the first time. "What is this all about?" He had a very strong German accent and Finn later remembered smiling—*This is John,* he thought. Hauptmann's questions went unanswered. His captors searched him for weapons. They found none. They then searched him more thoroughly, pulling from his hip pocket a wallet that contained twenty-nine dollars, including a twenty-dollar gold certificate. Justice Department Agent William Seery turned away from Hauptmann with the bill so that the prisoner could not see it was being checked against the Lindbergh ransom list. Seery turned back, facing the other officers. He nodded. The bill matched.

A question flashed into my mind as I read through the several accounts of Hauptmann's arrest. *Was that bill folded?* Great emphasis had been placed on the fact that the bill-passer had been folding the ransom bills into a tight wad that could fit into his pocket. In fact, at the urging of a Hearst reporter, Detective Lieutenant Finn had consulted a young New York psychiatrist, Dr. Dudley Shoenfeld, and asked him to etch a psychiatric portrait of the Lindbergh kidnaper-extortionist.

The psychiatrist told the detective that he was certain the Lindbergh child had been kidnaped by a lone man, not a gang of professional criminals, and that the kidnaper was impelled by acute psychic drives. The kidnaper saw Lindbergh as all-powerful, the world's hero, Shoenfeld said. The kidnaper himself felt inferior, was in actuality very inferior to Lindbergh, but believed that he was omnipotent and that Lindbergh was a rival who had so completely monopolized the world's attention that the world could not understand that the kidnaper was the greater man.

And so, acting out his fantasies, gratifying his need to demonstrate that Lindbergh wasn't as strong as believed and his need to attack Lindbergh, the kidnaper attacked the father's virility by stealing the child. The killing of young Lindbergh, which Shoenfeld claimed to have predicted, was no surprise: "For if the crime were governed by unconscious drives, these forces would be gratified only by the death of the child," Shoenfeld later wrote.

But more important to me at this time, as I read all I could find about Hauptmann's arrest, was something else that Shoenfeld had told Lieutenant Finn. When he was finally arrested, the doctor had predicted, police would find in John's pocket at least one ransom bill, which he would carry as a reminder of his omnipotence, and that bill would be folded; tightly folding the bill was a subconscious manifestation of John's personality—methodical, extremely cautious, inner-directed, and probably struggling to hold back his homosexual tendencies(!).

The ransom bills that had been passed in 1933 and early 1934 had indeed been folded. But the bill recovered when Hauptmann was arrested was in his wallet, laid out flat in the bill pocket. The bill he passed at the gas station, which had led to his arrest, had not been folded. The bill he passed in the grocery store two weeks before his arrest, which had provoked an argument with the owner, had not been folded. And as I read quickly on, I learned that Hauptmann had passed still another ransom bill, in a Bronx shoe store one week before his arrest; that bill had not been folded.

While following this tangential lead, this search for information about the compulsively folded bills (as the psychiatrist had called them), I was driven off on an even further side trip by a paragraph in George Waller's *Kidnap*. What Waller had written was farther down the road than I'd reached in my chronology, but I made notes anyway and thought about it for hours.

By now, in Waller's chronicle, Hauptmann had finally been told he was under arrest as a suspect in the Lindbergh crime and he had attempted to explain how he'd come into possession of Lindbergh ransom money: a shoe box full of it had been given Hauptmann for safekeeping in December 1933 by a friend who had gone back to Germany to visit his family; the friend had died there and when Hauptmann discovered the box contained money he'd begun to spend it for household expenses because the friend had owed him several thousand dollars. What lured me into this tangent forking off another tangent were two sentences in Waller's text. They came at the end of a long recitation about the witnesses who would be asked by police to attend a lineup and try to identify Hauptmann. The witnesses were vital, Waller wrote, for possession of ransom money was not nearly enough to convict Hauptmann of kidnaping or extortion, or both; witnesses must place Hauptmann in the vicinity of Lindbergh's home on the day of the kidnaping or in the cemeteries during the negotiations, to construct an unassailable case against him. After listing the possible witnesses, Waller had written:

> Of equal importance now was an East Side storekeeper who had been given one of the ten-dollar gold certificates as far back as March 1, 1933; he might prove that Hauptmann was lying when he said that the . . . gold notes had been turned over to him . . . in *December* of '33. The storekeeper had told detectives that he'd remember his customer if he saw him again.

Waller did not name the East Side storekeeper, nor did he give any details of the transaction in which the ransom bill was passed. Checking through several books which provided a complete list of witnesses at Hauptmann's trial and a brief summary of their testimony, I realized that that "East Side storekeeper" had not testified.

He could not identify Hauptmann, I thought. I was certain of that. If he had been able to identify Hauptmann, the prosecutor would certainly have put him on the witness stand to destroy Hauptmann's main defense, that he did not begin passing the ransom bills until the summer of 1934, following the death of the friend who'd given him the box of gold notes. The only possible reason that witness was not called is because he had been unable to positively identify Hauptmann or, perhaps, had even said that Hauptmann was most definitely not the man who had passed him the Lindbergh gold note.

As I filtered my suspicions through my mind the other piece that had almost screamed out at me fell into place—the folded bills. According to Waller and other writers, *all* the ransom bills that had been passed between the date of the payment to John by Dr. Condon and the summer of 1934, when Hauptmann claimed he had discovered his friend's cache of gold notes, every single one of those bills without exception had been folded in that peculiar, mathematically precise manner that had so annoyed the Greenwich Village theater cashier and many others. But none of the bills that Hauptmann was very definitively known to have spent, and which he later admitted spending, was so folded.

My mind leaped to the obvious conclusion—Hauptmann had been telling the truth. Immediately I pulled back: at the very most, the flimsy evidence I'd discovered pointed to the thin possibility that Hauptmann only stumbled upon the money a month or so before his arrest. I would need much firmer proof than a deduction based on secondary sources; I would have to find documents to sustain that conclusion so hastily arrived at. I forced it from my mind for now, because of the need to continue my reading. But the feeling had begun to grow on me that I would find many more holes in the fabric of the case against Hauptmann.

I picked up the thread of the narrative where Hauptmann was standing in handcuffs next to his car, in the Fordham section of the Bronx. Police began to question him about the gold note. Fast questions, insistent.

"Where did you get this gold certificate?" one officer demanded. And another, before Hauptmann could reply: "How long have you had it?" And another: "Do you have any more?"

Hauptmann waited until the questions ceased. He then replied that he had made a habit of collecting gold notes for the past two years. He was afraid of inflation, he'd seen inflation in Germany make paper money valueless and he didn't want to go through that again. Every time he was offered a gold note in transactions at banks, shops, or brokerage houses, he'd accepted it. At one time he'd collected about three hundred dollars' worth but he'd been spending them after deciding his fears had been groundless. This one, taken from his wallet, was the last one he had left.

"Why did you tell the man in the gas station you had about a hundred left?" Lieutenant Finn asked.

Well, Hauptmann said, he wasn't really telling the truth just now. He did have about a hundred left. They were at his house, in a tin box.

Nothing was said about the Lindbergh case. As I read the questions Hauptmann was asked, and his answers, it became rather obvious that he believed police and federal agents had arrested him as a gold hoarder. That he had begun the first in a series of lies because he was afraid he would be charged with a federal offense.

After phoning Inspector John Lyons and waiting in the street for more than an hour so that he could join them and share credit in the arrest, police drove Hauptmann to his apartment. There he showed

Finn the tin box with his gold hoard—six twenty-dollar gold coins.

"Where are the gold certificates?" Finn asked. "Like the one in your wallet?"

Hauptmann said he had no gold certificates, he had been talking about these coins all the time. He didn't know what Finn meant.

One of the police officers gave Hauptmann a sudden push and he sat down heavily on his bed. The questions came fast again. Where are the gold notes? How did you get hold of them? Isn't it true you extorted them from Charles Lindbergh? You are the kidnaper!

"What are you saying?" Hauptmann replied. "I know nothing about ransom money."

Other investigators in the meantime were tearing Hauptmann's five-room apartment apart, searching for evidence. Drawers were opened and the contents scattered on the floor; the nursery of the Hauptmann child, eleven-month-old Manfred, was ransacked, clothes and toys piled in the center of the floor, the child's mattress torn open, the rocking chair, high chair, and playpen that Hauptmann had made for his son toppled over and thrown aside.

Downstairs, in the backyard, Anna Hauptmann sat on the grass with her son, both enjoying the warm autumn sun. A man walked into the yard from the back, from the area of the garage. Anna picked up her son and held him to her as the man approached.

"What is your name?" the man asked.

"I am Mrs. Hauptmann," she said.

The man flashed a detective's badge. "Come upstairs," he said. "The police want to ask you some questions."

On the way up, Mrs. Hauptmann saw the tenant who lived in the ground floor rear apartment peering from her window. Manfred was left with the woman, and Mrs. Hauptmann followed the detective upstairs.

She cried when she saw the shambles her apartment was in, strange men almost tearing down walls, viciously (she felt) throwing her possessions onto the floor. The detective took her into the bedroom. She saw Richard sitting on the bed in handcuffs, and ran to him.

"Richard, what is this?" she cried. He didn't answer. "Richard, did you do anything wrong?"

"No, Anna," he said.

"Tell me if you did anything wrong!" she almost shouted.

Inspector Lyons ordered her out. The detective who had brought her up now led her downstairs again, past the ravaged nursery, living room, and kitchen.

The questioning and the search continued. A Justice Department agent pushed a new pair of women's shoes in Hauptmann's face: Didn't you buy these shoes with a twenty-dollar gold certificate? Hauptmann admitted he had, about ten days earlier. Two gold notes were thrust toward Hauptmann: Didn't you give these notes to Mrs. Rauch, the landlady, as part of your rent payment? Hauptmann admitted doing so. Then how could he explain the fact that these notes, and other notes connected with him, were part of the Lindbergh ransom money?

Hauptmann explained again that he had collected the gold notes in various places: maybe the bank tellers and shopkeepers could explain how they came by the gold notes.

The search of Hauptmann's apartment and the attic above, reached through a small opening in the ceiling of a closet, turned up several interesting items—a box of more than a hundred Hudson sealskins, which Hauptmann explained by saying he had been speculating in furs with a friend for about two years; seventeen memorandum books with notations in German and English, apparently an account of Hauptmann's trading in furs and in the stock market; and a pair of expensive German field glasses, which police believed Hauptmann might have used to spy on the Lindbergh home while he was plotting the kidnaping.

But they could not find the ransom box into which Lindbergh had forced the bundles of ransom money; they could not find any other gold notes secreted in Hauptmann's apartment. The search of the bedroom continued, Hauptmann watching indifferently as police sliced open his mattress and pulled out the stuffing, then shoved him back onto the bed. Special agent Thomas Sisk was in the closet, tapping the woodwork and plaster to find a hidden safe, watching Hauptmann to check his reaction. There was none. Hauptmann didn't seem to be concerned at the destruction of his home.

Occasionally, however, when he thought no one was watching him, Hauptmann raised himself slightly off the bed and peered out the window. Sisk saw him do this several times. He left the closet and walked to the window. All that he could see of possible interest was the small frame garage about fifty feet away.

"Is that where you hid the money?" Sisk asked.

101

"I have no money," Hauptmann said.

Sisk alerted Inspector Lyons and the senior New Jersey trooper present, told them he suspected the ransom money was hidden in the garage. The three went outside, broke the lock on the garage door, and began to look around. The garage floor was made of heavy planks and two of them tilted under Sisk's feet. He pried the planks up with a crowbar. The soil underneath appeared to have been dug up recently. Sisk spaded into it, digging for ten or twelve inches until he struck metal. He dug it out: a heavy metal jar. The officers pried off the lid. A few inches of water lay in the bottom; nothing more.

Hauptmann was led out of his apartment at about twelve-thirty, shoved into a police car, and driven to the Greenwich Street police station in Manhattan. Police took him to this out-of-the-way precinct house, rather than to headquarters, to keep the news of a break in the Lindbergh case from reporters. They began to question him in a windowless room, dozens of police officers and federal agents demanding to know where he had hidden the $45,000 in ransom money still missing, accusing him now of kidnaping and murder as well as extortion. "Why did you kill that baby?" one officer shouted, and others asked the same question in a variety of ways: "Why did you leave the body in the woods?" "Did the baby die when the ladder broke?" "Why lie? Tell us who helped you steal the baby."

Lieutenant Finn left the interrogation room after a little while and went into the detective commander's office. He phoned Dr. Shoenfeld, the psychiatrist who had constructed a psycho-profile of the kidnaper. "This man fits into your picture," Finn said. Shoenfeld asked for details and Finn told him all that he knew of Hauptmann, everything that confirmed Shoenfeld's theories. Finn was elated at the capture, Shoenfeld later wrote, and the detective told the psychiatrist: "This is the parting of the ways. You're a doctor and you're interested in saving a man. I'm a cop and I'm interested in hanging him."

The questioning went on. Where were you on March 1, 1932? A Tuesday? Hauptmann asked. The police did not pounce on that, on how he could remember the date was a Tuesday: because for years afterward almost everyone in the United States remembered exactly where he was when he first heard the news of the Lindbergh kidnaping.

Well, Hauptmann said in his difficult-to-understand accent, he knew that on that date, March 1, he had been working on the construction of an apartment house, the Majestic, at Central Park West and Seventy-second Street. He'd started work at eight. But first he had driven his wife to Fredericksen's bakery and lunchroom on Dyer Avenue, about a mile from their home. Anna, he explained, was working there as a waitress. He then drove back home, put the car in the garage—he had built it himself more than a year earlier, he said—and then he took the subway downtown to his job. He had returned home around six and had driven over to the bakery some time before seven. His wife had to work late every Tuesday and Friday so he always took his supper there on those nights and waited until she was done, at nine. Then they drove home together.

Inspector Lyons nodded and a few detectives left the room, to check out Hauptmann's alibi. The questioning continued.

"Where were you on the night of April 2, 1932?" he was asked. That was the night Condon handed the ransom money to John.

During the day, Hauptmann said, he was working at the Majestic. He remembered it was a Saturday because that was the day he quit his job. He got home at six, as usual. At about seven his friend, Hans Kloeppenburg, had come to the house with his guitar. Every first Saturday of the month, without fail, they got together for a musical evening, Kloeppenburg on the guitar and Hauptmann on the mandolin, singing old German songs. Around midnight, sometimes a little earlier, Kloeppenburg would leave.

Now one of the police held before Hauptmann a tightly folded bill. Do you recognize this? he asked. Hauptmann didn't reply.

The bill was unfolded. Recognize it now? Hauptmann studied it and said he didn't know what they were driving at.

"Don't you always fold up your bills like this?"

"No," Hauptmann said, "I carry my money in my wallet. Like the gold note you took from me."

Hadn't he gone to a movie house in Greenwich Village about ten months ago and thrown this bill, folded this way, at the cashier?

"I've never been to Greenwich Village in my life," he said.

It was a Sunday night, Hauptmann was told, last November 26 . . .

"My birthday," Hauptmann said. "That's my birthday. I was at home that night, Anna gave me a party, a few friends came over . . ."

While Hauptmann continued to be questioned in the Greenwich Street station house, annoying the police with his calm in the face of a murder accusation, detectives began to investigate his alibi.

Anna Hauptmann: She couldn't remember March 1, 1932, it was too long ago. A Tuesday, the detective said. A Tuesday? Of course. Richard must have been with her because back then she was working with Christian and Katie Fredericksen, a waitress in their bakery. Katie took off every Tuesday night and every Tuesday night Richard came to take his supper there and drive her home at nine. Richard was with her that night, he never failed to come for her on Tuesdays. Then what about Saturday night, April 2, 1932, what were you doing that night? Saturday nights were Richard's music nights, she said, answering without hesitation. Kloeppenburg was there, a regular thing, they made music and sang and she served coffee and cake. And November 26, last year? That was Richard's birthday, she said. A little party for him, nothing special, a few friends and relatives to help him celebrate.

Then what about the money? she was asked. Richard had not worked since the spring of 1932 and Mrs. Hauptmann had told them she had stopped working in December of that year. Where did the money come from? They had saved, of course, Anna said. Their expenses were low, they had saved thousands since they were married on the tenth of October, 1925. And Richard was making money in Wall Street.

"Didn't he tell you his money is from the Lindbergh kidnaping?"

Anna put her hand over her mouth, biting at the knuckle. "What do you mean?" she asked.

They told her: Your husband, Bruno Richard Hauptmann, kidnaped the Lindbergh baby. Killed that baby. Extorted $50,000. Had been arrested with some of the money. Probably had the rest of it hidden away somewhere.

"No! It is not so. My Richard could do no such thing."

They began to question her again, trying to break down her spontaneous corroboration of her husband's alibi. They questioned her for several hours, then told her to meet them at her apartment at nine the next morning; Mrs. Hauptmann would spend the night, and the next several months, at the nearby apartment of her niece,

Maria Mueller. That arrangement suited police well. The Hauptmann lease was broken and a new tenant claimed the apartment: New Jersey State Trooper Lewis J. Bornmann.

Hans Kloeppenburg: Yes, he remembered that first Saturday in April, back in 1932. Saturday was the night he and his old friend Richard always got together to play music, to sing, to laugh.

Katie and Christian Fredericksen: Yes, every Tuesday night for as long as Anna Hauptmann had worked for them, she worked until closing. Richard always came for her and drove her home by nine.

Maria Mueller: Richard Hauptmann's last birthday? Last November? Certainly she remembered. She went to her aunt's home in the afternoon and in the evening some of the Hauptmanns' friends came by for the party. One of the friends was Isidor Fisch. Uncle Richard said Isidor was his business partner, in the fur business and the stock market.

Downtown, in the police station, Richard Hauptmann sat in the same chair, ten hours after he had been ordered into it. He had been questioned almost without a rest during those hours, teams of fresh detectives spelling each other every hour or so. Richard appeared tired, he blinked a lot, his body sagged, but he never lost control.

Now, around midnight, Inspector Lyons decided to spring the trap, as he had called it since May 1932. It was then that Albert Osborn, the outstanding authority on handwriting in the country, had devised a test to betray the writer of the kidnap notes. It was a simple paragraph that sounded innocent enough on the face of it. But within those sentences were key words, syllables, and letters that, Osborn had said, would tell him beyond a doubt whether the writer had written the ransom notes.

Hundreds of suspects had taken the test and had been cleared by Osborn. In all previous cases the suspect had not been told that his writing was being analyzed against the writing on the ransom notes—it must be that way, Osborn had warned police, for otherwise the suspect who was warned in advance would attempt to disguise his handwriting, would make it that much more difficult to determine with accuracy whether he had written those notes to Colonel Lindbergh.

Inspector Lyons decided to ignore Osborn's instructions with this suspect. George Waller and other writers said he did so because he did not want Hauptmann to later claim, if and when he went on trial, that he had been tricked and his rights had been violated.

I can't believe that, I thought. *Lyons must have had another motive. He ripped apart Hauptmann's house, his garage, his car. Why such concern with the legal niceties now? I filed my suspicion away for later investigation and continued to read about the handwriting test.*

Lyons, it is said, advised Hauptmann that he could clear himself very easily if he would submit to a handwriting test. The test was designed to prove or disprove his claim that he had not written the ransom notes. Would he be willing to take the test?

Hauptmann said: "I will be glad to write because it will get me out of this thing."

A New Jersey state trooper dictated Osborn's paragraph, reading slowly as the prisoner wrote. Over the next six or seven hours those dozen or so sentences were dictated to Hauptmann again and again. Never, it was stressed by all writers, did the police tell him how to spell a word. Never did they instruct him in the arrangement or placing of the words on the page, or the use of capitals, or punctuation.

And when he was done, by early morning, even police untrained in handwriting analysis were certain this man was the kidnaper. The strange transposition of *g*'s and *h*'s as in "nihgt"; the spelling of the word "boat"; the hyphenation of the words "New York." At last, at long last, they had found the killer of the Lindbergh baby.

The next morning, Anna Hauptmann returned to cry again at the destruction of her home, crying without shame as they continued to pull the apartment to pieces. After a time, police led her down to the garage. She watched as the men pried up floorboards, tore apart Richard's workbench, ripped off the roof. Eventually a detective tore down a board that was nailed above the workbench across two uprights. There was a narrow shelf behind the board. On the shelf were two bundles wrapped in newspaper. The detective lifted them down and opened them. Inside each package was a thick wad of gold notes. They were checked against the ransom list: all were Lindbergh gold certificates.

Mrs. Hauptmann continued to watch, appearing more anxious, more disturbed, as the search went on. Beneath the workbench, behind another board nailed across uprights, they found a one-gallon shellac can with several bundles wrapped like the first ones: Lindbergh gold notes, almost $12,000 worth. The garage was now ripped to the earth. No other ransom bills were found. The total yield was $13,760. Counting $5,100 that had been previously recovered through banks, $18,860 of the ransom was now accounted for. Another $31,140 was still missing (none of it would ever be found, so far as the public record discloses).

What do you know about this money? an officer asked Mrs. Hauptmann.

She shook her head. She could not speak.

Did you see your husband place it there? Where did he get it?

Again the dark blond hair danced as she shook her head vigorously. Her blue eyes seemed clouded with tears.

"I know nothing," she said. "Nothing. But Richard could not have done this thing."

By two o'clock that afternoon, September 20, Hauptmann was still being questioned in relays. He had not slept for twenty-four hours. No sooner did he seem to doze than a fresh group of questioners would begin hammering at him again. The same questions, for twenty-four hours.

But now they had a new line of attack. Why had he lied about the money? Where did these gold certificates, found in his garage, come from? You know they're Lindbergh money? You must know because you kidnaped the baby and got the money from the old man, in St. Raymond's Cemetery.

No, Hauptmann said, he had never been in St. Raymond's in his life. He had lied about the money, he had lied from the very beginning, because he was afraid he would go to prison if it was learned he had so many gold notes. Now he would tell the truth. The money wasn't his.

Whose money is it? How did you get it?

From a friend, Isidor Fisch. Isidor had asked him to take care of the money while he was away, in Germany.

And the story flowed out of Hauptmann: He and Fisch had been business partners. They had invested several thousand each in the partnership. Fifty-fifty. Fisch knew furs, he had been a furrier in the old country, so he bought and sold for the partnership. Hauptmann knew the stock market, he had made some money since the crash. So he bought stocks for the partnership. He also bought

107

stocks for Fisch, personally; Fisch didn't have a brokerage account of his own so Hauptmann traded for him. But Fisch's selections had turned out badly and he had lost much money. Hauptmann had had to lend Fisch several thousand, the last time just before Christmas, last year, when Fisch decided to visit his parents in Germany. Fisch was a Jew and he was so concerned over what he had been hearing about Hitler that he went back hoping to convince his parents to emigrate to America.

The money? someone demanded.

Well, several weeks before Fisch was scheduled to leave he came to Hauptmann with two suitcases containing personal effects and several hundred fur pelts that Fisch had recently bought for their partnership. You know, Hauptmann said, the furs you found in my house. Well, Fisch had asked him to store them. And only a couple of nights before he sailed, Fisch brought to Hauptmann a shoe box that was wrapped and securely tied. He had said they were important papers and asked Hauptmann to safeguard them. Hauptmann had put the box on a closet shelf and forgotten about it.

But three or four weeks ago there had been a heavy rain. The roof had leaked and water had soaked the closet. By accident, he had discovered the shoe box. Soaking wet. He had opened it and was surprised, shocked, to find it contained a large amount of money. He didn't even realize they were all gold notes because they were soaking wet and stuck together. He took the money down to the garage where he wrapped most of it in newspapers and hid it away. A few bills at a time, he put in a bushel basket to dry, hiding the basket on a shelf way up near the garage ceiling. He began to spend the money because Fisch owed him thousands, for the loans. He spent only about a dozen bills before he was caught.

And where is this Mr. Fisch now?

He died in Germany last March, Hauptmann said. He was a very sick man, tuberculosis.

Do you expect us to believe that?

Well, it's true, Hauptmann said, every word is true.

His story did sound too fantastic to believe. Police refused to believe it; seasoned criminals frequently blame their crime on a "dead friend" when they are trying to alibi away the evidence against them.

Investigators were even more certain Hauptmann was lying, was

108

undoubtedly the kidnaper, murderer, and extortionist, after they learned about his background. A rather sordid criminal career, they later told the press.

He had been born in Kamenz, in Saxony, on November 26, 1899. He had served as a machine-gunner in the German army; conscripted at seventeen, wounded and gassed at eighteen, released from the army at nineteen. He sought work—he'd had eight years of academic schooling and two years in a trade school, where he had learned carpentry—but there was no work to be had in postwar Germany. There was very little food and not much hope for the future.

Hauptmann's mother was widowed. His two brothers had been killed in the war. In March 1919, two months after returning to Kamenz, Hauptmann and a young friend from his regiment walked to a neighboring village and, in the hour after midnight, climbed by ladder through the second-floor window of the burgomaster's home and stole several hundred marks and the man's silver watch. In the next week, in Kamenz, they burglarized two shops. Several days later they stopped two housewives who were pushing prams loaded with groceries. While his friend held a pistol on the women, Richard took their groceries and food ration cards.

They were arrested at the end of March and convicted of the three burglaries and a charge of highway robbery. Richard was sentenced to serve four years and nine months at hard labor. Paroled in March 1923, he returned to Kamenz. He was arrested again a few months later on charges of stealing a bale of leather strips. He was jailed to await trial. Two days later, while exercising in the jail yard, Hauptmann walked through an open gate and escaped. In a wry touch, he left his prison clothes on the doorstep with a note: "Best wishes to the police."

Hauptmann went to Hamburg and stowed away on the SS *George Washington*, bound for New York. He was discovered at sea and forced to return to Germany. A month later he attempted to board the same ship but was recognized; he leaped into the bay to escape police. Finally, in July 1923, he went to Bremen and stowed away aboard the SS *Hannover* and this time successfully made it ashore in New York.

In the United States, he had had no criminal record. He found work as a dishwasher immediately upon landing. After several months he got a job as a carpenter, working on the construction of a new home development in the Bronx. Through friends he met Anna Schoeffler, who had arrived legally in New York early in 1924. She was twenty-six, a few months older than Richard. They were married a year after being formally introduced.

Both were thrifty and hardworking. From the beginning of their marriage both worked steadily and saved every penny above their basic living expenses. By their first anniversary they were saving almost all of Richard's earnings as a union carpenter—eighty to ninety dollars a week. They watched their savings grow and planned one day to buy their own home, have children, and lead a quiet, happy life.

For days police tried to punch holes in this portrait of the later Richard Hauptmann, thrifty, industrious, noncriminal. Files were checked, descriptions of uncaptured bank robbers and burglars were carefully sorted, former employers were questioned. A blank, all of it. Richard Hauptmann could not be connected to any crime between his illegal arrival in New York and the Lindbergh extortion nine years later.

Police investigated the relationship between Hauptmann and Fisch. That such a man had existed and was a friend of the prisoner was beyond doubt. Police had found a few letters from Fisch to Hauptmann, sent from Leipzig before he died. That Hauptmann actually did have some dealings with Fisch in fur pelts was confirmed by investigation and by the fact that Fisch had left a large number of sealskins with Hauptmann before sailing.

But, police said, it was unlikely that Fisch had been financially able to invest thousands of dollars with Hauptmann in a joint stock market speculation business. Fisch was a poor fur cutter who lived in comparative poverty, renting the cheapest room in his landlady's house, owning very little clothing and no car, no luxuries. Most damning of all, while Fisch had sent small sums of money home to his parents through the years, they in turn had to help him out by sending money to him in 1932—the kidnap year, the year Hauptmann wanted police to believe Fisch had come into a fortune in ransom money. In the years since 1932, Fisch had had to borrow several thousand dollars from friends, and he borrowed two thousand from Hauptmann to finance his trip to Germany.

The most significant evidence to prove Hauptmann a liar was his brokerage account records. Hauptmann had insisted to police, and had told his friends, that he had quit work in April 1932 because he

110

was making money in the stock market. But an analysis of his accounts proved that he had lost thousands of his and his wife's savings in the market, and considerably more beyond that traceable money.

A thorough accounting of Hauptmann's finances showed that his total known assets on April 2, 1932, when the ransom was paid, were $4,941. From that date until he was arrested, he and his wife had jointly earned $1,168. Yet Hauptmann had lost nearly $6,000 in the stock market, had spent more than $15,000 on living, travel, a trip his wife took to Germany in 1932, and other luxuries, and still had, when arrested, total assets of $26,000—which did not include the ransom money found in his garage.

Hauptmann insisted he could explain that remarkable affluence. Between September 1932 and the end of July 1933, Fisch had given him sums of money in cash to deposit in Hauptmann's brokerage accounts. Those sums, which Hauptmann pointed to on his brokerage statements, amounted to a little more than $14,000. Furthermore, Hauptmann said, he and Fisch had made profits in the thousands of dollars in their fur dealings. You will find the record of that in my account books, Hauptmann said, everything we bought and sold is listed in those books and they will prove I am telling the truth. There were no records of those fur dealings with Fisch, police said, not in Hauptmann's ledgers, not in the letters Fisch wrote to Hauptmann; in no record, further, could Hauptmann show he had entered sums from Fisch for stock market investment that totaled more than $2,000.

Quite clearly, Hauptmann was lying. It was all lies, police said, most especially Hauptmann's claim that another four or five thousand in assets did not show up on any records because of his habit of keeping those sums hidden at home; when the banks started to fail at the beginning of the Depression, Hauptmann said, he began hiding his money at home, as so many Americans were doing.

Rubbish, police said when they explained to reporters why they were certain Bruno Richard Hauptmann was the kidnaper, killer, and extortionist they had long been seeking. The word of Hauptmann's arrest leaked to reporters on the afternoon of September 20, the day after police had stopped his car and begun to question him. Immediately reporters and photographers rushed to the Greenwich Street precinct house, and soon there was a mob of the curious and the bitter; talk of a lynching became so loud, was ex-

111

pressed in such angry tones, that squads of police were called from other precincts to maintain order.

But late in the afternoon there was a diversion, and the mob's temper changed. A squad car pulled up in front of the station house and out stepped a tall, erect, dignified man with grey hair.

"Jafsie!" someone in the crowd shouted. "It's Jafsie!" the people on the street began to shout in chorus.

And as John F. Condon climbed the steps to the station house, another cry went up: "Jafsie will burn him!"

At this early stage in the Hauptmann investigation, Condon's word on whether or not the suspect was John, the man in the cemeteries, was more critical than any documentary evidence. Condon had talked to the extortionist for more than an hour. He had seen the man's face. He had felt the peculiar deformity on John's left hand. Condon, of course, would identify Hauptmann and put an end to the few remaining doubts police had.

Before an audience composed of most of the highest police officials of New York and New Jersey and J. Edgar Hoover himself, Hauptmann was placed in an identity lineup with thirteen police officers. Not one of them resembled Hauptmann in any way. Not one of them spoke with any kind of accent.

It is axiomatic that identity lineups can be completely objective only when all the other men on stage with the suspect have the same general characteristics that he does. If an eyewitness has described the suspect as tall and thin and if the suspect is placed in a lineup with short and stocky men, then the witness will most naturally be influenced; similarly, a suspect with a foreign accent should not be the only person in a lineup who speaks with an accent. This lineup was stacked against Hauptmann, no doubt because police were certain he was the kidnaper and desperately wanted him identified. Condon himself later wrote: "My eyes ran down the line. Twelve or more men! And perhaps eleven of them were broad-shouldered, florid-faced, bullnecked chaps who could not by any stretch of the imagination have been confused with the man I had described, over and over, as John."

Condon nevertheless went ahead with the charade. He spoke briefly to each of the men in the line, then asked four of them to step forward. Hauptmann, the only man with an accent, was of course among them. Condon stepped directly in front of Hauptmann and lectured the group to "tell the truth." He asked to see

112

the hands of each of the four, looking for the distinctive muscular development near the thumb. He found it on Hauptmann's hand, he later claimed.

He then wrote something on a slip of paper and handed it to Hauptmann. "Read it aloud, please," Condon asked. Hauptmann read, in his dreadful English: "I stayed already too long. The leader would smack me out. Your work is perfect."

Condon questioned Hauptmann for several minutes, examined his hands once more, then started questioning him again. Hauptmann responded to all questions, denying they had ever before met or spoken to one another. Getting a little annoyed by it all, Inspector Lyons broke in and asked Condon:

"Would you say he is the man?"

"He resembles the man," Condon said. "I can see a resemblance, but I cannot swear to it."

Condon was later taken to the office of District Attorney Samuel J. Foley in the Bronx, where the extortion had occurred. Authorities badgered him for hours through an entire evening, trying to convince him to identify Hauptmann. They showed him photos of the prisoner, profiles, three-quarter profiles, full-face views, "refreshing his memory," as one writer of the time put it, "almost imploring him to say definitely and finally, 'Yes, this is the man.'"

It seemed strange to me that Condon, so positive in his identification of Hauptmann from the witness stand later, was not able to identify him at the beginning. But I decided to let it pass for now, to analyze it more carefully when my chronology reached his testimony at the trial.

A little more than two weeks after he'd been arrested, Hauptmann was delivered to New Jersey authorities to stand trial for murder. An extradition order had been signed by New York Governor Herbert Lehman. Hauptmann, finally hiring an attorney, fought extradition. The hearings were held in Bronx County Court on October 15, 1934. Yet not one of the dozen books and magazine articles I consulted at this time went into the details of the extradition hearings. And I wondered why.

By law, in order to dissolve an extradition order, the burden of proof falls on the accused; he must demonstrate beyond doubt that he could not possibly have been in the state in which the crime was committed at the time it occurred. Hauptmann had been so very positive when he told police that he'd been working at the Majestic apartments on the day of the kidnaping. He had said he always took the subway to work, and that statement had been confirmed by several people police questioned. Since it took him forty minutes to travel to the Majestic by subway, it wasn't likely that he could have quit work at five o'clock, washed up and changed, caught the subway home, and then, probably, had something to eat, placed the homemade ladder in his car, and driven to Hopewell by nine o'clock.

His alibi had been nearly perfect, but not perfect enough to influence the judge at the hearing to deny extradition. What, I wondered, had happened to that alibi? Were police able to prove Hauptmann had been lying? Or did something else happen to destroy his alibi?

Once more I made a note for future investigation: to locate a copy of the extradition hearing and study it; also to study newspaper accounts of the hearing.

Murray Bleefeld called around this time and asked that we postpone our second interview for three or four days; he was going to be tied up with federal men and a grand jury. I told him that I'd discovered that John Condon had been unable to identify Hauptmann in the police lineup, that he had been badgered and still refused to make a positive identification. "I have a feeling the man was lying when he identified Hauptmann at the trial," I told Murray.

"Of course he was," Murray said. "He was the biggest liar who ever took the stand. That's what Parker told me, and that's what I've always believed. Parker told me that Condon had always said the kidnaping was the work of a gang, but when he gets into the courthouse he picked out Hauptmann and everybody ignored the gang theory. Even after Hauptmann was put in the chair and killed, Condon still insisted a gang was involved.

"Parker told me, 'The man lied, Murray. He couldn't identify Hauptmann. He lied because police threatened to arrest him as an accomplice. He lied to save his own skin.' That's what Ellis told me."

"I hope I can prove that."

"You will, you'll prove it."

"I'm glad you're so confident about it," I said, "because I'm not. If I'm going to write this book I have to be able to prove Hauptmann's innocence to the most experienced criminal lawyer around. Not just the public, but cops and lawyers and judges."

114

"You have to nail the evidence so tight that nobody will doubt you."

"Exactly. I need documentary proof."

"You'll get it. You'll get it."

Murray's assurances hung heavily on me. A thought that had darted below my consciousness each time I'd made a note to explore further some element in the case, now surfaced. How on earth would I ever find the documents—the objective truth—that would overcome the illusions of history? Despite Murray's confidence, strong feelings of futility came over me.

6 The trial of Bruno Richard Hauptmann on a charge of murdering Charles A. Lindbergh, Jr., began January 2, 1935, in the century-old Hunterdon County Courthouse in Flemington. It ended on the night of February 13, 1935, when the jury found Hauptmann guilty of murder in the first degree and made no recommendation for mercy. Between those two dates the country was treated to a spectacular circus that angered even *Editor and Publisher*, the normally uncritical organ of the journalistic profession. The magazine complained, after Hauptmann was convicted:

No trial in this century has so degraded the administration of justice. If the life of one man and the unhappiness of hundreds are to be commercialized for the benefit of entertainment, of radio broadcasters, newspaper publishers, newsreel producers; if a public trial means protection from star-chamber tyranny but not from the indignities of the mob, then the ancient institution of trial by a jury of peers is without meaning.

Most certainly it was spectacle more than trial; low camp theater masquerading as justice. For about a month before the trial opened, technicians were busily decorating Flemington with telephone and telegraph cables in order to transmit to the world what every journalist called the story of the century.

Several American newspapers established branch offices in the little town, enriching the citizens who threw open their spare bedrooms to reporters at five dollars a night. The more affluent papers announced with pride that they had acquired the services of Edna Ferber, Fannie Hurst, Damon Runyon, Adela Rogers St. Johns, Alexander Woollcott, Walter Winchell, Kathleen Norris, and a dozen other journalists of equal rank and popularity to write "special reports" in their own inimitable styles. The *Daily Mail* and *Daily Express* of London were sending special correspondents. So were *Paris-Soir* and a score of equally important European publications. The goal of all was commerce, the boosting of circulation. Before the trial, the papers and radio stations conducted advertising campaigns to boast about the enormous effort and expense the publication or broadcaster was going through for the benefit of the public, trying to convince that public to buy this paper or listen to that station. An example from one of the Hearst papers:

NATION ITSELF ACTS AS JURY TO TRY HAUPTMANN

Adela Rogers St. Johns is at Flemington to write a special daily article on the trial of Bruno Richard Hauptmann for the kidnap-murder of the Lindbergh baby. Read her story every day in the *New York Journal.*

In these circumstances, justice and the determination of truth were incidental to the entertainment of the masses. There were, as Alan Hynd wrote, several Hauptmann trials occurring simultaneously but separate and distinct from one another. There was the relatively minor trial in the courtroom, a drama whose climax was known to all, since every citizen had been told for months that Hauptmann was beyond doubt the baby-killer. There was the trial in the newspapers in which experts, especially psychiatrists, most of whom had never seen nor spoken with Hauptmann, explained the compulsion that had led him to kill the son of the nation's hero. There was the trial over the radio in which the "hacks of the airwaves" distorted the evidence with their vocal nuances; one of the more popular of these commentators was the noted defense attorney Samuel Leibowitz, later a New York State supreme court justice, who repeatedly told his radio audience that the evidence made it increasingly clear Hauptmann was guilty.

"All four trials had one thing in common—an arresting switch applied to the tenet of American jurisprudence that holds that a man is innocent until proven guilty," Hynd wrote. "Hauptmann was presumed guilty unless proved innocent. The only question was: how guilty was he? The suspense over the outcome of the four trials was confined to speculation as to whether Hauptmann would get the chair or life imprisonment."

The spectacle most definitely affected the jury. Under New Jersey law, a jury in a capital case must be sequestered. The Hauptmann jury was housed on the third floor of the little Union Hotel, across the street from the courthouse. The hotel was the nerve center of newspaper and radio journalists. During its meals the jury was seated in the public dining room, separated from other diners by only a flimsy cloth screen. At each meal they heard the boisterous newspaper men and women commenting on the events in court; most reporters, with the exception of Damon Runyon, were vocal in their condemnation of "Hauptmann the baby-killer." To Eddie Mahar, the Hearst chain's bureau chief at Flemington, Hauptmann was a Nazi monster, and most other writers agreed.

"Bruno Richard Hauptmann looks like this new guy they have got over in Germany," Mahar told St. Johns and other Hearst writers as the trial was about to begin. "The one they call Der Fuehrer, that Hitler. You got to remember Hitler and Hauptmann had exactly the same experience in the war, they were both corporals in the German army. They must have learned the same kind of brutality. Same type, you look and you'll see it."

Loud enough to be heard by everyone, Runyon said, "That doesn't make him guilty. I think we'd better keep open minds."

A strange silence fell, St. Johns later recalled.

Four times daily, on its trips between the hotel and courthouse, the jury was required to pass through a carnival of reporters standing on the courthouse steps making bets on how long it would take the jury to convict Hauptmann; citizens participating in the curbstone trial, rendering the popular verdict by shouting at the jurors, "Burn Hauptmann"; newsboys shouting headlines about Hauptmann's impending doom; souvenir sellers hawking reproductions of the kidnap ladder. And at night the jurors could hear from the

119

broadcasters' room, directly over their own, radio commentators like Leibowitz and Gabriel Heatter informing their audiences that Hauptmann had come one day closer to the electric chair.

Through it all, the fiction was maintained that the jury was intelligent and sophisticated enough to ignore the mob and reach an impartial verdict. When a change of venue was demanded by Hauptmann's attorneys, it was denied by the trial judge, Thomas W. Trenchard, who obviously felt, as Waller rather naively expressed it in *Kidnap,* that the jury, "well-balanced, soberly respectable, seemed qualified" to order their minds unaffected by the circus atmosphere outside. In truth, however, twelve Solomons could not have withstood the demands of public opinion.

Edward J. Reilly was the chief defense counsel. For more than a quarter century Reilly had been the leading criminal lawyer in Brooklyn. He hadn't lost an important case. But in these latter years of life this flamboyant showman, who had usually won his clients' acquittals by orating a jury into mass confusion, had become a heavy drinker. He appeared, even to those reporters who had no doubt Hauptmann was guilty, more interested in his liquor and his "secretaries"—a succession of busty blondes—than in the welfare of his client. Through the machinations of Jack Clements, once a police reporter and now, in 1935, an executive of the Hearst papers, Mrs. Hauptmann had been persuaded to dismiss the attorney who had represented her husband in the Bronx extradition hearing and to retain Reilly. The Hearst organization had actually paid Reilly's fee, in advance. Assured of his wages, Reilly had little interest in the case except for the publicity it brought him. The moment he banked his fee, Reilly commissioned a printer to make up some new stationery for him. The letterhead read:

The Hauptmann-Lindbergh Trial

Edward J. Reilly

Chief Counsel

And running down the left-hand margin of the expensive paper was a drawing of the kidnap ladder in brilliant red ink—the color of blood, some critics noted.

"What was I doing here in this madhouse?" Adela St. Johns re-

120

members asking, when she learned the night before the trial was to open that Reilly, instead of being deep in preparation for saving a man's life, was still passed out from the New Year's Eve party of the night, morning, and afternoon before.

Reilly was a man from whom rhetoric flowed and flowed, to be stopped only by the sharp rap of a judge's gavel. But when delivered before hostile jurymen who knew he considered them hicks, his words seemed artificial and fell flat. His effect on the jury of simple and religious rural citizens was disastrous. "From the start Reilly did all he could to show his contempt for us," the jury foreman said after the trial. Hauptmann understood that Reilly was more interested in the trial as theater, as drama, than in the man whose life was being judged. Whenever he had anything to say to his attorneys he said it not to Reilly but to C. Lloyd Fisher, a highly regarded local lawyer who was second in command of the Hauptmann defense.

By hiring Reilly, the Hearst papers had purchased an exclusive right to all interviews with Mrs. Hauptmann and all the sob-story mileage they could get out of her visits to her husband in his jail cell. Such a paternalistic interest on the part of William Randolph Hearst might have been helpful to Hauptmann had the Hearst papers been sympathetic to a man against whom the entire world seemed to be aligned. But the sympathy was lacking, on orders from the Chief, as Hearst was known.

"We cannot endure the kidnaping of our children," Hearst told St. Johns as part of her instructions on how she must write about the trial. "In this trial," he continued, "I am sure we can produce a flame of nationwide indignation that will deter other criminals. As you know, crime is the most dingdong [!] repetitive thing in the world; we must not allow this to become a *wave*." To Hearst, who had financed the defense, Hauptmann was guilty beyond all possible doubt. Every Hearst paper hammered that fact home to its readers, as did the hundreds of papers across the country that used Hearst's International News Service in their coverage of the trial.

The Hauptmann trial-cum-theater began with the selection of the jury, eight men and four women, farmers, mechanics, housewives. And then the oration by the principal player, Attorney General David Wilentz. As for Hauptmann, he was but a symbol, a stage prop who was expected to remain mute until after the superstars had performed.

121

Wilentz was thirty-nine, young for that office. He had never tried a criminal case of any kind. By tradition, the county prosecutor or an assistant on his staff prosecutes all cases that go to trial. But Wilentz was an ambitious man. He had made it plain he wanted to be governor one day. Serving as chief of the prosecution team was an opportunity that would come only once in his lifetime, bringing instant national recognition and an unlimited political future.

Wilentz's photograph, published on the front pages of most newspapers in the country, showed him to be a handsome man with a thin dark face under glossy black hair. He usually wore slightly loud suits (for that era), a pearl-grey felt hat with the brim snapped down in front and on one side, a velvet-collared Chesterfield coat, and a striking white scarf. But now, as required by his starring role, his costume was a conservative dark suit and dark tie.

Wilentz's oration started off slowly, a short, dry recitation of the law: they would prove that a burglary was committed in the act of entering Lindbergh's home, and that a killing during a felony burglary is murder in the first degree. Warmed up, he came quickly to the point: "And the state will prove to you jurors that the man who killed and murdered that child sits in this very courtroom." He pointed toward Hauptmann and all eyes focused on the accused, who did not appear to react in any way.

The state would prove, Wilentz continued, that Hauptmann had planned the kidnaping for weeks, that he had been seen in the vicinity of the Lindbergh home before the crime, while he was plotting this foul deed, and on the day of the crime—their witnesses will swear to that. They would prove also that Hauptmann climbed through the window with his homemade ladder, lifted the sleeping child from his crib, and left the ransom note on the windowsill. He began his descent to the ground. Suddenly, the ladder broke and Hauptmann fell to earth with his victim. The child was probably killed when his head hit the side of the house during the fall. There was a gasp from the audience at this point.

Hauptmann removed the ladder from the wall and began his flight. But after seventy yards under the double burden of ladder and child, he halted. He dropped the ladder. He "ripped and tore away the baby's sleeping suit, even before he left the Lindbergh grounds." And Wilentz cried out: "And Lindy, Lindy, who could find a speck at the end of the earth, Lindy couldn't find his child because Hauptmann had murdered it."

Wilentz continued his speech. "Then, at the very first convenient spot, he scooped up a hastily improvised and shallow grave and put this child in face downwards, and he went on his way to complete the rest of his plans in this horrible criminal endeavor." Then the body was discovered. "The moisture in the ground had still preserved the face a little bit, so that it was white when it was turned up, and twenty minutes after the air struck it, it had turned black. The body was horribly decomposed. . . ." Another gasp from the spectators. Anne Morrow Lindbergh's head was bowed, as it had been from the beginning of the speech. Lindbergh and Hauptmann both stared straight ahead, impassive. Anna Hauptmann bit at the knuckle of her right forefinger and turned away from her husband so that he would not see her anger at this man Wilentz's terrible words about Richard.

"We will prove to you beyond a reasonable doubt," Wilentz went on, "that the man who committed this crime was Bruno Richard Hauptmann, and that it was Hauptmann alone."

As I read, several questions flitted through my mind: *What had happened to the police certainty that a gang working with a member of the Lindbergh household staff had kidnaped the child? What had happened to the Italian shouting "statto citti" during the telephone call? And the Italian woman who had asked Condon to meet her at the Tuckahoe depot for a message from the kidnapers? And what had happened to the gang that Commodore Curtis had been convicted of dealing with?* Had they all been shoved aside in the rush to convict Hauptmann?

The Lindberghs were the first important (and newsworthy) witnesses. Anne Lindbergh described in a low, tense voice the events of March 1, 1932. She was shown and identified pieces of her child's clothing, particularly the sleeping suit. Her testimony was brief. She left the stand after Reilly had the good sense not to cross-examine her, and she was driven home, never again to return to the courthouse.

Lindbergh also testified about the night when his child was stolen, his appointment of Condon as intermediary, the long negotiations, the trip with the ransom money to St. Raymond's Cemetery, his wait in the car as Condon went alone to deal with John.

"I heard very clearly a voice coming from the cemetery, to the best of my belief calling Dr. Condon," Lindbergh testified.

"What were the words?"

123

"In a foreign accent, 'Hey, Doctor.' "

"How many times?"

"I heard that voice once."

"Since that time have you heard the same voice?"

"Yes, I have."

"Whose voice was it, Colonel, that you heard saying, 'Hey, Doctor'?"

"That was Hauptmann's voice."

And Lindbergh looked at Hauptmann directly for the first time since the trial had begun. Hauptmann shifted uneasily in his oak chair and a faint flush touched his cheeks. Anna Hauptmann stared at Lindbergh, with, it seemed to some writers, accusation in her eyes and on her barely moving lips: You lie.

That afternoon Adela Rogers St. Johns wrote, for the Hearst papers:

> For the first time, Lindbergh swung in the witness chair and looked square at Hauptmann. He had done it. He had made the positive identification. He had named *Hauptmann* as the kidnaper.
>
> My first reaction was Lindbergh is *sure.*
>
> Watching Lindbergh today in this ordeal I cannot believe he would swear away the life of any man unless he was sure. Automatically, I looked at the jury, even before I looked at Hauptmann.
>
> Yes.

Yes, she was certain the jury believed. If any writer in that courtroom was able to gauge a jury's reactions, it was St. Johns. She was the daughter of Earl Rogers, a brilliant lawyer, "the best of all" even Clarence Darrow had called him. She had grown up in the courtrooms, was schooled during conferences between her father and his clients, had learned the art of cross-examination by watching the master, as well as the art of reading a jury, all the dramatic art and artifice a trial lawyer must possess. And now, looking at the Hauptmann jury, she knew: Hauptmann was guilty, the verdict sealed.

Later, after the trial ended, she questioned the jurors. Yes, she had been right: Lindbergh had convinced them on the third day and the following twenty-nine days of theater were anticlimax.

So much for the appearances, for the script written by police and skillfully directed by Wilentz. I turned once more to Alan Hynd for, I hoped, the reality. Hynd had written: "Lindbergh himself, asked before the Bronx grand jury whether he would be able to identify Hauptmann as the man he had heard calling 'Hey, Doctor!' the night the ransom was paid, replied, 'It would be very difficult for me to sit here and say that I could pick a man by that voice.'"

If Hynd's statement was true—how often that phrase, "if true," leaped into my mind—then Charles A. Lindbergh had lied. *That's too harsh,* I thought. *From everything I've learned about Lindbergh I don't think he would have deliberately lied in order to convict Hauptmann. He must have convinced himself first, or allowed himself to be convinced by the "overwhelming evidence" police said they had collected against Hauptmann. The truth was plain to everyone, police said, the prisoner is guilty of this callous crime. And Lindbergh, in his grief, must have believed, and identified Hauptmann.*

Yet I wondered how anyone could identify a man's shout, from two hundred or more feet away, more than two years after hearing it. Lindbergh had heard two words: "Hey, Doctor!" Two words that were shouted, that must therefore not have sounded like a man's normal voice. And the jury believed. I recalled and turned again to an editorial in the *New York Law Journal,* the official daily newspaper of the state appellate courts. Published a couple of days after Lindbergh's testimony, the editorial said:

The question of identification by voice, concerning which there is not an abundance of authority, has received new interest from Colonel Lindbergh's testimony in the Hauptmann prosecution for the murder of the Lindbergh child. . . .

While such testimony of identification is entirely competent, in the sense that it may be received for the consideration of the jury, its weight is at best doubtful, even conceding to Hauptmann's voice certain peculiarities of tone and pronunciation. With such evidence of identity standing alone and without corroborative proof, we doubt its legal sufficiency to establish any substantial link required for a conviction of capital crime. . . .

There was, however, an interesting case in New York, decided some years ago (*Wilbur* v. *Hubbard,* 35 Barb. 303), in which it was held a question for the jury to determine whether the dog of the defendant, sued for damages for the killing and wounding of the plaintiff's sheep, could be identified by witnesses who had only heard the dog's bark the night of the killing, and who had not seen the dog kill the sheep. In this case it was held (by the court) to be for the jury to determine from the evidence, whether the dog had such a peculiar bark or voice that witnesses *acquainted* with the animal could satisfactorily identify it by its bark.

After repeating the key paragraph of the court's decision, that a dog may be identified by its bark if witnesses were familiar with that bark before the incident involved, the editorial continued:

But here it will be noted that the point was made that the identification of the dog was based upon the testimony of persons who had become familiar with the bark of the dog to be identified; and the court's reference (in its ruling) to the identification of human voices contemplated that it should be made by "acquaintances."

In the Hauptmann case Colonel Lindbergh had never before heard the voice which uttered the words "Hey, Doctor!" the night of April 2, 1932, and was from two to three hundred feet away. He did not claim to have heard the voice again for more than two years, or until after the arrest of Hauptmann in connection with the crime.

In a Massachusetts case (*Commonwealth* v. *Best,* 180 Mass. 492) testimony of witnesses that they could identify horses by the peculiar sound of their footfalls upon the roadway was held admissable upon the issue of the identity of the horses, the weight and sufficiency of such testimony being for the jury. But here again, familiarity was shown.

In another Massachusetts case, which was a prosecution for arson, a woman who claimed to have heard the same voice *twice on the same day* was allowed to testify that the voice she heard in the evening was that of "the same man that spoke to me at noon." The evidence was held competent. . . .

In the case of *Pilcher* v. *United States* (113 Fed. 248), however, it was held that the admission of the testimony of a witness that he was "under the impression" that one of the voices which he had overheard in a conversation relating to the commission of the crime, was that of the defendant, was erroneous; and in a Texas case the testimony of the complaining witness that in "his opinion" (the defendant's voice was that of his assailant) was held insufficient to support a conviction, where the assault took place in the darkness and the witness testified that he had known the defendant for but a few hours.

Colonel Lindbergh did not testify that it was merely his "opinion" that the "Hey, Doctor!" voice was the voice of Hauptmann, whom he heard speak after an interval of more than two years, though such a conclusion could be, at best, only an expression of opinion. Colonel Lindbergh's testimony as to identity of voice was unqualified, and it is believed that . . . the surrounding circumstances and other facts in evidence would not justify so positive a statement.

In effect, the editor of this journal of the legal profession was saying that Lindbergh had been as carried away as everyone else with this "trail of the century." And there had indeed been enormous hatred directed at the man Hauptmann, because of public revulsion at what had happened to the Lindberghs. And I wondered: Did Hauptmann hate just before he was killed by the state? Or had he been able to transcend hatred? I pulled from my files a copy of Liberty magazine which had recently been revived in an attempt to capitalize on the wave of nostalgia for the twenties and thirties. In a 1971 issue was reprinted an article Hauptmann wrote only days before he was executed and which was published a month after his death. Searching for an indication as to how this man felt when he knew he was about to die, I read:

And so I sit, ten feet removed from the electric chair, and unless something can be done to aid me, unless something can be done to make someone tell the truth, or unless someone does tell it, I shall at eight o'clock Friday evening, in response to the call from my keepers, raise myself from my cot for the last time and shall walk that "last mile." I suppose there will be in that chamber some of those who have had a part in the preparation of my case for the prosecution. It is my belief that

127

their suffering, their agony, will be greater than mine. Mine will be over in a moment. Theirs will last as long as life itself lasts.

That crowd shouting for death is history. The Lindbergh who rose above his suffering to perform his duty for society is history. Hauptmann the baby-killer is history. The man himself is buried in the pages of an obscure magazine, his words translated into English, probably edited, but still his words, a final, vain, eloquent protest:

> When I rise to join in that last deathly procession, I shall walk as any man walks, striding along one foot ahead of the other. I shall breathe the air my guards are breathing. I shall hear things that are being said, with ears that are the ears of other men. I shall say with a voice that is the same as voices of other men that a tragedy is being enacted, that a life is being wantonly taken, that I am innocent of the crime of which I have been convicted, as innocent as anyone in the world; and then, if the decision of the court is carried out, I shall be strapped into the chair, and in a few fleeting seconds this body that is mortal will be no longer living and breathing but just a mass of clay.

I found it too painful to continue reading Hauptmann's last words as he prepared to confront death. Instead, I returned to the more predictable formal drama of his trial.

Lindbergh was still in the witness chair. During a long cross-examination, defense attorney Reilly showed how greatly his mental powers had diminished: he made the novice's mistake of reinforcing the prosecution's evidence by asking Lindbergh whether he believed that "the defendant . . . is guilty of the kidnaping"; Lindbergh, of course, replied, "I do." Hauptmann groaned. Fisher, the other defense lawyer, winced. Unperturbed by his error, Reilly then made plain that his chief line of defense would be to throw before the jury the accusation that everyone in the world except Hauptmann could have committed the crime. Among those he implied were suspect, during his questioning of Lindbergh, Reilly included John Condon, Betty Gow, Violet Sharpe, Red Johnson, Whately the butler, and several others who were by now conveniently dead. (Back in the Union Hotel at the end of the day, reporters snickered at all the potential murderers lurking about the Lindbergh household. "I bet Reilly wishes Betty Gow was dead," one reporter shouted. The jury heard, of course, and the impact was lost: just another defense smokescreen.)

Reilly attempted to be specially caustic in his questioning of Betty Gow. She was a spirited Scotswoman, however, and her ability to deflate Reilly and to deflect each of his thrusts brought waves of applause through the courtroom. Until, in exasperation, Reilly was forced to shout:

"You are a very bright young lady, Miss Gow, aren't you?"

Saucily she answered, "I am." (Greater applause.)

But Reilly did succeed in raising doubts about a story she had told in direct examination, that one day about a month after the kidnaping she and Elsie Whately had found in the driveway of the Lindbergh estate the thumb guard the Lindbergh boy had worn the night he was stolen. The discovery of the thumb guard was important to the prosecutor, Wilentz, for it permitted him to claim, as he did in his opening statement and in his summation, that Hauptmann had caused the child's death and then callously ripped off the sleeping suit to help him extort the ransom from Lindbergh. By hammering at Betty's story about the thumb guard, Reilly seemed to have planted a seed of doubt in the spectators' minds and perhaps in the jurors'. Reilly had asked her: "Yet with all these police officers around and with all the inclement weather for a month, and with everybody searching those grounds day after day, night after night, you would have this jury believe that you could pick up in broad daylight on that road this bright, shiny thumb guard . . . ?"

Reporters told Wilentz that Reilly had scored two important points. He had made it seem possible that Betty Gow was lying. And, as a corollary, he had made it seem possible that perhaps she indeed had some guilty knowledge of the kidnaping. Wilentz was so concerned that he called out of their scheduled turn several eyewitnesses who could place Hauptmann within yards of the Lindbergh house; the script required that he drive from the jury's mind the possibility that Gow had been lying.

To the stand was called Amandus Hochmuth, a small and frail man with thick grey hair and beard, who said proudly that he was eighty-seven. Wilentz asked him to recall the day of the crime, more than thirty-four months before, and Hochmuth said he remembered it clearly. Shortly before noon he was sitting on the front porch of his home, gazing at the junction of the county highway and the lane leading to the Lindbergh estate. "I saw a car coming round the corner, pretty good speed, and I expected it to turn over in the ditch. And as the car was about twenty-five feet away from me, the man in there looked out of the window like this"— imitating the driver's expression—"and he glared at me as if he saw a ghost."

"The man you saw, is he in this room?" Wilentz asked.

"Yes, alongside the trooper there." Hochmuth pointed his finger at Hauptmann.

"Please step down and touch the man you pointed at," Wilentz said. Hochmuth walked unsteadily toward the defense table. Hauptmann's face was blank as Hochmuth stopped before him, reached over, and put one hand on his knee.

Hauptmann leaned across the state trooper guarding him and whispered to Anna, *"Der Alte is verrückt"* ("The old man is crazy"). Upstairs in the courthouse garret, where telegraphers sat at their machines to flash the journalists' reports to their newspapers, bulletins went out over the wires that Hauptmann had been positively placed near the scene of the crime on the day of the crime.

Continuing his testimony, Hochmuth said the "dirty green car" Hauptmann was driving had a three-section ladder inside, stretching from the front seat to the rear window. When he took the witness, Reilly tried desperately to shake his story, but failed.

Alan Hynd, again, cast serious doubt on another element of Wilentz's case. Hynd wrote that Social Security records turned up after the trial disclosed that in June 1932, shortly after the events Hochmuth swore he witnessed, a welfare investigator had reported about him:

"Health is very poor, applicant partly blind."

In early August, slightly more than a month later, another investigator noted on his report about Hochmuth: "Frail. Failing eyesight due to cataracts."

Where did Hynd learn about those reports? Were they accurate? I would have to track them down, of course, because if the old man was "partly blind" and suffering from cataracts, his identification of Hauptmann was worthless.

On that same day, the fifth day of the trial, Wilentz called another eyewitness to the stand. He was Joseph Perrone, the cab driver who had been given the ransom note to be delivered to Doctor Condon. Quickly, Wilentz led Perrone to the point: the man who had flagged him down on a Bronx street corner, and had given him the envelope with Condon's name and address on the front, was Bruno Richard Hauptmann. Perrone, too, stepped across the courtroom and touched Hauptmann in identification.

"This is the man," Perrone said.

Softly Hauptmann said, "You're a liar."

Only a few people near him heard the comment. Reilly, who had heard it, asked Judge Trenchard to place Hauptmann's words in the record as his answer to the accusation. Trenchard refused. Reilly then cross-examined Perrone; once more, he was unable to damage an eyewitness's testimony.

The next day Wilentz called to the stand his "star witness," as the newspapers and broadcasters called him, Dr. John F. Condon, Jafsie himself. Several hundred spectators had stood around the courthouse doors in a cold drizzle through the night, to hear the testimony that the papers and commentators had said would decide the entire case and probably put Hauptmann in the chair.

Wilentz, all writers explained in their articles and columns, was not really certain Condon would play the role everyone was ascribing to him. Jafsie probably would finger Hauptmann, they wrote, but on the other hand the prosecution was caught up in a terrible suspense. Condon was believed too unpredictable to depend upon to aid the case against Hauptmann. The good doctor had given the newspapers so many different stories since the kidnaping that it was impossible for Wilentz to know what he would say under oath. He had not positively identified Hauptmann after the arrest and for that reason was not called to testify at the extradition hearing. He had been chasing around the country after Hauptmann's arrest, apparently still looking for the kidnaper, and he had told reporters that Hauptmann was not the man. A month before the trial began, Condon had gone to Florida to "run down certain clues" that had only recently come to him, and told reporters in Palm Beach that Wilentz was making a mistake in trying to convict Hauptmann of murder because at most the man was guilty of extortion. All writers stressed that Condon was so eccentric, Wilentz was afraid he would demolish the prosecution's case.

Those stories were simply another part of the drama, the creation of suspense for several purposes, mostly to sell newspapers, but also to carry through on the illusion that Hauptmann stood a chance of acquittal because he was being fairly judged by his peers. As for Wilentz worrying about Condon's testimony—absolute nonsense. No trial lawyer with the least intelligence would risk his case by putting on the stand any witness who had not been thoroughly interviewed first, so that every answer he would give would be known to Wilentz before he asked a question. And Wilentz was plainly a very intelligent man.

Condon was called to the stand. Dressed in black as if in mourning for young Lindbergh, he appeared younger than his years because his frame was still sturdy, evidence of daily workouts in a local gym. Wilentz guided Condon through a recitation of his public career and accomplishments and then brought him suddenly to the evening of April 2, 1932, the night he paid the $50,000 ransom.

"Whom did you give that money to?" Wilentz asked.

"John," Condon said, apparently stretching out the interrogation for the maximum dramatic effect.

"And who is John?"

In a loud voice, separating each syllable of the name, Condon replied: "John is Bru-no Rich-ard Haupt-mann!"

Up above, in the garret, the telegraph keys clicked out the news for the evening's headlines: JAFSIE IDENTIFIES HAUPTMANN.

It seemed to me, as I read about the telegraph-key clatter resounding through the courtroom each time a headline-provoking statement was made by a witness, that here was one further gross influence on the jury. The reporters covering the trial were almost unanimously convinced of Hauptmann's guilt from the start. So convinced, they seized upon every piece of prosecution evidence that would confirm their judgments and dashed off new leads for their stories to create new and startling headlines. And in so doing they signaled to the jury what they, jointly the thirteenth juror on the panel, considered significant. From my own experience in reporting criminal and civil trials in the New York courts, I know that every time a reporter rose quickly and ran from the courtroom to phone in "a startling new development," most of the jurors snapped wide awake, shot glances at one another, were made to understand that what they had just heard was important. Occasionally, such reporters' actions were beneficial to the defendant. But in this trial, in which most details of the ransom negotiations and payment and the arrest of Hauptmann were revealed for the first time, the bias leaned heavily against the defendant.

Wilentz ignored the electrical chatter that punctuated Condon's statement and said: "Now let's get back to where we *should* start. In March 1932, as the result of a letter or advertisement you inserted, did you receive a note?"

"I did."

"What was it that you received?"

"I received a letter with a peculiar signature on it."

Wilentz then produced from the mound of evidence on the prosecution table, and had admitted into evidence, the letter that Perrone had delivered to Condon's home and the letter to Lindbergh that had been inside it. During the next several hours remaining in that sixth trial day and over most of the following day, Wilentz led Condon through his experiences in his attempts to negotiate the return of the child. The 500-page edited trial transcript I was consulting fairly closely followed Condon's story as I had made notes of it from the several books I'd been reading. But there were additional details that I was certain could be vital to my reexamination of the case.

As I compared the transcript with the books and magazine articles I'd been consulting, I realized that all writers, with the exception of Hynd, took Dr. Condon's testimony at full value and without reservation. Yet Condon obviously had an enormous stake in supporting the prosecution's case. He had been suspected as a member of the extortion plot by several police officials. He was later to write that he had been abused by police, threatened, his telephone tapped, the walls of his study ripped open, his summer retreat searched. He had been attacked in the press, some papers insinuating that he knew more than he admitted, and he had received crank letters calling him a scoundrel and a murderer. In short, this old man (he was seventy-four at the time of the trial), a man full of ego and self-importance as to his place in the community as an educator, patriot, orator, and intellectual, had seen serious cracks developing in the structure of his life that he had so carefully built. Was it not possible that Condon felt he had been ridiculed sufficiently to empty the breath of his triumph, and was now intent on restoring the glory that had once been his? Certainly Condon, more than anyone else in the case, was vulnerable to police pressures to produce for the state. I didn't know as I read the transcript whether he had so produced, whether he had distorted his testimony in any way because of police threats, yet my intuition told me it was highly likely.

And as I read I also felt that writers like the author of *Kidnap,* particularly, should have examined Condon's role a bit more cynically instead of blindly accepting his testimony on faith.

One example of this lack of critical judgment especially troubled me. That was the manner in which Condon explained his refusal (inability?) to identify Hauptmann in the police lineup even after speaking with him at length, questioning him, and shaking his hand. During his cross-examination, Reilly asked Condon about the numerous times he had told reporters that Hauptmann was not the John of the cemeteries, that the police had not yet found the real kidnaper. Condon denied making those statements. The cross-examination of Condon went like this:

"Did you tell reporters at that time that Hauptmann was not John?"

"Oh, I never did," Condon replied. "I never told or mentioned his name to them in public, never. . . . I make a distinction between *identification* and *declaration of identification.* "

"In other words, I am to understand that you split hairs?"

"No hairs at all. A man's life is at stake and I want to be honest about it."

"In Greenwich Street, New York, police station you said it was not the man, did you not?"

"No sir. Get all the people that were there; I did not."

"You never said it *was* the man?"

"I never said it was or was not."

"Because you know you are not sure?"

"Because I made the distinction between declaration and identification. The *identification* meant what I knew mentally. The *declaration* meant what I said to others."

"You didn't identify him at the police station, did you?"

"No sir. Beg pardon, there is the word *identification* again. I take exception to your language. It would make a mistake to begin to divide the identification and the declaration and denial. You would make it appear that I am dishonest and I am not. . . . I want you to know, counselor, that the identification is purely a mental process after the senses have known, after the senses have distinguished. And unless it is taken *that* way, then to answer

134

quickly might be a kind of trap that you were getting me into. The *declaration* is where I tell it to others. *Identification* is what I know myself."

The cross-examination continued on that point for a while. Then Reilly, exhausting the subject without further enlightenment, turned to other matters. I read those pages again and closed the book with the feeling that, even for a doctor of pedagogy, as Condon called himself, the distinction between "declaration" and "identification" was indeed splitting hairs. And that if Alan Hynd's article was accurate—if Condon was so certain Hauptmann was not John that he continued to search for the extortionist after the arrest—then Condon was lying. I began to suspect, further, that the prosecution knew Condon was lying and bolstered that lie—how else construe the prosecution's assertion to reporters that Condon finally identified Hauptmann because in the months that the prisoner was behind bars he had lost thirty pounds, and now looked as he did in 1932?

And yet all the writers believed Condon and lustily embraced his story. Waller, most of all: in the definitive work on the case, the result of twenty-five years of research, Waller strove mightily to rationalize Condon's failure to identify Hauptmann. He wrote that, after speaking with Hauptmann in the police lineup and failing to get a confession from the prisoner:

It was a bitter moment for Dr. Condon, but he had done his best. He returned to the inspector's desk and said that he was finished.

Almost at once, it seemed, the quiet room turned into a carnival. Police officials and a swarm of reporters and photographers surged around Dr. Condon, flash bulbs flared, excited voices rang in his ears—"Which one is John? . . . Look this way, Jafsie! . . . Dr. Condon, look at me! . . . Which one is John? . . . Jafsie, Jafsie, look this way!"

Dr. Condon barely kept his temper in check. A man's life hung on the words he would speak, and the appalling atmosphere in which he was asked to say them was a disgraceful parody of the processes of law and justice he revered. He determined to teach these shouting men, the police and the press, a good lesson. He knew that Richard Hauptmann had been arrested with a ransom bill on him and that a great many more had been found in his garage. That was plenty of evidence for the police to charge him with extortion.

And so he said that for the time being he was withholding his identification.

A voice loud enough to be heard above the tumult bawled at him that either he could pick out John or he couldn't. *Which of the four men was John?*

Dr. Condon said firmly that at the present time he would not declare an identification.

Those paragraphs troubled me. It was evident that Waller had ingenuously accepted the state's case and Condon's testimony and later writings to compose his book, a best seller which probably convinced most of its readers that Hauptmann was unquestionably guilty. Waller certainly must have discovered, during his years of research, that Condon had repeatedly said Hauptmann was not John; Waller ignored that. His research must have disclosed that Condon actually told police, after viewing Hauptmann, that the prisoner "resembled" John but he couldn't swear he actually was John; Waller ignored that, and distorted Condon's comments of September 1934 to make them correspond to what Condon said four months later.

I kept going back again and again to the transcript of Condon's trial testimony. As I checked it against other sources, especially Condon's own book, a number of rather serious questions came to mind. Those questions demanded answers, and they'd have to be explored in depth later, when I began my search for original documents in the case, because the questions created broad gaps in Condon's testimony.

For example, in recreating the trip he made with Al Reich to Woodlawn Cemetery, where he met John for the first time, Condon testified: "I got out of the car with the letter that I had picked up at the frankfurter stand and went over to the middle of that space, like a little piazza or area in front of the gates. I took the letter out. One man walked down from 233rd Street in the direction of the automobile, between me and the automobile. Mr. Reich was in the automobile and I saw this man come down there, but I didn't pay any attention or any account to him."

Almost immediately, he said, he saw a handkerchief being waved inside the gate. The man waving it turned out to be John.

But who was the first man? I wondered. Condon was convinced he was dealing with a gang, including the Italian who had said *"statto citti"* and the Italian woman who asked him to meet her at the Tuckahoe station. I thought: *If he was so convinced a gang was involved, wouldn't he have believed this man he first saw at the cemetery was a lookout? Wouldn't he be very curious about this man? He most certainly would have been. Then why did he skim over it so lightly in his testimony and in his book?*

Again, I wondered once more why there was no mention of the Italian man Condon had heard over the telephone and the Italian woman who had approached him at the charity bazaar. But now my suspicions went even further. Obviously, the defense didn't know about these two incidents which established that more than one man had been involved in the extortion plot. Just as obvious, the prosecution had suppressed this evidence because it would have made a mockery of the claim that Hauptmann had acted alone. And if that evidence was kept from defense and public, how much other evidence helpful to Hauptmann had been similarly concealed?

Another question: During Condon's long recital of his experiences with John, he again slid quickly past an incident which could be vitally important. After the ransom had been paid, Condon told federal agents, John had climbed a low railing in the cemetery and leaped to the other side, landing on a freshly dug grave. Perhaps he had left his footprint, Condon suggested. Condon returned to the cemetery accompanied by his son-in-law, Ralph Hacker, and federal agent Thomas Sisk. They found a print where Condon said it might be. A plaster of paris cast of the footprint was made. But it was never introduced into evidence. Had it matched Hauptmann's shoe, I was certain, the prosecutor would have put it into evidence because he held back no evidence in his files that could have convicted Hauptmann. His failure to use the plaster cast against the prisoner must have meant that it didn't match Hauptmann's shoes. Was this also deliberately suppressed?

Another thing that further aroused my curiosity about Condon's honesty was his strange inability to speak Hauptmann's name. Early on, Condon had identified Hauptmann as John. Yet during all his long recitation about his meetings and discussions with the extortionist, Condon never called him "Hauptmann" from the witness chair but always referred to him as "John." Perhaps I was over-

137

reacting, searching for flaws in his testimony. Perhaps I was too anxious to destroy Condon's story. Fearing so, I reread his testimony for perhaps the sixth time. And I knew I was absolutely correct: on page after page the question is asked of Condon, "Who said that?" and Condon replies, "John." In one instance Wilentz attempts to give him an opening by asking, "Who asked who was up there, the defendant?" And with the defendant, Hauptmann, sitting only a few feet away, Condon replies, "John asked me who was up there."

Wilentz finally found it necessary to ask Condon, "And John is who?" in order to get the desired response, "Hauptmann." And to remind the jury that Hauptmann had really been identified by this witness who was so reluctant to utter that name.

Several times Condon insisted that he was "an honest man," and I suspected that he was finding it difficult to truly associate Richard Hauptmann with John, that deep in his psyche he had the gravest doubts. There seemed to be a conflict between his memory and the public ritual he was being required to perform at Flemington. My intuition told me Condon was lying. When he identified Hauptmann as John, his very being must have been affected, because he valued so highly his reputation for morality and honesty. He could not continue to lie and so he called the extortionist "John" even after saying it was Hauptmann.

Finally, one thing more made me suspect Condon of lying. Made me believe, in fact, that his testimony had been rehearsed. I returned again to Reilly's question, "Did you tell reporters at that time that Hauptmann was not John?" And Condon's reply: "Oh, I never did. I never told or mentioned his name to them in public, never—note the words—of affirmation or denial. I make a distinction between *identification* and *declaration of identification.*"

Immediately after denying he had made such a statement to reporters, Condon leaped into his explanation of his distinction between mentally identifying someone and verbally declaring that identification. It all came too fast, I felt. Condon had not been asked why he had failed to identify Hauptmann at the police lineup. He volunteered his explanation. It was as if he had struck upon the perfect explanation, or rationalization, only very recently and couldn't wait to relay it to the world that was so anxiously awaiting his testimony.

And so I constructed in my mind a scenario that might have been

138

acted out in the prosecutor's office. It is several weeks before the trial. Condon is sitting in the office of Attorney General Wilentz (a meeting that actually occurred). Several police officials and assistant prosecutors are with them. Condon is being asked the details of the story he will tell from the witness chair, for it is accepted practice to determine in advance what your witness will testify to. And someone at the conference asks: "Reilly will want to know why you didn't identify Hauptmann at police headquarters. What will you tell him?"

Condon: "I wasn't too certain at that time."

Voice : "Was it because of uncertainty or because you wanted to be absolutely fair?"

Condon: "Oh, I want to be fair when a man's life is at stake."

Voice: "Then you decided to withhold your *verbal* identification for a while?"

Condon: "Yes, that is correct. I knew it was Hauptmann the moment I saw him. I just did not want to say it until everyone calmed down."

Voice: "Then you simply refused to declare your identification because . . ."

Condon: "That's absolutely correct. There is a distinction between the identification I make in my mind, and the *declaration* of identification I make to the world . . ."

Was I so anxious to prove Hauptmann's innocence that I was reading too much into words a man had spoken under stress? Perhaps so. Yet the weight of my own certainty was too heavy to ignore: Condon had been lying; the police and possibly the prosecutor had known he was lying. I hoped I could eventually prove it, but I was afraid that the old man may have had, as Thomas Carlyle once put it, "the talent of lying in a way that cannot be laid hold of."

7

The trial continued. The river of words pursued its course. Through the courtroom, along the miles of telegraph wires, words soon edited, condensed, bulletined and headlined, transformed into mauve prose for the evening papers. Fingers were keeping things going, court stenographers transcribing the script and the audience reaction—(Applause), (Laughter)—and the elevators of public opinion remained stationary because the performance was so closely following the promptbook.

Yes, I've seen Bruno Richard Hauptmann before, when he bought a movie ticket from me on November 26, 1933, Cecile Barr swore. Hauptmann threw a bill at me, a strangely folded five-dollar gold note, "folded three times in eight parts." And I looked at him, I asked him which of the three price-class seats he wished to buy and as he stood there, trying to make up his mind, "all that time I looked at him." Yes, sir, I am certain it was Hauptmann.

Oh, certainly, I remember Hauptmann, Millard Whited swore. I lived about a mile from the Lindbergh place and I knew everybody in the neighborhood. A stranger showed up in February, a couple of weeks before the kidnaping. Twice I saw this stranger. The first time was about the eighteenth of February. I was driving home for dinner and he stepped out of the bushes at the side of the road and I saw him good through my open window and after I passed I looked through the rearview mirror and wondered why and where he came from. The second time was about a week later, around the

141

twenty-fifth to the twenty-seventh as near as I can recollect now. I was driving my truck and I saw him on the crossroad that leads to Zion, just standing there. I passed no more than six feet from him. It was Hauptmann, sure enough, and I wondered what this stranger was doing around there.

Well, it was about eight o'clock on the Saturday before the kidnaping, Charles Rossiter said. I was a salesman back then and I did a lot of driving around the state. That night I was driving along Route Thirty-one, right near the Princeton Airport, when I saw that man—Hauptmann—standing at the back of a car at the side of the road. I stopped and got out, to see if he needed any help. He said he didn't need any help but I didn't leave right away, "I stood there and looked the man over pretty well." The next time I saw him it was his picture, the day after his arrest. So I told police about it and they took me over to the Bronx. I saw him there, Hauptmann. The same man.

With these three, there were now six eyewitnesses to place Hauptmann near the Lindbergh home at the time of the kidnaping, in and around the cemeteries during the extortion, and in the act of passing a Lindbergh ransom bill. Each of them, all of them, multiplied the impact Lindbergh had on the jury: Hauptmann was both the kidnaper-murderer and the extortionist.

And to firmly and devastatingly place Hauptmann in the nursery on the night the child was stolen, Wilentz called a string of expert witnesses, the handwriting analysts. Albert S. Osborn, white-haired, somewhat deaf, the most expert of all the experts, was the first of seven men called to swear that Hauptmann had written every single one of the ransom notes.

Wilentz led Osborn through a lecture on the art and science of identifying disputed writings, as one journalist of the day put it. Art and science? Nonsense. American courts have held repeatedly that the testimony of so-called handwriting experts represents the lowest degree of evidence, and with good reason. The analysis of questioned documents is neither science nor art. It is a very subjective process in which the examiner looks for "similarities" between two sets of writings and, depending on whether or not he finds enough similarities, renders his *opinion*. Legal scholars to this day question the value of such opinions, primarily because each side in a legal dispute always manages to find enough experts to support its particular contention.

142

The value of handwriting analysis is questionable, moreover, because so many "experts" have so often been proved dead wrong. For example, a short time before the trial one of the handwriting experts who testified against Hauptmann had helped convict an innocent man by swearing the defendant had forged a number of checks. Again, Albert S. Osborn's son, who also testified against Hauptmann, still headed the family firm in 1971 when it reported there wasn't "the slightest question" that Clifford Irving's forgery of the handwriting of Howard Hughes had actually been written by Hughes; further, the Osborns said, it was "impossible as a practical matter, based on our years of experience . . . that anyone other than" Hughes could have written the letters written by Irving. Further evidence from the Hughes-Irving fiasco shows how "scientific" this field is, even with improvement in techniques in the forty years since the Hauptmann trial. Alfred Kanfer, another handwriting authority, was asked to compare Irving's forgeries with authentic handwriting by Hughes. After studying the materials, Kanfer said they'd been written by Hughes and asserted: "The chances that another person could copy this handwriting even in a similar way are less than one in a million." Finally, another piece of evidence attesting to the extreme fallibility of handwriting experts emerged in 1970, during one of Hughes's many court battles. In this one, the former commander of the FBI forgery school gave it as his expert opinion that a document purportedly signed by Hughes was a forgery. Later events in court proved that Hughes had indeed signed it.

But to return to the transcript of the Hauptmann trial: Bulletin boards are wheeled into the courtroom. On them are dozens of photographic blowups of letters, words, sentences. Osborn the elder steps down from the witness chair and over to the photos, takes pointer in hand, and begins his lecture. He is questioned only occasionally by Wilentz.

He explains to the jury: The thirty pieces of script before us include fourteen ransom notes and sixteen specimens of Hauptmann's known writings. Among his known writings are some of the pages he wrote as police dictated to him at Greenwich Street in the days after his arrest. We will break down all these writings into three categories: the disputed ransom notes; the "conceded writings," such as Hauptmann's automobile license applications; and the "request writings," done at the dictation of police.

143

"Have you made a careful comparison and examination of the so-called ransom notes with the conceded writings and the request writings of Bruno Richard Hauptmann?" Wilentz asks.

"I have."

"Based on your examination and comparison, what is the opinion you have reached?"

"My opinion is that the ransom notes were all written by the writer of the various papers signed 'Richard Hauptmann.' "

"Explain the reasons."

In the first of several lengthy, rambling lectures, Osborn said he'd found all the writings were connected with each other in a large number of ways, a number of which were outside the question of handwriting. By that he meant, he said, a discernible pattern in the use of words and the peculiar spelling connecting them; the fact that the second note referred to ideas expressed in the first note, such as the amount of ransom, and each note that followed made reference to something previously written; the crude symbol with the three circles and three holes found on all notes, so that when all the notes were placed one upon the other, the three holes matched so perfectly that by holding them to the light "you can see right through the holes." Here the reporters scribbled more quickly to record his implication that the kidnaper had punched holes through a pad of paper at one time, tearing off a sheet whenever he wanted to write another note.

Through almost all the eighth day of the trial and into the morning of the ninth, Osborn went over individual letters in the ransom script and in Hauptmann's writings to show that peculiarities in the ransom notes were the same as peculiarities in Hauptmann's writings. The witness dissected individual words to demonstrate that they appeared in all sets of writings. He summed it all up by saying the evidence proving Hauptmann had written the ransom notes was "irresistible, unanswerable, and overwhelming."

Reilly took the witness for cross-examination. Handing Osborn two of the ransom notes, he said: "I ask you whether there is, in your opinion, a visible difference between them?"

"Oh, there is a *little* variation," Osborn replied, "but in my opinion they are substantially the same."

Another note was handed him, one sent to Dr. Condon. "Isn't the phrasing of the letters, the general outline, a little clearer than the preceding notes?"

"I would say that it is clearer than the nursery note and perhaps a little more freely written than some of the others, but it is essentially the same."

"Well, is this disguised, in your opinion?"

"I think they are all disguised, all the ransom notes. That is, they are all disguised to a certain extent. That is, they are not natural, free writing."

Disguised. I turned back now to the earlier part of Osborn's speech, where he had originally brought up the theory of disguised writings. He had said: "In my opinion the ransom letters are all written in a disguised hand, somewhat disguised." Then he explained that it is customary, when taking a handwriting sample from a suspect, to have him write the same material three times. And he went on:

"The writing is taken away and another sheet is supplied and the same matter dictated. Now, if they differ from each other it is not the habitual genuine honest writing of the writer. And that is exactly what we find in this request writing. In one instance we find it on the same sheet of paper. In my opinion these ransom notes are disguised writings, part of the request writings are disguised writings, and the writer didn't have but one disguise. So that when the request writings were asked for, part of them are written in the style of the ransom notes and part . . . are like the writings of the automobile registrations" and a promissory note Hauptmann had signed.

Wait a minute . . . wait just a minute, I thought. From everything I'd read, Hauptmann had been forced to write "from dictation" for many hours. "From nine that evening until early the next morning," one handwriting authority in the employ of the prosecution later wrote, "he covered page after page with writing." Scores of pages, no doubt, perhaps a hundred or more, in those hours; on the ten pages of that dictation I was able to find reproduced in several books, police officers present had written the precise time of dictation, and they ranged from nine in the evening of September 19 to ten the next morning. It seemed plain that only a small portion of the pages he had written had been introduced into evidence and were used to demonstrate similarities between those writings and the ransom notes. Would it be unfair to suggest that prosecution witnesses had been very selective? That only those samples with the greatest similarities would do for their demonstration?

Disguise? Or had it been weariness? The elder Osborn had said it was customary to have a subject write three times under dictation. One reason not to have a man write dozens of times would be the distortion in the handwriting that repetition naturally brings. There was also something else, I remembered from my readings in the Clifford Irving forgery. One of the Osborns who had wrongly attributed Irving's writings to Howard Hughes, while attempting to explain to interviewers how they'd made the error, had stressed two important procedures that an analyst must follow. One is to obtain samples of the subject's writings that have been written at roughly the same time as the questioned documents, because the style and character of handwriting changes; that, of course, was not done in the Hauptmann case if only because his arrest came more than two years after the ransom notes had been written. Second, the analyst must make certain the samples have not been done deliberately for a specimen. "Writing is a semiconscious act and it's as difficult to do naturally if you have been asked for a specimen as it is to walk into a room naturally if you are being filmed," a member of the Osborn firm explained. The Hauptmann samples, then, were doubly unnatural: they were written under dictation as handwriting samples to be submitted to an expert, and they were written after Hauptmann had been told he was a suspect in the Lindbergh murder.

The train of thought leaps back further as the mind filters and digests, as it recognizes nuances. Osborn had said the ransom letters were written in a disguised hand. "Part of the request writings" were similarly disguised, he said; Hauptmann "didn't have but one disguise." The logic is defective: building a positive identification by placing disguise upon disguise with no glue to bind them is like building a house by placing brick upon brick and omitting the mortar. For if Hauptmann was the criminal genius Wilentz etched for us and had actually written the ransom letters in a disguised hand, would he then attempt to disguise the words he was writing for police? Hardly. He would write as naturally as possible so that the dictated writings wouldn't accidentally resemble the disguised writings in the ransom letters. To repeat the disguised writing would defeat the very reason for disguise. It would be absolute lunacy.

Osborn and the other six witnesses agreed that Hauptmann wrote every one of the ransom notes. And as I read through their

146

testimony I was struck by an odd omission. Osborn had said at the very beginning that the ransom note which had been left in the nursery was written by the same man who had written all the other notes. But he had made the statement, "That first letter was written with more deliberation than any of the other letters, written somewhat more slowly and with more deliberation. . . ." He quickly added that he was certain it had been written by the same man. Yet his statement quite explicitly pointed to differences. When I looked through all the handwriting testimony for a discussion of the first ransom note, I realized that every one of the prosecution's experts had ignored the letter found in the nursery. They made general statements that it had been written by the man who wrote all the later notes, but they offered no specifics. In all their charts breaking down the notes into sentences, words, and individual letters, only a single word, "is," was taken from the first ransom letter. They ignored thirty-nine other words and nine numerals. Was it because they could not say Hauptmann had written them? I found it all rather strange. My thoughts returned again to Mickey Rosner, the bootlegger and Lindbergh's "secretary," and the assertion that he had displayed the first ransom letter all over Manhattan, permitting it to be copied and recopied until many con men and thieves had an exact reproduction of it. Could that event, if it indeed occurred, be an explanation for something else Osborn said? "The first two lines of the second letter are written with great deliberation," said Osborn, "and very distinctly like the writing in the first letter. The rest of the second letter is written somewhat more freely."

Was it possible that one man, the kidnaper, wrote the first letter and was then frightened off by the death of the child? And then a second man, the extortionist, got a copy of the first letter and began to write the second one in the style of the first, and then, growing slightly careless, wrote the remainder of it "somewhat more freely"? Could Hauptmann have been the extortionist, the writer of all the later ransom notes? Perhaps Condon wasn't lying . . .

Damn the experts! I was beginning to feel like a yo-yo, thrown down and yanked back up again. Hauptmann didn't do it . . . well, maybe he did part of it . . . no, he couldn't have, they're lying . . . on the other hand . . . damn. It was all too complex to worry over at this early stage. I would return to the handwriting later.

But I couldn't let go, not immediately, because a phrase in the testimony of Osborn's son, Albert D., one of the experts for the prosecution, leaped out at me. He, too, swore Hauptmann wrote all the ransom letters. But when asked for specific reasons, he fell back primarily on the fact that certain words which had been misspelled in the ransom notes had also been misspelled by Hauptmann when the test paragraph was dictated to him again and again. Osborn was asked whether any of the words had been deliberately misspelled by police as they dictated. He replied he didn't know "of my own knowledge," but insisted that could not have happened because he had the utmost confidence in the police and especially the federal agents. "Of my own knowledge": how many witnesses have I heard or read about who avoided a direct perjury charge by denying personal knowledge of an event they have heard, secondhand, did take place? Men accustomed to testifying under oath and wise in the ways of legal deception repeatedly use that expression or variations of it—"to the best of my recollection" is another example—and though I could not know whether Osborn was deliberately fudging, those phrases have always been a warning signal for me. (Hauptmann, of course, swore when he took the stand in his own defense that all the misspellings had been dictated by police. I could no more take that as truth than I could take Condon's stories, for the defendant more than anyone else can be expected to lie. I would have to find other evidence to prove or disprove my suspicions.)

Handwriting experts concluded their lectures, the charts were taken away, and Wilentz moved on to negate in advance an expected defense attack. It was the opinion of Lloyd Fisher, the second-in-command of the defense staff, that the strongest possible defense was to attack the identification of the child's body found in the woods months after the kidnaping. If the jury could be made to doubt the body was that of young Lindbergh, then they could not bring in a murder conviction. At the very least, they would be forced to recommend mercy so that Hauptmann would remain alive while those who believed in his innocence—Fisher and Mrs. Hauptmann were almost alone in that belief—could search for new evidence to free him. Fisher had taken over from Reilly in the examination of every witness who testified about the corpse, and the thrust of his every question had been whether the state had absolutely unalterable proof the body was correctly identified. Had the issue been pressed, Wilentz might have had difficulty proving the *corpus delicti.*

Mrs. Elmire Dormer was called to the stand. There had been stories in the papers that the body found in the shallow grave was actually the corpse of a child who had died at St. Michael's Orphanage, across the road from where the corpse had been discovered. Bootleggers anxious to end police searches of their trucks took that body from the graveyard and placed it where it was found, the articles suggested. Fisher knew that in that part of New Jersey people might be made to believe anything about a Catholic orphanage, and he had prepared a long and hard cross-examination of Mrs. Dormer, the institution's custodian.

Wilentz asked: "Was there a child unaccounted for in that orphanage in February or March 1932?"

"None were missing. They were all accounted for."

"How about May 12, 1932?" (The date the body was discovered.)

"No, every day we know all the children and we account for them every day."

"So that in the year 1932 there were no children unaccounted for in your orphanage?"

"No, sir."

Wilentz strode to the prosecution table and picked up the school's attendance books for 1932. If there was any dispute about the attendance, he said, he would offer these books in evidence.

Reilly replied: "There is no dispute." Fisher nodded agreement; he wasn't paying close attention, for he was busy making notes for his cross-examination. Besides, the prosecutor had asked only about *live* children missing, while the report he had received was that the body of a child resembling the Lindbergh child had been stolen shortly after its death, around the time of the kidnaping.

Wilentz pressed on. "If there is any claim about it," he said, "I will offer the books in evidence."

Reilly: "I will say now that there has *never* been any claim but this was Colonel Lindbergh's child that was found there."

Fisher, rising to answer, but too late, appeared as if struck in the face with a club; Reilly had just destroyed the slimmest chance to save Hauptmann's life. Even if he protested and tried to correct the record, the jury had heard the concession. Fisher shot up straight now and shouted at Reilly, "You are conceding Haupt-

149

mann to the electric chair!'' Then, with an inaudible word that was a short sharp hiss of contempt, he rushed from the courtroom. Hauptmann started to rise, as if to flee with the lawyer he most trusted, but thought better of it as his guards stirred. He sat heavily and whispered, "You are killing me." Anna Hauptmann sat, the wrench of recognition twisting at the edges of her mouth, understanding that a crisis had been reached—and lost.

Mrs. Dormer was followed by Justice Department agent Thomas Sisk. He related the events following Hauptmann's capture: While searching the closet in Hauptmann's bedroom he noticed the prisoner glancing furtively from the window to the garage; eventually, it was in the garage that the cache of ransom money was found. Hauptmann leaned forward in his seat, turning round to see whether Fisher was returning, growing more agitated as the import of Reilly's blunder stabbed home. And now further agitated by Sisk's testimony, vigorously shaking his head at every one of the federal agent's assertions. They had dug under the floorboards in the garage, Sisk swore. They had found the metal can buried a foot below the soil. It was filled only with water. Sisk went on:

"We questioned Hauptmann as to that jug. He denied knowing anything about it, but the next day when we questioned him he admitted that he had that money in there three weeks before he was arrested."

"Mister! Mister!" Hauptmann shouted. He jumped up and started toward the witness. "Mister, you stop lying. You are telling a story!"

His guards, seized by surprise for a moment, finally leaped after Hauptmann and pulled him back to his chair. Lindbergh turned to look at him. Each day, Lindbergh sat at the prosecution table as a silent accuser, a constant reminder to the jury that he was the grieved father and that *he,* Charles Augustus Lindbergh, was a member of the prosecution team. He glared at Hauptmann now.

Judge Trenchard banged his gavel. "One moment," he commanded. "Let me suggest to the defendant that he keep quiet. If he has any observations to make, let him make them quietly through counsel."

Hauptmann's head fell to his chest. He understood what was being done to him. Reilly had thrown away a major part of his defense in a single brisk sentence. Now Sisk was destroying in advance another piece of his defense. During the days of questioning after his arrest, Hauptmann had told police he remembered

Fisch's shoe box with "important papers" only after rain had dripped into the closet and soaked that box. He had accidentally found the money, soaking wet. Police lab reports confirmed the bills had been water-soaked. Now Sisk, in a swift thrust like an infantryman slashing his bayonet to the enemy, sliced and punctured Hauptmann's defense: the gold notes had been soaked because Hauptmann had placed them in a jug that later became partially filled with water.

Yes, Hauptmann understood this personal disaster: "Mister . . . you stop lying. . . ." He must have also understood on this twelfth day of his trial something even more terrifying to the marrow of his life: he had been a fool. He'd been dealing in reality, in the facts of his predicament, and he obviously believed the truth would see him vindicated, because he assumed everyone else at the trial was a part of the real world. He must have believed all the evidence and truth would be brought out in court as it is in Europe, including Germany. In Europe, criminal justice is derived from the Roman law. The judge, armed with all the evidence amassed by police, examines and cross-examines witnesses. There is little distinction between the people's attorney (who is not considered a prosecutor) and the defense attorney. Both are bound in theory and usually in practice to present to the court all material relevant to the case, and it is most especially the duty of the people's attorney to present the true facts rather than press for conviction. A trial in Germany and most of the Continent is a fact-finding expedition, not a ritual twisted to the artifice of legal formality as it is in our courtrooms, which dance to the tune of English law. Hauptmann, having had some experience in German courts, must have felt his soul corrode at this shock of recognition that our trials are formalized contests, with victory to the lawyer who can throw the hardest punches, who can feint and jab and block and deceive with greater skill than his opponent. "Mister . . . you stop lying. You are telling a story"—words of a man who suddenly realizes the bars keeping the lions from him are built of twine.

And now flowing over me was an aching need to know, a hunger of the mind. Was Condon lying? Was Lindbergh, even Lindy, the hero, was he lying? Was Sisk lying? Would Hauptmann have been so grievously provoked had Sisk been telling the truth? Were they *all* lying?

But why? Anti-German feeling because of Hitler? It had to be more than that. Perhaps . . . let us suppose that each of them, each man and woman of them, knew with absolute certainty that Hauptmann was guilty. The police said so; there was the money in his garage; the "Fisch story," as they so cavalierly dismissed Hauptmann's explanation of how he came by the ransom money; his profession, carpenter; his resignation from his job the day the ransom was paid; his weak alibi. Each of these witnesses knew Hauptmann's alibi had collapsed, for police and press had told them so. And so, for the glory of being part of a well-publicized justice, of official retribution, of carnival and theater, a chance to step onto center stage for a brief moment of media fame, perhaps, for those with a longer view, to become a footnote in history, a need for immortality of sorts, or even possibly to share in the $25,000 reward—each of them believed that a little embroidery in the official fabric couldn't hurt. Hauptmann was so guilty that a little piece of distorted evidence, a small lie, would not be very dreadful. The other witnesses are convicting this man, not me, each of them might have thought, the burden of his doom falls on everyone else . . . me, I'm just adding a drop to an ocean, I'm just a minnow among larger fish . . . what's the harm?

"Yes, Hauptmann was the man who . . ."

Another piece of evidence was introduced by Wilentz. Gingerly he handled a small piece of board wrapped in cellophane. His witness, Inspector Henry Bruckman, chief of Bronx detectives, was asked to explain its significance.

On the morning of September 24, the fifth day Hauptmann was in custody, Bruckman went with carpenters to the prisoner's apartment. He had decided to give the place the same close examination that had been given the garage where the money was found—raze the walls, if necessary, to locate other clues to prove Hauptmann was a kidnaper and extortionist. While carpenters were stripping the plaster in the living room, Bruckman had explored in the nursery. He looked into the closet, empty now except for a clothespole and a shelf. He called one of the carpenters to remove them so he could squeeze inside, for it was a very shallow closet. The obstructions removed, he stepped inside and, with a flashlight, sought evidence of a hollow where more money could have been hidden. The beam of his light fell on the inside trim above the doorway. Something was written there. Bruckman put on his glasses.

"2974 Decatur," Condon's address. Inside Hauptmann's house! Beneath it: "S"—the second letter was blurred—"DG 3–7154."

Of course, Sedgwick 3–7154, Condon's telephone number. Here was proof Hauptmann had been in contact with Condon during the ransom negotiations. The earliest stages, in any case, for Bruckman remembered that Condon had changed his number to a private listing ten days after the kidnaping. Hauptmann, then, had been the German who called a couple of times in the first days of negotiations.

Bruckman examined the inside of the closet more closely. There were other pencil markings on the inside of the door: the notation "$500," followed by what appeared to be the serial numbers of two bills. But the numbers didn't match any of the Lindbergh ransom bills. Anxious to confront Hauptmann with his discovery, Bruckman ordered the trim and door removed. Behind the trim he found a shallow recess in the wall. Perfect for hiding ransom money, Bruckman thought. He took the wood and the door to the Bronx district attorney's office, where Hauptmann was being questioned for the sixth day.

Bruckman stepped down and District Attorney Samuel Foley's stenographer was called to the witness chair. He brought with him his stenographic notes of Foley's interview with Hauptmann about the writing in the closet. The stenographer read to the jury:

Q. Hauptmann, I want to ask you some questions about this board. You know it is from your closet in your own home, don't you?
A. It must be.
Q. It is the same kind of wood, your handwriting is on it.
A. Yes, all over it.
Q. What did you write on that board? Read it to the stenographer.
A. I can't read it anymore.
Q. Who rubbed it out? Can you read the address on it?
A. Two-nine-seven-four. I can't make out the first. I can't make out the first . . . I read the number down below, 37154.
Q. What else can you read on that board that you wrote yourself?
A. I can't read . . . that's a *T-U* and *R* . . . another one I can't make out.
Q. That is Dr. Condon's address, isn't it?

153

A. I don't know.

Q. Why did you write it on the board?

A. I must have read it in the paper about the story. I was a little bit interest, and keep a little bit record of it and maybe I was just on the closet and was reading the paper and put down the address.

Q. How did you come to put the telephone number on there?

A. I can't give you any explanation about the telephone number.

Q. Your only explanation for writing Dr. Condon's telephone number and address on this board is that you were probably reading the paper in the closet and you marked it down, is that correct?

A. It is possible that a shelf or two shelfs in the closet and after a while I put new papers always on the closet and we just got the paper where this case was in and I followed the story of course and I put the address on there.

Q. Do you remember the day you wrote this on the board?

A. No.

Q. You remember that you did write it?

A. I must write it, the figures, that's my writing.

Q. The writing is yours too, isn't it?

A. I hardly can read it.

Q. From what you see of it, it is your writing, isn't it? It is your figures and your writing?

A. I really can't remember when I put it on.

Q. Regardless of when you put it on, it is your figures and your writing, isn't it?

A. The writing I can't make out so very clearly. I don't know.

Reading that transcript, several things become as clear as anything can over a span of forty years. Hauptmann, in his answers, seemed genuinely to believe he had written at least the figures on the trim board and perhaps the letters. Rather than being evasive or attempting to lie, he responded as a man would who believed he must do all he can to help authorities clear up this strange set of circumstances so that he could return to wife and child; he even offered a farfetched suggestion out of his naive notion of justice in America: maybe he'd been reading in the closet where he always stored newspapers and jotted down the information about Condon

154

out of interest in the case. Farfetched, not because he was lying but because he apparently didn't understand which closet the trim board had been removed from. The nursery closet had only a single shelf, not "two shelfs"; Hauptmann was thinking of some other closet in which he could stand with ease, probably the large kitchen closet in which police found a pile of newspapers when they searched his apartment. The nursery closet was extremely shallow and it was dark, without artificial light, for Bruckman had to use a flashlight to discover the writing on the trim board.

(The writing on the door, which was more likely Hauptmann's, is another matter. Swing the door open and it is possible to read something on it in the natural light of the room. That writing, on the door, was not put into evidence by Wilentz because it would not have helped his case. Hauptmann had explained that the numbers on the door were records of two large bills Isidor Fisch had turned over to him to buy stocks. Five-hundred or thousand-dollar bills, he didn't remember which. But he was worried about being responsible for so much of his friend's money so he wrote the serial numbers on the door and hid them in the little hollow behind the trim board until he could get down to his broker's office and execute Fisch's order. The serial numbers, federal agents discovered, were indeed for a five-hundred and a one-thousand-dollar bill. That evidence would have helped Hauptmann, so Wilentz, a part of the advocacy system, did not introduce it.)

As I thought about it, the trim board with Condon's address and phone number made less and less sense, made no sense at all after a time. Not only was the closet dark, but it was so small Inspector Bruckman had to have a shelf and clothespole removed and even then he had to back into it to see out because there wasn't enough room to turn around. Even a carpenter, accustomed to jotting down measurements and memoranda on boards, on walls, on any handy surface, would not have written these letters and figures in a place where he would have difficulty seeing them and where he could not comfortably stand to read and write. And writing Condon's phone number anywhere in his apartment made absolutely no sense, since Hauptmann did not have a telephone. To make telephone calls, he went out to a public phone booth. In New York City, all phone booths were equipped with telephone directories. Condon was listed in the directory. Would you write a number in a dark closet when you had to go down into the street to make a call from a booth with a directory inside it? And would you leave that number in your closet for more than two years after its usefulness ended, to haunt you as evidence of your crime?

Even John Condon, the most dramatic witness for the state, the only man ever to talk to John of the cemeteries, questioned the authenticity of the writing on the trim board. (While suspecting that Condon had lied in his testimony for the defense, I could not afford to ignore a lead that reinforced my intuition even if the source was otherwise corrupted; I'll accept it as a possibility now in the early stages of my search, I said to myself, and either prove it or discard it later on.) Said Condon after the trial: "To this day I cannot bring myself to accept the written telephone number and address in the kidnaper's closet. . . ." For Condon, a man so convinced that Hauptmann was guilty, to question an important piece of evidence, made it highly likely that evidence had been faked. That likelihood raised many other possibilities. Assuming Condon—and my own intuition—to be correct, the closet writing was counterfeited. Yet Hauptmann, examining it in the district attorney's office, seemed almost convinced it was his writing. Could that mean his handwriting was so common that the writing of any number of other immigrants schooled in certain areas of Europe could have been similar to his? If so, what does that do to the opinions of handwriting analysts who so heavily stressed the European and Germanic constructions and writing techniques linking the hand of Hauptmann with the hand that had written the ransom notes? Once more the questions could not be immediately answered—if ever, I thought with a sinking feeling. The question would have to be pushed aside for now, along with so many others.

Back to the courtroom once more, or rather, to a strange incident that took place about this time in the trial, an incident not related to jury or public until years afterward. It concerned John Hughes Curtis, the swindler who'd been convicted of obstructing justice by refusing to help police find the kidnapers he had claimed to be in contact with before a child's body was found. Curtis had been reading newspaper accounts of the trial and was working out angles that could be of benefit to him. His jail sentence had been suspended, but he'd been forced to pay a $1,000 fine and his good name had been sullied. How to correct that? And get back his money?

An idea occurred to him: he would offer to go to Flemington and

156

testify that Bruno Hauptmann was one of the kidnap gang he'd been dealing with. Yes, he could positively identify Hauptmann. In return for his help in convicting the defendant, all he wanted was a small reward: exoneration and the return of his $1,000.

Curtis telephoned Colonel Schwarzkopf, head of the state police, and offered his testimony against Hauptmann. If he could be exonerated by the state, if Lindbergh would pose with him, shaking hands, to restore his reputation, he would testify against Hauptmann.

And Schwarzkopf, that honorable man, that upholder of the law and the dignity of justice, said it sounded like a brilliant idea and he would put the proposition to Lindbergh. But Lindbergh said no and that was the end of it.

Unbelievable! Schwarzkopf was willing to go along with an absolute lie in order to further condemn Hauptmann. The head of the police, the man whose morality or lack thereof sets the tone for every member of his force, would have helped put a perjurer in the witness chair. And I remembered something else I'd read about Schwarzkopf. Shortly before the trial began he had told reporters he considered Lindbergh one of his dearest friends and said he "would do anything for that man." Including, obviously, accepting a concocted story from an admitted swindler. Schwarzkopf's attitude most certainly must have been communicated to every one of his investigators: convict Hauptmann at all costs. Is that why the closet board had turned up? Could I be far wrong, then, in suspecting Wilentz's witnesses were lying? No . . . my suspicions only touched the surface, of that much I was certain. And the lies probably went beyond an individual here swearing he saw Hauptmann in the cemetery, an individual there swearing he saw the man near Lindbergh's home. The few discrepancies I had uncovered so far gave promise of a total fraud, a broad conspiracy by dozens of men and women acting out of varying motives, all intent on convicting Hauptmann. Conspiracy? I'd always shuddered at that word, so much a part of the paranoia of the sixties that became reality in the seventies, but now it sounded right.

Another expert was called by Wilentz. An accountant, William Frank of the Treasury Department. His testimony, aided by exhibits filled with figures, balances, debits, and bottom lines, nearly put jurors, reporters, and spectators to sleep. But his conclusions were highly damaging to Hauptmann. Some of the figures he recited

157

startled quite a few people in the courtroom, stirred them from their midday naps. In 1933, he said, Hauptmann traded with three stockbrokers and the total amount of money passing through his accounts was $256,442.15, over a quarter of a million dollars! Another figure was equally impressive. Between April 2, 1932, when the Lindbergh ransom was paid, and September 19, 1934, when the defendant was arrested, if you total all the wealth Hauptmann amassed in that period and add to it his known expenditures, you arrive at the figure $49,950. Just a few dollars shy of the $50,000 ransom. Hauptmann had possessed and spent the fifty thousand!

Reilly took the witness on cross-examination. He had Frank read a long list of stock transactions upon which he'd based part of his accounting. Frank admitted Hauptmann had traded on margin, had been in and out of the market day after day.

Didn't all this show that Hauptmann traded in a great many stocks?

Yes, sir, it did, Frank conceded.

That he was constantly in the market, buying one day and selling the next?

Yes, it did.

That he frequently made small profits in a two- or three-day period?

Yes, sir.

Actually, hadn't the defendant earned $8,000 this way in just one month?

Yes, sir.

Then doesn't it appear you've credited Hauptmann with a sum of cash he never had? That the huge sums his brokerage accounts showed at various periods, wasn't that just paper figures, churning, buying and selling? In actual cash, wasn't the figure only a few thousand?

No, sir. My accounting is correct.

That is all, Reilly said. With exasperation, no doubt.

Reilly's questions and their implication sounded logical to me. I'd been caught with the fever during one of those boom markets of the sixties, gambling in stocks and feeling superior to friends who gambled on horses because they were *gambling* and I was . . . well, part of the great American mainstream. I took a beating, of course. Just a couple of thousand. But because I was buying

158

for the fast three-point profit (and often "cutting losses" at three points on the downside, so often I was soon wiped out, never to return), because of the almost daily trading on margin, any accounting of my transactions would make it appear I had $100,000 in that account. It looks so lovely on paper . . .

I jumped out of sequence now in my readings and moved ahead in the trial transcript to learn precisely what Hauptmann said about those figures which indicated he had possessed $50,000, presumably the ransom money. And as I read, I realized Hauptmann sounded like a liar, a rather inept liar, even under the careful guidance of his own attorney. With all the evidence so far introduced against him making it plain to everyone that he was guilty, his explanations sounded empty.

On this date, he said, the $900 deposited in his stock account was money supplied by Fisch. On April 28, 1933, $2,500 in cash—Fisch's money. On July 24, $4,500 in cash—Fisch's money. Except for the reinvestment of his dividends, Hauptmann testified, every penny actually added to his brokerage account had come from Fisch.

From his testimony, I tried to follow Hauptmann's almost daily stock trading, but it was too much for me, all those figures. I'm still unable to balance my checkbook, and the new math they were drilling into my kids at school created a panic within me. I couldn't terrorize my head with Hauptmann's figures, not right now. Later, I would try. I went back to the place where I had left the trial.

"I call as my next witness Lewis J. Bornmann."

"Detective Bornmann, please!"

Bornmann rises from the prosecution table and steps to the witness chair. He has not been outside, in the corridor or in an anteroom, not kept segregated from the proceedings so that his recollections, his mind, would be uninfluenced by the testimony of witnesses who preceded him. He has sat day after day at the long table of the prosecution, with Lindbergh and Wilentz and a half dozen prosecution lawyers.

Bornmann. The cop who took over Hauptmann's apartment hours after his arrest, who cheerfully agreed with Mrs. Hauptmann that she should move in with relatives and then confiscated the apartment. The man who still lived there, keeping out defense lawyers and investigators who sought entrance; mistrustful, they wanted to see where Bornmann had located certain evidence they

159

heard he had found, how he had come across it, what the apartment now looked like. But Bornmann turned them back, an officer of the law protecting the law's castle, repelling the outsiders. For after all Bornmann had exercised a peculiar brand of annexation and he wasn't going to permit the dispossessed to interfere with the sovereign states of New York and New Jersey.

Wilentz asked: And did you again search that apartment?

Yes, I did, Bornmann said. It was on September 26 (seven days after Hauptmann's arrest) that I conducted another search of said premises with other police officers. Said search took us to the attic. We gained access to the attic by entering a small linen closet, pushing up a trap door in the ceiling, climbing up the closet shelves, and pulling ourselves through.

When you got into the attic what did you find?

Well, first we searched for money and during the search I noticed that a length of one of the attic floorboards had been removed. About eight feet of it had been sawed off one end of this long floorboard. I knew it had been cut off because there were nail holes still in the beams and between the seventh and eighth beam there was a small pile of sawdust lying there. Also, on the floorboard adjoining the end of the piece that had been sawed away, you could see a small saw cut where the saw bit into the adjoining board.

So, he continued, I called for Arthur Koehler, a wood expert for the U.S. Forest Service. Koehler had been helping us trace wood in the kidnap ladder for two years. And he came as soon as he could get away and on October 9 we returned to the attic of said premises.

What did you do when you arrived there?

Well, we brought with us one of the side rails in the ladder, one of the uprights. It's marked Rail 16, that's what we marked it when we tagged each piece of it for lab analysis. Rail 16. There are four nail holes in Rail 16. Up in the attic, we put Rail 16 down on the beam that also had four nail holes. Then we pushed nails into the holes in Rail 16 and they went right in with just a little finger pressure and they went right in and right down into the holes in the attic beam. They fit perfectly, no doubt about it.

The prosecutor paused, turned to the jury with a smile, let it sink in. An earlier witness, the owner of the house, had testified that

160

...ursery note. It was signed with a ...uliar symbol that police claimed ... was so distinctive it couldn't be ...cated. Which may not have been ...e the truth. (*Author's collection*)

The first (below left) and second (below right) ransom notes. Do long-suppressed documents prove that even the prosecution handwriting experts realized the handwriting on these notes differed from that in the nursery note? (*Author's collection*)

The corpse found in the woods and identified by Lindbergh as his child. The infant's doctor said he couldn't identify the remains "if you gave me a million dollars." *(UPI Photo)*

The morning after the kidnaping; police search for fingerprints outside the nursery from which the child was abducted. *(UPI Photo)*

Hundreds of thousands of these posters were distributed across the country. Tacked up in public places, they were quickly stolen by souvenir hunters. *(Author's collection)*

WANTED

INFORMATION AS TO THE WHEREABOUTS OF

CHAS. A. LINDBERGH, JR.

OF HOPEWELL, N. J.

SON OF COL. CHAS. A. LINDBERGH

World-Famous Aviator

This child was kidnaped from his home in Hopewell, N. J., between 8 and 10 p. m. on Tuesday, March 1, 1932.

DESCRIPTION:

Age, 20 months   Hair, blond, curly
Weight, 27 to 30 lbs.   Eyes, dark blue
Height, 29 inches   Complexion, light
      Deep dimple in center of chin
      Dressed in one-piece coverall night suit

ADDRESS ALL COMMUNICATIONS TO
      COL. H. N. SCHWARZKOPF, TRENTON, N. J., or
      COL. CHAS. A. LINDBERGH, HOPEWELL, N. J.

ALL COMMUNICATIONS WILL BE TREATED IN CONFIDENCE

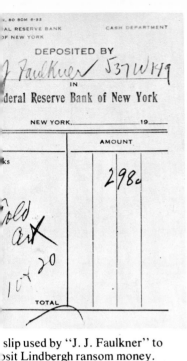

slip used by "J. J. Faulkner" to
?sit Lindbergh ransom money.
?e traced the pseudonym to one of
?up of men and women who
?me chief suspects—and who had a
?ection with Dr. Condon. That
?rmation was suppressed. *(Author's*
?ction)

The garage behind Hauptmann's home, stripped to the
framework in search for ransom money, is being
shoved to the ground. *(UPI Photo)*

?key Rosner (c.), bootlegger, stock
?ndler, and Lindbergh's "private
?retary," one of several gangsters called in
?help recover the child. *(UPI Photo)*

Dr. John F. Condon, who negotiated with the
extortionists, leaves Bronx courthouse after
questioning by D.A. Behind him is his
bodyguard, Al Reich. Most investigators, and
even Lindbergh, suspected Condon was part
of the extortion gang. Lindbergh lied about
his suspicions at Hauptmann's trial. *(UPI
Photo)*

Hauptmann and his wife, Anna, at the beach on a Sunday in 1929. Photo is from the Hauptmann album, confiscated by police. *(UPI Photo)*

Hauptmann (r.) and his close friend Hans Kloeppenburg flank Anita Luxemburg at Hunter's Island in 1933. Police and prosecutor claimed, without proof, that Hauptmann was having an affair with Anita. *(Author's collection, print by Brian Gaumer)*

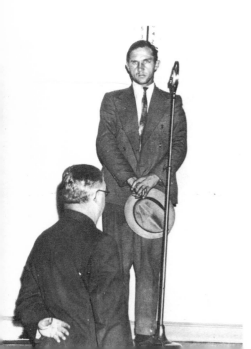

Hauptmann is questioned by police official at line the day after his arrest. Moments after this photo was taken, Dr. Condon spoke with Hauptmann f almost an hour and then said prisoner was *not* the extortionist. Why did Condon later change his story? *(UPI Photo)*

Anne Lindbergh, 1928. She was close to a breakdown at the time of the trial. Did Charles Lindbergh lie and distort—as hidden documents prove—to protect her? *(Wide World)*

Lindbergh enters the courthouse with State Police Superintendent Schwarzkopf, who said, "There is no oath I would not break," to help Lindbergh—and who tried to get a witness to commit perjury. *(UPI Photo)*

Hauptmann examines ransom letters during his extradition hearing in the Bronx, October 1934. *(Wide World)*

The circus atmosphere surrounding "the greatest trial of the century" extended into the courthouse, souvenir vendors hawking replicas of the kidnap ladder scant yards from the courtroom where Hauptmann was fighting for his life. *(UPI Photo)*

Left: Arthur Koehler, the "wood expert" who swore Hauptmann ripped a piece of wood from his own attic in building the kidnap ladder, stands with the ladder and the other half of the board taken from Hauptmann's attic. Right: A close-up of the ladder and the attic board. *(Wide World) (UPI Photo)*

Hauptmann confers with his chief defense counsel, Ed Reilly. Once Reilly received his fee from the Hearst papers, he no longer cared what happened to his client. *(Wide World)*

Lindbergh on the stand as a witness for the prosecution. His testimony, some jurors later said, convinced them that Hauptmann was guilty. *(Wide World)*

Betty Gow, the nurse, the last person known to have seen the Lindbergh child alive. *(Wide World)*

Wilentz tips his hat to cheering crowd as he enters courthouse. Reporters told him his attack on Hauptmann would bring an unprecedented confession from the stand. Wilentz, in trying for that confession, used every dramatic device ever seen in cross-examination. *(UPI Photo)*

A film camera sneaked into the courtroom captured one of the dramatic moments of the trial—prosecutor David Wilentz, arm upraised, demanding of Hauptmann, "Didn't you lie when . . .?" Behind Hauptmann are the kidnap ladder and handwriting exhibits. *(UPI Photo)*

Richard and Anna Hauptmann lean across police officers to talk for a few moments before the prosecution rested its case, January 24, 1935. *(Wide World)*

Hauptmann in his cell the morning after the verdict. *(Wide World)*

Anna Hauptmann, supported by two friends, leaves her home for the chapel where her husband's remains are to be cremated. On the left is Gerta Henkel. The prosecutor said, without proof, that she was having an affair with Hauptmann. *(Wide World)*

At the moment jury foreman Charles Walton mumbled, "Guilty . . ." one of several photographers permitted to bring cameras into court snapped this photo. *(Wide World)*

HAUPTMANN

JUDGE TRENCHARD

DEFENSE ATTY. REILLY

WILENTZ

SCHWARZKOPF

FOREMAN WALTON

when the Hauptmanns moved into the apartment in October 1931, the attic floor had been intact. A couple of the jury members nodded. It was plain now. Hauptmann had run short of wood and had removed a length from his attic to finish the kidnap ladder.

Now, Detective Bornmann, I show you a board. Did you take this board from Hauptmann's attic?

Yes, sir, I did. That's the board that had a piece cut from it.

Who removed that from the attic floor?

I did.

Was it the same color that it is now?

Oh, yes sir, it is.

And what was the color of Rail 16?

The same color as the attic board.

Your witness, the prosecutor said. He sat down, quite pleased. The kidnap ladder had now been rammed home—right into Hauptmann's attic.

Frederick Pope, a local lawyer, one of the assistants to Reilly and Fisher, rose to challenge for the defense.

He asked: "Before you put Rail 16 into place there was nothing between the attic board and the end of the building, was there?"

No, sir, Bornmann replied. There was about eight feet missing from the floor, the board that was cut out was about eight feet long.

Now, even after you put Rail 16 into place it didn't reach from the end of the floorboard to the end of the building, did it?

No sir, there was a space about an inch and a quarter between the board on the floor and the beginning of the ladder rail. When we put the ladder rail into place with the nails, there was this gap of more than an inch.

Yes, the defense attorney said, but I'm talking about the other end also. The missing length even after laying Rail 16 down is about thirty-six inches, isn't it?

Well, Bornmann said, about eight foot of it had been taken out and Rail 16 is about six foot, eight and a half inches.

The implication was clear to the spectators and the jury. Hauptmann, a skilled union carpenter, had removed a board from his attic that was between fifteen and thirty-six inches too long and had to later cut a foot or more from it. Or, perhaps—another inference that could be drawn—was it that Bornmann had been so sloppy in

161

manufacturing his evidence he cut off and threw away a length of attic floor a couple of feet longer than the board he was going to claim had come from Hauptmann's attic?

But it wasn't made sufficiently clear to the jury. The cross-examination had been too brief. Nowhere in it does the lawyer shout: "Do you expect this jury to believe this ladder upright, Rail 16, came from that attic? Let us see what you expect this jury to believe. Wasn't there a lumberyard two blocks from the defendant's home? Didn't you find enough wood in his garage and in the basement to make this upright? Is it your expert police opinion that Hauptmann climbed into his attic in search of a length of wood to complete his ladder? He knows he needs precisely six feet, eight and a half inches. He is a carpenter, he measures his work, he knows the length he needs. In his attic, he begins to saw. Without measuring. Is it your expert opinion he sawed off a piece about eighteen inches too long? That he took it down through the trap door into his house and then down into his garage and sawed off the eighteen inches? And then, finding it was still too long, he cut off another inch and a half from the *opposite* end? Is that the expert police opinion you expect this jury to believe? Or is it more logical to believe there was an inch-and-a-half gap between the ends of those two boards in the attic because that was the only way to get the nail holes to match up? Did you, Detective Bornmann, drive nail holes in the beam so they'd match the holes in the rail?"

But the questions were not asked. The information received by the jury was that the board had come from the attic. More than a foot off one end, an inch and a fraction off the other. Nuances never highlighted by questions to force the jurors to think. Nuances suggesting manufactured evidence.

Coils of suspicion uncoiled in my mind. Eyewitnesses, suspect. Handwriting analysts, suspect. A board from the attic, suspect. A commander of police willing to suborn perjury, suspect . . . suspect. Was it all like this? Layer upon layer of perjury, a meandering river of lies that swallowed Hauptmann and carried him over the abyss?

8

David Wilentz speaks: "The state calls Arthur Koehler."

I remembered from my readings in the past that Koehler had convinced even those who could not be convinced by all the other evidence. Koehler the wood expert. A scientist. Men of logic and experience, unmoved by eyewitness testimony for they know eyewitnesses are unreliable, unmoved by Lindbergh's voice identification because it is so open to doubt, unmoved by handwriting experts for they have so often been wrong, unmoved by most of the evidence—men of reason were made to believe by Arthur Koehler.

His story, as I found it in his testimony and in two magazine articles he'd written shortly after Hauptmann was executed, was that of the scientist-detective.

Koehler was at breakfast in his home in Madison, Wisconsin, on the morning of March 2, 1932, reading the first reports of the Lindbergh kidnaping. And as he read about that homemade ladder he grew excited; perhaps I can help police trace the wood to the kidnaper, he thought. He wrote to Lindbergh and offered his help as a wood technologist at the government's Forest Products Laboratory, as a man who was an authority on the properties of wood.

He received no response until the following May, shortly after the body presumed to be young Lindbergh's was discovered, when police sent him tiny slivers of wood that had been shaved from the ladder and asked whether he could identify them. What kind of wood was it? Where did it grow? Could it be traced to retail out-

163

lets? He examined the slivers. They were of wood from all parts of the country. Pine that grows in North Carolina and adjoining states, known in the trade as common pine; Douglas fir from the Northwest; a strip of birch and one of Ponderosa pine, both from Western forests. He made his report. Weeks later Colonel Schwarzkopf asked him to come to New Jersey and help the police.

When he was shown the ladder in the state police laboratory in Trenton, Koehler realized immediately that the man who had built it was a sloppy carpenter. The ladder, he said, was shamefully made. "It had cleats—crosspieces—instead of rungs, and the notches mortised by the chisel in the side rails were uneven; it clearly was a job no man had taken pride in."

In places, Koehler saw, the kidnaper's chisel had cut much deeper than was necessary, something a good carpenter would not have done. But there was worse, Koehler noted. One of the ladder's upright rails and every one of the cleats had been trimmed by a plane with a dull and nicked blade. And almost every piece of wood used in that ladder had been scarred by the careless dragging of a dull handsaw whose teeth caught in the wood. A good carpenter, a man taking pride in his work, keeps his tools sharpened.

Koehler dismantled the ladder, marking each piece of wood and each nail very carefully, so that it could be reassembled as it was when found. For four days he studied the wood under his microscope, measured with calipers the scars left by unsharp tools, until he had memorized the several distinct patterns of the carpenter's careless scarring.

The kidnaper's chisel had been sharper than the other tools and police had the chisel—the one found under the nursery window. Where the chisel had made its bite into the wood, Koehler said, he found right-angle lines. The recovered chisel matched those lines.

One more thing Koehler noted in his growing reports. The pine upright of one section of the ladder, now called Rail 16, had four nail holes in it. They were square holes that had been made by old-fashioned cut nails. There was no trace of rust. To Koehler, this meant the board had been previously used in some place that was sheltered from the weather. He told Police Chief Schwarzkopf: "Whenever you get a suspect, look around his premises for a place indoors where there are empty cut-nail holes, and possibly some boards to match with the ladder rail."

Now Koehler was ready to try and trace the wood to its origin, the mill that dressed it, and from there to the lumberyard which had sold it to the kidnaper. And from there? The Carolina pine offered the greatest hope. Koehler had found that two side rails of Carolina pine matched end to end, meaning they had once been part of a longer piece. Under his microscope he detected marks of the machine planing these two pieces had received in some unidentified mill. What excited him was evidence that the cutting edges of two knives in a machine used to trim lumber before shipment each had a perhaps unique imperfection. Along each edge of the boards Koehler could detect a series of shallow grooves scarring the surface at regular intervals of eighty-six hundredths of an inch. The flat surfaces of the boards showed still another imperfection: every ninety-three hundredths of an inch there was another scar, evidence of another defective knife in the edge trimmer. Koehler photographed all the blemishes, enlarged them, studied them, thought about them.

Through these studies of the cutting marks made in the wood at the mill, Koehler was able to determine that the planing machine used to dress the lumber had six knives in the cutter that trimmed the edges and eight knives in the surface cutter. He then arrived at an estimate of the speed at which the lumber had been fed through the planer, about 230 feet a minute. That speed, he knew, was more than double the speed of planing machines normally used in Eastern mills which handled this type of pine. With luck, then, he might not have too much difficulty tracing the mill that had dressed the kidnaper's lumber.

He wrote to every one of the 1,600 pine mills in the Atlantic Coast states. Do you have any planers, he asked, that feed as fast as 230 feet per minute, have six knives in the side cutter heads and eight knives in the top and bottom cutters? Twenty-three mills responded that they did have such a planer. Koehler asked them to send him samples of pine from those planers.

The mill of the Dorn Company at McCormick, South Carolina, forwarded a sample that Koehler decided had been passed through a planer at almost precisely the rate of speed of the wood in the kidnap ladder. But the sample didn't show evidence of the slightly defective knives because they undoubtedly had since been sharpened many times. Koehler went down to the mill.

There he confided his mission to Joseph J. Dorn, a state senator

165

and one of the millowners. Dorn ordered all operations halted and had his workers begin a search of the mill for every scrap of one-by-four Southern pine they could find. Perhaps, he told Koehler, some wood was lying around from before the kidnaping, twenty months earlier, that would match the wood in the ladder.

No scrap was found. But while Koehler was waiting he inspected the planer and satisfied himself it was indeed the one which had dressed the common pine in the kidnap ladder. From company records he learned this particular planer had been operating at its slightly too fast speed since September 1929, when an off-sized pulley had been installed. That meant he'd have to trace every shipment of wood from that planer in the thirty months between that date and the kidnaping.

Because the ladder was connected to a crime in New Jersey, Koehler felt it sensible to begin his search for the ultimate purchaser of that wood among Dorn customers north of the Potomac. He copied from the Dorn ledgers the date and destination of each shipment to the north. The completed list showed that forty-six carloads had been sent north to twenty-five firms. And it was obvious where he would have to start: eighteen of the carloads had gone to two firms in New Jersey that were within a twenty-five-mile radius of the Lindbergh home. These were a box factory in Trenton and the Johns Manville plant at Manville.

Koehler took the next train north to Trenton. He told Chief Schwarzkopf of his findings and Detective Lewis Bornmann was assigned to accompany Koehler on his search. At the Johns Manville plant, Koehler and Bornmann were told that all the wood from the Dorn mill had long been used up in making crates for Manville products. None was sold to the public. High fences around the plant had protected the lumber from theft. The wood, when used, had been cut into lengths too short to have later been used in making the ladder. At the box factory in Trenton the story was the same.

"So with relief," Koehler later said, "I crossed off shipment after shipment, to leave but twenty-eight."

Koehler's assumption that none of the lumber in those eighteen carloads could have been stolen because of "high fences" ignored a common event, employee theft. Even back in those more innocent times workers would not have been above stealing a few lengths of lumber from the boss. The ladder, built as it was of three

166

distinct types of wood and one piece showing prior use, made it likely the kidnaper had picked up the lumber wherever he could find it and had not bought from a lumberyard the precise quantity he required. (Which creates another thought: Hauptmann, building a ladder, would have known as a carpenter precisely how much lumber he needed and would have bought from a lumberyard a consistent type of lumber.) For Koehler to arbitrarily cross those shipments from his list was naive. There is no evidence—in fact it would be highly unlikely—that the shipments to both plants were cut into shorter lengths as soon as they were received; no doubt, the lumber was cut as needed and the original lengths were on hand for quite some time. Koehler must have eliminated those firms only because there was no possibility of tracing the wood they'd been shipped, only because the wood had been so thoroughly dispersed it was impossible to trace.

And as long as I found myself indulging in that favorite pastime of skeptics, poking holes in someone's story, I decided to take it from the beginning, point by point.

Koehler, a wood expert, said the ladder showed evidence its maker was a dreadful carpenter. The construction of the ladder was amateurish. The carpenter's tools were unsharpened. His chisel bit much too deeply. But Hauptmann was a skilled union carpenter, and had been for at least six years before the kidnaping. He had helped build some of those tacky houses that dot the Bronx. He had built for his newborn son several pieces of well-constructed and finely detailed furniture, a rocking chair, high chair, and playpen. On the last job he held, at the Majestic apartments, around the time of the kidnaping, he was employed as a finisher, the carpenter responsible for putting into place door and window trim, kitchen cabinets, moldings, all the small details of carpentry that require skill and patience and in which the slightest carelessness would glare like a full moon on a cloudless night. No, Koehler's assertion that the builder of the kidnap ladder was a poor carpenter doesn't fit what we know of Hauptmann. The record seems to be speaking of two different men.

And the chisel? At one point during his examination Wilentz asked Koehler to step to Hauptmann's toolbox and see whether it held a three-quarter-inch chisel. High drama for the jury's benefit: Koehler rummaged around and then grandly announced the chisel was missing. That could only mean Hauptmann had dropped it while descending the kidnap ladder. Koehler later went to great lengths to stress that the chisel found under the nursery window matched the "right-angle lines" left in the kidnap ladder by a chisel. What did that mean, exactly? I consulted the trial transcript, Koehler under cross-examination. Well, he said, it meant the mortise cuts in the ladder had been made by a three-quarter-inch chisel, and a three-quarter-inch chisel had been found under the nursery window. That's all. Of perhaps several million chisels of that size in use at that time, Koehler was trying to imply both chisels were one chisel—when he possessed no such evidence.

Why was everyone stretching so hard to fill in every single gap in the Hauptmann case in an attempt to convince us all that he was indeed the guilty one? So many people, during the trial and for many years after, from John Condon to George Waller, distorted the evidence, attributed to Hauptmann a personality he didn't seem to own, tried to make us believe the case against this man was superperfect. No murder case is ever perfect, obviously, for only the victim might tell us the truth (perhaps) and the victim cannot be present. Even seeing on our television sets Jack Ruby kill Lee Harvey Oswald could not bring into the courtroom a case so brilliant in its perfection, in its wholeness and completeness, that it would absolutely satisfy. For what would we learn of motive? Had Ruby testified about his motive we could never be certain he was being truthful. We would never have been certain he had acted alone and not as the agent of some dark conspiracy. And by attempting to bring such perfection to the case against Hauptmann, all writers and all witnesses automatically damn their own stories and damn the truth. Michelangelo may have been correct when he said that trifles make perfection. But only in art. If, in a criminal trial, every trifle is absolutely perfect and all trifles add up to a perfect whole, then we must assume the trifles have been deliberately shaped to attain the perfection of art. But a courtroom is not an artist's canvas or a sculptor's block of marble. To create, in a trial, an artistic masterpiece so perfect there can be no question the result is truth, means truth has been shaped and distorted to fit the artist's concept.

To return to Koehler, then, still testifying. He had searched high and low for the wood from the Dorn mill, in lumberyards, in chicken coops and garages where some of the wood ended up, climbing fences with Bornmann like a couple of weird burglars with badges.

Always disappointed. Until one day he arrived at a lumberyard in Ozone Park, Queens. The dealer told him all the lumber from the Dorn shipment had been sold months before. The familiar tale, to Koehler's ears, he was much too late. But, said the dealer, now that I think about it, I'm pretty sure we used some of that pine here in the yard, to build storage bins. He led Koehler and Bornmann to the bins and sawed off a length of protruding board. Koehler walked into the sunlight with the strip of pine and studied it under his magnifying glass.

Along one edge of the board were the familiar scars of the defective cutter knife. But there was a slight difference. The blemishes on this board were a trifle farther apart and nearer the center of the board edge than were the scars of the ladder rail. Koehler thought about it for a while, as Bornmann drove them back into the city. The only possible explanation for the wider spacing of the blemishes was that this piece of wood had been fed through the planing machine at a slightly faster speed than the wood in the ladder rails. The pulleys, of course, Koehler surmised. This board had gone through the planer either just before or just after the Dorn mill hands changed the pulley on the machine. Perhaps then the shipment he sought, the shipment from which the kidnaper had bought his common pine, had gone to a firm on his list either immediately before or immediately after the shipment to the Ozone Park lumberyard.

He consulted his list. The subsequent shipment had been made to a lumberyard in Youngstown, Pennsylvania. But Koehler had made a note next to that yard's name which indicated the wood it had received had been trimmed an eighth of an inch narrower than the ladder board. Clearly, he saw, "I could rule it out!" Now, Koehler said, he was certain the shipment he had sought for so many months had gone to the customer on the list prior to the lumberyard they'd just left. That was the National Millwork and Lumber Company, in the Bronx, which had received a Dorn shipment nine days before the Ozone Park firm.

Bornmann drove directly to the Bronx yard. The date was November 29, 1933. Once more the sleuths were disappointed. All the pine from the Dorn shipment, they were told, had been sold long before. Koehler later wrote: "But then occurred another lucky break. It might be, the yard foreman thought aloud, that he had made his molding bins out of that Dorn mill one-by-four-inch stuff.

169

He looked just once, then got a saw. A piece projected; he cut it off and handed it to me. One look was enough! The marks on the edge were the same!''

It seemed strange. Two lumberyards somehow managed to have a piece of that Dorn pine and each yard employed such sloppy carpenters that a piece of wood projected from the bins constructed of them. Was every carpenter as careless as the man who'd made the ladder? Does every lumberyard contain bins with projecting pieces so that employees might scrape and tear skin, overalls, lumber? Even stranger is Koehler's assertion that he and Bornmann had searched in upstate New York, Connecticut, and Massachusetts for almost a month and only after many disappointments found the wood he was seeking in the Bronx. If it were true, then Detective Bornmann wasn't a very smart cop. He knew the extortionist almost certainly lived in the Bronx. All the evidence pointed to it and all police authorities were certain of it. Why on earth didn't Bornmann *start* with the Bronx lumberyard? Why give the kidnaper more months to dispose of his ransom money? And, since the criminal was known to be a German, according to all accounts, why give him more time to perhaps flee to Europe?

Koehler never explains. He wrote and testified that he was now positive he'd traced the lumber to the yard that sold it to the kidnaper. That detective work was a vital point for the prosecution because Hauptmann always purchased his lumber at that yard. He was well known there, had in fact been employed by the yard, sent out to work for customers who needed a carpenter. The implication was stunning: Hauptmann had bought the lumber used to make two of the ladder uprights.

Koehler testified and wrote that he now had come up against a solid wall hampering further search—the lumberyard dealt in cash. It had stopped giving credit long before the Dorn shipment was received and therefore no names of customers were available. That is the reason, we must all infer from Koehler, he was unable to personally arrest Hauptmann by sleuthing in wood.

However . . . and however and however. Another contemporary writer, Sidney Whipple of the United Press, who reported on the search for the kidnaper as a police reporter, published a complete cops-and-robbers account of the case immediately after Hauptmann's conviction, and later edited and annotated the trial transcript published by Doubleday in 1937, provided some enlight-

170

ening information in just a few sentences in his books. Whipple had written:

> The known customers of National Millwork & Lumber were then thoroughly investigated and one by one eliminated from the case. . . . And at this point [a reporter] made the logical suggestion to the authorities that every one of the automobile license applications from within a certain well-defined zone of the Bronx be examined for comparison with the ransom notes. Such a search was conducted. Of the thousands of such documents on file, all but 480 were eliminated, and there remained only forty-eight possible suspects by the end of 1933. All of them were closely shadowed by Lieutenant Finn's men.

Known customers of the lumberyard. Licenses issued to drivers living in a certain area of the Bronx. Hauptmann's name must have appeared on both lists since he was a steady customer and occasional employee of the lumberyard and since, at his trial, the handwriting experts claimed the writing on his license applications was the same as the writings in the ransom notes. Why was he "eliminated" from both lists and cleared of all suspicion? Had his name appeared on either list—and it must have—he certainly would have been kept under surveillance as forty-eight men had been. Most especially since all the minute details of the description Condon swore to at the trial fit Hauptmann. The mind leaps with questions, the questions stumble over each other like kittens playing with string and getting tangled in it. Is it possible Hauptmann didn't fit the description of John in 1933 and that Condon revised his description a year later to fit the man who'd been arrested? Was this further support for my instinctive feeling that Condon had lied? Is it possible Hauptmann's handwriting was ruled out in 1933 as unlike the writing in the ransom notes, then was made to match by mental gymnastics in 1935? Could it be possible Hauptmann was eliminated because he was not passing ransom money in 1933? Had not begun to pass it until August 1934, as he claimed, because that's when he discovered the gold notes in Fisch's shoe box? Doesn't it seem more likely now that Hauptmann was telling the truth and the witnesses against him lied?

Including, perhaps, Arthur Koehler, the wood expert now in the

171

witness chair. In fact, another major discrepancy in Koehler's story now became clear to me. In one section of an article he wrote for the *Saturday Evening Post,* he said National Millwork and Lumber could not provide names of its customers because they sold only for cash. But later in that same article he said that after Hauptmann was arrested police had found in that lumberyard a sales slip showing the prisoner had bought nine dollars' worth of lumber late in December 1931, little more than three months before the kidnaping. That purchase most certainly would have placed Hauptmann in the list of customers Whipple says were thoroughly investigated. Why wasn't Hauptman arrested in 1932, when Condon's memory of the extortionist would have been much fresher? Why, most of all, did Koehler contradict himself? Police most certainly found the sales slip, for it was introduced as evidence against Hauptmann at the trial. Koehler's claim that the lack of such a sales slip made it impossible for him to trace Hauptmann in 1933 forces us into the man's mental processes, the workings of his mind. He could have been gratifying his own ego, a sleuth who failed only because of forces beyond the control of science. Koehler took such pride in his role as detective that he published a learned article in the *Journal of Criminal Law* describing his achievements and suggesting that the techniques he had employed in the Hauptmann case could be useful to other detectives and to prosecutors. If Koehler was motivated by vanity, by a delight in valuing himself and his creations above all other things, then all he contributed to the case against Hauptmann becomes as small as all vanities. If . . . that's an enormous qualifier, that word, I thought. I can't prove ego and vanity ruled Koehler and twisted his reasoning; I'm only thinking that was possible. And, thinking that, I must examine Koehler's story with a sharply critical mind.

Back I went to something he'd written in his detailed report of his detective work in tracing the Dorn shipments. I could rule it out! he had exclaimed. The shipment to a lumberyard in Youngstown, Pennsylvania, could be eliminated because the wood involved was an eighth of an inch narrower than the ladder board. If so, it was strange that Koehler included this yard in his list in the first place. For Koehler had written, in his article for the professional journal: "Two of the North Carolina pine rails were cut from one board which was fourteen feet long originally. It could be determined that it had been dressed to three and three-quarters inches in width, which made it unnecessary to pay any attention to similar stock dressed to three and five-eighths inches in width. In fact, that eighth of an inch difference in widths narrowed down the tracing of lumber from sixty-three to forty-five carloads." Certainly, if Koehler was eliminating wood that had been dressed a mere eighth-inch too wide, an even greater logic would have demanded he eliminate lumber trimmed narrower than the ladder boards. Koehler testified he had eliminated all shipments of board that had not been dressed to the precise measurement he sought. Why had he listed the Youngstown shipment, only to dismiss it later? I didn't know and since Koehler died many years ago, I'd never find out. But I knew what I suspected—Koehler ignored the Youngstown shipment because he was in New York, 300 miles away; he lied about it later because he didn't want to be left open to the criticism that lumber with the same scarring he'd been searching for might have been found hundreds of miles from Hauptmann's home.

The circuits of the mind make further connections. Those two pieces of pine in which Koehler claimed to have found telltale mill scars enabling him to trace them to the Bronx lumberyard clearly were not planed or sanded by the man who built the ladder. Had they been, the marks of the Dorn mill's planer would not have been visible. Would Hauptmann, a skilled carpenter, have neglected to sand smooth the lumber in his ladder? Doesn't a total amateur carpenter like me sand every piece of wood I work with? Most certainly, if only to avoid splinters. When I built the bookcases that fill two complete walls around me, didn't I sand each board, even the edges that were to go flush against the wall? And I am not a meticulous man, as Hauptmann is said to have been. I am known for being careless and sloppy, yet I sanded. And I am sure a professional would have planed and then sanded his lumber before putting the pieces together as a ladder.

As I read on, I found that Koehler was again stretching to bring to his case the perfection of detail that damns it all in my mind. He claimed that after tracing the Dorn pine to the Bronx lumberyard and reaching the end of the road in his investigation, he set out to similarly trace the Douglas fir that had also been used in the ladder. One day in December 1933, he and Detective Bornmann sat in the

173

rear office of a lumberyard at 149th Street and the East River, also the Bronx. The sleuths were copying from a ledger names of customers who had bought Douglas fir of the size found in the ladder.

As they worked, two men entered and bought a forty-cent piece of plywood. One of the men offered a ten-dollar gold certificate in payment. The clerk asked the customer whether he had a smaller bill, a five perhaps. Retrieving the ten, the customer handed her a five-dollar bill. She accepted it and went into the rear, where Koehler was sitting, to get change. The men must have glanced over the low partition that separated him from the front of the shop and noticed his Forest Service badge, ordinarily concealed under his jacket but now possibly exposed, Koehler later wrote, because when the clerk returned with the change the men acted extraordinarily suspicious. One of them said: "Never mind, I have the change." As he threw forty cents on the counter the other man took from the clerk the five one-dollar bills she had brought out front. Muttering something about going to a nearby restaurant to eat, promising to return later, the two men left without the plywood they'd just bought. So suspicious were their actions, the foreman of the yard went into the street and took down the license plate number of the small green car they drove away.

After Hauptmann was arrested, the clerk and the foreman saw his picture in the newspapers and recognized him as one of those two customers who had behaved so strangely. Hauptmann and his associate fled the lumberyard because the gold certificate was undoubtedly, a ransom bill, police told newspaper reporters. Surely this was further evidence of Hauptmann's guilt. Koehler agreed. That little incident was important to everyone who condemned Hauptmann because it punctured a facet of Hauptmann's alibi, that he didn't know the gold notes he'd been passing were Lindbergh money. That story told by the murderer had to be proved a lie; showing his guilty behavior proved it was a lie. And now I understood the motive behind another anecdote police had related to the press, which had made banner headlines—BRUNO TRIES SUICIDE! I had ignored the story before, that Hauptmann while in jail in the Bronx had stolen a pewter spoon and sharpened it into a blade with which he could slit his wrists or his throat—because it seemed an aberration of a tale. Now it became all of a piece. Hauptmann had plotted suicide because he was guilty. But even writers absolutely certain Hauptmann was guilty commented after

174

his execution that the suicide tale was no more than a bit of dramatics by police, nothing more than coming up with a harmless little story to satisfy reporters' demands for more color.

That the authorities were stacking the deck against Hauptmann long before his trial I had no doubt. Consider the police story about the two men who acted so suspicious that the foreman of the lumberyard took their license number. Yet neither the foreman nor the clerk was ever called to testify at the trial. No doubt even police realized they were mistaken, no doubt the physical evidence didn't support their eyewitness testimony. Had the license number been Hauptmann's number; had the bill given in payment been folded in that unusual way all the ransom bills were folded; had it matched a serial number on the Lindbergh list—had even one of these facts been true, prosecutor Wilentz most certainly would have called the lumberyard employees to testify in order to prove Hauptmann's guilty behavior months before he claimed he found the ransom money. Yet police, prosecutor, and Koehler-as-detective, knowing they were distorting the truth, publicly stated that the link had been connected. (Further evidence of the falsity of the story: police said it had happened around noon, but Hauptmann's stock market accounts show he made several trades that day in his broker's office about ten miles away.) The police and Koehler, trying so hard to create that artistic masterpiece, the perfect case.

Another thought lights the mind. These men, all of them, were making so great an effort to convince us of Hauptmann's guilt because they were trying to convince themselves, hoping to relieve their own doubts.

And now the really vital evidence from Koehler was about to come. Koehler, wood detective, on the Flemington stage for his second day of glory, was asked by the prosecutor: After you removed from the ladder this section of wood, Rail 16, what did you find?

Detective Bornmann and I took it to Hauptmann's attic, Koehler said, and I found that the nail holes in the rail corresponded exactly with four nail holes in the joists in that attic, and I found that the grain of the wood in Rail 16 corresponded exactly with the grain in the piece of wood still in the attic.

Then you say there is a relationship between Rail 16 and the board found in Hauptmann's attic?

Yes, there certainly is, the witness responded. Those two pieces at one time were one piece. They were cut in two in the attic. I know that because there are a number of similarities between the two that make me believe they had been one.

Is one of the similarities the nail holes?

Yes, exactly, Koehler said. I took nails from the board still in place in the attic, because they would most naturally be the same as the nails which had once been in Rail 16, and I lined up Rail 16 over the beam on the attic floor with the nail holes in it. I pushed down on the nails and each of them went through Rail 16 and into the holes in the beams. They fit perfectly into those holes.

Tell us, what is your opinion as a wood expert?

In my opinion, he said, that rail had at one time been nailed down on that beam in the attic. The nail holes in the rail and in the beam are irregularly spaced, both in distance between holes and in direction, and even in the slant at which they were originally hammered into place. It would not have been possible that there could be another board somewhere, spaced exactly as those nail holes are spaced. The same distance apart, the same direction separating them, the same slant to the nails. No other board *anywhere* could have fit into that attic.

Wilentz turned to the jury and smiled; I have driven this ladder directly into Hauptmann's home, his eyes and mouth seemed to be saying. Upstairs, in the upper gallery of the courtroom, the din of teletype machines again emphasized the prosecutor's point: guilty, guilty, guilty. Wilentz returned to the witness.

"What other reason do you have," he asked, "for giving as your opinion that Rail 16 and the board from Hauptmann's attic were at one time the same piece of lumber?"

Because, the witness explained, speaking directly to the jury, when the rail was laid down in the attic and the nails inserted and fit perfectly, the rail was perfectly parallel to the adjoining board. If it had been an accident that these nails fit perfectly, it would not be expected that the board would necessarily be parallel to the other boards in the attic floor. That it was parallel proves even more conclusively that it had once lain in the attic, as part of the floor.

And now Wilentz glided into his spectacular dramatic scene: Koehler had said earlier he was certain the ladder rail and the attic board had once been a single piece. Will the witness please explain to us further why he stated that?

Well, when I was up in the attic with Bornmann I had peered

176

down at the board still nailed into place and saw that a piece had been roughly cut away from it, Koehler said. I could see that a saw cut had been made at the end of the attic board, the end of what remained of the original long piece of board. Looking closer, I discovered on the adjoining floorboard a small cut of a saw directly in line with the board that had been cut out. Furthermore, there was a little pile of sawdust on the plaster of the ceiling below the board, directly under the end which had been cut. And furthermore, the piece of board left behind, still nailed down after the builder of the kidnap ladder had taken away the length he required, projected over the beam into which it had been nailed. Now, a carpenter wouldn't let the end of a board overlap and hang free that way. He would have placed the edge across the joists and finished it off perfectly. That indicates the board was not in its original condition.

Not only that, he went on, but by matching the grain from the upright rail in the ladder with the board remaining in the attic, I find that it matches up practically perfectly, considering there is a gap between the two. The gap, of an inch and a quarter, can easily be explained, Koehler said. After the board had been removed from the attic it had been trimmed slightly at that end, doubtless because the ladder-builder decided it was too long for his purpose.

"Will you show us on these photos," Wilentz said, "the grain and how you matched the grain?"

Koehler, handling several enlargements of the two pieces of wood, explained why he was certain the grain of the ladder rail corresponded precisely with the grain of the floorboard. Every year, he told the jury, a tree produces a layer of wood under the bark. Those are known as the annual rings and by measuring them we can determine the rate of growth and the age of the tree. There are the same number of annual rings in the floorboard as there are in the ladder rail.

"Does that indicate the two boards are of the same age?"

It indicates that it took the same number of years to produce that much growth, the witness said. Further evidence the two boards were once a single piece, Koehler said, is that the *variation* in the width of the rings is the same. There are three narrow rings in the floorboard and then the next two are thicker and the next two are narrower again. And as you can see—pointing to the photo of the ladder rail—the pattern here is precisely the same. But there is one apparent inconsistency, he went on, again touching each photo

177

with his pointer. In this part of the floorboard the rings are wider and more distorted than they are in the end of the ladder rail which had once been attached to this board. The reason for that—a knot.

Just a minute now, Wilentz said. Can you show us on this next photo?

Another enlargement was introduced and mounted on the bulletin board. Koehler stood before it, his pointer down at his side, waiting for the next question.

Can you show us the knot you are talking about?

Yes, this is the knot right here, at this end of the attic floor board.

Proceed from there, please, Wilentz said.

The witness: You see, knots distort the grain in wood. And the closer you get to a knot the more the grain is distorted. Here, in this corner of the floorboard from the attic, you see the grain is greatly distorted. But you will notice that on this edge of the ladder rail that was sawed from the floorboard, the annual rings are wider. That shows there was some factor influencing their growth right there. And that factor, in my opinion, is the influence of the knot in the floorboard extended over into the end of the rail of the ladder. The reason the grain is not so greatly distorted in the rail is because it was farther away from the knot.

And on and on Koehler went. The "inconsistency" in the grain is due to a knot. Since there is an inch-and-a-quarter piece missing between the two lengths of board, we must "imagine" the manner in which the grain traveled along the missing piece and was changed somewhat by the knot before it got to the ladder rail. No inconsistency if one is able to "imagine" as I have done the natural course of the grain over that missing piece.

Wilentz said: "I notice that the ladder rail is not as wide as the attic board. Will you explain that?" He was quite skillful, this Wilentz, for a man who had never tried a criminal case. By asking the question now, with great candor, he deflated a defense attack. "Why is the rail narrower than the attic floorboard?" he asked again.

"In examining the ladder rail," Koehler said, "I noticed that both edges were planed with a hand plane." And the witness went on quickly, not giving any juror a chance to wonder why a carpenter who was so slovenly about his work he didn't plane or sand the other uprights in the ladder would have planed this particular board

178

on both edges: "The plane," Koehler rushed on, "was not in very good condition and left ridges."

Wilentz stepped to a table on which were spread out several of Hauptmann's tools and his metal toolbox. He lifted an old wooden-bodied plane and carried it to Koehler. "Can you tell us whether or not this plane was used in planing the ladder rail?"

"It was," Koehler said.

"Is there any question in your mind about it?"

"Not the least."

"Why do you say that? Will you explain it?"

"Because on the ladder rail there are a number of ridges of different sizes and when I plane a piece of wood with that plane it makes similar ridges of the same size and same spacing apart as are found on the ladder rail."

"Would any other plane, in your opinion, make those ridges and those marks?" Wilentz asked.

"No, that would be out of the question."

Wilentz asked Koehler to demonstrate for the jury why he felt so certain Hauptmann's plane and only Hauptmann's plane could have left the marks found on the ladder rail. The witness planed a piece of wood, using Judge Trenchard's bench to work. He then placed a sheet of paper over the newly planed area and rubbed lightly with a pencil—"A very simple method I learned as a youngster," Koehler said. The impression of the plane marks that came up in the pencil rubbing was precisely the same as the impression of marks left in a piece of the ladder, Koehler swore. Hauptmann's plane had been used to trim wood in the ladder! And the teletype machines chattered in the attic above.

The prosecutor moved on to the chisel found under the nursery window and once more I read of Koehler's dramatic discovery: there was no three-quarter-inch chisel in Hauptmann's toolbox. And now Wilentz moved to link the chisel even more closely to Hauptmann. He asked Koehler to carry the ladder to the edge of the jury box and show the jurors the places in the wood where a chisel had gouged. Koehler did so, pointing to chisel marks in several places. Then, using the chisel found under the nursery window, the chisel which the state had just proved must have been Hauptmann's because his toolbox lacked a chisel of that size, Koehler gouged into another sample piece of wood. Once more he rubbed his pencil over a sheet of paper to get an impression of the

179

marks. Once more the impressions matched. "Hauptmann's chisel" had been used on the ladder. Actually, what Koehler had proved was that a three-quarter-inch chisel had gouged into the wood of the ladder, *any* chisel of that size and not necessarily the one found outside Lindbergh's home. But the subtlety was undoubtedly lost on the jury, for it escaped reporters, most of whom wrote that the wood detective had proved Hauptmann's own chisel had been used to build the ladder.

It didn't much matter, of course, in the long run. Hauptmann was so demonstrably guilty, according to the script, that a distortion here or an exaggeration there made little real difference. Yet Koehler's testimony was highly significant, for if he was willing to go along with the charade and distortion of the meaningless chisel evidence, if he was willing to tailor his later writings to fit the prosecution's carefully woven garment, if he could justify in his own mind a minor falsification in this instance and a bit of glossy misrepresentation in that instance—then all his testimony could be a lie. I would have to prove it, not through intellectual analysis alone but with hard facts. Somewhere, perhaps in police files, would be the cold documentary evidence I needed to demolish the state's case against Hauptmann.

Koehler, whose offense is the most reprehensible since he claimed to be a man of science, was given over to Frederick Pope, associate defense counsel, for cross-examination. Pope questioned him for a couple of hours. It was futile. Koehler could not be budged. The best Pope could do was get him to admit everything he had sworn to had been his "opinion"—as if any juror distinguishes between the *opinion* of an expert witness and the *facts* shown in a document or in a scientific analysis. Pathologists, for example, may be called to tell a jury certain medical facts which are not matters of opinion, perhaps that the victim died of a bullet wound in the heart. Doctors can hardly disagree on such facts. But in the area of mere opinion the experts differ so widely among themselves that little credit can be given to expert opinion as such. Lawyers know or should know the difference between fact and opinion, judges know it, seasoned observers do also, but few jurors are sophisticated enough to sort it all out.

And I remembered now that that was one of the things about the Hauptmann case always nagging at my mind, that he was convicted most of all on the testimony of self-styled experts. Years earlier, when I had come to understand that if justice were the pillar of society, as some wise man had written, then it was a pillar rotten within from the gnawing of termite-minded men, I began to look into the reality behind appearances of expert witnesses. It was the performance of a psychiatrist that got me started. A man was on trial in Nassau County, Long Island, charged with the kidnaping and murder of an infant, a crime in many details similar to the Lindbergh crime. His defense was insanity, that he did not know the difference between right and wrong. Defense attorneys brought in a noted psychiatrist who testified that after analyzing the defendant for many hours, he had determined that no other possible conclusion could be reached: the defendant didn't know the nature of his act. The prosecution countered with its own psychiatrist, a man then in charge of the criminal psychiatric ward of Bellevue Hospital. The prosecutor's psychiatrist sat in court for days before he was due to testify, studying the defendant. During lunch hours and in the evenings before taking a commuter train back to the city, the state's psychiatrist got drunk on martinis, sipped slowly at first but poured down faster after the second or third. Toward the end of his first lunch hour in the commuter town he told reporters, in confidence, that the defendant was absolutely sane. We wondered how he had arrived at that conclusion since he hadn't examined the man, whose death the state was demanding, and had watched him in court for only a few hours. By his third day the psychiatrist was arriving in court in the morning drunk, sat through the morning sessions in a near doze, and fortified himself further over lunch. And then, drunk in that barely noticeable manner of the long-time alcoholic, he testified that in his opinion the defendant was as sane as a man can be. The defendant was convicted and eventually electrocuted.

So I asked a lawyer friend to recommend a book or two that might enlighten me about the way the law views expert witnesses. "That they're all worthless bums," my friend said. He pulled several volumes down from his shelves and underlined passages. Wrote one authority: "Skilled witnesses come with such a bias on their minds to support the cause in which they are embarked that hardly any weight should be given to their evidence." And another: "Expert witnesses become so warped in their judgment by regarding the subject in one point of view that, even when conscientiously disposed, they are incapable of expressing a candid

181

opinion." And, finally, one of the more famous trial lawyers of this century: "It has become a matter of common observation that not only can the honest opinions of different experts be obtained upon opposite sides of the same question, but also that dishonest opinions may be obtained upon different sides of the same question."

So much, I felt, for expert opinion, whether on wood, on handwriting, or on a man's mental state. I don't mean to imply that the general distrust in which the experts are held made them liars in the Hauptmann case, but that distrust taken together with all the discrepancies I'd so far uncovered made me feel certain the thematic discords in the expert testimony were no accidents, but deliberate lies and distortions.

9

"The state rests," Wilentz said a little past noon on the seventeenth day of the trial. The evidence was in, the verdict assured. The formality of defense was all that remained.

Lloyd Fisher, the local lawyer who could at least command the respect of this country jury, made the opening defense speech. We will prove, he said, that the defendant can account for all his movements on the three dates in question: kidnaping; extortion of ransom in the cemetery; visit to the Greenwich Village theater in 1933 where a ransom bill was passed. Hauptmann will tell you of his movements himself, and he will bring witnesses to support him. We will also attempt to prove, Fisher said, that the ransom letters were not written by this defendant, "not by sheer force of numbers in handwriting experts, as the state did, for we are unable to procure such an array of witnesses as the state had because we are without funds. The funds of this man Hauptmann are totally and completely exhausted and his defense has been almost entirely financed through members of his counsel. And I say to you that we cannot bring you eight or nine or ten or twelve outstanding experts from the far parts of the world. We have no money to bring an expert from Los Angeles . . ."

"Just a minute," Wilentz shouted. "We object to this, of course." Small things hurt this man who was achieving so large a victory. There had been newspaper criticism of the cost of the state's handwriting experts, who had submitted bills totaling more

183

than $30,000; some writers had tartly commented that that sum was more money than the defense had available for its entire case.

"We expect the defense to prove that remark," Wilentz said, "that the reason they haven't got more handwriting experts is a lack of funds."

The defense will go further than that, Fisher replied. We are without funds because the state has confiscated every penny the Hauptmanns had, even money that couldn't possibly have anything to do with this case. (No objection from Wilentz; it was true.) Limited that we are, the defense lawyer continued, we will prove the handwriting in the ransom notes is not that of Bruno Richard Hauptmann. As to finances, we will prove the state has overestimated and distorted the amount of money they claim was traced through Hauptmann's accounts. We will prove it is *repeat* money, the same money moving in and out of the various accounts. We will further prove that Hauptmann did have a partnership with Fisch, in stock trading and in fur speculation. We will prove to you that eyewitnesses such as Hochmuth are unreliable. We will prove to you that the state has utterly failed to make out a case against Hauptmann, and we shall expect you to return with a verdict acquitting this man. Fisher sat down and Reilly arose.

"Bruno Richard Hauptmann, take the stand," he called out.

Hauptmann walked quickly, with long strides, to the witness chair, appearing almost anxious to be sworn and to tell his story at last. He crossed his legs and watched Reilly intently. Hauptmann had been closely watched in turn by reporters, including Adela Rogers St. Johns. She later wrote:

> What struck me full as he walked within a table width of me on his way to the stand was his self-possession. Self-hypnotic it may have been, not one trace of the pre-cross-examination tremors and tensions, not one sign of I-walk-toward-life-or-death-for-me, these next hours I go free or I go to the electric chair.

"Self-hypnotic." So loaded a word, Ms. St. Johns. I still can't understand how you, of all journalists, could have so completely lost your ability to see beyond the emotional press-agentry of police and prosecution. You were a mother, yes, and of course deeply moved by the Lindberghs' personal tragedy. Yet you were also

Earl Rogers' daughter. Having read your memoir of your father, I expect and demand more from you than from other writers. You had grown up believing, as your father said to you when you were a little girl becoming involved in your first murder case as the child-woman whose intuition complemented the adults' logic:

> The presumption of innocence is the best thing in the jury system. Having acted with full power to find the guilty man, we will now lean over backwards to be fair to him. . . . So the jury in the box starts with This man before us is *Not Guilty* yet. The state can now throw everything it's got at him, they must make us believe he's guilty before we, the twelve good men and true, vote that he is. You and I, *we* are always on the side of the accused. He has a moral and a legal right to have us on his side, to show his side, his defense, whatever it may be, so the jury has that before them as it considers its verdict. That's our job. Our—life. Everything's against him except the presumption of innocence and the best defense. Only then does he get a square deal.

Yet Hauptmann had not even begun his defense and you, long weeks before, had decided he was guilty. How could you have forgotten those words your father spoke, words which made so great an impression on you that you repeated them from memory in your book about him some fifty years later? It is still hard for me to believe that you, Earl Rogers' daughter, were caught up in this unreasoning hatred of Hauptmann. Forgive me, please, Ms. St. Johns, but you have written so often about how much you learned from your father, yet in this case at least you brushed aside everything he had taught you. And please understand that a tangential aim of my research is to warn my contemporaries in journalism that those who came before us and many still among us are blinded by lies and illusions, and so infect all of society with their blindness—and men lose their freedom or their lives, as a result, in prisons and in obscene wars.

Reilly stepped toward Hauptmann. He began his examination slowly, gently, bringing him through his formative years in his native Saxony, his apprenticeship to a carpenter at fourteen, the war and the injuries he sustained, his return home and his inability to get work. And then to Hauptmann's several "offenses," as Reilly called them, which had led to his arrest and imprisonment in Germany. The lawyer brushed over Hauptmann's "offenses" lightly, like a man ashamed to admit insanity in the family.

Finally, Reilly said, in 1923 you left Germany . . . ?

Yes.

. . . and entered the United States after hiding on board a ship?

Yes, Hauptmann said. He described his two unsuccessful attempts to enter the country illegally, and smiled, almost proud of the memory, it seemed, as he spoke of the third time he stowed away and landed successfully in New York City.

Hauptmann ran through the jobs he had held, one menial job after another until he found work as a carpenter at eight dollars a day and joined the union. And met his Annie a few months later and married her in October 1925. The times were good, he testified. He was seldom without work because carpenters were in demand in the twenties and he often worked overtime. His wife worked steadily as a waitress, earning more than thirty dollars a week with tips. The household expenses, all living expenses, were paid with the money Annie earned and all of Hauptmann's earnings were saved. Including the thousand dollars or so extra he made in 1929, working Saturday afternoons and Sundays to help a friend build three houses in the Bronx.

Reilly asked: "And how much of that did you save?"

"Well, I took some to the bank and some of the money I always keep in the house." Plainly, he had been waiting to tell about the money he kept in the house, an important feature of his alibi, for a long time, because he spoke of it now before Reilly had a chance to ask.

"Did you keep some of the money in the house?" Reilly said, trying to underline the point, impress it upon the jury.

"Yes, always," Hauptmann said. "That is a habit I have."

"Do you remember about how much you had in your house at the end of 1929?"

"In 1929 I would say three thousand."

"Three thousand?"

"Three thousand, three thousand five hundred."

"In cash?"

"In cash."

"And that was money you made as a carpenter and saved?"

"Yes."

Reilly's natural flamboyance was held in check as he permitted Hauptmann to hold center stage. He asked: In 1931, did you decide to take a trip to California? Hauptmann said he and Annie had been planning that trip since their marriage because he had a sister living in California. He and his wife and their best friend, Hans Kloeppenburg, had left in July. They drove to California and back, taking three months. Kloeppenburg, of course, shared expenses.

And how much money did Hauptmann have in his apartment at the time of the trip? Approximately a little bit over $4,000, he said. He also had in the bank about $500 or $700, he couldn't remember precisely, and a few months before the trip he'd bought a 1930 four-door Dodge for $700. And he and Annie also owned a $3,750 mortgage. All told, their wealth in September 1931 was over $9,000, including the money hidden in a trunk at home.

At last Reilly came to the year of the crime. He asked: Did you meet a man who worked in an employment agency in Manhattan? Hauptmann said he had. He was in Fredericksen's bakery where his wife worked and mentioned to another customer that he was out of work. The customer said the company he worked for, Reliance Employment Agency, had jobs available for carpenters. On Saturday, February 27, Hauptmann said, he went to the agency. He paid a ten-dollar fee and was sent to the Majestic apartments for work. There, he was told to report on Tuesday, the first day of March. On Monday he got up at his usual hour, six in the morning. He sharpened his tools, drove down to the Majestic, and put his toolbox in the carpenter's shop. Then he went home. The next morning he returned to the Majestic at eight and waited for the construction superintendent. After a half hour he saw the man, who told him there would be no work until March 15. He returned on that date, was hired, and worked through April 2, quitting at the end of the day because he had thought he was to be paid a hundred dollars a month and discovered he was getting only eighty.

Reilly rephrased his question several times, making Hauptmann emphasize that he had worked on that Saturday, April 2. "Positively," Hauptmann said, he did work that Saturday. The date was significant; it was the day the ransom was paid in the Bronx. Hauptmann also swore he had gone back to the Majestic the following Monday, but simply to get his check for two days' work in April.

I flipped back through the trial transcript to the testimony of a prosecution witness I'd ignored earlier because I'd wanted to read Hauptmann's explanation of his employment first. That witness, Edward Morton, was the timekeeper at the Majestic. He had testified that Hauptmann did *not* work on April 2; his employment time book showed Hauptmann was absent April 2, worked on April 4, and never returned, quitting without giving notice. The testimony pictured Hauptmann as a man so certain he would be getting $50,000 of Lindbergh's money, he didn't bother going to work that morning.

Hauptmann, the timekeeper also swore, had been paid one hundred dollars a month, not eighty. Wilentz asked, Here, on this payroll record in evidence, does this figure *one hundred* prove Hauptmann was paid one hundred a month? Certainly, the witness said, he got a hundred dollars a month.

The prosecutor then asked Morton: "Will you tell us whether or not Bruno Richard Hauptmann worked on any day from March first to March twenty-first for your company?"

"No, sir, he did not."

"Does that mean he did not work for your company on the first day of March?"

"It does."

And the prosecution had put into evidence an employment card which indicated Hauptmann had been hired on March 21, 1932.

Now, however, Hauptmann was insisting on dates, on a rate of pay, absolutely contrary to what the timekeeper had said and what the employment records disclosed, records the jury had seen and could look at again during deliberations. Was Hauptmann lying? If so, they were awkward, dumb lies, the lies of a foolish man. When he was first arrested Hauptmann had claimed he'd begun working at the Majestic on March 1, 1932, the day of the kidnaping. The prosecution apparently proved through the evidence of the employment card that he hadn't started work until March 21. But now Hauptmann was certain he was on the job on March 15. What made Hauptmann revise his starting date of employment and destroy a vital part of his alibi—that he was on the job in midtown Manhattan the day of the kidnaping? Strangest of all, why did he then pick out March 15, a date absolutely useless as an alibi? By continuing to insist he had begun work on the fifteenth, when the timekeeper had already testified otherwise, and that he had been paid eighty dollars and had worked on the day the ransom was paid, Hauptmann branded himself a liar. The "proof" was against him; mentally, I placed quotation marks around *proof* because I doubted the evidence, particularly of employment dates. Would this master criminal Hauptmann have been so stupid as to substitute a lie valueless to his defense (the fifteenth) for a lie that supported his alibi (the first)? If he were going to lie he would have held onto the more serviceable lie—"I was working at the Majestic the first of March"—and stayed with it all the way.

Something had happened between Hauptmann's arrest and his trial to force him to revise his employment date in this way. Perhaps his memory had been refreshed. Perhaps, I thought, the payroll cards and the employment record had been tampered with. And I thought: Hauptmann's alibi is where you start when you look for documentation. Find evidence the payroll records were faked to destroy his alibi and you have the backbone of a case against police and prosecution. It wouldn't surprise me to find such evidence, for it has happened in hundreds of cases that have become public knowledge and in thousands that have never surfaced. Only hours earlier, during a brief break from my researches, I had read a story in the *Times* about a man who had spent more than two years in prison for a California bank robbery; after his parole he proved that the key evidence against him, fingerprints supposedly found on the bank counter, had been falsified by a policeman hungry to establish a brilliant arrest record. No, tampering with Hauptmann's employment record would not surprise me at all.

Reilly was still leading Hauptmann through those critical dates in 1932. He asked the defendant to detail for the jury precisely what he had done on that Saturday, April 2, that the ransom was paid. On that Saturday, Hauptmann said, I left the house at the usual time, seven in the morning, and took the subway to work. One hour for lunch starting at noon, and then I worked until five o'clock. An hour later, roughly, I arrived at home. At around seven Hans Kloeppenburg came by for our usual musical evening, the first Saturday of every month. It was me, my wife and Hans, and perhaps a fellow named Jimmy, I don't know his regular name and I'm not certain he was there or not.

Reilly asked: "What do you mean by the first Saturday of every month was your regular musical evening?"

"Well," Hauptmann replied, "Hans was playing the guitar and I was playing the mandolin and we used to play together and enjoy

189

ourselves for about an hour, an hour and a half, to keep in practice. Then Annie would make coffee and serve cake and we'd talk for a couple more hours."

Hans, he said, usually left between eleven and midnight. The only time I left my apartment that night was at the end of the evening, maybe eleven-thirty, when I drove Hans to the subway station. I came right back and went to bed.

Lindbergh, reporters noted, leaned forward in his chair and studied the witness. Lindbergh's eyes gave nothing away, but the journalists were quick to guess what he may have been feeling. Three weeks earlier he had sworn that Hauptmann was the man who had shouted "Hey, Doctor," from inside St. Raymond's Cemetery. Now Hauptmann was denying it and, by inference, saying Lindbergh was either mistaken or a liar. The glances of the journalists swung between Lindbergh and Hauptmann, some of the reporters hoping the testimony would create a confrontation. But it was four-thirty and Judge Trenchard declared the session adjourned until the next morning. Hauptmann left the witness chair with his head high, appearing quite confidant his explanations would now and forever settle the question of his innocence. He quite plainly believed he could convince the jury he was telling the truth.

January 25. The eighteenth day of the trial. Reilly had told reporters the evening before, in his daily press conference at the Union Hotel bar, that when Hauptmann returned to the stand he would prove that Isidor Fisch had been his friend and partner, had given him thousands of dollars to invest in the market, had bought furs with some of their joint funds, and had died owing him many thousands. The newspapers that morning contained long stories about Fisch and all that was known of this mystery man, as some writers called him.

Hauptmann would have great difficulty trying to shift the ownership of the ransom money to Fisch, most articles said, because Fisch's financial records indicated he was too poor to have received ransom money and certainly too close to poverty to have advanced Hauptman funds for stock speculation. In the years between his arrival in New York in 1925 and up to 1932, Fisch had sent his relatives in Germany occasional small sums. But in 1932 they had to rescue him from starvation by sending him money. He had borrowed several thousand dollars from friends to invest in a pie-baking firm, which apparently went bankrupt, and he had borrowed other sums from friends for living expenses. Members of a religious-fraternal club to which he belonged had told police Fisch was so broke in 1932 he couldn't afford to see a doctor about the illness that eventually killed him, and club members forced charity on him so that he could pay the rent on the single dreary room in which he lived. After Hauptmann's arrest a New York City detective who was in Europe on another case was diverted to Leipzig to interview Fisch's family. There, he heard the same story—Fisch was too poor even to pay for medical attention, he died because in America he had no money for doctors and by the time he returned home it was too late to save him. These facts, all writers said, fragmented Hauptmann's alibi even before he could tell it from the stand.

However, one curious note did turn up in the Fisch investigation. He had originally applied for a passport to return to Germany on May 12, 1932—the day the body identified as young Lindbergh was found in the woods near Hopewell—and had planned to sail in July but had to put it off because the friend with whom he was traveling lost his job and didn't have enough money for the tickets. Fisch and his friend did finally sail on December 6, 1933. At the end of the following March, Fisch died of tuberculosis in a Leipzig hospital. And, the news articles pointed out, when Hauptmann was first arrested police had told reporters they were seeking one Isidor Fisch as "an accomplice." Later, police explained they had simply wanted to question Fisch as a *possible* accomplice because Hauptmann had brought up his name and they felt there was a chance he was involved in the crime. When further investigation disclosed Fisch was dead, as Hauptmann had said (one of the few times he didn't lie, police said), it became obvious Hauptmann was simply attempting to divert suspicion from himself to Fisch.

Hauptmann, on the stand, seemed alert but relaxed as his lawyer approached to begin his examination. Reilly began with a few questions about Hauptmann's financial condition up to the end of 1931, then slid directly into the heart of their defense. He asked: "When did you first meet Isidor Fisch?"

"Suppose the early part of March or the early part of April, 1932," Hauptmann said.

"Where did you meet him?"

"Hunter's Island."

"Who introduced you to him?"

191

"Well, nobody," Hauptmann said. He had earlier explained that he and a group of fellow-Germans spent much time both summer and winter on Hunter's Island, a spit of land jutting into Pelham Bay off the North Bronx. They'd go boating—Hauptmann owned a canoe—play volleyball and soccer, fish, picnic, and sit around making music and singing German songs. In winter they'd rough it on weekends, in lean-tos and tents, with huge bonfires to keep them warm. It was very casual. Any stranger who came along, any German immigrant, was quickly brought into their circle. About meeting Isidor he said: "He was just on our place, where we used to be always. He was a German and we got in conversation."

They talked about Germany and America, about the need to make money and the hardships of the Depression. Fisch said he was a fur trader, making profits speculating in raw pelts. Hauptmann said he was also a trader, in the stock market. He had quit his job because he could make more money in the market than the four or five dollars a day he could earn as a carpenter in these times of Depression. Fisch asked a lot of questions about the stock market, Hauptmann said, during their meetings on Hunter's Island and back in the Bronx; they had grown close and were seeing much of each other, particularly since Fisch had a room in a house where friends of the Hauptmanns also lived.

In early May, Fisch proposed a partnership. Each would invest an equal amount to be placed in a fund. Hauptmann would use some of the money to trade in stocks and Fisch some to trade in furs, and they'd split the profits and losses fifty-fifty. The partnership started off slowly, Hauptmann said. In the middle of May, 1932, he gave Fisch $600 to invest in furs. During the summer, probably August, Fisch gave him the first of several payments to buy stocks.

Wilentz and his aides were almost frenetically scribbling notes on their yellow legal pads as Hauptmann testified. He had originally said, during those days of questioning following his arrest, that he'd first met Fisch in the summer of 1932. Now, faced with the necessity of explaining where he got the money he was investing in stocks and depositing in his bank accounts in May and later, and faced with what would have been an implausible story, that he and Fisch had become business partners immediately after their casual meeting in the summer, Hauptmann had moved up by several months the date of his meeting Fisch. Plainly, the prosecution team felt, Hauptmann was lying.

I jumped forward in the transcript now, trying to weave together all the witnesses who testified on a particular phase of Hauptmann's alibi. The problem with trials is the lack of continuity—evidence comes in spurts instead of being concentrated topically. For my purposes, a working version of the testimony to help further investigation, it was necessary to leap around among the witnesses. First, Gerta Henkel, a friend of the Hauptmanns. She testified that Hauptmann sometimes came by to have coffee with her because Fisch had rented a room in the apartment—from her husband—and Hauptmann occasionally picked up Fisch to take him down to the stockbroker's office. She said she had introduced Hauptmann and Fisch in her home in the summer of 1932, but later learned they had actually met in March or April; Fisch had told her that, she said. Gerta's husband, Karl, testified that it was he who had introduced Hauptmann and Fisch, some time in the summer of 1932. When Reilly tried to develop whether Henkel's wife or Fisch later told him that Fisch and Hauptmann had known each other before the introduction, the court refused to allow the answers because they would have been hearsay. There it was: Hauptmann most certainly seemed to be lying in order to explain large sums of cash flowing through his stock and bank accounts.

Hauptmann's testimony continued. The partnership flourished, he said. He wasn't certain just how much money he'd made from the fur business in the first year because, he testified, "I didn't check it up yet" in the notes he had made from memory of his partnership with Fisch. Later he testified he had to work from memory because the "big book" of accounts which would show all the transactions in the fur business and would prove he and Fisch had been partners and also that Fisch had given him large sums to invest—that large ledger was missing. Police had taken it from his apartment and he never saw it again. I put another note in my files: search for that "big book" or, at least, evidence it once existed.

Reilly now asked: "Did you ever receive any money from the fur business?"

"Oh, yes."

"Large sums?"

"Large sums and small sums."

"What was the largest sum you say you received as your share from the fur business in any one year?"

"I guess the largest sum over a thousand dollars."

"How much?"

"Over a thousand."

Reading this exchange, I couldn't help thinking that Reilly should have clarified it. Did Hauptmann mean a thousand-dollar profit in an entire year? That wasn't very large considering the impression left on the jury by the Treasury agent who had testified Hauptmann was speculating with a quarter of a million dollars. Or did Hauptmann mean a thousand dollars in one particular transaction, one of those large sums he mentioned? If the latter, Reilly should have developed it further.

Quickly now, Reilly moved to the key point at issue: Fisch's box full of money. In December 1933, Hauptmann said, Fisch sailed for Europe. On the Saturday night a few days before he sailed, the Hauptmanns threw him a farewell party.

"Did Fisch have anything with him," Reilly asked, "any bundles or anything with him the night before he sailed?"

"No, sir."

"Well, before he sailed did he leave anything with you to take care of while he was in Europe?"

"Well, he left two suitcases."

"What else?"

"Four hundred skins, Hudson seal."

"What else?"

"And a little box . . . I find out later it was a shoe box."

"Now, will you describe to the jury under what circumstances it was that he left this shoe box with you, what he said and what you said?"

"Well, at Mr. Fisch's request it was, he was throwing a party when he left for Germany. It was at his request in our house. We invited a couple of friends and about nine o'clock or a short while before nine o'clock Fisch came and he got a little bundle under his arm. I answered the doorbell, my wife was in the baby's room. He came and we went in the kitchen and he said, 'I leave it, I leave something, if you don't mind keep care of it and put it in a tight place.' I didn't ask what was in it. He only said that is papers in it. I thought maybe they are bills . . ."

194

Wilentz objected to the witness describing his thoughts and Reilly said: "Tell us what you did, not what you thought."

"I put it in a broom closet," Hauptmann said.

The broom closet had a top shelf that was seldom used, Hauptmann said, so he put the tightly wrapped box on that shelf and forgot about it until August 1934.

Reilly asked: "And what caused you to disturb it?"

"I was looking for—it was Sunday, it was nasty weather outside—and I was looking for a broom. I took the broom. The broom is on the left side of the closet. And when I took the broom I must hit the box with the broom handle, and I looked up and that way I saw that it is money. I damaged the box."

For a man who must have been living with this story, this alibi, for so many months, Hauptmann seemed to be having great difficulty thinking and speaking about it clearly. He had neglected to mention the most important part of that occurrence and Reilly had to prompt him.

"Well, now, had there been any moisture or wet or anything in that closet?"

"All soaking wet."

"Were there some kind of pipes that ran through the closet?"

"Yes."

"What kind of pipes? Were they water pipes or gas pipes?"

"No, no water or gas pipes. That is, I guess that is ventilation pipe, I guess, for toilets."

"Did you take the box down?"

"I put it in the boiler and took it down to the garage."

"What money did you see in the box?"

"Only gold certificates."

"About how much?"

"I didn't count it from the beginning."

"Is that the money you afterwards started to spend?"

"That is the money."

"Is that the money found in your garage?"

"It is."

"And was Fisch dead at this time?"

"Yes."

Again trying to keep it in order, I went skimming through the trial record for testimony about the water-soaked closet I remembered from previous readings. Yes, the landlady's son testified, the Hauptmanns had complained about a leak from the roof that soaked their closet in August 1934. Yes, a plumber testified, he had been called that August to repair a leak in the roof that permitted a large amount of water to run down into the Hauptmanns' closet. Yes, Anna Hauptmann testified, that Sunday in August Richard was working in the kitchen when he discovered the leak over the closet. Finally, Reilly put into evidence Weather Bureau records showing that sudden storms had struck the city that weekend, dumping seventy-seven hundredths of an inch of rain.

So it wasn't a *story*, as when Hauptmann shouted at a witness, "Mister, you're telling a story." It had definitely rained on a weekend in August, causing the roof to leak and flooding the closet. But it was still possible Hauptmann had selected the known fact of the rainstorm and the wet closet shelf and woven it together with a lie about Fisch's shoe box, to create a plausible story about the ransom money.

Once more, I jumped forward to other witnesses. Hans Kloeppenburg, whose testimony I'd already skimmed through earlier, testified he was at the farewell party for Fisch. At about six o'clock, the witness said, Fisch came in and talked at once with Hauptmann. "He carried a package in his arm. It was about, I would say, five to six inches high and seven, eight wide, and the length was about fourteen inches." He said the last time he saw Fisch with the package was when he and Hauptmann went into the kitchen together. When they joined the others in the parlor, Fisch no longer had the package. And Mrs. Katie Fredericksen also swore she had been at the party for Fisch, but she had arrived later and didn't see any package. However, she drove Fisch to the subway station at the end of the party and he showed her a roll of bills. Wilentz objected and the judge ruled out further testimony on the subject, but the point was made. Fisch did have money to spend. More important, Fisch was at Hauptmann's apartment that evening and did leave with him a package the shape of a shoe box.

Reilly now broke off his questions about Fisch and the money and carried Hauptmann through the necessary formality of denying all the charges against him. He did not kidnap Lindbergh's child, he said; was never in the child's nursery; had never in his life seen the child; did not write any of the ransom notes; never met Condon. Those denials were not enough, Reilly knew. He asked

Hauptmann to describe for the jury in detail his precise movements for the first of March. Hauptmann did so, once more staying away from his original alibi that he had begun working that day, once more saying he was told there was no work. So he went back to the employment agency in an attempt to retrieve the ten-dollar fee he'd paid, but he didn't get it because the agency said other jobs would be coming in soon that he might fill. He then went to Radio City, which was under construction, but could find no work there. He was home around five and a couple of hours later he went to Fredericksen's bakery to have his supper and wait for Annie to finish work. They returned home about nine o'clock and "went right away to bed."

Reilly stepped to the kidnap ladder leaning against a wall near the jury box and asked: "You have seen this ladder here in court, haven't you?" Hauptmann said he had.

"Did you build the ladder?"

"I am a carpenter." The crowded courtroom trembled with laughter and Hauptmann smiled, like a straight man slipping in his first joke. Asked to come down and look more closely at the ladder, Hauptmann walked briskly over to it and said: "Looks like a music instrument. To me it doesn't look like a ladder at all. I don't know how a man can step up."

At last Reilly came back to the money in the shoe box. He asked: You testified you took the money down to the garage, what did you do with it then?

Well, Hauptmann said, when I saw it was money I took the box down from the shelf and put it in a pail to carry it out because the water was running down my arms. It was four bundles of money in there, wrapped in brown wrapping paper and also in newspaper. In the garage I took the money out, squeezed the water out, put it in a wooden basket and the empty box and paper I put in the garbage. The money in the basket, I covered the basket and put it up on the ceiling behind some boards where nobody could see it. Put it on an upper shelf that reached the ceiling and nailed two strips in front of it and put another basket on top of the basket where the money was lying in. As it dried, I took a few bills and spent them for living expenses and hid the rest where the police found it three weeks later.

Reilly interrupted Hauptmann's story to get to the question on everyone's mind—the newspapers had been asking about it—why did he steal nearly $15,000 from the estate of a friend? The question wasn't asked so bluntly; Reilly led Hauptmann slowly and gently through an accounting of their partnership. Again, Hauptmann had enormous difficulty explaining clearly; his English was so dreadful the jury no doubt didn't understand his figures. Only after reading his testimony several times, quite carefully, does it finally become clear. When they settled accounts just before Fisch sailed, it was determined he owed Hauptmann $3,500. But Fisch didn't have any cash to square the debt, so he suggested selling some of the $21,000 worth of furs he claimed to have stashed away in a warehouse. Hauptmann said that would be foolish, if they held onto the furs they'd make a greater profit later because of inflation. Fisch then asked for a $2,000 loan for his boat passage and living expenses in Germany and Hauptmann agreed to lend him the money. He took $2,000 from his own stock account, the equity in stocks he was trading solely for himself and not for the partnership; he could borrow that sum without selling any stocks because he was trading on margin and had much leeway due to an increase in the value of his stocks. All told, then, he said, Fisch owed him $5,500 when he sailed. Hauptmann said after he was notified about Fisch's death he went looking for the furs supposedly in storage but could find no trace of them. Fisch had cheated him, had lied, he started to say, but Judge Trenchard refused to permit that kind of testimony after Wilentz objected.

"Now," Reilly said, "when you were taken to the New York City police station, were you beaten by police?"

Wilentz again leaped up to shout his objection but it was too late: "I was beaten," Hauptmann said. Legal arguments, now, over the materiality of a beating in New York on a case in New Jersey. "I will show it is material," Reilly said. It is material, he added, whether documents introduced against this defendant, the handwriting samples, were beaten out of him. The question is material, the judge agreed.

Reilly led into it slowly. Tell us about the request writings, he asked.

Hauptmann said that as best he could remember he was first asked to write the specimen paragraph some time after dark on the day of his arrest. Police dictated to him, yes, but they ordered him to spell certain words in a certain manner. When he wrote the word *not*, they dictated it with an *e* at the end of it.

Reilly asked: "How do you spell *signature*?"

"S-i-g-n-u-t-u-r-e."

"Did they spell it s-i-*n*-g . . ."

"They did," Hauptmann interrupted.

". . . n-a-t-u-r-e?"

"They did."

Here an editor's note in the trial transcript made it clear Reilly had just destroyed another part of the defense, that Hauptmann was forced to misspell several words—for the word *signature* doesn't appear in any of the request writings. It was never dictated to Hauptmann. Once more, Reilly blundered. Not only was trial-as-theater stacked against Hauptmann, but he didn't seem to have received even a minimal defense; Reilly, I was certain from his actions and from the way he phrased certain sentences, believed Hauptmann was as guilty as hell and couldn't be bothered trying to help the man tell his story as clearly as possible. And this blunder was even worse than casually accepting identification of the child's body. This time Reilly gave the prosecutor an opening to confuse, bewilder, and embarrass Hauptmann. But Reilly plunged on, unaware that his error put the lie to all Hauptmann's testimony about police dictation of the specimen sentences.

"Some of the notes were written that first night, weren't they?" he asked.

Hauptmann said they were.

"And they kept on for how many hours?"

"I can't remember exactly the time of the request writing, but I know real well it was late. It was really late in night time, probably after twelve o'clock. I refused to write any more."

"What did they do to you?"

"They forced me. They said, 'You won't get any sleep, you got to write.'"

"Did they do anything to you physically?"

"Not exactly, but they didn't give me any chance to sleep. They made me write to around two o'clock in the morning the next day." (Actually, the dictation apparently continued until at least ten the next morning.)

"How many times did they request you to write? Many times?"

"Many times. I fell asleep on the chair and they poked me in the ribs and said, 'You write.' I got a couple of knocks in the ribs when I refused to write."

Reilly asked Hauptmann about the statement he'd made to the

199

Bronx district attorney concerning the closet trim board with Condon's address and phone number allegedly in Hauptmann's hand. At the end of the statement the DA asked whether Hauptmann had been treated fairly in the Bronx and he had said he had been, indeed. Did that statement about treatment in the Bronx, Reilly asked, cover what had been done to you downtown in New York?

Hauptmann said: "When Mr. District Attorney Foley was asking me how did they treat me, the coppers in the Bronx, I said the treatment in the Bronx jail and in the courthouse was fair, but it covers only the Bronx. The treatment in the police station in New York, it was different, it was just the opposite way. I got the effect from this treatment for two months. That is the reason I lost over thirty pounds." (And not, Hauptmann implied, because his guilty knowledge of the crime had caused him to stop eating, as police had claimed.)

"No further questions," Reilly said. "Your witness." Hauptmann had testified for six hours.

Strange, so much of Hauptmann's testimony sounded like the words of a liar. Yet he rang true to me, in a very subtle way. Every trial I've ever reported on or read about in which police brutality was charged by the prisoner, the brutality was described as the most dreadful ever inflicted on any man's body. Hauptmann, however, "got a couple of knocks in the ribs," wasn't permitted to sleep, and lost weight as a result. Had he been a liar, reaching for any tale that might possibly save him, he would have done much better than that. Intuition combined with experience made me think it possible that most—perhaps all—of his testimony was truth.

10

Wilentz began to pull his notes together as he rose to cross-examine. There were typewritten sheets prepared long before, plus newly scribbled reminders of the areas in Hauptmann's testimony to be attacked. As Wilentz got his papers in order, some reporters whispered about Hauptmann's testimony. A few felt Reilly had cut it too short, even after six hours, by not exploring more fully the relationship between Hauptmann and Fisch. What had been developed was obscure and hard to follow. The defense had not kept the promise made in the opening address, to prove that the enormous sums flowing in and out of Hauptmann's accounts had been *repeat* money. All Reilly and the witness had succeeded in doing was to bore the jury with figures, so that it probably ignored all that testimony. Yes, Reilly should have coached Hauptmann on how to tell his story clearly. Other reporters said the jury wouldn't have understood no matter how clear it could have been made for them, and that Reilly had stopped at that point in order to protect his client. It was three o'clock in the afternoon. Judge Trenchard always ended the trial day at four-thirty. Should Wilentz's cross-examination begin to get to Hauptmann and really nettle him, the clock would run out and Hauptmann could escape total disintegration. And over the weekend, bolstered by talks from Lloyd Fisher on how to respond to Wilentz, Hauptmann might be able to recover and survive the assault.

There was no question that the cross-examination would be an assault. The night before, Wilentz had called Adela Rogers St. Johns to his office for any advice she might remember from her father's cross-examinations. She told him, she later said, "All the things my father did ahead of cross-examinations. How he knew every single thing so completely, was so familiar with everything the witness had ever said or done, was so informed on all places, laws, times, religions, backgrounds, that he never had to hesitate. He saw instantly if any answer was a lie, an evasion, a quibble. I told him how my father worked out special questions, and spaced them . . ."

And Wilentz had said: "I must shake Hauptmann's story."

Wilentz did, he most certainly did. St. Johns would describe it later that evening in this Hearstian prose:

> Lightning struck Hauptmann on the witness stand and he shriveled under it, cowering, gasping, livid.
>
> It struck without warning and those of us in the courtroom shrank from the sight of a man being electrocuted it seemed before our eyes.
>
> We saw a man weak now under the lash, we heard the lash strike again and again and Hauptmann fought back in his chair to get away from it, the death sweat gleaming on his forehead and deadly fear in his eyes. I could smell the fear. So complete was his breakdown that I could hardly bear to watch it and once I actually put my hands over my eyes to shut out the sight of a human being brought face to face with his own acts, his own words, his own past that was so damning—any moment—I thought, he may scream out anything—a confession, an admission—anything to *stop* this. If there had been another hour of it, that might well have happened.
>
> Every reporter felt this.

Wilentz had started off graciously enough, quickly taking his cue from Hauptmann, who surprised everyone by speaking before the prosecutor could ask his first question.

Hauptmann said: "Mr. General, may I go back to my financial transactions?"

"Yes?" Wilentz asked.

"All I said about my financial transactions, that is to be how I remember because there is no exact bookkeeping to keep Mr. Fisch and myself apart; that is the way I remember. And it may be some difference in one way or another."

"What you mean is that everything you have said about your financial transactions, all that testimony—you mean that is your best recollection; there may be a difference here or a difference there, is that what you mean?"

"The difference isn't very big, but that is the best recollection I have."

"Yes. You have had an opportunity in this court today, and you still have an opportunity this minute to tell the whole truth. Have you told the whole truth?"

"I told the truth already."

"So you now stand on the story you have given today."

"I do."

Wilentz had seemed kind during that first exchange. His voice was soft, his questions and manner unthreatening, getting Hauptmann to relax, lulling him. Now Wilentz suddenly shifted the scene back to Germany. Reilly had used the word *offense*. Wilentz's tone changed completely, as he used much harsher words, stressing the words as he questioned Hauptmann about his criminal past.

You *escaped* jail? he demanded in mock surprise. Hauptmann said he had simply walked through an open gate, then conceded that was an escape. Convicted of *only one crime*? Yes, only one, Hauptmann said. Well, what about *breaking and entering* a home through a *window*—you crawled into the house through a *second-story window*, didn't you? Hauptmann licked at his lips and said he had. His eyes shifted toward the jury and St. Johns thought of "a cornered rat."

And isn't it a fact, Wilentz went on, that you and another man were convicted of *holding up two women with a gun*? Yes, that's true, Hauptmann said. Women wheeling *baby carriages?*

Hauptmann, flushing now: "Everybody wheels baby carriages." He brought his handkerchief to his mouth, cleared his throat, and held the neatly folded white cloth over his lips for a moment, as if trying to hide tremors there.

Wilentz shouted: "*Everybody* wheels baby carriages, and you and this man with the gun held up these two *women* wheeling *baby* carriages, didn't you?"

Hauptmann was about to answer but one of his lawyers object- ed. As a brief argument broke out, Hauptmann lifted his handkerchief to his face again, wiping the perspiration from his forehead. The witness chair had lost its comfort for him. He had wanted to explain, he later wrote in his death cell, that there were no babies in the carriages; in Germany, prams were used as shopping carts. But he wasn't given time to explain. The questions had come so fast there was no time for thought. And St. Johns, in her report for the Hearst papers that evening, wrote that no one in the courtroom dared move because they all understood now that the man accused of kidnaping Lindbergh's child "had robbed babies—in their perambulators." Wilentz's half-truth had become fact, even in St. Johns' mind—in the minds of every juror, spectator, and newspaper reader flashed an image of Hauptmann's friend shoving a gun into a baby's mouth while Hauptmann stripped the carriage bare. Yes, St. Johns wrote, Wilentz had proved to them all that Hauptmann was capable of killing the Lindbergh child.

The prosecutor continued with a recitation of crimes he said Hauptmann had committed in Germany. Trying to sell stolen goods to a policeman. "I will say what you are reading there is something new to me," Hauptman protested. But Wilentz's harsh voice overrode him: "When you told this jury you were out on parole you knew very well Germany *wanted* you for *years,* didn't you?" Giving Hauptmann no time to explain that the statute of limitations had run out, if he could have found the words, Wilentz raced on, getting Hauptmann to concede he had been planning to return to Germany this year of his trial and leaving the impression he was going to flee with the Lindbergh ransom money.

Now Wilentz turned to one of Hauptmann's small memo books, found in his home by police. Look at it, the prosecutor demanded. Hauptmann took it, opening to a page Wilentz wanted to discuss. Yes, Hauptmann said, it is my book in my handwriting.

"Take a look at this word. Tell me if that is your handwriting, that one word there."

Hauptmann did not answer.

"Or did some *police*man write it?" Wilentz sneered, again stressing a word and, as one reporter later noted, tearing down in that single sentence the last shred of possibility that police had dictated the request writings as the defendant had claimed.

"Well?" Wilentz asked.

Hauptmann: "I—I can't remember every word I put in there."

Two, three, four questions and to each Hauptmann responded: "I can't remember." Always fatal words from a witness, pointing to a lie, not an honest inability to recall. Jurors, reporters, and audience leaned forward, wondering at the word in the book which made Hauptmann's memory fail and condemned him as a liar. Wilentz asked:

"Tell me, how do you spell *boat*?"

Hauptmann spelled it properly.

"Then why did you spell it here, b-o-a-d?"

"You wouldn't mind to tell me how old this book is?" Wilentz said: "You tell me." Hauptmann studied the book a moment and said it was at least eight years old.

"Why did you spell, b-o-a-d?"

"Well, after, you make improvement in your writing."

Wilentz pressed it with several questions on why he had misspelled the word and Hauptmann said that he didn't think he had written it that way and then, "I am not quite sure I put the word in."

Wilentz leaned toward him now, pointing an anger-waving finger. "*You* tell the *truth* now," he shouted. "Didn't you spell it in there?"

"Now listen," Hauptmann said. "Listen, I can't remember I put it in there."

Wilentz, sounding almost shrewish, nagged after him and Hauptmann said he couldn't "say yes or no that I ever put it in there." The prosecutor shouted:

"The reason you don't say yes or no is that you wrote the word *boad* when you got the fifty thousand from Condon, isn't that right?"

"No, sir."

Wilentz strode angrily to the prosecution table and returned with the last letter written by the extortionist, containing instructions on how to find the kidnaped child. "*Boad* Nelly," he almost shrieked. "Look at it." Hauptmann took the letter. Wilentz came even closer now, almost touching the defendant.

"Do you see the words, *boad Nelly*?"

"I see it, certainly."

"Look at it again, *boad,* do you see that?"

"I see it."

"B-o-a-d?"

"I see it," Hauptmann said, sounding exasperated. Worried, perhaps.

Wilentz asked whether in Saxony, where Hauptmann was schooled, don't they substitute a *d* for a *t* in most words of this kind? Hauptmann said only with some words and Wilentz demanded whether he'd written *boad* because that's how it is spelled in Saxony. "Oh, no . . ." Hauptmann began and Wilentz cut in, his voice edged with irony-surprise:

"That *isn't?*"

No, Hauptmann explained, maybe they pronounce it with a *d* but they write it with a *t*.

A few questions about Fisch which Hauptmann answered without difficulty and Wilentz's manner seemed to have been transformed. He had become courteous, gentle, a nice man asking questions that were easy to answer because there were no tricks in them, no hidden meanings and insinuations. *Space your questions,* St. Johns had advised. Now Hauptmann relaxed in that brief space of sensible questions. Without signal, Wilentz suddenly returned to the attack:

"Did Fisch help you kidnap the Lindbergh child and *murder* it?"

Hauptmann appeared as if struck by a stone, unable to believe such a question could be asked. For a moment he raged at the prosecutor with his eyes, but said nothing. Finally he whispered:

"I never saw the Lindbergh child."

A quickened pace, once more. Wilentz forced Hauptmann to admit—reluctantly, so reluctantly he was clearly hiding something—that he had hidden a pistol in his garage (a small pistol someone had given him years before, he explained days later when Reilly took the witness again and attempted to repair the damage wrought by Wilentz; he had put it in the garage because he didn't want it in the house and he couldn't bring himself to throw it away). The prosecutor forced Hauptmann to admit he had used an alias, Perlmeyer, when he stowed away on the boat, and the next question stunned Hauptmann again. What was the first name, Wilentz asked several times, wasn't it *John?* "I can't remember," the witness repeated. A common trial technique: a question becomes fact and an unsophisticated witness strengthens the *fact* by falling back on the lack of memory instead of denying it. So, those in the courtroom felt, Hauptmann had been "John" at another time, on the boat coming to America—and in the cemeteries extorting Lindbergh's money from Condon.

It was a quarter of five when Judge Trenchard called an end to the day's proceedings, fifteen minutes past the usual time of adjournment. With relief, Hauptmann stepped down and was led away between his two guards. The spring had gone from his step. He did not look at his wife.

Wilentz's step now had the bounce in it. Walking back to his office, surrounded by scores of reporters and photographers, he seemed to be trying to hold down a too obvious pride as several of those nearest him congratulated him on his performance. They were certain, they said, that on Monday he would break Hauptmann and actually get him to *confess.* Right from the stand, a confession of murder from the killer. Over the weekend Hauptmann would create in himself such terror that by Monday he would unravel before their very eyes, they told Wilentz. What an incredible victory, to back the victim into the ropes and destroy him with sledgehammer blows until he could do nothing else but collapse and cry and scream out: "Mr. General Wilentz, I did it, I killed the Lindbergh baby!"

It didn't work out that way, of course. But several times during the nine hours of cross-examination over the next two days, Hauptmann seemed close to an absolute breakdown. Wilentz employed every known technique of the cross-examiner to get the jury to hate this man Hauptmann and to break his spirit.

Wilentz was questioning Hauptmann about one of the notebooks police had seized at his apartment. You kept accounts in your book about all the money you earned and all you saved, didn't you? No, Hauptmann said, not everything, all the money he earned and all his wife earned, but not everything. Money you loaned to people? Yes, I kept a record of that. Did you keep an account every year of how much you and your wife were worth? Yes, that is so, the witness said.

"I suppose when you put the figures in the books that you put the correct figures in, didn't you?"

"Well," Hauptmann said, "I saved every week about ten dollars."

"No, never mind, we will get to that . . ."

"I did not put . . ." Hauptmann tried to say, but Wilentz cut him off: "No. Just one minute now. You *just answer* the question.

207

You see, you know what I'm going to ask you but I will come to that later. What I asked was, did you when you put the figures in the book, did you put correct figures in? Were they *truthful* figures?"

"You mean . . ."

"When you wrote in the books you kept, were the figures honest figures, were they *true* figures?"

Clearly upset now, Hauptmann said: "I said he was, them figures were true, but I will—left some of them out."

Wilentz refused to let him escape from the trap being set, by permitting an explanation. There was a script—Wilentz's questions which would show Hauptmann claimed to have falsified his own ledgers—and the prosecutor couldn't allow the defendant to explain, right now, as Hauptmann appeared to be trying to do, that he saved every week "about ten dollars" which he did not record in his ledgers. The form was more important than any possible truth—first show Hauptmann lied and then his explanation that he had put aside that unrecorded money in his trunk would also sound untrue. Following the form, cutting off all attempts at explanation, Wilentz propelled Hauptmann through a series of questions, forcing him to answer that when he had written this figure of $100 in his book it was an accurate figure, this one of $500 was accurate, each individual figure was accurate.

"So that the figures in the book," the prosecutor asked, "whatever the figures in those books are they are correct, honest, and true, isn't that right?"

"Yes."

"When you wrote into your own books in your own hand, you didn't try to fool anybody but you were putting the truth in there?"

"Yes . . ."

"All right . . ."

". . . but there is only one thing that I did not put . . ."

"*No buts.* Is it the *truth?*"

At last, Fisher rose to object that Wilentz wasn't permitting the prisoner to answer and Judge Trenchard agreed he "should be permitted to make his explanation now, *if* he has any"—a doubt in the judge's voice not lost on jury and press.

Hauptmann finally was able to say: "I saved money besides that my wife should not know. I put nothing in the book."

"*Oh!*" Wilentz shouted. "In other words *you were hiding it on your wife?*"

Hauptmann nodded and Wilentz went on: "You were hiding a *lot* of things on your wife, weren't you?"

"No, sir. It is only the money I kept."

"When is the first time you met Mrs. Henkel?" Wilentz asked. Hauptmann appeared surprised, as if thinking, what does she have to do with the charge against me? He then grew upset. Gerta and Karl Henkel were good friends. Isidor Fisch had roomed with them. Hauptmann occasionally picked up Fisch at that apartment to drive him down to the broker's office and he'd have coffee with Fisch and Gerta first. While he seemed to be thinking about how to respond to this meaningless question, Wilentz demanded again: "When did you meet her?"

"Summertime, thirty-two," Hauptmann said.

"Where?"

"Hunter's Island."

"Was Mr. Henkel there when you met her?"

Hauptmann didn't answer and Wilentz shouted: "What are you *thinking* about? You *know* whether he was or not."

"I guess her sister was there."

"I am asking you about *Mister* Henkel, not her sister."

"I can't remember if he was there."

"Who introduced you to Mrs. Henkel—nobody?"

"Well, it doesn't need much introducing out there."

"That was when your wife was away, wasn't it? She took a trip to Germany that summer?"

"Yes, that is right."

Wilentz turned and smiled at the jury. This man, he had just proved to them, this defendant was hiding money from his wife and was interested in another woman.

The prosecutor returned to the $14,000 in gold bills Hauptmann swore he had found, asking whether he'd told his wife about their sudden riches. He repeated his question with variations several times, forcing Hauptmann to squirm: "No, I didn't tell her." And Wilentz piled on layer after layer of righteousness and indignation with questions designed to become facts in careless minds. Was Hauptmann *honest* with his wife about the money? Didn't his wife *work and slave* in a bakery and give you her earnings, and her savings when you were first married? Didn't *she* buy the furniture in your apartment? You were *partners,* weren't you, except when it came to the $14,000.

"Why should I make my wife excited?" Hauptmann replied to that last question.

"Oh, I *see,*" the prosecutor said, his sarcasm growing heavier. "When you were keeping your books and you were cheating her with your books of accounts and you wouldn't tell her about the money, why did you *keep that from her?*"

"Should it be a pleasant surprise for her sometimes," Hauptmann said.

"You were keeping a *surprise* for her?"

"Yes, because my intention was to buy her a house, build her a house sometime."

Wilentz jumped into another area now, keeping Hauptmann off-balance. He established that one of Hauptmann's stockbrokers was a man named Brent. Hauptmann said he knew the man well.

"Do you remember saying to Mr. Brent, 'Mr. Brent, if my wife ever asks you where I was some night tell her I was with you.' "

Hauptmann said he didn't remember that and, when pressed, said he had never done such a thing. But in the act of asking the question Wilentz implied he had a document to prove Hauptmann a liar. Brent was never called to testify, however; Wilentz had successfully made unproved statements to the jury implying Hauptmann not only cheated his wife out of money but was also setting up an alibi for his philandering—no doubt with Mrs. Henkel.

Wilentz shuffled through his papers, consulted one of them, then began to question Hauptmann about stock market losses in 1931. Why, he asked, did you ask your broker for more time to pay a seventy-four dollar margin call and risk having some stocks sold out from under you when, as you claim, you had more than four thousand hidden in the trunk? Isn't it because there was no more money left? Hauptmann said no, he just didn't think seventy-four dollars was worth going to the bank for or dipping into the trunk.

Wilentz asked: "When it came to losing money, you were losing Annie's money?"

"Just the same my money."

"But what you were saving was your money from the trunk, wasn't it."

"Yes."

"Did you want to get away from Mrs. Hauptmann?"

"No, it just happens that . . ."

"Didn't you say, when Mrs. Hauptmann came back from Germany, that you *couldn't live with her any more?*"

"What?" Hauptmann asked. He leaned forward, appearing amazed at what he'd heard.

"Didn't you tell that to Mr. Brent? That you can't get along with Annie?" Hauptmann simply stared at him. "Well, you did or you didn't."

Straining forward now, Hauptmann looked frightened, like a man who suddenly feels a sliver of ice glide along his spine and smells the smell of death. He shouted: "Do you know what you are talking about?"

"I am talking about you and your *wife. Did you say that?*"

Hauptmann slid down in his chair, shock visibly clouding across his face. "No," he said simply. His body trembled.

Wilentz released the tension by turning to another subject. And, during cross-examination about the closet trim board with Condon's address and phone number on it, Hauptmann made a statement which brought into focus the reason he'd been such a poor witness. The prosecutor insisted that Hauptmann tell the jury whether he'd been speaking the truth when he said the writing on the board was his. Hauptmann appeared to be thinking the question over and Wilentz thundered at him, "Why do you hesitate?" "Why don't you answer?" "Can't you say yes or no?"

"You will have to give me a chance," Hauptmann said.

"I will give you all day but you ought to know whether you told the truth."

And Hauptmann said: "No, I have to trans—I am thinking in German and I have to translate it in American language, and it needs quite a bit of time, so excuse me."

And I remembered something Murray Bleefeld had said, during one of the conversations we'd had so far. Murray had called Hauptmann "a poor bastard who couldn't even speak English and should have had a translator in court." Ellis Parker, I think, had said that to Murray. And it began to make sense now—Hauptmann was stumbling all over himself because he was mentally "translating" and Wilentz was whipsawing him around the courtroom, keeping him in a state of confusion by demanding he give only *yes* or *no* answers, shouting, Just say yes or no and you explain later,

211

and then rushing forward without waiting for the explanation except on those rare occasions—much too rare—when defense lawyers objected that Hauptmann should be permitted to explain.

At the end of this particular demonstration of that roundly applauded courtroom tactic, Hauptmann finally sat up straight, ignoring Wilentz's repeated demand that he give a yes or no answer, and said: "Well, I guess I explain it first."

Wilentz, affronted, said: "Will you *please* do us the kindness of abiding by the rules of the court and answer first yes or no? Did you tell the truth about this board when you were being examined in the Bronx County Courthouse under oath?"

"Then I say no."

"You *didn't* tell the truth there?" A victory. Wilentz had got him to admit he'd lied. Now the prosecutor tried to rush on. "All right," he said, "now just . . ."

"Wait a minute," one of the defense lawyers said. And Hauptmann, a dark-veined anger swelling his throat, asked: "You want to give me a chance to explain?"

"He may have it," Judge Trenchard ruled.

The explanation—that he'd never said he had written on the board, just that it looked like his writing but he couldn't be certain—fell absolutely flat. Wilentz had stuck another lance into his victim and the jury could see blood, and in a courtroom only liars and the guilty bleed.

I thought at first that Wilentz could be excused his excesses for he was simply performing in the manner expected in the staged combat of a courtroom; his assistants and the reporters had told him he might break Hauptmann down on the stand and that was a goal worth shooting for because it was all part of the game. At times, however, Wilentz seemed to be torturing Hauptmann. For example:

"You are really having a lot of fun with me, aren't you?" Wilentz demanded after Hauptmann had stumbled through still another lengthy explanation of his finances.

"No," the witness said.

"Well, you are doing very well. You are smiling at me every five minutes."

"No," Hauptmann said again, his handkerchief clenched in his hands.

"You think you are a big shot, don't you?"

212

"No. Should I cry?"

"No, certainly you shouldn't. You think you are bigger than everybody, don't you?"

"No, but I know I am innocent."

"Yes, you are the man that has the willpower. That's what you know, isn't it?"

"No," Hauptmann said once more. His blue eyes slid back and forth between Wilentz and Fisher, like a deer caught in a trap, seeking help but fearing it.

Wilentz shouted: "You wouldn't tell if they murdered you, would you?"

"Nooo . . ." A moan, Hauptmann's usually straight body beginning to slump and to twist from side to side. His hands gripped the arms of his chair until the knuckles turned pain-white, and he gripped harder still, as if trying to fight faintness with pain.

"Willpower is everything with you, isn't it?"

Hauptmann attempted to speak but could not, then gasped air and said carefully: "No, it is—I feel innocent and I am innocent and that keeps me the power to stand up."

"Lying, when you *swear to God* that you will tell the truth. Telling lies doesn't mean *anything* to *you."*

"Stop that!" Hauptmann was near hysteria now. His right arm shot out as if to hold back bullets.

"Didn't you lie in the Bronx Courthouse?"

"Stop that!"

"Didn't you lie under oath, time and time again? *Didn't* you?"

"No, I did not." His body straightened, the tremors ceased. He seemed to have drawn on some inner strength to get himself under control.

"Lies! Lies! Lies!" the prosecutor shrieked.

"Well, you lied to me too."

"Yes? Where and when?"

"Right in this courtroom here." The English was poor, the thrust lost. Another witness might have put it, You lied about Mrs. Henkel, you lied about me and my wife, you lied with a lot of your questions.

And I wondered what on earth the defense attorneys were doing during this tormenting of Hauptmann. And the judge. At the trials I've covered, every lawyer and every judge would have stopped Wilentz long before. This was more than cross-examination, this

213

was torture, attempts to degrade Hauptmann, to jam the circuits of his brain so that he would collapse, in full view of the hundreds in the audience and those surrogates of millions of spectators, the journalists. The reporters scribbled and silently cheered Wilentz on. The spectators were fascinated that this man of iron will—so they'd read, a man who thought he was superior to everyone in the world, the pop psychiatrists had said in newspaper interviews—seemed to be crumbling to pieces. And the judge and defense lawyers: what vise gripped their vocal cords? Wilentz must have put on a hypnotic performance; how often in your life do you see a man peeling and splintering right before your eyes?

"You are not smiling anymore, are you?" Wilentz asked, his question almost a boast.

"Smiling?"

"It has gotten a little more serious, hasn't it?"

"I guess it isn't any place to smile, here."

Wilentz stepped closer. *"I am a carpenter,"* he said, quoting Hauptmann's words, mocking him.

"I am," Hauptmann said.

"That was funny, wasn't it?"

"No, sir, there was nothing funny about it."

"You had a good laugh, didn't you? Did you *plan* that answer in the jail there? Did *someone tell you* to give that answer when I asked you about the ladder, to stand in front of the jury and say, I am a carpenter?"

"No, sir."

"You thought that out yourself?"

Frederick Pope, associate defense counsel, finally got to his feet. "Well, I think this has gone just about far enough," he said. And I had the feeling someone finally objected to the brutalization of Hauptmann only because the prosecutor had indeed gone too far—he had suggested that the defense lawyers had coached Hauptmann in a jocular answer. The lawyers felt threatened, and so they finally objected.

"I will withdraw the question," Wilentz said. Another illusion of trials—strike out the prejudicial question and pretend the jury will automatically forget it and be unaffected by it. Turning to the bench, Wilentz asked: "May we have a recess, if your honor please?"

214

Pope continued his objection: "I think we ought to come back into a courtroom and see if we can't get down . . ."

Wilentz: "Now, *I* object to *that*. I think it's a reflection on the court."

The judge hadn't seemed to notice that his court had been insulted until Wilentz spoke, and now Trenchard said: "What did you mean by that, Mr. Pope?"

"I mean this patent abuse of the witness! It's about time we protested against it. It has been going on for quite a while."

"Whenever you have any occasion to protest, make your protest to the court and the court will deal with it," Trenchard said. "It always has and will continue to do so. We will now take a recess."

Could Wilentz have been that brilliant? I wondered. He had pushed his interrogation over the edge of legal propriety, he had committed an offense against trial procedure by stepping beyond the bounds even of cross-examination. He likely would have been criticized from the bench had he not caught an intonation in Pope's voice and cut him off with a counterattack which turned Pope into the loser. And Hauptmann also lost, of course—a much greater loss.

And so it went, through the rest of that day and through most of the twentieth trial day—Wilentz attacking for more than eleven hours, seeming to be trying to drive Hauptmann to collapse and then losing that elusive prize, a full confession, as Hauptmann pulled his soul together right at the edge of complete disintegration.

Still, although he got no confession, Wilentz destroyed Hauptmann's defense. Every explanation the prisoner had offered, during his direct examination, Wilentz managed to make seem a lie. The "Fisch story" is impossible to believe, after reading the cross-examination. Hauptmann's explanation of why he had written to Fisch's brother in Germany, after learning of Isidor's death, why he explained they'd been partners and Isidor owed him $5,500, but then neglected to notify the brother that he'd found more than $14,000 in Isidor's shoe box—the explanations sounded like lies. After reading through Hauptmann's testimony on cross-examination I was certain of one thing—no jury in the world ever would have acquitted him. He was guilty, on the face of it. The evidence against him, although so tarnished after filtering through my mind, seems overwhelming because Hauptmann's explanations ring so

215

false. Yet even after suffering with Hauptmann through the savage cross-examination, that strong thread of truth I felt I detected in his story remained with me.

I glanced quickly through Reilly's redirect examination, the defense lawyer's attempt to knit together the broken chain of his defense. Reilly failed, most naturally. But, in reading, I did come across another item for further investigation. Hauptmann claimed that when police arrested him they had confiscated along with his ledger book several letters he'd received from Fisch before his death in Germany, letters that would also have proved they did indeed have a very extensive partnership. Reilly asked Wilentz to produce those letters and he said he would; later he informed the court that police could locate only a single postcard that said anything bearing on the case. Where are the letters? I asked myself. I must find them.

Anna Hauptmann followed her husband to the stand. She wore a navy blue dress with a cowl neck, and a small black felt hat. On her fingers were a gold wedding band and a white-gold engagement ring set with small stones. She seemed terrified as Reilly led her through the same story her husband had told—their introduction by mutual friends, marriage, her work as a waitress, their frugality.

Yes, she said, she had worked on the night of March 1, 1932, and Richard had called for her sometime around seven o'clock. He was in the bakery with her until they left together for home, about nine-thirty, and he remained at home with her until they awoke the next morning. The night of April 2, the night the ransom was paid, there was a "musical evening" at her apartment, she testified. And that night on which Richard was said by a witness to have been at a movie house in Greenwich Village, he was actually at home with friends who dropped in to celebrate his birthday. After questioning her for a time about Mrs. Henkel, Reilly asked whether Anna had the slightest suspicion Richard might have been unfaithful. Mrs. Hauptmann flushed and said:

"Mrs. Henkel was not only a friend of my husband, she was my friend, too." Never, she added, did she doubt Richard's fidelity. On point after point, she supported her husband: Fisch was his business partner; rain had leaked into the broom closet that Sunday last August; she had saved most of the $7,000 she had earned since coming to America. Reilly's direct examination ended with the question: "Do you trust your husband, Mrs. Hauptmann?"

She replied: "Who shouldn't trust a husband?"

Wilentz took the witness. He was gentle in his questioning, almost respectful toward this woman who had suffered as much as Mrs. Lindbergh, as some writers put it. He asked obvious questions, those to which the answers were well known by now, and he got the expected responses—a recitation of the materials Fisch had left behind when he sailed for Europe, ten or fifteen minutes devoted to a complete inventory of Fisch's possessions, Wilentz's tone that of a neighbor chatting over the back fence. In the same disarming manner he asked about the closet where rain had leaked in. No, she said, she never saw a shoe box on the top shelf because she never used that top shelf.

Wilentz's neighborly manner quickly changed. He brought out a photograph of the broom closet and asked if it correctly showed the position of the shelves. I think so, she replied. This apron hanging on the nail there—it was a hook, she protested—well, he said, a hook, she used to take her apron off the hook and put it back without trouble, wasn't that correct? Oh, Anna said, I could hang it up.

"Now see if that hook isn't above the top shelf," Wilentz said, pointing at the photo in her hand.

"I see that," she said.

"And you know that if you stood a few feet away from it you could see everything on that top shelf?"

"Why should I stay away a few feet and look up there? I didn't stay away a few feet. When I went to the closet I went over, opened the door, and got whatever I needed from the closet."

Wilentz's manner now reverted to prosecutor; he cried: "Will you *please* tell me if it is not a fact that if you stepped away from the closet a few feet, if the door was open you could see *everything* on the top shelf, *couldn't you?*"

"I don't think so."

He shook his head in disbelief. "You were the lady of the house and I take it you did your own cleaning, Mrs. Hauptmann?"

"I did."

Wilentz asked several questions about whether she cleaned closets, and did she clean this particular closet, and Mrs. Hauptmann parried them, not about to permit him to set her up for a trap as he had done to her Richard time and again. Finally she insisted she never cleaned the top shelf because "I didn't use it."

"You don't really *mean* that, do you, Mrs. Hauptmann?"

"I didn't use that shelf."

His voice colder and tougher now, Wilentz asked a long series of questions about the closet and finally got Mrs. Hauptmann to admit she had kept several of her things on the top shelf, including a tin box with soap premium coupons. Through repeated questions edged in tones of disbelief, Mrs. Hauptmann maintained she had never seen the shoe box in the eight months her husband claimed it had lain on the top shelf. Wilentz made it plain he *knew* she was lying—from loyalty, of course, to help her husband, but lying nonetheless.

I'd grown weary now, reading through Hauptmann's defense. I closed the trial transcript because that defense had been so futile, so disastrous for Hauptmann. For the remainder I turned to several brief summaries of the trial; I wanted to end this as quickly as I could. Reilly, I read, paraded a series of witnesses to the stand to testify that they had seen Hauptmann on the three key dates in question, that he was a long distance away from Lindbergh's home, the cemeteries, and Greenwich Village. But most of the witnesses proved to be former inmates of mental institutions, former convicts, or simple liars, men and women apparently suffering from the same fever afflicting most of the people in this case, a need to leap into the spotlight for a brief moment of fame on the world's stage. "You are killing me with these witnesses," Hauptmann cried to Reilly at one point. And even those few witnesses who sounded as if they were sincerely telling the truth were confused and disoriented by Wilentz's brilliant cross-examination.

Anxious as I was to wrap it up and get to sleep so that I could start tracking down Murray Bleefeld, who hadn't called in many days, I couldn't resist studying the last day of the trial—the judge's charge to the jury and the courtroom scene when the verdict was brought in.

Judge Trenchard read his instructions to the jury on the morning of February 13, the thirty-second day of the trial. Unlike most states, New Jersey permits a judge to review the facts of the case rather than simply advising the jury on the law. Trenchard began reasonably enough:

"The evidence must establish the truth of the facts to a moral certainty, a certainty that convinces the understanding and satisfies the reason and judgment of those who are bound to act conscientiously on it. . . . The state, in order to justify a verdict of guilty, must establish beyond a reasonable doubt that the death was caused by the act of the defendant. . . .''

And then, assuming the arm of God, Judge Trenchard reached out and condemned Hauptmann to death.

"It is argued," he said, "that Dr. Condon's testimony is inherently improbable and should in part be rejected by you. But you will observe that his testimony is corroborated in large part by several witnesses whose credibility has not been impeached. . . . Of course, if there is in the minds of the jury a reasonable doubt as to the truth of any testimony, such testimony should be rejected. But, upon the whole, is there any doubt in your minds as to the reliability of Dr. Condon's testimony?''

He went on: "If you find that the defendant was the man to whom the ransom money was delivered, the question is pertinent: Was not the defendant the man who left the ransom note on the windowsill of the nursery and who took the child from its crib?''

And on: "It is argued by defendant's counsel that the kidnaping and murder was done by a gang and not by the defendant. . . . Now, do you believe that? Is there any evidence in this case whatsoever to support this conclusion?''

And on: "The defendant says that the ransom money was left with him by one Fisch, a man now dead. Do you believe that?''

Trenchard paused when defense attorneys stirred as if to object, then continued: "The defendant says that he found the ransom bills in a shoe box which had been reposing on the top shelf of his closet several months after the box had been left with him, and that he then, without telling anybody, secretly hid most of the bills in the garage where they were found by the police. Do you believe his testimony that the money was left with him in a shoe box, and that it rested on the top shelf of the closet for several months? His wife, as I recall it, said that she never saw the box, and I do not recall that any witness excepting the defendant testified that they ever saw the shoe box there.''

And still on: "There is evidence from which you may conclude, if you see fit, that the defendant built the ladder, although he denies it. Does not the evidence satisfy you that at least a part of the wood from which the ladder was built came out of the flooring of the defendant's attic?''

And: "The defendant denies that he was ever on the Lindbergh premises, denies he was present at the time the child was seized

219

and carried away. He testifies that he was in New York at that time. . . . This mode of meeting a charge of crime is commonly called 'setting up an alibi.' " Reilly rose to protest, but Fisher pulled him back into his seat. Setting up an alibi, Trenchard went on, "is not looked upon with any disfavor in the law . . . and if a reasonable doubt of guilt is raised, even by inconclusive evidence of an alibi, the defendant is entitled to the benefit of the doubt. . . . You, of course, should consider the testimony of Mr. Hochmuth, that on the forenoon of that day, March 1, 1932, he saw the defendant driving rapidly from the direction of Hopewell, that he had a ladder in the car. . . . Do you think there is any reason, upon the whole, to doubt the truth of the old man's testimony?"

For an hour and ten minutes this elderly man in black, this judge some called a living legend, lectured the jury in a paternal manner, guiding them to their verdict: "Do you believe that?" "Is there any reason to doubt that prosecution witness?" "Is there any reason to believe the defendant?"

One by one by ghastly one, each point condemned Hauptmann to die. "He just strapped Bruno in the chair," Damon Runyon said at the conclusion of the charge to the jury. Even Lindbergh, later that evening during dinner, told a guest that Trenchard's summation was biased. The judge's repeated phrase, whenever he discussed Hauptmann's defense, "Do you believe that?", did not appear as horrible in print in the evening paper, Lindbergh said, as it did in the courtroom. For what the judge actually said, what Lindbergh and everyone in court had heard, were icy intonations calling Hauptmann a liar—"Do *you* believe THAT?"

The jurors deliberated into the night; they had voted Hauptmann guilty the moment they entered the jury room and the long delay in reporting their verdict was caused by the demand of several jurors to recommend mercy. Hauptmann sat in his cell directly beneath the jury room, watched by two guards. On orders of the sheriff, the prisoner was not permitted to speak to his guards and the rule of silence was enforced during the long hours waiting for the verdict. But Hauptmann could hear. And the jury could hear. Outside, the night had become a forest teeming with life. Ten thousand men, women, and children, the result of thousands of years of civilization, filled the streets around the courthouse. A holiday spirit vibrated from them, in the beginning. But as the night wore on and the February cold bit deeper, some in the crowd grew impatient. A few began the chant, and then many, and then almost all the crowd, until with a single voice the chant came strong into the jury room and into the prisoner's cell below: "Kill Hauptmann! Kill Hauptmann! Kill Hauptmann!" A man rushed to the courthouse steps and threw a rock at the building; he shouted with pride as it smashed the delicate fan-shaped window over the portico. The crowd cheered him and moved close to prevent police from seizing him. These are the people, as some poet has written; God's botched experiment run wild.

The jury returned eleven hours and fourteen minutes after they had filed out of the courtroom around noon. Another ten minutes for defendant, judge, lawyers, and audience to reassemble. Lindbergh was absent for the first time; the hero who had sat at the prosecution table and reinforced the contrast between good (of victim) and evil (of defendant) was with his wife at her mother's home in Englewood, going to her after the judge's charge, apparently understanding that Anne Lindbergh desperately needed his strength at this hour of lead.

The English writer, Harold Nicolson, who was preparing a biography of Anne's father and was a guest at the Morrow house, during this period, wrote the next morning to his wife, V. Sackville-West: "The jury had been in consultation for five hours when we sat down to dinner and a verdict was expected at any moment. They (the Lindberghs) knew that the first news would come over the wireless, so that there were two wirelesses turned on—one in the pantry next to the dining-room and one in the drawing-room. Thus there were jazz and jokes while we had dinner, and one ear was strained the whole time for the announcer from the courthouse. Then after dinner we went into the library and the wireless was on in the drawing-room next door. They were all rather jumpy . . ."

The courtroom was now filled, and Judge Trenchard took his position behind the high bench. "Let the defendant stand," he said. Hauptmann rose.

"Mr. Foreman, what say you? Do you find the defendant guilty or not guilty?"

"Guilty," foreman Charles Watson said, a frog-croak of a whisper. Then he remembered a paper in his pocket and drew it out.

The clerk said: "Read it in a louder voice."

Watson read: "We, the jury, find the defendant, Bruno Richard

221

Hauptmann, guilty of murder in the first degree." He sat down quickly. Hauptmann blinked: no recommendation for mercy; he must die.

The defense requested a poll of each juror and now each of them, asked individually how they found, repeated the words the foreman had spoken.

"The state moves for immediate sentence," Wilentz said.

From the floor above, a man who had somehow slipped out of the locked courtroom shouted from an open window to the mob below: "Guilty—death!" The mob screamed approval, joyous, dancing for the newsreel cameras; blood-feeding beasts in all their hunger—only Madame Defarge was missing. Judge Trenchard appeared surprised at the cries of the crowd. Lloyd Fisher, defense counsel, murmured: "A cry for blood."

Miles away, in Englewood, Betty Gow stepped into the room in which Harold Nicolson was sitting with a friend and said: "Hauptmann has been condemned to death without mercy." Nicolson joined the Lindberghs in the drawing room. Hours later he wrote

The wireless had been turned on to the scene outside the courthouse. One could hear the almost diabolic yelling of the crowd. They were all sitting round . . . Anne looking very white and still. "You have now heard," broke in the voice of the announcer, "the verdict in the most famous trial in all history. Bruno Hauptmann now stands guilty of the foulest . . ." "Turn that off, Charles, turn that off." Then we went into the pantry and had ginger-beer. Charles sat there on the kitchen dresser looking very pink about the nose. "I don't know," he said to me, "whether you have followed this case very carefully. There is no doubt at all that Hauptmann did the thing. My one dread all these years has been that they would get hold of someone as a victim about whom I wasn't sure. I am sure about this—quite sure. It is this way . . ."

And then, quite quietly, while we all sat round in the pantry, he went through the case point by point. It seemed to relieve all of them. He did it very quietly, very simply. He pretended to address his remarks to me only. But I could see that he was really trying to ease the agonised tension through which Betty and Anne had passed. It was very well done. It made one feel that here there was no personal desire for vengeance or justification; here was the solemn process of law inexorably and impersonally punishing a culprit.

"The main points" of Lindbergh's private summation for his wife and for Betty Gow, trying to ease the doubts they apparently still had, were, Nicolson wrote, the handwriting testimony; the "brilliant piece of detective work" in tracing the ladder wood to Hauptmann's attic; Condon's telephone number found in Hauptmann's apartment; the prisoner's possession of the ransom money and the fact that he began to invest heavily immediately after the $50,000 had been paid; recognition of Hauptmann's voice by Condon, Lindbergh, and the taxi driver, Perrone; and "the fact that his alibis were all proved fraudulent."

Nicolson concluded his letter:

> I feel that they are all relieved. If Hauptmann had been acquitted it would have had a bad effect on the crime situation in this country. Never has circumstantial evidence been so convincing. If on such evidence a conviction had not been secured, then all the gangsters would have felt a sense of immunity. The prestige of the police has been enormously enhanced by this case.
>
> Poor Anne—she looked so white and horrified. The yells of the crowd were really terrifying. "That," said Lindbergh, "was a lynching crowd."
>
> He tells me that Hauptmann was a magnificent-looking man. Splendidly built. But that his little eyes were like the eyes of a wild boar. Mean, shifty, small and cruel.

In the courtroom the judge said abruptly: "The defendant may stand."

Hauptmann rose once more, his face as white as Anne Lindbergh's must have been.

"Bruno Richard Hauptmann, you have been convicted of murder in the first degree. The sentence of the court is that you suffer death at the time and place and in the manner prescribed by law. . . . I sentence you to die in the week beginning Monday, March 18, 1935. You are now remanded to the custody of the sheriff."

Anna Hauptmann watched her husband led away, handcuffed to

223

two guards. She had seemed calm, almost impassive, during the long hours of waiting for the jury, through the verdict, through the sentence, as if to reassure her Richard with her own stoicism. But now he was through the door, gone from sight, her face sagged heavily and she wept.

In his cell, Hauptmann's handcuffs were unlocked from his wrists. He doubled over and fell, as if his bonds had been broken by despair. His face hit the stone floor. The guards lifted him to his cot. He carried his hands to his face and cried, perhaps for the wife, child, friends, the trees and beaches and oceans he would never see again. The guards left, locking him in; they were embarrassed because they did not believe he could ever cry.

11

I roughly shoved the books and magazine articles across the scarred oak table. Climbing the stairs from my office to the bedroom above, I noticed for the first time that dawn had long since come and the sun was now playing in the top branches of the ancient twisted elm down the hill. I turned away from it, turned my mind to the story of Bruno Richard Hauptmann. That story fascinated me by its incompleteness, by the unwillingness of its chroniclers to excavate beneath the monument to justice constructed by the Condons, the Wilentzes, the Trenchards, by all those policemen and "experts" and, yes, by Lindbergh the hero and surrogate victim. All the "main points" of his attempt to quiet the rumble of doubts in Anne's mind were questionable, I knew now; not one of them stood up as the positive sign of guilt Lindbergh had attributed to them. I didn't agree with Nicolson that Lindbergh wasn't seeking vengeance and wasn't attempting to justify his own responsibility. Like Wilentz and everyone else involved, Lindbergh could not permit the very real weaknesses in the case against Hauptmann to intrude upon illusion. Lindbergh summoned all his powers of suasion to justify what he had helped the prosecution to do, and denounced Hauptmann by comparing him to a fearsome animal.

What fascinated me most of all was the friezelike quality of the trial and the unreality of the man, Hauptmann, as he had been pre-

225

sented to us. Hauptmann, as an individual, does not exist except as defined in terms of the world that prosecutor Wilentz created, the narrow world of a man of evil. In my years as a newspaper reporter, I had sat through several murder trials, but I had only dimly perceived back then what I now understand clearly through my readings in this case: a trial is a distortion of reality because it does not resemble life. It deals in human relationships, certainly, and in psychological processes, but within so constricted a vision that it is divorced from the real, turbulent physical life we all—including the defendant—live day by day.

Wilentz, and all the writers of the era, saw Hauptmann as unredeemably evil, a man who held up women and babies at gunpoint, a man who burglarized, robbed, jumped ship, murdered a child—a man of absolute evil. But, I wondered, did he ever love? Fornicate? Defecate? Did he write to his mother in Germany, as a dutiful son would? Did he send her money? Did he love his newborn son? His wife? Did the fluid of life flow through his body?

Wilentz would have none of this. The ceremony of the trial demands, and so reality must be abandoned. Thus the real Hauptmann was refined out of existence. He became the Defendant, a symbol, an icon in the temple of Justice. Wilentz could not permit any of the reality to spoil the illusion, for Wilentz also was a prisoner, his mind shackled by the role he accepted; that of Prosecutor, one who has come to believe his duty is to convict at all costs. The anger now rising in me as I made ready for bed was directed not so much at Wilentz, not in this special instance, but at our adversary system of justice which so often creates injustice.

Prosecutor and defense attorney are caught in a world of combat, leaping to the contest with a crash of rhetoric against rhetoric, attempting to destroy the enemy in a battle whose prize is the admiration of the legal profession, the plaudits of the crowd, enormous ego-gratification. And the prisoner in the dock, whether going free or to prison or to his execution, is no more than the silver cup awarded the victor; no one cares that his life and liberty have been sealed in that very cup.

It is advocacy, courtroom as boxing ring, which required Wilentz to portray Hauptmann as purely evil and to convince the jury to send to his death this vicious man. It is advocacy, at least in part, which made witnesses lie—for I felt certain that many had lied. It is advocacy which made the police or prosecutor withhold the letters and the "big book" of accounts that Hauptmann had asked for to prove his relationship with Fisch.

Advocacy is essential to our lawyers and our prosecutors. It creates drama. Without drama there are no headlines. And lacking headlines, the lawyer lacks the stroking of ego so necessary to all actors; it is as if the actors would cease to exist if no one praised them. Trial lawyers are indeed actors. Sam Leibowitz, a criminal court judge in Brooklyn when I was a young reporter, once graciously lectured me on how to understand what is really happening in a trial, saying: "Always remember every trial lawyer is a ham, he's playing for the applause." Leibowitz, perhaps the greatest actor-lawyer of his time, most certainly was an authority on trial as theater.

But as I finally slipped into bed after long hours of work, I was troubled less by the immorality of defendant as incidental to legal procedure and legal theater than by the more specific questions raised in my mind. Those questions had been brushed aside during my first readings, but they came back to me now.

The piece of lumber from Hauptmann's attic, for one. How that attic board troubled me. Hauptmann was arrested September nineteenth. The ransom bills were discovered in his garage on the twentieth. The board with Condon's telephone number, that mute evidence that even Condon said was likely a fake, was discovered on the twenty-fourth, during a search of Hauptmann's apartment by a police official who ordered the very walls razed until he found every scrap of evidence that existed. By their own words, their own testimony, police told us of the extensive search for evidence from the moment of Hauptmann's arrest and through the twenty-fourth. Why then did it take Detective Bornmann until the morning of the twenty-sixth to discover that a length of wood had been cut from the floorboards in the attic? It wasn't possible the attic had been neglected by Justice Department agents, Treasury agents, New York City police, and New Jersey state troopers. No, that attic must have been run through the filters of dozens of police eyes and minds and hands. In the search for the ransom money still missing, the floorboards must have been pulled up. Hauptmann's garage was torn to the ground and the earth beneath excavated. But not the attic? Absolutely ridiculous and without logic—since in the

227

tremors of excitement at discovery, police destroyed garage, furniture, mattresses, every conceivable place where evidence might be found. The attic must have been searched thoroughly before Bornmann made his find. Where does that lead us? Down that inevitable path I had seen traced in my mind so early—Hauptmann was the victim of manipulated evidence and had been sacrificed on the altar of retribution: cleanse this stain on society and destroy the stainer as a warning to other men of evil.

Yes, warning. To my mind came the words Adela St. Johns had written for the Hearst press in a flood of emotion immediately after the verdict—journalistic emotion, certainly, but also authentic feelings, for she was a mother and as with all parents the Lindbergh kidnaping touched a personal chord. I searched in one of her books of memoirs and found this:

KEEP YOUR HANDS OFF OUR CHILDREN

The Lindbergh jury didn't say guilty, though that is the technical verdict brought in after eleven hours.

They didn't only say Put to Death. What they really said was

Keep Your Hands Off Our Children.

Leave Our Children ALONE.

Keep the Bloody Hands of Crime Off Our Babies.

This is what we tell you now. You Can Never Get Away with It. We will always send you to Die in the Chair *if you touch our children.*

Yes, warning and retribution. And a psychic-religious cleansing of society.

As I lay in bed my mind returned to this son of the prince of darkness, this Hauptmann who as characterized in Wilentz's official script was a depraved offender against all humanity. And I came to realize what it was that had long flickered like the flame of a candle just below my consciousness: it was the disconnectedness of the case against Hauptmann, the discontinuity of the script.

Hauptmann was said to be the master criminal who conceived, plotted, and executed this abominable crime. From the day in November 1931, when the prosecutor claimed he bought the lumber

228

for the kidnap ladder, until his arrest almost three years later, Hauptmann's sole concern had been to abduct the child, murder it, extort the ransom money while pretending to have placed the boy in excellent care, and then conceal his crimes and his booty.

But where were the antecedents? Where were the past actions, the dynamics of a criminal personality? Hauptmann had, indeed, been a criminal in Germany in the aftershock of the Great War. How many others among us, warped by war and sick with hunger and futility, became criminal in the immediate aftermath of war and then gradually slid into society's broad stream? In Germany, Hauptmann had robbed. But between his arrival in New York in 1923 and the kidnaping more than eight years later there is not a shred of evidence that he had ever engaged in an unethical act, much less a criminal one. He had, in fact, been a hard-working, thrifty man, saving for a future with his wife and the children they planned to have. Yet Dudley Shoenfeld and other psychiatrists for the mass newspaper audience said, *without ever having met Hauptmann,* that he was a schizophrenic, had homosexual tendencies, believed he stood alone on a mountain top above all men and all morals. The long-distance dissection of personality by psychiatrists, repeated in the recent present by the author of *Kidnap* jarred me. There was no indication Hauptmann was homosexual, whether latent or practicing; Wilentz, in fact, attempted to prove Hauptmann was a womanizer, as they called it in those days, so smitten by a younger woman that he planned to leave his wife.

But to return to the main point: Hauptmann for more than eight years was law-abiding. To me, those orderly eight years made the drama of Hauptmann as kidnaper a moment in time without roots, because the audience never is told how the present, the kidnaping, has become what it is. I don't mean motive; any man who is hungry enough and has lost enough control may be capable of kidnaping or extortion, bank robbery or murder. Motive is not the point. Although the motive in Wilentz's drama, that Hauptmann required large sums of money because stock market fever was depleting his savings may have a certain logic, motive still concerned me little. The defect in the Hauptmann case, I realized, after abandoning my attempt to sleep, was the lack of psychological continuum—neither Attorney General Wilentz nor anyone else could present a believable thread connecting past and present. How and why did the present flow out of the past? The question was never asked and never answered in Wilentz's theater. And his script failed because it required of me a greater suspension of belief than I was willing to give.

12 Murray seemed slightly embarrassed when I pulled up in front of the big, old, still fashionable midtown hotel in which he was staying—whether embarrassed by the age and decrepitude of my nine-year-old station wagon with plastic "wood paneling" and several layers of spring mud on the faded blue paint, or by the contemptuous expression on the face of the hotel doorman, I wasn't certain. But when he got settled, after hiking his trousers above his knees and fussing with the crease, then kicking aside some tools and crumpled cigarette packs at his feet, Murray said, "It's a great old car—clean it up a bit and it'll look as good as a Cadillac."

We were driving to New Jersey, to Mt. Holly, where Ellis Parker had ruled as chief of detectives of Burlington County for two decades, where Murray had been drawn into the Lindbergh case thirty years before. On a long shot, I had called the office that Parker had once inhabited and reached the present detective chief, Harry McConnell. I am writing a book on Ellis Parker, I told him—a slight fib, a reporter's tool for skirting the main point until you can be certain of a man's cooperation—and I'm very interested in Parker's role in the Lindbergh case. I think Parker got a bad deal and I'm hoping to vindicate him. Can you help me?

"Sure, come on out," McConnell said. "There's drawers full of material that Parker left behind. Mostly newspaper clippings. I haven't gone through it, really, so I'm not certain what's here."

231

"I'm trying to locate Ellis Parker, Jr. Is he still living around Mt. Holly?"

"Young Ellis died a couple of years ago," McConnell said, "but his younger brother is still living around here and so are some of Ellis, Sr.'s sisters. If you come down I'll put you in touch with some people who will know where to find them."

"What do you think of the Hauptmann case?" I asked. "Was Parker right about Wendel being the kidnaper?"

"Well, I'll tell you. A lot of people down here believe Hauptmann was innocent. They're certain Parker had proof of that. As for Wendel being the real kidnaper, I don't know. But there's an old reporter down here who's been working for years on a book about Parker and Hauptmann. He swears Wendel did it. His name's Frank Fitzpatrick. You should call him."

I made a date to drive down and see McConnell the next day, then phoned Fitzpatrick. He had, he said, spent all of his spare time in the past twenty years researching a book about Parker, about the Lindbergh crime, a book that would prove Parker had been right—Hauptmann was innocent and Wendel was the actual kidnaper. But he didn't know whether he could help because we were now competitors. Still he agreed to have lunch with me and Murray. He remembered Murray, he said, and he appeared a little upset about it—"Bleefeld is the man who sent Ellis and his son to prison." Still, he agreed to meet with us. One o'clock Thursday at the Washington House Hotel in Mt. Holly.

Driving out that morning, the tape recorder on the seat between us, I continued the interview with Murray that had been postponed by my emotional involvement in the Hauptmann trial.

"We left off," I said over the slightly raucous sound of an automobile engine with 120,000 miles of use, "with Parker asking you to help arrest Wendel. Why did Parker need you for that?"

"What was important, Parker said, was that he was waiting for Wendel to come to New Jersey so he could apprehend him, but Wendel did not want to come to New Jersey. Parker tried to get him to come out a dozen different times in a dozen different ways. He didn't just tell him to come in, he led him to believe he really needed him to come in. But Wendel wouldn't come. He always used the warrants as an excuse, the warrants that were out for worthless check passing. And Parker told me, 'Time is getting short, Murray, we must apprehend this man.' So I got together

232

with Ellis Parker, Jr. And I should tell you, at this point, that Parker swore in Harry Weiss as his deputy and Martin Schlossman, my brother-in-law."

"How did they get into it?"

"When I was deputized, we left Trenton and went right to New York. And before I left Ellis said to me, as a continuation of what he said the night before, that it might be necessary for me first to find a place where we could take Wendel, once we apprehended him. He said they were working on it, they didn't have any place in mind yet, and maybe I could help them. That's why he needed me in New York."

"But why couldn't Parker and his son arrest Wendel themselves?"

"Well, for one thing he didn't want to go to New York himself because protocol would have made it necessary to bring in the New York police and he was afraid of a premature newspaper story. That would have ruined it all. But most of all it was part of the genius of Parker the detective, his knowledge of psychology and how people would react. Especially how Wendel would react. You see, he didn't want Wendel to know that he was behind the arrest. For the whole thing to work, Wendel had to believe Parker was still his friend and would protect him, that he was in danger from us and that Parker would get him out of it. That way, Wendel would fall right into Parker's hands . . ."

"What were Parker's plans, precisely?"

"I'll get to that, but first I have to tell you the thing that led Parker to me through Jack Arbitell was that I could do whatever he felt had to be done because I lived in New York and that's where Wendel was. So he told me about finding a place to take Wendel and also that he would need somebody to work with me and I should start thinking about somebody who could help me with Wendel.

"And I told him that the only place I could consider taking Wendel once we apprehended him was to my father's home in Brooklyn, on Voorhies Avenue, because I lived in an apartment, but my father's house had a finished basement. And Ellis said, 'That's perfect.' I said the only problem was my sister and her husband lived with my parents and he said, 'Well, maybe your brother-in-law can help us out.' That's how Martin Schlossman, my sister's husband, became involved. Parker asked, 'You have anybody else can help you?' And I said I have a friend of mine who used to work for me,

Harry Weiss, a young fellow I'd known for a long time. Parker agreed about Schlossman and Weiss.

"So the next day I spoke to my father and said I was Ellis Parker's deputy. Of course, my father had met Parker because he went to visit my brother with me on the prison farm, and my father asked me what I had to do for Parker. I told him everything, about the Lindbergh case and Hauptmann being innocent and Wendel, the real kidnaper, walking around loose in Manhattan. How I was going to apprehend him.

"My father listened to this with his hair standing on end, just the way mine was standing on end when Parker first told me the story. I was his favorite son and my father knew Parker had done all of those things for Jeff, getting him out of Trenton prison, and that he would do more for Jeff. While this may have been an inner motivation for his agreeing to let us use his home to keep Wendel, more important was that I told him this man was the kidnaper of the Lindbergh baby. I spent hours telling my father everything and he felt the way I felt, that this was a great thing for me to be doing, and for him to help with, to get the real kidnaper and save an innocent man.

"I said we have to take this man when we pick him up, bring him some place to question him, and Ellis Parker thinks bringing him to your house would be the best thing. He said, 'Well, if you think it's right, Murray, I'll do it.' Just like that. Then I spoke to Schlossman and Weiss, introduced them to Ellis, Jr., and we all went out to Mt. Holly and Ellis, Sr., deputized them. Now we were all working on this thing together.

"Where can I find Weiss and Schlossman?" I asked. "I must interview them."

"Weiss is dead. Martin, well, we don't really have much contact. We all went to prison for this and Martin changed his name and he's still sort of blaming me, so we haven't seen each other except for a couple of family affairs over the years."

"I still want to talk to him," I said. "You have to understand something—wherever possible I'm going to check your story out with other people who were around and with any documents I can find. Schlossman is important. Where can I find him?"

Murray gave me Schlossman's home and office numbers and offered to call him, even though Schlossman might get upset at Murray and refuse to see me. No, I said, don't take that chance.

Actually, I wasn't worried about the risk of upsetting Schlossman; I wanted to keep Murray away from his brother-in-law so that there would be less chance of Murray influencing Schlossman's recollections.

"Now I'm Parker's deputy and I'm like his right arm," Murray continued, "and Parker is relating to me many things that took place in the past and many taking place right then. Ellis, Jr., and myself were really working with him like around the clock. Because it was getting close, Hauptmann was due to be electrocuted. This is February 1936.

"As a digression, Hauptmann is convicted. Picture yourself as the attorney general of the state of New Jersey. You decide, because it's within your power, to go in and try the case yourself even though the county prosecutor should be doing it. This man Wilentz goes in for the obvious reason, that it's the talk of the world and Wilentz's name will then be the talk of the world. So he goes in and he's got all the power he needs to convict Hauptmann. George Waller wrote a bad book, *Kidnap*, because he made it appear everybody was equal when they weren't. When Hauptmann's lawyers had to get a witness, they didn't have any money so they didn't get their witness. But when Wilentz wanted something to be done it was done the next morning. He had the money, he convicted a man with all the money and power of the state behind him, based not on pure circumstantial evidence but on inconclusive circumstantial evidence. I tell you again and again . . ."

"I know, Murray, I've just been reliving it all," I interrupted. "Let's get to the arrest of Wendel."

"Okay, but I have to go back to that first day I was sworn in by Ellis. After he made me his deputy we went to New York to the Hotel Stanford on West Thirty-second Street where Wendel was living. The Parkers had already been there, they looked the place over and decided they wanted to keep Wendel under surveillance. Right next to the Stanford was another hotel, it's still there, the Martinique, and they thought we should get a room in the Martinique in such a position so that we could look into Wendel's room with binoculars. They knew the room Wendel was living in, they knew his window faced the back of the Martinique, so we took a room that gave us a clear sight into his room. And we watched him with binoculars to see what he was doing.

"And we talk a lot more as we're watching Wendel's movements. Ellis talks and he tells me more things. And I'll never forget the way he broke it to me. He said: 'Now, Murray, you're the kidnaper of this baby. You're the master criminal of this century. You conceive and you execute the crime of the century. Now you have fifty thousand dollars from it. You got it all, now, you got all the money. Okay. Here it is: Isidor Fisch is a friend of Hauptmann. He gave the money to Hauptmann. And where did Fisch get the money? Well, Murray, Isidor Fisch is also the man who at one time was represented by Paul Wendel, when he was a lawyer in Trenton, in a case that's on record. I have the record. Isidor Fisch and Paul Wendel were connected.'"

"You're kidding," I said.

Murray laughed. "Right. That's exactly what I said to Ellis. And Ellis wasn't kidding."

"Can you prove it?"

"Parker said he had the court records. You'll have to find them. Okay. Paul Wendel was Fisch's lawyer. Parker knew this. He was putting the pieces together. He knew Fisch left the money with Hauptmann and he was sure Fisch got the money—the gold notes—from Paul Wendel."

"What kind of case was Fisch involved in?"

"I think, if memory serves me right, Parker told me it was something to do with narcotics."

"Narcotics?" I searched back in my memory for something I'd read over the past several days, not paying any attention to Murray as he continued talking about Fisch and Wendel. And then it came to me: Adela Rogers St. Johns had written that in his testimony Hauptmann said he and Fisch had smuggled furs from Germany. "I took it there were other lines, probably drugs," she wrote in one of her books of memoirs. "Fisch took hot money paid him for his smuggled wares back to the Continent. . . . According to Hauptmann on the witness stand, Isidor Fisch had been called back to Germany in a hurry" and so was forced to leave the "hot money" with Hauptmann until his return. St. Johns was wrong about every fact in those few sentences. Fisch had been planning his trip to Germany for almost a year. Most important, there was no mention of drugs or hot money in Hauptmann's testimony or anywhere else in the trial record or in the dozens of books and magazine articles I had read. Originally, I had dismissed her recollections as a further example of poor reporting, but now I began to wonder. She had

236

been very close to Wilentz, had been practically instructing him in the techniques of prosecution. Could she have heard about Fisch's involvement with drugs from Wilentz? Was the prosecution aware of Fisch's criminal past and did it suppress that information?

Murray was saying: "I'll show you the meaning of the connection between Wendel and Fisch. Paul Wendel gets the money from old man Condon. Nobody but Paul Wendel. He has the money now, but in a year or so the gold notes are called in by Roosevelt. Now if I was your lawyer and I represented you in a narcotics case and got you off, and I knew you were capable of certain criminal acts, what would I do? What Wendel did. He gets hold of Fisch and says he's got counterfeit money. Can Fisch pass it for him? Sell it for him? Fisch says, sure, give me some samples. He brings Fisch samples. Fisch takes a look at them, the first thing he notices is they're gold notes. The papers are full of the Lindbergh ransom numbers, every day. Fisch says, Goddamn it, this is ransom money, where the hell did this guy get it from? Fisch makes a deal, Wendel brings him the money, they agree on the price, Fisch is going to sell it for him. Fisch, of course, lets Wendel think he really believes it's counterfeit money. Hot money. Not kidnap money.

"So Fisch takes the money, I think about twenty thousand in gold notes. Now comes a time when Fisch has to come back and give Wendel clean money for the gold notes and when Wendel tries to get paid Fisch says, Get lost, you bum, this is kidnap money. And Wendel gets lost, he can't holler to the cops, he can't do a damn thing except get lost. Now Fisch has the money by possession and . . ."

"How do you know this?"

"Wendel told me, in his confession. Part of it, Parker guessed. And when Wendel started spilling his guts to me and Schlossman and Weiss, this is what he told us. Anyway, the rest is obvious. Fisch gives the money to Hauptmann to hold while he goes to Germany. Hauptmann puts it on the shelf in the closet and he finds it later, when the rains came in and the box split open. Maybe Hauptmann didn't tell the truth, maybe he opened the box when he heard Fisch died in Germany, opened it to see what was in the box and saw money there and decided to keep it. Either way, this poor dope doesn't know about gold kidnap notes, he doesn't know about anything."

"Tell me about the arrest of Wendel and his confession," I said.

237

"I'll get to it. But let me just tell you a little more about this poor dope Hauptmann. Parker is telling me this, during one of those talks before we apprehended Wendel, Parker is showing me how dead certain he was that Hauptmann couldn't have done it. He goes out one day, Parker tells me, this master criminal Hauptmann, this genius, he gets in his car and goes to a gas station. The gold notes have been called in for a long time. So he buys gas and pays for it with one of his gold notes, that he's supposed to know is ransom money, that he should know is listed in the banks and stores and gas stations because it was in all the papers about the list of ransom bills. And when the guy in the gas station starts to talk to him about how rare the gold notes are this master criminal says, 'Oh, I got plenty of those at home.'

"Let me ask you, and that's how Ellis put it to me, let me ask you something. If you were the kidnaper of this baby, if you had the brains to collect this ransom, would you take a gold note and go to a gas station with your own car, your own face, your own license plate number, and give this guy a gold note and add insult to injury and tell him you got more like this at home?"

"I know, that's one of the major defects of Wilentz's case," I said. I decided against trying to cut off Murray's speech. How could I stop a man who so deftly dropped Parker's name in the right places, to forestall interruption? Murray went on:

"That's what Hauptmann did in the gas station. But he didn't just do it that once. He went out shopping with his wife. Bought her a pair of shoes with a gold note. He went to a fruit market, paid for a couple of pennies' worth of fruit with a gold bill, the genius kidnaper calling attention to himself that way. This poor guy was passing the bills little by little. What he thought he was doing was using the money Fisch had hoarded that nobody knew about and he was just feeding it out a little at a time. The kidnaper would never do that. Only somebody who didn't know it was Lindbergh money."

"Absolutely," I said. "Now can we get to Wendel?"

Murray laughed. "When you start telling me to just answer yes or no, then I get out of the car," he said. "Okay, back to Paul Wendel, the real kidnaper. At the Hotel Martinique, Schlossman, Weiss, and I took a room with windows that look out on the Stanford Hotel, across a courtyard. Ellis Parker wanted us to do this so we could watch Wendel's movements. Frankly, we didn't get a clear picture of his movements, we didn't have the clearest kind of view that Parker would have liked us to have. But anyway, in that room from time to time were the three of us and Ellis, Jr., watching Wendel.

"Finally there comes a time, in the middle of February, Hauptmann is scheduled to die but Governor Hoffman gave him a stay of a week or so, and Parker tells us to move. We moved. Wendel comes out of the hotel. Weiss and myself walked up to Wendel and said we were detectives and that Jim De Louie wants to see you. De Louie was a detective in New Jersey and Wendel knew the name and that's why he came along, thinking he's finally caught and going back to New Jersey. I sat Wendel in the back of Schlossman's car, between Weiss and myself, and we started driving to my father's house."

"Was there any conversation on the way?"

"Very little. We drove downtown and just after we went across the Manhattan Bridge, Weiss told Wendel to lie down on the floor. We didn't want him to know exactly where we were going. We went down Flatbush Avenue and then to Ocean Parkway and finally got him to my father's house. We put him downstairs in the basement, we put a blindfold on him. While we had him we bathed him, fed him, took him upstairs to the bathroom. We even gave him a radio so he could listen to music, and he had a cot to sleep on. The things he later said about being beaten up and tortured are entirely false. That's what he said at our trial in federal court in Newark and what he wrote in his book that made him out to be a hero, but . . ."

"Murray, please keep it chronological now. Tell me what happened from day to day. Did Parker tell you the questions to ask him?"

"Well, we brought him to the house and put him in this furnished room."

"Was he tied up?"

"No. Just someone guarding him all the time. Me, Weiss, Schlossman, and Ellis, Jr. But Ellis, Jr., was on the outside, behind the door leading upstairs. Wendel didn't know he was there but Ellis, Jr., was always there listening and waiting for him to break down."

"Break down how? Did Parker instruct you in how to break down?"

239

"Parker not only told us what to do but he predicted what would happen and when it did happen it was as if old man Parker was pulling strings from out in Mt. Holly telling Wendel how to behave and what to say. And when Wendel finally did break he just dropped his head . . ."

"Wait," I almost shouted. "I'm not going to let you run on like this. What instructions did Parker give you?"

"Ellis, Sr., said to me, 'You and your two deputies tell Wendel a story. Tell him that you're mobsters. And tell him that because of what he did, kidnaping the baby—and tell him you know he was responsible for it because you got the word from the people you know in New Jersey—because of what he did, he's curtailing your activities. You can't make any money, you can't move because the police are all over everybody, jumping on everybody. The police want to solve this crime, they know Hauptmann didn't do it and they want to find the men who did.'

"And that's what we did. When we picked him up at the hotel we tell him our names. Schlossman is Hank. Harry Weiss says his name's Spidella. They tell him I'm Tony. I don't tell him anything, he thinks I'm the head man and I acted like the head man because I did the talking and I asked the questions. And Wendel right away figured 'the Italian Mob' because of the names we give ourselves and the way we act tough and the stuff on the Italian mob is in all the papers. Luciano and his boys—although a lot of them were Jewish—but Wendel figures he's been grabbed by the real mobsters."

"You said you asked the questions. What kind of questions?"

"Mostly it was demanding to know how he kidnaped the baby, and why he did it. But he just wouldn't say anything and we were getting pretty frustrated. During this time I was running out to Mt. Holly a lot, talking to Ellis, telling him that this guy Wendel wasn't ever going to break down. I said, 'Ellis, this man is sitting there and he's eating and sleeping, he's listening to music, he bathes every day and he shaves, but he doesn't tell us anything.' And Ellis said, 'Don't worry. One day, Murray, when you least expect it, this man will break down and tell you the whole story. This man is dying to tell the story to somebody. He wanted to tell it to me, Murray, but he was afraid. I know he'll tell it to you because he thinks you're criminals and he'll want you to know that he's the master criminal who did this thing. I know how his mind works, I've known this man for a long time. Just keep telling him how tough he's making it for the boys to make a living because the police are putting the heat on them and he'll eventually break down and tell you the whole story.'

"Now, on the fifth or sixth day Wendel breaks down hysterically, he cries and cries and he tells a story from beginning to end, how he kidnaped the Lindbergh baby. Of course, this man was in a room in the basement. There were electric lights but there was no sun, no outside environment. Whether the man realized he was going to be held there until he told us what he did, or whatever reason, just the way Parker described it was the way it happened. He just broke down and started telling us all about it. Nobody hit him with a baseball bat. Nobody mistreated him, nobody . . ."

"Come on, Murray. That kind of psychological mistreatment has made a lot of innocent men confess."

"I know, I know," Murray said. "I've met a few guys in my time who confessed to things they didn't do and nobody ever hit them with a rubber hose. But this was almost forty years ago. That's how police did things back then. So we weren't enlightened, we didn't have the Supreme Court telling us it's wrong. The police beat up Hauptmann, they beat up that guy Curtis, they threatened to beat up Condon. And they probably even beat up Violet Sharpe. We didn't beat anybody. Ellis didn't do things that way, he used psychology."

"But it is possible Wendel confessed because there was no outside environment, as you said, because he thought he'd be held there forever?"

"No way," Murray said, with a large dose of fervor. "I was there, I heard him, I saw him. I believed every word that man said, I know every word was the truth. I can't explain any better than that—just that I *knew* he was telling the truth."

"Okay. What did he say?"

"Crying hysterically, he said, as though he were talking to a thousand people, as though no one were there, oblivious to everything and everybody: he was going to do something that the world would take notice of. He decided that Lindbergh was an international hero and he waited and waited, until that baby was born, until such time that he felt he would have an opportunity to kidnap that baby. And doing this he was going to get even with the world. The world! He was going to kidnap Lindbergh's baby and get

241

money to boot, so he would get everything that he felt the world owed him."

"Why did he want to get even with the world?"

"Because of what he felt the world had done to him, how the world had treated him."

"His father was a minister. Did he say his father forced him to go into the ministry?"

"'My father,' he says, 'was a minister. My father wanted me to be a minister. I went on to school and I became a lawyer.' He studied for the ministry under his father. I don't know if he told me he was a pharmacist before he was a lawyer, or worked in a pharmacy while he was going to law school, but there was a period during this time that he was a pharmacist."

"He said he was a failure in everything he had done?"

"A failure in everything he had done. Not in the sense that he failed, but it seemed that everything he was trying to do he was always being opposed, there was always an obstacle for him. The world was screwing him. And then he talked about studying medicine . . ."

"Let's get to the actual kidnaping. What did he say about it?"

"He talked about watching the house with binoculars for months on end, while the house was being built, when the Lindberghs go, when they come back. And he watched them, he watched them coming back to the house with that baby. He said, 'The world believes that somebody went up the ladder and came down the ladder. I went up the ladder. I made those ladders. They were makeshift ladders but they were enough for me to go up to the bedroom. And they were a little too short because I made pieces, three pieces that fit into one another. And they were short but I was tall enough to get over the windowsill and get inside.' He didn't go up to the house to measure the height, he measured it by watching the house and estimating the height. And he said, 'I put stockings over my shoes and I had a laundry bag around my neck and gloves on my hands. The laundry bag had strings and the strings were around my neck.' When he went up the ladder he broke the rung. He was a big man, he knew he couldn't come down that ladder with the baby around his neck. And when he was in that house he closed the window and left the note on the radiator.

"He says, and he's crying, not semi-hysterical but he's reduced to a point where the hysteria left him and he's sobbing, and he says, 'Those fools think that I pried open the window with a chisel. I opened it with a screwdriver.' Ellis Parker always told us that his people in looking over the place knew it was a screwdriver and not a chisel. Schwarzkopf and Wilentz and all the so-called experts called it a chisel. Never stopped calling it a chisel. Wendel said, 'I lifted that window up with a screwdriver. Then I took the baby, the baby was fast asleep in that crib. I went over and I took my finger with plenty of paregoric on it and I rubbed it on the baby's lips while the baby was sleeping. The baby continued to sleep.' He said the baby was sickly, he knew the baby had a cold when he brought it to his house. He said, 'Then I put the baby in the laundry bag.' "

"What did he say about the ransom note?"

"He had written the note, prepared the note, everything at home. And he said, 'The symbols on the note, I took from my lawbooks. You look at the outside of some lawbooks, there are books that have a key on them. The end of the key is half a circle with a red dot in the center. I took those two circles and I enlarged them and I locked one over the other.' Wendel, not Hauptmann, did this because Wendel was the lawyer, he was looking for an identification that could identify all his notes as coming from one man. All he had to do was to go to the lawbooks and keep using that key, enlarged. That has a lot of meaning for you, doesn't it?"

"Yes," I admitted. "I've got lawbooks back home published by the company that used the key. It's a trademark. And what Wendel told you solves one riddle—what the hell the symbols on the ransom notes meant. All the writers were trying to guess at it back then but nobody came up with a good explanation."

"Wendel did," Murray said. "Wendel, in his confession, told us that the symbols on all the notes were done together. 'I made a whole batch of those symbols on paper and lined up the paper and punched the holes through the paper at one time. All the sheets of paper at once.' He said he took the key from the lawbooks and put one part of the key's circle against the other so the long part of the key would face in opposite directions, and then used just the circles of the key. And after drawing the circles he punched the holes through the paper."

"One thing bothers me, Murray. His telling you he did this doesn't prove he did it. When those symbols were published in the papers everybody was trying to guess what they meant. Maybe Wendel was speculating back then and when it came to the crunch of being held prisoner he used the result of his speculations in his confession.''

"Sure, that's possible," Murray conceded. "But I believed Wendel then and I still believe it to this day. Because he told us so many other things that made it all fit together.''

"Like what?''

"The writing in the notes. He said he wrote the notes in such a way as to disguise the person who kidnaped the baby, to make everybody think he was an illiterate or a foreigner. He was *German,*" Murray almost shouted. "Paul Wendel's father was German. And Paul Wendel wrote those notes like a foreigner would and of course he ended up using German. The notes, the spelling in them, the guttural connotations in the notes and in the voice of the man in the cemetery, all of that was Paul Wendel using something from his heritage. All the things about being German that they attributed to Hauptmann belonged to Paul Wendel.''

"Was he born in Germany? Did he have an accent?''

"I don't know where he was born. But he was German through descent and heritage. He had no accent. He spoke the King's English. Wendel, I think, was a Lutheran, his father was a Lutheran minister. I don't know if his father was born in Germany but he definitely had German around him, he knew German and that's why he used it in the notes. That's what he told us in his confession.

"Now, the note in the nursery. He says when he got in the bedroom he closed the window but didn't pull the shutters tight. He left the note on the windowsill, on the radiator there. He put the paregoric on the baby's lips—he thought of paregoric because he had been a pharmacist—giving the baby enough to keep him sleeping soundly. He put the baby in the laundry bag around his neck and walked out the nursery door. He said, 'I didn't go down the ladder because it was broken.' He goes out the door in his stocking feet, stockings that were over his shoes, quiet, very quiet, and the floors were carpeted, the staircase was carpeted. He went down that staircase, kept to the side wall, the living room was off to the left and he could look in the living room. The door to the outside is on his right, and he goes out the door with the baby and leaves the door ajar. He doesn't close it tight so they shouldn't hear it snap. He said, 'Sure I broke one of the rungs of the ladder, that's what Lindbergh said he heard. He was right.' Lindbergh said he heard a

244

snapping of something. It could have been a tree branch, but it was the rung of the ladder Wendel broke on the way up. Wendel left the door slightly ajar. The baby in the meantime is in the laundry bag around his neck so his hands would be free to do whatever he had to do. And he goes out the door and goes to his car. Takes the ladders away from the house. Dead quiet. He found he couldn't manipulate the ladders with the baby, so he left the ladders, he threw them on the side. He said he couldn't manipulate them, he couldn't maneuver them into the car the way he had brought them so he left them on the side. No fingerprints, he was wearing gloves. And away he went, with the baby. And he brought the baby right to his home. His wife knew he had the baby, his daughter knew. He said, 'I drove to my home . . .' I didn't say anything, he was just talking, nobody interrupted him, everybody was spellbound, as a matter of fact. He says, 'My home was a twenty-minute ride, less than twenty minutes from the Lindbergh home. I got to my home, I took the baby upstairs, put him to bed, went downstairs, and listened to the radio announcing the kidnap of the Lindbergh baby.'

"He said he brought the baby upstairs, to the bed in the attic bedroom. The baby was sleeping. They took care of the baby. The wife would take turns with the baby, the daughter, the son.

"The bed was old-fashioned, very high, not the normal bed. They came up one day and found the baby on the floor, the baby was dead. It fell out onto its head. See, the baby was sick for a few days or a week. The baby was sick. And he didn't take the baby to a doctor, he wasn't a doctor, he didn't know what to do. The baby was sick with a cold when he took him, and when he took him in a laundry bag he might have enhanced the sickness, maybe he couldn't breathe, or the paregoric, maybe the baby was on the way out when he put him up on the bed. There was no crib, they didn't do anything to insure that the baby wouldn't fall out. The baby was a walking baby, twenty months old at the time, and the baby fell out on a bare floor and got the skull fracture and that's how the baby died. See, the baby could have died from . . ."

"What was his reaction when he found the baby dead?"

"He didn't tell me. He just made arrangements to take the baby back to the area. One night he took the baby back and buried the baby in the ground. He knew the area. He was born and bred in that Trenton area."

"Did he discuss his family's role in it?"

"No, except that they helped him take care of the baby. They knew what he did, knew it was the Lindbergh baby. He dealt with them very lightly in his confession only to say that they knew that it was the baby, they helped him take care of the baby. The man was a typical German boss man in the home. I know from the way he talked about his family, the things that he did at home, that his family obeyed him. Whatever he told his family to do they would do. He told them that they had to take care of the baby, that he was going to bring the baby there. He had it all planned in advance. He made that trip he said at least a dozen times up and back. Made the trips to find out how long it would take. Watched the house going up, knew when they came back from Englewood, knew when they went."

"Did Wendel tell you about getting the ransom money?"

"He sure did. He told us he had a sister living in back of St. Raymond's Cemetery. In his confession Wendel said, 'They didn't know that, nobody knows.' This is behind the cemetery where he met Condon. The reason he told us in his confession about his sister living in back of St. Raymond's Cemetery is that he chose that spot for the payment of the money when Condon showed up with the money. He knew that when he got the money he didn't have far to go with the money, to hide somewhere. The sister didn't know what he was doing there. So if he came with a little box with $50,000 she wouldn't know what it was.

"Wendel told us how he got the money, and told us how he lost the money. How Fisch was the man who done him in. When he gave Fisch the money he told him it was counterfeit money. Fisch knew it was the ransom money and said, 'Get lost, you bum.' Wendel told us that. But he never even talked about Hauptmann, he pooh-poohed it, he knew the conviction was a farce. He said that he was the man that did the job, he didn't even want to talk about Hauptmann because it would rob him of his meaning, his fame. He's talking about being compared to Lindbergh. Lindbergh became an international hero, he flew the Atlantic. Wendel was better than Lindbergh because he took Lindbergh's son. And got away with it. He wasn't saying it in those words, that's the basic feeling I got out of it. He wouldn't mention Hauptmann, why should he mention Hauptmann? This is a psychotic man with a criminal twist to his mind, and an intelligent man with all the talent and educational background that I described to you. This is a man who knew how to write a note, and disguise his writing. A man who knew how to write a note the way he wanted to write it, the German thing, and those circles from the lawbooks. He was practically bragging about it all.

"Now, that's as far as we got in the confession. Of course he detailed it more and then I said to him, when I started to talk, I said, 'Paul, I think now you've solved everything, for us and for yourself. I'd like you to sit down, Paul, I'll give you some paper and pencil, I'd like you to put down on paper everything you've told me.' This was during the afternoon. So he sat down and started to write the story. As he was writing the story, we were watching him, we took one page at a time, and he started to leave out certain things that he had said.

"We said, 'Listen, you remember what you said, you didn't put it in there.' So he took the page and rewrote it. It seemed he probably realized he had made a confession and he wanted to change it a bit, for whatever was going through his mind. This is a great mind, with all the criminal tendencies, so now it occurred to him that maybe he should write something different. So now Weiss jumps in and he says, 'Hey, you lying bastard, you left out what you said,' the chisel or the stockings over the shoes, something that he left out. But eventually he got all of it in as we all remembered it. And he signed it.

"Then I said to him: 'Now Paul, there's one final step.' I said, 'Paul, we want to send this to somebody, somebody who could help you. You mentioned people that you knew.' Ellis told us, 'You just tell it to him this way and slowly but surely he'll come and tell you that he wants this confession to go to his friend Ellis Parker.' And don't you know we talked, 'Should we send it to the governor?' 'No.' 'Should we send it to Schwarzkopf, he's handling the investigation?' 'No.' 'How about Wilentz?' 'No. My friend that helped me when I was disbarred.' 'Who's your friend?' 'Ellis Parker.' 'You want us to send it to Ellis Parker? Address that envelope to Ellis Parker.' He wrote out the envelope, he knew the address. We told him we were going to send it to Ellis Parker. We didn't. We gave it to Ellis, Jr., and he went out right away, called his father, and his father said, 'I told you he was going to break down.'

"He wrote out the confession. Ellis, Jr., and I took it to Parker. He said, 'All right, now you tell him that you mailed it and you wait a day until it reaches his friend Parker, then you can ask him what he wants to do, you're finished with him. Because for all the obvious reasons he was brought there, this is going to clear up the whole picture now. So ask him where do you want to go, Paul?' We ask him and Wendel says, 'Why don't you take me to my friend Ellis Parker?' Just the way Parker said it would happen.

"We told him we mailed the confession to Parker, we wanted to let him know we're waiting for Parker to get it. So we wait two days. Then we get him cleaned up, he wanted his clothes cleaned and his shirts and laundry done. So it was the third day after the confession, at dusk, that we get into the car. Schlossman, Weiss, and myself. Ellis, Jr., goes back ahead of us to tell his father we're on our way and he's waiting at his father's house for us to bring Wendel there. We drive out to Mt. Holly. We get there at night, maybe eight o'clock, it's dark because it's February. We park across the street from Ellis Parker's house, Wendel tells us how to get there, he directs. We knew where it was but we're pretending we don't know.

"He says, 'Park right here,' and we said to him, 'Okay, Paul, walk across the street. Which house is it?' He points to the house. He walks across the street. Not with a gun pointing at him, not telling him he's gonna get killed if he doesn't go to the house. He couldn't walk fast enough to get to Parker's house. He rang the bell, we saw the door open, we saw Parker and somebody alongside Parker, it might have been his son, and when he went in we drove away.

"The next evening I was in his office and Ellis was telling me what was happening, the steps that he was taking to insure that this was going to become a matter of world knowledge. There was a man in the death house sitting and waiting to be electrocuted for this crime that another man honestly confessed to. So now I met with Parker and his son in his office. Parker said, 'What I did, I took Wendel over to the New Lisbon Colony.' That was a state mental home. He had told us, a few days before, when he knew we were bringing him in after the confession, that he arranged with Superintendent Jones to bring him to the New Lisbon Colony. They prepared for him a living room and bedroom, a two-room apartment there. And they arranged through Hoffman to get Gus Lockwood, Hoffman's chauffeur, to stay with Wendel and guard him at New Lisbon.

"So the first night Wendel slept at Parker's house and the following day after breakfast they drove to the New Lisbon home. That's where Wendel knew he was going, he agreed to stay there. They told him where he was going."

"Did they suggest any sort of insanity as a defense?"

"No, no. Parker says to him, 'Paul, I'm going to try to work this out in your best interests. I know what you've been through. I'm going to try to protect your family, everything I can do in my power through friends and contacts, to see that your wife and son and daughter are not involved.'"

"Was it your feeling or Parker's that Wendel had an urge to let the world know he kidnaped the Lindbergh child?"

"Yes. Parker said, 'Murray, this man wants to tell me the story in the worst way, he wants to tell it to somebody. He did something that he knows is the greatest thing in the world, the crime of the century. This is what he wanted to do and he did it. Now that it's out he's glad it's out, he's glad some people know he did something he considers so brilliant.'

"I don't think I covered a very important part of this," Murray went on, appearing to hurry now as we saw the sign "Mt. Holly" on the New Jersey Turnpike. "This is a very important thing for your book because it is substantiating evidence that Wendel did this thing. The day after we brought Wendel to Parker's home in Mt. Holly, I went back there, as I already mentioned. I was still working for Ellis. Schlossman and Weiss are out of it now because their roles are finished, but I'm still working with the Parkers. Ellis was forever showing me all the things he was doing because he was so positive in what he was doing. So he sent Ellis, Jr., to go to Trenton to get Paul Wendel, Jr., Wendel's nineteen-year-old son. When they pull up in front of the house Parker says to me, 'Murray, I want you to listen to this.' And he tells me to go into the dining room, stay just behind those big old-fashioned sliding wood doors and listen. Which I did.

"Paul Wendel, Jr., is brought into the sitting room. Parker says to him, 'Paul, sit down.' The kid sat. 'Paul, I brought you here to tell you that I'm holding your father. He's sound. He's safe. He's in good health. I'm holding him because he confessed to the kidnaping of the Lindbergh baby.'

"This is the son, now. Just like Hauptmann told the truth when he said, 'I know nothing, I'm innocent,' so Paul Wendel, Jr., was telling the truth when he answered; '*I always knew they'd get my father for this.*' I heard it myself. The man's own son said he knew his father would get caught for kidnaping the Lindbergh baby. If I couldn't believe anything else about this case I could believe that, the son admitting his father was involved.

"Then Parker says, 'Don't worry, Paul, I gave your father my assurance that I would do anything in my power to see that nothing happens to you or the family.'

"The next day Parker and Wendel discuss his confession and Parker told him, 'Paul, I don't know what I can do for you because this is a serious crime you've committed. You're going to have to be punished for what you've done. I suppose with Hoffman, my friend, as the governor, it may be possible to get you a life sentence because you've told the truth about how the baby died and it was an accident. However, your confession makes your wife and children conspirators in this because they helped you. Even though they're conspirators there will be a way to get them off legally. And I'll help you do that.'

"This is the kind of guy Parker was. I didn't know it until Wendel's confession was finally made public later, but in the confession that was finally delivered to the pardons board, Wendel is quoted as telling Parker that he took the Lindbergh baby to a tenement house in Trenton. Not to his home, where his wife and children were helping him, but to a tenement house. Despite what Wendel had done, despite the kind of man he was, Parker still had enough feeling for his wife and children to protect them by letting Wendel change the location and keep them out of it.

"But I'm running ahead of my story. Wendel is in the New Lisbon Home. Parker, Ellis, Jr., Mrs. Bading, and a few others are there with him every day, for weeks, getting him to fill in as much detail as he can remember about it. Parker questions him, brings out fresh details, fills in the holes, and goes around investigating Wendel's story. And then Parker made a serious mistake. I don't know why he did it the way he did, maybe because of the political situation between Hoffman and Wilentz, maybe because Hoffman could only act through the board of pardons, but for whatever reason Parker sent copies of the confession through the mails, anonymously, to every member of the pardons board. If it was me today, knowing what I know, I would have called a press conference and broadcast it to the world and refuse to give up my prisoner until a

250

new and complete investigation was done by someone outside the people controlled by Wilentz and Schwarzkopf. But Parker sent the confession anonymously, which hurt him a lot. Because just at the moment these people were getting the confession by mail and probably getting the shock of their lives, the story broke in a Trenton paper that Parker was holding someone who confessed to the Lindbergh crime."

"How did that leak out?" I asked.

"Gus Lockwood, the governor's chauffeur. He'd been guarding Wendel at New Lisbon for a week or two and he was going crazy there. Finally, they gave him a night off and he drove into Trenton to his favorite gin mill near the State House. And he got drunk and started bragging about the prisoner he was guarding, the man who kidnaped the Lindbergh baby. Well, this place was a hangout for politicians and reporters and some young reporter overheard Gus and went running to his editor with it. And the next morning the paper published a story—not a story, more like an editorial, but on the front page—it didn't really have any facts but it asked a lot of questions. Like, who is Ellis Parker holding for the Lindbergh killing? And, what right does Ellis Parker have to be keeping this news from the public?

"This is only a day or two before Hauptmann is scheduled to die, that's probably why Parker rushed it up and sent the confession through the mails, because he felt he was running out of time. So when that article came out, what is Ellis Parker hiding, Wilentz jumps right on top of Parker to protect his reputation and to make certain that Hauptmann went to the chair. He sent Parker a telegram demanding he turn his prisoner over to the proper authorities, since Parker had no jurisdiction, and after consulting with Governor Hoffman who was behind him in this all the way, they decided Parker had to give up Wendel. Parker tells me he's forced to turn Wendel over, and he said he's calling Jim Kirkham, Mercer County chief of detectives, to tell him he's bringing in a prisoner. 'Murray, I'm still going to do everything in my power to see the truth comes out,' Parker told me. 'Even though Wilentz now holds all the cards and will try to make Wendel appear a hero, I'm going to fight this until my dying day. An innocent man's life is at stake.' When Kirkham gets Wendel he has to tell Wilentz about this prisoner he's holding for the Lindbergh crime. Wilentz, in his not so innocent way, and Schwarzkopf in his not so innocent way, let everybody know that there was a man lodged in the Mercer County jail and he was going over to see him.

"So by the time he goes to see him there are cameras, lights, a Hollywood setting. Now he comes to the jail. The entrance is lit up like daylight. Mobs of people surrounding this jail. The public believes they finally got the kidnaper. Now Wilentz comes to the jail. Imagine you're in that jail house, you're Wendel, the guy that was disbarred because you were convicted for embezzlement of a client's funds. You're the guy that Mercer County has warrants out for your arrest for issuing worthless checks. You're a criminal. You're in the jail but you're not in a cell, they got you in a reception room. You're waiting for the attorney general of the state to come in and greet you. And greet him he does. When they walked into the jail they walked up to Wendel, Wilentz, Schwarzkopf, and others. And Wilentz says, 'Hello, Paul.' And Paul sticks out his hand and Wilentz takes the criminal's hand and shakes it. And Wendel now becomes instead of a criminal a hero, overnight. Wendel said to him, 'Am I glad to see you.' And Wilentz says, 'Don't worry, Paul, nothing is going to happen to you.' Sure as shooting it's not gonna happen. Not with the attorney general having tried and convicted a man who is in the death house. He isn't going to turn around and tell the world he made a mistake. Not after having fought on the record to tell the world he was convicting the kidnaper of the Lindbergh baby. He isn't apt to tell them that he made a mistake and now he has the real kidnaper. Because if he admits this he makes a complete fool of himself, he'll never be governor, he's liable to be an office boy. Now the camp represented by Wilentz, Schwarzkopf, and all, they go to work to disprove everything that Parker and Hoffman and everybody else did.

"Right away Wendel began to deny his confession. He said, 'I'm glad you're here now, this is what was done to me, this is what I've got, a broken leg and a broken head and a broken mind.' And Wilentz is going to accept it all because he's not about to tell the world that this is the man even if it is the man. And it was the man. And Parker was right and went to his death believing it, and Hoffman died believing it, and my father died believing it. And I'll die believing it. Because it was the truth. Wilentz says to Paul, not Wendel, Paul, sit down Paul, in the Mercer County jail—Parker told me, Hoffman told me, I was talking to these people all the time, I was the active deputy—Wilentz told him to sit down and write everything out, repudiating his confession. He shot it full of holes. The whole thing. He's talking to a criminal to sit down and write it. Imagine telling you or me to do something like this. Then Wendel became a hero. They allowed Wendel to be taken from Mercer County after they got through and Hauptmann was electrocuted . . ."

"Wait. They have a repudiation and a confession. Doesn't it go before a grand jury?"

"Hoffman is still trying to save the pieces. He gives Hauptmann a reprieve for seventy-two hours and he goes before the pardons board begging them to commute the sentence since there is so much evidence of Hauptmann's innocence and so much evidence of Wendel's guilt. All he can get for Hauptmann by law is those three days, he can't give the man more time, during which time a new grand jury will hear the evidence against Wendel and decide whether to indict. If they indict, then the pardons board can't let Hauptmann die.

"But they don't indict. Because Wilentz—the man who would be made a complete fool of should Hauptmann be proved innocent, the man who might even be in a lot of trouble himself if it could be shown that he had a hand in framing Hauptmann—Wilentz is the guy to present the evidence to that grand jury. And what does he do? He makes sure that the official sheet of paper charging Wendel with the murder of the Lindbergh baby, the paper filled out by Mercer County chief of detectives Jim Kirkham, never gets to the grand jury. Since there is no official charge, the grand jury has nothing to investigate."

"Did you hear anything about how Wilentz handled that grand jury?" I asked. "You know as well as I that grand juries are guided and controlled by the prosecutor who's presenting evidence. Did Wilentz control that grand jury?"

"Parker later told me, he knew because the foreman of the grand jury was his close friend, he said Wilentz handled it like he handled the Hauptmann trial. He told them the confession was a lot of poppycock. The man was beaten and tortured, there was no confession, this isn't the man. So they didn't vote an indictment. The case against Wendel is dead.

"And so is Hauptmann. He was executed a couple of nights later. The poor bastard never had a chance. Not with Mr. Wilentz and the honorable Colonel Schwarzkopf, that frame-up artist, and all

253

the power of the mighty state of New Jersey doing their damnedest to spill the blood of the first fall guy who comes along and can be pinned with the kidnaping. And now that Hauptmann was dead a new face entered the picture to finish up Wilentz's dirty work by . . ."

"Wait a minute," I interrupted. We were entering Mt. Holly now, a medium-sized town whose charm had long before been renovated out of existence, the old Victorian houses stripped of their verandas and bastardized with counterfeit-stone facades. I pulled over to the curb. We had a few minutes before our lunch date with Frank Fitzpatrick so I kept the tape recorder running. "Very quickly, tell me about your arrest. You can fill in the details on the way home."

"That's what I started to talk about," Murray said. "The new face in the picture was this other honorable guy, Francis Geoghan, the Brooklyn district attorney. This bum should have been in jail himself, and I call him a bum with his great big shock of white hair because he was a bum. Geoghan had just been rapped all over the place by the Amen investigation, that's long before your time but it was a special investigation, like the Knapp Commission in New York, headed by John Harlan Amen. The investigation was into Geoghan's dereliction of duties as DA, especially in cases involving the mob and Murder, Inc. And especially in a very famous scandal at the time, the Drukman murder case. This man Drukman was murdered by the mob and Geoghan got a lot of money to make the files disappear so nobody would have to stand trial for murder.

"In fact, after Amen's report Geoghan had been superseded on all racketeering cases and Amen put into his job. Geoghan could only handle regular criminal cases. He was fighting for his political life and to stay out of jail, because they had enough on him to put him away for a long time. And if you think Wilentz got into a three-ring circus to demolish all the work we did on the Wendel case you should have seen what this white-haired Geoghan bastard did when he learned Wendel had been held in Brooklyn."

"How did they discover that?"

"Because Wendel, with his shrewd mind, he outsmarted us. Before we took him out to Ellis, right here in Mt. Holly, we had Wendel's clothes dry-cleaned. And when he got his suit back he found the dry cleaner's tag in it and he stuck it in his pocket. So when Wilentz helps him repudiate his confession and start screaming he was tortured, Wendel gives him the dry-cleaning tag and tells him he thinks it was in Brooklyn. And Geoghan gets into it and tracks down the dry cleaner on some street near my father's house and they trace it to that house and then figure out it was me and Schlossman and Weiss. So now this man Geoghan has all the whitewash he needs to cover his own crimes. He's going to become the number two hero in America, right behind Wilentz. He's going to show what he will do to kidnapers. Now we're the kidnapers.

"So the three of us take off. Parker tells us to take off until this thing dies down and he can straighten it all out. Parker still believes that whatever is happening may be a little bit disconcerting but he thinks he's going to get the truth out anyway and save Hauptmann. Little does he know the power Wilentz and Geoghan have to mess him up. We take off, Parker gave me some money to go away with and I spoke to Jack Arbitell and he sends me down to Savannah, to stay with an old-time rumrunner he knew. I stayed there and this thing is gaining momentum and Geoghan is screaming about fugitives from justice.

"And my father is sick. He went into a hospital just before this all blew up, with a kidney problem. Geoghan has him arrested right in the hospital room, a formal arrest and he makes it sound like my father had an operation to avoid Geoghan's law. And so from the hospital he goes to a prison ward and then when he's bailed out he goes back to a private room. And he died right there. Geoghan should have died and Wilentz should have died for what they did to people who were trying to do what was morally right.

"Anyway, and thank God it was before my father died, but I got word through Jack Arbitell that the lawyers said the best thing was for me to come back and surrender. The lawyers make the arrangements and I fly into Albany. There I meet a detective from Geoghan's office at a restaurant, with my lawyer. That detective, incidentally, was Frank Bals, the cop who later threw Abe Reles out the window, Reles the informer on Murder, Inc. But I want to make it clear I surrendered voluntarily, I wasn't arrested like that bad-book writer, Waller, says in *Kidnap*. It was voluntary. So we take the train to New York and I walk into Geoghan's office. Talk about torture. They didn't allow me to go to sleep, they didn't allow me to eat. There were forty-nine cops there, one guy swing-

255

ing, another guy threatening, 'Listen, you little bastard.' And they started to hit me. I demanded to see Geoghan and finally the DA came in."

"What's been happening to Wendel all this time? Was he jailed in Jersey on the old bad check charges?"

"Are you kidding? This guy Wendel is a criminal, spent time in prison, has been dodging criminal warrants against him for a year, two years or more. So what do they do to him? They take him to Brooklyn and put him in a suite in the Towers Hotel, the best hotel in Brooklyn, the best foods from the best restaurants. This Geoghan takes Wendel and puts him in the Towers. Geoghan grabs onto Wendel like another long lost brother. If you saw a love deal between two people—what they did, now they got the kidnapers. They got Murray, Weiss, Schlossman, and my father.

"I got to see Geoghan. I said, 'Listen, I came in voluntarily. I surrendered to come in and tell you this story as it should be told. Truthfully. I don't have to be subjected to constant interrogation, third-degree tactics. If this is what you intend to do, I got nothing to say. You might as well start right now, get your bats, get your pipes, get your men, and you can bang away because nothing's gonna happen. Call them all off.' He says, 'What do you want?' I said, 'I wanna eat, I wanna go to sleep. Like a man. I want to get up in the morning and sit down and do things like men do.' And that's the way it was done. I ate and slept and then, the next day, I told him the whole story.

"Then he told me, 'Murray, I want you to plead guilty to what you've done. We call it kidnaping. You did kidnap a man. You took a man across a state line. That's kidnaping a person interstate.' He said, 'I want you to go into court, Weiss and Schlossman are not going to plead guilty, they want to go to trial.' He said, 'All I want you to do is tell the truth. I want you to plead guilty and nothing will happen to you.' 'What do you mean nothing will happen to me?' He said, 'I want you to go into that courtroom and tell the truth because Schlossman and Weiss won't listen to a thing.' They didn't. They went to trial. And I went into that courtroom and told the truth. And my truth reversed their conviction and dismissed their case. Because when I was on the stand the judge began to question me. I brought out that I was a deputy appointed by Governor Hoffman and working with Ellis Parker. The judge said, 'You're a deputy?' I said yes. He asked how did it happen. Now the judge was questioning me and I had a beautiful opportunity to tell a story in narrative form, without lawyers objecting, opposing counsel and all that. And I told him, 'If you were an officer in civilian clothes running out of a building chasing a man and said to me, as a citizen, help me catch that man, he just hit a woman or he robbed a woman, I would go with that man not knowing he was an officer, just the fact that he said he was an officer chasing a thief or a murderer. These men on trial did exactly that very same thing. They were deputized. They were told to pick up a man, they picked up that man, thinking they were within their moral and legal rights as deputies. And I did the same thing.' This testimony is what upset their conviction. They were convicted and they were sentenced to twenty-to-life and I pleaded guilty to that very same crime and I got a suspended sentence because Geoghan kept his promise. But Geoghan got his piece of cake because he got all the publicity he wanted."

"What about the federal trial?" I asked.

"Wilentz, you see, wasn't going to give up. He was a Democrat, the President was a Democrat, the Justice Department was controlled by the Democrats. And they were going to get that Republican Hoffman, by getting the Parkers, if it took a century. So they get a federal grand jury in Newark to indict all five of us—both Parkers thrown in the pot this time—on charges of violating the kidnap law. The Lindbergh Law! What an irony.

"But there was a guy in Newark as United States attorney, John Quinn, who didn't want to screw Ellis Parker, he really wanted to get Parker off. When I'm brought over to Newark to plead to the indictment, Quinn calls me into his office. And he tells me, 'Murray, I want you, Weiss, and Schlossman to plead guilty and nothing is going to happen to you. My word of honor you'll get off the way you did in Brooklyn.' I said, 'Good, you've got a deal.' And he said, 'But there's something else I want you to do, Murray. I want you to go and see Ellis Parker. His lawyers are advising him and his son to fight this all the way, to deny everything. He can't beat it, not after everything that came out in the Brooklyn trial. We do not want this man hurt, he is an internationally famous figure and a person who is well-thought-of in this state. I'd like you to talk to him, tell him what you're going to do. Tell him that if he comes in here and pleads guilty with his son, that'll be the end of his case.' I went to see Parker. Arbitell arranged a meeting, it was in the middle of the night. I went to his home in Mt. Holly. And he cried like a baby. I said, 'Ellis, please do what I ask you to do. We tried, God knows we tried. We failed, but maybe someday the truth will be known. But certainly nothing should happen to you or to any of us. My father died, Ellis, as a result of this. Let's go in there and plead guilty, Ellis, and then forget this thing for the moment.' He said, 'Murray, I can't do it. I was told by Hoffman, who's putting up the money for me, that I should listen to everything that my two lawyers tell me. And they're telling me to go in there and fight it, and fight it I will.' I asked, 'Ellis, are you going to tell the story?' He said, 'I'm going to try and tell the story.' He cried like a baby. He said, 'I'm going to try to bring out the story, Murray, help me if you can and do whatever you think you have to do.' And I said, 'I will, I'm only going to tell the truth.' The truth I told."

"Why did the Parkers fight it?"

"Parker told me he had two of the best lawyers in the state, paid for by Hoffman, and he had to do what they told him. And they were telling him to deny the whole story, to deny he'd ever met any of us. But how could he deny it? Everything was there, our telephone calls to Parker's house from a phone around the corner from where Wendel was kept—telephone records in black and white—and Wendel's story, and my testimony at the Brooklyn trial. Even if I went in and denied it all my original testimony would kill me.

"Parker and his son did fight it. And they were convicted. Parker got six years and his son three. Parker died in Lewisburg Penitentiary. They say he died of a brain tumor, and I'm sure he did. But it was more than that. Maybe a brain tumor contributed to it, but I think he died of a broken heart. Whenever I think of Parker I think, 'Poor Ellis.' "

"And Wendel?"

"He became a hero for a while. He sold his story to the newspapers and magazines, the pack of lies he cooked up with Wilentz and they eventually were put out in book form. We have to get that book so I can show you all his lies. And that lying bastard went to his grave—if he is dead, I don't know, maybe he's alive, he'd be about eighty-five now—but he went along the rest of his life knowing that he had done the spectacular thing he always dreamed of doing and he got away with it. But best of all, he did come to the world's attention and he didn't have to pay a penalty for it. He gained a great deal, in fact. Parker died knowing in his heart that

Hauptmann was innocent. My father died knowing. I'll die knowing it. Worst of all, Hauptmann died knowing it."

"You were promised another suspended sentence," I said, "how did you end up in prison?"

"Well, five years after Ellis's trial I went to jail, so did Weiss and Schlossman. What happened was, the U.S. attorney, John Quinn, died a couple of years after the trial. The judge at the trial, Judge Clark, had gone into the army because by now it's World War II. Both these men knew of the understanding that we'd get suspended sentences. But during all those years we were never called for sentencing and we were talking to our lawyer about it one day and he said that we should go in, get the suspended sentence, and clear the record. But now there's a new judge and a new U.S. attorney. They don't want to know from promises. We all get sentenced to two years and go to Lewisburg and serve out a good piece of our time."

13

As we walked into the restaurant where we were to meet Frank Fitzpatrick I began to grow disheartened about the Wendei story. Murray's story. Assuming every bit of it were true, assuming Wendel made his confession because, as Parker had said, he had a compelling need to tell someone how great a criminal he was—still, every word he told Murray could have been the result of his fantasizing, his need to inject himself into the case as demonstrated by his earliest stories to Parker about having contact with the actual kidnapers, a need to become involved that seemed to afflict an enormous percentage of the American population. Or he might have manufactured a confession in order to be released from captivity. Everything that Wendel had spoken of had already been written about, in millions of words in newspapers, magazines, and even a couple of fast books churned out to meet the public's insatiable demand. All Wendel had supplied were variations on the basic facts already made public. The "key" on the spines of his lawbooks could have been the result of his speculation as to the meaning and derivation of the symbols on the ransom notes. The Germanic construction of the notes, the details about the ladder, even the question as to whether a chisel or a screwdriver had been used to pry open the nursery window—none of it was new, not a single piece of information was absolutely, stunningly new. In a novel, in a film, even, surprisingly enough, in real detective work, the actual killer would have said something like "I left a black kid

261

glove, right-handed, with a Saks Fifth Avenue label, under the crib that night." And the police, having withheld that information, would have known the confession was total truth.

Perhaps I was demanding too much from Murray and from Wendel. I must try to find any Parker relative still alive, and try to get my hands on Parker's documents. And I knew there was one enormous obstacle to overcome before I could believe Wendel's story: the baby's body. The accuracy of Wendel's confession depends, in part, on his statement that after the baby died he had taken the body back to the area and buried it in the woods where it was later found. But Parker himself had said the body identified by Lindbergh could not have been his son. And, after my research, I agreed with him almost completely. Charles Lindbergh, Jr., most likely was not found in that shallow grave.

"Is Frank Fitzpatrick around?" Murray was asking the bartender. "We have a date with him."

The bartender looked over to plastic booths and Formica-top tables lining one long wall of the restaurant. "That's him over there," he said. A tall slim man in his sixties stood up and came toward us, very slightly bent over from the waist as if he had long suffered from back trouble. "I'm Fitzpatrick," he said, "come on and sit down."

We talked for over an hour, jumping around from one area of the case to another. I've been working on this book for years, Frank said, and after I nail down one more piece of evidence I'll be ready to look for a publisher. What kind of evidence? I asked.

"There are photos of the body found in the woods that will prove it wasn't the Lindbergh baby," he said. "Medical photos and medical reports that have never been made public. I think I'm going to be able to convince the widow of the man who had them to let me use them in my book."

There it was again: the hole in Wendel's story. "I take it you don't believe that was the baby?" I asked.

"No one around here does. Everything old Ellis said about the body is the truth. No doubt about it."

Another thought flashed across my mind. There's a man up in Connecticut who says he's sure *he's* the Lindbergh baby. Know anything about him, a man named Harold Olson?"

"Never heard of that," Frank said. "But you never know but maybe he's right. The Lindbergh baby didn't die the way every-

262

body claims he did. So maybe he's still alive. And maybe this man is Lindbergh's kid. You never know."

For most of the hour that we talked Murray was reminiscing again, covering for Fitzpatrick all the ground he had gone over with me, into my tape recorder. I broke in as often as I could, trying to draw information from Frank, trying to overcome his reluctance to give even a small part of his twenty years of research to a competitor. I didn't get very much from him. Except that, when the conversation somehow swung away from Wendel and over to Hauptmann and the evidence against him, Fitzpatrick said:

"Hauptmann was framed, I know he was."

"How do you know it?"

"The things they claimed they found in his house. For example, that board in his closet with Condon's phone number written on it. You know how it got there?" I shook my head. "It was put there by this guy Cassidy, Tom Cassidy, he used to work out here for the *New York Daily News* and he went into the Bronx to help cover Hauptmann's arrest. And after they took Hauptmann away and his wife moved out, the police confiscated his apartment. And one day Cassidy is up in the apartment with a photographer and he needs a fresh story for his first edition. So he goes into Hauptmann's closet and writes that stuff on the closet board and then has his photographer take pictures of it. Then he calls the inspector or whoever was in charge and he says, 'Look what I found.' Front-page pictures and story in the *News* that night."

"Can you prove this?"

"Hell, Cassidy was bragging about it all over Mt. Holly. Ask anybody in town who goes back that far and they'll tell you how Cassidy was bragging about it. He even showed us how he wrote it and when he showed us it looked the same as the writing on the board they brought into the trial to nail Hauptmann."

"Why didn't Reilly put Cassidy on the stand?"

"I don't know. Probably because he knew Cassidy would deny it and maybe because Reilly always worked with reporters and got a lot of publicity from them, so he wasn't about to get them mad at him."

"And the inspector swore that *he* found the board?"

"Sure. They all lied about the evidence. I mean, Hauptmann never admitted he wrote those numbers. He was confused because he was trying to tell the truth and he just didn't recollect putting

263

those numbers on the board. Because he didn't put them there, Cassidy did. And that's how the whole trial went."

Murray swung the conversation back to Wendel again and Fitzpatrick said: "There are a lot of reasons I'm certain Wendel was the real kidnaper. You see, I was working for Parker at the time. I was just a kid, doing a little newspaper work and doing some stuff part-time for Parker. Old Ellis taught me how to take fingerprints, how to read them and compare them, things like that. And he had me doing undercover work for him on the Lindbergh case, from the beginning."

"What sort of things did you do?"

"Well, a lot of things. But I'll never forget the one thing that made old Ellis feel certain Wendel was the kidnaper. It was before that body was found in the woods, when Paul Wendel had come in and said he could help get the baby back. Parker was playing along with Wendel, giving him enough rope, as he called it, and on one of the errands Wendel was running on in connection with the case, Anna Bading drove him. And when she came back, after dropping Wendel off somewhere, she was white as a sheet. I asked her what the matter was and she said to me, 'I never thought I'd get home alive.' What happened? And she said, 'We were driving around and as a joke I told him, Paul, I think you have the baby at home in Trenton. And such an expression came over his face the likes of which I've never seen. It was fright, at first, and then it was hatred. He looked like he was wanting to kill me.'

"I'm convinced Parker was right, Wendel did it. See, there's another thing in all of this that people don't realize. It got lost in the shuffle when they were letting Wendel go and accusing Parker and Hoffman of interfering with justice. Wendel repudiated his confession after Wilentz got to him. But if you read that repudiation, it's a confession in itself. He said in his repudiation that he'd be willing to plead guilty to kidnaping but not to murder. There was no death penalty for kidnaping at that time and Wendel being a lawyer knew it. He in effect admitted the kidnaping."

"Do you have copies of the confession and the repudiation?"

"Yes," Fitzpatrick said, "but everything is stacked in boxes and it'll take me a while to find it. Maybe if we talk again I'll try to dig it out for you."

We left Fitzpatrick without getting more from him than a confirmation of my own deep conviction that at least some, perhaps all, of the physical evidence against Hauptmann had been constructed by police. Or, in this particular instance, by a headline-hungry reporter. Fitzpatrick was of no further assistance in my research for he did not have any of Parker's original papers. His own study of the case was based exclusively on the evidence presented at the Parkers' trial and on interviews with contemporaries, none of which satisfied the standards I had set for myself: conclusive documentary evidence which would withstand the most rigorous test. Fitzpatrick, in fact, had never made an attempt to talk to Parker's heirs or to retrieve whatever papers old Ellis may have left behind.

Murray and I went over to see Chief McConnell. He gave us the names of a dozen or so old-timers who would enjoy reminiscing about Ellis Parker and the Lindbergh case and who might have some documentation about Wendel's role in the crime. McConnell also gave us some rather disappointing news when we asked where Anna Bading was living. "She died last year," he said. "Her husband is still alive but he's a funny guy and he just doesn't want to talk about it at all.' Ellis, Jr., was dead but, McConnell said, "He has a younger brother, Eddie, still living down around Haynesport." A quick check through the telephone directory—no Eddie Parker listed. McConnell, after graciously running through his files—Ellis Parker's old files—without turning up a single document that could help me prove Wendel indeed was involved in the kidnaping, suggested we search out Hoppy, Russell Hopstatter, another retired newspaperman, who he said usually sat around at the Elks Club during the afternoons.

Over to the Elks we went, another building dating back to the Victorian Era, but this one untouched by the Holiday Inn renovation mentality: fireplaces, enormous leather armchairs and couches, original wood paneling never touched by paintbrush or Formica, the ambience of a London club for gentlemen.

"Eddie Parker?" Hopstatter asked. "Sure, I'll find him for you. A few of the Parker girls are still around, Ellis's daughters, I'll check with them." Another member of the Elks offered to make the calls while Hop talked to us. "I worked with Ellis on the Wendel case," Hop said. "Ellis believed Wendel was the brains behind it and he had help somehow from the inside. I don't remember if he said exactly how, but I remember he used to insist that the maid, that Violet Sharpe, she didn't commit suicide just because she was ashamed that she went out drinking beer with a man as the cops claimed. She was involved in it. And Wendel was the brains. That's what I remember Parker saying."

"I've heard a story about the board in Hauptmann's closet . . ." I started to ask, and Hop broke in: "Cassidy. The *Daily News* reporter. Sure, he wrote that phone number, whatever it was, he admitted that to me and to Ellis, he told everybody about it. He was sure Hauptmann was guilty so it didn't matter very much, that's how he felt about it."

"You said you worked with Ellis on the case?"

"Sure. I did a lot of running for Ellis. I'll never forget the day I picked up Wendel's confession from the mailbox for him. I brought it to Ellis and he opened it and read it and he just hit the ceiling. He was overjoyed, surprised, cussing his head off he was so happy."

"How could he be surprised?" Murray asked.

"He was. 'Hop, look at this, we broke the Lindbergh case. Can you believe getting a confession in the mail like this?' On and on, like he was surprised."

"He was playing it cagey," Murray said. "He knew that confession was coming but he wanted you to think it was a surprise."

"Could be," Hop conceded. "Ellis worked that way."

Another one of the elderly men in the club came over. "Got to a couple of the sisters, they don't know where Ellis's papers might be. Said to try Eddie Parker. Here's his address."

We drove over to see Parker, a few miles south of Mt. Holly. He didn't have his father's papers, but he suggested that the widow, Ellis, Jr.'s second wife, might have them. She's since remarried and living down in Clearwater, Florida. She's Mrs. Blair Rodman now. I called her and asked if she had the Parker papers.

"They've been destroyed," she said.

"Oh, my God, no."

"I'm afraid so. My husband was so discouraged about everything that happened to him and his father, after that Wendel thing blew up in their faces, he ordered me to burn everything after he died."

"But why?" I asked.

"Ellis told me, 'No good will come out of any of this now, it's too late. No one will ever believe Hauptmann was innocent and my father was right.' So I burned the papers after he died."

Even Murray was growing discouraged. "I should have started this two, three years ago," he said. "Everybody's dying off on me." I felt the same way. But more disheartening than the deaths of so many who had been involved with Ellis Parker in the Wendel arrest was the fact that Parker's papers, the nearest thing to documentary evidence against Wendel I could hope to find, had been burned and were irretrievably lost. A participant's memory, forty years later, is at best unreliable; only documents could satisfy me.

Yet I went through the motions of interviewing participants. Murray and I stopped in to see Jack Arbitell, the former bootlegger who had originally brought Murray and Parker together. On the whole, his memory confirmed Murray's account of the Wendel case, with slight variations and some additional anecdotes about Parker and Wendel. As I play back the three hours of tape now, listening to the voice of an ailing man in his early eighties admitting his memory has been fading of late, I smile broadly again as I did that day, when Arbitell would sit up straight as something flitted through his mind and then suddenly launch into a long anecdote almost as if he had total recall.

"I remember Ellis telling me how he got wind that Wendel was mixed up in this kidnaping. Ellis said to me, 'Jack, this guy Wendel was in my house one day and we went over to my office and we talked a lot and he said, "You know, Ellis, I'm getting damned tired of trying to save some money, five-dollar bills and ten-dollar bills. I want to make fifty thousand dollars at one time. Fifty thousand, fifty thousand . . .' Wendel kept going on about fifty thousand. And you know, Jack, when I heard about the kidnaping and the fifty-thousand ransom, it came into my mind that Wendel did it. That's when I started watching him.'"

A few minutes later Arbitell was pouring us some brandy and laughing because his doctor told him he had to stop drinking and as a former bootlegger he still objected to anyone being a teetotaler, when he remembered something else from those days:

"Parker did a lot of investigating about that ladder. He said it was a homemade proposition and the lumber came from a church in Trenton. He said he was sure the wood didn't come from Hauptmann's attic at all. 'Jack, that was a frame-up with the wood man, that Koehler fellow,' he said. 'They tried to frame Hauptmann. He didn't make that ladder, he didn't get the wood from out of his house. Wendel got it from some church they were building over in

Trenton. I can prove it,' he said. He always considered . . ." Arbitell paused for a moment, searching for the words. "There was a woman in Hopewell," he went on. "She ran a candy store and Wendel used to go in and buy things out of this woman's place. Parker questioned this woman but she didn't know anything about this kidnaping. But he was there, Wendel was there. She told Parker that Wendel used to come in a lot just before the kidnaping, she didn't think much of it because he was just another man coming in for cigarettes and stuff. But Parker had good information about Wendel being in the area just before the baby was snatched. Least that's what Parker told me."

Another few feet along the tape, Murray is talking about Wendel once working in a pharmacy and then as a lawyer and then . . . "Wait!" Arbitell shouted. "The drugstore, sure. You see, when I was running a hotel in Trenton I had a young fellow working for me. I don't remember his name. He used to work in a drugstore around the time of the kidnaping and later on in that year, must have been 1932, he worked for me. And we're always talking about the Lindbergh case, this is before Hauptmann is arrested, and this young fellow says to me that when he clerked in the drugstore he used to bring medicine to Wendel's house, baby medicine, and he always wondered about that because Wendel didn't have any small babies. This fellow worked in a drugstore around the corner from Wendel's house and he said they used to make prescriptions for a baby at that address. The clerk didn't know Wendel had anything to do with it, this is long before Wendel got into the papers. I told Parker about it." But the clerk could never be traced after so many years; all the records connected with the hotel were long since destroyed, and all other employees of the hotel were dead. Another trail that would be impossible to follow.

"There's something else I remember about Wendel. When I read the book he published, after Wilentz and the Brooklyn DA made him a hero," Arbitell said at another point, "I got a big laugh out of something Wendel wrote. He claimed he was an inventor and he was such a good one that he invented something the Capone mob was interested in. But he didn't say in his book what the invention was. I'll tell you about that to show you what kind of a louse and con man and how crazy this Wendel was. He met me one day on the street, he knew my business and that I had a lot of contacts with the people in bootlegging and all that. And he said, 'Jack, I

268

want you to come over to my house, I want to show you something. We can make a lot of money with this thing.' So like a jerk I went with him. And he took me down to his cellar and picked up a half dollar and showed it to me. He said, 'What do you think of that?' and I said, 'It's a half dollar.' He said, 'Yeah, but how does it look to you?' I said, 'What is it, a phony?' And he said, 'No, not a phony, I make them.' I said, 'If you make them, they're counterfeit.' He said, 'But I invented something so that they're as real as what comes out of the mint. I can turn out so many of the things in one day it'll make your hair stand on end. Any time you're ready you let me know and we'll both do it together.' I started to go, to get away from the guy, and he said, 'Wait a minute, I wanna show you something else.' He got a little bottle of alcohol and he said, 'Taste that.' So I put a drop on my tongue and he said, 'What is it?' I said, 'Alcohol.' He said, 'I made that.' And I told him a lot of people are making alcohol. And Wendel said, 'Sure, but I made that out of water.'

"Well, the guy was half nuts. I said, 'You made this out of *water?* How the hell could you make alcohol out of water?' He said, 'That's what I did, I invented a way to make alcohol out of water. It's going to make me rich.' And I said, 'All right, I'll see you tomorrow, Paul,' and I got the hell out of there and never saw him after that. I figured the guy was crazy, making alcohol out of water and making half dollars that ain't phony, you know damn well they're both impossible. That's the last time I talked to him. But I heard he suckered somebody else into his crazy inventions and got into trouble with some pretty rough people here in New Jersey and with Al Capone himself—he tried to rob Capone with his crazy inventions, I hear."

Murray was rather quiet driving back to New York City, occasionally dozing off in the car. He was disheartened that we hadn't found solid evidence of Wendel's involvement in the kidnaping, but most of all, I knew, he was upset that Arbitell had aged so much in the years they'd been out of touch, was now a semi-invalid with a serious heart problem. I dropped Murray at his hotel and promised to call him the next evening, after I interviewed Martin Schlossman, his brother-in-law, and did a little more legwork.

I sat with Schlossman in his office the next day. Like Arbitell, Schlossman confirmed almost every element of Murray's story, with some variations. He, too, insisted Wendel was not beaten, that Parker had demanded no one lay a hand on their prisoner because Parker's "psychology" was to frighten Wendel into believing he was a captive of mobsters who were angry because police were harassing them. He was threatened—"We'll rip you limb from limb," Schlossman remembered warning Wendel, if he persisted in remaining silent, or, alternately, "Look, if you don't tell us what's what in this case we're going to push you in some cement and throw you in the river." Wendel was badly frightened, Schlossman admitted; he actually believed they were mobsters and would kill him. But his admissions made it plain to them all, Schlossman maintained, that Wendel was the kidnaper.

"I became convinced of it after we had him write out word for word what was in the ransom notes. What we did, we wrote out a few of the ransom notes, but we printed them and we left out the German twist to the notes. We put them in fairly decent English, with the proper spelling. And we said, 'Write this.' He did and when we took it upstairs to compare it to copies of the real ransom notes we had, it looked like the same writing. We weren't experts, of course, but we laid one note on top of the other and they were practically the same. The notes that he wrote had the same type of German twist to them that the ransom notes had. That's what convinced me.

"I remember him saying that he didn't mean to hurt the baby and that he never even meant to get the ransom. Our theory was that this fellow did this thing and then didn't know what to do afterwards and somebody else got the ransom."

"Just a second," I said. "It seems very possible that the first ransom note, the one in the nursery, was written by one person and then all the others were written by someone else. Did you have Wendel write out several notes, or just the first one?"

"I really don't remember," Schlossman said. "It wasn't more than a couple, it could have been just the first one, but I can't remember."

"It's pretty important," I said. "Please try to remember."

"Hell, I couldn't remember after so long. What I do remember is that Wendel did admit to some of the notes and some of the notes he didn't admit to. In other words, I got the impression that somebody else got the ransom. I remember that impression very clearly—that Wendel had nothing to do with the negotiations, or they were a separate transaction, somebody else he maybe spoke to who got the idea to make himself fifty thousand. It seemed to me to be a disconnected thing.''

"What about Fisch?''

"Fisch was part of my impression that the kidnaping and the extortion were separate. He said he had a connection with Fisch, very definitely some contact with this guy Fisch. I remember him saying that Fisch got the money at the cemetery. How, I don't know. That's the reason the money never came back, it was buried somewhere. Our theory after listening to Wendel was that Fisch got all the money, either at the cemetery or Wendel gave it to him, I really can't be sure now. But I think it was at the cemetery because why would he give Fisch *all* the money? You see, as far as we know none of the other money besides what Hauptmann had and what was passed ever showed up, but they had a list of all the bills, not just the gold bills. So it had to be buried somewhere, whoever got it never got a chance to use too much of it. But my impression then and my impression now is that Fisch got the money in the cemetery.''

I couldn't take that bit of information much further, just then, except to wonder whether Wendel had been Cemetery John and Fisch, perhaps, had been with him, keeping out of sight of Condon or, possibly, deliberately omitted by Condon in his official recitation of his experiences because Wilentz was insisting that only one man, Hauptmann, had been involved. Only one other piece of potentially useful information came out of my interview with Schlossman. I asked him what Wendel had said about the ladder and he replied:

"That he got the wood from his father's church in Trenton, a Lutheran church his father was pastor of. Some construction work was going on there, renovation of the church or something like that. He told us he just took the wood from the piles of lumber being used.''

The next day, in trying to track down documents concerning Wendel, I called a half dozen federal offices in New Jersey because the Parkers had been convicted in federal court there. The United States District Court in Trenton, to which the Parkers had appealed their conviction, could not locate the trial transcript or the appeal papers that should have been in its possession. The federal warehouse on Washington Street in Manhattan located several cardboard cartons in which the court papers and the raw file from the U.S. Attorney's office should have been stored; the cartons were empty. The U.S. Attorney's office eventually conceded it had a small file, with a few documents, from the Parkers' trial. I went over to Newark to take a look at it.

Again I was disappointed; I suppose I had been hoping to find documents that had been suppressed and that would have demonstrated Wendel's guilt. Even Wendel's confession and the repudiation to which Fitzpatrick attached such importance were missing. All I found was a synopsis of the testimony in Parker's trial and an application by Parker for executive clemency, written in Lewisburg Federal Penitentiary in January 1940, two weeks before he died. None of the material was helpful, although some was titillating and perhaps revealing.

Attorney General David Wilentz testified for the prosecution at Parker's trial. He said that while he was preparing his case against Hauptmann, in the weeks before that trial began, he had heard Ellis Parker "was to be a witness for the defense in the Lindbergh case." So he summoned Parker to a meeting and warned the detective "that he did not want state officials testifying for the defense." Further, Wilentz told Parker "that if he knew anything about the case he would have to testify for the state regardless of what his testimony would be."

"Of course," I wrote in my notebook as I made notes of the material I wished Xeroxed, "here's another example of Wilentz making certain there would be no flaw in the script he was writing."

Parker's application for executive clemency made it plain Wendel was a scheming con man who was either very daring or absolutely lacking in sophistication or sanity, because he twice attempted to swindle Al Capone. Attached to Parker's clemency application was an affidavit sworn to by his lawyer, Harry Green. In it Green said that on the first or second Sunday after the kidnaping, Paul Wendel visited a Frank Cristano of Leonia, New Jersey, apparently knowing Cristano had some contact with underworld figures. Wendel told Cristano he knew where the baby was being kept, he could produce the baby, and they'd both share in the $50,000 ransom. He asked Cristano to get in touch with Al Capone and he'd arrange for the baby to be turned over to Capone so that the Chicago Mafia leader would get credit for the return of the child

and "get out of his income tax troubles with the government."
Cristano absolutely refused to get involved in Wendel's scheme
"because he regarded Wendel as a faker and a swindler by reason
of a transaction several years before, in which he embarrassed
Cristano seriously with Capone."

The affidavit went on to explain that in 1929 or 1930 Wendel
came to Cristano with a stunning proposition that would make
them both wealthy. Wendel explained he had invented a process
enabling him to convert common tar into alcohol for four cents a
gallon, which could be sold "commercially and lawfully" for
fifteen cents a gallon—and, although it isn't stated, could be sold to
bootleggers for twice that amount. Wendel asked Cristano to contact Al Capone. Cristano did so and Capone told him to come out
to Chicago right away and bring this inventor with him. Before going to Chicago, Cristano, who must have been rather ingenuous for
a man who could get through to Capone with a proposition of this
kind, was persuaded by Wendel to buy five tons of tar to get their
business rolling. It seems Wendel had demonstrated his process by
sprinkling some powder into a can of tar before Cristano's eyes
and when Cristano returned some hours later, the tar had turned
the color of water and when analyzed by a chemist was said to be
"alcohol." So Cristano, highly impressed, ordered his five tons of
tar and boarded a train with Wendel for Chicago.

Capone also was impressed by Cristano's story and by Wendel
the inventor, on the surface. Wendel was housed in the Lexington,
the hotel in Cicero that Capone had taken over and converted to his
private fortress and from which he dominated Chicago-area crime
and politics. Scarface Al, as he was known to moviegoers and
headline writers, treated Wendel "royally," says the affidavit, and
actually advanced him $700 as a down payment on their partner-
ship. At the time, however, Capone quietly sent his troops out to
investigate Wendel and quickly learned "he was a crook and a faker and that he had conned Cristano by switching the tar for alcohol." Capone got his money back and "threatened to take Wendel for a ride." Cristano must have been a persuasive talker for all
he got from his role in Wendel's little swindle was "embarrass-
ment." He must also have been conducting a vendetta against a
man named Calabrese, because when Wendel came forward with
his latest scheme, to turn the Lindbergh child over to Al Capone,
Cristano said he didn't want to get involved and he sent Wendel to

Calabrese, not further identified in the affidavit. Calabrese apparently contacted the Capone gang with Wendel's proposition and was told that if Wendel's name was so much as mentioned in front of Capone, bodies would be falling all over Chicago and New Jersey. So ended Wendel's escapade in trying to con Capone a second time, and I marveled at the man's gall or insensitivity or absolute insanity.

And so, also, ended my attempts to prove Wendel was the Lindbergh kidnaper, at least for the moment. I knew I could probably spend many weeks finding and interviewing people who had been privy to Parker's machinations in his attempt to prove Wendel guilty, but further confirmation of Murray's story would still be valueless without documentation. And the documents had been burned. Even if I could convince Frank Fitzpatrick to share with me the evidence he said he had amassed over the years, which I felt was unlikely after telephoning him again and meeting further resistance, I knew he didn't have any documents that could be considered unassailable proof.

As I thought about it, trying to fight feelings of weariness and disappointment, I realized that Wendel's possible guilt was, in a way, beside the point. It was Hauptmann's innocence that concerned me most. In those long days and nights of reading through the trial transcript and the other published material on the case, I had felt almost confined in an orbit around Richard Hauptmann and had longed to escape. The Wendel investigation, though important and once potentially fruitful, had been a form of escape. But now I had to return to Hauptmann's orbit.

14

The place for me to start, obviously, was with Hauptmann's alibi. Had he begun working as a carpenter at the Majestic on March 1, 1932, as he originally claimed? Or was it March 15, as he said at his trial? Or March 21, as his employment card seemed to prove?

Documents on the Hauptmann case, I thought, probably existed in the files of four law-enforcement agencies which had been involved. The Justice Department—the FBI, actually—was out for now; even with passage of the Freedom of Information Act, I knew from reading about lawsuits filed by Alger Hiss and by the Rosenberg sons, the FBI would resist opening its files. The New Jersey attorney general's office would also have to be put aside for later because David Wilentz, although aging and reportedly no longer very active, was still an influential political figure in the state. Perhaps it was paranoia, but I did not want to risk Wilentz's learning of my investigation prematurely; I was afraid he could order files closed in Trenton and even in Washington and New York. That left the other two possible repositories of documents, the New York City police department and the Bronx district attorney's office. I decided to start with the latter because as a feature writer for the *Post* I had several contacts in the DA's office, and because a year or so earlier I had received a large amount of cooperation from the chief assistant in that office, Seymour Rotker, when I was researching an article for *Playboy* on a major Mafia figure.

275

I decided to make a direct approach to the district attorney, Mario Merola. I told him I was doing a book on the Lindbergh case and would appreciate permission to go through the files of the extradition proceedings that had been handled in his office four decades earlier. "If the files are still around," Merola said, "you're welcome to see them, spend whatever time you need to copy them. I'll put a Xerox machine at your disposal," he added. "But let me check first to see whether they're still here."

They were, and within a couple of days I had a desk outside Sy Rotker's office and four very large folding envelopes tied with purple ribbon which didn't appear to have been loosened in many years. One of the envelopes had hand-printed across the face the legend: "Hauptmann—Reports, Letters, Etc. Important." I untied the bow on that one and pulled out the contents, a six-inch thickness of documents. The first document was a letter from a New Jersey police official to the Bronx district attorney at the time, Charles McLaughlin, dated May 24, 1932, and my spirits rose: that date was less than two weeks after a body identified as young Lindbergh had been found; it meant that some New Jersey authorities, at least, were cooperating very early on with officials in the Bronx, where the extortion took place. And that increased the possibility of finding, in these files, official reports made too early to have been bent to the will of those who pushed aside all evidence in their haste to convict Hauptmann.

One such document virtually jumped out of the pile at me a few moments later. In an envelope addressed to Edward D. Breslin, assistant Bronx district attorney, I found a letter from the district attorney of upstate Albany County, enclosing reports from Albert H. Hamilton, "Chemical and Microscopical Investigators, Auburn, N.Y." The first item from Hamilton was a letter dated August 29, 1933, more than a year before Hauptmann was arrested. In it, Hamilton requested specimens of the handwriting in the ransom notes so that he could compare them with the writings of suspects. There was and still is a state prison at Auburn and I suspected Hamilton was one of dozens of investigators across the country who had been hired since the kidnaping to find the kidnaper by comparing the ransom writing with the writings of men and women in prison.

Attached to that letter was a report, dated some months later, but still long before Hauptmann had been arrested. In it Albert H.

Hamilton said he had compared the handwriting characteristics of the person who wrote the Lindbergh ransom notes with specimens taken from a man named "Manning Strawl"—Hamilton himself put quotation marks around the name—and after careful study he concluded that:

> The person who wrote the request writings and then signed the name "Manning Strawl" to same was the person who wrote all the "kidnap" letters and envelopes.
> This finding can not be modified by any other standard.

The document was signed Albert H. Hamilton.

Now I know how Schliemann must have felt when he discovered the ruins of Troy, or Sutter when he came up with gold in the Sacramento hills, I thought. The cloud that had hung over me since I realized I could never satisfactorily establish Wendel's guilt lifted; this brief document made a mockery of Osborn and all the handwriting experts whose services had been purchased by the State of New Jersey. Albert Hamilton, whoever on earth he may have been, was obviously respected enough by New York law enforcement officials to have been employed in the search for the man who wrote the ransom notes. He was, no doubt, a recognized handwriting expert. And in August 1933, long before anyone even suspected the existence of Bruno Richard Hauptmann, this expert had examined some suspect's handwriting and opined that that man had written the ransom letters.

Putting aside "Manning Strawl" for the moment—I would try to dig up some information about him later—the important thing was that Hauptmann had been convicted at least in part on the testimony of seven handwriting authorities who swore he had written every ransom note, yet here was another authority who swore that some other man had written those letters. And Hamilton didn't know a man named Hauptmann lived; he had no interest in helping convict or acquit Hauptmann.

I returned to the covering letter from the Albany district attorney to the Bronx district attorney and realized it was dated December 22, 1934, three months *after* Hauptmann's arrest and a few weeks before his trial. Plainly, this report was kept secret by the prosecution. In reading through the records in the Hauptmann case I had come to suspect that some evidence had been suppressed so that there would be no flaw in the prosecution script. But here, in my hands, was the first tangible proof to support that suspicion. And I knew it was likely that within these files I would find many other documents that had been kept hidden from Hauptmann's lawyers back then and from the public for forty years.

I resisted the temptation to dance on my desk, and also fought down the urge to continue riffling through the files at random. Hauptmann's alibi, I decided, was my main goal for now; I'd have plenty of time later for the other aspects of the case, for Merola and Rotker had both said I could use the records as long as necessary.

That alibi demolished by Wilentz's witnesses still disturbed me enormously. It seemed peculiar that Hauptmann had originally claimed to have been working on the day of the kidnaping, then changed his starting date on the construction job to March 15, even though the prosecution claimed to prove he did not begin work until March 21. I thought that perhaps in the transcript of Hauptmann's extradition hearing, the first opportunity the prisoner had to test the state's evidence against him, I could find some evidence to support my feeling that the payroll records had been altered to damage Hauptmann's alibi. I began reading the transcript of that hearing, held in Bronx supreme court on October 15, 1934. Hauptmann's lawyer was James Fawcett of Brooklyn. The state was represented by District Attorney Samuel Foley and by Mr. Wilentz, the New Jersey Attorney General, appearing in a New York court apparently to chalk up some experience in this skirmish before the big trial in Flemington.

Hauptmann's lawyer called to the stand Howard Knapp, assistant treasurer of Reliance Property Management, the agents of the Majestic apartments, on which Hauptmann had worked. Knapp brought with him the payroll records for March and April, 1932—but he did not have the records for the first half of March, the critical period from March 1 to March 15.

"Where are the records for the first half of March 1932?" Fawcett asked.

"Our records do not indicate that any such records exist at this time—or at that time, either," Knapp quickly corrected.

"Any records at all respecting the first half of March 1932?"

"Chronologically speaking, this is the first payroll that we have."

"You have no payroll records before that date?"

"Nothing before that on the Majestic apartments."

Hauptmann's lawyer pressed Knapp on the point and practically called him a liar as the witness continued to insist, "To my belief there is no payroll record in existence." Yet Knapp admitted his company had been in charge of employment at the Majestic since long before March 1, 1932, and employed more than one hundred men and women on any given day. How can you expect us to believe, Fawcett obviously was stating in his questions, that the payroll records for this particular date do not exist?

I certainly couldn't believe it. I felt strongly that Knapp had been lying: the slip of the tongue in which he said no "such records exist at *this* time" made me feel certain they had existed at least until Hauptmann said he'd been working on that day. And I wasn't imagining a slip of the tongue, because in the transcript the stenographer used both a comma and hyphens to mark a distinct pause between that phrase and Knapp's attempt to cover his lie by adding, "or at that time, either."

The folder in which I had found the 240-page transcript contained a file envelope marked: "Hauptmann—Notes taken during extradition." If the payroll record was not produced in court, it could only mean those records would have supported Hauptmann's alibi and been harmful to the prosecutor. So I began searching through the folder with notes of the extradition, looking for a copy of the payroll record or any evidence that it had once existed.

I was certain I wouldn't find it. It didn't make sense that a prosecutor would deny the existence of an employment record and then leave it in the files—unless he was so arrogant he felt certain his files would never be examined by an outsider.

The small sheet of yellow legal paper on which someone had hand-written a receipt almost escaped my notice. That receipt read:

Received from Asst. D. A. Breslin, the following records:
Employment card record of Richard Hauptmann,
Carbon copy of payroll Feb. 29, 1932,
Carbon copy of payroll March 15, 1932 . . .

The payroll record *had* existed, for here was some kind of receipt for the semimonthly records which would cover the dates surrounding the kidnaping. Damn it, I said to myself, the bastards did suppress it and lie about it—Foley and Wilentz and Knapp and everybody else involved, they had to know those records existed and they had to know they were dooming Hauptmann by suppressing them.

I looked around me, at the secretaries in an adjoining room and the assistant prosecutors and policemen strolling around the offices. Should I slip this evidence into my pocket and walk out with it? Or should I ask someone to Xerox it? The first would be illegal, stealing city property. The second could be disastrous, for if anyone in that office learned I was discovering material which could prove Hauptmann had been wrongfully convicted the files might be sealed on me. I couldn't be certain Merola would cooperate in what could eventually become a condemnation of an earlier DA and I wasn't about to test him. Besides, the receipt proving the payroll records had existed and had been in the hands of the district attorney was unsigned. It was either a rough copy of a formal receipt or, more likely, the prosecutor's note to his secretary to type out an official receipt. Somewhere, the original receipt must exist, or at least a carbon copy of it.

I rummaged quickly through the papers in this file folder but could find no receipt. Still, I did find other material of even greater significance. One of these was an affidavit made three days after the extradition hearing by a man named Joseph M. Furcht. He swore that he had been hired as supervisor of construction at the Majestic in September 1931. Shortly after he came on the job, he said, the contractors who were working to complete the building suddenly quit and Furcht was put in charge of construction. His first need was for carpenters to fill the jobs vacated by the contracting firm, so he called upon E. V. Pescia, an employment agent on Sixth Avenue, to supply him with the necessary skilled carpenters.

"On or about the twenty-fifth of February, 1932, it became necessary for me to hire two skilled carpenters," Furcht's affidavit continued. "I thereupon again called Mr. Pescia's office and he sent me Gus Kessenes and Bruno Richard Hauptmann. . . . I hired Gus Kessenes on February 26 and Bruno Richard Hauptmann on February 27, 1932, both of whom were directed by me to report to work on March 1, 1932, at eight o'clock in the morning.

"On March 1, 1932, at 8 A.M. Bruno Richard Hauptmann and Gus Kessenes reported for work at the Majestic apartments and worked through that entire day until five o'clock; subsequent thereto they worked there the second, third, and fourth days of March from 8 to 5 A.M. The work of Bruno Richard Hauptmann was such that he was constantly at the premises of the Majestic apartments from eight to five during that period." Furcht ended by stating that he remembered Hauptmann and Kessenes because he was in such "great need of two carpenters" at that time and he clearly remembered Hauptmann because Hauptmann was "a skilled carpenter who, much against my wishes, I was forced to put on maintenance work, which is ordinary work instead of skilled carpenter work."

There it was—Hauptmann, according to the construction superintendent, had begun work on March first as he had originally told police when he was arrested. There was no doubt any longer in my mind that the Majestic employment records had been doctored because it would not have been possible for Hauptmann to have worked until five, taken the subway home, put the kidnap ladder in his car, and drive out to Hopewell in the time span involved. Even if it were possible, police and prosecutor clearly recognized this as a grave defect in their case, but instead of considering the possibility that Hauptmann was telling the truth, they bent the evidence to fit the guilty verdict they had already reached.

Furcht's affidavit was sworn to three days after the extradition hearing. In the transcript of that hearing I read that Hauptmann's lawyer, Fawcett, had asked several witnesses connected with the Majestic whether they knew where to find Furcht, the superintendent, and each said they had no idea where he was because he had quit the Majestic years before. Plainly, Furcht had read about the hearing in the papers and had come forward. But why, I wondered, didn't his testimony force a reopening of the extradition hearing? What happened to Furcht's testimony?

I found a telephone and again called Lenny Katz at the *Post*. Please pull out the clips on a Joseph Furcht, I asked, in connection with the Lindbergh case—especially clips from October 1934, during Hauptmann's extradition hearing in the Bronx. Lenny said he'd call me back in a little while. I continued going through the file of material concerning the extradition. And I promptly came across a second page of Furcht's affidavit, separated from the first for some reason. His statement continued: "At the time that Bruno Richard Hauptmann and Gus Kessenes were employed under me, during that period, I signed their payroll sheets.

281

"On October 17, 1934 [that is, two days after the extradition hearings] I personally went to the offices of the employment agent, Mr. Pescia, and again examined the records in connection with my request for two carpenters which I made to him in February 1932. His records clearly brought out the fact that Bruno Richard Hauptmann worked for me on March 1, 1932. Annexed hereto is a photostatic copy of the record of E. V. Pescia."

The photostatic copy was missing, probably turned over to the Jersey prosecutor along with the Majestic payroll records. Although I still did not have in my hands the actual document, I was certain it once existed because Furcht would not have attached to his affidavit a document that would have shown him to be mistaken or lying. Yes, all those documents proving Hauptmann had worked on the day of the kidnaping most certainly did exist at one time.

Following this second page of Furcht's affidavit was an affidavit from Pescia, the employment agent, who confirmed that his records showed Hauptmann had come to him for a job in the closing days of February, paid a ten-dollar fee, and was sent to Furcht on Saturday, February 27. Pescia's records also showed that Hauptmann was scheduled to begin working on the following Tuesday, March 1, and that Furcht had so informed Pescia. "If Bruno Richard Hauptmann had not started work on that day I would have been notified by Mr. Furcht, for he was quite in need of a carpenter," Pescia added.

Lenny Katz called and read me a clipping from the New York Times about the "new evidence" provided by Furcht and Pescia. Reporters assigned to the Hauptmann case asked Wilentz and Bronx District Attorney Foley to comment on this evidence and in their comments lies further proof that the payroll records which "didn't exist" were indeed in the hands of the prosecutors. Foley said, according to the Times, that "he believed the employment records showed that Hauptmann had quit work at the Majestic at 1 P.M. on the day of the kidnaping." Wilentz told reporters: "The police know definitely that Hauptmann did not work those hours, nor did he put in a full day of work on March first . . ."

Both Wilentz and Foley admitted in those statements that they knew of some records reflecting Hauptmann's employment on March first. In effect, both admitted the prosecution had not been truthful at the extradition hearing and that it had suppressed the records. Both men, sworn to uphold the majesty of the law, to protect the innocent as a priority over convicting the guilty, not only condoned the lies of Mr. Knapp at the hearing but indulged in further verbal contortions to buttress the official position, that Hauptmann was the killer of the Lindbergh child. Sure, they said, Hauptmann worked on March first, but he quit early so that he could get out to Hopewell. No reporter, not even chief defense attorney Edward Reilly, asked why Hauptmann would call attention to himself by leaving work early on his very first day on the job simply to get out to Hopewell in time to kidnap a baby while the baby's parents and their servants were still awake. Hauptmann did no such thing, I was positive. And I began to understand now that when he wrote his script and got his witnesses to swear Hauptmann did not begin working until March 21, David Wilentz knew it was all a lie, every bit of it.

Lenny read me another newspaper clipping, an article about a second affidavit signed by Furcht in which he "retracted" his first, the alibi for Hauptmann. The story said that after Furcht's original affidavit was made public, Wilentz immediately began to inquire about this disturbing news. And so it was that a few days later Furcht was summoned to the office of District Attorney Foley where, in the presence of prosecutor Anthony M. Hauck and several police officers, Furcht made his second sworn statement. In it he said:

"I am not positive at this time whether or not Hauptmann worked at the Majestic apartments on March 1, 1932. . . . At this time I wish to state that I do not know whether or not Hauptmann worked on March 1, 1932, at the Majestic apartments, as the only information I have is the record of the employment agency. . . .

"The system that we used for keeping a record of the time that the men worked was as follows: There was a bimonthly time book which was kept by me and also by Edward Morton. This book showed the names of the men working, and next to the names the date, and in the evening either Morton or I would mark whether the men worked that day. If I were to refer to this book *as of March 1, 1932, it would be possible for me to determine whether or not the particular workman worked a full day.* . . . I do not know whether or not those records are still available, but they were when I left in December 1932."

According to the receipt I had just found in the district attorney's files, those records were available. And it becomes plain, once more, that prosecutors of two states were distorting their evidence to fit their preconceived certainty that Hauptmann was guilty. For what clearly happened is that Furcht was called into Foley's office and was questioned about the affidavit he had given to Hauptmann's attorney. During that questioning he was no doubt made to concede that his first affidavit had been based on memory and on the employment agency's files. Then, told the only real evidence to support his statement would be the actual employment records—"and they are missing"—he was forced to say he was "not positive" whether Hauptmann had worked on the day of the kidnaping. That is the only logical explanation for this "retraction" that was not quite a retraction.

I found further evidence within the next documents in the folder that someone had tampered with Hauptmann's time sheets in order to prove he had not begun to work until March 21. Those documents were photostatic copies of sheets from that portion of the Majestic's time book which the prosecution did produce in court. The time sheets demonstrate that several prosecution witnesses had lied about Hauptmann's employment.

Hauptmann is said to have begun work on March 21. Several witnesses connected with the Majestic or with Reliance Property Management testified at the extradition hearings or at the later trial that the construction workers were paid at the end of the month for the two-week period ending the last Saturday of the month. In this case, that would have been March 26; one witness, in fact, specifically said he had prepared the payroll checks based on the work the men had performed up to March 26. Hauptmann therefore should have been paid for working six full days his first week on the job.

But he was paid for eleven days. According to all the witnesses against him, Richard Hauptmann was paid for eleven days when, the state claimed, he had only worked six days.

I examined the time sheets more closely now—and there was no notation next to Hauptmann's name, as there was next to the names of several others, that Hauptmann had put in any overtime. Plainly, the extra five days' pay could not be attributed to time and a half.

There was further internal evidence of tampering within the time sheets themselves. It appeared quite likely that whichever police officers altered these time sheets went even further. Those time sheets are divided into columns. The left-hand, widest column lists the names of the employees, seventeen of them including Hauptmann on the sheet in question. To the right are the columns for the dates. When a man was marked present and working on any specific date, a check mark was used, according to several witnesses. A man who was absent on any date would have a zero entered in the column for that date.

Along the line following Hauptmann's name there are, for the sixteenth through the twentieth—dates during which Hauptmann had not yet been employed, according to the prosecution—zeros entered in the columns for each date, indicating Hauptmann did not work on these days. But the zeros are more than zeros. They are heavy blobs of ink, circles with no center holes. Of all the zeros on these pages only those circles proving Hauptmann had not yet begun work are solid black dots. All the others are neat and round, proper doughnut-shaped zeros. Leading me to the inescapable conclusion that those blobs of ink were affixed to the page after Hauptmann's arrest in order to cover up the original check marks that would have shown he was working. That's the only possible explanation, I felt, for the suddenly sloppy penmanship. Taken together with the fact that he'd been paid for eleven days when it was claimed he had worked only six, this evidence, I was certain, proved the time sheets had been altered.

But there was more. Two other men had begun working on the twenty-first. While the column next to Hauptmann's name for the five days before the twenty-first contained these questionable zeros, the columns for those dates next to the other two names had lines drawn through them. Only in Hauptmann's case were "zeros" used to indicate he had not yet been employed. Why? Because a simple line would not have erased the check marks of employment; only a round blob of ink could do that.

Also, something else became clear. I remembered that the timekeeper who testified at the trial, Edward Morton, had sworn Hauptmann was not hired on March first and had been told to return in two weeks "because we only hire on the first and fifteenth." Yet Hauptmann, it was said, was hired on the twenty-first. And in the time sheets two other carpenters, Angus Morrison and William Bowie, are listed as having been hired on the sixth. Clearly, another lie to convince jury and public of Hauptmann's guilt.

Further, the documents I was now studying shed some fresh light on when Hauptmann resigned his job. It was a vital question. Condon had turned the ransom money over to Cemetery John the evening of April second. Hauptmann swore he had worked that day, a Saturday, and then quit, effective immediately. His payroll checks showed he did work for two days in April. The prosecution insisted, and "proved" through the time sheets, that Hauptmann had worked on the first, been absent on the second, then worked the following Monday, the fourth. That "proof" permitted Wilentz to say that Hauptmann, so busy preparing to collect the ransom money and so confident he would get it, did not come to work that Saturday. Once again, however, the "zero" alongside Hauptmann's name for April second is a solid ball of black ink and not one of the perfect circles that appears throughout the time sheets. Also, there is additional evidence that someone tampered with that date of resignation. The last column of each time sheet is headed "Remarks." On Hauptmann's line there is the notation "Out 4/4." That is, it shows he quit April fourth, not on the second as he claimed. But the second "4" bears no resemblance to the first. It quite clearly was written over another number.

Similarly, the last element of Hauptmann's explanation of why he had resigned in early April had obviously been doctored. Hauptmann said he quit when he realized that instead of being paid one hundred dollars a month, which he thought was to be his salary, he was receiving only eighty. Prosecution witnesses said he was lying; he was being paid one hundred dollars. There is, in the time sheet, a column devoted to each man's rate of pay. Every single one of the figures—whether "70" or "90" or "100"—is written very clearly beside each man's name. Except for Hauptmann. There is a small stroke for the numeral "1" and then another of those very strange ink blots that seemed to drop out of the time keeper's pen only when that pen was being used on Hauptmann's line in the ledger. Not only that, but Furcht in his affidavit had said he was forced to assign Hauptmann to "ordinary work, not skilled carpenter work." All the skilled carpenters on the time sheets are recorded as being paid one hundred dollars. Hauptmann, on "ordinary work," must have been paid less.

All those coincidences of leaky pens and the unbelievable discrepancy between the number of days Hauptmann worked and the number of days for which he was paid were simply too much.

Hauptmann, beyond question, had been victimized by police who altered the time sheets to fit their belief in his guilt, by witnesses who went along with the alteration, and, most of all, by David Wilentz, who had conceded to the press that Hauptmann had indeed been employed at the Majestic on March first and then later presented "evidence" to prove he had not begun work until three weeks later.

Was Hauptmann also victimized by his defense attorney, Ed Reilly? I wondered now why Reilly did not point out to the jury all of the discrepancies and alterations I had found, why he did not question Morton, the timekeeper who testified at the trial, more thoroughly and more harshly? Did Reilly feel so certain his noted powers of oratory would seduce the jury into a verdict of acquittal that he neglected to defend his client properly?

And I remembered now that when I was writing out my summary of the trial a couple of weeks earlier I had told myself that if I could find evidence Hauptmann's employment records had been faked I would have the backbone of a case against police and prosecution. Now I had found that evidence. And now I was thoroughly convinced I would find documents to refute, point by point, every piece of evidence used against Hauptmann. I had already, in an afternoon of work, found a document that cast further doubt on the expertise of handwriting experts and documents proving Hauptmann's employment record had been doctored. I knew I would find a great deal more over the following days. But it was now late afternoon in the DA's office and the staff were preparing to leave. I returned the files to Rotker's secretary, Frances Shulman, and said I would be back in the morning. I went down into the street, located a telephone booth, and began calling around town in an attempt to find one man in the New York City police department who might help me locate the police files on the Lindbergh case and perhaps copy at least part of those files for me. Although the district attorney had said I could Xerox anything I found, I didn't want to risk someone's recognizing that a document I was copying might deflate the established wisdom that Hauptmann was guilty. Besides, the police files would probably be even more complete than the DA's.

I located Lieutenant Arthur Scanlon after several calls to police headquarters. Scanlon—which is not his actual name, for obvious reasons—was a young foot patrolman in a Brooklyn precinct when

I was a young reporter assigned to headquarters in that borough. Years before, I had written a story about an arrest he had made and when he was later advanced to detective he insisted the publicity I'd given him had played a large role in his promotion. We kept in touch over the years, but I hadn't seen him since long before leaving the *Post* at the end of 1970.

When Scanlon's voice finally came on the line I asked him to have dinner with me, to meet me at Forlini's in a couple of hours. "I need an enormous favor on a really big story," I said. "For a book, not the newspaper, so it'll be nothing current that could kick back at you."

"You're buying the dinner." A statement, not a question.

"Of course," I said.

"Buying me dinner is a bribe."

"The hell it is. The Scotches you belt down are the bribes."

"Bribe me at seven, Forlini's."

When we were seated a couple of hours later, I told Scanlon I was researching the Lindbergh case. I told him about my conversations with Murray and our visits to New Jersey and my researches in the trial transcript, but I didn't mention my explorations in the Bronx district attorney's files.

"I'm getting to feel pretty certain Hauptmann didn't kidnap the Lindbergh baby," I said, "and now I want to be legally certain. I want to find documentation that'll make even lawyers and police lieutenants say I'm right. I have to get into the department's files on the Hauptmann arrest."

Scanlon smiled. "What you're asking me to do is steal department property so you can prove the department framed this man."

"Just about that," I conceded. "But I don't want you to steal anything 'cause that's a crime. Just photocopy them."

"You're out of your mind. If the stuff hasn't been thrown out there's probably dozens of boxes filled with papers on the Lindbergh case. And you want me to pull them out."

"I'm just asking you to Xerox them."

"*Just* asking! You're really nuts. No way I can do that. It would take me weeks. Everybody in the department would know about it before I got past the first box and I'd be back pounding a beat in Brooklyn. No way."

"There has to be a way. I need those files. I really need them." I was practically begging him by now. And it got through to him.

288

He thought about it for a moment, then said: "I can probably spend a few hours going through the stuff quickly and pull out one or two items at a time and Xerox them. But you have to tell me exactly what you're looking or. If I find something that looks close to what you want, I'll make a copy. But I can't copy everything in the warehouse."

"It's a deal," I said.

"Tell me right now what you're looking for. I'll get over there tonight and spend a couple of hours on it. It's better at night. Fewer people around to ask questions."

I didn't respond immediately because I had to think it through, so we ordered dinner and Scanlon remained quiet for a time while I tried to decide what was most important to me at the moment. I wanted Scanlon to find the missing payroll records for the first two weeks in March 1932, which, I was certain, would be the final proof Hauptmann had been working the day of the kidnaping. Yet I also needed more time to dig further into the DA's files so that I could give Scanlon several things to be looking for simultaneously. But I was afraid that if I asked him to wait a couple of days he might change his mind about helping me. I decided to throw at him everything I'd found so far that had confirmed my original suspicions.

"The most important thing right now," I told him, "is anything that looks like a payroll record for February and March, 1932, especially March first on." He began making notes, ripping a page out of his duty notebook. I explained the significance of the employment record and showed him my copy of the receipt indicating the record existed. "There's probably something around, on DA or department letterhead, that corresponds to this. That's what I need even if you can't locate the actual employment record. Just the fact of its existence proves someone suppressed it and lied about it."

I asked him to look for several other specific items. "Anything involving Dr. John F. Condon and a guy named Sam Perrone is really important," I said. "They both saw the kidnaper—or the extortionist, I don't think they were the same—but they saw this man and they later swore it was Hauptmann. What I need . . ."

"Their original descriptions of the guy," Scanlon interrupted, "because you think they changed their stories."

"Exactly. Perrone I don't trust because he saw the man very briefly at night. And Condon was a Goddamn liar."

289

"What makes you so sure of that?" he asked.

I summed up what I'd discovered so far, how Condon spent a half hour or more examining Hauptmann in the police lineup and couldn't identify him, and how he later explained it away by launching into his nonsense about the distinction between identification and declaration of identification. And Scanlon agreed that the old man had behaved rather peculiarly.

"That's why I have to find the first statements these jokers made to the police," I said. "One other thing, because I don't want to load you down with too much"—Scanlon smiled. I had already overburdened him. I went on—"Hauptmann always insisted he had a lot of money in the stock market because half of it was the money of a man named Isidor Fisch, the guy Hauptmann says he got the ransom money from only he didn't know it was ransom money. Half of it was Fisch's investment, Hauptmann said, and some of it was the profits from their fur speculations—they had a partnership in that too. Hauptmann testified he could prove all of it with letters from Fisch or Fisch's brother, sent from Germany, and most of all from Hauptmann's own account book. He called it a big book, some kind of large ledger, I guess."

"How the hell can I Xerox a large book?" Scanlon asked.

"Just Xerox any part of it dealing with Fisch. But my guess is that the book is over in Jersey. What I'm hoping is that someone, like an accountant, summarized it in a report. Anyway, the police took the letters and the book when they arrested him and the prosecution claimed they never existed. I'm sure the prosecution suppressed that evidence, but it's possible Hauptmann was lying about it."

"Most killers do," Scanlon said.

"You're sounding like a cop."

"And you're sounding like a defense shyster grabbing for anything that'll get your client off. Or any decent lie."

I got a little angry at that one, but the smile on Scanlon's face said, *You know I'm right but you can't admit it.* I thought about it for a moment.

"Did I insult you?" Scanlon asked, salting the wound a bit more.

"Not really, but please pull the knife out. Look, I know I've become too personally involved in the Hauptmann case. But you're right. I shouldn't play defense lawyer until I have solid evidence to back up my case."

290

"Okay," he said. "Now that you're a good reporter again I'll find you that proof. If it exists."

We separated about an hour later, Scanlon promising to drive directly to the warehouse in Brooklyn and search out the Lindbergh file. I told him I'd be staying in the city overnight and gave him a phone number where he could reach me. Call me at any time, I said, no matter how late, because I would be anxious to know whether he'd located anything.

His call came about 3 A.M.

"I hit pay dirt," he said. "One hundred percent pure gold."

"What did you find?" I asked.

"Oh, nothing more than a lot of stuff that shows both Perrone and Condon are liars," he said.

"Anything else?"

"You bastard," he said. "Won't even give me the satisfaction of getting excited."

"At three o'clock in the morning? Hey, I'm really excited, honest. What makes them liars?"

"Well, from what I've copied, Perrone was running around identifying dozens of guys who didn't resemble the extortionist in any way. And Condon—ready for this?—Condon not only gave a different description of the extortionist, but he was tied in with a few guys who could have been the *real* kidnapers."

"You're not kidding me?" I asked, now suddenly awake.

"Absolutely no gag. In an official report, signed by some lieutenant or captain, there's a summary of an investigation of a German family, the Geisslers. They were good suspects. And Condon was linked to them, officially. But detectives couldn't get any kind of solid evidence so they just kept watching these people. Then they bagged Hauptmann and forgot about the Geisslers."

"Where can I meet you?"

"I'm going to bed," he said. "I'll give you the stuff tomorrow."

"You Xeroxed it?"

"No, the machine is broken or was stolen or something," he said. "All I have are my notes. That'll have to do for now. There's something more. I found a carbon of that receipt for the employment records. It shows that the records for February and March did exist, so they were lying about it like you guessed."

"Did you find the records themselves?"

"No. From the looks of the receipt, they went over to New Jersey 'cause the receipt is signed by an Inspector Walsh of some Jersey police department, I think Jersey City.''

"Did you make a copy of that?''

"I told you, there's no copying machine. But I'll go back in a couple of nights and lift it out and get it copied for you. Also, I found another big one. The ledger book, Hauptmann's ledger . . .''

"You *found* the thing?'' I interrupted.

"No, that's probably in Jersey, too, but what I did find is a Justice Department summary of the book, an analysis of the records in the book. From what I can see they show that Hauptmann and Fisch were partners and did put a lot of money into the partnership. Like you said Hauptmann claimed. It's all there, dates that stocks were bought and sold, dates that furs were bought and sold, the whole works.''

"I have to meet you right now,'' I said.

"No way. I'm on duty pretty early tomorrow. Besides, I don't have the receipt and I don't have the summary of the book. I'll go back and get them copied for you.''

We made a date to meet the next afternoon. And the next evening I was studying the notes Scanlon had made from the police files. (Scanlon eventually photocopied all the documents he was able to find in police files.) I started with Perrone, the cab driver who swore Hauptmann had handed him a ransom note on a Bronx street corner and gave him a dollar to deliver it to Condon's home. And as I read, several things about Perrone came through with great clarity: The man who handed Perrone the note vaguely resembled Hauptmann but differed from him in several vital features; Perrone also had an experience that made him suspect more than one extortionist was involved; and Perrone was "identifying" so many men as the extortionist, men who bore no resemblance to Perrone's own first description or to Hauptmann, that even police believed he was mentally disturbed and absolutely unreliable as a witness.

The first official statement taken from Perrone was on May 12, 1932, the day the body of a child was found and identified as Lindbergh's son. Perrone was asked by a New York City detective to tell him precisely how he had described to Dr. Condon the extortionist with the letter, on that night he delivered the letter—that is, he was asked to get on record his recollection of what he said the extortionist looked like on the very night he saw the man. Perrone said the man was "German or Scandinavian, about thirty-five, one hundred seventy to one hundred eighty pounds, blue eyes, brown felt hat, brown double-breasted overcoat." There was no further description, not of the man's coloring, hair, facial structure.

Eight days later Perrone was taken out to Hopewell, to the Lindbergh home, which was still being used as the headquarters for New Jersey investigators. He was again asked to repeat, for the record, precisely what the extortionist looked like. Perrone repeated his story—that the extortionist asked whether he knew the Decatur Avenue address on the envelope and then gave him a dollar to deliver the letter—and once more described the man. He again said he was about thirty-five and German or Scandinavian. But now he added that the man had dark-blond hair and "He had a full face and had heavy eyebrows about the same color as his hair." Hauptmann's face has always been described as, and can be seen in photographs to have been, long and triangular, coming to a point at his chin; "a hatchet shape," most observers wrote. That contradiction makes it likely that Perrone was not handed the note by Hauptmann. Further, Perrone's now adding the man's hair coloring to his description is rather curious, because he said the man was wearing a hat. Hauptmann, like most men in those days, wore his hair trimmed close to his head, and it isn't likely Perrone could have seen the color of his hair. It must be remembered Perrone claimed he got a good look at the extortionist because their conversation took place under a streetlight. But a light some twenty feet above the street would have cast shadows on the face of a man wearing a hat and most certainly would have made his short-cropped hair almost impossible to see.

In this same statement made in Hopewell on May 20, Perrone is asked by police to explain a rather remarkable incident which occurred the day before and which may have been the reason he was driven to Hopewell for questioning. Perrone said that on the afternoon of May 19 he was in an American Legion hall in the Bronx "and there was one man there that looked like" the extortionist. So Perrone engaged the man in conversation "and I found out he lived in New Jersey for three years, he said he was a carpenter, and he also lived in the Bronx for fifteen years." Perrone took the man's name and address under some pretext or other and then promptly went to the Bronx Park police station and told a Lieutenant Dynan "that the man I saw pretty near answers the description of the man that gave me the note." And, the report goes on, Perrone said:

"The man in the American Legion told me he was a Scandinavian and that's why I reported it."

On May 19, 1932, therefore, Perrone believed the extortionist had been Scandinavian.

That Scandinavian carpenter no doubt had nothing to do with the extortion plot, for he immediately sinks out of sight and is never referred to again.

But Perrone, pressing his search for the extortionist, continually identified men who could have had nothing to do with the crime and who bore not the slightest resemblance either to Hauptmann or to the man Perrone had originally described.

For example, an FBI report of July 11, 1934, summarizes another incident involving Perrone. The FBI agent who investigated, Thomas H. Sisk, wrote: "Joseph Perrone, witness in this case, observed a man he believed resembled the kidnaper walking along the street in the upper Bronx. . . . Investigation developed that the man's name was William Chetel, a Russian Jew, whose description in no way fits that of the kidnaper or other suspected persons. Dr. Condon failed to identify Chetel; his handwriting does not compare with the ransom notes."

After that summary at the beginning of his report, Sisk went on to explain that on the previous May 25, less than four months before Hauptmann was arrested and positively identified by Perrone, the cabbie saw the man "he thought gave him the note" at the corner of Mosholu Parkway and Jerome Avenue in the Bronx. Perrone followed the man, who kept turning around and walked into a theater lobby apparently to get away from Perrone and to seek the protection of a policeman standing in the lobby. Perrone followed his suspect. He went up to the policeman, identified himself as a witness in the Lindbergh case, and asked the cop to seize the man and get his identification.

The officer, no doubt overwhelmed, did just that. When Chetel, the suspect, gave his name and address on Giles Place in the Bronx, Perrone told the cop that the address is in a "Communistic neighborhood" and the number of Chetel's apartment house is a building "largely inhabited by Jewish Communists." Chetel began to insist he was not involved in the Lindbergh case with such vehemence that Perrone conceded he "might be" mistaken. His suspect was released.

But, thinking about it over the weekend, Perrone decided he had not been mistaken and he reported his sighting of the suspect to the FBI. He said that Chetel was about thirty-eight years old, five ten and one hundred sixty pounds, and "rather bald." Sisk must have wondered how a rather bald man could be the extortionist when neither Perrone nor Condon had ever mentioned baldness. But he followed through by interviewing Chetel. And Sisk noted that Chetel "in many respects does not fit the descriptions furnished by Perrone and Dr. Condon. . . . Chetel is forty-nine, at least ten years too old, he is a couple of inches too tall, he is too dark. . . ."

Nonetheless, Chetel was taken down to the agent's car, where Perrone was waiting. The two men "were allowed to talk to each other face to face for at least an hour." And Perrone, after an hour with his suspect, admitted there was some doubt in his mind whether Chetel was the extortionist, but also insisted he was "a ringer for him and an awfully good likeness. . . . Perrone said he looked more like the man who gave him the ransom note than anyone he has seen to date. . . ."

There are, in the files made available to me, several other examples of Perrone's identifying men who, upon investigation, were absolutely ruled out by police and FBI agents. In every case, none of Perrone's suspects come near fitting the physical characteristics of Hauptmann. The precise details of each such case are repetitious and I simply skimmed over them. But there was one further document relating to Perrone that I could not ignore because it absolutely destroys Perrone's credibility and makes it obvious he lied when he identified Hauptmann. At the same time, this interview with Perrone makes it even more possible that the "gang" which Condon believed was involved did exist.

The interview was conducted by FBI agent William Seery on March 9, 1934, again months before Hauptmann was arrested. In it, Perrone is asked to relate once more the events of two years earlier, when he was given the ransom note addressed to Condon. Perrone is quoted by Seery as saying that just before he was flagged down by the man with the ransom note he had a rather strange fare in his cab, a man of about thirty-five, medium height and build. This man waved him down at Jerome Avenue, had Perrone drive him just one block, and got out. The fare was only fifteen cents, the meter's minimum. As Perrone began to drive on again to look for another passenger, he had gone less than one block when the man with the ransom note waved him down.

"He says the man was running north on Knox Place," the FBI report continues, "and Perrone can't understand how he knew Perrone was approaching because a building on the southwest corner prevented anyone on Knox from seeing a car" along the intersecting street. Perrone told Seery, according to the agent's report, that "it appeared to him at the time that this strange man must have known that he, Perrone, was approaching this intersection." That is, Perrone was saying the first fare appeared to be in league with the second, the man with the note.

Seery's report doesn't indicate any follow-up investigation of Perrone's story. By this time, after so many wrong identifications by Perrone, investigators probably doubted everything he said. Especially after Perrone, on one occasion, said the extortionist looked somewhat like New Jersey police chief Schwarzkopf. But in this same report by agent Seery there is another statement by Perrone which absolutely damns his identification of Hauptmann. Once more, Perrone gives a description of the note-passing extortionist. He again says the man was German or Scandinavian, about thirty-five, medium height and weight. And, in Seery's words, Perrone said:

"He spoke English correctly but with a slight accent; the accent was not noticeable when the man said 'Decatur' and 'Twentieth Street.' Perrone stated that his reference to this man's accent was rather to the manner in which he emphasized certain words than to the pronunciation of them, his impression being that the man may not have been born in the U.S. but undoubtedly had been here many years."

Hauptmann had been in America only nine years at the time of the kidnaping. Like most immigrants, he lived and worked among people of his own nationality. His accent was so thick, so guttural, that many had difficulty understanding him. But Perrone said, before Hauptmann's arrest, that the man he saw "spoke English correctly" and had such a slight accent that it could be detected only in emphasis placed on certain perhaps unfamiliar words and not on a basic mispronunciation.

Not only was the man's speech as described by Perrone totally at variance with Hauptmann's, but in this statement to the FBI Perrone once again said the extortionist looked like someone other than Hauptmann—this time he picked out photographs of two men with criminal records as resembling Cemetery John and also said that a man whom he was trailing with police "somewhat resembled" the extortionist.

So much for witness Perrone, for the moment. The documents on John F. Condon are even more startling. For Condon was, as Scanlon had said over the phone, linked by the police with at least one member of a group of men and women who were major suspects until Hauptmann's arrest. The portrait of Condon as both a liar and a suspect in the extortion grew very clear over the next several weeks as I continued to search through the Bronx district attorney's files and as Scanlon kept sending me photostatic copies of material from the police files.

15 We must return to Condon's first contact with the extortionist. You'll recall that on the evening of March 9, 1932, after the newspaper story had appeared announcing Condon was willing to act as an intermediary, he received a letter from the extortionist announcing he was acceptable as a "go-between" and enclosing a sealed envelope to be turned over to Lindbergh. Condon testified and later declared in interviews and wrote in his memoirs that he called the Lindbergh home and spoke to someone who asked him to read the first note, addressed to the doctor. After doing so, Condon said, the voice on the other end asked him to open the envelope addressed to Lindbergh and read the note inside. Condon read it aloud and only then began to describe the "secantal circles" which seemed to be a signature. Until he opened that envelope, of course, he knew nothing about the strange overlapping circles that the extortionist signed to most of his letters.

But that was not quite true. Because of a report made by New Jersey state police lieutenant Keaton on May 16, 1932, a few days after the body was found, police began to suspect Condon may have been deeply involved in the extortion plot. The report states that the man who answered the phone at Hopewell when Condon called was Robert Thayer, one of Lindbergh's friends and advisers. Thayer was a partner in a most prestigious New York law firm and was married to an heiress to the Standard Oil millions. He was also an associate of "Wild Bill" Donovan, one of the four colonels directing the show. In his statement to Lieutenant Keaton, Thayer said:

". . . a voice on the telephone stated that he was Doctor John Condon and that he had received a letter addressed to Colonel Lindbergh. . . . I asked Doctor Condon how the letter to *him* was signed. He stated that it was *signed with the sign of the Mafia* [emphasis supplied]. I then asked him to open and read the letter addressed to Colonel Lindbergh."

Thayer quite specifically said he was told the first letter had the "Mafia" symbol, for he asked Condon to open the letter to Lindbergh only after hearing about the symbol. As a matter of fact, the letter to Condon bore no symbol or signature whatsoever. How, then, could Condon have known about a symbol before he was instructed to open the second letter, the one to Lindbergh which did have the symbol? Was it, police wondered, because Condon had advance knowledge of the symbol, even perhaps helped prepare it? Was he a member of the extortion gang?

But it is in other statements Thayer made to police in several interviews that the form and structure of a deliberate design to suppress evidence in order to convict Hauptmann begins to take shape. Although he played a major role in strategy conferences at Hopewell during the first weeks and although he had vital information which would have given jury and public a more accurate picture of the kidnaping, Thayer was never called to testify. All the evidence he could have supplied was filed away and kept from the defense.

Thayer's statements reinforced police suspicions that Condon was a part of the extortion plot, for in these documents is proof that Alan Hynd, the one writer to question the established version of the crime, was accurate when he wrote that the ransom letters with their "secret symbols" had been taken to New York by Mickey Rosner, where they were copied by con men and other criminals.

Thayer was known as a "sportsman," as it was discreetly called by the press in those days, a man who was free with his money at the best speakeasies in Manhattan and who enjoyed rubbing shoulders with underworld characters. It was through Thayer that Rosner, the bootlegger and speakeasy operator, was brought into the case. On the morning of March 2, only hours after it was announced the Lindbergh child had been kidnaped, Thayer went to see Rosner in the central jury court, where Rosner was facing charges of a stock swindle. According to a statement Thayer gave Inspector Walsh of the Jersey City police, Rosner "had professed to know a great deal about the underworld and on various occasions had taken me to underworld hangouts and pointed out various members of different gangs." Thayer asked Rosner to go with him to Hopewell and help Lindbergh get his son back. Rosner accepted the offer.

After making his demand for $2,500 expense money and extracting a promise he would not be followed during his negotiations with the underworld, Rosner asked to see the ransom note left in the nursery. Thayer told Inspector Walsh:

"Mrs. Breckinridge went and got it from someone and brought it to us. Rosner gave it to me and told me to make an exact copy of it, imitating the handwriting as near as possible and also the signature." Thayer said he did so and handed the copy to Rosner. "I have not seen it since the day I gave it to him," he added.

Rosner took the copy of the nursery note to New York City, police reports say; the next day he was in the office of his attorney in downtown New York and in the evening he was seen in conference with Bitz and Spitale, who were appointed his assistants by Rosner. There can be little doubt, and police reports indicate they believe it so, but Rosner most certainly displayed to several men of the underworld that note with the symbols which had supposedly remained secret.

Rosner was present at the Lindbergh home on the morning of March 5, when the second ransom note was delivered. It was dusted for fingerprints by Trooper Kelly and then opened. Thayer continues:

"I read the note over his shoulder and later Captain Lamb came into the room and read it with a magnifying glass. Colonel Lindbergh brought the note into the living room and showed it to Rosner who, the minute he read it said: 'Get me two troopers. I must take this note to town at once.' He left with the note in his pocket. I did not see this note again until about ten days later."

According to police reports, Rosner met Bitz and Spitale in the Cadillac Restaurant at Broadway and Forty-third Street and showed them both notes.

By March 9 at least one of these notes was in such wide circulation that the city editor of the New York *Journal,* in a telegram to

Chief Schwarzkopf complaining of police treatment of the press, had said: "Disposition of newspapers is to print accurate information and only such things as are helpful. Journal has proved this by not making public contents of ransom note which is in our possession."

Governor Hoffman, who gained access to most of the police files and was fed information by a few state troopers who didn't agree with the established wisdom in the case, later wrote: "Photographic copies of the original note were being offered for sale, through sources close to the state police, to newspapers."

The first two ransom notes or very close copies, then, were definitely in circulation by March 9, the day Dr. Condon received his first contact from the extortionist. The possibility that these notes may have been used as the basis for ransom negotiations entirely separate from the crime of kidnaping is a very strong one. And police suspected Condon of being at the center of the plot. As Lieutenant Finn later wrote:

"The feeling grew in many high quarters that the old schoolmaster knew a lot more about the kidnaping than he was letting on. But nobody could do anything about it. He was protected by Colonel Lindbergh's confidence in him."

Charles Lindbergh's testimony at Hauptmann's trial appears rather curious once you realize Thayer had told police he saw Lindbergh personally hand the second note to Rosner and heard the bootlegger shout that he was taking it to New York. During questioning of Lindbergh by defense attorney Reilly, there is this exchange:

> Q. When you contacted Rosner, did you give him a copy of the symbol?
> A. No, I didn't. Now, I don't know whether he had one or not. As a matter of fact, my recollection is that he had seen the symbol.
> Q. He had seen it?
> A. That is my recollection at this time.
> Q. Had the symbol been printed in the papers?
> A. No, not to the best of my knowledge.
> Q. Who had seen it up to that time . . . March the ninth?
> A. Why, members of the New Jersey state police, some of the members of the Jersey City and Newark police. . . .

As I say, my recollection is that Mr. Rosner saw one of these letters.

Yet Lindbergh knew Rosner had physically taken the original of the second note, with its symbol, away from Hopewell. He may honestly have forgotten that event although it is unlikely that after pinning such great hopes on Rosner's ability to effect the safe return of his child he could have erased from his memory Rosner's excitement at seeing the second letter and his demand for troopers to chauffeur him into New York. Especially since Lindbergh professed to have such an elephantine memory he could identify a man by his voice two years after having heard someone shout only two words.

As we shall see in connection with other documents concerning Lindbergh's role in helping convict Hauptmann, it seems probable Lindbergh distorted his trial testimony several times because, perhaps, he so firmly believed in Hauptmann's guilt he could permit no word from his lips to mar the prosecution's case.

Among police and FBI reports are several bearing on Lindbergh's attitude toward Dr. Condon. During the trial Reilly asked Lindbergh a long series of questions suggesting that Condon, who first entered the case because of publicity in a small local paper which drew an unusually prompt reply from the extortionist, may have himself been the "mastermind" of an extortion plot. After about a half hour of trying and failing to get Lindbergh to admit he had not trusted Condon, Reilly asked:

"Did it ever strike you that the mastermind might insert an ad in the paper and answer it himself?"

"I think that is inconceivable from practically any practical standpoint," Lindbergh replied.

However, Lindbergh was even less accurate in that ringing affirmation of his faith in Condon than he was about Rosner's possession of the ransom note. Despite the public stance of Lindbergh and everyone else, he had grave suspicions of Condon from the very beginning. It was never brought out at the trial (of course), but Colonel Breckinridge, the chief adviser out at Hopewell in the first week, drove Condon into the Bronx after the old man had delivered the ransom note and moved into a spare room in Condon's home because Lindbergh insisted Condon must be watched at all times. And more than a year after the ransom was paid, federal agent Hugh Larimer wrote in his report of a meeting between Lindbergh and Justice Department officials:

"Colonel Lindbergh made the remark that were Dr. Condon a younger man he would be immediately suspicious of him, but that in spite of Condon's age there were several little things that raised doubt as to Condon's sincerity." Among them, Larimer wrote, Lindbergh was suspicious because of the very prompt reply from the extortionist to Condon's offer of assistance in the *Home News* and because of Condon's barely believable story that at the age of seventy-one he had vaulted a fence and run after and caught a man half his age. The agent's report continues: "The Colonel was suspicious of Al Reich, who claimed he had observed John jump the fence and run. . . . Lindbergh was not impressed with the arrangement whereby Condon and Al Reich were to make the contact and deliver the money."

Finally, Lindbergh also doubted Condon's "sincerity" according to another report, because of the enormous number of discrepancies in the doctor's accounts of his negotiations with John. The story which disturbed Lindbergh the most, one report states, is that in which Condon said that during his long conversation with John at their first meeting, March 12, John had said:

"Tell Colonel Lindbergh he is wasting his time with those people down South. They are not the right parties. That Curtis knows nothing. The baby is not in Norfolk."

The Norfolk trio—Curtis, the dean, and the admiral—did not come into the case until March 19, a full week after Condon's meeting with John. How, then, Lindbergh and investigators wondered, could John have been aware of Curtis's activities? Was it possible that since Curtis had admitted his story was a fraud and he was a swindler, then Curtis, John, and Condon were part of the same plot?

Although Lindbergh knew about the discrepancies in Condon's stories and mistrusted him from the very beginning, he deliberately hid that fact during his testimony at the trial.

Police suspicion of Condon was heightened enormously after investigation of the "J. J. Faulkner" deposit of almost $3,000 in Lindbergh gold certificates. You'll recall that in the last-minute rush to convert gold notes into regular currency, someone turned in a part of the ransom money at the Federal Reserve Bank in New York, on May 1, 1933, without being noticed. The name and address on the exchange slip were traced to a Jane Faulkner, who had married a German immigrant. Jane's husband and her sister's husband, and other relatives and friends, were suspected by police of having taken part in the extortion and perhaps the kidnaping itself. But after being thoroughly investigated it was determined they had no connection with the case. That, at least, is what the official accounts claimed. Only Alan Hynd had suggested the possibility this group actually was involved in the crime because, he had written, one of them had committed suicide after being questioned repeatedly by police.

The official document that my friend in the police department copied for me told a much different tale. In a summary of the case made for his superiors by the man in charge of the investigation by New York police, Lieutenant James Finn, on January 23, 1934, at least a part of the real story is told in some detail.

Jane Faulkner, the report states, was located because her sister had married a man named Alvin Weigner. Police asked all banks in the area to comb their records to see whether Weigner had a bank account and to report on his current address. A bank near the address given on the "Faulkner" deposit slip reported it was doing business with Weigner. He was now living on North Chadsworth Avenue, Larchmont, a short distance above the Bronx-Westchester county line. A "confidential investigation" was begun at that address, the report continues. And police learned it was the residence of Carl Oswin Geissler, who had married Jane Faulkner. Weigner and his wife, Jane's sister, also lived there.

Geissler's marriage license was obtained by police, as were several other records, and, the report says, "the handwriting of Geissler was compared with that of J. J. Faulkner on the bank deposit slip by Albert D. Osborn and found to be similar." These documents and a few others were then "given to special agent Wilson to be forwarded to the government handwriting expert, Mr. Saunder, Washington, D.C., who had been assigned to the Lindbergh case since the beginning. The following day he notified this department that he compared the handwritings on all these papers and found they were all written by the same person."

Now certain they were zeroing in on a man who had deposited almost $3,000 in Lindbergh gold bills, dozens of police and federal investigators began an intensive investigation. Carl Oswin Geissler, chief suspect because of his handwriting, was found to have

305

two grown children by a previous marriage. His son, Carl D. Geissler, immediately became a suspect along with his father because he customarily did business in a store in which one of the ransom bills spotted by a bank teller had been passed. The clerks in the store, unfortunately, could not remember which customer had given them the bill, and police could get no substantial evidence against young Geissler.

Attention also turned to Geissler's daughter, Phylis, who was married to a man named Henry Liepold. Almost as soon as police began inquiring into her background, Phylis Liepold bought a train ticket to Canada under an assumed name. When investigators learned about it they kept her under surveillance, following her to the border and then searching her for the ransom money before she could cross over. No ransom bills were found.

The Geissler family was now most definitely aware police had them under surveillance. Had they been the Lindbergh kidnap gang or the extortionists, as Finn's report makes clear police suspected, then the search of Phylis Liepold now put them on their guard. The investigation continued. Among other things, police checked telephone records of the Geissler and Liepold households and learned that Henry Liepold had sent a cablegram to a man named Willie Krippendorf, in Munich. The cable urged Willie to take the "cheapest steamer rate possible . . . even third class." That cable had been sent shortly after the search of Phylis Liepold.

Clearly, police felt, Willie was being cautioned against making an ostentatious display of wealth. That probably meant Willie was a member of this gang. Perhaps, it was suggested, he had disposed of the money in Europe.

Willie Krippendorf was now investigated. Immigration Bureau records at Ellis Island disclosed he had originally entered the United States in 1923. He had sailed back to Germany in the spring of 1932, shortly after the ransom had been paid. His description in Immigration files disclosed that in 1932 he was thirty-five years old, was five-eleven and weighed one hundred fifty-five pounds, had gray eyes and blonde hair. In short, his sketchy description was close enough to that originally given by Perrone and Condon to mark Krippendorf as a suspect.

The more police inquired into this family of Germans and their friends, Lieutenant Finn later wrote in a magazine series, the greater became official excitement. Police discovered that when Krippendorf returned to the United States on May 5, 1933, shortly after getting the cabled "warning," he told officials at Ellis Island he was going to live with a friend, Leo Rodel, in Fort Lee, New Jersey. And, quoting Finn's report:

"Investigation revealed that Krippendorf and Leo Rodel were closely associated with Ralph Hacker, Palisade Park, New Jersey, who is a son-in-law of Dr. John F. Condon."

And Condon's son-in-law had been very much involved in the ransom payout. He was at Condon's home through part of the ransom negotiations. When it came time to pay out the ransom it was Ralph who drew up more detailed plans for the wooden box into which the money was to be placed. When Condon wanted a cast made of the extortionist's footprint, left in the soft earth of a freshly dug grave, it was Hacker who made the plaster of paris impression.

As Finn later wrote: "The Lindbergh murder case was getting hot."

It had come full circle—directly back to John Condon. A man identified by two handwriting experts as the man who may have cashed Lindbergh ransom notes was directly connected through relatives and friends with the Lindbergh emissary who had paid out the ransom money.

The circle now seemed to be closing in on this group. Joseph Perrone, the taxi driver, told police that Henry Liepold "bore a marked resemblance" to the fifteen-cent fare who Perrone believed had deliberately taken him to the intersection where John flagged him down. Perrone, according to FBI agent Seery's report of March 9, 1934, claimed to have spotted the man who actually handed him the extortion note while he was watching Geissler's Madison Avenue florist shop from an unmarked police car. The man entered the store and left a few minutes later, Perrone said, but because of the heavy traffic he disappeared before police could follow him. "This man is identical with the man who handed him the ransom note," Seery reported.

Although Perrone was hardly credible by this time, police were convinced they had located the kidnap gang. Willie Krippendorf's description matched John. Liepold looked like John's accomplice. A man who visited Geissler's shop was "identical" to the man who gave Perrone a ransom note. Geissler's handwriting matched the Faulkner deposit slip. And Condon was at least tangentially connected with Krippendorf. All that remained was to find solid evidence linking all of them to the kidnaping and extortion.

Police questioned everyone thoroughly, again and again. They searched for the ransom money, searched for tools that might have been used to make the ladder, even sent an investigator to Germany to trace Krippendorf's movements. And although Dr. Condon conveniently neglected to mention it in his own account of police suspicions against him, they searched his home and his retreat on City Island and dug up the grounds around that shack because they believed he was part of the Geissler gang and might have buried his share of the ransom.

The investigators concentrated most heavily on Liepold because he seemed to be weak and might be expected to break down and confess. In October 1933, after four months of constant harassment by police, Henry Liepold committed suicide. To police and federal agents, his death was an admission of guilt.

But police were unable to force admissions or obtain information from any members of the Geissler family or their friends. They could find nothing in bank accounts, tax records, personal property, or real estate purchases to indicate any of them had suddenly amassed a large amount of money. Then again, police reasoned, the ransom could have been transported to Europe by Willie Krippendorf, or buried almost anywhere in the country. Simply because they lacked proof to positively tie these suspects to the kidnaping didn't mean they were not involved. To the contrary, there was the handwriting evidence and the cryptic telegram that Liepold never explained before he died, and there was the curious relationship between Willie Krippendorf and Condon's son-in-law.

For more than a year dozens of federal agents and New York City and New Jersey detectives were engaged in a frustrating attempt to find proof against the Geissler group. The investigation was still going forward when Hauptmann was arrested in September 1934 and almost $15,000 in Lindbergh gold notes was found in his garage. The moment that money was discovered all other suspects were forgotten in the rush to convict Hauptmann and send him to his death. It appears now, looking through old investigative reports forty years later, that police were so frustrated by Condon and Perrone and their antics, so frustrated by their inability to connect the Geisslers with the crime, that they pounced on Hauptmann with a sense of relief because they could at last mark "closed" the most difficult criminal case any of them had ever worked on.

Lacking further documents about the Geisslers, I turned to a closer examination of what the records disclosed about Condon's identification of Hauptmann, an identification which was one of the foundation stones of the prosecution's case.

Among the police and FBI reports in the files were several bearing on Condon's description of Cemetery John. They are vital because Condon was the one man who claimed to have had a very good look at the extortionist. He had said publicly that at his first meeting with John in Woodlawn Cemetery he had "studied him" for more than an hour and "plied him with questions." At the second meeting, when he turned the ransom money over to the extortionist, Condon claimed he also got a close look at the man's features.

Yet in the days immediately after a child's body was discovered and police took control of the case away from Lindbergh and his advisers, Condon repeatedly told investigators he never actually saw the man's features too clearly.

For example, in a sworn statement given at the Bronx district attorney's office on May 14, 1932, Condon described his conversation with the extortionist in Woodlawn Cemetery and then said:

"He kept his coat lapels, his collar, turned up to cover part of his face . . . holding it up with his left hand. I said, 'What is the good of hiding your face? I am the one that ought to be afraid, not you.' I told him to take down his lapels from his mouth and he said he had a terrible cold. I told him I would get him medicine. He pulled his lapels down from his face *for a second* to cough. . . . He brought his collar down once from his face and coughed and *I got a glimpse of his face, just for a moment.*" [emphasis supplied]

Six days later, again under questioning in the Bronx, Condon was asked whether he could give a description of the man in the cemeteries. He replied: "Yes, allowing for the darkness and holding his coat up. Only once did it come down. He took down his coat for a moment and that was *the first and only time* I got a glimpse of the full face. His hat, fedora, was down over his forehead. . . ." [emphasis supplied]

Rather than studying the man carefully, at one time aided by light from the moon, as Condon later so vociferously claimed, he caught no more than a brief glimpse of the man in the darkness,

309

with a hat pulled over his forehead undoubtedly creating shadows.

In spite of this enormous handicap, Condon did supply police with a very full description of Cemetery John. The descriptions he gave in the first months after his meetings with John, when his memory must have been freshest, are almost completely at variance with his later descriptions, those he gave after Hauptmann began passing ransom money and those he gave during the trial and in his memoirs.

Condon's earliest descriptions of the man in the cemetery were given during his testimony in the Bronx on May 14 and again on May 20, 1932. In those statements he said John was about five foot nine and between one hundred sixty and one hundred sixty-five pounds. "It seemed to me he was about thirty years of age," Condon said. And the doctor testified on both occasions, the extortionist had "wide almond-shaped eyes . . . such as Chinese or Japanese have . . . eyes wide apart." In all his descriptions of the extortionist during those early months of the investigation, Condon also referred repeatedly to John's "hacking cough." In a statement to Inspector Walsh of the Jersey City police on June 2, 1932, Condon said John obviously was dreadfully ill. "The skin was smooth," he said of the extortionist's face, "and it gave me the impression that pulmonary disease had started its inroads into his body. He had a hacking cough." To other investigators he said "John coughed continuously."

In 1932, according to his driver's license application for that year, Hauptmann was five foot ten and weighed one hundred seventy-five pounds. His eyes were not almond-shaped, did not in any way resemble Oriental eyes. He did not have a hacking cough at that time and was not ill with pulmonary disease—police asked that question of everyone they interviewed about Hauptmann after his arrest; several times, in transcripts of Hauptmann's interrogations, he is asked: "Have you ever been sick? Ever had TB? Ever been in a hospital?" Hauptmann replied he'd always been in perfect health except for a few months the summer of 1932 when he had a touch of phlebitis in the leg. Police were excited about that, because John had leaped from a cemetery wall when he saw a guard approach and investigators believed Hauptmann may have hurt his leg in the jump. But two doctors who treated Hauptmann said it had indeed been phlebitis. And when police checked all doctors in the Bronx and Manhattan and all New York City hospitals, trying to find evidence Hauptmann had once had an ailment that caused the "hacking cough," they drew a complete blank.

Police had also asked Condon to describe John's accent and the quality of his voice. Although police summaries of Condon's description say he believed the man was either German or Scandinavian, in all the documents in my possession Condon says repeatedly he was certain John was Scandinavian. When asked by Inspector Walsh, "What makes you think John is a Scandinavian?" Condon replied, "Because he told me—and his accent . . . I figure he is not German." At another time he told Bronx investigators: "The accent was Scandinavian, not German." Like cabbie Perrone, Condon was positive in the months immediately after the ransom was paid that the extortionist was Scandinavian.

As for the voice, Condon repeatedly told police and federal agents that it was "a husky voice." In fact it would appear from the transcript of the police lineup in September 1934, at which Condon failed to identify Hauptmann, that one of the things troubling him so much was Hauptmann's voice. In that transcript is this exchange:

Inspector Lyons: "Would you say he is the man?"
Condon: "I would not say he is the man."
Lyons: "You are not positive?"
Condon: "I am not positive."
Lyons: "Do you recognize the voice?"
Condon: "The voice was husky."

But Hauptmann's voice was high-pitched, almost squeaky. And Condon refused to identify him as Cemetery John.

Condon's actions, both before he went to that lineup at the Greenwich Street police station and immediately after he failed to identify Hauptmann, appeared rather strange even to an FBI agent who firmly believed Hauptmann's guilt. Leon Turrou, a member of the FBI's "Lindbergh Squad" from the beginning, wrote in his book, *Where My Shadow Falls,* published in 1949, that he was assigned to pick Condon up at his home and drive him to the lineup. Turrou wrote:

311

I told him we had a suspect we wanted him to try to identify.

"Who?" he asked. "The kidnaper?"

"I don't know, Doctor. It may be."

"Don't worry, son," Condon said. "If he's the fellow I met, I'll know him. If I live a million years, I'll know him." Then he quizzically tilted his head toward me and whispered: "Now look here, describe this suspect you've got."

That surprised me. "I'm sorry, Doctor. I can't tell you that. The whole point of this is that you pick him out yourself."

"Why? Just tell me why. That's a fool notion," he protested.

On leaving the lineup room, Condon was asked by Turrou why he wouldn't identify Hauptmann. Condon said he was furious at the way the lineup had been conducted, one German among a lot of "bullnecked cops," and incensed at the way Inspector Lyons tried to pressure him into making a positive identification. "I wouldn't identify him for those insolent morons," he told Turrou.

"But *have* you seen him before, Doctor?" Turrou asked.

"No," Condon said. "He is *not* the man. But he looks like his brother."

In his official report, written several weeks later, Turrou said he had spoken to Condon several times since the lineup fiasco and he went on:

Doctor Condon impressed the agent that he had no desire, for some reason, to identify Hauptmann. . . . Several times he asked me that he be permitted to talk to Hauptmann privately for half an hour, following which he would render a definite opinion as to whether Hauptmann is the man known to him as John. . . . He remarked on one occasion that Hauptmann is *not* the man because he appears to be much heavier, different eyes, different hair, etc.

By now I could no longer grow angry, not even with documentary evidence of this official suppression of facts by agents in the field and no doubt by J. Edgar Hoover himself. For the FBI chief kept a close watch on the Hauptmann case and he was, in fact, present at the lineup. Turrou must have told him Condon said the suspect most definitely was not John. But by now I couldn't even bring myself to become angry at J. Edgar, who had made the wrath rise in me so often in the past.

It didn't surprise me to find proof that the only person ever to come close enough to John to shake his hand quite positively and without equivocation ruled out Richard Hauptmann as the extortionist. Condon appears to have been trying to act honestly, ethically. His early descriptions of the extortionist most certainly did not fit Hauptmann in any way, not the physical characteristics, the accent, the pitch and timbre of the voice; even the height and weight were somewhat off for a man like Condon, who claimed to be able to guess such things closely because he had trained many athletes in his day.

Why, I wondered, did Condon change his mind three months later and finally agree to testify against Hauptmann and identify him as the man in the cemeteries?

It seems rather clear that Condon was coerced by police into making that identification. Condon himself had said, on a number of occasions, that he had been mistreated by police, that the police accused him of being a member of an extortion plot. And he had expressed the fear of being indicted in New Jersey, in a statement to the Bronx district attorney when he had said: "I would not like to be indicted in New Jersey by the grand jury for they would choke you for a cherry, in New Jersey." Governor Harold Hoffman later wrote in a magazine series, the unedited typescript of which was photocopied for me, that he had been told by several Jersey state troopers that Condon was threatened with indictment on charges of obstructing justice if he continued to insist Hauptmann was not the man to whom he passed the ransom money. And federal agent Turrou, to whom Condon always insisted Hauptmann was not the man, later wrote: "Whether the doctor's change of heart was prompted by senility or a simple allergy to New York City's policemen is anybody's guess."

The precise reason for Condon's change of heart will now never be known. But once he did agree to go along with the lie, he distorted his testimony so that it would fit the prosecution script perfectly. Every one of Condon's original statements, which would have gravely damaged Wilentz's portrait of Hauptmann as a "lone wolf" kidnaper and killer, was suppressed by the doctor and by the prosecution. The jury was never given any of the statements Con-

313

don had made indicating he believed a gang was involved in the extortion, it never learned about the extortionist's cough, his husky voice, or any details of the descriptions by Condon which would have made it plain Hauptmann had been incorrectly identified. Instead, Condon perjured himself and corrupted the lofty principles about which he always boasted when he identified Hauptmann and claimed he had simply withheld his "declaration" until the proper moment.

In these documents I also found some confirmation of my earlier suspicion that Condon had so readily accepted John as the authentic kidnaper because his ego could not permit him to admit he was perhaps being duped by John. Condon, it will be recalled, said he had showed John the safety pins from the child's crib in an attempt to verify that he was dealing with the kidnaper. He said at the trial and wrote in his book that he had asked John, "Have you ever seen these before?" And John promptly replied that those pins had been used to fasten the child's blankets to his crib. Condon said he was "jubilant, there could be no doubt, now, that I was dealing with the proper person."

However, when Condon testified in the Bronx in May 1932, he swore: "I am here to tell the truth. I spoke to Colonel Lindbergh and asked him if I might take the two safety pins for this reason . . . I had an object in view. I didn't show that to the kidnapers as stated in the papers. I mentioned it many places to attract attention."

As far as can be determined from about a dozen documents I've read in which Condon related his meetings with John, he at no other time mentioned the safety pins after saying he had never shown them to the man in the cemetery. He omitted mention of them in statements to New York and New Jersey police officers and federal agents through the spring and summer of 1932. It appears the first time he told his story about having John identify the pins was at the trial, when the object was to blunt a defense attack as to whether John was actually connected to the kidnaping and murder, or was perhaps party to a separate extortion plot.

One document I was given made it appear even more likely Condon had indeed been dealing with several men. In his earliest statements—and the distinction must be kept in mind because Condon was probably telling the truth as best he knew it in the first months after the body was found and did not begin to tailor his stories to fit police and prosecution theory until much later—in those early statements Condon gave one vital detail about the night he handed John the ransom which he omitted from his later accounts. New Jersey state police chief Schwarzkopf, according to the transcript of a conference on May 18, 1932, attended by all ranking officials of the state police and several federal agencies, described Condon's account to him of the conversation with John moments before he had turned over the ransom money. Condon said he told John he must be informed immediately as to the location of the baby. And, according to Schwarzkopf, "John said, 'I will have to talk to my partners' and he went off to two men standing in the background some distance off. . . ."

Another document indicates quite clearly that Lindbergh himself knew there was more than one man involved in the extortion when he testified at the trial and swore Hauptmann's voice was the voice he had heard the night the ransom was paid. And that document seems to indicate Lindbergh actually *saw* the man—he never testified about that at the trial—and the description he gave of the extortionist was more unlike Hauptmann than even the "balding man" Perrone practically arrested on the street.

The document is undated, unsigned, and is on a flimsy sheet of paper bearing no heading or identification of any kind. However, there can be no doubt it is an FBI document. The sheet has two holes punched into it for mounting in a looseleaf folder and the holes, which are at the top of the sheet, correspond precisely with the holes in similar flimsy sheets used by FBI agents to write other reports which have been copied for me. Most vital in confirming authenticity is that the typeface on this sheet matches in every respect the typeface on a sixty-three-page FBI report on Hauptmann's finances, the summary of the "big book" Hauptmann requested at his trial. Both reports were found by Lieutenant Scanlon in police department file boxes.

This document is a chart of sorts which breaks down into fifteen separate components the descriptions of suspects given by three men—John Condon, Al Reich, who was Condon's friend and acted as his chauffeur, and Charles A. Lindbergh.

The headings at the top of the first two columns are: "Dr. Condon's description of man, possibly lookout, seen at Woodlawn Cemetery" and "Al Reich's description of possible lookout at Woodlawn."

315

The "lookout" at Woodlawn, the scene of Condon's first contact and long conversation with John, was dismissed by the doctor in his testimony and later writings as of no consequence. In his book, Condon had described the stranger in this way:

> Al nudged me. "Do you suppose that could be. . . ?"
> I followed his glance. A man was approaching south on our side of the street. I got out of the car, began walking in his direction. He passed me without a sign, passed Al's parked car. I returned to the cemetery entrance, resumed my vigil. . . . Between the bars of the gate, a man's arm was waving a white handkerchief up and down . . .

And at the trial, when asked about the man who appeared sometime before John began waving his handkerchief, Condon swore, "I saw this man come down there, but I didn't pay any attention or any account to him."

Yet according to documents I found, Condon, Reich, and the police had paid sufficient attention to this man to have called him a "lookout" and an "accomplice." In several statements made to federal agents and police of two states between May 1932 and June 1934, both Condon and Reich stressed that this man's actions made them certain he was working with the kidnapers. Rather than simply walking past them, as Condon stated publicly, the man was standing across the street from the cemetery gates with a handkerchief up to his face as if trying to hide his features. He suddenly dropped the handkerchief—a signal, both Condon and Reich said they thought—and just as suddenly Condon's attention was drawn back to his side of the street by the flutter of a white handkerchief; the man waving it turned out to be John. Condon and Reich both said the presence of the first man was, in their minds, proof that a "gang" was involved in the crime.

So strong was their belief this man was an accomplice that they both claimed to have studied his features, and gave police the rather complete descriptions summarized in the document about a "possible lookout at Woodlawn." Under each of the components of description in this document, Condon described the man as about thirty, five foot seven, one hundred fifty pounds, with an oval face and dark features. The man, according to this chart, was believed by Condon to have been Italian or Hungarian. (At another

316

time, while being interviewed by an FBI agent named Seykora, Condon said the lookout was "apparently a Calabrese Italian, short and swarthy.") Finally, the chart indicates that Condon, asked about the man's "carriage," replied it was "noticeably stooped; held head to left side."

Reich's description, though less complete, agrees with Condon's in every important respect except that Reich said the man's complexion was "healthy, ruddy, not dark as usual with Italian-Americans." But he did agree the man was "Italian-American."

The third column of this chart is rather startling. It indicates that Charles Lindbergh, who claimed to have identified Hauptmann's voice on the basis of two shouted words, actually saw someone at St. Raymond's Cemetery the night the ransom was passed. Lindbergh did not mention this at the trial. It has not been written about by any of the dozens of men and women who churned out books and magazine articles on the case, nor does it appear in any of the newspaper files which I've consulted. A search of the documents in the Bronx district attorney's office and in New York City police files was fruitless. It appears all other mention of this man seen by Lindbergh has been destroyed; in fact, there are no other documents in those files that would indicate he had ever been questioned by police in New York.

That third column is headed: "Col. Lindbergh's Description of Man at St. Raymond's."

Under the heading, Lindbergh is said to have described the man he saw as "not over thirty," with a height and weight corresponding to the description of the accomplice seen by Condon and Reich at the first cemetery. And, like Condon, Lindbergh described the man's complexion as "dark." Along the line for carriage, Lindbergh's description is summarized in this fashion:

"Had pronounced stoop. Walked with an unusual gait described as rolling gait somewhat similar to a sailor's walk and somewhat awkward."

So far as the jury was told, and the public, Lindbergh's sole contact with anyone involved in the kidnaping and extortion was in the two words he heard someone shout at a distance from behind a wall of St. Raymond's Cemetery. He testified at Flemington for several hours and never brought up this man he had seen well enough to have described his complexion, his height and weight, and his peculiar walk. He apparently did not mention the incident in the presence of Harold Nicolson, the biographer of Lindbergh's father-in-law who was living at the Morrow home in Englewood during the period between Hauptmann's arrest and his conviction. To be doubly certain any possible reference had not been edited from Nicolson's published letters, I requested of his son, Nigel, and received from him a copy of all the material which had been edited. There is no reference to the man at the cemetery in the diary entries and letters.

By withholding this information, Lindbergh would seem to have played a more deliberate role in the construction of the obviously false prosecution script making Hauptmann sole kidnaper and extortionist. It doesn't matter whether he knew Condon, Perrone, and police were guilty of lies and distortions whose sole purpose was to send Hauptmann to his death. The fact is that Charles Lindbergh, by going along with the prosecution, was as guilty as every one of the perjurers and the manufacturers of evidence and those on the prosecution staff who must have known the state's case was a lie.

Lacking further documents, it is not clear whether the man Lindbergh saw at St. Raymond's was John, who received the ransom, or the "lookout." If it was John then it is further proof Hauptmann could not have been the extortionist and Lindbergh knew it. Hauptmann was taller and heavier than the man Lindbergh saw and was very fair-skinned. Most vital, his carriage was straight and erect and he walked with what most writers called "a German military bearing."

But even if the man Lindbergh described was but an accomplice, then Lindbergh lied, morally if not legally, when he left the world with the belief that he'd only heard a voice in the darkness. And it begins to appear that Lindbergh also was untruthful about his identification of Hauptmann's voice.

The fact that such an identification of an unfamiliar voice heard after more than two years filled the editors of the *New York Law Journal* with disbelief has already been pointed out. But Lindbergh's voice identification can be challenged on more substantive grounds. A more careful exploration of the circumstances surrounding the identification that had so compelling an effect on the jury makes one begin to question whether Lindbergh distorted everything to which he swore at Flemington.

According to Bronx District Attorney Foley, as quoted in the

New York Times and other newspapers, Lindbergh went to Foley's office on the morning of September 27, 1934, wearing a cap and dark glasses. He entered through a private door to evade reporters and photographers. He took a seat in Foley's large private office in the middle of a group of investigators, surrounded by others so he would not attract notice. Hauptmann was led into the room at 9:50 A.M. and was kept there for about ten minutes while Lindbergh "observed him in different poses and attitudes." Hauptmann was first told to sit in a chair placed in the center of the room. He was questioned by Foley and others, some of the questions having been suggested by Lindbergh. Hauptmann was ordered to walk back and forth across the room several times, while more questions were asked and he responded to them. Lindbergh never spoke.

Lindbergh, it is obvious, had come to Foley's office to answer one or two questions. Was Hauptmann the man with the "rolling gait similar to a sailor's walk" who was at the cemetery the night the ransom was paid? Was Hauptmann's voice like the voice of John, shouting, "Hey, Doctor!"?

After Lindbergh left the building and was driven away, Foley told startled reporters about the brief visit. The district attorney announced:

"Colonel Lindbergh was here this morning in my office by arrangement, and at his own request he was confronted with the prisoner. He was in the room with Hauptmann for about ten minutes, and the prisoner was unaware of the colonel's presence. The purpose of the meeting and its outcome will not be disclosed by anyone concerned."

Reporters asked whether Lindbergh had identified the prisoner, but the district attorney refused to comment further. Some of the others who were present, among them members of Foley's staff, the New Jersey state police, and the Bronx sheriff's office, provided details of the so-called confrontation between Lindbergh and Hauptmann and confirmed the obvious—Lindbergh had come in an attempt to identify Hauptmann.

One official who had been in that room, Charles F. Brodie, the chief clerk of the district attorney's office, told reporters Lindbergh had made no comment of any kind while Hauptmann was on display and Lindbergh "didn't say anything after the confrontation."

There was silence for more than a week, a strange silence. Had

Lindbergh identified Hauptmann's voice at that time it seems likely the district attorney would have immediately announced it. That announcement did not come until October eighth, almost two weeks later, when Colonel Schwarzkopf told reporters in Trenton that Hauptmann's voice had been identified by Lindbergh. Schwarzkopf would say no more about the identification. The next day, District Attorney Foley confirmed reporters' speculation that the identification had been made when Lindbergh viewed and listened to Hauptmann on September 27. Foley said he had asked Hauptmann to say the words, "Hey, Doctor," in "different degrees of loudness and at various distances from Colonel Lindbergh." He added that Hauptmann had not hesitated to do so.

Lindbergh had sat silent, his face expressionless, as he watched and listened to Hauptmann, the district attorney said. After the prisoner was taken out of the room, Lindbergh said he was certain that was the man who had shouted to attract Dr. Condon's attention.

That's what Foley now said. And yet within minutes after Lindbergh had left the building that day, Chief Clerk Brodie had told reporters Lindbergh hadn't said a word after the confrontation. Reporters didn't question this curious contradiction. They did, however, ask Foley why he had delayed so long in announcing this identification which so damaged Hauptmann's chance of escaping with his life. Foley replied that he had been waiting for state police chief Schwarzkopf to make the announcement; an act of courtesy, that's all. So far as I can determine from newspaper files, Schwarzkopf was never asked about the delay.

That delay is extremely suspect. It is, in fact, difficult to believe Foley's explanation for waiting almost two weeks to make so important an announcement. The evening before Lindbergh sat in Foley's office to view Hauptmann, the Bronx grand jury had indicted Hauptmann on extortion charges. Foley was moving swiftly to bring Hauptmann to trial for extortion, asking the court to "set an early trial date." This was a Bronx case at the time, Foley's case. He had been announcing in the press all the evidence that was slowly being "found" to prove Hauptmann had been the extortionist and he was systematically denigrating everything that turned up in Hauptmann's favor, including the "Fisch story." And he was, as I discovered after going through his files, suppressing all materi-

320

sidor Fisch, whom police originally called an "accomplice," paddling Hauptmann's canoe t Hunter's Island in 1933. Gerta Henkel is at the helm. Mrs. Victor Schussler and her aughter, Violet, neighbors of the Hauptmanns, are seated in the center. *(Author's ollection, print by Gaumer)*

Isidor Fisch (r.) and Henry Uhlig sit in the lounge of the liner *Manhattan* before it departed for Germany. A few nights before sailing, Hauptmann claimed, Fisch left him a shoe box filled with Lindbergh ransom money. *(Author's collection, print by Gaumer)*

One of the envelopes that contained a letter from Fisch's brother to Hauptmann. On the reverse, in Hauptmann's handwriting, are notes he made while investigating Fisch's finances, notes that made him understand he'd been swindled by his partner. The letters were suppressed because they would have aided Hauptmann's defense. *(Author's collection, print by Gaumer)*

NAMES	1	3	4	5	6	7	8	9	10	11	13	14	15	Total Time	Rate	Amount	Remarks
JAMES HACKETT	✓	✓		✓	✓	✓		✓	✓	✓	✓	✓	✓				
DAN DUNNE	✓	✓		✓	✓	✓		✓	✓	✓	✓	✓	✓				
Jos CUEVAS'	✓	✓	✓	✓	✓	✓		✓	✓	✓	✓	✓	✓				
William RICHTER	✓	✓	✓	✓	✓	✓		✓	✓	✓	✓	✓	✓				
LAWRENCE FARLEY	✓	✓	✓	✓	✓	✓		✓	✓	✓	✓	✓					
JEREMIAH SMITH																	
CONSTRUCTION																	
JM FURCHT	✓	✓							✓	✓	✓	✓					
CARPENTERS																	
JAMES DAVIE	✓	✓	✓	✓	✓	✓		✓	✓								
ROBERT LOCKHEAD	✓	✓	✓	✓	✓	✓		✓	✓	✓	✓	✓					
ALLEN WILKINSON	✓	✓	✓	✓	✓	✓		✓	✓	✓	✓	✓					
GUSTAV KASSENS	✓	✓	✓	✓	✓			✓	✓	✓	✓	✓					
Jos. BURNSIDES	✓	✓	✓	✓	✓	✓		✓	✓	✓	✓						
Richard HAUPTMANN	●	●		✓													out 4/4
ALEX HAMILTON				✓				✓	✓	✓	✓	✓					
John FORDYCE				✓				✓	✓	✓	✓						
Handy MEN																	
JAMES CROSBY	●	✓	✓	✓	✓	✓		✓	✓	✓	✓						
JAMES CULLEN	●	✓	✓	✓	✓	✓		✓	✓	✓	✓						

The employment time records that destroyed Hauptmann's alibi. Note heavy blobs of ink next to Hauptmann's name, supposedly representing zeroes, and the obvious alteration in the "out 4/4" under "Remarks"—evidence the time sheets were tampered with. (*Author's collection, print by Gaumer*)

NAMES	1	2	3	4	5	6	7	8	9	10	11	12	13	14	15	Total Time	Rate	Amount	Remarks
JAMES HACKETT	✓	✓	✓	✓	●	●	✓		✓	✓	✓	✓	✓	✓			9c		
DAN DUNNE	●	●	✓	✓	●	●	✓		●	●	✓	✓	✓	✓			90		
Jos. CUEVAS	●	✓	●	✓	✓	✓	✓		✓	✓	✓	✓	✓				70		
William RICHTER	✓	✓	✓	✓	✓	✓	✓		✓	✓	✓	✓	✓	✓			90		
LAWRENCE FARLEY	●	✓	●	✓	✓	✓	✓		✓	✓	✓	✓	✓	✓			90		
William BURNS	●	✓	●	✓	✓	✓	✓		✓	✓	✓	✓	✓						
J.M. FURCHT	✓	✓	✓	✓	✓	✓	✓		●	✓	✓	✓	✓				20		
CONSTRUCTION																			
CARPENTERS																			
JAMES DAVIE	✓	✓	✓	✓	✓	●			✓	✓	✓	✓					115	3/18/bks	3/13-16
ROBERT LOCKHEAD	✓	✓	✓	✓	✓	✓	✓		✓	✓	✓	✓	✓				100	3/18/bks	3/13-16
ALLEN WILKINSON	✓	✓	●	✓	✓	●			✓	✓	✓	✓	✓				100	3/18/bks	3/13-16
GUSTAV KASSENS	●	●	✓	✓	●				✓	✓	✓	✓	✓	✓			100	3/18/bks	3/13-16
Jos. BURNSIDES	✓	✓	●	✓	✓	✓			✓	✓	✓	✓	✓				100	3/18/bks	3/13-16
Richard HAUPTMANN	●	●	●	●	✓	✓			✓	✓	✓	●					90		
Handy Men																			
JAMES CROSBY		●	✓	●	✓	✓	✓		✓	✓	✓	✓					20		—
JAMES CULLEN	●	✓	✓	✓	✓	✓	✓		✓	✓	✓	✓					20	3/18/bks	3/13-24
DAVID DAVIE	●	✓	✓	✓	✓	✓	✓		✓	✓	✓	✓					85	3/18/bks	3/13
John R. CORIR	●	✓	✓	✓	✓	✓	✓		✓	✓	✓	✓					90	3/18/bks	3/13

The receipt, signed by Jersey City
police official, proving the payroll
record for the first two weeks in March
did actually exist. In denying
Hauptmann access to those records,
police and prosecution destroyed his
alibi for March 1, 1932, the day of the
kidnaping. *(Author's collection, print
by Gaumer)*

The FBI report on a "possible
lookout" and the man Lindbergh saw
the night the ransom was paid.
Lindbergh suppressed his knowledge
that more than one man was involved,
helping police hide evidence that would
have aided Hauptmann. *(Author's
collection, print by Gaumer)*

Rail
No. 16

oard from
ttic floor

Board from
ttic floor

Rail
No. 16

Koehler's photos "proving" that Rail 16, an upright from kidnap ladder, was cut from Hauptmann's attic. Top: To show similarity in grains, Koehler laid Rail 16 on attic floorboard as if they'd been one board cut in two, then hinged back. Bottom: Photo shows Koehler distorted truth. He superimposed photo of end of Rail 16 over end of attic floorboard to show they were once connected. But the grains appear to match only because Koehler *lifted* Rail 16 a fraction of an inch. His rationale was that one surface of Rail 16 had been planed by that fraction. Even so, it should not jut out so far above floorboard in Koehler's composite. That it does, other wood experts say, indicates Koehler was fabricating evidence. *(Author's collection, print by Gaumer)*

Paul H. Wendel, after his arrest as killer of Lindbergh child. Days before Hauptmann was to be executed, Wendel signed a confession that he alone was the kidnaper, but later he said he had been coerced. *(Wide World)*

UNITED STATES BUREAU OF INVESTIGATION

Form No. 1

THIS CASE ORIGINATED AT NEW YORK CITY   NY FILE NO. 62-3057   IW

REPORT MADE AT:	DATE WHEN MADE:	PERIOD FOR WHICH MADE:	REPORT MADE BY:
NEW YORK CITY	10/18/34	9/20-10/6/34	J. A. GENAU

TITLE:	CHARACTER OF CASE:
BRUNO RICHARD HAUPTMANN with aliases	KIDNAPING AND MURDER OF CHARLES A. LINDBERGH, JR.

SYNOPSIS of FACTS:

ACCOUNTING REPORT

DETAILS:

Investigation discloses Richard Hauptmann had account with
Carleton & Mott, brokers, from 11-1-29 to 5-25-32; $622.75
cash deposited therein; net loss from transactions $1,543.59.
Richard Hauptmann had account with Steiner, Rouse, & Co.
from 8-8-32 to date; $3162.50 cash deposited therein; net
profit from transactions $413.26; on 9-24-34 account had
credit balance of $111.21 and 100 shares stock worth $775.
Anna Schoeffler had account with Steiner, Rouse, & Co.
from 3-27-33 to date; $13,157.50 cash deposited therein;
net loss from transactions $5,689.94; on 9-24-34 account
had credit balance of $1,242.41 and 400 shares of stock
worth $3775. Anna Schoeffler had commodity account with
Steiner, Rouse, & Co. from 10-9-33 to 2-27-34; no cash
deposited, but funds transferred to and from brokerage
account; net loss from transactions $188.60. Richard Hauptmann
had account with E. A. Pierce & Co. from 1-18-34 to
7-24-34; no cash deposits made, but stocks and funds transferred to and from other brokerage accounts; net profit
from transactions $602.50. Net result stock market trans-
actions of Hauptmann and wife: Net loss $6369.29. Ernest
Schoeffler had account with E. A. Pierce & Co. from 1-26-34
to date; $1225 cash deposits; on 9-24-34 account had debit
balance of $2.67 and had 50 shares of stock worth $400.
Hauptmann and wife had several savings accounts in Central
Savings Bank; $7,085.50 cash deposited therein; on 9-24-34
had credit balance of $2578. Hauptmann had savings account
in Mount Vernon Trust Co. from 6-1-32 to 8-18-34; $1787.75

DO NOT WRITE IN THESE SPACES

APPROVED AND FORWARDED		SPECIAL AGENT IN CHARGE		RECORDED AND INDEXED
				CHECKED OFF:
COPIES OF THIS REPORT FURNISHED TO:		UNITED STATES		JACKETED:
4 - Division				
5 - New York		BUREAU OF INVESTIGATION ROUTED TO: FILE		

First page of suppressed FBI report. Note in eight and ninth lines from bottom the summary of Hauptmann's profits and losses in the market. In five years he lost less than $6,000, not the "enormous sums" the prosecution cited as motive for kidnaping. *(Author's collection, print by Gaumer)*

62-3057

A summary of these entries indicates net purchases and
profit as follows:

1933		Bought	Sold	Profit
May 5		1680.00	2600.00	920.00
26		2798.00	3600.00	802.00
"		3085.00	4000.00	915.00
July 15		5000.00	6900.00	1900.00
Aug 8	1600 @ 5.50	8800.00	10400.00	1600.00
	400 @ 5.50	2200.00	-	-
Oct.24		3500.00	4000.00	500.00
Nov 3		21900.00	-	-
		48963.00	31500.00	6637.00

Total Sales	$31,500.00
Purchases 48,963.00	
Unsold 24,100.00	24,863.00
Profit on Sales	$ 6,637.00

It will be noted that the value of the net purchases, plus
a recorded payment of $2,080.00 to Fisch, equals the sum of $19,543.00.

Total Purchases $48,963.00	
Total Sales 31,500.00	
Net Purchases 17,463.00	
Cash to Fisch 2,080.00	$ 19,543.00

From the foregoing it will be noted that from the indicated
purchase of 2,000 Hudson Seal furs purchased on August 8, 1933, only
1,600 are recorded as having been sold on November 4, 1933, so that it
would appear that 400 of these furs had not been sold. Similarly, it
appears that the entire purchase of furs on November 3, 1933 ($21,900.)
had not been disposed of by sale.

It will also be observed that the first three entries
indicate that "Richard" had a one-half interest in the transactions

- 38 -

A page from the FBI report. Here an accountant summarizes Hauptmann's entries in his ledger concerning his fur speculations with Fisch. That ledger was suppressed so that Wilentz could call Hauptmann's alibi "the Fisch story." *(Author's collection, print by Gaumer)*

Ellis Parker, the detective who believed Hauptmann had been framed and who was certain Wendel was indeed the kidnap and extortionist. *(UPI Photo)*

Parker with his son (l.) and his secretary, Anna Bading, arriving at Newark federal court in 1937. The Parkers were convicted on charges of kidnaping Wendel and sentenced to prison. *(Wide World)*

al that could have helped Hauptmann. Like almost all prosecutors in the thirties, Foley was trying Hauptmann in the newspapers.

For Foley to have deferred to Schwarzkopf to make the announcement of Lindbergh's identification would have been politically naive for an elected official, as Foley was, and it would have been out of character for the man.

More likely, Lindbergh himself hesitated in making the identification because he was not certain. Only the day before viewing Hauptmann for the first time, Lindbergh is said to have told the Bronx grand jury that he could not identify any man's voice after so much time had passed. Yet the very next morning he did make such an identification, as Foley would claim more than two weeks later, despite the comment by one official who had been there that Lindbergh said nothing at the time.

Turn now to the diary of Harold Nicolson, who was a guest in the home of Anne Lindbergh's mother, where the Lindberghs also were living at the time. In his entry for October *ninth,* Nicolson wrote:

"Yesterday Hauptmann was identified by Lindbergh as possessing the voice he had heard calling in the cemetery. Yet this dramatic event did not record itself upon the life here. Lindbergh was at breakfast as usual and thereafter helped me to unload my Leica camera. . . ."

The identification, then, was not made on September 27 but more than a week later. For more than a week, Lindbergh was apparently uncertain. For more than a week he must have thought about that voice; he must have considered whether it was a fair test to require a man to repeat the words that had been shouted out in the open air, from about two hundred feet away, in a room no more than thirty feet in either direction, heavily carpeted and filled with furniture and a dozen men.

During that week he was, according to newspaper reports, conferring with police and prosecutors. Foley himself, in confirming the identification and adding details to Schwarzkopf's brief announcement, said Lindbergh had based his decision "on a lot of other evidence besides the prisoner's voice." That implies quite strongly that officials laid out before Lindbergh the evidence they had amassed against Hauptmann in order to persuade him to identify their prisoner. If so, then the identification is valueless and

Lindbergh, a logical and intelligent man, must have known it. Either the voice he had heard was Hauptmann's or it was not—and no other evidence, whether handwriting, eyewitness identification by Perrone or anyone else, or the so-called closet board with Condon's phone number, should have played a role in his decision.

I have been unable to find any documents relating to Lindbergh's visits to the Bronx, with the exception of the report about the "lookout" Condon and Reich saw and the man—lookout or extortionist—seen by Lindbergh. All other material on Lindbergh seems to have been removed from the files to which I had access.

Still, it appears highly likely from the reporters' accounts of events surrounding Lindbergh's identification and from Nicolson's diary, that Lindbergh's identification of Hauptmann is tainted well beyond the legal questions raised by the *Law Journal* editors. That taint, taken together with Lindbergh's suppression of what he had seen the night the ransom was paid; with Thayer's statement that Lindbergh knew at least one of the ransom notes had been taken away by Mickey Rosner, while Lindbergh testified he thought Rosner simply "saw" the notes and their symbols; with his testimony that he trusted Condon when he in fact was suspicious of him; with Nicolson's account of how Lindbergh recreated the evidence against Hauptmann for his wife in order to assure her that justice had been done—all of this makes it quite possible Charles Lindbergh was a willing participant in the wrongful execution of Richard Hauptmann.

And I wondered why. Could it have been that his wife was in such fragile emotional condition he felt it necessary to close out this case and this tormenting period in their lives, even if it meant convicting a man who was probably innocent?

16

That Hauptmann's execution was "wrongful" becomes much more likely when other documents are examined, for it grows even clearer that each of the six eyewitnesses lied, or, to be absolutely fair, were mistaken when they identified Hauptmann. Condon, we have seen, did lie again and again. Perrone probably believed Hauptmann was the extortionist because Perrone was so obsessed with his role in the case and his desire to find the kidnaper that he behaved almost dementedly; "a screwball," Lieutenant Finn called him in one report. But Perrone also committed perjury in his testimony, at least once so far as I can determine; and a man capable of lying once is capable of lying in his every statement. The lie was designed to make his identification of Hauptmann more credible. Asked to describe the lineup from which he picked out the defendant, Perrone said it was composed of six men in civilian clothing. But a transcript of that lineup shows Hauptmann was flanked by only two men, both of them Irish and one of them actually wearing his police uniform. The police, after their shock at Condon's inability to identify Hauptmann, were not about to take any chances with the unreliable Perrone so they stacked the lineup for him.

The testimony of the other four eyewitnesses who identified Hauptmann is similarly demolished by official documents.

First, Mrs. Cecile Barr, the easiest of the lot for hardly anyone except Wilentz and the jury, perhaps, seemed to believe her story:

323

that Hauptmann had thrown a strangely folded ransom bill at her to buy a movie ticket at a theater miles from his home the night of his thirty-fourth birthday. Her identification of Hauptmann as the man passing a gold note in November 1933 was vital because it permitted Wilentz to say Hauptmann had lied when he claimed he hadn't found the ransom money until late the following summer. Mrs. Barr said she was able to identify Hauptmann because he had been so rude to her, practically tossing the folded bill at her. Certainly, in the dozen words she said Hauptmann had spoken, she would have heard his thick accent. And yet, in a report by Lieutenant Finn, who questioned her, she is quoted as saying the customer was "apparently an American."

To prove Hauptmann was more than just an extortionist, which is really all that Condon, Perrone, and Barr were able to do with their testimony about events in New York City, the prosecution had to prove Hauptmann's presence near the Lindbergh home on March 1, 1932. To do so, Wilentz called three other witnesses whose veracity is also open to question, as the documents in my possession demonstrate.

Charles B. Rossiter, for one. He was the salesman who swore he saw Hauptmann near the Princeton airport on the Saturday night before the kidnaping, when he noticed a stalled car and stopped to offer assistance. "I stood there and looked the man over pretty well," he had testified, and he was certain that man was Hauptmann.

As it turns out, however, Rossiter was a thief who had been dismissed from several jobs for stealing company funds; the last time he was fired was shortly before he called New Jersey state police to report he'd seen Hauptmann's photo in the newspapers two days after his arrest and said "this man looks very much like the man I saw in front of the airport." He was rushed to state police headquarters, where he gave a statement describing the events near Princeton airport just prior to the kidnaping. He was then shown several photographs of Hauptmann, but couldn't identify them, according to Detective Bornmann's report. Rossiter quickly added, however, that the man in the newspaper photo "bears a striking resemblance."

He was then taken to New York for a personal look at Hauptmann. He immediately identified him. Later, he was questioned in the Bronx district attorney's office about what he had seen the night he offered "Hauptmann" assistance. Rossiter was asked to describe the man he had seen and the description fits Hauptmann rather well—not too surprising, since he'd just viewed Hauptmann. He was asked: "What did the car look like?" And he replied:

"It was a sedan very much resembling a Buick, but the rear of cars all look alike. It had New York license tags. I looked on the taillight for the name of the car but there was none there. There was a tire on the back and a three-prong tire rack to hold the tire."

Hauptmann's car, in fact, was a Dodge, purchased the year before the kidnaping and still owned by him when he was arrested. On the back of the car, at the top of the frame holding the license plate, was a large and clear name tag identifying it as a Dodge. Further, the car never had a three-prong tire carrier on the rear. The spare tire was carried in a well in the front left fender. On the back of Hauptmann's car was a wooden trunk he'd made himself for his trip to California in 1931 with his wife and his best friend.

Another witness who placed Hauptmann in New Jersey around the time of the kidnaping was Amandus Hochmuth, the eighty-seven-year-old man who had testified that around noon of the day the child was kidnaped he had seen Hauptmann driving a car near the Lindbergh estate; there was a three-section ladder in the car. Alan Hynd had claimed Hochmuth was almost blind in 1932.

I found verification of Hynd's statement among the documents given me. Amandus Hochmuth, client #14106 in the Division of Old Age Security, Department of Public Welfare, New York City, had claimed he lived in New York and had given the addresses 595 East 134th Street and 370 Willis Avenue, both in the Bronx, in order to collect public funds while he apparently was actually living at Hopewell. It is even possible that he was in the Bronx the day of the kidnaping, but too many years have passed to determine that.

In these copies from Hochmuth's files are two items under "health." On June 29, 1932, four months after he claimed he saw Hauptmann, an investigator, Edward Carey, reported: "Health is very poor, applicant partly blind, suffering from a complication of diseases." And on August 4, 1932, another investigator, Joseph McGovern, noted in Hochmuth's file: "Frail, failing eyesight due to cataracts." Hynd had been accurate; Hochmuth was nearly blind.

Governor Hoffman, responsible for determining who should collect the reward offered by the state for the conviction of the kidnapers, took advantage of the opportunity and questioned several of the witnesses long after Hauptmann was executed. He had Amandus Hochmuth brought to his office on December 15, 1937. Hochmuth sat in a chair about ten feet from a file cabinet on top of which was an eighteen-inch-tall silver cup filled with flowers. The old man was asked to identify the object. He said it was a woman wearing a hat. Then, realizing he'd given the wrong answer because of the reactions of the governor, a criminologist who was also present, and several of Hoffman's aides, Hochmuth said it was a bowl of fruit "sitting on a piece of furniture."

Hoffman and his aides then began to question the old man rather severely, making it plain they thought he had lied at the trial. Hochmuth could not remember why he waited until two months after Hauptmann's arrest to come forward with his story and he could no longer remember which of two versions of his story was correct: that Hauptmann's car had "almost" gone into a ditch, as he testified, or that it actually "slid into a ditch," as he told state trooper W. O. Sawyer, the first investigator to interview the old man. Now certain he was not believed and afraid he would not share in the reward, Hochmuth launched into a rather fantastic story.

"Well," he said, "when the baby was killed, that was on March first, and before that I saw a fellow hanging on the bridge there—this is the first time I have mentioned it. He was hanging on the bridge, and we have a good many Germans coming to the neighborhood, and I said, 'Are you looking for a job?' And I didn't get a satisfactory answer but I saw he was a German and I spoke German to him and we had quite a talk. I said, 'I am from Hamburg,' and he said he came from Saxony. I said, 'What is your name?' and he said, 'Hauptmann.'"

As Richard Hauptmann had said about Hochmuth, *"Der Alte ist verrückt* ("The old man is crazy"). Hochmuth, almost blind on the day of the kidnaping, lying about his place of residence in order to cheat a New York City welfare agency of a few dollars a week, was so anxious to share in the reward, he tried to convince the governor that Hauptmann, slinking around Hopewell planning this terrible crime against the only child of the world's hero, told a stranger his name and place of birth.

The final self-styled eyewitness at the trial was Millard Whited.

He had sworn he saw Hauptmann twice near Lindbergh's home, once about ten days before the kidnaping when he saw the man stepping out of the underbrush "and wondered why and where he came from," and several days later standing at a country crossroads.

Under cross-examination Whited claimed he had first told his story to several state troopers who, accompanied by Lindbergh, were waking up neighbors around dawn of March second, asking whether they had seen anything suspicious. He was certain he had been interviewed by the policemen for more than fifteen minutes, he swore, and had told them in great detail about his encounter with the stranger he was later to identify as Hauptmann.

Official documents reveal another story, however. In his report about that morning state police corporal Joseph Wolf wrote: "I was later detailed by Lieutenant Keaton to accompany himself, Sergeant Haussling, Detective Horn, and Colonel Lindbergh in an attempt to secure information from nearby neighbors. No definite information was secured and we returned without success in finding any clue or securing any information from persons interviewed regarding suspicious cars or persons having been noticed in this section at any time previous to the time crime was committed."

And in another report, dated April 26, 1932, when police were requestioning all residents of the Sourland Mountains two months after the crime, Whited is quoted as saying he "didn't see anything out there" in the weeks and hours before the kidnaping.

Sergeant Sam Leon of the state police and Detective Robert Coar of Newark, questioning Whited, asked:

"Have you noticed any persons walking through the woods in the vicinity of the Lindbergh home before March 1, 1932, that acted in a suspicious manner?"

"No, I have not," Whited said.

"Is there any information that you can give that would assist us in this investigation or help the police recover the Lindbergh child?"

"No," Whited said.

After Hauptmann was executed, Governor Hoffman looked more closely at the serious discrepancies between Whited's first statements to police and his later ones in which he suddenly remembered he had seen Hauptmann. The governor questioned Detective William Horn about the interview with Whited some eight hours after the kidnaping. And Horn said he clearly recalled talking to Whited that morning and was certain the witness "at no time mentioned seeing a suspicious person in the vicinity of the Lindbergh home before the night of the crime."

When Whited himself was questioned by the governor he admitted he had testified against Hauptmann because he'd been promised a part of the reward. And he told an involved story to explain why he had denied seeing anyone in the area until Hauptmann had been arrested and police showed him photographs of the suspect. He had, he claimed, told one state trooper all about seeing the man he later identified as Hauptmann, and he made that statement before other police questioned him that first morning. He wouldn't say anything about it to the other officers—not even to Lindbergh, the famous Lindy—because the first trooper had warned him to be quiet so that news of his story wouldn't leak out to the press.

Hoffman searched state police files and could not find any report indicating Whited had claimed to have seen a suspicious man in the neighborhood on two occasions before March 1, 1932. And, as Hoffman put it in summing up his conviction that Whited was a liar, it is beyond belief "that the state police would have made Whited's *false* statement a part of their official records while eliminating from the files all mention of the important prior disclosures he claims to have made."

At the best of times, even when given by men of absolute integrity and unsullied by the sensational atmosphere that smothered the Lindbergh case, eyewitness testimony is notoriously untrustworthy. One of the more famous illustrations of this is still cited in law schools. Many years ago a professor of criminology performed an experiment on his unsuspecting class, which was composed of police officers, lawyers, and law students—an intelligent and at least somewhat trained group of men.

Without prior warning, a stranger burst into the classroom in the midst of a lecture. Waving a pistol, he shouted something and then fired directly at the professor's chest. The lecturer crumpled to the floor.

For a moment his students sat there, stunned, and then made an attempt to capture the man with the gun, who had already dashed out into the corridor. But before the students could race from the room, their professor rose and ordered them back into their seats.

He then explained that the pistol had contained only a blank and had been fired by a friend in order to test his students' ability to recall the details of an event which they had personally witnessed. And he asked them to write out as complete an eyewitness description of his "assailant" as they possibly could.

The results were astounding. Not one of the more than thirty students came even near to remembering what the intruder had looked like, only moments after they had seen him. Color of hair ranged from black to blond, height varied by as much as twelve inches, and weight by fifty pounds. Some said he had been a German, others Italian, and two described him as Oriental. The single student who had come closest to an accurate description still was not accurate enough to provide a description that would have been useful to police.

That experiment came to mind when I read an article by David Davidson, a reporter for the *New York Post* who had covered the arrest of Hauptmann and his trial. Davidson, who believes firmly in Hauptmann's guilt, recalls his own experiments with eyewitnesses in the Sourland Mountains forty years ago. Writing in the February 1976 issue of *American Heritage*, Davidson recalls:

To test the fundamental reliability of eyewitness testimony, a fellow reporter on the *Post*, the late Henry Paynter, devised an impish experiment in which I had the pleasure of accompanying him one weekend. Equipped with a batch of photos of nine nationally prominent persons, we went on a tour among the farmer neighbors of the Lindberghs in the Sourland Hills. In each case we showed the photos and asked whether any such person had been seen in the neighborhood at the time of the kidnaping. The responses were fairly astonishing. For instance, a photo of General Hugh S. Johnson, former chief of Roosevelt's National Recovery Administration, brought the following comments:

"I remember him all right. He was coming up the road dressed like a tramp."

"Isn't he that Whately fellow, the English butler of the Lindberghs?"

"That's a tough face. That's one I'll never forget. If ever I see that colt a-foolin' around my traps, I'd sure as hell go for my rifle."

Concerning the notably mild-mannered Dr. Rexford Guy Tugwell, New Deal economist and assistant secretary of agriculture, one witness remarked: "He has a criminal face. Isn't that the Mr. Schmidt who killed himself around here?"

Other photographs, Davidson reports, brought similar results. That of a New York City judge who disappeared in 1930 and was never found brought comments such as: "Oh, yes, he was prowling around here with that other fellow, asking the way to the Lindbergh place." The "other fellow" was the mild-looking economist, Tugwell.

A photo of Mayor Fiorello LaGuardia of New York led one witness to declare: "I saw him driving in a blue sedan with something, maybe a ladder." And to Davidson, one of the more surprising results of his experiment was that not one of the persons questioned was able to identify Al Capone, who had been page-one news for a decade and was at that time called America's Public Enemy Number One.

Police investigating the Lindbergh kidnaping had one other witness who they hoped could identify Hauptmann as having been near the Lindbergh home on March 1, 1932. But the witness disappointed them. He was Ben Lupica, the prep school boy who had come forward on March second and said he'd seen a man erratically driving a Dodge sedan along the road running past the Lindbergh driveway on the afternoon of the kidnaping. Inside the car, Lupica had said, he'd been able to see at least two sections of a ladder stretching from the front windshield to the rear window.

In none of the accounts of the Lindbergh case is there any mention of young Lupica from the period between the time he made his statement to police and almost three years later, when he testified in Hauptmann's behalf. Lupica was in the courthouse throughout the days of the trials, under subpoena as a state witness. But Wilentz never called him to testify and the reason became clear when he did take the stand as a defense witness.

Lupica told the jury about seeing a man in a car with two sections of a ladder, and said he later identified the ladder as the one found on the Lindbergh estate. But the car, he said, had New Jersey license plates.

Defense attorney Fisher asked the witness: "Have you at any

time said to anybody that you can definitely recognize the defendant, Hauptmann, as the man you saw in that car?

"No," Lupica replied.

"Can you identifv Bruno Richard Hauptmann as the man you saw in the car . . . ?"

"I cannot."

Wilentz took the witness and, incredibly, was permitted by Justice Trenchard to show Lupica a newspaper clipping and to read to the jury a statement he was said to have made to the reporter; at other occasions during the trial, particularly when the defense was attempting to show that Dr. Condon had made dozens of contradictory statements to the newspapers, Trenchard would not permit any of those statements to be introduced. But Wilentz was able to read what were purportedly Lupica's words in the days after the kidnaping.

"Bruno Richard Hauptmann is the same man that I saw at the foot of the lane leading to the Lindbergh home only a few hours before poor little Baby Lindbergh was killed and murdered. . . . He was driving a black Dodge sedan, had a ladder inside the car."

Wilentz then questioned Lupica very briefly. You have told me, the prosecutor said, and you have told five or six other aides of the prosecutor, that the man you saw on March first resembled Hauptmann. Isn't that true?

"That Mr. Hauptmann had a resemblance to him," Lupica said.

"And you have always said that he resembled Hauptmann, haven't you?"

"Yes, it is the truth."

"And you say so today, don't you, Ben?"

"Yes."

"You told everybody in the world that the man you saw on March first in an automobile with a ladder in it looked like Hauptmann, isn't that right?"

"He has a resemblance, yes."

To an unsophisticated jury, David Wilentz made it appear Lupica had indeed seen Hauptmann on March first but because of some aberration, perhaps, refused to make a positive identification. Few jurors ever make the distinction between a positive identification and a "resemblance," and certainly not in a case in which the prosecution evidence is so damnably overwhelming.

In truth, however, when Lupica was taken to the Bronx district attorney's office after Hauptmann's arrest and a statement taken from him, the first comment he made was: "I'm sorry about that story in today's *Daily Mirror*. The reporters talked to me and showed me pictures of Hauptmann and I told them he looked something like the man I saw that day. But I never said he is the man or any of the other things they wrote." And the district attorney said: "It's all right, Ben, I know how those reporters make up things."

The transcript shows that Lupica, after viewing Hauptmann in his cell, said flatly that he was not the man he saw in Hopewell that day. "He looks like him," Lupica said in the Bronx, "but he is not the same man."

Wilentz surely knew Lupica would so testify at Hauptmann's trial, for why else did the prosecution fail to call him as a witness? And Wilentz's act, in making it appear the witness had indeed named Hauptmann as the man he saw that day but had backed away from so positive a statement for reasons of his own, was absolutely irresponsible in a man sworn to seek truth and justice. This act, and so many others by David Wilentz, recall what Felix Frankfurter wrote in his book *The Case of Sacco and Vanzetti*. Discussing the testimony of a woman who identified one of the prisoners when it was likely she could not have seen his features, Frankfurter wrote:

"And what shall we think of the animus and honesty of the state that introduces such testimony to convict, knowing that the jury is too ignorant to disbelieve?"

And what are we to think of the honesty of the state when one of its investigators lies with great flair and drama and other investigators know he is committing perjury but remain silent, at least until Hauptmann is convicted?

The witness who lied was FBI agent Thomas Sisk. It was Sisk who swore that he first suspected Hauptmann had hidden the ransom money in his garage when the prisoner, sitting on the bed in his second-floor apartment, constantly glanced out the window toward the garage. Sisk testified that he informed his superiors of his suspicions and when the garage was searched almost $15,000 in gold notes was found.

That story was not true, it was later conceded by Lieutenant James Finn, the New York City police officer who worked on the case from the beginning and took part in the arrest of Hauptmann. Finn wrote a series of articles for *Liberty* magazine while Hauptmann was awaiting execution. And in one of those articles Finn said:

> Much has been made, for instance, of the alleged fact that the prisoner's glance, continually straying out of the window toward the garage, gave detectives the bright idea of extending the search to that building, where . . . the ransom money was hidden.
>
> That's a good story. It may have seemed to be a true one. But the truth of the matter is that when we first came into the house, Hauptmann was deposited at the edge of the bed in the middle of the room, and as the search proceeded he was moved over into the corner; and in either case Detective Wallace, being greatly attached to the prisoner by reason of a pair of steel handcuffs, would have had to rise and take a bow each time the prisoner wished to look out the window; and Wallace was in no mood at the moment to furnish comic relief.

Another investigator, FBI agent Turrou, also made it plain that Sisk had lied. Turrou was the only person involved in the case to admit publicly, years later, that John Condon had said Hauptmann was not the extortionist he'd met in the cemeteries. And in his memoirs Turrou also discussed how the money had been found in Hauptmann's garage. He wrote that FBI Director Hoover had ordered his agents to make another search of the house and garage after New York and New Jersey police said they could find nothing. The search was conducted, the garage was torn to the ground, and the ransom money recovered.

All of this, Turrou said, happened *after* Hauptmann was taken from his home and down to the Greenwich Street police station, *after* Hauptmann had been placed in the lineup and questioned by Condon.

Thus, two other investigators who were present later indicated Sisk had committed perjury; Hauptmann had, no doubt, correctly characterized Sisk when he shouted at the witness: "Mister! Mister! You stop lying. You are telling a story."

Hauptmann's outburst was directed not so much at Sisk's story about how the money was discovered, as at the agent's statement

333

that the first thing they had found when they began to dig in the garage was a metal can filled with water, and that Hauptmann had "admitted that he had that money in there three weeks before he was arrested." Sisk's statement enabled the prosecution to blunt Hauptmann's defense, that the ransom money was watersoaked because rain had leaked into his closet and had made him aware for the first time that there was money in Fisch's shoe box.

Yet in all of Hauptmann's statements to the police during the two days he was questioned at Greenwich Street, he made no such statement to Sisk nor to anyone else: I have copies of all the interrogation sessions, from the Bronx district attorney's files. Once the money was found and he was confronted with the discovery, he offered only one explanation to police, to the district attorney, to the court during the extradition proceedings, and at his trial—that he dried out the wet bills he had found in the shoe box and then placed them in dry containers in his garage.

As I go through the documents to analyze and write about them, there is a temptation to say that *this* particular piece of manufactured evidence is the one that convicted Hauptmann, or *that* particular evidence most influenced the jury and the public. In reality, each item played a special role in the crime that was committed against Hauptmann. No single facet of the evidence, no single bit of testimony, can be singled out and given special weight—with the exception, perhaps, of Lindbergh's voice identification of Hauptmann and of his silence about the man he had seen in St. Raymond's Cemetery.

Sisk's lie about the manner in which the money came to be watersoaked, however, touched Hauptmann deeply and provoked his only angry eruption during the trial. To Hauptmann, at least, those lies and distortions seemed more damaging than any others.

I learned, from the documents copied for me, that Hauptmann had been telling the truth when he described how he had found the money in the shoe box because of leaking rain on a Sunday in August and, more important, that he'd been telling the truth when he said he did not begin passing ransom notes until after that rainy day one month before his arrest.

That evidence is contained in reports by Lieutenant Finn and other New York City police officers. From the very first ransom bill recovered from banks and merchants, and up to June 1934, all Lindbergh ransom money that came into Finn's office was sent to the police laboratory for analysis.

The lab report on four of the bills which were submitted for analysis in June 1934—two months before Hauptmann says he found his particular cache of money in the shoe box—is similar to most of the previous reports. In it, the police chemist reports the frequent presence of lipstick and mascara on the bills, and police noted that earlier bills sent for analysis had also revealed the presence of blond, brunette, and red hair. Taken together with the fact that several bills had been passed at burlesque houses and restaurants, this finding indicated the man who was spending ransom money was living a somewhat flashy existence. These details, of course, did not fit the very conservative Hauptmann. Microscopic examination also disclosed that these four bills, like many tested earlier, were found to have stuck to them "a number of gold or brass dust particles" and a "fatty substance, apparently oil or grease." Police surmised, according to Lieutenant Finn, that the bill-passer was a mechanic of some kind, probably a machinist who had a lathe or drill press and who worked with metal; oil applied to the work probably flew off the machine with the metal particles and both were transferred to the bills, perhaps by the man's hands.

This report concludes: "All of the four bills apparently fold straight through the center lengthwise and then through the center crosswise and once again crosswise, making a double fold crosswise, resulting in a compact arrangement—apparently to fold them in such a size as to be carried in a vest pocket or a watch pocket."

Once more, we can see that these bills passed up to June 1934 had been placed in circulation by the man Cecile Barr, the theater cashier, had seen, the man who folded his money and kept it in his watch pocket. The bill recovered from Hauptmann on the day of his arrest, we've already noted, was found in his wallet and was lying flat. During one of the interrogation sessions at the Greenwich Street station, when Inspector Lyons pressed Hauptmann on the point, asking: Where do you keep the bills you carry around with you? Hauptmann replied, "Here, in my wallet," and it appears from the transcript that Hauptmann pulled out his wallet to demonstrate. Lyons does not call him a liar, does not press the point. He seems to be satisfied Hauptmann is telling the truth.

The bills discovered in Hauptmann's garage were also submitted for laboratory analysis. Those bills showed entirely different characteristics than the bills passed earlier.

The garage bills, the lab report stated, were "in a rather damp condition . . . watersoaked . . ." Lieutenant Finn said in one of his summaries that "there was a strong musty odor" on these Hauptmann bills, "as if the bills had been buried in the ground or in a damp receptacle." Since none of the earlier bills recovered had been wet or possessed a musty odor, it is possible Hauptmann did not come into possession of that money until shortly before the first one he is known to have passed, in early September.

And what is just possible, at first examination of the documents, approaches likelihood as the search continues. For one of the lab reports on Hauptmann's bills says that they had been wrapped in newspapers dated June 25, 1934, and September 6, 1934—Hauptmann had said that after he dried out the bills in his garage at the end of August and beginning of September he wrapped them in newspapers lying around the house. Most telling of all, in these reports, are other different characteristics of the bills discovered by the lab technicians. The early bills had traces of lipstick, mascara, and several shades of hair, indicating they'd been in the presence of women. Hauptmann's bills lack these substances. The early bills had on them gold or brass particles, suspended in what appeared to be machine oil. Hauptmann's bills also had on them a fatty substance that was probably machine oil, but clinging to it were traces of emery dust. In Hauptmann's garage was an emery wheel which he used for sharpening his tools. There was no lathe or drill press or any equipment on which brass or gold could have been worked, nor was there any trace of brass or gold dust. Seemingly, the earlier bill-passer was a different sort of mechanic than Hauptmann was and caused different kinds of particles to become fixed to his collection of ransom money.

There is further circumstantial evidence indicating Hauptmann did not begin to pass the ransom money until late August or early September, 1934. An examination of the testimony of federal agents, bank employees, and brokerage house customer's men at the trial and a study of documents relating to Hauptmann's bank accounts and stock market transactions show that of dozens of people to whom Hauptmann passed money, and who were later questioned, not one of them—without exception—could say they had ever received a Lindbergh ransom bill from Hauptmann. Most of them, in fact, stated that they had never been notified by the banks in which their firms made deposits that Lindbergh ransom money had been turned in. In a number of cases, the banks specifically said that no ransom money had ever been found in the deposits by Hauptmann's brokerage firms.

336

To cite but one example, found in an FBI report on the tracing of money which Hauptmann deposited in either banks or brokerage accounts. The report, Bureau of Investigation File Number 62-3057, made by agent J. A. Genau on October 18, 1934, says of currency Hauptmann deposited to his brokerage account:

In regard to the $1,000 deposit of currency appearing in the account on January 26, 1934, Mr. Allan Wilcox, clerk in the cashier's cage of E. A. Pierce and Company, who accepted and counted this deposit, stated that he cannot remember the denominations of this currency; that he cannot remember if any gold certificates were contained therein; that no record was kept of gold certificates.

This $1,000 was deposited in the main office of the Bank of Manhattan Company, 40 Wall St. Mr. M. W. Williams, cashier of the bank, stated that the deposit was not made up of gold notes; that the bank kept a record of all gold notes in deposits in excess of $100.

Throughout this and other documents relating to an FBI search for evidence that Hauptmann had used gold certificates in his stock market trading, investigators state that no such evidence was ever developed. The reverse, in fact, seems to have been true—when Hauptmann needed money to purchase stocks or respond to a margin call for more cash, he invariably took those funds out of one of his bank accounts. On January 18, the week before the $1,000 transaction quoted above, Hauptmann opened his margin account with E. A. Pierce by withdrawing $2,500 from a savings account.

Hauptmann, of course, had he been the extortionist who received all or part of the Lindbergh ransom money in April 1932, might have been acting very cautiously by getting rid of the gold certificates elsewhere and depositing "clean" money in his accounts. But then, how does one explain his absolutely stupid behavior in passing notes in 1934 in stores where he was known? Such illogical behavior is inconsistent with what we know of Hauptmann.

The FBI also considered the possibility that Hauptmann deposited ransom money in a bank account and then withdrew untainted money to deposit in his brokerage account. But the banks reported that no ransom bills had ever been deposited by Hauptmann.

There is further evidence, in this FBI report by agent Genau, that Hauptmann was telling the truth when he maintained he did not find the money until August 1934, at which time he began spending small sums for living expenses.

On March 27, 1933, Hauptmann opened an account with the brokerage firm of Steiner, Rouse and Company, in his wife's maiden name, Anna Schoeffler, although he had full control over the account: (Hauptmann told police he put the account in Anna's name because he had had an auto accident in which he broke a man's leg, and an attorney had advised him to transfer his assets in the event the man sued. The accident victim settled for a few hundred dollars, but Hauptmann didn't bother changing the name on the account. His story was verified by police.) Hauptmann was doing a lot of short-term trading in this account; it is the account which permitted a federal agent to testify that Hauptmann had $250,000 in the stock market when, in actuality, the "largest credit balance appeared on June 6, 1933, in the amount of $8,431.39," to quote this FBI report. But the distorted testimony is unimportant, for the moment. The main point is that, because it was a margin account and because Hauptmann frequently had a large credit balance, he was in the habit of periodically withdrawing sums of money from this account. Most of those withdrawals were of small sums ranging from $30 to $150, which Hauptmann said was for living expenses since he did not have a steady job.

The last two withdrawals, totaling $175, were made in the final week of July 1934.

In the following month, Hauptmann claimed, he discovered the gold certificates in Fisch's shoe box. The FBI accounting document makes it seem likely he was telling the truth, for he stopped taking money from his brokerage account at the end of July even though at the time of his arrest that account had a credit balance of $1,242.61 and also held shares of stock with a market value of close to $4,000.

Further, Hauptmann went on a hunting trip to Maine in the summer of 1933. No ransom bills ever turned up in Maine. He took a vacation with Anna in Florida; no ransom money was recovered in Florida. He went to Canada some time later, according to Lieutenant Finn, "but he spent nothing but good money across the boundary." If anything, Hauptmann would have been unloading Lindbergh money where he was unknown, rather than spending it, as he did, near his home in stores where he customarily shopped.

One piece of negative evidence helps support the conclusion that

338

Hauptmann was not the man, or one of the men, who had been passing the ransom money in the first couple of years after the kidnaping, that he did not begin passing money until he says he did, in September 1934. That evidence is found in a laboratory analysis of all the bills then in possession of authorities, almost $5,000 worth. The analysis by the Justice Department, dated August 7, 1934, goes into exhaustive detail about the gold particles, lipstick, mascara, and other substances found on the bills. And two paragraphs leap out:

> Three hundred and ten of the individual bills were chemically treated in an effort to develop latent fingerprints invisible to the naked eye.
> In all, five fragmentary latent prints were developed and on such prints appeared *sufficient characteristic ridge detail to permit identification* upon direct comparison with fingerprints or palm prints of the person who left them [emphasis supplied]. There was not, however, sufficient characteristic ridge detail to permit a classification of these prints for the purpose of search.

When Hauptmann was arrested less than two months after this report was made, his fingerprints were compared with those found on the bills. They did not match.

There is still another laboratory report of interest. After Hauptmann was arrested, Lieutenant Finn personally supervised an examination of Hauptmann's car. Police assumed it transported Lindbergh's gravely injured child from Hopewell to the point four miles away where the boy was dumped into the woods. Finn ordered the lab technicians to test "every inch of Hauptmann's car" for bloodstains, for the autopsy report indicated the child had probably been bleeding as a result of his skull fracture. No trace of blood was found.

At this point in my review of but a small part of the foot-high pile of documents on my desk I suddenly recalled something that Sidney Whipple had written in his introduction to the Hauptmann trial transcript that he edited and published. In attempting to answer the charges Governor Hoffman had made after his own investigation into the case, Whipple ignored the evidence Hoffman had made public and dismissed it in its entirety with this statement:

* * *

339

The governor, while not shouting "frame-up" as loudly as defense counsel had shouted it, nevertheless indicated that he was seriously considering that possibility. Again he ignored the obvious argument that such a frame-up, assuredly unparalleled in American jurisprudence, would have entailed collusion between: all the prosecuting authorities of the State of New Jersey; the investigating authorities of the United States Department of Justice [here Whipple went on, naming six or eight agencies] and all the minor officials engaged on the case from 1932 to 1934. Such a conspiracy would have necessitated collusion among some six hundred individuals. In the words of Mr. Justice Trenchard, now do you believe that?

A terrible choice of words, that last sentence, considering Judge Trenchard's obvious bias. But those were simpler times, those days when most reporters had absolute faith in all institutions of government. Watergate was forty years into the future; criminal acts by men in power, whether Presidents, prosecutors, or police, were beyond the imagination of most journalists. But it should not have been so. Only a couple of years before Hauptmann was convicted a special presidential commission, known as the Wickersham Commission, reported after long study of court records that police frequently beat confessions from prisoners and sometimes manufactured evidence to buttress false confessions, and that prosecutors too often were guilty of employing perjured testimony and counterfeit evidence to win at all costs, in violation of the canon of ethics. The commission's findings received wide publicity, but Whipple managed to ignore them as he ignored the work of one of his colleagues on the New York City police beat published around the same time. The book was called *Third Degree.* Based on the Wickersham Commission's documents and on personal research, it was a series of fast and breathless chapters by Emanuel Lavine, a police reporter who set out to prove, and did a fairly good job of it, that "seventy percent of all convictions obtained in our courts is achieved by what is known as the third degree."

Whipple was wrong. It did not require "collusion among some six hundred individuals" to construct the script which sent Hauptmann to his death. It did not require a "conspiracy" in which Lindbergh, Schwarzkopf, Sisk, Condon, and all the rest came together to plot against Hauptmann. All that was required was for some

340

dozen or so prosecution witnesses to lie, individually and for their own peculiar motives. And no single man or woman among them had to know all the others were lying or had to be in collusion with any others.

That there were lies, distortions, and suppression of evidence was clear from the documents that I had so far examined. Those documents show that:

1. Hauptmann's original alibi, that he had worked a full day at the Majestic apartments on the day of the kidnaping, was destroyed by police and prosecution. The "missing" employment books did exist, proved by the receipt for the employment records that I found in official files and by the statements to reporters, made by Attorney General Wilentz and Bronx District Attorney Foley, that police knew Hauptmann had worked *only* half a day. His alibi was further destroyed by police tampering with the time sheets that were permitted into evidence, those curious blobs of ink that were said to be circles proving Hauptmann was absent from work on certain key dates but were most likely made to blot out proof that he *had* worked on those dates.

2. John Condon most definitely had said to FBI agent Turrou that Hauptmann was not the man who received the ransom money. He probably identified Hauptmann, as Turrou later wrote, because police forced him to do so. Condon's connection with those who had been the major suspects before Hauptmann's arrest, the Geissler family and their friends, was suppressed. So was the statement by Lindbergh's aide, Robert Thayer, that Condon described the symbols on the ransom note before opening the envelope in which was the note with the symbol. Condon was a suspect, was believed to have had a role in the kidnaping and extortion, and that information was suppressed by police.

3. Lindbergh lied and distorted on several occasions. He testified he had complete faith in Condon, but privately he had told investigators that he suspected Condon. Lindbergh testified that he didn't think Mickey Rosner, the bootlegger and stock swindler, had taken the second ransom note away with him, while Thayer had told police he saw Rosner take it from Lindbergh's hands and dramatically demand two state troopers to drive him into New York City with it. Lindbergh permitted investigators to spread the lie that his identification of Hauptmann's voice had been made on the spot, when he actually didn't identify the voice until a week lat-

341

er and only after police had influenced his decision by summarizing all the other "evidence" they claimed to have had against Hauptmann. Lindbergh also withheld the fact that he had seen another man at the cemetery, for that would have undermined Wilentz's concept of one man as both kidnaper and extortionist.

4. All the other eyewitnesses were liars. Perrone, the cab driver, picked Hauptmann out of a lineup composed of two police officers, one in uniform, after months of identifying men who bore no resemblance to Hauptmann. Barr, the theater cashier, had said the man who threw a gold note at her appeared to be an "American" and had no accent. Hochmuth, the old man who said he saw Hauptmann near the Lindbergh home, was almost blind at the time. Whited, the other resident of the area, had originally told police he had seen nothing suspicious the day of the kidnaping and then concocted the unbelievable tale about withholding information from police and from Lindbergh because the first police officer who questioned him had warned him to be quiet. Rossiter, the salesman who claimed to have seen Hauptmann near the Princeton airport, was totally wrong in describing the car he claimed Hauptmann was driving.

5. The evidence from every eyewitness to the extortion plot in the Bronx—Lindbergh, Condon, Perrone, and Al Reich—that a "gang" had indeed been involved, was kept from the defense, the jury, and the public.

6. Finally, police suppressed their lab reports. Those reports showed quite clearly that the ransom bills definitely known to have been passed by Hauptmann differed, under microscopic examination, from ransom bills passed earlier. Only the bills spent by Hauptmann or found in his possession had once been watersoaked; the unique condition of Hauptmann's bills created a strong inference that he'd been telling the truth about discovering the box of money after it had been soaked by a leaking roof.

Thus far I had found evidence that about a dozen men and women, among them police officers, had lied, and that police and prosecution hid from the defense evidence that would have supported Hauptmann. And now I turned to what was perhaps the most crucial of the suppressed evidence.

The "Fisch story," police and prosecutor called it, thereby dismissing Hauptmann's alibi in advance and destroying his main chance—to prove Isidor Fisch had been his business partner in the stock market and in fur trading and had given Hauptmann large sums of money to invest. On this part of his alibi hung Hauptmann's primary defense, that Fisch had also given him the gold notes found in his garage. Wilentz, at the trial, said that of course there was a man named Fisch, we concede that, Mr. Hauptmann didn't simply pull his name out of the air. But what proof is there that Fisch was anything more than just a poor German immigrant, sickly and dying? None, none whatsoever. When Hauptmann asked for his ledger book, for letters from Fisch's brother, the prosecution said they did not exist or, alternately, that it was too much trouble to search for such evidence.

That ledger, the "big book" Hauptmann begged for when he was testifying, did exist. And so did the letters from Pinkus Fisch which show that Isidor told his brother that back in America there was a man named Hauptmann and he, Isidor, and Hauptmann were speculating as partners and growing wealthy together.

Among the files are dozens of official FBI and police reports about Hauptmann's finances, his memo books, his letters, and his dealings with Isidor Fisch. There are also a handful of reports on an investigation into Fisch's life in America. Reading through those reports, one thing becomes clear: Isidor Fisch was a confidence man who borrowed money from friends to invest in firms that did not exist and who seems to have cheated Hauptmann out of more than $7,000 by counterfeiting receipts to show he had bought furs which actually didn't exist.

But before exploring Fisch's character and his business partnership with Hauptmann, I was led by certain documents into an examination of David Wilentz's evidence that supposedly explained why Hauptmann had committed so brutal a crime.

In trying to prove motive for the kidnaping, the state demonstrated through its expert witnesses that Hauptmann had lost heavily in the stock market by the end of 1931, was almost without funds, and kidnaped the Lindbergh child a few months later in order to extort $50,000.

But that "proof" collapses upon an examination of several memorandum books found in Hauptmann's desk the day he was arrested and of FBI accounting reports on Hauptmann's bank and brokerage transactions.

In one of those memo books Hauptmann kept a meticulous record of his and his wife's income and savings from January 1, 1926, three months after he and Anna were married, to January 1, 1930. In each of those four years the Hauptmanns' joint income ranged between $3,000 and $4,000. At the end of that period, on New Year's Day, 1930, they had accumulated savings of $7,666.

The accounting demonstrates that the Hauptmanns were both hardworking and exceedingly frugal. Hauptmann worked through 1931 and part of 1932 and his wife worked into 1933. If their earnings and savings pattern continued, as he claimed it did when he testified that he had saved a great deal of money from his salary, then by the date of the kidnaping it is likely the Hauptmanns were worth about ten thousand dollars. Anna Hauptmann, in fact, had told one friend that they'd saved that amount or a little more.

There is no evidence and it had never been suggested in the newspapers or at the trial that Mrs. Hauptmann was the kind of woman to flaunt her wealth or boast about her savings. On the contrary, she was usually very circumspect about her personal life. Several of Anna's friends, questioned by police about her personal life or her finances, replied: "I don't know, she never told me." There is, however, one exception, and it bolsters the other evidence indicating Hauptmann had saved a large sum of money up to a year before the kidnaping. In a report by FBI agent John Seykora, dated a few weeks after Hauptmann's arrest, he summarizes an interview with Mrs. Otto Wollenberg, who came from the same town in Germany where Anna Hauptmann was born and who had grown friendly with her over a few years before Hauptmann was arrested. During the interview Mrs. Wollenberg said, in the FBI man's words:

"That before the Hauptmanns' California trip, early in the spring of 1931, Mrs. Hauptmann told Mrs. Wollenberg that they had saved about ten or twelve thousand dollars since they were married; that both of them worked all the time and that she hardly had time to sleep."

There is additional evidence that Hauptmann's memo books faithfully and accurately recorded the amount of savings he and his wife were accumulating. An FBI report on Hauptmann's bank accounts notes that he had savings of $5,700 at the end of January 1928. Hauptmann's memorandum lists savings of $5,780 on January 1, 1928—only an $80 disparity. It is likely, from the evidence contained in FBI documents, that Hauptmann was worth more than $10,000 by the spring of 1931, less than a year before the kidnaping.

But it is true, as Wilentz said in explaining to the jury why Hauptmann had kidnaped the Lindbergh child, that he had begun to use his savings for stock market speculation. He opened a trading account with a brokerage house on November 1, 1929, by withdrawing $2,800 from his bank account and adding $200 in cash. According to the FBI accounting report, Hauptmann was required to deposit another $1,500 in cash in June 1930, because he had "suffered large losses."

However, the accountant's characterization of Hauptmann's losses as "large" and Wilentz's statements to the jury that the defendant kidnaped young Lindbergh because he had gone broke in the stock market are patent falsehoods. The FBI report states that this stock market account "was inactive during 1931" and continued to be inactive up to the time of the kidnaping. And at the conclusion of the report on this account, in the final summary of Hauptmann's losses, the accountant reported: "Losses—$363.65."

Hauptmann's total stock market losses from 1929 through the early part of 1932 were *less than $400.*

Plainly, if he had a net worth of perhaps $10,000 at the end of 1931 and suffered stock market losses of under $400, Hauptmann had not been so completely impoverished by his speculations that that can serve as a motive for kidnaping. Another part of Wilentz's script collapses.

This FBI document, sixty-five pages of single-spaced type, is unfortunately only a synopsis of Hauptmann's finances. Its main goal was to demonstrate the amount of cash flowing into Hauptmann's various accounts in an obvious attempt to prove he had been spending well above his means and could only have done so because he had received $50,000 in Lindbergh money. A federal accountant who testified at the trial, William Frank, had sworn his figures showed Hauptmann had possession of more than $49,000 that could not be accounted for through his income and savings before 1932. The writers of the day threw kudos at the federal agents who had proved "to within a few dollars," as they put it, that Hauptmann had had his hands on every bit of the Lindbergh money.

345

"How could they say they proved I had fifty thousand dollars ransom money," Hauptmann asked Governor Hoffman during that visit to his death house cell, "when the police came to me after the trial and said they would help me stay out of the chair if I told them where the other thirty thousand is to be found?"

This FBI document makes plain why the New Jersey state police were still trying to find $30,000 in ransom money after Wilentz had proved Hauptmann dumped every cent of it into his stock market binge. The truth is that in all Hauptmann's market trading, even in the transactions which took place before the kidnaping, he suffered a total loss of only $5,216.03. Not $49,000 or $35,000, but a rather modest $5,200 in almost five years of activity—little more than $1,000 a year.

To sum up this point because it must be stressed, this FBI document shows that Richard Hauptmann suffered a loss of less than $400 before the kidnaping, which is hardly motive for purse-snatching when a man has thousands in the bank. And it shows that Hauptmann, rather than losing in market speculations all the Lindbergh money, with the exception of the gold notes found in his garage, actually suffered a loss of only $5,216.03.

One other thing must be noted. When he testified at Hauptmann's trial the federal accountant, Frank, swore that "my figures are accurate" and that he wasn't simply counting the same few thousand dollars that Hauptmann withdrew from his bank to buy stocks on margin, then withdrew from his brokerage house when his equity built up and returned to his bank account, and then back again, many dozens of times. No, Frank swore, Hauptmann was playing around with enormous sums of money, cash money. The FBI report, however, shows that in his accounting, Frank was bending the truth somewhat. Hauptmann had certainly bought nearly $400,000 worth of stocks. He had made deposits of more than $21,000 into his brokerage accounts. But an examination of the document proves conclusively that Hauptmann was moving money from bank to brokerage house and back again, and was churning his stock account on margin; at no time did the amount of equity in his accounts exceed $11,000 or $12,000, and when it did come anywhere near that figure it appears from the records to have been, as Hauptmann said, because Isidor Fisch had become his investment partner and was funneling money in.

And then something else suddenly leaps out of these pages and condemns the prosecution again for its distortions. A great deal was made by Wilentz at the trial of the date Hauptmann and Fisch first were introduced. Hauptmann had said it was March or April, 1932, and, the police and prosecution said, he was lying, he did not meet Fisch until July or August of that year. He lied because he had to fabricate an earlier date of introduction to Fisch to explain how he came to possess the enormous sums which he deposited in cash in his bank and brokerage accounts.

What enormous sums? Reilly never asked that question and even Hauptmann accepted Wilentz's argument. Hauptmann was at a disadvantage because his own ledger was suppressed and the records of his bank and stock accounts which were subpoenaed by the prosecution remained in Wilentz's hands at all times. Reilly and Hauptmann had little time to study those records in preparing for direct examination of the defendant.

Had there been time, it would have become obvious Hauptmann had not lied, but the prosecution had distorted. Here in this FBI report there is a boringly complete list of every cent in cash that Hauptmann deposited to his bank and stock accounts after the day the ransom money was paid. Through the months in question, April to August, 1932, Hauptmann was putting into a bank account small sums that never exceeded $200 and were most often less than $100. The only money deposited in his single brokerage account at the time was $600 on April 8 and $22.75 on April 11. Hardly enormous sums.

Hauptmann and his defense counsel had fallen victim to a hoary courtroom trick—make a statement supposedly based on accounting records, but don't permit your opponent time to examine those records so he will be forced to accept that statement as truth.

That the police and the prosecution knew Hauptmann and Fisch were business partners—in spite of Wilentz's implication that it was a fishy story—can be found in the final pages of this lengthy FBI report. There, the FBI agent lists the names of all potential witnesses to Hauptmann's transactions, including customer's men, bank clerks and treasurers, and investigating police officers. One of those listings includes the names of Inspector Lyons of the New York City police department, FBI agent Sisk, and Captain Lamb of the New Jersey state police. They would be needed at the trial, the report states:

347

"To testify as to finding record book or journal in the home of Richard Hauptmann and the questioning of Richard Hauptmann relative thereto and the general questioning of Hauptmann as to stock market trading and other transactions."

But the official fiction was that "the record book or journal" did not exist and that "other transactions"—meaning fur trading with Isidor Fisch—were part of the defendant's manufactured alibi. So Wilentz said, again and again.

From page 31 of the FBI report:

> During a search of the premises occupied by Hauptmann, Inspector John A. Lyons of the New York City Police Force and Special Agent T. H. Sisk found, in a desk in the front room of the house, a record book or journal which was exhibited to Hauptmann and identified by him as his property. The book contains a number of entries which appear on pages 4 to 9, 50, 51, 72 to 77, 100 to 107, all of which entries Hauptmann admitted were in his handwriting. The book was later examined by Special Agent W. C. Dickson who has reported that it is evident that the book is a personal record of Hauptmann's interest in numerous transactions. . . .

The first pages cited are Hauptmann's record of stock transactions between May 4, 1932, and August 8, 1932, listing the name and quantity of a particular stock, price paid, and price realized when sold. The FBI report does not duplicate Hauptmann's lists, simply summarizes them, and so it is not possible to analyze them. But there is some interesting information to be gleaned from the later pages.

"The entries on pages 50 and 51 constitute a record of stock market transactions similar to the record on pages 4 to 9," the report says. It goes on to state that pages 4 to 9 had lines drawn through them, as if Hauptmann was starting a fresh accounting of his stock portfolio. Page 50 lists one new stock purchase, made on June 6, 1933. It is the only transaction noted on that page. And significantly, the FBI agent wrote in his report, there is a notation at the bottom of the page which indicates that on July 10, Fisch gave Hauptmann a little over $2,000 to buy into a partnership on a "20 percent basis."

While that notation is not fully explained, the FBI analyst makes it plain he believes that sometime in the early summer of 1933 Hauptmann and Fisch became partners in stock market speculations. That belief is strengthened by the next series of entries in the book, on two fresh pages. Those entries are headed "17,500—Richard Account" on one page and "17,000—Isidor Account" on the adjoining page. The FBI report says the headings and the entries that follow are probably "accounts in a partnership's books."

What appears to have happened is this: In June or July, 1933, Hauptmann "canceled" his own stock market accounts in his ledger and, on a fresh page, placed the stocks he already owned into a partnership account with Fisch. The FBI analyst suggests this is what occurred. And it conforms to Hauptmann's explanation to police, when he was questioned about this ledger, that he had begun trading in stocks for his partnership account with Fisch while Fisch was trading in furs.

During that questioning by police in the first days after his arrest, and in his testimony at the trial, Hauptmann conceded that he had deposited large sums of money into his brokerage account in the spring and summer of 1933. Most of that money, he said, had come from Isidor Fisch. The prosecutor labeled this alibi the "Fisch story." And yet, based on Hauptmann's ledger, it seems to have been the truth.

There is another transaction in the ledger that indicates Hauptmann and Fisch had become partners in speculation as early as May 8, 1933, a date which is important because it lends greater support to Hauptmann's explanation. The brokerage account in which Hauptmann did most of his trading was not opened until August 1932. But according to an officer of Hauptmann's brokerage house, whose affidavit is reprinted in full in this FBI analysis, Hauptmann did not begin speculating heavily until May 1933 (and not in 1932, as Wilentz had claimed at the trial). The largest deposits Hauptmann made to this trading account were between April 28 and August 10, 1933. They came to a little less than $12,000. After September 1933, Hauptmann's account became inactive. And on October 21, 1933, on still another page of this ledger, Hauptmann calculated the balance in the partnership account as if he "desired to make a determination of his position" on that date, the FBI agent comments.

Isidor Fisch bought his ticket for Germany the following month. It appears likely the stock trading activity slackened in September and Hauptmann calculated his position in October because Fisch was preparing to leave the country. The evidence in Hauptmann's ledger, confirmed at least in part by the records of the stock brokerage house, indicates Hauptmann's major stock market trading began after the date he and Fisch had entered into a partnership of some kind, and that trading activity greatly diminished very shortly before Fisch returned to Germany.

This section of the ledger alone, had it been shown to the jury and released to the newspapers, would have raised some serious questions about the prosecution's case against Hauptmann. That it was hidden—suppressed—can only be attributed to a deliberate decision by one or more officials to deny Hauptmann a fair trial.

But an important question comes to mind: Did Hauptmann's ledger and memo books reflect an accurate accounting of his savings and of a partnership with Fisch, or were they documents carefully planned to create an alibi should he be arrested as the extortionist?

All the evidence laid out in this accounting report indicates the books are exceptionally accurate in every area where the FBI was able to check entries against documented sources, such as bank and brokerage house statements. Hauptmann's notation in a memo book that he had over $7,000 in savings on a certain date, for instance, is confirmed by his bank statements; a notation that he had a certain amount in equity in his stock account on a given date is confirmed by statements from the brokerage house. In each case, when the FBI was able to check Hauptmann's figures against original sources, his figures were accurate.

Furthermore, two pages in his ledger are devoted to an accounting of funds that Hauptmann and Fisch either deposited to the stock account or withdrew for personal expenses. The account was begun by Hauptmann on November 1, 1933. It ends July 28, 1934, three months after Hauptmann was notified that Fisch had died— an indication that Hauptmann was meticulously accounting for every penny he withdrew from their partnership account for the day Fisch's brother would arrive to settle the estate. By checking these items in Hauptmann's ledger against bank and stock market transactions analyzed by the FBI, it is clear that Hauptmann's records

350

are accurate and it becomes likely that this ledger was not composed as a future alibi.

The FBI summary of Hauptmann's ledger continues with an analysis that makes more obvious the reason this book had to be suppressed. The report states:

"Pages 74 to 77 are given over to a record of the *purchases and sales of furs* and it is indicated . . . that the transactions are for the *account of Isidor Fisch and Richard Hauptmann*" [emphasis supplied]. Hauptmann set up his ledger, the FBI report goes on, so that when it was opened to the pages concerning fur speculations he could promptly determine their financial position. The left-hand page showed the purchase of a specific lot of furs. When that lot was sold, Hauptmann followed the line across to the right-hand page and noted the details of the sale. The FBI agent wrote:

"Because of the relative importance [!] of these transactions and of the fact that they are comparatively few in number, the record as it appears in the book is shown hereunder. . . ." It doesn't have to be said, but I intend to stress it—the transactions were so important to Hauptmann's defense that the book was suppressed.

Precisely how this partnership worked, who contributed what funds and to which account, furs or stocks, is not clear from the ledger. Even the notation by Hauptmann indicating he had $17,500 to his credit and Fisch had $17,000 is deceptive. It is possible that was their investment on paper, for the stock account was margined as high as 80 percent and the furs that were purchased did not have to be paid for, in many cases, for ninety days; the ledger indicates most of the furs were sold at a profit within ninety days, in some cases within three days.

Yet Hauptmann, when arrested and asked to explain why he had been "stealing" money from his late partner, Fisch, maintained he had simply been taking what was his because Fisch owed him $7,500. How Hauptmann arrived at that figure is impossible to determine at this point, because the original documents in the case are locked away at state police headquarters in Trenton and no writer is permitted to examine them. We know Hauptmann withdrew $2,000 from his brokerage account to finance Fisch's trip to Germany. The other $5,500 he said he was owed is hidden in this ledger book.

But there is a clue. The accounting of fur purchases and sales

351

shows that between May 8 and November 10, 1933, when trading seems to have ended at almost precisely the time stock market trading fell off, the partners had bought almost $51,000 worth of various skins, from Hudson seal to Russian caracul. (Again, it must be made clear that, as in the stock market account, the total sum cited is not moneys actually invested in cash, but the result of repeated buying and selling.) The profits on sales made by the partners came to $6,637. But there is something rather curious here. The ledger shows that on August 8, 1933, they bought 2,000 Hudson seal pelts at a total cost of $1,100. On November 3, their last recorded purchase, they bought almost 3,300 pelts ranging from silver fox to mink, at a total cost of $21,900. Only 1,600 of the Hudson seals were sold, at a profit of a dollar a pelt. The 400 sealskins and the 3,300 assorted pelts were not sold when Fisch went to Germany. According to Hauptmann's ledger, $24,100 worth of furs were owned by the partnership and should have been in storage somewhere.

Hauptmann searched for those skins, but could never find them. And he slowly came to the conclusion that Fisch had cheated him.

Isidor Fisch, it appears from the documents available, was most certainly dishonest. He also seemed to have been persuasive enough to make one group of friends believe he was starving, so that he could cadge money from them and from an immigrant society to which he belonged, at the same time he was getting another group of friends (Hauptmann and his acquaintances) to believe he was a wealthy fur speculator and investor in small expanding businesses so that he could borrow money from them by claiming he was temporarily short of liquid capital but didn't want to miss out on a sure winner. None of the money Fisch borrowed was ever repaid.

It is possible, from the FBI and police files, to put together a portrait of Isidor Fisch. Born in Liepzig in 1905, he came to America around 1922 and got a job as a furrier. He was making about fifty dollars a week, at first, and by the late twenties was earning about a hundred a week. He went to night school, learning to read, write, and speak almost perfect English and winning a certificate of merit. He lived frugally, sending large sums of money to his parents in Germany, "of whom he was very fond," one friend told police. But he apparently had saved enough to enable him to buy a piece of land in Freeport, Long Island, in 1928. At the same time, however, he gave most of his friends in a fraternal lodge in which he was sergeant-at-arms the impression that he was always on the edge of destitution.

In 1931, Fisch invested $1,500 in a pie-baking corporation. The details of that investment cast a little further light on Fisch and the kind of men he was associating with. In tracing Fisch's background, police interviewed Lamber D. Brush, who was the brother-in-law of New York City's coroner but who was estranged from his family because, it appears, he was continually involved in questionable businesses.

Brush conceded that police information was accurate, he had once been a partner with Isidor Fisch in a pie company. That partnership came about, he said, when the pie-baking company he had begun in October 1930 had grown short of capital and was near collapse by the following January. At that time he was visited by an old business acquaintance, Charley Schleser, who suggested they form a corporation and seek an infusion of new capital. Charley said he would find a couple of investors among his contacts but, as a finder's fee, he wanted a share in the new corporation even though he couldn't personally invest anything. Brush agreed to the proposition although he was fully aware of Charley's rather tainted business credentials. Brush had met Charley around 1918, when Schleser was running a delicatessen in upstate New York and Brush was general manager of a meat-packing firm in Brooklyn. Charley had had business reverses and had fallen behind in paying his bills to the firm Brush worked for, so Brush bought him out and assumed the debts. Apparently, Brush had been involved in manipulating the books in Brooklyn so that the debts in upstate New York would appear diminished, and eventually he was fired.

Brush says he saw Charley occasionally up to 1925, then lost contact with him until he appeared with his offer to help the pie business. But, Brush said, he'd heard a few things about Charley. Charley had gone to prison for a couple of years for swindling a woman out of thousands of dollars. Most recently, Charley was involved in a crooked real estate business with a man named Joe De-Grasie, a *real* hoodlum—implying Mafia connections. As the FBI agent relates Brush's account:

"Brush said that he considered Charley as a trickster very capable of successfully putting over a shady deal and undoubtedly closely identified with the criminal element. . . . During the time

353

when the pie company was in operation, on several occasions undoubted gangsters had visited Charley and gave every evidence of being intimate with him. As a matter of fact, Brush says it was Schleser's boast that he could get gang assistance at any time should he need it."

DeGrasie was only one member of that criminal element that visited Charley at the pie company, Brush said. And DeGrasie loved to boast about how great a team he and Charley had been in their real estate swindles. They had a legitimate real estate office on Beekman Place, near City Hall, DeGrasie told him. And DeGrasie said "that the plan of operation during their real estate days was for him to dig up the suckers and turn them over to Schleser, who was the office man and who would put through the deals by which several people were victimized."

Brush told police that DeGrasie left New York in March 1931, shortly after the pie company was incorporated, because he had swindled someone out of about five thousand dollars. DeGrasie had fled to Germany; his wife was German. Investigators seemed to grow rather excited about that information and they asked Brush to describe DeGrasie. Well, Brush said, he was about thirty-five years old at this time, 1934, short and stocky with black hair and quite clearly of Italian descent and, "There was something wrong with one leg, causing him to limp slightly at times."

That description, one police report dryly noted, "seems to match the possible lookout seen in the cemeteries."

But DeGrasie had left a year before the kidnaping and FBI agents were assigned to check with immigration officials on whether he had returned. That particular trail ends, for us, because there are no further reports concerning DeGrasie's movements after March 1931 in the files to which I had access.

It was DeGrasie and Schleser who brought Isidor Fisch into the Knickerbocker Pie Company. Whether Fisch was one of their "suckers" or whether he was associated with them in other ventures cannot be determined from the small number of documents available to me. But that Fisch himself became a swindler—of Hauptmann and others—soon becomes apparent.

Schleser told police that when Isidor Fisch came to him and offered to invest in the new enterprise, Fisch said he was prepared to put about $800 into the corporation. Charley said that wasn't nearly enough, and about two weeks later Fisch returned with

$1,500. He said it was all his savings, but Schleser felt certain it was borrowed money.

Actually, Fisch had borrowed the money from Mrs. Augusta Hile, the mother of Karl Henkel. Fisch roomed with Karl and Gerta Henkel and it was Gerta who testified she introduced Fisch to Hauptmann in the summer of 1932.

Schleser also told police that when Fisch first came into the pie firm as a stockholder in the corporation, "he was in a run-down condition and no doubt already the victim of tuberculosis." Fisch said he had become ill because of his years in the fur business, dressing fur pelts in chilled rooms until his lungs were affected. He wanted to get out of furs, he said, and into some other form of occupation, which is why he was going into the pie business.

But Fisch also told Brush, the man who operated the original pie company until it was incorporated as Knickerbocker in January 1931, that he was still working as a furrier and making eighty to a hundred dollars a week. Brush said Fisch finally lost that job months later when the pie business interfered with his fur trade. And when the pie business folded around August 1931, because of a dispute between Schleser and Brush, Fisch's entire investment was lost.

A couple of months later, according to Mrs. Hile, Fisch borrowed another $1,850 from her "to put in the pie business so we can expand," he said. To the day he sailed for Germany, Fisch told one group of friends that the "pie business was doing fine."

After meeting Hauptmann in the summer of 1932, Fisch began hanging around with him at the brokerage office on East Eighty-sixth Street where Hauptmann watched the tape almost every day. Several customer's men told police they'd been introduced to Fisch by Hauptmann. Gerta Henkel, with whom Fisch roomed during 1932, told police shortly after Hauptmann's arrest: "Isidor got on my nerves, he always get me nervous, pacing up and down the floor and looking out of the window to see if Hauptmann come or not. He was always there until about half-past nine in the morning. He would go away with Hauptmann, but sometimes Hauptmann didn't come and he go away alone. I said, 'Where you go, working or what?' He said he go down to the stock market."

By the beginning of 1933, which is several months before Hauptmann's ledger indicates they had become partners, he was telling friends that he and Isidor were going into business together. Hans

355

Muller, who was married to Anna Hauptmann's niece, told police that some months after Mrs. Hauptmann returned from a trip to Germany, in October 1932, Richard was talking about going into business with Fisch. Each of them would invest $17,500 in a partnership, Hauptmann to speculate in stocks with part of the capital and Fisch to buy and sell fur pelts, "everything on a fifty-fifty basis." In the statement to the FBI by Mr. and Mrs. Wollenberg, they said they had gone to the Hauptmanns' apartment some time in the early morning hours of January 1, 1933, to wish them a happy new year, and they met Fisch for the first time. "Hauptmann seemed to show considerable respect toward Fisch," Wollenberg was quoted in the FBI report. Wollenberg said he'd been drinking and at one point, forgetting his manners, he pointed toward Fisch and asked Hauptmann, "Who is that little shrimp there?" And Hauptmann replied, "That guy is worth thirty thousand dollars. He is my partner in furs and in the stock market. We have an agreement that we go half-and-half on everything." Mrs. Louisa Schussler, who lived downstairs from the Hauptmanns, said she began to get friendly with Anna when the latter was growing large with her pregnancy, in the summer of 1933, and would come and visit and ask questions about giving birth and raising a child. At one point, Louisa told police, Mrs. Hauptmann began talking about Fisch. "She said she thought Fisch is a nice man, he speaks nice English and she likes to talk with him, and Fisch and Richard are going in business together."

While cultivating the Hauptmanns as friends and business associates, Fisch was warning Mrs. Hile not to tell anyone he had borrowed money from her because "he didn't think it was anybody's business but ours." She agreed—and Fisch promptly borrowed another $1,000 from her "to buy furs with Richard."

In June 1933, a month after the deadline for converting gold certificates into other paper money, a month after Wendel had said Fisch tricked him out of the gold notes, Fisch rented a safe-deposit box at the North River Savings Bank branch on West Thirty-fourth Street, in the fur district. When that box was opened by court order in August 1934, after Fisch's family had hired an attorney to seek out any assets in his estate, it was empty. In September, when Hauptmann was arrested, police verified that the box had indeed been empty and they wondered—in several reports—whether Fisch had been Hauptmann's "accomplice" in the kidnap and extortion and whether he had hidden his shoe box of gold notes in that bank until just before sailing for Germany. In August 1933, a few months after renting the box, Fisch started a trading account with a brokerage house on Broad Street, far removed from the East Eighty-sixth Street brokerage office he frequented with Hauptmann, and he began to trade in a relatively small way, in hundred-share lots never worth more than $1,000. Hauptman evidently did not know about Fisch's solo market trading.

By the autumn, shortly before buying his ticket for Germany with money borrowed from Hauptmann, Fisch was boasting that he was a wealthy man. Hans Muller remembered that the only time he ever saw Fisch in Hauptmann's house was after Fisch had definitely decided to return to Germany before Christmas. Muller told police:

"Richard was at his desk and Isidor came in and they spoke about the fur business. They were talking that when Isidor came back from Germany they can start to buy fur from the trappers and I said to Isidor, 'That cost a lot of money.' He said, 'Oh, we make the money. We almost missed ten thousand today. If I would have bought the right furs and have money for it we could have sold it right away and make ten thousand dollars on it.' And at that point I was sent out of the room because Richard, he want to talk business with Isidor Fisch."

Fisch boasted to a number of other friends of the Hauptmanns' that he was "getting rich in furs" and that he "had already a big bundle of money from fur profits." At the conclusion of his going-away party, a few days before sailing for Germany in early December 1933, Fisch was driven to the subway station by Mrs. Katie Fredericksen, whose husband owned the bakery in which Mrs. Hauptmann had worked until her pregnancy. And Fisch practically propositioned her, she said, apparently trying to demonstrate that he had a great deal of money. "I don't know if it was a joke," she told the Bronx district attorney, "but Fisch said, do you want to go downtown and raise the roof some place?" Mrs. Fredericksen said she couldn't possibly do that, she wanted to go straight home. "And Fisch took some bills from his pocket and held them up and said we be spending that for a good time." She replied that he'd go broke before getting to Germany if he carried on like that. Then they arrived at the Pelham station and Fisch got out without any further conversation.

Yet at the same time he was causing members of the Hauptmann circle to believe he was wealthy, Fisch was presenting another face to another group of friends. The members of his lodge, the Chrzanower Young Men's Association, interviewed by FBI agent P. M. Breed during a meeting several days after Hauptmann's arrest, all swore that Fisch was always broke and nearly destitute, so broke that he was unable to seek medical aid for his pulmonary condition and on two occasions was unable to pay one-dollar assessments by the lodge. At the same time, most lodge members said he appeared to live at a near-poverty level because he was sending large sums of money to his parents. One member of the group told agent Breed "that Fisch did a lot of overtime work as a furrier and had a small machine in his room. On this he frequently used to work until one or two o'clock in the morning stitching furs, explaining that he needed the extra money to send to his family in Europe. He also stated that he used the money secured from overtime work to pay his passage to Europe."

Another lodge brother said he had met Fisch on the street shortly before he sailed for Germany. Although it was very cold Fisch was wearing only a raincoat, and the friend remonstrated with him. Fisch said he had no money, "that he was having hard work paying his room and board expenses which amounted to thirteen dollars a week." The friend gave Fisch an old sweater to keep warm.

Charley Schleser, the man with mob connections who brought Fisch into the Knickerbocker pie firm, although himself a confidence man, seems to have been conned by Fisch. He said that he saw Fisch occasionally after their business closed down and "things had gone from bad to worse with Fisch. . . . He practically lived from hand to hand, earning a few dollars here and a few dollars there in the repairing of furs on small individual orders, his health getting worse by the minute." Charley offered to take Fisch in, he could come and live with Charley and his wife until things improved, but because of his "sensitiveness" over his financial condition Fisch refused. Eventually he took a thirteen-dollar-a-week furnished room in the building in which the Henkels lived. But, Charley told police, Fisch had been evicted from that room some time in the spring of 1933 and "thereafter Fisch slept wherever he might find it possible to do so, including the benches in the Grand Central depot." Charley was certain of that, because Fisch had told him so. However, police learned Fisch had moved out of the room, voluntarily, to take a larger place on East Eighty-sixth Street, in the German community of Yorkville, near the brokerage office where he would frequently watch the tape with Hauptmann.

Schleser said he gave Fisch money during this period, a few dollars at a time, to help him out. Still, Fisch was getting much worse. Several weeks before Fisch sailed for Europe, Charley met him outside the Pennsylvania Hotel in the fur district "and because of Fisch's weakened condition took Fisch to a restaurant in order that they might sit down, Fisch having seemed to be about to faint while they were standing on the sidewalk. Fisch was very much depressed at the time, as he had been on recent earlier meetings, and renewed previous threats to commit suicide, stating that he felt there was nothing else left for him to do." Schleser and another friend who had been helping Fisch with small sums of money during this period argued with him and suggested he return to Germany. Fisch said he would very much like to do so, but he couldn't afford the boat passage. Schleser and the other friend gave Fisch thirty-five dollars "and with a few dollars raised here and there Fisch departed for Europe."

Up in the Bronx, meanwhile, Fisch was playing the rich speculator, borrowing money from Hauptmann and Mrs. Hile and several others, according to police reports, and leaving Hauptmann with the understanding that he had in storage more than $24,000 worth of furs on which they could expect a large profit when he returned from Germany, probably in March or April.

At least one of Hauptmann's friends did not trust Fisch, however. Hans Muller, married to Anna's niece, told the Bronx district attorney:

"Fisch didn't have no place of business, Richard told me. I asked him if they go partnership together don't they want to have office or storage house, or if they shouldn't go to a notary public if he is going to invest so much money in Fisch's fur business. They speak about thirty-five thousand dollars, each party seventeen five, and I said, 'If you want to invest so much money, Richard, you got to go to notary and have agreement and go to bank and have bank account so you know how much money you got and how much money you pay out.' And then he tell me later they wanted to get everything down on paper before Isidor went to Germany but they never did, they never make the agreement.

"I ask him one time, I said, 'Richard, if you go in storage business and you buy so much furs, don't you have to have storage house or loft?' He said, 'No, that is not done in business like this, the furs is bought in lots and stored in storage house and we get paper for it and we don't have to have our own place for that.' "

Fisch sailed on December 6, 1933, with a friend, Henry Uhlig, who had known Fisch as a child and who remained close to him when both emigrated to New York. Over the next months Fisch sent a couple of postcards to Hauptmann—which during Hauptmann's trial David Wilentz said was "all the letters we could find"—and then there was silence. At the end of April 1934, Hauptmann received a registered letter from Pinkus Fisch, Isidor's brother. It said, in part:

> I am writing you in great sorrow the sad news of my brother's death. My brother, Mr. Isidor Fisch, died at the Leipzig Hospital on March twenty-ninth at 2 P.M.
>
> Now that we are back again to normal functions, I have taken time to let you know about it, although I have not been able to write sooner. . . . I feel it is my duty to let you know about it in America as *my brother has often talked about you and your business connections with him,* which I imagine were not only business but of a more friendly nature. I am saying that because of conversations between me and my brother about you.
>
> [Isidor] has told me about several business enterprises in which you were also active, and still are. He advised me that you and my brother used to *speculate with stocks and silver fox furs.* He also told me of a will which is supposed to be in the safe of a New York bank. That safe is supposed to contain all papers in regards to his business and private matters.
>
> In *his last few hours he mentioned your name* and I supposed he wanted to say something to us about you, or *something for us to tell you,* but he did not have the strength, and so I beg you please in the name of my relatives and dead brother, let me know what your connections were with my brother in business and also in private matters. Please do not misunderstand me to write such a letter shortly after my brother's death but evidently you were his close friend and I presume that you are willing to help us in getting the estate of my brother, for which he has worked so hard, so it will not get into someone

else's hands. He advised us that *the stocks and merchandise would amount to quite a bit of money.* He also mentioned that again on his deathbed and the same confidence my brother had in you is still good with me in memory of my brother. . . . I would be pleased to have a complete list of all the goods belonging to my brother, to your knowledge, knowing that you will do this as a last favor to my brother. If you believe that the *news of my brother's death should be kept from some persons,* in regards to creditors, I will leave that entirely up to you.

The emphasis in this letter has of course been supplied, for police and prosecutors knew of the letter and others to follow. They knew that Pinkus Fisch had been told by Isidor about his business arrangements with Hauptmann, but all officials denied the letters' existence, doubtless because to have produced them at the trial would have raised questions slashing at the fabric of Wilentz's case. To reemphasize it: Pinkus Fisch said that Isidor told him he and Hauptmann speculated in stocks and furs, and talked about it often. Pinkus Fisch suggested that Isidor had attempted to say something to be told to Hauptmann—and the defense could easily have drawn the inference that it was a warning about the Lindbergh ransom money in Fisch's shoe box. Pinkus said he'd been told by his brother that the stocks and furs were quite valuable. Pinkus suggested others should be kept in the dark about Fisch's death so that, presumably, they would be denied any claim against the estate. All these statements in the first letter from Pinkus were so completely the reverse of what Wilentz "proved" that the letter had to be kept from the jury and the public.

Hauptmann replied to Pinkus on May fourth. His letter was introduced at the trial; Wilentz was able to attack it as lies and fantasy, since it appeared to exist in a vacuum, without connection to the letters from Pinkus or the material in Hauptmann's ledger books. In his letter, Hauptmann first expressed his grief "that I will never see Isidor again" and then went on to detail their business arrangements:

In the spring of 1933 I bought stocks for Isidor, which I knew would bring a profit and they did. We used to talk about his business and I loaned him money several times, when he

361

wanted to buy furs. In the summer of 1933 he gave me two thousand dollars for stock market speculation, with an agreement that he would get 20 percent of all winnings and also share 20 percent in money lost. This was my unlucky year and I have lost heavy. Isidor knew what it means to play the stock market, it is always a gamble. After this experience we decided to go into business and build up a future as he figured that we would make 20 to 25 percent on the capital invested in the business. . . .

On November the first, 1933, we started the business with a capital of $35,000 which was supplied by both of us, each one putting up half the money. We figured out the value of my stocks which on November the first, 1933, amount to $12,000. Isidor's supply in furs is $21,900. I gave him $5,500 cash out of my private bank and my interest in the business would be $17,500.

On November the thirteenth, 1933, Isidor asked me to take $2,000 out of the business as he needed money for traveling expenses to Germany, otherwise, he would have to sell furs to get the money, and we decided that it would be unwise to sell them as they will bring more money later on, and on November the fourteenth I took $2,000 out of my business and gave it to him. . . .

Our business standing is as follows: My interest in full is $17,500. Isidor was not in a position to pay the full amount as he had other expenses. . . . Amount of stocks—$10,000— Isidor one half, Richard one half. Amount of furs—$21,900, Isidor one half, Richard one half plus $7,500 on Isidor's half. . . .

Isidor also told me he was interested in a bakery business in which he invested $10,000. For the past few days I have been running around trying to locate this bakery, but all I could learn was that the bakery went bankrupt about two years ago. I can hardly believe it because Isidor had told me, just before he left on the boat, that everything was all right. I think there is something wrong. I personally believe that this bakery is operated under a different name, or probably Isidor changed the name to cut the income tax, but I think that there are papers in his bank box which should explain everything.

Now, dear Mr. Fisch, I beg you to write to me in the near

future giving me information on the most important things. Would it be possible for you to copy the bills, and also send the address of the warehouse where the furs are stored, and also the address of the bank. I don't know what warehouse he used in storing the furs, everything is in his name. I would like to have everything locked, also his bank box. After his visit to Germany we intended to write the business in both names, but as it stands now I am unable to get into the warehouse or the bank. . . . Our business was built up in trusting each other. I have kept books on all items bought and sold but I don't know where it is stored. . . .

In his letter, Hauptmann appears to be somewhat anxious about his inability to trace his late partner's assets. But the letter also appears to be self-serving. The most serious question about it, one which Wilentz stressed in his cross-examination, is Hauptmann's statement about the amount he and Fisch had invested in their partnership. "We figured out the value of my stocks which on November the first, 1933, amount to twelve thousand dollars. . . . I gave Isidor $5,500 out of my private bank. . . ." But Hauptmann's own ledger and the FBI accounting summaries make it plain that he didn't withdraw $5,500 from his bank or brokerage accounts during that period. And there has never been any evidence that Hauptmann had cash hidden in a "private bank"—that is, money hidden in his trunk as he claimed at his trial. Although I've discovered that most of what Hauptmann told police when he was in custody and later swore to at his trial was indeed the truth, in this instance I must assume, perhaps unfairly, that he did not have money hidden away. Making that assumption, one must ask how he built up his assets from the $12,000 he may have had before the kidnaping to the claimed $17,500 he invested in the partnership, while losing about $5,000 in the market.

It isn't possible, with the small number of documents available, to understand Hauptmann's figures or to attempt to answer the question with certainty. But some inferences can be drawn from the material at hand.

To start, the evidence clearly demonstrates that Hauptmann did not possess Lindbergh ransom bills until after Fisch had died. Condon stated positively that Hauptmann was not the man who received the ransom money; none of the Lindbergh bills were ever deposited in Hauptmann's brokerage or bank accounts, nor did any turn up when Hauptmann traveled out of the city, where he most logically would have disposed of such dangerous currency; police laboratory reports show conclusively that the ransom bills found in Hauptmann's garage differed from those passed during the two years before Hauptmann says he found Fisch's shoe box. In sum, it isn't likely that the $5,500 he claims to have given Fisch was part of the Lindbergh money.

If Hauptmann did not have $5,500, the only logical explanation for his statement in the letter to Fisch's brother is that he lied.

But why did he lie? And why settle on $5,500 and not some other sum, such as $10,000?

There are clues in his ledger. By the time he wrote that letter to Pinkus Fisch, Hauptmann had learned that he'd been fleeced by his business partner and friend. And from the transactions listed in the ledger and from statements he made to friends, it is plain that Hauptmann believed he had made many thousands of dollars in profits from Isidor's fur trades. In fact, Hauptmann's ledger indicates that he and Fisch had made profits of almost $7,000 speculating in furs and, based on past experience of a 25 percent profit on investment, should have realized gains of another $4,000 or $5,000 on the furs Isidor claimed to have bought and were supposedly stored in warehouses when he left for Germany.

The figures in the ledger bring a little sense to Hauptmann's claim that he "gave Isidor $5,500. . . ." Hauptmann believed that Fisch had made a total profit of about $11,000. Hauptmann's share should have been $5,500. No doubt knowing that Pinkus, as executor of his brother's estate, would not admit that Isidor had been a swindler and would not recognize a claim based on unrealized profits, Hauptmann apparently decided to claim he had actually given Isidor the money in cash.

Such a claim on Fisch's estate would not have been too unethical for Hauptmann, or for many men, under the circumstances. Hauptmann was buying stocks for their partnership through his own stock market account, using his own funds; the ledger clearly indicates stock purchases for the partnership. During the span of the joint venture, the stock trading account suffered thousands of dollars in losses. Hauptmann, as the partner who had put up his stocks, absorbed those losses. He must certainly have felt that to balance his loss, he should have been compensated by the "profits" from Isidor's fur trading. When he could not find those furs that had not been sold, Hauptmann in effect established a claim on Isidor's estate for the amount he believed he would have received had Isidor been honest.

That Hauptmann knew, before writing the first letter to Pinkus, that Isidor had been a swindler is obvious from the documents at hand. After Isidor's death Hauptmann began to discuss his partner's finances with their friends. He learned Isidor was not a wealthy man, as he had claimed, but that he owed money to several people, including Mrs. Hile. Most distressing, for Hauptmann, is that Henry Uhlig, Isidor's childhood friend, who sailed with him to Germany and who was at his bedside when he died, told Hauptmann in this period that Fisch had cheated him. In an interview in the district attorney's office in October 1934, another friend of Fisch, Max Falek, said that he and Uhlig were at Hauptmann's house discussing their fruitless search for Fisch's furs and other assets. Hauptmann showed them a fur price book and Uhlig, who was also a furrier, looked through it and said, "Isidor claimed he paid more for the furs than they really cost. He was cheating you." Falek told the district attorney: "I never knew Fisch to be that kind of fellow. I trust him with everything I did."

These events, and the transactions recorded in Hauptmann's ledger, make it possible to understand why he falsely claimed that he had given Fisch $5,500 in cash.

Pinkus Fisch responded to Hauptmann's letter on June third, once more confirming in a few sentences that Isidor had said he and Hauptmann were business partners. "He spoke very well of you," Pinkus wrote, "saying that you were his best friend and adviser with whom he talked over his private and business maters. . . ."

In this second letter, Pinkus asked a number of questions about the partnership and wrote that he'd given Henry Uhlig a letter which, he hoped, would have the force of power of attorney so that Uhlig would be able to get information from banks in which Isidor had safe deposit boxes. After Uhlig conducted a search and compiled information on Isidor's assets, then Pinkus would come to America to settle the estate. And he supplied Hauptmann with a list of furriers and warehouses in which, he said, Isidor's $21,000 worth of furs were no doubt stored.

By his next letter Hauptmann seems to have been growing frantic. He has, he said, investigated at the warehouses and furriers Pinkus named, but either the firms do not exist, or the warehouses never heard of Isidor Fisch and never had any of his furs in storage. "We attempted to locate the firms you mentioned in your letter, but we could not find them," Hauptmann complained.

Richard was unable to locate those firms because Isidor had manufactured them. It is impossible at this date to know whether Richard understood the extent of the fraud Isidor had perpetrated upon him—although it is clear he suspected—but, after his arrest, police investigated those firms and learned that Fisch had been a confidence man. The safe-deposit box, which had been opened by court order a month before Hauptmann's arrest, was found to be empty. The largest furrier that Fisch claimed to have been doing business with, Klar & Miller Brothers, on West Twenty-eighth Street, was investigated by Detective Max Leef of the 32nd Squad. In a report dated October 5, 1934, Detective Leef says his inquiries in the fur district disclosed that the firm never existed; further, the telephone number for the firm listed on a bill left with Hauptmann by Isidor Fisch belonged to another furrier at a different address, and that furrier had never done business with Fisch.

The strongest evidence that Fisch was a swindler is found in a report by Detective Leef dated October 7. In it he says that he had interviewed a Louise Helfert, "a lady friend of Isidor Fisch," who admitted that for the last year or so she had been making out for Fisch "bills in the thousands of dollars on the letterhead of Klar & Miller, doing it because Fisch did not have a typewriter." Detective Leef notes: "Klar & Miller Brothers is the nonexistent fur company."

With Fisch proving to be a thief, police told the newspapers that he was believed to have been Hauptmann's "accomplice" in the kidnaping and extortion. But by the time David Wilentz came into Bronx Supreme Court to fight Hauptmann's attempt to overturn the order extraditing him to New Jersey, all discussion of Fisch as a thief and a probable extortionist was forgotten. All information on the partnership between Richard and Isidor was suppressed so that the state could label Hauptmann's defense "the Fisch story."

The evidence in these dozen or so police and FBI reports appears to confirm rather conclusively that Isidor and Richard had indeed established some kind of stock market and fur-trading venture, that Fisch was a rather unprincipled rogue with criminal connections, that he swindled Hauptmann and others, and that Hauptmann was owed several thousand dollars by Fisch, as he had claimed from the moment the ransom money was found in his garage.

None of this evidence was ever presented to the jury at Flemington, or to the public.

17

When Albert S. Osborn and his son, Albert D. Osborn, testified at Hauptmann's trial as the foremost experts on questioned documents the prosecution could find, they unequivocally declared Hauptmann had written all the ransom notes; there could be no question about it, they said, and there was no other possibility.

But there are, in the documents at hand, several questions which make their conclusions less than perfect.

To start, the elder Osborn in all his published work over more than thirty years had always maintained that any handwriting expert worthy of carrying the title would not attempt to arrive at an opinion until he had studied a large sampling of the suspect's undisputed writing and compared those writings with the originals of the writings in question, in this case the ransom notes.

Yet the elder Osborn, testifying at Hauptmann's extradition hearing three weeks after his arrest, said that he had worked from photographs of the original ransom notes when analyzing Hauptmann's writing; photographs, the handwriting experts have always said, tend to distort and should be avoided at all times. More revealing still is a letter from the elder Osborn to State Police Superintendent Schwarzkopf, dated September 21, 1934, the day after Hauptmann had completed his dozen hours of writing in the police station. In it, Osborn says he has "examined a large number of writings" by Hauptmann and concludes that Hauptmann was the

369

writer of the ransom notes. But in this brief report, as Osborn called it, he lays particular stress on Hauptmann's "automobile registration cards" and mentions no other documents in the "large number" of writings he examined. Lieutenant Finn has written that the morning Hauptmann was arrested, on September 19, Hauptmann's auto registration applications were sent to Osborn for his study. Handwriting authorities have repeatedly said that a proper analysis of questioned documents requires days and sometimes weeks of study. Osborn himself, in a letter to Bronx Assistant District Attorney Breslin dated October 5, 1934, asked for all the material in the "Hauptmann matter" so that "I will not have to rush my preparation" for the extradition proceedings, more than a full week away. It appears quite likely Osborn identified Hauptmann's handwriting on the basis of the very incomplete writings on the automobile registration forms.

Did Osborn commit himself so early that he could not easily declare he'd been in error, assuming he later reached that conclusion? That he was uncertain of his ground more than two weeks after Hauptmann's arrest is illustrated by a letter he wrote to District Attorney Foley on October 5. In it, Osborn asked, "Do you have any of the handwriting of Mrs. Hauptmann? If she is examined again, I think it would be a good plan to have her do some writing, especially of figures."

This rather strange request makes it appear Osborn is suggesting that although he would be willing to swear Hauptmann had written the ransom letters, he was having difficulty with the numerals in those letters. Could Osborn have possibly believed Hauptmann had written the *words* and Mrs. Hauptmann was called in to write the *numerals*? Or is he in doubt about Hauptmann's hand in writing any part of the notes? In either case, he does not appear to be as certain in this private letter to Foley as he was at the trial. And that letter takes on added significance when one reads through the trial transcript and realizes that not a single one of the handwriting experts testifying for the prosecution mentioned any of the numerals in any of the notes. Not one of their enormous number of photographs illustrated any of the numerals that were liberally sprinkled through all the ransom notes.

Every one of the prosecution's experts conveniently ignored the first ransom letter, the one left in the nursery, when comparing

Hauptmann's writings with the letters sent to Lindbergh. In all their charts they took from the first ransom note only a single word, "is," and declared it looked similar to Hauptmann's writing of that word. They ignored thirty-nine other words and nine numerals because, it seems clear, they could not say Hauptmann had written them. Which brings us back again to Mickey Rosner and the ransom note he displayed all over Manhattan, raising the possibility that if Hauptmann were guilty of anything it was at the very most of being an extortionist.

But even that seems unlikely, not only because of all the evidence which shows rather conclusively that he had nothing to do with the Lindbergh case until finding the money Fisch left in his care, but also because of compelling evidence that the handwriting experts were less than scientific in their methods of analysis.

The truth is that those experts based their identification of Hauptmann as author of the ransom notes almost exclusively on the writing that he produced in the police station after his arrest. The point is worth emphasizing: Hauptmann was called the writer of all the ransom notes almost entirely as a result of comparing those notes with the specimen paragraphs he wrote at the dictation of police, and *not by comparison with his natural handwriting.*

Like all writers who had come before me, I had originally accepted the assertion of the elder Osborn and the other experts that they had examined "a large number of writings" by Hauptmann before arriving at their opinions. Those witnesses and all contemporary writers said Hauptmann was proved to have been the author of the ransom letters after the experts had made a careful study of the "conceded writings"—that is, Hauptmann's writing during the normal course of his life and in the police station. It hadn't occurred to me earlier that in lumping all Hauptmann's writings into a category called "conceded," the prosecution and its experts could have falsified even this "scientific" evidence. But now, after having read police and FBI documents relating to Hauptmann's notebooks, I realized I may have accepted too much on faith. I returned to the trial transcript to learn precisely which of Hauptmann's writings from the years *before* his arrest had been analyzed by the experts.

There was one promissory note, with Hauptmann's signature only. One insurance application, with his signature only. Nine automobile registration applications, each of them containing his signature and several other words such as address and descriptive characteristics, his height, weight, color of hair and eyes.

That was all. Eleven examples of Hauptmann's natural writing before his arrest. Eleven signatures. Perhaps one dozen other words, not counting repetitions of "blond" under a question about his hair coloring and "Bronx" in the space for his address. And some of those words were not written in script, but were printed in block letters.

According to all contemporary newspaper and magazine stories, however, police had seized in Hauptmann's home between fifteen and nineteen notebooks in his handwriting. In the relatively few official documents in my possession there are discussions of at least eight such books—ledgers, address books, memo books—with hundreds of words written in them. I've counted the words in police and FBI reproductions of several of Hauptmann's notebooks. There are, in Hauptmann's hand, 235 separate words, omitting repetitions. Police also retrieved from Hauptmann's home copies in his own hand of the letters he had written to Pinkus Fisch, five pages of script with another couple of hundred words. Thus, there were available to the handwriting experts many scores of pages of Hauptmann's natural writing, filled with hundreds upon hundreds of words in both English and German.

And yet the handwriting analysts ignored all of that material. They condemned Hauptmann almost entirely on the "evidence" of the police station writings.

It is difficult to understand why the expert witnesses did not consult the enormous body of writing by Hauptmann which was available. There are two possibilities. Either the police withheld from the experts all of Hauptmann's natural writings because they realized from a visual examination that those writings wouldn't support their contention that Hauptmann was the author of the ransom notes. Or the expert witnesses saw those writings and pushed them aside because they couldn't be made to fit the only conclusion acceptable to the prosecution, which was paying their fees: that Hauptmann was guilty.

In either event, the handwriting evidence against Hauptmann was as twisted and dishonest as every other piece of evidence and testimony presented by the prosecution.

It must again be stressed that Albert D. Osborn, in discussing

372

with reporters many years later why his firm committed such a dreadful error when it authenticated Clifford Irving's forgery of Howard Hughes's signature, described the two basic techniques of handwriting analysis which his firm had embarrassingly ignored in that case.

To be absolutely accurate, Osborn said, a handwriting expert must obtain samples written at about the same time as the questioned documents so as not to be deceived by changes in the style and character of writing that usually occur as time goes by. That condition was not met in Hauptmann's case. In Hauptmann's writings for the period 1931 to 1933 that were consulted by the expert witnesses, there were three auto registration applications, one promissory note, and one insurance application—documents containing only seven or eight individual words. The amount of writing involved was much too sparse to permit anyone, no matter how expert he claimed to be, to render a valid opinion.

Osborn's second prerequisite for an accurate opinion is that the analyst must be certain the samples he's studying are in the subject's "natural" handwriting. How natural could Hauptmann's writings in the police station have been? From all the evidence available, Hauptmann and his wife were up late the night before his arrest, seeing a friend off on a trip to Germany; there had been a bon voyage party and the Hauptmanns didn't get home until past midnight. They were awake by their usual time, 6:30 the next morning. Arrested several hours later, seeing his home torn apart and his wife in a state of shocked bewilderment, being hammered by police with questions about the gold notes and then being told he was a suspect in a horrible child murder, Hauptmann must have been under enormous stress and in great fear. And then, for at least thirteen hours that night and through the next morning, he was made to write at least sixteen specimen letters (that number were introduced at his trial) and probably three or four times more than that. Furthermore, police had told Hauptmann that the writing they demanded would be used to prove or disprove his guilt, even after the Osborns had warned investigators not to inform any suspect about the reason for wanting his handwriting specimen.

And finally, in his memoirs of the case published in *Liberty*, Lieutenant Finn wrote that the specimen paragraph "was handed to Hauptmann" in the police station. *Handed*, Finn said, not dictated, and Finn was there.

373

Under those circumstances would any person's handwriting be natural? Most decidedly not. Given the intense mental stress that Hauptmann must have felt as he wrote those specimens, even if he had not been beaten as he had charged, his writings would have certainly been as unnatural as the handwriting of someone whose mind was fogged by alcohol or drugs; his writings would have been so far from natural as to have been useless for honest comparison. Yet Hauptmann's writings were used for comparison, they were used to convince the jury and the world of his guilt.

If Hauptmann had been made to write several dozen pages of the specimen paragraph, as I believe was done, and only sixteen were introduced at his trial, that selectivity was a deliberate attempt by police or the handwriting experts to suppress any of those writings which didn't appear to match the handwriting in the ransom notes. Even after such selectivity the experts were forced into some strange contortions to make their opinions more believable. The experts, especially the two Osborns, swore Hauptmann had written "in a disguised hand" when he produced the police station specimens. They didn't seem to be troubled much by the patent absurdity of their logic: that a man who wrote several ransom notes in disguise would later use the same disguise in writing specimens for the police. Most naturally, they did not consider the more logical possibility: the "disguise" they saw was the result of Hauptmann's stress and fatigue.

The handwriting evidence fails on every count. The standards required for accuracy, cited by the Osborns and other experts before the Lindbergh kidnaping and over the subsequent forty years, were violated in Hauptmann's case. The handwriting analysts not only drew their opinions from a stacked deck by relying almost exclusively on the specimen writings for comparison, but each expert also ignored the fact that the ransom notes are written in a system of penmanship completely different from the one Hauptmann had always used in all his writings. The ransom notes are written in the vertical round hand system. Hauptmann wrote in the Palmer-Zaner system, according to Samuel Small, a scholar of penmanship. Small conferred with Governor Hoffman after the trial, begging him not to permit Hauptmann to be executed. Spreading out magnifications of all the writings before the governor, Small declared:

"The shadings are different—the downstrokes and the up-strokes. Every letter has different characteristics—they are started

374

in different places. The smartest criminal in the world, with all the writing in the ransom notes, couldn't do that, couldn't disguise his writing in that way.

"It isn't a question *if* Hauptmann wrote those letters. It is a question whether he *could* write them. I tell you that if you went to the prison and said to Hauptmann, 'I will let you free if you can write a single sentence the way it is written in the ransom letters,' Hauptmann would have to stay in prison the rest of his life. Any expert who has studied types and methods of writing will tell you that."

The vital point is that the elder Osborn, in his own published writings, had himself maintained that no person could ever disguise his handwriting from one system to another. Although Osborn did state at the extradition hearing that the ransom notes had been written in a style "very similar to our old round hand in English," neither he nor any of the other men who testified about Hauptmann's handwriting at Flemington ever pointed out that the defendant's basic penmanship style differed from the penmanship of the person who wrote the ransom note.

The elder Osborn went to some absurd lengths to defend his original judgment, that Hauptmann wrote all the notes. At the extradition hearings he said that one of the important similarities between Hauptmann's writing and the ransom letters is that in both cases "there is hardly an *i* dotted." Hauptmann's lawyer asked:

"There are thousands and thousands of people who don't dot their *i*'s when writing, isn't that so?"

"I would say," Osborn replied, "that there are thousands and thousands of people that occasionally omit it but to omit it entirely, for instance, is an individual characteristic in my opinion."

Pressed on whether there weren't "hundreds of thousands of people" who do not use the dots, Osborn replied, "Well, I think they are very, very scarce."

That, of course, just isn't so; any manuscript collector could point to dozens of specimens in his collection in which the *i* is undotted. Further, although Hauptmann did not dot his *i*'s in the request writings dictated by police, he did occasionally do so in his automobile registration applications—a further hint that perhaps police did tell him precisely how to write those specimens.

That both Osborns were heavily involved in working with police, as amateur detectives, to prove Hauptmann's guilt and were thus

375

ignoring the objectivity expected of scientists, can be seen in several letters found in the files.

On October 2, 1934, the younger Osborn wrote to District Attorney Foley and enclosed photographs of the writing on the door and the closet panel in Hauptmann's apartment "which I made last Friday." Osborn continues: "If this writing on the jamb did not mean anything, why did someone smear it over, as was clearly done?" Yet that writing, which Osborn-as-detective considers so vital to the prosecution's case against Hauptmann, is demonstrably a fraud. In that same letter, Osborn makes another suggestion in his role as sleuth: "In the photograph of the figures on the door there seems to be part of a fingerprint. Perhaps this is Inspector Bruckmann's. I understand he discovered this, but it might be interesting, at least, for one of your fingerprint men to compare it with Hauptmann's."

And in the same letter in which the elder Osborn implied he was having trouble tying Hauptmann into the "figures" in the ransom notes and asking the district attorney to get samples of Mrs. Hauptmann's writing of numerals, he also came up with a brilliant idea for detectives to investigate. "I have suggested to Lieutenant Finn," he wrote, "that if it hasn't been done, it would be a good plan to check up the gas and electric bills of the Hauptmann household, which would show when they were both absent and might give some useful information."

There are other examples, in police and district attorney files, which show rather strongly that the Osborns, rather than being independent scientists, behaved like members of the prosecution team gathering evidence against Hauptmann.

What was it that some legal scholar once said about "scientists" such as handwriting experts? "Skilled witnesses come with such a bias on their mind to support the cause in which they are embarked that hardly any weight should be given to their evidence." Or to quote again a famed trial lawyer: "It has become a matter of common observation that not only can the honest opinions of different experts be obtained upon opposite sides of the same question, but also that dishonest opinions may be obtained upon different sides of the same question."

While exploring the evidence of the handwriting experts, I considered gathering photographs of all the ransom notes and Hauptmann's conceded writings that I could find, and submitting them to

376

one or more authorities on questioned documents for a fresh analysis. But the first man I called, a man who was recommended by my friend in the New York City police department who had secured many of the documents from which I'd been working, told me I'd be wasting my time. "Anyone in this business of questioned documents" he said, "has cut his teeth on the Lindbergh case. Even someone who disagrees with the Osborns' opinion—and that's all it was, an opinion—will not say so publicly. The accepted verdict is that Hauptmann did it and to swim against the current might mean a man's losing his standing in the field. His very career could be jeopardized if he disagreed with the findings of history."

"Do you disagree?" I asked.

"I will not give you an opinion and I will not permit my name to be used in your book. I'm sorry. But I will say this—if I were free to give an opinion it would run counter to old man Osborn's testimony. That's all I will say about it."

Theo Bernsen, a European writer who has been conducting his own investigation of the Hauptmann evidence, did have photographs of many of the writings examined in London. During a trip to New York Bernsen discussed the findings.

"Through a friend," he said, "I made contact with language experts for the German embassy in London. The man I went to is in charge of translating English to German and German to English, getting the proper language and syntax and grammar, all that sort of thing. He is an authority on German writing, a recognized authority.

"I showed him certain parts of the ransom letters. Enough to get his opinion but not enough to make him aware this was the Lindbergh case; I insisted it was historical, had nothing to do with current affairs in any way.

"He said the letters—he didn't know they were kidnap letters—but he said they were not written by a German who had been taught English. They were written by a man who knew English, was brought up in English, and was trying to write the way a German would. The language structure is so peculiar that even the most illiterate German wouldn't make those mistakes, he said. All of it was written by a man who thinks in English and is trying to write Germanic. The grammatical errors show it clearly, the attempt to make a Germanic construction by a man thinking in English.

"He particularly stressed the word 'boad,' the word that Osborn and the others claimed was German. But in German it is written with a *t—boot*—and it's not possible a German just learning English would make that mistake. It was someone who knew English and who believed, from pronunciation he'd heard, that that's the way Germans spelled it."

Although it isn't possible at this date to get a fresh comparison of Hauptmann's handwriting with the ransom notes, because the originals have been locked away by New Jersey state police officials, my research has developed enough evidence to make it possible to state that there is absolutely no proof he wrote any of the ransom notes. I can't claim, from the materials available to me, that there is evidence proving Hauptmann *didn't* write those notes, but simply that the state did not actually prove what it claimed to have proved. Most important of all, from the legal point of view, is that the state's contention that Hauptmann was the kidnaper because it was proved he wrote the first ransom note (and so was proved to have taken the child from the nursery) is a lie. The experts used only one word from the nursery note. They used only seven or eight words from Hauptmann's natural writings. Their conclusions proved nothing except to reaffirm the accusation that some handwriting experts will swear to anything their employers demand.

All the evidence, including the elder Osborn's difficulty with the numerals in the ransom notes, the fervor with which both Osborns became detectives aiding the prosecution in its search for evidence, and, most of all, the peculiar omission from the experts' exhibits of the notebooks written in Hauptmann's hand, leads to only one conclusion: the testimony of the prosecution's handwriting analysts was deliberately and grossly distorted to help police and prosecutor rush Richard Hauptmann into the electric chair. Those experts were not impartial scientists, as they claimed. They were detectives, they were avengers, they were a part of the mob; their vaunted clinical detachment collapsed in the face of the intense need of the police to convict Hauptmann and thus expiate their guilt over not being able to solve the case for more than two years, the need of the public and the press to avenge this foul deed against the heroic Lindy, and the need of Lindbergh himself for . . . I'll leave that to the psychiatric theorists. What is undeniably plain is that, when considered with all the other documentation showing Hauptmann was the victim of an enormity of contrived evidence, the handwriting experts in this case appear to have been as lacking in ethics as Colonel Schwarzkopf, who encouraged perjured testimony, and as all the police and FBI men and eyewitnesses who fabricated evidence and who lied repeatedly.

That charge attains greater validity when we examine documents relating to the testimony of another expert, Arthur Koehler, and the floorboard that was "missing" from Hauptmann's attic and was proved to have been used to make the ladder.

Cut through all of Koehler's testimony about his remarkable (though questionable) feat in tracing the common pine used in a part of the ladder to a lumber mill in the South and eventually to a lumberyard in the Bronx, and we are left with the attic floorboard. That is the heart of Koehler's evidence against Hauptmann, that a floorboard in his attic precisely matched, in the pattern of its grains, the ladder upright called Rail 16. If Koehler was honestly mistaken, or if he lied and distorted, then all of the state's evidence about the ladder falls to pieces.

To go back to the trial. New Jersey State Police Detective Lewis J. Bornmann had testified that when he searched Hauptmann's attic on the eighth day after Hauptmann's arrest he noticed that one of the rough pine boards at the extreme edge of the attic floor was shorter than all the rest. Upon closer examination he realized that a piece which must have originally been eight feet long had been sawed off and removed from the attic; proof to support that observation was then found, a small pile of sawdust under the remaining piece of flooring. He also noted "that there were nail holes still in the beams" across which the missing attic board had once lain. Bornmann then took Rail 16, the only piece of lumber in the ladder which was not new and which apparently had once been used indoors, and laid that piece across the beams. He inserted into the ladder rail four nails of the type that had been found in the ladder and, he swore, "those nails fitted perfectly into the holes that were still in the beam."

I had instinctively questioned Bornmann's testimony on reading through the trial transcript because it seemed likely that in those eight days during which police had searched the Hauptmann apartment for money, had torn the garage down to the ground, and had ordered the very walls stripped down when they could find no more than the $14,000 or so in gold notes—it seemed to me that in those first days of the search someone would have noticed a piece of attic board was missing.

379

The materials I copied from the files of the Bronx district attorney and which I received from police files disclose that the attic had been repeatedly searched in the week before Bornmann made so startling a discovery of a piece of tangible evidence that prosecutor Wilentz could promise the jury he would "hang the ladder around Hauptmann's neck."

On the nineteenth, the day before police found the ransom money, a day during which they frantically searched for that money, State Police Trooper Horn went through the entire building from attic to basement, accompanied by a half dozen New York City detectives and Justice Department agents. Trooper Horn does not mention anyone noticing the missing piece of attic floorboard in the report he wrote the next morning.

On September twentieth another group of investigators from each of the three police agencies involved were sent to Hauptmann's home "to conduct a thorough and systematic search of the entire premises, including the basement, *attic*, and garage. . . . A thorough canvass of the floors was made. . . [emphasis supplied]." Once more, there was no mention of the missing floorboard and the telltale pile of sawdust.

On the same day State Police Corporal Samuel Leon made another search of the home with one other officer from the New York police and from the FBI— each team was always composed of at least one member of each agency—and he later wrote in his report: "We then searched the kitchen, bedroom, nursery, parlor, *attic*, and cellar, but were unable to find anything connected with the Lindbergh case [again, emphasis supplied]."

This is still the morning before the gold notes were found in the garage. And Agent Turrou later wrote that on that morning J. Edgar Hoover, waving aside Colonel Schwarzkopf's protestations that the Hauptmann place had been thoroughly searched, dispatched other teams to take still another crack at it. After the ransom bills were found in the garage, at least two other searches of the attic were made. In neither report of those searches is there any mention of the unusual attic floorboard.

Those reports indicate clearly that evidence other than ransom money was being sought by the police but nothing of value was discovered. Yet on September 22, when it was apparent no further money would be found in and around Hauptmann's home, police were specifically sent to make another search for evidence other than currency. Three New Jersey state police sergeants and four New York City detectives were given the assignment. Specifically, Sergeant A. Zapolsky wrote in his report, "We were assigned to search the attic." A thorough search was made, he wrote. "In the attic we picked up a mason's bag containing two trowels, two pieces of pipe, one ruler, one plane blade, and one empty fiber suitcase." After what Zapolsky called "a very thorough and minute search," that is all the evidence seven investigators came up with; there is no mention of the partially missing floorboard.

These police reports continue day after day, and not one of them makes any mention of this board which later turned out to be the most important piece of evidence directly linking Hauptmann to the kidnaping in Hopewell. At least two other reports in this week after Hauptmann's arrest state, in fact, that the attic contained no evidence at all.

Turning now to the day of Bornmann's remarkable discovery, the files available show that in his own initial report setting out his activities on September 26, he wrote: "This date detailed by Captain Lamb to continue the search on the above-captioned home. Meeting Detective Tobin, two police carpenters, and Supt. Wilson on the premises at 9 A.M., we immediately proceeded to make a thorough search of the attic. *Nothing of value was found*, with the exception of several small pieces of wood and shavings and several cut nails that may possibly have a bearing on the case [emphasis supplied]."

In several later reports of the same date, Bornmann does describe his discovery in the attic. But it is difficult to understand why Bornmann went through the trouble of writing the first report which says five police officers combed the attic without success when, if he is to be believed, he had not completed his search. A report for the files is a summation of a detective's activity during the day or on one specific assignment. None of the police and FBI reports in my possession was written until the day following an assignment and some were written days later. For Bornmann to write a report about a 9 A.M. search of the attic, and then to write follow-up reports of the same date, is at least to be viewed with suspicion.

Such suspicion intensifies on a reading of all the reports on searches of the attic I've been able to find. For it becomes clear that at the very least, thirty-seven different police officers searched Hauptmann's attic on at least nine separate occasions before Bornmann discovered a piece of flooring was missing, yet not one of those other investigators was capable of noting that a board in the attic had been sawed in two. For such a thing to have occurred, each of those thirty-seven men, and possibly many others whose reports I do not have, must have been as blind as the witness Hochmuth.

No, it seems rather likely Bornmann manufactured that evidence. Certainly, were any competent defense attorney in possession of these files detailing the week-long search of the attic that turned up no evidence of the missing length of wood, Bornmann's testimony would have been impeached and he would have been absolutely discredited. And Wilentz could not have then called Arthur Koehler to "hang the ladder around Hauptmann's neck."

The first line of Bornmann's report reminded me to turn to other documents I'd skimmed through, concerning fingerprints on the ladder, which I'd intended to explore in greater depth later. Bornmann had written: "This date detailed by Captain Lamb to continue the search. . . ." Captain Lamb? A rather interesting gentleman, this Captain Lamb.

Back during the first week of the kidnaping, long before Hauptmann had been arrested, New Jersey state police told newspaper reporters that not a single fingerprint had been found on the kidnap ladder. Upon reading those stories about the peculiar lack of prints, Dr. Erasmus Hudson, a respected New York physician and criminologist, volunteered his services to the police. Hudson had been experimenting with the relatively new silver nitrate process, far superior to older fingerprint "dusting" technology. He persuaded State Police Superintendent Schwarzkopf to permit him to demonstrate the process, and was able to raise over five hundred prints from the ladder. Most of them were the prints of policemen and reporters, for by then the ladder had been handled by a great many people. But at least twenty could not be identified as the prints of anyone known to have touched the ladder. These unidentified prints were photographed by Dr. Hudson, for use in the event a suspect was later arrested. Police confiscated the photographs and negatives. FBI Director J. Edgar Hoover later told Governor Hoffman those photographs were never sent to Washington for comparison against the prints of thousands of known criminals.

Hauptmann's fingerprints no doubt were not found on the ladder; had they been, Wilentz would have used that evidence in court. After his arrest, state police repeatedly fingerprinted Haupt-mann, forcing him to let them ink his fingertips and even his palms and the edges of his hands. Hauptmann protested that he had been printed many times in the several days since his arrest, but the New Jersey troopers insisted none of his earlier prints had been clear enough.

After those prints had been taken from Hauptmann, two New Jersey police officers consulted Dr. Hudson. They asked: Is it pos-sible to counterfeit fingerprints? And how do we go about it? Those officers seemed quite disappointed, Hudson later said, when he told them that although counterfeiting was possible, "I would be able to detect the difference between real and counterfeit finger-prints."

One of those officers was Trooper Kelly, the fingerprint man for the state police. The other was the superior investigating officer on the case, the man coordinating the work of all New Jersey police and detectives, Captain John Lamb.

That name, of the man who was seriously asking whether it was possible to counterfeit fingerprints—Hauptmann's, no doubt—seemed familiar. Someone, perhaps Murray Bleefeld, had men-tioned Captain Lamb in connection with the other famous New Jersey criminal case of this century, the Hall-Mills murder. I did a little research in some of the crime books on my shelves. The Rev. Edward Wheeler Hall and Mrs. Eleanor Mills, his choir singer and his mistress, had been found murdered in a lover's lane in New Brunswick, New Jersey, in September 1922. Both had been shot several times and Mrs. Mills's vocal cords had been slashed. Strewn around the bodies were fragments of letters from Mrs. Mills to Rev. Hall—"I want to look up into your dear face for hours as you hold my body close"—and the murders became, most naturally, a newspaper sensation. But after a rather casual investi-gation by police and a purple-prosed one by reporters, the case was closed. Four years later, as a result of a campaign by the *New York Daily Mirror*, during a circulation war against an upstart paper, the *Daily News*, the investigation was reopened. One of the leading in-vestigators on the case was then Sergeant John Lamb. It was Lamb who persuaded the sluttish, middle-aged Mrs. Jane Gibson (known as the Pig Woman) to belatedly come forward and swear she had witnessed the murder while she was out on her mule, Jenny, look-ing for the thieves who'd been raiding her corn bin. The Pig Woman testified that the killers were the reverend's wife, Frances, two of her brothers, and her cousin. As she testified, Mrs. Gibson's elderly mother sat in the front row of the court muttering, "She's a liar, she's a liar, she's a liar." The jury reached the same opinion, especially after other witnesses testified that she was home in bed when the murders occurred, and the four defendants were acquitted. Sergeant Lamb's reaction was never recorded.

(As an aside, the investigator who convinced Mrs. Gibson's relatives to testify for the defense and who was directly responsible for ruining Lamb's attempt to convict the defendants on patently perjured testimony was the chief of detectives of Burlington County, Ellis Parker. An old friend of Mrs. Hall's family, Parker felt strongly that "this here's a frame-up," and he conducted his own investigation. Years later, when the Lindbergh child was kidnaped, Colonel Schwarzkopf and his chief investigator on the case, Captain Lamb, refused to permit Parker to join the investigation even though the governor at the time, A. Harry Moore, had ordered Ellis to participate.)

All in all, the circumstances surrounding Bornmann's claimed discovery in the attic of a missing piece of floorboard, and Captain Lamb's propensity for contriving testimony against murder suspects makes it highly probable the attic evidence was contrived—as fingerprints would have been had Dr. Hudson not discouraged Captain Lamb. What I believe most probably occurred in the attic is that either Lamb or Bornmann, remembering the comment of the wood expert, Arthur Koehler, that Rail 16 had once lain indoors and that a search of any suspect's home should be made for a place where the rail had previously been used, decided to fake the evidence once it was clear all prior searches were fruitless. Bornmann then went into the attic. He laid Rail 16 down across one of the floorboards so that the nail holes in the rail would lie above one of the joists. Measuring only roughly, he cut off a length of lumber that would approximately correspond to the length of the ladder rail, but he cut it at least eight inches too long, forced to do so, perhaps, because of the sixteen-inch spacing between joists. He threw that length of lumber away. He then placed Rail 16 over the joist nearest the remaining piece of floorboard, took four of the square-cut nails which he had found in Hauptmann's attic, and slid them into the nail holes in the ladder rail. He then hammered them home, so that they would create holes in the

384

joists precisely corresponding to the angle and spacing of the holes in the rail. When he removed the nails, he had his evidence to directly link Hauptmann to the ladder.

There can be no other explanation. As has been pointed out, a carpenter who works in a lumberyard which is only two blocks from his house, a man who is supposed to be a criminal genius, does not take wood from his own attic should he be lacking a piece. If Hauptmann had made that ladder, he no doubt would have made it in his garage, where he had a workbench and tools, and where he could work in secret. It would have been easier for him to walk two blocks to a lumberyard and buy a piece of lumber of the proper length and width, than to climb into the attic and cut a piece that he later had to plane down on both edges to bring to the proper width.

There is other circumstantial evidence which tends to further support the conclusion that Bornmann created the attic scenario. For one thing, through all the days in which Hauptmann was questioned by police and the Bronx district attorney's staff—questioning that continued after the date Bornmann claims to have found the attic proof of the prisoner's guilt—no investigator ever questioned Hauptmann about it. He was repeatedly interrogated about the ransom money, about the board with Condon's telephone number which had been found in his closet, about his tools and his purchases of lumber, and dozens of other questions connected with the ladder. But not once was he asked to explain the missing board in the attic. From a close examination of transcripts of those sessions in which Hauptmann was questioned and from the memoirs of FBI Agent Turrou, it becomes rather clear that the investigators were absolutely convinced of the prisoner's guilt and were throwing bits of "evidence" at him in an attempt to break him down and get a confession; for some, especially federal agents, the greatest interest was to wear him down so that he would confess and tell them where he'd hidden the remainder of Colonel Lindbergh's money. But it is peculiar that the most dramatic piece of evidence police later claimed to have found, the attic floorboard, was never used to destroy Hauptmann's obstinate disavowal of guilt.

Similarly, it is difficult to believe that if the attic evidence existed at the time of Hauptmann's extradition hearing in mid-October, District Attorney Foley and Attorney General Wilentz would not have produced it in the Bronx court. Hauptmann was suing to overturn the extradition order signed by New York Governor Leh-

385

man. The prosecutors had to show that Hauptmann had been in the area of Hopewell on the day of the kidnaping. The only proof they had was the eyewitness, Millard Whited, who testified he had seen Hauptmann near the Lindbergh estate on two occasions, the last of which was a couple of days *before* the kidnaping. And Hauptmann's attorney put on the stand three men from Hopewell who had known Whited for many years; each of them said his reputation in the area was dreadful, he was a liar and a cheat. Albert S. Osborn had testified that Hauptmann wrote all the ransom notes, but that was not evidence Hauptmann had been in the Lindbergh nursery and personally left the note there; even if he had written it, someone else could have performed the actual abduction. Had the attic evidence been discovered on September 26, it seems logical to conclude that the prosecution would have presented it at the extradition hearing even if Arthur Koehler had not yet made the very thorough study he later swore he did make. With so relatively weak a case against Hauptmann in the Bronx, the prosecution would probably have introduced the attic evidence had it truly been discovered almost three full weeks before the Bronx hearing.

Bornmann, who lived in the Hauptmann apartment from the day after the arrest until the trial, must have manufactured the attic evidence long after September 26 and then back-dated his reports so that it would appear he had simply decided to make another search of the attic on that date. He could not pretend to have found the evidence before September 26, because his report and the reports of other investigators said that up to that date nothing of interest had been found. And he could not have filed a report a week or a month after that date, because the delay would have been more suspect. So he filed his fake report with a date and time immediately following his last authentic report of his fruitless search of the attic.

The evidence discovered by Bornmann is probably the most demonstrably false of all the evidence against Hauptmann. And it is Bornmann's evidence upon which the credibility of Koehler's testimony hinges. Without that ladder rail, none of Koehler's testimony can be considered even circumstantial evidence connecting Hauptmann with the kidnap ladder; without that ladder rail, in fact, Koehler's testimony is absolutely valueless.

That Koehler's testimony, the evidence Wilentz himself considered the most vital to the prosecution, is indeed worthless can be demonstrated even without resort to the overwhelming proof that Bornmann was a liar. The physical properties of Rail 16 itself provide proof it could not have come from that attic in spite of Koehler's assertion that it did.

Koehler, you will recall, asked the jury to follow the surface grain of the attic board, to "imagine" where the grain would have traveled along a piece of wood of almost two inches that was missing from one end, and then follow the grain to Rail 16. Koehler was able to "imagine" it and he asserted the grain continued in a common pattern from the attic board to the ladder rail.

But after the trial two other wood specialists working for the federal government, Arch Loney and Roy Knabenshue, came forward and said that when they read of Koehler's testimony and studied photographs of the boards, they immediately contacted the defense and offered to testify that by no stretch of anyone's imagination could they have come from the same lumber stock. But chief defense counsel Reilly told the two men they were not needed.

One of the things these two wood specialists cited, according to newspaper reports, was a knot in the wood of Rail 16 on which Koehler leaned heavily. Koehler had testified that this knot created a distinctive pattern that could be traced over to the attic board despite the missing piece. However, Loney and Knabenshue maintained, Koehler had minimized the significance of the difference in quality of the knots in each board, and that difference alone would make it unlikely the boards had once been connected. The knots in each board produced clearly defined rings around them. But the rings in Rail 16 were in no way as distinct or similar to the rings that could be seen in the attic board. They were flatter and fuzzier. Had the boards once been connected, the two men said, the knots and their rings would surely have looked more alike. That they were dissimilar made it likely they had not been part of the same length of lumber. This lack of similarity, it must be pointed out, was not a defect of the photographs the two wood specialists studied; Koehler mentioned it in his testimony as he handled the two boards, but he passed hurriedly over it.

Koehler had used other photographs to back up his conclusion, and Loney and Knabenshue separately pointed to them as even greater evidence Koehler was distorting the truth. One of the photographs showed the butt ends of the ladder rail and the attic board. One was placed on top of the other to demonstrate that the annual rings of the tree from which the boards had been cut were precisely the same on each edge, indicating they once had been connected. The photographs seem to show the same curvature, the same arc in the annual rings, and their evidence can be convincing. But then Koehler carried his demonstration an unnecessary step further, and damned his own evidence.

What Koehler did was to take the portion of the photograph showing the butt end of the ladder rail and cut off the left side of it. He then superimposed the remaining right side of the butt upon the photograph of the floorboard's butt end. This demonstrated, he said, that the rings which could be seen in one board matched perfectly the rings seen in the other—"the grain in the end of the ladder rail matched that in the end of the floorboard," as he put it in his testimony.

In truth, the photographs demonstrate most clearly that Koehler was forcing his "scientific" evidence to fit his need to prove Hauptmann guilty. As one can see upon examining the pictures, Koehler had to lift the ladder rail, the right-hand section in his reconstruction, perhaps as much as a quarter inch in order to get the rings to match. There is no possible way that a board, cut in half across its width, can have its grains matched up unless the surfaces of each piece are flush.

However, there was testimony that the ladder rail had been planed across one surface so that it was about one sixteenth of an inch thinner than the attic floorboard. Is it possible that planing had removed enough wood so that Koehler was justified in lifting the ladder rail section of board in his photograph to take into account the missing wood? A close examination of the pictures shows that is not possible. The right-hand board, the ladder rail, juts out far above the attic floorboard, much too far to be accounted for by the planing of the other surface. A precise measurement, even in the reduced-sized photographs, makes it clear that for Koehler's speculation to be accurate, then the upper surface of the board from the attic floor must also have had some of its surface removed. And that never occurred.

Still, the annual growth rings do appear to match rather precisely. If my conclusion was correct, that the two boards had never been one piece of lumber, is it possible that two pieces of wood cut from different trees at different times—even years apart—could produce growth rings that would match almost precisely?

I remembered that there had been an article in my town's local newspaper, the Ridgefield *Press,* about a rare botanical event, the growth to maturity of an American chestnut tree. Once quite common, the chestnuts were decimated soon after the turn of the century by a fungus bark disease that usually kills the trees off before they attain more than fifteen or twenty feet in height. But a forty-foot chestnut was found growing in the town and the paper ran a long article on it. The reporter interviewed J. Mortimer Woodcock, who had run a nursery in the town for several decades and who was also "a former U.S. forester."

I called Mr. Woodcock. He remembered Koehler's testimony very well, he said. He had graduated from Syracuse University's School of Forestry in 1927 and had of course been interested in the wood expert's detective work in the Lindbergh case. I asked: Do you remember what you thought about his testimony at the time?

"Certainly," he said. "You can't match up grains of wood and say this board came from the same tree as that board. You can tell what type of tree it was. You can tell how good the growth was in one year compared to another year, by the annual rings in the board. But matching up the grain the way he says he did is not possible."

I went over to see Mr. Woodcock, bringing with me copies of Arthur Koehler's photographs. He studied them for a time.

"You see," he said, "each tree grows according to the weather. If you had a stand of this pine down in Carolina, growing in the same area, each tree would reflect the climate . . ."

"So you might have a number of trees in the same area with precisely the same growth, the same configuration of annual rings?" I asked.

"I would say so. But then again there could be variations because of soil variations. Still, if you cut a number of pine trees from the same area of the same woods it would be very difficult to ever identify one board as coming from a certain tree or to say that two pieces are from the same tree. It is always going to be possible to have one board and then find another board from a different tree that has the same size rings as the first, the same grain, the same good growing seasons and bad growing seasons. Especially if both trees that the boards came from were growing in the same area under the same climatic conditions."

I had brought with me a couple of pieces of common pine which

389

I had cut from one length of lumber, to help demonstrate what Koehler had done with his photographs of the board edges. Woodcock began examining them. He held the edges toward me.

"You can see the rings here are both running the same size," he said. "If you trimmed this piece off another board that had the same size rings, the same growth, I wouldn't know that they'd come from two different boards or from the same board. And I don't think anyone could swear to that for certain."

We discussed Koehler's photograph, in which he superimposed a part of the ladder rail on the attic floorboard in order to show that the grains matched. I explained my deduction, that by lifting one board in order to make its grains match with the second, Koehler actually proved they had come from different stocks of lumber.

"It certainly would be logical that by raising this piece higher than the other," Woodcock said, "he's forcing grains to match where they really don't. The only time that could happen is if one piece had been planed across the surface . . . but that can't be in this case because the top surface of one board is lifted up above the surface of the other. If these pieces were supposed to be attached and there wasn't a really large gap between them, then it can't work the way Koehler claimed it did."

"Let's go back to the surface grain that Koehler said he could trace from one board to the other. You said it would be difficult for anybody to say that one piece of wood was cut from the same long board that another piece came from."

"Very difficult," Woodcock said.

"Another way of putting it is that grains of wood are nowhere near as distinctive as, let's say, your fingerprints. In theory, no two people have the same sets of fingerprints. Is that true of wood grains?"

"Absolutely not. You can identify varieties of wood easily enough and you can tell from the rings a great deal about the growth of the tree. But to come down and identify individual trees and individual boards of lumber and match them, that's not possible. A lot of trees have the same growth and a lot of lumber is going to be easy to match up. There isn't enough variety among growths, especially from the same forest, to be able to say that this board came from the same tree as that board and from no other tree, or that this board was once attached to that board. It's just not possible."

As I was leaving, Woodcock stopped me at the front door. "You know," he said, "if Koehler did that to make the end grains match, well . . . he was highly respected, he was the leading authority in the field. How he could have done it is beyond knowing."

I drove home and returned to the reports that involved Arthur Koehler. And what I found in those documents helps impeach Koehler's testimony even further, for they make it plain that Koehler, like so many others, was distorting truth in order to create a more perfect case against the defendant.

Koehler had testified that Hauptmann's plane and only that one plane could have left the distinctive marks in the ladder's wood that he had found there. At his trial, several carpenters testified in Hauptmann's behalf that almost any plane would leave the marks Koehler claimed were so distinctive, if the tool was held in a distorted position no carpenter would use. I consulted several carpenters in town, and tried it myself, and in every case it was demonstrated that by holding the plane at an unnatural angle to the surface of wood being worked on, any gouge you're trying to make will show up. Koehler's experimental gouges with Hauptmann's plane in court appear to be the result of his need to reproduce for the prosecution the patterns he claimed to have found in the ladder's wood.

Koehler's demonstration of those gouges was based on the premise that after making the kidnap ladder some time in late 1931 or early 1932, until his arrest in September 1934, Hauptmann neither used nor sharpened that plane blade. But it is clear from police reports that Hauptmann did use that plane on several occasions after the kidnaping. And since he was a skilled carpenter, with an emery wheel in his garage, it is likely he had sharpened the blade at least once. Had he sharpened it, this part of Koehler's testimony would collapse. It isn't possible at this time to learn whether it had been sharpened during that thirty-month period. But even if the blade had never been laid against the emery wheel in that period, the nicks that existed in it before the kidnaping would have assumed a completely different character during its quite frequent use up to the day of his arrest.

For Hauptmann used that plane during his work at the Majestic apartments. (And he had told police several times during their days of questioning, before he ever learned of the existence of Arthur Koehler, that when he was hired to work at the Majestic he sharpened all the tools in his toolbox the day before reporting for work.) In October 1932, Hauptmann made a door for another tenant in the building in which he lived. That tenant, Victor Schussler, told police without possibly knowing the significance of his remark that he frequently went into Hauptmann's garage "to borrow a chisel and a plane and other tools." Hauptmann built a wardrobe closet and a crib for his son after the child's birth in November 1933. He also said, and it was confirmed by police, that even after quitting work to concentrate on his stock market speculations, he occasionally did carpentry for customers of the lumberyard near his home who had projects they couldn't handle themselves and who asked the yard foreman to recommend a good carpenter. In all of these carpentry projects, and possibly many more that I have not learned about, Richard Hauptmann must have used his plane. And it is inconceivable that he did not sharpen it at least once.

Koehler, you'll remember, also testified at the trial that Hauptmann's toolbox was lacking a three-quarter-inch chisel. Conclusion: Hauptmann had dropped his chisel under the nursery window, where it was found by police.

During the questioning by police on September 20, a full day after his arrest, Hauptmann was asked whether he owned any chisels and he replied that he had a mixed but full set of National Tool and Stanley chisels ranging in size from one-quarter inch to two inches. Koehler knew the chisel found on the Lindbergh property was a Bucks Brothers brand, manufactured before 1900. Yet he blithely reported a chisel missing out of Hauptmann's set of more modern chisels. If he were the absolutely disinterested man of science he claimed to be, Koehler would have questioned that curious discrepancy and would, perhaps, have wondered about the other evidence—for certainly it is difficult to conceive that a carpenter who had lost his chisel early in 1932 would by late 1934 have failed to replace it, even though he had worked for at least a couple of weeks at a professional construction job.

I have found further evidence that once again either the police or the prosecution committed an illegal act against Richard Hauptmann in order to convict him. A New York City police department document dated September 29, 1934, is an inventory of the tools found in Hauptmann's toolbox. In that list of several dozen handtools is the line: "1—cold chisel ¾"—National Tool make."

Hauptmann did have a three-quarter-inch chisel on September

29. Some time between that date and Koehler's theatrics at Flemington, police or prosecutor removed it.

There is additional evidence that Hauptmann had a *second* three-quarter-inch chisel which was hidden from the jury. At around this time in my investigation I was told that all the evidence in the Hauptmann case which was once in the possession of Attorney General Wilentz was stored in a small basement room at New Jersey State Police Headquarters in Trenton. I called the Superintendent of Police, Major George Quinn and, after giving him my background as a newspaper reporter and free-lance writer, I asked permission to examine the Hauptmann material.

"I'd just like to see the ladder and the wood and other exhibits used in the trial," I said, "and maybe take fresh photos for my book."

"That can be arranged," Quinn said. "Unfortunately, there is no one currently on the force who was connected with the case, no one who is still on top of it. I'll assign someone to help you go through the material, but it's going to be difficult.

"You know," he added, "the file is still marked open because there's a feeling that others were involved."

I wanted to say, *you people convicted him as a lone killer,* but I held it back and instead said, "Yes, from what I've been reading it seems pretty certain this man Fisch was Hauptmann's accomplice. And there's also the question of the ransom money."

"That's correct," he said. "A large part of it has never been recovered. For a lot of reasons, the case is still open. No one is actively working on it, of course, but it is still open in the event something develops or some new information comes in."

I drove down to Trenton a few days later. Major Quinn was not in that day, but he had assigned Major William Baum, the chief of the Criminal Identification Bureau, to assist me in my search. And Major Baum disappointed me. Because all the documents on the case were haphazardly piled in a small room, he said, it would not be possible for me to go through them. Any documents filed in an orderly manner, in several file cabinets, could not be seen "because I don't know what happened to the keys, it's been so many years since anyone's been in that room that it's all a mess." He quickly added, cutting off my obvious suggestion: "And I don't want to take responsibility for breaking the locks on the files." The upshot was that Baum would assign one of his aides to accompany me and to help me take photographs of the ladder and the wood from the attic. I didn't care about the photographs, that had been simply a ruse to get into the files. "But Major Quinn said I could look through some of the documents," I said. "When we were talking the other day we discussed the fact that Hauptmann must have had accomplices and I said I'd like to see the files because I wanted to make an intelligent guess in my book as to who those accomplices were. He agreed about that."

"I don't care what he said then," Baum replied, but very politely. "We've decided it would be too much trouble giving you access to everything, considering the condition of that storage room."

He took me across a courtyard to an old building he said had been the first barracks erected on the grounds. We went down into a basement, along a dingy corridor to the end, then stopped at what appeared to be a prison cell. On the heavily padlocked steel bars securing the cell was a small hand-lettered sign that read: "Lindbergh Case File." Beyond the steel bars I could see four locked file cabinets on top of which were dozens of cartons of investigative reports, and several score other cartons similarly filled with material. Resting on top of a stack of cartons that lined one wall were the original kidnap ladder, the attic floorboard, and other lengths of wood. Much as I hated to admit it, Major Baum had underestimated the "trouble" which would have been created were I given free access to all the files; it would take me at least six months simply to sort everything.

A trooper was called to assist me. "Mr. Scaduto wants to take photos of the ladder and perhaps the handwriting exhibits," the Major said, pointing to a dozen or so large display cards with photographs of the handwriting that had been used by Osborn and others to explain their opinions to the jury. "Just those things, nothing else," the major added. He left us.

I took my pictures. When I was done I took a chance and began to rummage through Hauptmann's toolbox, rusting on top of one of the cabinets. I'm looking for chisels, I said, evidence that Hauptmann made this ladder. There were several chisels in the toolbox. I measured them with a tape measure I had brought along. None of them was a three-quarter-incher. A few moments later the trooper, his curiosity apparently overwhelming the orders he'd been given to restrict my researches to the ladder and the fingerprint exhibits, pulled from a tall metal locker filled with boxes a rolled-up manila envelope. "This could be it," he said. There was some writing on the outside of the envelope. It said: "Two old chisels found in Hauptmann's garage."

We opened the envelope and discovered two chisels inside. I measured their cutting edges. Both were three-quarter-inch chisels. One of them was a Bucks Brothers brand similar to the one found under the nursery window. But this one was almost new, definitely not the chisel which had been found and was introduced at the trial, because it wasn't old enough and it didn't have a tag attached with an exhibit number as it would have had were it the one placed into evidence. The other chisel was much older, a Stanley. One surface of the wooden handle had been whittled flat: a carpenter's technique for preventing a round-handled tool from rolling off a shelf.

It was possible the Stanley was the chisel police had taken from Hauptmann's toolbox so that the prosecution could claim it was missing, but since the notation on the envelope said the chisels had been "found in Hauptmann's garage" it is more likely I had located two *additional* three-quarter-inch chisels. Either way, the evidence was strong: on the day Hauptmann was arrested police had confiscated two or three of his three-quarter-inch chisels so that Arthur Koehler could add one more piece of damning but false evidence to his testimony "proving" Hauptmann had built the ladder and had killed the child.

(I also found a small box filled with photographs of "Latent fingerprints—Hauptmann case." There were possibly two hundred photos. Most of them appeared to be of prints found on the ladder; some were prints which had been lifted from smoother surfaces, perhaps in the nursery. Prints the police denied they had ever found.)

Koehler's scientific objectivity and his impartiality are open to question in still another incident connected with his work in "tracking Hauptmann to justice," as the newspapers put it in those days. Apparently to demonstrate to his readers that Hauptmann was guilty beyond all doubt, Koehler had written in the *Saturday Evening Post* that a man later identified as Hauptmann had come into a Bronx lumberyard with a companion on a day that Koehler and Bornmann were poring over the records in an attempt to find the customer who had bought common pine of the size and type used in the ladder. The men acted very suspiciously, offering a gold note in payment and then fleeing without taking their purchase, after they glimpsed the badge on Koehler's vest as he sat in an open office behind the counter. The foreman of the yard, Koehler said, later identified one of the men as Hauptmann. This event, in late 1933, was absolute proof that Hauptmann possessed gold notes long before he claimed he had found the horde in Fisch's shoe box and that he had guilty knowledge those bills were from the Lindbergh ransom payment. Otherwise, why would he have run away?

The foreman was never called to testify, a curious omission because it was so vital that Wilentz prove Hauptmann's possession of ransom money before August or September, 1934. The reason he did not become a prosecution witness can be found in the transcript of the questioning of this foreman, William F. Reilly, by Bronx Assistant District Attorney Breslin and Captain Lamb.

"Can you relate to us this transaction with reference to a gold certificate?" Breslin asked.

Reilly said, "I couldn't say it was a gold bill. I never seen the ten-dollar bill."

"Do you think you can identify Hauptmann as the man in the lumberyard that day?"

"Yes, I think I can identify him," Reilly said.

"What did the other man, his companion, look like?"

"He was a little guy, short, skinny, and dark. He might be of Italian descent, but *he speaks perfect English. In fact, they both did* [emphasis supplied]."

Later, after failing to identify Hauptmann, foreman Reilly said: "He looks something like the man, but not exactly the same. There's just a resemblance to the man. But the man didn't have the accent this Hauptmann has."

And yet, long after the trial, the impartial scientist Koehler said it was Hauptmann who had fled the lumberyard that day, distorting truth so that he could further establish Hauptmann's guilt in the minds of his readers.

The pile of documents on my desk was dwindling now. Only two other items remained, both relating to the events of the night the Lindbergh child was kidnaped.

Police witnesses had testified at the trial that only two footprints had been found around the Lindbergh home, directly under the nursery window. One was large and indistinct, presumably the kidnaper's. The other was Mrs. Lindbergh's. The police lied.

Official documents show that many other footprints were found—and they were not made by the dozens of state troopers and the hundreds of newspapermen who trampled all over the area within a couple of hours of the alarm. Joseph Wolf was the first trooper to reach the scene after the arrival of the Hopewell police chief and his constable. He went looking for footprints in the mud before anyone else began wandering over the grounds. And he wrote the first major report in the investigation. In it Wolf said:

"The kidnapers consisted apparently of a party of at least two or more persons. . . . Apparently two members of the party proceeded on foot to the east side of the Lindbergh residence and assembled a three-piece homemade extension ladder. . . . Two sets of fresh footprints led off in a southeast direction. . . . Kidnapers arrived in a car which was left parked some distance from the house either in Lindbergh's private lane or a rough road known as Featherbed Lane. . . . I detailed several troopers *so that footprints would not be destroyed* [emphasis supplied]."

Trooper Nuncio DeGaetano, in his report, wrote: "We traced rubber boots or overshoes impressions from the ladders down an old road toward the chicken coop. The footprints went across the road and appeared to stop alongside impressions from an auto."

None of those footprints could have been Lindbergh's because he ran only to the road, which was in another direction. And yet, at the trial almost three years later, both troopers swore the only footprints found in the mud were the two directly under the nursery window; no one bothered to make casts of those impressions, they swore. Although I have been unable to find any report about casts of all these footprints leading away from the nursery window, it seems highly unlikely that Wolf would have assigned several troopers to guard the footprints so that they "would not be destroyed," and then destroy them without taking impressions. One must assume casts were made, or at least careful measurements taken. That evidence was never introduced at Hauptmann's trial. The only inference to be drawn is that it was not produced because it was detrimental to Wilentz's case.

As Trooper Wolf was safeguarding the footprints that were later suppressed by police and prosecution, other troopers were telegraphing and telephoning requests for assistance, contacting police forces throughout New Jersey, New York, and Pennsylvania. Lieutenant Finn, who was instrumental in capturing Hauptmann more than two years later, was to write, as Hauptmann waited to die:

"Do you realize what this meant to Bruno Hauptmann? It meant, among other things, that long before he could possibly reach Holland Tunnel or the ferries, every car coming into Greater New York was being searched for the missing child! The teletype having done its work, the telephone got busy. Within the hour every policeman in New York was on the lookout for the kidnaper."

Finn neglected to disclose that within the hour extra policemen were assigned to the tunnel and ferries with orders to note the license plate number of every car crossing into New York City. When Hauptmann was arrested in 1934, his license number was not among those that had been noted and filed. His car could, of course, have been missed. But it is more likely he was never in New Jersey that night.

That was the full extent of the documentation I was able to recover from law enforcement files. I felt certain those police and FBI reports made a compelling argument that Richard Hauptmann was innocent of the crime for which he was executed. Not only did it seem probable that all eyewitnesses lied, including Condon and Lindbergh, that police suppressed and tampered with evidence that Hauptmann had been at work on the day of the kidnaping and on the day the ransom was turned over to an extortionist, but beyond all that, I had uncovered documents which almost totally demolish the case David Wilentz presented to the world.

Isidor Fisch, those official investigatory reports showed, had most certainly been Hauptmann's business partner in stock market and fur speculation. And Fisch had swindled Hauptmann. Because the available evidence would have so badly damaged the prosecution's case, that evidence was suppressed. Hauptmann's ledger, the letters from Fisch's brother to Hauptmann, the phony bills that Fisch had a woman friend type out to convince Hauptmann he had been buying furs—all these and more had been hidden away so that Hauptmann's defense could be ridiculed as the "Fisch story."

True, not one of my documents proves conclusively that Fisch brought a shoe box filled with Lindbergh ransom money to the Hauptmann apartment in December 1933. But the circumstantial evidence leans heavily in Hauptmann's favor. There was a party for Fisch; even David Wilentz did not attempt to deny that known fact. Fisch had left two valises with Hauptmann for safekeeping while he was away in Germany; police found those valises when they arrested Hauptmann. Fisch had moved out of his furnished room before sailing and he had most definitely asked Hauptmann to store some of his most personal belongings. But was the shoe box among them? The meager evidence available to me suggests that it was. Police laboratory reports reveal that the bills Hauptmann passed and those found in his garage differed from all other ransom bills that were recovered. Police investigation was unable to turn up a single person who could swear that Hauptmann had passed a ransom bill before late August or early September, 1934, when he said he found the money, dried it, and began spending it. And at least one of those potential witnesses, the foreman of the lumberyard whose records Arthur Koehler was examining when two men passed a ransom bill, said that Hauptmann was not one of those men. Finally, Hauptmann's actions in almost deliberately calling attention to himself on those few occasions that he did spend one of those bills quite strongly suggest that he did not know they were part of the Lindbergh ransom.

When the evidence of official lies and distortions, running through every aspect of this case, are placed in balance with the mass of evidence demonstrating that Hauptmann had been telling the truth in every area that it is possible to corroborate, the scales tilt inexorably in Hauptmann's favor.

The materials in my possession also demonstrate that the men involved in the two so-called scientific disciplines in this case, men used by Wilentz with such telling effect, also distorted and lied.

The Osborns and the other handwriting experts were so unscientific in their analytic technique that their testimony was virtual fraud. Recall what these self-styled scientists did: Ignoring many dozens of pieces of Hauptmann's natural writing, these men condemned Hauptmann to death by basing their comparisons almost exclusively on his very unnatural handwriting, those specimens extracted from him during more than twelve hours in a police station where he was probably beaten and where police officers had possibly dictated the grammatical and spelling errors of the original ransom notes. To again use Justice Frankfurter's remark about another case, what does one make of the animus of the elder Osborn, swearing in Flemington that there was no doubt Hauptmann had written all the ransom notes, after indicating in the Bronx that he suspected the prisoner had written the words and his wife had stepped in to write the numerals?

Of Detective Bornmann, who almost certainly contrived the evidence of the floorboard missing from Hauptmann's attic, the best that can be said of him is that he was a cop working in a corrupt police force, working under a superintendent of police who had been quite willing to permit the swindler, Commodore Curtis, to perjure himself by testifying against Hauptmann, and working under Captain Lamb, who apparently attempted to frame three people in the Hall-Mills murder case and who was exploring the possibility of counterfeiting Hauptmann's fingerprints on the ladder.

But Arthur Koehler is another matter. A respected wood technologist, Koehler seems to have been so carried away with his role of detective and with the climate of vengeance against Hauptmann that he lied about his search for the shipments of common pine. He lied in his too-fantastic testimony about matching the wood grains to prove one rail from the ladder came from Hauptmann's attic. He lied about the chisel, the plane, about Hauptmann fleeing from a lumberyard after spotting Koehler's badge—he lied, fabricated, twisted, in almost every respect.

All right. I had, I believed, developed strong proof that Hauptmann was innocent, that every major piece of evidence used against him was either perjured or manufactured. But I wanted even more documentation, I hoped to develop a still stronger case. Most of all, I desperately wanted to find evidence that would solve one way or another whether the real kidnaper and extortionist, had been Wendel, or Fisch, or the Geisslers and Condon, or all of them, working together. I wanted to "solve" this case, although I knew the odds against me after forty years were many millions to one. But I decided to try. And the place to start was at FBI headquarters in Washington.

18

Governor Hoffman had written in his *Liberty* articles that J. Edgar Hoover appeared to have been disturbed by the counterfeiting of the case against Hauptmann. After Hauptmann's conviction, the governor had asked Hoover for assistance in his own investigation. Hoover replied that he could not provide any help because "the Bureau of Investigation withdrew from the case on October 10, 1934"—that is, three weeks after Hauptmann's arrest. Hoffman, who had also received from Hoover some veiled criticism of state police activities, particularly in not sending to Washington the photographs of the fingerprints found on the ladder, believed Hoover had withdrawn his men because he knew state troopers were concocting a case against Hauptmann.

Perhaps the FBI file would provide even greater evidence as to Hauptmann's innocence. Perhaps those files would permit me to speculate on the identity of the actual kidnapers or extortionists. I wrote a letter to Clarence Kelley, the FBI director, requesting permission to examine his agency's files on the Lindbergh case. In that letter I described my newspaper background and the cooperation —authorized by J. Edgar Hoover—I had received from the New York office of the FBI on several investigations into Mafia activities. I also mentioned that Hoover had once sent me a thank-you note for a series of articles on kidnaping that I had written for the *New York Post* which pointed out that "no matter what you may think about the FBI," it must be acknowledged that the bureau had

401

stopped the wave of kidnapings which plagued wealthy families during the twenties and thirties.

Kelley responded by sending me a copy of the Attorney General's order of 1973 which provided that "certain information, with specific deletions, which in the past this Bureau had not made available to the public, would be released as a matter of administrative discretion." By law, he said, the bureau is authorized to charge a fee "for furnishing copies of information and for time spent searching and screening our records." The files on the Lindbergh case, he added, contain more than 41,000 pages and would cost me a little more than $10,000. If I was serious, he in effect said, please send a $2,500 deposit. And then the needle—the hurdle that would stop me from further annoying the FBI:

"If you desire us to process your request, please indicate your willingness to pay fees as high as are anticipated, enclose a deposit as indicated, and submit a *notarized authorization letter from Hauptmann's heirs* granting their approval to utilize any information we will be able to provide you. . ." [emphasis supplied].

Hauptmann's heirs? There was no sign in the newspaper clippings that anyone had interviewed Mrs. Hauptmann since 1937 or so. The last article I had found said she would soon be remarried, and her new husband would adopt Hauptmann's child and give the boy his own name; the article did not print the new name. There was no way I could find them, and Mr. Kelley must have known it.

I made some calls to friends in the FBI and to a couple of congressmen, but the only help I got was the advice: sue him. I responded to Kelley's letter by saying I didn't understand his condition that I must have an authorization from Hauptmann's heirs. "Hauptmann was convicted of murder after a lengthy public trial," I wrote, "and executed, and he certainly no longer has any right of privacy. As for his widow and his son, who was an infant at the time of the trial, I am not seeking any information about them. Certainly any material that may invade their right to privacy can be withheld from me. Since the Bureau will be screening the records and will be making certain 'deletions' in any case, I would imagine that any documents concerning Anna Hauptmann and her son can also be deleted at that time."

Kelley replied: "As you are aware, the release of any material from our investigatory files is discretionary. . . . Even in a case such as Hauptmann's, it is our view that the potential invasion of privacy which could ensue from any release of FBI files extends to the immediate family of the subject involved. It has been our policy to request notarized authorization from the immediate family where the subject of the file is deceased."

Mr. Kelley was telling me: Stay out of my life and out of our files. I didn't like his attitude but I could understand it; the freedom of information act had made it necessary for the FBI to put many dozens of agents and clerks to work processing requests for documents suddenly opened to the public. So I had to find Anna Hauptmann, if she were still alive, or her son. On the chance that she had not remarried, or that the story had been planted so that other reporters would stop looking for her, I consulted the telephone directories for New York and every major city between Boston and Washington, D.C., and out as far as Chicago. There were no listings for Anna or Manfred Hauptmann.

The next long-shot idea was to consult a man who I knew had been looking into the Lindbergh case for almost a decade, Harold Olson, the businessman who believed he might be the child whose body was allegedly found almost three months after the kidnaping. I had avoided Olson because, frankly, he appeared from our brief conversations and from his long and rambling letters to be so completely obsessed with his search for identity that I was afraid he'd turn out to be some kind of nut.

I called Olson at his home in Westport, Connecticut. Despite a habit of rambling on about the Al Capone gang and about how his dreams had provided him with clues for further research, he did tell a rather lucid and somewhat incredible story about the coincidences and circumstantial evidence which made him believe he was Charles A. Lindbergh, Jr.

In brief, this is his story, the result of eight years of personal investigation. Olson was raised in Escanaba, Michigan, near the Canadian border. A birth certificate filed in that town gives his birth date as April 8, 1928, which would make him two years older than the Lindbergh child. His childhood in Escanaba was normal and unremarkable, he says, except for several incidents that did not assume a larger significance until much later. One of these involved his age.

"I was nowhere near big enough to be an average six-year-old when I entered school in February 1934," he says. "I was only forty-two inches and weighed thirty-eight pounds, hardly the size of a healthy six-year-old. It's about right, however, for a four-year-old, which was the Lindbergh baby's age at the time."

He was so small, in fact, that his teacher, whom he remembers only as Miss Lind, insisted he was too young to be in the first grade and should be put back into kindergarten. "She died not long after that," Olson says. "Her replacement told me she had committed suicide." A sister of Miss Lind came from New York to take the body back for burial, but local officials refused to release it and she was buried there.

Olson never had any reason to question that he was the son of Roy Olson and his wife, Sara, until some time in the mid-forties when his mother, after a heated argument with his father, threatened to leave and to take the child with her. During this argument, his mother said Roy Olson was not his actual father. By the summer of 1958, Harold got up enough courage to ask his father about his paternity but all the old man would say was that Harold was "legitimate." He would not supply any other information.

Olson was married in New York in 1959. He went East despite warning from his mother against leaving Escanaba and going to New York. "She said that I would be killed because certain people didn't want me there." His wife, Angie, is the granddaughter of a man who had fought with Garibaldi and came with him to America to live, and it began to trouble Olson that he was uncertain about his own antecedents. But, he said, he did not begin actively searching for the truth about his parentage until 1967, when Roy Olson suffered a severe stroke. As he lay dying, Harold says, "he tried to tell me something important about my past," but he could not make himself understood and he died without being able to speak again. Harold then decided to undertake a serious investigation into his background.

He began to consider the possibility that he is Lindbergh's son when he learned about the very serious doubts about the identity of the body found in the Hopewell woods, and when he began to look into his own skull fracture. He has X rays which show his skull once received an extensive fracture which, according to doctors he's consulted, could have occurred only in very early childhood. The X rays also indicate that extensive reconstructive surgery had been performed on his face, particularly below the eyes. Olson wondered: Could I have been the Lindbergh child and suffered a skull fracture when the ladder broke? And he also wondered

404

whether the plastic surgery had been performed to change his features so that he would not be recognized as Charles A. Lindbergh, Jr. Olson does bear a marked resemblance to the elder Lindbergh and he also has several of Anne Morrow's features.

"My mother had told me that a Dr. Clarence Olson, who was no relation, operated on me when I was a baby to correct a drooping eyelid," Harold said. "But the X rays show there was also surgery done on my chin, probably to erase a cleft—and the Lindbergh child had a pronounced cleft—and there was also plastic surgery done on my nose. One of my aunts, who saw me before the operation, once told me I was a perfectly lovely baby and she couldn't understand why plastic surgery had been done. If she was right, I want to know why it was done."

His search for the answer eventually led him to Dr. Olson's sister, Ida Dalton, who told him that her brother had died in 1965. Ida Dalton's other brother, Olson says he learned, was involved with the Al Capone organization in Chicago. Ida's husband, Bill Dalton, is a former New York bootlegger who dropped out of sight in the 1930s. Harold found a man he is certain was Bill Dalton and, after five years of begging him to tell what he knew about the Lindbergh kidnaping, he says Dalton reluctantly admitted he had been involved.

"He gave me some names, described the route taken after the kidnaping, described the original hideout, discussed the financing, and explained how Hauptmann was framed. He also confirmed that the baby was dropped during the kidnaping and received a severe skull fracture when the ladder broke. He told me no one thought the baby would live after the fall. Then he felt the dent in my head. And he said, 'You're lucky to be alive.'"

Harold began to form his theory that the Lindbergh baby had been kidnaped by the underworld, a theory many police and much of the nation gave credence in 1932. But the motive for kidnaping was not the paltry $50,000 ransom, Olson feels: Bootleggers kidnaped the son of the most famous flier in America because Lindbergh and many other airmail pilots were helping the Treasury Department during Prohibition by reporting stills they sighted from the air; the kidnaping was a warning to all airmail pilots. And, Olson believes, the Al Capone gang was behind it.

The baby was taken to northern Michigan, to Escanaba, then a major stop on the pipeline of liquor coming in from Canada and considered Al Capone territory. At around the time the remains of the body identified as the Lindbergh child's were found in Hopewell, a fisherman named Jim Nelson "found" a child of about the same age. The little boy was in a bag in the bow of a fishing boat docked at Escanaba. That little boy, Olson believes, was the Lindbergh child, and Roy and Sara Olson "adopted" it as their own.

"Before she died my mother admitted that my birth certificate is a fraud," Harold says. "She told me it was the birth certificate of a child she'd had in 1928 and who died before I came along. They just gave me the dead baby's identity because it was easier that way."

Olson had undergone sodium pentothal treatment several times in an attempt to pull from his subconscious the uncertain terrain of his past, but the "truth serum" has not helped him remember much more than he is able to recall while conscious. The psychiatrist who administered the treatment, H. Ezell Brenham of Stamford, Connecticut, however, does say that although "there would usually be good reason to question the stability of a person giving a past history such as Mr. Olson gave . . . he is a very well balanced, emotionally stable man who is undergoing a considerable amount of frustration in establishing his true identity, a frustration which is absolutely normal in such a situation."

As we talked, as Olson told me his story, it was obvious that the only possible way he would ever know for certain whether he is Lindbergh's son is through comparison of fingerprints. Regardless of what state police claimed, I felt certain from what I'd seen in Trenton and for several other reasons, that fingerprints of the infant had been found in his nursery. Governor Hoffmann said he had seen the prints. Dr. Hudson said that he had found infant's prints in the nursery. Evalyn Walsh McLean, the Washington society woman, owner of the Hope diamond, had become involved in the case when she was swindled out of $100,000 by a confidence man who said he could return the child; after Hauptmann's trial she hired a private detective who, she claimed, gave her a set of the child's fingerprints. Harold agreed that he had to locate a copy of those prints if he was ever to prove—or disprove—his claim to be the Lindbergh child.

I told him about the demand by FBI Director Kelley that I get authorization from the Hauptmann heirs before he'd permit me to examine the files on the case, said that if fingerprints exist a copy would be in the FBI files, and asked whether he could help me get into those files. "Do you know where to find Anna Hauptmann or her son?" I asked. Harold told me about a woman in England who claimed she had once been in contact with Anna Hauptmann, as recently as 1973. I telephoned her in London, wrote her, hounded her, and eventually she gave me an address in an Atlantic Coast city where, she said, "Mrs. Hauptmann was living with an elderly woman until about a year ago, and then she moved away. Perhaps the woman still lives there and can help you." She added: "But Mrs. Hauptmann has become very religious and she will no longer discuss the case. She believes the Lord knows Richard was innocent and it is no longer important that the world be told the truth. You'll never break through that defense."

Before beginning my search for Anna Hauptmann, I returned to an area of Richard Hauptmann's story that I had avoided—his last year of life in a small cell only a few yards from the electric chair. I wanted to familiarize myself with those last months of life so that, if I were lucky enough to find Mrs. Hauptmann and could persuade her to cooperate with me, I would have a clearer understanding of what she and her husband had gone through. Governor Hoffman had written about Richard's last months and I turned now to his typescript and to some published material that I had come across and had laid aside.

A couple of days after his conviction, Hauptmann was secretly moved from his Flemington jail cell to the Trenton State Prison. His lawyer, Lloyd Fisher, notified of the transfer, was waiting at the state facility when Richard arrived. They talked for a few moments and, when the warden said the prisoner had to be taken to his cell in the death house, Richard shook Fisher's hand and said:

"Lloyd, I come in here today a man. Maybe some day soon I go out just a piece of clay."

He was taken to Cell 9, the cell nearest the door leading to the execution chamber. It was a large cell, with a comfortable cot, a writing desk, sink, and toilet. Immediately, Richard pasted photographs of his son, Manfred, and his wife against the wall. Anna moved to a hotel in Trenton with their baby for a time and visited Richard every day; the son was cared for by one of the several Hearst reporters who continued to haunt her movements in order to protect their boss's financial stake in the Hauptmanns; the Hearst papers, however, still did not publish any articles that would have raised doubts about Richard's guilt.

Within a few weeks Hauptmann began to write, in German, his autobiography, apparently at the suggestion of Lloyd Fisher. The lawyer brought him the eleven volumes of trial transcript and Richard relived the trial through its pages; the last half of his autobiography was an analysis of the evidence used to convict him. Only a few pages of it was published, in the *New York Mirror*, after his execution.

That execution was stayed by an appeal to the New Jersey Court of Errors and Appeals. While the court considered its judgment, Governor Hoffman was being harangued by Ellis Parker to force a new investigation into the kidnaping. Almost from the moment Hauptmann had been arrested and through his conviction, Parker had repeatedly warned the governor: "Harold, they got the wrong man. They're faking the evidence against him." And then, Hoffman wrote, he received a telephone call from Charles Curtis, former Vice President of the United States, whom Hoffman had known from a few official and social contacts when he'd been a congressman several years earlier.

"Governor, are you looking into this Hauptmann case?" Curtis asked. The appeals court had upheld the conviction and although Hauptmann was appealing further, to the United States Supreme Court, Curtis was certain that court would not overturn the verdict. As governor, the final decision will be yours, he told Hoffman, and as governor you should look carefully into the case before you receive Hauptmann's final appeal for life.

"I'm only one member of the Court of Pardons," Hoffman said. "In New Jersey the governor has no authority to commute a capital sentence."

"No matter," Curtis said, "you must look into it. I think that there are a lot of funny things about that case. I've read a lot of testimony and it doesn't seem to me that Hauptmann was adequately represented, or that he got a very fair deal."

Hoffman claims he began to think seriously about the case for the first time as a result of Curtis's call and because of the ever-increasing number of letters protesting the electrocution of Hauptmann and a telegram from Clarence Darrow begging for commutation to life because "no man should be executed on such flimsy evidence."

It was around this time that Hoffman received a visit from Mark Kimberling, the warden of Trenton State. "Governor," he said, "Hauptmann has asked to see you."

"*Me* see Hauptmann? What for?"

"I don't know exactly, Governor. But he keeps asking for you."

On the night of October 16, 1935, Hoffman visited the condemned block at the prison and sat with Hauptmann in his cell for more than an hour.

"Governor," Hauptmann began after they shook hands, "why does your state do to me all this? Why do they want my life for something somebody else have done?"

"Well, you have been found guilty," Hoffman said. "The courts . . ."

"Lies! Lies!" Hauptmann pointed to the trial transcript. "All lies! Would I kill a baby? I am a man. Would I build that ladder? I am a carpenter . . . I have told the truth. They have a lie detector. Why don't they use on me that and on Dr. Condon also use it? They have too some kind of drug, truth drug, I have heard. Why don't they use on me that drug? And on Dr. Condon use it too?"

Hoffman later wrote that Richard's attitude surprised him. He had almost expected "a cringing criminal begging for mercy," but instead he found a man with dignity, protesting his innocence, logically analyzing the defects in the evidence against him, occasionally bitterly denouncing his chief defense counsel.

"Could a man do for dollars what Reilly has done to me?" Hauptmann asked. "Only once, for about five minutes, did I have a chance to explain my case to him, really. Sometimes he came to see me, not often, for a few minutes. How could I then talk to him?"

Hauptmann lifted one of the transcript volumes. "Why did they take from me all my shoes?" he asked. "When I was arrested they took, among many things, all my shoes. What for I could not imagine, but now I have found out. Because they have a footprint. . . . There was a footprint of a man who, according to the prosecutor, climbed the ladder to get the unfortunate child. It is to me a riddle, for the prosecutor said it was many feet from the window to where the ladder was found and all soft earth—how could it have been but one footprint?'' [Neither Hauptmann nor the governor was aware of state police reports that *many* sets of footprints had been found.] "Why did they not produce at the trial the impression of which they cast a model? Why? They cannot say that my foot has become larger or smaller. So too the footprint which was found in the graveyard from where Dr. Condon swore that he gave to John fifty thousand dollars. Also here my shoe certainly did not fit. Why did they not produce the plaster model that was made?''

Hauptmann also asked why the prosecution never produced a phonograph record that Condon reportedly made for FBI agents after passing the ransom money to the extortionist known as John. I had not read of this recording before, but it was one further reason for getting into the FBI files because, Hoffman said he had learned, Condon is supposed to have recorded his conversation with John and to have also mimicked his voice. "Why don't they play for us that record?'' Hauptmann went on. "Does anyone think that these footprints and this record has been held back out of pity for me? Oh, no. For me, no pity!''

Hauptmann demanded to know why the fact that his fingerprints were not found on the ladder wasn't introduced at the trial, how the prosecutor could be permitted to lie about the missing chisel in his toolbox, why the court did not force the introduction of the missing letters from Pinkus Fisch, and how police could lie about the closet trim board with Condon's address and phone number written on it. Hauptmann turned, picked up another volume of the transcript, and quickly located the testimony of Inspector Bruckman about finding the board: "This man lied,'' Hauptmann said.

"I want to ask you about that,'' the Governor said. "You did admit that it was your writing, didn't you? And that it was Condon's telephone number? How do you account . . .''

"That is one of the things they have done to me,'' Hauptmann replied. "A few days after my arrest my Annie and the child could stand it no longer in the house because the baby could no longer sleep because of all the police and people who were there. So they went to relatives. Now I can see it was the wrong thing to have done, for the police could manage to do as they wished.

"Some days after I am arrested, when everything seems so mixed up, the police appear with a board on which is some writing. They say the board is from a closet in my home and when I look through a magnify glass at the writing it looks like mine and I say it must be mine because often it is my custom to write down things like many carpenters, on pieces of wood. But then they tell me it is Dr. Condon's telephone number and the number of his house. Dear God! If I that number had written and knew what it was, would I be so stupid to tell the police? No! With my dying breath I would have said I have never seen it before.

"Besides, if I have commit this crime, would I have marked down in my own house this number? Because in my house I have no telephone and must go some distance to telephone. What good would be to me a number written inside my closet which is the broom closet and very small and which I would have to get inside to see the number? And too, the closet is dark. . . . I am now certain that the numbers on the closet wainscoting have been made either by police or by reporters who tried to write like me."

Hauptmann returned again and again to the ladder during this conversation, almost as if he had been grievously insulted that anyone could think he, a skilled craftsman, could have made such a piece of junk.

"Is it not unbelievable that to make one support for the ladder, out of six, I would have from the floor of my own house torn up one of the boards? This is the one they call Rail Sixteen. In the first place, it had in it some large knots which alone would prevent a carpenter from making a ladder of it. Anyway, it is not altogether a ladder—it is only a wooden rack. Its construction shows that it did not come from the hand of a carpenter, not even a poor one. The prosecutor tried to say I was not a good carpenter, but I say I have often worked for myself and as a foreman. Every master could depend on me. I have often figured out whole requirements for wood for new construction and order materials, and often I was responsible for the whole job. I have built a whole garage myself, the one behind my house that they tore down.

"But the ladder rail. It was said to the jury, and by experts, that it came from my house. Whether it really came from the house I do not know, but if it did then I make responsible for that the persons who were there after my Annie left the house.

"Listen," Hauptmann went on, rising to stand before the governor. "Wilentz says I am a smart criminal. He says on these hands I must have worn gloves, because there are not fingerprints. He says on these feet I must have worn bags, because there are not footprints. If I was a smart criminal, if I would do all those things, why would I go in my own house and take up half of one board to use for one piece of the ladder—something that always would be evidence against me?

"If I wanted to make a ladder could I not get around my yard and around my garage all the wood like this that I would need? I have lots of boards like that. Besides, only about one block from my house is a lumberyard where for a few cents I could buy such a board. This expert, this Koehler, he says I bought all the wood for the ladder from the lumberyard. But not this one piece, I took that from the attic. Listen, would I, a carpenter, buy wood for five rails only and not know I need for six?"

Hauptmann condemned Koehler's testimony at great length and concluded: "Why would the jury believe Koehler? I know why. It is because, even though a piece is missing that must be supplied by the mind, they want to believe this one thing which will help take my life. Because when my life may depend on a mistake of Koehler's, that is not important. Oh, no! The poor child has been kidnaped and murdered, so somebody must die for it. For is the parent not the great flyer? And if somebody does not die for the death of the child, then always the police will be monkeys. So I am the one who is picked out to die."

Speaking rapidly, but only occasionally growing excited, Hauptmann jumped from one piece of evidence to another, and then finally came to the statement he'd made from the witness chair that he had been beaten by police.

"Wilentz, he showed from what I say in the Bronx, that I was treated nice in the jail up there, I was never hit by the police. Nobody believe me when I say downtown, before I go to the Bronx, they hit me. I was handcuffed in the chair and the police give me such a terrible licking that I fall downward to the floor. They showed me a hammer and then they put out the lights and started to beat me on the shoulders, the back of the head, and the arm. Then, too, they kicked my legs with their feet and kept yelling, 'Where is the money?' 'Where is the baby?' 'We'll knock your brains out!' "

(*Where is the baby?*—had police said this, it is further evidence investigators doubted the identification of the corpse found in the woods.)

Hoffman here interrupted his narration of Hauptmann's soliloquy to say that some time later he obtained a copy of a physical examination of Hauptmann by Dr. Thurston H. Dexter on September 25, 1934, several days after Hauptmann was arrested. The examination was made in the presence of Hauptmann's lawyer at the time, James M. Fawcett, and Louis L. Lefkowitz, an assistant medical examiner. In part the report said:

"Scab and abrasion between left eye and molar region, and under the lid a faint yellow discoloration . . . on right shoulder a tender lump, an inch and a half, and a lump on the spine of the left scapula and above it . . . all of lower shoulder blade shows a swollen welt with discoloration and abrasions . . . a large mark and discoloration, yellow and blue, extending into the axillary region . . . in the lower left quadrant of the abdomen, close to the groin, an area of three by five inches of faint greenish-yellow discoloration . . . in the upper chest region, involving principally the sternum, a large irregular region discolored yellow and faint blue, superficially abraded . . . right thigh much swollen, very tender, and markedly discolored."

The doctor ended his report with the statement: "I conclude from this examination that he had been subjected recently to a severe beating, all or mostly with blunt instruments. The injuries resulting from this are general and include the head, back, abdomen, and thighs."

Throughout his talk, Hauptmann broke in again and again to wonder about the motivation and the sanity of Dr. Condon. "He holds the key to my cell," Richard said. "If he will tell the truth, I will be a free man." His main point concerning Condon was that both the chief witness and the accused spent a lot of time at City Island. During the summer following the kidnaping and the summers of 1933 and 1934, Hauptmann was at City Island between three and five times a week, and certainly was there every weekend. He kept his canoe at Dixon's boathouse. During those same summers Condon spent much time at his "shack" on City Island and to get there from his home he had to walk past the boathouse. Condon had told reporters that he frequently rented a boat from Dixon during the summers.

"For three full summers we are both on the same place, we must pass each other sometimes. How could anybody believe that Dr. Condon was looking as he says all over the country for John—who he now says is me—without coming face to face with me? Condon says that he could identify John when John was walking along a

413

street and Condon was on top a bus, yet on City Island nearly every day he would not see me and pick me out as John.

"If I was the kidnaper and I got the money from Condon would I not know, too, that the doctor was on City Island many, many times? And would I not have stayed away from City Island because I would have been afraid of being identified by Condon? Even after the doctor had seen me in what they call the police lineup in New York, why would he keep going around all over trying to find John to whom he paid the colonel's money?"

Hauptmann said that while he was being held at the Hunterdon County Jail, about a month before his trial and before Condon had identified him as John, the doctor came to visit. With him was Anthony Hauck, the county prosecutor from whom Wilentz expropriated the case. Hauck remained in the corridor with a guard, Hauptmann said. Condon asked him a lot of questions, many of them the same he had asked during the police lineup in Manhattan. And at the end Condon rose from the bench and began to hop around. "I can't identify this man," he said. "I cannot testify against this man." The guard and the county prosecutor rushed in and escorted Condon away.

"When Dr. Condon did not identify me as John in New York and again in Flemington, what should so suddenly make him change his opinion and say quickly that I am the man to whom he has given the money? Can it be like the man Curtis, who has been condemned for having contact with kidnapers, that the police too have made the doctor say I am the man or they will also prosecute him? For surely he, too, must have had contact with the kidnapers, since he paid to them the money."

By now Governor Hoffman was "anxious to bring the interview to a close," but Hauptmann continued to fire questions at him, questions he said Reilly never even asked during the trial. Finally, Hoffman called to the warden to let him out. The cell door was unlocked. The governor stepped outside, then turned to shake hands. Hauptmann was staring at him "hopelessly," the governor wrote. And then Hauptmann said:

"What harm could I do anybody behind these bars? When they kill me they kill an innocent man. But I know—they think when I die, the case will die. They think it will be like a book I close. But the book, it will never close."

Hoffman fled back to his hotel room.

414

As I read through the governor's account of that death cell meeting, only a part of which I've reproduced here, I tried to imagine what Hauptmann had been going through, confined to a small cage, soon to die in a chamber into which six other men had passed in recent months, spending almost every hour reading and analyzing the trial and recalling all that had happened to him since that morning his car was forced to the curb in upper Manhattan. No man can pay as much attention to himself, his predicament, his enslavement, as Hauptmann was forced to do, without living in hell all the time. I wondered how he managed to hold onto even a shred of decency and sanity.

Lloyd Fisher, the one defense attorney absolutely convinced of Hauptmann's innocence, was a frequent visitor. One afternoon, when he arrived, he found Hauptmann terribly agitated about something. "Look," he said, pointing through his bars to the large skylight in the roof of the death house. One of the frames of the skylight had been opened slightly to admit a little air. A sparrow was caught in the wire mesh place just below the glass to prevent prisoners from escaping. "Do something, Lloyd," Richard said. "A free thing like that should never be in there." Fisher called one of the guards, who got a long pole and tried to free the bird, without success. Through the rest of the afternoon, Hauptmann barely paid attention to his lawyer's discussion of appeals to the courts and the Pardons Board. "His mind and his eyes seemed to be continually on the imprisoned bird," Fisher later said.

In December, several weeks after the governor's visit to his cell, Hauptmann learned that the United States Supreme Court had refused to hear his appeal. The next step was to the Court of Pardons, to beg for clemency. Hoffman was a member of the court and the prisoner wrote him a personal plea:

> With clear conscience I have fought my case. In my heart I cannot believe that this State will break the life of an innocent man. I assure your Excellence, had I any guilty feeling in this terrible crime I would not trouble you with this request. But since it is my deepest desire to prove to your Excellence and the world that I have spoken the truth, I would be very thankful for permitting any able persons, whom are free of any opinion in this case to give me a test with a so-called lie detector,—Serum, or whatever Science may offer.

I hope for myself and in the course of justice that this my wish may inspire Dr. Condon to do the same. . . . I have a deep interest, in what kind of force made him change his saying. Because when he was visiting me in my Flemington cell, he said all excited to the prosecutor,—"I can not testify against this man."

I hope that I went not too far in my writing, or have overstepped any regulations, but I assume your Excellence will understand my feeling.

I plea to your Excellence to give my request your favorable consideration. It certainly will inspire other persons, especially Dr. Condon, to do also. I only fighting for my honor and against the disgrace of my family. . . .

By now Governor Hoffman had met Murray Bleefeld and was aware of the plans to seize Paul Wendel in Manhattan, although he does not mention it in his script. Nor does he admit he went to visit Hauptmann again, with Parker and Murray, although it is highly likely that he did so. According to Hoffman's account, on the night of January 15, 1936, he took a suite at the Hotel New Yorker in Manhattan because "several people had expressed a desire to see me in relation to the case." Both Bleefeld and Martin Schlossman, his brother-in-law, independently remembered that they had gone to the New Yorker in mid-January, so that Schlossman could meet the governor and be sworn in as another of Parker's deputies. They did not see the governor that night, as they both recalled it, although they did confer with Ellis Parker, Jr., who was also at the hotel.

Governor Hoffman was busy in several conferences. David Wilentz was there, "without prearrangement," Hoffman claimed, and they talked in the governor's suite. They had gone to the same school, had each managed the high school basketball team at different times, had worked for the same newspaper, and then had joined rival political parties, Wilentz to become Democratic county chairman of Middlesex County and Hoffman his Republican counterpart in the same county. Both men were ambitious, highly motivated, had large egos. They became rivals, the two most powerful officeholders in the state, although "remaining friends," Hoffman said. The rivalry made itself felt in what was by now the Hauptmann case. Wilentz knew Ellis Parker was guiding the governor in his maneuvering to save Hauptmann's life. He knew the governor had visited the condemned man in his cell—Hoffman inadvertently admitted it to reporters and the New Jersey Democrats had attacked Hoffman rather viciously and even began a move to impeach. Wilentz wanted to be the next governor. Their conversation, this night in Manhattan, must have been a bitter one—Hoffman would only go so far as to write that neither of them had to "pull our punches."

Hoffman said he believed the eyewitnesses, all of them, had been lying, and that evidence had been suppressed by the police. Wilentz countered that Condon's phone number in Hauptmann's closet and the spelling of the word boat as "b-o-a-d" in the ransom notes, and in one instance in Hauptmann's own writing long before the kidnaping, was sufficient physical evidence to convict.

"But that evidence would support only the crime of extortion," Hoffman argued. "Even if it were unanswerable, it would not put Hauptmann at the scene of the kidnap and murder."

"Then why in hell doesn't he tell the truth?" Wilentz said.

"How can we get at the truth?"

They talked about it for a while, and a plan evolved. Wilentz argued, and the governor came to agree with him, that only when Hauptmann's last hope to remain alive was gone would he finally reveal everything he knew about the crime. If he had been involved only in the extortion plot and admitted it and named his accomplices, he would save his life. Even if he admitted that he had kidnaped and murdered the child, alone, he would be given an out: Both Wilentz and Hoffman agreed that in exchange for the entire truth, they would jointly go before the Pardons Board and ask that the sentence be commuted to life imprisonment. To get this word to Hauptmann, the governor agreed to see his wife and try to persuade her to carry the offer to him.

After Wilentz left, Hoffman met with J. Edgar Hoover, who also happened to be at the same hotel "without prearrangement." They talked until well past midnight. The governor doesn't go into detail about their talk. The next morning, the day before Hauptmann was scheduled to die, he returned to Trenton and quietly made arrangements to see Mrs. Hauptmann in her hotel, the Stacy Trent.

"Mrs. Hauptmann," he said, "tomorrow is the day when, under the law, your husband is to die. I wanted to help him, but he has not been telling me or anyone else the truth."

"No! No! No!" Anna screamed. "That isn't so. Richard did tell the truth. He is telling the truth."

Her face, Hoffman later wrote, had become very pale, then suddenly reddened with anger and she began to poke her fists against his chest. And the governor wondered whether he was doing the proper thing, following the plan he and Wilentz concocted, behaving rather cruelly to this woman in an attempt to get her to force her husband to tell the truth, as Wilentz demanded. But Hoffman continued his psychic assault upon her.

"Things look bad for your husband," he said. "Everyone seems to believe that he is guilty. There is only one way he can save his life."

"What way is that?" she asked, her eyes lighting up.

"Well, Mrs. Hauptmann, last night I met with Attorney General Wilentz, over in New York." Mrs. Hauptmann's expression turned bitter at the mention of the prosecutor's name, but Hoffman went on: "He thinks it is important—I do, too—to get the whole story of how this thing happened. If your husband committed this crime . . ."

"He didn't! He didn't! He didn't do it, I tell you—he couldn't do it."

"Listen until I finish, Mrs. Hauptmann. Your husband had some of the money. No one believes his story as to how he got it. He has been convicted; he has been sentenced to die tomorrow. But you can save him. The attorney general says that if Richard will agree to tell the whole story, he will go—or send one of his assistants—to the prison with me, and if he is convinced that the story is true, even if it shows that your husband was the only one who committed the crime, he will go with me before the Court of Pardons and ask to have his sentence changed to life imprisonment. There is no doubt that the court, with both the governor and the attorney general making this request, will commute your husband's sentence.

"You must go to the prison this morning," he continued. "You must see your husband. You must tell him to tell the truth."

Anna Hauptmann leaped from her chair, shrieking, the governor wrote. She screamed: "No! No! No! I couldn't do that. He would turn his back to me. He would think that the last one in the world to know that he is innocent should think, too, that he have commit this crime.

"My husband have only a few hours to live. Could I do that to him—make him think I, like that judge, like that jury, believe too

418

that he would kill a baby? Would I make Richard think I too have believed those lying witness who for money would send a good man to die? No! Never would I do that! Not even to save my Richard's life would I do that!''

She walked away from him, pacing to the window, trying to hide the handkerchief she brought up to her eyes. Then she turned back to the governor. "How could he do a thing like that without me—his wife—knowing he was doing it?" she asked. "How could he cut from the attic floor a board and take it out and make such a ladder? No! Without me he couldn't commit this. Why don't your state take my life? If Richard is guilty I must also be guilty. I too should go to the electric chair.

"Without him I do not wish to live. My little boy . . ." She sat once more, falling heavily into her chair, sobbing now. "He is not guilty, my Richard. I swear it. Like almost every other night, that night he comes to the bakery. People saw him there—why would they not believe those good people who tell the truth? Yet liars they want to believe.

"That night Richard he go home with me together. I remember the next day a neighbor came to me like this, with a newspaper. 'Look what happened!' she said. And I too, like all women, felt terrible for the little child who have been took from his home. Why? Why? Why would they tell such lies to take my husband from me?''

Hoffman tried to interrupt, to reason with her, but every time he said the only way to save Richard's life was to get him to tell the truth, she erupted.

"The truth he has told! What more can he say? Yes, maybe he could make up lies to say he did it and save his life. But soon it would be found they were not the truth. No! Always I—and some day our baby—would be sorry that he would say he have done such a thing even to save his life.''

She mentioned the rumors, recently printed, that Richard would have confessed and involved his accomplices if it weren't for fears that his wife and his son would be harmed. "That, too, is a lie,'' she said. "Always we would be safe with the law until those people too could be put in jail. Besides, why should we want to live? My Manfred must some day have everybody point at him their fingers and say that his father have been a kidnaper and a murderer. So too they will always say of me, 'She is the wife of Hauptmann, who have killed a baby.' ''

Confronted with Anna's stolid trust in her husband's innocence with her refusal to compromise her faith in him even to save his life, Governor Hoffman abandoned the original plan and made a less cruel proposal. "Will you do this, Mrs. Hauptmann?" he asked, "go down to see your husband and ask him if he will talk to the attorney general and to me and answer any questions? Perhaps the attorney general will not go, but he will send one of his best men. Maybe Richard will say something to help. He might even say something that will save his life."

"That I will do," she said, "for Richard he have always said that gladly he will answer questions that anybody want to ask him. But I will not say to him, his wife, I will not say that at last he should tell the truth when always I know that he has told the truth that he did not do this terrible thing."

Anna Hauptmann went directly to the prison. An hour later she called the governor from the warden's office. "Richard says he will be glad to see you and Wilentz—he will be glad to see anybody," she said. "But, Governor, the story is just the same—he have told everything he knows—nothing more he can tell."

Hoffman immediately called Wilentz and told him everything that had occurred during his meeting with Mrs. Hauptmann. "She talked to him," he said, "and he told her his story would be just the same, he doesn't have anything else to tell us."

"The hell with it, Harold," Wilentz said. "If that's still his attitude I'm damned if I'm going to do anything to help him."

That afternoon, six hours before Hauptmann was to die, Hoffman announced he was granting a thirty-day reprieve. "A shocking crime was committed," he told reporters, "and in the interests of society it must be completely solved. A human life is at stake. As governor I have a duty to perform. It is my heart, my conscience, my job—and this is my decision."

Amidst renewed speeches in the New Jersey senate demanding the governor's impeachment and attacks in the press for even temporarily saving Hauptmann's life, the mail once more grew to a flood. Most of it was favorable, Hoffman said. But some of it upset him, for it demonstrated that Hauptmann was the object of an unreasoned hatred throughout the land. One letter, in particular, stood out. It was from a judge in the Midwest, a man to whom in theory truth was most sacred above all. The judge wrote:

"Is it not much better that this man, who, after all, is an alien, should die, even if there were some doubt as to his guilt or inno-

420

cence, than that there should be a reflection cast upon American courts?''

Although he does not admit it in his articles, for obvious reasons, Hoffman again visited the prisoner, accompanied by Parker, Murray Bleefeld, and Parker's secretary, Anna Bading. And Hauptmann again said he knew nothing, he had nothing further to say because he was absolutely innocent. On the date set for execution, March 31, Hauptmann wrote a final plea to Governor Hoffman. He said, in part:

My writing is not in fear of losing my life, this is in the hands of God, it is His will. I will go gladly, it means the end of my tremendous suffering. Only in thinking of my dear wife and my little boy, that is breaking my heart. I know until this terrible crime is solved, they will have to suffer under the weight of my unfair conviction.

In passing away, I assure your Excellence that I am not guilty of this crime. Over and over again I was trying to convince the prosecution that they murder an innocent man. I offered myself to any test what science may offer,—but I was begging in vain. I did this, not to force the prosecution to put me free, but only to convince the world that I am innocent . . .

May I ask fair-thinking people—would I have been convicted of this crime without the circumstantial evidence, and them false witnesses—No! never and never. Why did people say on the witness stand that they saw me near Hopewell? The motive can only be money and to play an important part in the Lindbergh case. Up to the present day I have no idea where the Lindbergh house in Hopewell is located.

Why did, and does Dr. Condon hide so many things he knows? It is not for the course of justice that this man says everything. Why did Dr. Condon say in my cell, he cannot testify against me? My God, Dr. Condon and your witnesses, did you ever realize what you did? In a short time I will stand before a higher Judge, you will live a little longer, but you and you can never leave this world with a happier inner feeling as I do . . .

My God, my God, I hardly can't believe on all that what happened by my trial. But it was necessary to convict me and so close the Books of the case.

Mr. Wilentz, with my dying breath I swear by God that you

421

convicted an innocent man. Once you will stand before the same Judge, to whom I go in a few hours. You know you have done wrong on me, you not only take my life, but also the happiness of my family. God will be judge between you and me.

I beg you, Attorney General, believe at least a dying man. Please investigate, because this case is not solved, it only adds another dead to the Lindbergh case.

Your Excellence, I see this as my duty, before this state takes my life, to thank you for what you have done for me. I write this with tears in my eyes. If ever prayer will reach you, they will come from me, from my dear wife and my little boy.

In all your effort to save my life and see that justice is done, I assure your Excellence, that your effort was spent to an innocent man.

I thank your Excellence, from the bottom of my heart, and may God bless you.

Fisher visited Richard the day he wrote that letter, March 31. The prisoner was "terribly broken up," the lawyer later said, because he had been moved out of Cell 9, in which he had pictures of his wife and child and some fairly comfortable furnishings, into an adjacent cell. Hauptmann asked why this had been done to him.

"I have been a good prisoner," he said. "I have never made anybody any trouble. I never have broken a rule. Why should they do this to me? The other prisoner who is tonight to die, Charley Zeid, he have not been moved from his cell. Why should I be pushed around when this is my last day to live?"

Fisher tried to explain it was a prison rule to move a prisoner on the last day, but Hauptmann insisted he was being deliberately mistreated.

Later that afternoon, Fisher returned for another visit, to tell Hauptmann that the confession of Paul Wendel was being considered by the grand jury and that he would return as soon as there was any news to report.

At about eight-thirty that night Fisher returned, to report that the warden had stayed the execution for forty-eight hours. Richard did not seem surprised; he apparently had heard it from a guard or a prison official.

The day of execution was now set for April third. A grand jury refused to act on the Wendel confession, because of the repudiation written in the Mercer County jail with the assistance of David Wilentz. There was no avenue of escape left for Hauptmann.

That afternoon, the third day of April, hours before Richard was to die, Fisher visited him. Again, Hauptmann said he was totally innocent and had told everything he knew.

"You don't know, Lloyd, what I went through three days ago, when they were supposed to kill me," Richard said. "Even now I don't know what to do. If I cry like often I want to do when I think of Annie and our baby, everybody they will say that I am guilty. If I fight with my heart and soul they will say I am cold-blooded fellow like one who would commit such a crime."

Fisher was in and out of the death house that afternoon, seeing the governor to plead for a further reprieve, reporting back to Richard that he had failed. Each time he left, Richard would ask him to go and see Anna and tell her he was all right. "Please, Lloyd, don't tell my Annie they moved me out of my cell," he said. "It would upset her."

Later, about a half-hour before Hauptmann was set to die, Fisher returned to the prison. As he approached the bars of the cell Hauptmann said:

"I can see by your face, Lloyd, that it is bad news. Have you seen the governor?"

"Yes, Richard, and his hands are tied. He can't do anything under this state's law. My God, isn't there anything you can tell me—anything at all you know? If you can say something maybe I can still stop this thing."

Hauptmann was again being asked to invent any story to save his life, but his reaction was a look of disappointment that Fisher could have implied he knew anything he had not already told. Hauptmann said:

"You know, Lloyd, there isn't anything I can say. You know me better as anyone down here, and you know I know nothing about that crime."

"Yes, I believe that, Richard," his lawyer said. He shook Hauptmann's hands through the bars. "I'm going to the warden's office, and I'll wait there."

Fisher had walked three paces when Hauptmann called his name. He stepped back to the cell and Hauptmann said, "Lloyd, I want to say goodbye to you again. You have been very kind to me."

423

Fisher smiled, walked down to the warden's office, and cried.

The Rev. John Gourley, the prison chaplain, and the Rev. John Matthiesen, a German Lutheran minister, sat with Hauptmann in his small cell just seven paces from the execution chamber. Hauptmann had about five minutes before he would be led to his death. The cell was silent, Hauptmann praying. He looked up suddenly and said:

"Ich bin absolut unschuldig an dem Verbrechen das man mir zur Last legt."

"What did he say?" Gourley asked.

"He says," replied Matthiesen, "that he is absolutely innocent of the crime that has been laid at his door."

The ministers took turns reading the Scriptures. Hauptmann turned, fell to one knee, and bowed his head. After a few minutes he got up and approached the ministers, smiling. "I am happy now," he said. "I am at peace with my God and I am not sorry to leave a world that does not understand me." In German, he asked Mattheisen to help his wife and child, to fight to clear his name, and then he said: "You may now open the door."

Two prison guards were standing outside, waiting to take Hauptmann to the electric chair. One of them opened the cell door and Hauptmann stepped out. "Thank you," he said to the guards. He turned and faced the death chamber. As the party started to walk toward its door, Hauptmann looked up at the skylight in which the sparrow had been trapped. He said: "Look, I see a star."

They passed his old cell, where he had spent almost thirteen months, and he turned toward it.

"Please," he said. The guards stopped. "Let me look once more at my baby's picture." They stopped in front of the cell for a moment, Hauptmann staring at his son's photographs on the wall. Then he said: "I am ready."

Seconds later Hauptmann was strapped into the electric chair, his face covered by a mask to hide the distortions of sudden death. The executioner, Robert Elliott, turned a wheel. There was a sudden creaking of straps. Several wisps of smoke. And a shout from a reporter who was one of seventy witnesses: "It's terrible!"

A few days later Anna Hauptmann went to the prison and signed a receipt for a toothbrush, some books, letters, and pictures, "the property of Inmate No. 17400."

19

Several days later I was traveling to the city where I hoped the elderly woman who knew Mrs. Hauptmann still lived. With me was Stevie Trudeau, an actress, singer, and writer. She was familiar with every aspect of my work on this case, examining documents that had been passed on to me, helping with research, even taking part in several interviews. Most of all, Stevie is warm and compassionate and has the good reporter's ability to inspire trust, to get even the most reluctant man or woman to become open and frank; I was hopeful that the woman we were going to see would not be able to resist Stevie's pleas for help.

We located the address, a small frame house on an older suburban street with densely leaved trees, and rang the bell. An elderly woman opened the door and asked, through the screen, "May I help you?"

"I'm a writer from New York," I said, "I'm doing a book about Bruno Richard Hauptmann and the Lindbergh case." We could see the woman wince. Stevie cut in: "We're trying to find Anna Hauptmann and we were told she used to live with you and you might know where she is."

"Maybe," the woman said. "What kind of a book?"

"I can prove Hauptmann was innocent, that he was convicted on fake evidence. I've found proof of that in police documents."

"Come in," the woman said. She unlatched the screen door and we stepped into her living room.

"I have all the proof I need," I said, "to show that Hauptmann was innocent. What I need to make my book a better book is Mrs. Hauptmann's story, her experiences. I really must find her . . ."

"I am Anna Hauptmann," the woman said. She smiled; our surprise must have been evident. "Didn't you recognize me?"

Stevie and I laughed at her question and at the absurdity of having been caught unprepared. "How could we recognize you?" I asked. "The last picture we've seen of you was probably taken in 1936."

"I was thirty-eight then," she said. "Now I'm seventy-six. But please, sit down." She hurried to a maple couch over which was thrown a quilt she had crocheted, and she folded it so that we could sit. "Everything is so messy," she apologized. "I've been writing letters." Her dining room table had a few papers on it and a chair was slightly out of place. Everything else was so neat it appeared she had spent the morning cleaning.

"I wish I knew you were still living here," I said. "I would have brought you all my papers to show your husband was innocent."

She began to ask questions about what I had found, and where I had found it, and I told her about the missing letters from Pinkus Fisch, the evidence that the employment time sheets for March first had existed, the summary of Richard's ledger book—rattling off everything I could remember about all the distortions and lies that had been told by police and prosecutor. And I realized she was not getting excited, as I expected her to, and she didn't seem to be very interested in my recital, in fact. I wondered whether she had indeed decided to forget about fighting to prove her husband's innocence, as I'd been told. But I was wrong.

"I think about this often," she said. "Sometimes, when I think about it, I can't sleep. Two years ago, I woke up in the middle of the night and suddenly remembered something important. Richard made a cabinet for Fredericksen's bakery, very primitive, just two shelves to hold bakery boxes. He made it with the wood he bought in the lumberyard that they said he made the ladder with. I woke up and thought, 'Why didn't I remember that during the trial? Maybe that could have saved Richard.' And I wondered whether there were other things Richard made with that wood that would have proved he didn't make the ladder."

We sat with Mrs. Hauptmann for about three hours that first day and she talked openly about Richard, their relationship, the trial, and Isidor Fisch. Later, after we'd visited her six or eight times, we understood why her recollections seemed to bubble from her. "It is so good to be able to talk to someone about this," she said. "I can't talk to my son, Manfred, about this. I can't talk to anyone. It is so good that you came."

But now, at our first meeting, she was still wary. "I have been made promises by reporters so many times," she said. "Years ago, they come to interview me and promise to print our side of it but they never do, they write how I'm living, how the wife of a famous murderer gets along. Never anything about Richard's innocence. So I don't trust writers anymore."

We asked Mrs. Hauptmann about Fisch, the man initially responsible for sending Richard to his death. Her eyes clouded for a moment, but then she straightened her shoulders and leaned forward in her easy chair.

"When Richard found Fisch's money, that Sunday in the summer," she said, "he was moving a snake plant for me, out of a small pot into a larger one, because the roots were coming through. Richard was working at the kitchen sink, transplanting, and he spilled a little dirt. He went to the closet to get the broom and dustpan from the nail on the wall and when he was taking down the broom the handle hit something on the top shelf. He told me, 'It was like electricity and I thought, Isidor's box.'"

"When did Richard say this?"

"In the Bronx jail, two days after his arrest, when I asked him about the money they found. He told me the box was falling to pieces from the water that leaked in, and when he saw that it was money he took it out to the garage to dry it. He told me, 'Annie, Isidor cheated me out of seven thousand dollars. I was drying out the money to take out my share, what he owed me, and I was saving the rest for Fisch's brother, for when he came to America.'

"Maybe, if I had been different, Richard would still be here," she went on. "A few days after he found the money I almost learned about his secret, but I didn't want to pry. I'm sorry I didn't. You see, Richard would take a few pieces of money out and hang them up to dry, and when they were dry he would put them away and hang up a new set. Every day before he went to the office, to the stock market, he would work in the garage with the money. One morning I went outside and Richard saw me from the garage. He shut the garage door very quick. I wondered, 'What's going on in there, he's so secretive?' I thought I would go and check later, I was so curious. You know what we women are," she said to Stevie, smiling at her, a girlish smile. "But I thought, 'What if it's a surprise like the wardrobe closet he built for the baby?' And then I felt so cheap wanting to look. I didn't look because I thought he was building something and I didn't want to spoil the surprise.

"This was after Fisch died, after we learned Fisch was a liar and a crook. He told us he loaned a friend two thousand dollars to open a delicatessen and I told Richard, 'How nice, Fisch lends that man his money like that.' I always liked Isidor, he was so smart and so nice. But after he died the man sent a note to Richard and asked him to come and see him, something about Isidor. Richard went to see him and the man told him that Fisch owed him two thousand dollars. Richard said, 'I thought Isidor lent *you* the money.' But the man had a receipt to prove that Fisch lied, that he borrowed the money, he didn't lend it to the man. The man wanted Richard to help him get the money back, but Richard said he didn't know where Fisch kept his money or the furs he was supposed to have. Later, the man was there when they opened the safe deposit box, but it was empty."

Stevie asked: "Why did Richard lend Fisch two thousand dollars before he went to Germany? I mean, I could never understand why he didn't get a receipt from Fisch."

"Before Isidor died," Mrs. Hauptmann said, "Hans Kloeppenburg warned Richard not to lend Isidor the money for going to Germany and for buying furs in Germany, to sell in America, because Hans felt Isidor was a crook. Richard said, 'What can I do? We're partners on trust, I can't ask him for a receipt now because he would think I don't trust him.'

"Later, we find out Isidor was a crook. The lady upstairs where Fisch lived, Louise Helfert, said she made out bills for furs, under Isidor's directions. She would take the bills Isidor gave her and type them out —'bought one hundred silver fox furs'—and those bills were fake. She told us she typed them out in her home."

I said I had found a police report of an interview with the Helfert woman, which confirmed what Mrs. Hauptmann had just told us.

"I know," she said, quite simply. And I understood why she didn't appear excited about the material I had worked so hard to get: She knew, without the need of documentation, that "they murdered Richard in the electric chair," as she put it at one point.

"I liked Isidor, but some things about him were very funny, very strange," she said as an introduction to a long anecdote. Shortly after Manfred was born she received a letter addressed to him. "I thought it was a card for him, something like that, and I opened it. It was a letter. I read it and I was very upset. It said such terrible things, 'I hope you live an awful life and die young,' things like that. It was typed, but I showed it to people and tried to find out who would do such an awful thing. I showed it to Isidor because he was always interested in writing and he said, 'Let me have it, I'll try to find out who did it.'

"He came back a few days later and he said, 'This is a joke for Richard, not for Manfred. See, up in the corner, in pencil, is November twenty-six. That's Richard's birthday.' I looked and there in the corner was the date. I didn't see it before. Isidor saw it. Then Isidor told me he was certain Gerta Henkel and her sister, Erica, wrote the letter. I couldn't believe that, but Isidor said he was certain. I went to Gerta and showed it to her and told her what Isidor said. She denied it, she couldn't understand why Isidor said that. Why was Isidor stirring up trouble like that!

"I feel certain Isidor had something to do with the ransom notes. I don't ever want to accuse anybody without proof because I know what they did to Richard without proof. But Isidor was always interested in handwriting and somebody disguised the ransom notes to look like Richard's writing. In the Bronx jail, when I talked to Richard, he told me, 'Annie, if I didn't know that I didn't write those notes, I would say they were my handwriting.' "

"But Richard and Isidor didn't meet until after the kidnaping," Stevie said. "He couldn't have copied Richard's writing."

"I know," Anna Hauptmann replied. "Isidor wrote in perfect English, he studied at school. Maybe he disguised the writing to look like German and it just happened to . . . I don't know, that's one thing I have never been able to understand, how it should look so much like Richard's writing.

"Isidor, we thought he was our friend. Still, Richard and I always thought there was something strange about Isidor's going-away party. Isidor never wanted to go to parties, never wanted to meet too many people. But he asked Richard to give him a going-

429

away party, for leaving to Germany. After Richard was arrested we began to think that Isidor asked for the party as a plan to give Richard the money, in the shoe box.

"There were many things a little strange about Isidor. When he was going down to the boat, to go to Germany, Gerta and Erica decided they would go down and say goodbye, to surprise him. They went aboard and they saw Isidor standing with four or five men. When Isidor saw them he left his friends and came over to Gerta and said, 'What are you doing here?' He was angry. Gerta said, 'We wanted to surprise you, to say goodbye and make you surprised.' Isidor showed them to his cabin, then told them he was busy and made them leave right away. Gerta and Erica told me this, after Isidor died and things began to come out about him. We didn't know it until later, but Isidor kept one group of friends apart from another and he even kept people in the same group away from other people in the group.

"That's why he didn't want Gerta to meet those men. He was telling you and your friends how rich he was, what a great businessman he was," I said, "and he was telling his other friends that he was poor and starving so he could borrow money from them. He was deceiving everyone."

"That's what Hans always said, that Isidor tries to keep everybody apart," Mrs. Hauptmann said. "He didn't want anybody to know what he was telling anybody else. Like when we play cards, just for pennies, you know, we had so much fun where he had that furnished room. And that lady who made the bills for him, Marie Helfert and the Henkels, we played cards there. And Mrs. Hile, she was a cook in rich people's house, she would come sometimes. And Isidor would go to the subway station, he was the one who took her to the station. He wouldn't let Karl Henkel do it. 'No, no, no, I'll take her,' he always said. See, nobody should know anything, she had no chance to say anything to anybody. And Hans always said that Isidor always had a split in between everybody, don't let them get together and find out. Because he was lying to everybody."

"You must have felt so terrible when they told you why Richard was arrested," Stevie said. "It would be such a shock to any woman."

"Oh, yes," Mrs. Hauptmann said. "They didn't tell me anything for a long time and I couldn't see Richard right away. The second

430

day, before I really knew what it was all about, reporters were in my living room and I heard one reporter keep saying, 'He's going to burn for this, he's going to burn for this.' Burn? What were they talking about? I didn't know.

"I was so dumb," she continued. "I trusted everybody, even the police. I believed they would get at the truth, that Richard was innocent and the police only wanted to learn the truth. When Richard was first arrested, Gerta said to me, get a lawyer, and I said, no, no, Richard will be home tomorrow. If I only knew what they were doing to him, how they planned to murder him, I would get a lawyer and I would never move out so they could fake the evidence in the attic. But I was too trusting, and Richard died."

"The attic evidence was faked," I said. "I have pretty strong proof of that from the papers I found, that the attic board was a lie and so much else was a lie. And all of it was done after you moved out. The police persuaded you to leave that apartment and stay with your niece, didn't they?"

"No, I decided to do that. There were so many people coming around to look at us, so many reporters and crazy people, I decided to go stay with Maria. Today, I wouldn't do that. I know better now. We always had respect for police, for judges and everyone in authority. We respect them like they were ministers. I was so naive. Today, it couldn't happen. I know, now. If they want to search the attic I would let them search. But someone would be with them. I would never let the police be all alone, to do what they do when they're all alone."

Like her husband, in his conversation with Governor Hoffman, Mrs. Hauptmann had nothing but contempt for Reilly, the chief defense attorney. A number of times we asked her why Reilly had not presented certain evidence in Richard's behalf, and Mrs. Hauptmann replied, "Who knows why Reilly did what he did? Who knows what that man was doing." And she said:

"Reilly wanted me to lie about the shoe box. I told him I never saw it there and that was the truth, but he wanted me to swear I did see it. I couldn't lie, I'd be red in the face and shaking." Her hand reached for the Bible on the table next to her, as if she were recreating the oath she swore when she took the witness chair. "As much as I loved Richard," she said, "to lie would be wrong. You could put all the money in the world in front of me and I couldn't lie for it. Nothing is as strong as the truth."

I asked how she felt about Lindbergh and his role in convicting her husband. Her face flushed. "I will never know why that man lied the way he did," she said. "After the trial, after Richard was gone, people used to say to me, 'Lindbergh should go up in his plane and fall from the sky.' I said, 'No, I can't hate him. Carrying hate around hurts you more than the person you're hating.' But I don't understand how people could lie, to murder Richard. How could Lindbergh live with a lie? I didn't want him to fall from his plane and die. That would be too easy. I wanted him to live for a long time, with his conscience telling him he murdered an innocent man, he murdered my Richard. And when he was dying, I hope Richard came and stood before him. I hope Lindbergh saw Richard, I hope Wilentz, when he is dying, will see Richard standing before him to remind him what he did to us."

We talked through the afternoon and Mrs. Hauptmann was clearly getting tired. She seemed to be an energetic woman, for her age, but we had touched a deep emotion in her, and made her speak about the things she could only think about over the years, and the experience had clearly worn her down. We rose to go. I had brought with me a copy of a report describing in detail the evidence I had found in district attorney and police files, a report I'd written to facilitate the writing of the last part of this book. I handed it to her and asked her to read it, so that she would know my book would reveal the concealed evidence.

"I think I want to help you," she said, "but I have to think about it. So many times reporters have promised me things, and so many times I have been disappointed. When Richard was arrested I got a letter from a lady in Jackson Heights. She wrote, 'I would like to help you, but I am afraid because I know what the police do to witnesses. But I must tell you that I was in Fredericksen's Bakery that night and from seeing your husband's pictures in the papers I am positive he was in the bakery talking to you at the counter. I was sitting at the counter having a cup of coffee and your husband came in and talked to you a little while and then he walked the dog.'

"That thing about the dog, and other things in the letter, could not be known by anybody unless she was there. None of these things came out until the trial, so we knew the lady was telling the truth. I gave the letter to a *Journal* reporter and he promised to find the woman. I never heard anything about it again."

We stepped out onto her porch and Mrs. Hauptmann held the

door open for a moment, leaning toward us. She was forcing back tears.

"I trust you," she said. "My heart has been broken so many times in forty years, but I think I trust you. Please don't break my heart."

"We won't, I promise," Stevie said. "Please read what Tony's written. We'll come back tomorrow."

"All right," Mrs. Hauptmann said. "But please don't stab me in the back . . ." she closed the door on the last words of her plea.

Stevie cried in the car, as we drove away. "That poor woman," she said. "I have a feeling she's stayed alive all this time, waiting forty years for someone to come along and believe her. To tell the truth. To vindicate her husband. And when she sees that done, then she can die in peace. Forty years, wondering if anyone will ever believe her Richard was innocent . . ."

We returned to her house the next day at around noon and she seemed pleased to see us. The writing materials had been cleared from the dining room table, and Anna Hauptmann seemed more comfortable having guests in her home now. She had a pot roast in the oven and after seeing that we were seated she ran back to the kitchen to lower the temperature. "I'm making it for a friend in the hospital," she said. "You know hospital food."

She had read my long report on the evidence, she said, had stayed awake until almost 3 A.M. to go through it. "I couldn't sleep," she said. "It was all going through my mind again. That used to happen a lot, and it still happens. I used to cry, back then. But sometimes, now, there are no tears left."

Once more, I had the feeling that none of my notes on the documents from official files surprised her—she had always known, with the faith of one who needs no documentary proof, that Richard did not do this thing.

"I do have one correction to make," she said as she sat across from us. "You wrote that Betty Gow was Red Johnson's girlfriend, but it was the maid, Violet Sharpe."

I told her that she was wrong, that it was Betty who had been dating Red, and Mrs. Hauptmann smiled and said: "Oh, my memory isn't as good as it used to be."

Stevie laughed. "Your memory is incredible. Tony forgets things that happened last week, but you remember what happened forty years ago."

"Only about Richard," she said. "I can see it like it happened yesterday. I remember it like it was yesterday. So many things in my life I can't remember anymore, but I never forget anything to do with Richard."

"Have you been thinking about it all these years?" Stevie asked.

"It's with me all the time. All the time I think about those things that happened. I feel I'm back there, living it all over again. And Richard is with me. I feel that, Richard is with me all the time.

"You see, the happiest days of my life were when I was married to Richard."

A small sound, a stifled sob, from Stevie, and I could almost feel some kind of force pass between these two women, an elderly woman who has stifled her grief for so many years and a younger one, almost young enough to be her granddaughter, now so emotionally involved in Anna Hauptmann's life. As she reminisced about Richard, Mrs. Hauptmann seemed to be speaking to Stevie, one woman pouring out to another woman her grief over what was done to the man she loved. And still loves.

"I feel Richard has been here with me all these years, he is always with me," Mrs. Hauptmann said. "It is like he is always over my shoulder, near me if I need him, if I need help. During the trial something like that happened to me. When it got so bad, all those lies, I wanted to scream out that everybody was lying, but I couldn't scream because I couldn't let Richard know how I despaired. And I felt a hand on my shoulder, comforting me. I turned around, but there was no one there."

"You felt as if someone was with you," Stevie said.

"Yes, someone was there, giving me courage."

She reached down to pat her elderly dachshund, Zepple. And she smiled as she remembered something about Richard. "How could they think my Richard could do such a thing, to a baby?" she began. "He loved children, and children loved him. They were always around climbing all over him. The neighbors' children, they would run to meet his car when he came home. They'd get in the car and ride with him to the garage in back of the house, just a little ride, but Richard loved to do it.

"The little girl downstairs, Viola, the Schusslers' child, asked to go shopping with us one day. Her mother said it was all right so we took her with us. On the way back, Viola was in the back seat with

434

all the bags of groceries next to her. I didn't see anything, but suddenly Richard stopped short. Viola and the bag of groceries fell off the back seat and I could smell that a bottle of ammonia broke. I rushed to get Viola out and after we got everything straightened up I asked Richard why he stopped so suddenly. He said, 'A little dog ran in front of the car, Annie, I couldn't run it over.' That's the kind of man Richard was. A good man who loved children and pets. Could he have done such a thing?"

"Especially something so horrible, murdering a baby," Stevie said. "I can understand murder when you're angry or crazy, but kidnaping and murdering a baby is something I can't understand anyone doing."

"I know my Richard couldn't do such a thing. And I know something else. You see, there were only two things that gave me the strength to continue through all this. One was the knowledge in my heart that Richard was innocent, because he was with me that night and nothing anybody said could change that. He was with me. The other thing that gave me strength was to protect my baby."

I noticed that she always called her husband "Richard" although police and Wilentz always used "Bruno." I asked her which was the correct name.

"Richard is what he always used. I didn't know about Bruno until he was arrested. He didn't like that name, so he used Richard. On everything, he was Richard."

Could the police have stressed the Bruno to take advantage of anti-German prejudice?

"That's what I always believe," she said. "They called him a German machine-gunner, as if there was never any American machine-gunners. Police called him Bruno to make him sound more German, to inflame the public. They wanted everybody to hate him, before the trial. So that they could murder him."

She lifted from her lap my report which had kept her awake for so many hours and a flash of anger passed across her face. "I still can't believe it, what they did to him. Those letters from Isidor's brother that you found. I remember sitting in a room in the Bronx, and District Attorney Foley asking me about Fisch. I talked about the things that were in the letters from Pinkus, that Isidor had mentioned to Pinkus about the fur and stock business. And Mr. Foley opened an envelope and spread out the letters in front of me and

435

said, 'Are these the letters?' I said they were. Those letters showed that Richard was telling the truth about everything to do with Fisch.

"But later, at Flemington, that *Wilentz* said the letters didn't exist, there were not any letters. How could he live with a lie?

"This Wilentz, is he still alive?" I nodded. "Good," she went on. "You go to see him and show him the proof you found, what he did to Richard, and I want to go with you. I won't say anything, I just want to see him and I want him to see me. I just want to stand before him and let him see the wife of the man he killed."

"I want to be there too," Stevie said. "I'd love to see his face when he reads this, when he sees Mrs. Hauptmann."

"How could these people do to Richard what they did?" Mrs. Hauptmann asked once more. "That Dr. Condon. I visited Richard in Flemington just after Dr. Condon left. Richard was so very happy. He told me Dr. Condon came to his cell, Richard had the only cell along the whole corridor, and Dr. Condon stood outside the cell and looked at Richard and talked to Richard. He was very upset. He walked up and down the corridor"—she leaped from her chair and paced rapidly between the dining room and living room, skipping occasionally to demonstrate Condon's agitation—"and he was waving his arms and jumping up and down and shouting, 'I can't testify against this man. I can't testify against this man.' And the guard was saying, 'Shhh, shut up.' And then, at the trial, Dr. Condon swore it was Richard in the cemetery. Why did he do this to us?"

She returned to her chair and I told her she shouldn't be leaping around the way she had just done. She laughed. "I'm fine," she said. "I'm a healthy woman. Two years ago I had an operation on my leg, but it doesn't bother me anymore. Except when I get up on the ladder to wash my windows."

Her energy and agility were amazing. Several times during our talk this day she'd leap up to pantomime something. Richard played soccer at Hunter's Island, and Mrs. Hauptmann ran and kicked to demonstrate; Richard told her about the way police beat and kicked him, and she rose and kicked out to show us precisely how it had been done.

"You know, it's ironic how upset Richard was when a man did to somebody what police later did to him." She had been working in a bakery and lunchroom, long before going to work for Fredericksen. The owner permitted a group of neighborhood toughs to hang around in the back room, playing cards and helping themselves to coffee and doughnuts.

"The baker usually fell asleep at night, at the table in the back," she said. "And the kids were always around. One morning I came in and the baker told me someone had taken all his money, that he kept on a shelf in the closet. I asked him, 'Who could do such a thing?' He said he thought it was this new girl, a very nice young girl who just came over, she started working two days before. I said, 'It can't be her. How can you say such a thing?' He said the girl spent a lot of time in that closet, where we hung up our coats, and she probably was trying to decide how to steal the money.

"I told him, 'What about the boys you let stay in the back? You fall asleep all the time and those boys are there when you're sleeping. What about them?' He said, 'No, no, it wasn't them, it was the new girl.' The baker had some friends who always came in, some detectives, and he said, 'The detectives are coming in a little while to question her. Now I want you to tell them you saw her take the money.'

"'I won't do that,' I told him. 'How could you ask me to tell such a lie? I never saw her take anything and if you were to ask me a guess I would say it was one of the boys.' He told me I was being foolish, that he was very certain it was the girl. 'So what's the difference if you say you saw her do it?' The girl came in a little late that morning, it was snowing and the trolley car was delayed. She was a happy girl, very sweet and always smiling. And she came in about a half hour later and apologized to the baker, and she was laughing and smiling.

"Then the detectives came and they took us to a back table and talked to us. They asked her why she took the money and she said she didn't know anything about it. And she didn't. They said, 'Do you want to go back to Germany?' She said, 'No, why should I go back to Germany? I like it here and I like my job.' They said, 'Well, maybe you're going to have to go back to Germany.' They had her in tears. I thought they shouldn't do things like that but I couldn't say anything, they were the police. The poor girl. They didn't arrest her, and she stayed on at the job.

"And when I told Richard that night, what had happened, he wanted me to quit the bakery. He said, 'I won't have you working for people like that.' I told him I couldn't quit, the man needed me

437

and I wanted the job, and Richard agreed I could stay. But after that, he thought very little of the man. He always asked how people could do such things like that. And then they did it to him."

She smiled, as she often did when she remembered something especially warm about her life with Richard, and she said: "When I went to Germany to visit my mother, in the summer of 1932, Richard wrote me love letters every day. When I arrived there were three of them waiting and my mother made some remark about it. I remember every word Richard wrote in those love letters. In one of them he wrote, 'If I live to be a hundred, I will love you more each year.' In another one, he told me he went down to the Battery and stared out for hours at the sea. And he wrote, 'If the waves could talk, they would tell you how much I already miss you.' He didn't really want me to go from him. At the boat, when I was leaving, he hugged me across the gate and he said, 'If you don't want to go, I'll pick you up now and carry you home.'"

She got up and went to a maple secretary in one corner of the living room, filled with Hummel figurines. "Let me show you what Richard sent me when I was in Germany," she said. She pulled a large flat box from the drawer, extracted a colored photo of Richard, and very proudly held it toward us. Hauptmann looked extraordinarily handsome. His blue eyes were soft and tender, not like the eyes in the photographs taken after his arrest, when he hadn't slept for many hours, dark-ringed sunken eyes in those newspaper pictures, almost-cruel eyes. A reporter had borrowed this picture after Richard's arrest, Mrs. Hauptmann said, to be used in a newspaper. I commented that I'd never seen this printed, and I had seen many photos of Richard. "That's because he looked too handsome, too human, for the newspapers," she said. She clutched the photograph against her body and said:

"It was taken in 1932, on East Eighty-sixth Street, after I went to Germany to visit. He sent it to me in a letter, while I was still there. The letter said, 'I send you this picture so I can be with you over there.' Somebody told me that the photographers who took the picture put it in his window, right out on Eighty-sixth Street where everybody could see it. Richard went to the stock market office on that street every day. He must have seen it. This was a few months after the ransom money was passed. Would a kidnaper who got all that money from Lindbergh allow his picture to be seen on one of the busiest streets in New York?"

"Was Richard a religious man?" Stevie asked.

"Oh, yes," she said. "He believed in God. In the prison he had his Bible. I remember one day I asked him, 'Richard, can I bring you any books, anything to read?' And he pointed at the Bible on his cot and said, 'That's the only book I need.' We used to drive through Bronx Park, along the road that had a lot of dips in them. And Richard would go a little fast so the car would bounce and I'd say, 'Oooh, Richard, stop that.' Because it made my stomach feel funny. And he'd laugh at that and do it again, and we'd both laugh. But, about God. Once, during the spring, Richard pulled over while we drove through the park. He pointed to a tree with white flowers on it and asked me, 'Annie, do you know what that is?' I said, 'I don't know. It's a tree with white flowers but I don't know what kind of tree it is.' And Richard said, 'That's God over there. You and I could never make that tree bloom with flowers—that's God.'"

She was close to tears. "They almost made him give up God, in the prison," she said. "He wrote me a letter, the day before they murdered him. It wasn't signed, it wasn't finished, it didn't even look like Richard's handwriting because he was in such distress. 'Annie, I almost lost my faith in God,' he said. 'You can never know how terrible the last twenty-four hours have been.' He almost stopped believing in God because of what they did to him, moving him out of the cell he was in, taking him away from his pictures of me and the baby, making him sleep practically on the bare stone floor. I think they did other things to him, and it almost made him turn his back on God. I found that letter when I went to get his things after they killed him."

"Do you still have it?" I asked.

"Yes, I keep it all these years. Maybe I'll let you put it in your book to show the world what they did to him. I want the world to know what they did to my Richard.

"Do you know Richard did not see his baby for a year and a half before he died? Manfred was less than a year old when Richard was arrested. He saw his baby in a big hall in the Bronx, and he never saw him again. Because he didn't want the baby to see him behind bars, in a prison, in a courtroom. 'I don't belong here, Annie,' he said to me. 'My baby will never come here, my baby will never see me in jail. I am innocent and I will be coming home to you and Manfred, and I don't ever want him to see me behind these bars.' See what that Wilentz did to him, taking from Richard his baby, making it impossible for Richard to see his baby for a year

439

and a half, until they murdered Richard. That's what they did to us.

"If I didn't have a child, when Richard was murdered, I would have fought and fought, I would never give up. But I had a child to raise and protect and I could not keep fighting because Manfred might have been hurt.

"You know, I always hoped, and sometimes I believed very strongly, that some day someone would write the truth about Richard. But after being disappointed so many times I didn't think it would ever happen. And Manfred would say to me, 'Mother, you must forget it. We are poor people. We can't fight it. What can we do? Who will listen to us?'

"But now," she added, "I think you will write the truth. And maybe I can fight again . . ."

Stevie broke in: "That was so sad, not seeing his baby for all that time. Especially, a baby that age is growing and changing all the time. Richard missed all that. And Manfred . . ."

"I think of that a lot, how he never had a father, and I wonder sometimes if Wilentz understands what he did to us. To Richard, to me, and especially to Manfred. He lives near here, with his wife. I see them a lot, Manfred is here all the time, but it was very hard on him when he was growing up. In school the children used to say to him . . . oh, I can't talk about that, it hurts too much. This is what Wilentz, and Lindbergh, did to us."

"How did you feel when Lindbergh testified against Richard?"

"I think what Mrs. Lindbergh said was the truth. My heart went out to her. In the courtroom I was thinking, 'Somebody took a baby and here is my husband on trial, who had nothing to do with it—and still my heart goes out to her.' "

"And Colonel Lindbergh?" I asked.

"Richard and I used to talk about how we felt, all the witnesses who lied. And when Lindbergh said he recognized my Richard's voice, I was shocked. In a simple way, to put it simply, knowing Richard had nothing to do with it you have no words, you're shocked. And Richard said he believed most of them *knew* they were lying, even Lindbergh."

"Did Richard ever talk about the day in the Bronx when Lindbergh is supposed to have identified him?" I asked. "I suspect very strongly that he couldn't really identify your husband at first, he only did it later because of police pressure or something."

"No, I don't know anything about that," she said. "I must be

440

truthful, I don't remember that Richard ever told me anything.

"But I do remember something connected. I had a letter from one of the Bronx jurors, a grand juror. He wrote, 'Mrs. Hauptmann, I am breaking my oath as a grand juror by telling you this, but I can't help it. I have to tell you. When Lindbergh testified before us, he said he couldn't identify the voice.' That's what this man wrote me."

"What happened to the letter?"

"I gave it to one of the reporters who said he was trying to help me, but I never heard anything about it again."

"Someone apparently saved it," I said, "because years later a man named Hynd wrote the same thing in a magazine article."

"I don't know about that," she said. "You see, I don't want to say anything wrong, not even the smallest thing do I want to say that is wrong. Even if it's to my advantage to say it, I don't want to lie or say something that's wrong. It's the only way I can live. That's why I'm living today—because I can't lie. Sometimes I wonder about those reporters, like the man who wrote in our closet—how they can sleep at night after what they've done. And I wondered the same way about Lindbergh."

I asked whether she had ever talked to Lindbergh during those long days out in Flemington, or if he ever tried to say anything to her. Mrs. Hauptmann said she decided to confront Lindbergh one day, "to look him in the eye" to see how he'd react, whether he'd say anything to her. "Also, I wanted to show him what I was like, that we're not the kind of people to do this, to say to him, 'How could you believe we could do something like this, that Richard could have done this thing?'" At the end of one trial session she hurried out of the courtroom and went down a private stairway that Lindbergh used in order to get in and out of the courtroom and avoid the crowds.

"I was waiting down there, near the sheriff's office, when Lindbergh came down. He saw me and he turned his face to the side and looked down when he walked past me. Like he was embarrassed and afraid to look at me. I followed him, I walked alongside him, but I never said a word. I just wanted him to look at me. He wouldn't. And the next day the door was locked and court people told me, 'Don't go there anymore.'

"But more than Lindbergh, it was the police and the reporters that were so horrible," she went on. "The police, not only what

441

they did with the fake board from the attic and the telephone number in the closet, but because they were so terrible to us in so many ways.

"They used tactics to try to trick me. Once, they asked me if I'd ever been to Hopewell and I said, 'No, of course not, I don't even know where it is.' They asked me if I'd like to see it. I knew that if I said no they would think I was afraid to go there, I was hiding something. I didn't have anything to hide—I always believed that telling the truth would make everything come out right.

"We went in a limousine, three or four detectives and me. We drove past the little house—what do you call it? the gate house—and drove up to the big house. I said, 'Yes, it's a big house.' Very calm and plain. 'Have you ever seen this house or been at this house?' they asked. I said no. We got back in the car and drove along the road a few miles and stopped. They asked me to get out of the car and we walked into the woods a little ways. A detective pointed to a spot on the ground and said, 'This is where the baby's body was found.'

"I said, 'Oh, so far away? I thought it was near the house.'

"I knew they took me out there because they hoped I would break down and cry and confess that Richard did it, maybe that I helped him. I knew that's why they wanted me to go out there. I went with them because I didn't want them to even think I was trying to hide anything."

"There's one thing I wanted to ask you about the police," I said. "Richard testified he was beaten and Governor Hoffman had a copy of a medical report that said he was definitely beaten . . ."

"You have a report about that?" she interrupted. "I'm so glad there's proof of what happened, because nobody would believe Richard got beaten. I knew it, I knew they beat him to make him confess. I saw Richard in the Bronx, after police had him for two days. He was sitting in a room with a detective and his eyes were swollen and black and blue. I went to him and touched his face, where his eyes were puffy. 'Richard, what happened?' He said, 'Nothing.' Very curt, shrugging his shoulders. Later, when we were alone a few minutes, he said, 'Annie, they punched me and kicked me.' The lights were out so he couldn't see who was hitting him. He said they strapped him to the chair and the police would kick him in the chest and stomach. Like this."

She rose quickly and showed us, with a few little kicks. "Don't do that," Stevie said, "you may get hurt." Mrs. Hauptmann laughed. "I can still kick," she said.

"You mentioned the reporters," I prompted.

"Yes, yes, more than anything I blame the reporters for permitting Wilentz and the police to murder Richard. Many of them knew what Wilentz was doing to Richard, with the fake evidence and the lies of the witnesses. I remember one of them so well, Pat McGrady, I think he worked for the Associated Press. He was one of them who believed Richard was being murdered by the police. I asked him why the newspapers wouldn't do anything to help us and he said, 'Mrs. Hauptmann, the newspapers are afraid to print the truth. They said so many terrible things about your husband that if they printed the truth now and Richard went free, he could sue every one of them for libel. So they won't ever print the truth.'

"They were also afraid of Wilentz," she went on. "Nobody would publish Richard's story when he was alive. He wrote his own story, after the trial, in German. I later dictated it to Mrs. Bading because she knew German, and she put it into English. The papers were going to print it, but Wilentz told them not to. They didn't print it until after Richard was dead, in the *Mirror*."

"Do you have that story, the original?" I asked.

"Yes, I have a copy," she said. "The one in German, I don't know what happened to it. But I have a copy of one in English. I'll let you have it before you go, if you promise to bring it back to me."

"Of course," I said. "I'll Xerox it and bring it right back."

"Then you can have it, you should read it. Richard explains a lot in it, that they wouldn't let him tell from the witness chair. That was awful, the way the trial was run. We thought we could come in and tell the truth and explain everything, but they wouldn't let us explain. 'Just answer the question, yes or no.' And no explanations."

"When the police asked me if Richard was with me that night the Lindbergh baby was kidnaped, I said I didn't know because I didn't remember it was a Tuesday night. Then when they told me it was a Tuesday, I said he *usually* was with me on Tuesday nights. I thought 'usually' meant 'always' because my English wasn't too good back then; I meant he was *always* there on Tuesday nights because he *was*.

"But when I tried to explain it in court, that Wilentz made me

443

say that I told the police 'usually' and he wouldn't let me explain, the judge wouldn't let me explain. They wouldn't let me explain why I said I didn't know if he was with me that night because I didn't remember it was a Tuesday, they wouldn't let me explain anything. That wasn't right. Why is the law like that? You can only say yes or no, you can't explain. They murdered Richard in the electric chair because we couldn't explain."

"I can understand the law doing that," I said, "because the law is made for lawyers and not for people. But what I can't understand is why the reporters ignored all the contradictions. The whole question of whether Richard was working on the day of the kidnaping—Wilentz and Foley said in the Bronx that he was working a half day, something like that, and then in Flemington, Wilentz proved he didn't start working until much later in March and he claimed the employment records didn't exist for the first week in March. I can't understand why the reporters didn't jump on that— it was so obviously a lie."

"Because all they cared about was sensationalism," Mrs. Hauptmann said. "That's what Jack Clements told me, the Hearst reporter who made me sign a contract so we could get a lawyer without charge. I remember one time I visited Richard, I think it was in Flemington just before the trial started. And Clements wrote in his story that I was crying when I came out. I never cried. I wanted to, many times, but I wouldn't show that to the reporters because Richard would read about it and it would upset him.

"I read the story the next day and I got very angry with Clements. 'This is a lie,' I told him. 'I didn't cry.' and Clements said, 'What difference does it make? The public wants sensationalism and it won't hurt you to give them a little sensationalism.'

"I knew Clements and the Hearst people were taking advantage of me. But what could I do? We had no money. The police took everything. We had two mortgages, and they took them, they took our bank book, my citizenship papers, they even took a silver spoon from the baby that was a christening present from my sister. So when Jack Clements came to me and said the Hearst papers would pay my expense in Flemington, my room in a private house, and give me a few dollars to live on, and pay for the best lawyer around—this Mr. Reilly—I accepted because . . . well, what was I to do? I had no place to turn."

During the trial, Anna Hauptmann said, a woman reporter from a Boston paper slipped past the Hearst men guarding the rooming house she was living in and knocked on her door. Anna opened it.

"She was very nervous, very frightened. She said she had just sneaked up the stairs and she wanted to talk to me. I told her to come in. She said she wanted to write a story about my life with Richard, what Richard was really like, a story in Richard's favor that no paper ever wrote before. I gave the interview because it would help Richard's case, I thought.

"Jack Clements was furious with me when he read the story the next day. He waved the paper at me and he said, 'Did you say these things?' I told him I did. He said, 'You can't do that, you can't talk to other newspapers. You have a contact with Hearst.' I told him, 'Why didn't you ever print this story? I told you all of this, but you never wrote a story like this.' He couldn't answer. All they cared about was the sensationalism, selling newspapers. They didn't care about the truth. Richard was killed because nobody cared about the truth. The newspapers were getting rich, Wilentz was getting famous, Lindbergh was getting . . . I don't know what he was getting, but he also didn't care about the truth."

It was again time to go. Mrs. Hauptmann went upstairs to get the "story" Richard had written while his appeals were being carried to a higher court—an autobiography consisting of seventy single-spaced typed pages.

We returned to Connecticut. Mrs. Hauptmann had given me the address of Hans Kloeppenburg, who had been Richard's best friend and who had testified at Flemington that he had seen Fisch bring the package which Richard later said turned out to be a shoe box filled with ransom money. I contacted Kloeppenburg and he agreed to see me. While Stevie put in order the notes of our interviews with Mrs. Hauptmann, which we reconstructed immediately after leaving her—we hadn't used a tape recorder because she had not yet officially agreed to cooperate, although it was clear she would—I drove to Kloeppenburg's home in southern New Jersey.

In brief, Kloeppenburg repeated in our talk his testimony at both the extradition hearing in the Bronx and the trial at Flemington concerning Fisch and the shoe box: He was there, in the Hauptmann apartment, when Fisch arrived carrying a package the size of a shoe box. Kloeppenburg in fact had opened the door to admit Fisch when the bell rang "and then he gave the package to Richard and they went into the kitchen together; when they came to the other room where the party was they didn't have the package anymore."

I asked him what he had thought of Fisch. "I couldn't say it to Anna and Richard at the beginning because they liked Fisch a lot, but I always felt Fisch was a crook," he said. "He was a foxy guy, that Fisch, he was so smart and foxy. He borrowed money from Mrs. Hile, Karl Henkel's mother, and he told Mrs. Hile not to ever tell Karl. Whenever she was coming to her son's place, where Fisch had a room, it was Fisch who would go get her at the subway station. He would never let Karl or anybody else get her. Then he would stick around when she was there and take her back to the subway station. He don't ever give them a chance to talk. Even her own son didn't know she loaned Fisch money until we got word Fisch was dead."

On the day Richard was arrested, police also arrested Kloeppenburg and took him down to the Greenwich Street police station. At first the detectives had said Richard had been hurt in an accident and Kloeppenburg's help was needed, but as soon as he was escorted into the police station he began to feel he was a suspect in some crime.

"They took me in a room and questioned me," he recalled. "I was there almost all night. And after they questioned me for a time, then I had to do handwriting. I had to copy something they had written down, just a few sentences they had on this piece of paper. At first they dictated it to me. But then, afterwards, they put it in front of me and had me copy it just the way it was written."

I pressed Kloeppenburg on this point: Was he certain police asked him to copy the specimen paragraph, with all the errors in spelling? He was certain, he said, that they had placed it in front of him and made him copy it; he could no more forget that night than the Lindberghs could ever forget the night their child was kidnaped. "They made me copy those few sentences again and again," he said.

Perhaps Hauptmann had been telling the truth when he swore police had forced him to misspell certain words in his specimen writings. Perhaps that specimen paragraph which the handwriting experts had used as practically the sole evidence with which to condemn Hauptmann had not been dictated to him but had been placed before him so that he could copy it precisely. If so, then the testimony of the handwriting experts was even more fradulent than

446

I'd believed. But why hadn't Reilly, the chief defense counsel, developed this detail when Kloeppenburg testified?

"Because Reilly didn't care," Kloeppenburg said. "Reilly never asked me questions about Fisch or the writing I did for the police. I went one Sunday morning to Reilly's office in New York, to tell him what I knew about Fisch being a crook and what the police did to me. Reilly was drunk. He asked me if I see this and this and that, the things he was most interested in I guess. I said no, I didn't see any of it. And he said, 'You're not a witness.' I went to Flemington to testify because Richard and Anna insisted I should be called. And Reilly never asked me the important questions."

With two brief anecdotes, Kloeppenburg brought into stark relief the dark underside of that concept called fair trial, demonstrating the lengths to which police and prosecutor went in order to create the perfect case against Hauptmann.

"When I was going to testify in the Bronx about the shoe box," he recalled, "the detectives or the DA's men took me in a private room and started talking about what electricity does to the body, all the terrible things that happen when a man is electrocuted. They were trying to scare me with the electric chair so I wouldn't testify. And they threatened to put me in prison. But I testified anyway. And then, during the trial, Wilentz did the same thing, he tried to scare me so I wouldn't testify."

Kloeppenburg explained that a couple of reporters for the *Journal* had asked him to see whether he could get Hauptmann to tell everything he knew about the kidnaping or the extortion. The reporters had to secure Wilentz's permission to get visiting privileges for Kloeppenburg. Wilentz agreed to see Kloeppenburg.

"The reporters took me to see Wilentz in his hotel suite in Trenton, where he was living during the trial. Then they left me and Wilentz alone for a private talk. Wilentz wouldn't let me go see Richard and try to talk to him because, he said, 'I have enough witnesses and evidence and I don't need any more.' This was just a few days before I was supposed to testify, and after telling me he won't let me into the jail to see Richard, he said to me:

"'If you say on the witness chair that you seen Fisch come in with the shoe box, you'll be arrested right away.'

"I was very surprised that he said that. I told him: 'But I seen it. I seen him come in the house with the shoe box. It's the truth.' And he said if I talk about the shoe box I'm going to be in a lot of trouble. Then a day or so later, I think it was the day before I testified, there was a story in the newspapers that police were about to arrest a second man in the kidnaping. That was me they were talking about. They were trying to scare me so I would shut up. And I was scared. So when I testified I never called it a shoe box. I described the size, I gave measurements the size of a shoe box, but I never used that word.''

When I later returned to my home and reread Kloeppenburg's testimony I found that he had indeed described the size of Fisch's package but had never called it a shoe box. And in going through the New York Times Index for the period of the trial I found that the newspapers had printed a story, the day before Kloeppenburg testified, about the "impending arrest" of a second man in the kidnaping; after his testimony Wilentz told reporters the story wasn't true.

How many other witnesses, I wondered, did not have the strength of Kloeppenburg and were frightened away by police and prosecution?

Back in my home, I now began to read through Richard Hauptmann's autobiography.

"On the twenty-sixth of November, 1899, I first saw the light of this world . . .'' he began. In great detail, Hauptmann described his home, his three brothers, his sister, his parents—a childhood no different from any other boy's first dozen years, except for a speech impediment. "It was very difficult for me to make all the usual sounds,'' he wrote. "There was something wrong either with my vocal cords or my tongue.'' But it was corrected during his first years at school and in his teens he sang with the church's male chorus.

I skimmed over the early part of the typescript rather quickly, because much of it had been told before although neither so affectionately nor in such fine detail. He wrote of the start of his father's drinking and how it affected and hurt his mother and the children; his "merry life'' as a Boy Scout leader; his desire to follow his older sister to America, to California, the America he read about in *The Last of the Mohicans* and other books of his childhood; his apprenticeship to a master carpenter. And the war: The death of his brothers; the Battle of Verdun, at which he was gassed and wounded. He wrote of the postwar hardships, his inability to find work, his burglaries and petty thefts, including several the police had never learned about. There were no babies or baby carriages when he and an old army comrade stole food from two women after "showing them a gun," he wrote; they were carts used for marketing.

He was in prison for four years. After his release early in 1923, paroled a year early, he again tried to find work, journeying as far as Nuremburg. But, still, no work was available. Another army comrade asked him whether he'd like to make a few marks delivering a pulley belt to a buyer. The man told Hauptmann he had gotten the belt legally, when he worked at a factory job putting in a new belt. Hauptmann agreed to deliver the belt but when he arrived at the destination he immediately suspected the man to whom he'd been sent dealt in stolen goods. "I suppressed this feeling," he wrote. "I needed the money." He was arrested.

"I knew perfectly well what was ahead of me now because in order to be honest I had to say that I know this belt was stolen. Even if I did not get any sentence, still I knew that I would have to go back and serve the last year of my previous sentence. Go back to prison? No! I knew I would be lost if I were again placed behind those walls. So I decided to run away. I saw the gate open and no guard in the yard. Providence could not have made it any easier for me. I simply walked out and went through the nearby fields to the woods. No one followed me. In the woods, I lay down on the ground and considered my desperate situation. I was clear about one thing. I had to go away—to forget and bury everything behind me—to build up a new life in some other country. I decided to go to America."

For many pages, Hauptmann described his two unsuccessful attempts to reach the United States by stowing away, and the final one: "Now I also walked down the gangplank and, without being stopped, I reached the pier—from which I immediately went out into the street. 'God, I thank you,' were my first words as I walked the pavements of the new world! I was without means, but this did not bother me. Did I not have the desire to work myself up?"

Several dishwashing jobs, then work as a carpenter, and then meeting Anna. "At this time I became acquainted with my future wife. The woman with whose sons I roomed did washing in the same establishment where Fräulein Schoeffler was employed. On one of her visits to my landlady, we saw each other for the first time. Just then I did not have the intention of going with a girl. I intended instead to save five hundred dollars and then go to California to my sister. Also, my past bid me to remain single. . . . In the spring of 1924 I took a room for myself. When I visited the family with whom I previously lived I often met Fräulein Schoeffler, and soon I realized I was pleased when she was present. We soon realized that we were in love. All during this summer of 1924 I knew that I had found my dear wife. All my intentions of remaining single were set aside by the finest thing in a person's life. . . .

"Before we talked about marriage, I told her all my past. I must say that I passed over everything as superficially as I could, for I was afraid that I might lose her love. How happy I was when she said: 'This lies behind you and the past shall not destroy our love and happiness.' "

Except when he writes about his wife and, later, about his son, the remainder of Hauptmann's autobiography is a flat, unemotional account of his dealings with Fisch, his understanding that he had been cheated by the counterfeit bills for furs, his discovery of the shoe box filled with money, and his arrest and trial. Most of it repeated what I had written from other sources, from Governor Hoffman's account of his conversation with Richard, and from Hauptmann's own disjointed testimony at Flemington.

But he did write an account of the pretrial visit to his Flemington jail cell by Dr. Condon, which was described to us by Anna Hauptmann. Condon had come to his cell accompanied by the county prosecutor, Anthony Hauck, and several state policemen, Richard wrote. He was admitted to the cell and sat on a bench with the prisoner. Hauptmann goes on:

"The first thing he asked me was if I had ever seen him before. I answered, 'Yes, yes, I saw you in the New York police station.' He then asked if I had ever seen him *before* I saw him in the police station. I answered, 'No, I never saw you in my life until that day.'

"Finally, he started to talk about the Lindbergh case. He told me that he was suspected by the police, of having something to do with the crime. He told me that he personally had been very roughly treated by the police because the police felt he knew something about the case. He asked me if I would do what I could to help him out of the mess he was in. I said to Dr. Condon, 'I would be glad to help any man who is in trouble in any way in my power, but I know absolutely nothing about the Lindbergh case and since that is true, I see no way that I can help you.' I said that it was a shame for a civilized nation to let their police abuse a man as I was abused—to

450

let them knock a man in the head with a hammer and when he falls, to let a half-dozen other big policemen assault him. I told him I certainly felt sorry for him if he got the same treatment from the police that I got.

"He shook his head and said he had had bad treatment, too. He hesitated for a minute and then asked me if when he was talking to me he could call me by the name John. He said it was a favorite name with him and he liked to call people John. I told him I didn't care what he called me.

"About then, Condon took from his pocket a piece of paper and a pencil. He made a circle on the paper and then divided the circle into four parts. In the first square he made a picture of a bench. In the second square he drew a cross. In the third square he put some sort of picture, but I have been unable to remember what it is. The fourth section he left empty. He held the picture in one hand and looked at it, and held the pencil in the other hand. Suddenly, without a word, he jumped up from the bench where we were sitting, threw the pencil and paper down on the bench and said to the prosecutor, who was standing just outside the bars:

"'No! I can not testify against this man! I will not testify against him!'

"The prosecutor seemed to be taken by surprise and he attempted to quiet Dr. Condon. He said to him, 'All right, Dr. Condon, go ahead, go ahead.'

"I looked at Condon sharply. His conversation did not seem to be making any sense. His mind seemed to be wandering and he seemed to find it difficult to stay clearly with one subject many minutes at a time. . . ."

Condon remained for about an hour, Hauptmann wrote, during which he described his conversation with John on a park bench and asked Richard whether he had been the man in the cemetery. "No," Hauptmann said, "you certainly know I am not the man you talked to. I know nothing of the Lindbergh case." Hauptmann continued:

"At no time during the conversation did he say I was the one he talked to in Van Cortlandt Park, or that I was the man to whom he delivered the ransom money. The prosecutor and the policemen seemed to be getting impatient with his rambling conversation with me. When he was ready to go, he asked if he might come to visit with me and I said, 'I am glad to have you come any time you please.'

451

"However, I never saw Dr. Condon again until I saw him at the courtroom in Flemington, sitting in a chair close by me. I was happy when I saw him there because I supposed, following his conversation with me, that he would go on the stand and say the same thing he had said in my cell. But the whole world knows my disappointment. The whole world knows how he completely changed his story.

"But what the world doesn't know, and what the world probably will never know, is what force was exerted upon Dr. Condon to cause him to so completely change his story. Apparently the power of the Lindbergh name and the power of the governments of the State of New York and the State of New Jersey, was too strong for him to withstand. And he took the easiest way out.

"When my trial began on the second of January, 1935, I was glad. I was entirely confident that I must be freed. . . . I will desist from a discussion of all the circumstantial evidence used against me. How easily it can be built up, and how I was convicted on it! I cannot write down how I felt when all these things came up and I saw my life being connected. If my lawyer had not continually admonished me to remain quiet I would have protested loudly against all these lies. At many times I could only keep myself back with a great effort. The question was asked me many times as to how I could hold out without breaking down. The reason was not only strong nerves, but a clear conscience. I may say that I can sleep more soundly than many of the people who were on the witness stand. Did I not have the strong conviction that I would return to my wife and child after the trial?

"The thought never occurred to me that I could be convicted, because I knew that my conscience was clear. But what was the verdict? I was condemned to death for murdering a little child that I had never seen in my life!

"I do not want to write of my own feelings as I left the courtroom; it would be an indictment and I would have to strike a sharper tone, in order to put it in the proper words."

Hauptmann ended his memoir a paragraph later, then added a postscript: "Nothing in my life has ever moved me so strongly and so unnerved me as the unfolding of my life story. It will be impossible for me to write it again. I have written everything down just as it occurred."

452

20

"Richard wrote that he was convinced he would return to you and Manfred," I said to Mrs. Hauptmann a few days later. "Did he still feel that way after all that happened at the trial?" Stevie and I had returned to see her again; we visited with her a number of times while I was writing this book, and what follows is a condensation, a compression, of perhaps a dozen conversations, including telephone calls.

"Yes, he was certain in his heart that he would come back to us," Anna Hauptmann said. "He never believed, until the last hour, that they would kill him. He always thought a miracle would happen. He always said, 'Annie, I'll be home again with you.'

"Look, I show you," she said, going to the secretary. "I have been reading through Richard's letters, I want you to see them, to publish some of them. Here is one, that talks about coming home to his family."

It was dated Trenton, 20 July, 1935, nine months before his execution. In English, he wrote:

My dear Anny:

It is nearly two weeks since I saw you last time, so therefore I will write you; if it would permit it to write in my mother tongue, you certainly would get one letter after another. But you know, dear Anny, I can not express myself as I would like to and as I feel in my heart.

453

The last time you was visiting me you said you like to bring our baby to me. O dear Anny, you know how I would like to see my baby, all my thoughts are by him and you. But I can not allow you to bring our child, our sunshine, behind these walls. Even when he don't know where he is when he see me, this would not give me any justification. As long as I can prevent it, our child shall never come behind these walls. So, therefore, I have to wait till I come home again.

Furthermore dear Anny, can you imagine how I would feel when I see you and the baby, my heaven on earth, going from me, and I have to stay in this terrible place. It would be a struggle against madness. I have stand a great deal of suffering already, but that would be the end. You said, people said I was never asking to see my baby. Of course, they will say I must be a madman. Did people ever understand me or was trying to understand me? They probably will better when they have read my life story.

Dear Anny, I know positive that I will be home again and then our happy family life will continue. Just now, I have to be satisfied to have only the picture from you and the baby in here. Every night between seven and eight, I kiss the baby and you, like before, as we did together. Brahms' beautiful lullaby, I know it is the time to put the baby to bed. To be in thought of my family is one thing nobody can take away from me; it is all what remains left and there is no possibility for stealing it.

My love for you and the baby and my belief in God, no one can lay his hand on it. These are two supremes that can not be stolen through circumstantial evidence.

Dear Anny, when I say I am positive sure, that I have to come home free, is based on my belief in God. I know He will never permit that some persons commit a murder on me. Just now, I am like a ball in a child's hands and they like to play with it. But the dishonour will not rest on my shoulder, but it will rest on the shoulder of the State. Because the State must be responsible on the group of men whom was working only in their own interest and not in the course of justice, this was only a matter of secondary consideration, but to win this case and so to climb higher on the political ladder was more important as justice. Therefore this false sentence never will stand, not before God and not before the American nation.

Dear Anny, you are wondering always when you come visiting me that I am so happy. It is not only the happiness in seeing you, it is also a quiet happiness that I have in my heart that I know the time will come when the truth comes out and then the people will say that I am innocent. For this time, my dear Anny, let us pray together and fold the hands up of our child to pray to God; God is with us, then we will soon be together in happiness and love.

Your Richard.

Kiss the baby from me and when possible bring some pictures to me.

"He wasn't just saying he'd come home," Stevie asked, "to keep your spirits up?"

"Oh, no, " Mrs. Hauptmann said. "I was strong, I could take it, all that Wilentz and the reporters did. After Richard was arrested and to the day they killed him, I was all alone. I told all my relatives to stay out of it. I tried to protect them, because I knew how terrible the reporters were. I could take it, but I was certain my relatives couldn't.

"When I went to visit Richard I was always careful to dress well and to keep myself up. The reporters criticized me for it, always writing, 'Mrs. Hauptmann was very well-dressed today. . . .' What was I to do. Wear rags? What would Richard think of me? I had to be strong, even in my despair, because I could not let Richard down."

Anna Hauptmann was an incredibly alert woman, during our lengthy talks with her, and her memory was remarkable. In perhaps fifty hours of conversation about Richard and those days between their marriage and his execution, she didn't repeat a single anecdote, not one fact, without letting us know she was doing it deliberately and remembered she had said the same thing earlier: "I know I told you this yesterday, but . . ." Many of the elderly men and women I met and interviewed during two years of research rambled and repeated themselves constantly, but not Anna Hauptmann; she seemed to have stored in her mind images of *everything* that ever happened to her and Richard in their dozen years together, and she seemed able to retrieve a specific image at will.

I asked her about Isidor Fisch, and about Paul Wendel: had she ever heard of any connection between them? Did Governor Hoffman or Ellis Parker tell her about the evidence they amassed during the Wendel investigation? No, she said, she didn't really know anything about Wendel. She met Parker only once. He had called her in the Bronx, long after the trial, and asked her to come see him. She did, one day on her way to visit Richard in Trenton. They talked, but Parker never mentioned Wendel; he seemed to be trying to make her understand that he, at least, knew Richard was innocent and that he was trying to prove it. Parker had told her: "I told the police they had the wrong man, they were bungling the case, so they shoved me out of it." And Anna came away with a feeling that Parker might be able to help. He did not, however, tell her about Wendel.

"But Isidor Fisch did have friends in New Jersey," she said. "He would tell us about visiting friends in New Jersey, I know that for sure. But I don't know where these people lived. We tried to find out if maybe they had something to do with the kidnaping, but we found out nothing.

"There are a lot of things I remember about Fisch, that I didn't have time to tell you before," she continued. "I read in your reports that some gold notes were passed at burlesque houses. Isidor liked to go to burlesque, he always went to those shows because he liked them so much. He told us that.

"He also told us a lot of times that he loved to go to the court house, he would sit and watch the trials. And he told me, 'Most of the time they convict the innocent.'" Mrs. Hauptmann repeated it in German, to get Fisch's words precisely, and then translated it more accurately: "He said, 'The people who get convicted are the ones who are not guilty.'

"Isidor was a strange man, I told you that already. He was a loner and everybody thought he was very peculiar. We would go to Hunter's Island and Isidor would always wander away by himself, vanish for a half hour at a time. And people would say, 'Where's Isidor?'"

"There's something Richard wrote in this letter . . ." I began.

"Oh, excuse me," Mrs. Hauptmann said. "I remembered something about Isidor that I have to tell you. Mr. Steinweg, the man with the travel agency that sold the boat ticket to Fisch, he said to me one day, 'Find out what time Richard gave Fisch the money. This is important. I won't tell you now what it's about, but find

456

out.' When I went to see Richard the next day I asked him about it. Richard said that Isidor met him at the broker's office. He said, 'I'll get a check for you from the broker,' and Fisch said, 'No, I want cash.' Fisch suggested Richard get the check and they cash it in Richard's bank. They rushed to the bank to make it in time, it was just before closing time late in the afternoon. Richard said he remembered they had to rush to get to the bank in time.

"When I told this to Steinweg he said Fisch had bought the ticket in the morning, before Richard gave him money. Fisch had a lot of money, Mr. Steinweg told me. He said he thought Fisch was wearing a money belt, filled with money, but of that he wasn't certain. He was certain Fisch bought his ticket and changed money into deutschmarks in the morning, a lot of money, before Richard gave him the two thousand. And Steinweg told me Fisch bought the ticket with gold notes."

I had not yet asked Mrs. Hauptmann about Steinweg; his statement didn't appear in the material I had left with her earlier. But Steinweg had been much on my mind in the days before this visit to Mrs. Hauptmann. Only a week or so earlier I had been told by Harold Olson, the Connecticut man who believes he is the Lindbergh child, that he had located a woman "with a lot of documents in the Hauptmann case." The woman was Grace McGrady, a writer and the wife of Patrick McGrady, the Associated Press reporter who had covered Hauptmann's trial; he was the reporter who had been described by Mrs. Hauptmann as one of the few sympathetic journalists she had met. I called Grace McGrady and asked her about the documents in her possession. They were, Grace said, depositions and investigative reports compiled by one of the private detectives Lloyd Fisher had hired to uncover new evidence on which Hauptmann could base his appeal for a new trial.

"The detective doesn't want his name used because his wife is afraid to let him get involved publicly," Grace said. "But he's an old friend from back in the Lindbergh days and he contacted me when he read something I wrote about Harold Olson. The detective's certain Hauptmann was innocent and he's sending me copies of everything he has."

Although she had already committed herself to write a magazine article based on the investigator's material, Grace offered to share a few of the documents with me.

One of those documents was a report by the investigator of an interview he had had with Steinweg months after Hauptmann was convicted. The report states that the records of Steinweg's ticket agency show that Isidor Fisch and his friend, Henry Uhlig, had purchased one-way tickets to Germany on the liner *Manhattan* on August 18, 1933. The investigation continues:

On November 14 at 11 A.M., Fisch again came to the agency and bought $600 worth of marks and two tourist-class return tickets for $210 each. Fisch paid for the German money and the tickets with gold certificates of ten- and twenty-dollar denominations. Steinweg told me that Fisch paid for his tickets in Lindbergh ransom notes.

The agent Steinweg remembered the transaction perfectly well for several reasons. First, he had been rather surprised to see so much money come out of the pocket of a fur cutter who had never looked as though he was very prosperous. Secondly, he remembered the gold certificates and saved most of them because they were nice and crisp and he wanted to give some of them to his wife on her birthday. But before this happened a friend of his, a Mr. Gartner, who also went to Germany, asked him for some of these bills and he paid by check for the amount. But when this man went to the Federal Reserve Bank to pass some of the bills he was arrested on the suspicion that he was J. J. Faulkner, and he had to write his own and Faulkner's name a good many times to convince the police that he was not this man nor the kidnaper of the Lindbergh baby. . . .

The police claim that on November 14, 1933, Hauptmann gave Fisch $2,000 which Fisch then used to buy tickets and marks. But Fisch paid for all this at 11 A.M. but Hauptmann did not take out the money which he gave to Fisch until a few minutes before 3 P.M. that day. Therefore Fisch must have paid with his own money and not with that that he received from Hauptmann. . . .

That report confirmed Mrs. Hauptmann's recollection of what Steinweg had told her. And it made it plain to me that the authorities, perhaps by frightening Steinweg as they had tried to frighten Hans Kloeppenburg, had suppressed this evidence that Fisch was in possession of ransom money before he sailed to Germany. For I had read about this purchase of tickets and marks with gold certificates early in my research, but I had dismissed the story because all later published accounts had said it was proved false. After talking to Grace McGrady, however, I returned to the original publication of the anecdote. It had been written by Sidney Whipple, the United Press reporter who was considered by his contemporaries to be the unofficial historian for the police and prosecution. Whipple had access to police files, he'd written a fast melodramatic account of the case called *The Lindbergh Crime,* and he later edited the trial transcript for trade publication.

In *The Lindbergh Crime,* written as the case progressed and published less than a month after Hauptmann was convicted, Whipple had said that Fisch had paid for his tickets and the marks with gold certificates of ten- and twenty-dollar denominations. Whipple then wrote:

> George Steinweg, the steamship agent, remembered the transaction perfectly for many reasons. First, he had been rather surprised at seeing so much cash come out of the pockets of a fur cutter who had never appeared to be overprosperous. Second, he remembered the gold certificates. Third, it appeared to him that Fisch was financing his friend Uhlig's trip abroad.
>
> When Steinweg, therefore, read in the newspapers that Fisch's name had been brought into the case, he went to the police and divulged what he knew about the transaction. And after that, his mind going back to the flutter of gold notes over his agency counter, he went to his own bankers and asked if they had a record of a deposit in such certificates, on or about November 14, 1933.
>
> The bank officials also remembered the matter very well. They had discovered, upon checking over the certificates, that they were a part of the Lindbergh ransom money. But at that time they had no means of tracing them back to the depositor, and although the federal government was notified, the trail was lost.

Except for the lack of reference to Gartner, the man who was sold some of the gold notes and was suspected of being the kidnaper when he tried to cash them, Whipple's account of the incident is remarkably similar to that in the investigator's deposition. Yet the investigator didn't interview Steinweg until September 1935, more than six months after Whipple's book was published. There can be little doubt that Whipple got his story, including the fact that bank officials had notified the Treasury Department about finding Lindbergh ransom bills in the steamship agency's deposit, from the police *before* Hauptmann went to trial; later the authorities denied the story because it would have marred their portrait of Hauptmann as the lone kidnaper and murderer and would have helped Hauptmann's defense.

Most important, there can be no doubt at all that Steinweg was telling the truth: Isidor Fisch gave him more than $800 in ransom money a year before Hauptmann passed *his* first gold certificate. If his story were not true, Whipple would never have been given the vital detail that the ransom money had been discovered by bank officials. Isidor Fisch had most definitely possessed and spent gold notes from the ransom before the going-away party at which Hauptmann said he was given the shoe box.

Another document given to me by Grace McGrady strongly supports that conclusion. In a deposition taken by the private detective, a man named Arthur H. Trost swore that he had known Isidor Fisch since the summer of 1931, about eight or nine months before the kidnaping. Trost said he met Fisch frequently in a billiard parlor at Eighty-sixth Street and Third Avenue, in the Yorkville section of Manhattan. Between the summer of 1931 and through January 1932, he saw Fisch in the billiard parlor two or three times a week. In February, the month before Lindbergh's son was kidnaped, Fisch stopped going to the billiard parlor. Trost did not see him there again until the following summer. His deposition concludes with that last meeting:

My occupation is painter and I have been acquainted since March or April, 1931, with a man who is also a painter and who I knew only by the name of Fritz. . . . In June or July, 1932, I met Fritz at a restaurant at 1603 Second Avenue at which time he asked me if I wished to buy some 'hot money' for fifty cents on the dollar from a friend of his. I told him that I would go with him to see the people who had it for sale and he then took me to the same billiard parlor and when we arrived there he started to introduce me to Isidor Fisch. I then

460

told Fritz that I was already acquainted with Isidor Fisch and needed no introduction to him. I also told Fritz that Fisch was already indebted to me for borrowed money and that I could not believe any of Fisch's stories. I was led to believe by Fritz that this 'hot money' was in the possession of Fisch and that Fisch had it for sale.

Mrs. McGrady gave me one other deposition from her files. In this one, two witnesses gave the investigator information that indicates Fisch had a very direct involvement in the kidnaping and that he was in close contact with two employees of the Lindbergh and Morrow households—the "insiders" who police were certain had participated in the crime. But the problem with this deposition, with all such statements, is that there is no possible way to verify the accusation at this late date. Lacking full access to police and FBI files, I was unable to determine whether there is independent evidence confirming any particular statement made by a witness. I publish this statement anyway, however, for two reasons: the information it contains about Fisch and at least one of the "insiders," Violet Sharpe, does not defy credibility, for it is of a piece with everything we have learned thus far, and its publication may eventually pry loose further information.

The deposition was sworn to by a man named Gustave Mancke and his wife, Sophie. The Manckes lived in the Bronx and owned an ice cream parlor and lunchroom on Main Street in New Rochelle, a suburban town a few miles north of their home. They swore that during an eight-week period in January and February, 1932, and up to the Sunday before the kidnaping, Isidor Fisch ate in their shop on several occasions. Each time, Fisch was accompanied by Violet Sharpe, the maid who committed suicide after repeatedly lying to police about her movements in the days before the kidnaping, and by Oliver Whately, Lindbergh's butler. In this brief statement the Manckes appear to have identified at least some members of the "gang" which police had always believed planned and executed the kidnaping. Gustave Mancke swore and his wife verified that:

During these eight weeks and I believe usually on Sundays at about 9 P.M. or later, a man and a woman who I identify positively from photographs as Ollie Whately and Violet

461

Sharpe came to my place four or five times to eat. On three or four occasions they were accompanied by a short thin dark man who looked like Eddie Cantor only with much larger ears. He coughed badly and I slapped him on the back, saying, 'You resemble Eddie Cantor.' His friend said, 'No, his name is Fisch.' I said, 'Why not herring?' They laughed and went out. This man who coughed always spoke to me in German. I positively identify this man as Isidor Fisch. The man who I identify as Whately . . . limped slightly and had blond hair thinning at the temples.

The woman who I identify as Violet Sharpe always ordered tea and sandwiches. She was hard to please and was always disagreeable. The whispering of these people attracted my attention and the attention of my wife. The man Fisch never came to my place alone. He was there with Violet Sharpe and Whately three or four times. None of these people who I have mentioned above ever came back to my ice cream parlor after March 1, 1932.

I cannot characterize the Manckes' statement as absolute proof that Isidor Fisch was in contact with the two servants, for I have no corroboration. But I most certainly did have very firm evidence from a number of sources that Fisch had been spending ransom money and police had known it and suppressed it. By all official accounts Hauptmann was the only man of whom it could be said that he definitely passed Lindbergh gold certificates. But the conclusion that has always been drawn, Hauptmann as kidnaper and extortionist, is absolutely false.

Hauptmann claimed he did not find Fisch's hoard of gold notes in the shoe box until late August 1934, and never passed a ransom bill until early the following month. All the suppressed evidence in the police laboratory reports supports the truth of his statement: The gold certificates he is known to have passed in the two weeks before his arrest and those found in his garage were water-soaked; they had attached to them microscopic particles that differed in every way from the particles attached to all other ransom bills recovered before his arrest, and none of those he passed were folded in the tight wads that had become a characteristic of an earlier billpasser. The earliest gold certificate that even the police were able to claim had been put into circulation by Hauptmann was the one

462

that Cecile Barr, the theater cashier, said he had given her the night of his birthday in November 1933, and Cecile Barr was demonstrably lying—she had, remember, originally told police that her customer was "an American" without an accent. Between the time the ransom was paid and up to Hauptmann's arrest, more than 500 bills from the ransom had been turned over to authorities, but not one single person could be found to swear that Hauptmann had passed a ransom bill before the month he was arrested and not one ransom bill was ever recovered from any of the several banks and stock brokerage firms to which he was constantly bringing cash.

All the evidence I've found about the Lindbergh ransom money points along two parallel roads: Richard Hauptmann didn't have any of that money until he discovered it in Fisch's shoe box; Isidor Fisch, on the other hand, had a large amount of the ransom before he sailed to Germany, and from the day he sailed until Hauptmann says he began passing the shoe box bills the following summer, almost no Lindbergh gold notes were put into circulation. The evidence demonstrating that Fisch possessed the ransom money, that he gave a box full of it to Hauptmann for safekeeping, and that Hauptmann never passed any Lindbergh ransom notes until he found the shoe box, is overwhelming.

Unfortunately, I had been unable to find in the files I examined any descriptions of others who passed ransom bills before Hauptmann began spending Fisch's money. I had hoped to uncover evidence that Fisch had been identified by others as having spent some of the ransom. I had hoped to find descriptions of bill-passers who might match Fisch or Wendel or other suspects. But if any other eyewitness descriptions existed they weren't in the documents to which I had access. If there was further evidence of Fisch's handling of ransom money—and perhaps even independent confirmation that he had been in close contact with Lindbergh "insiders" before the kidnaping, or proof he had known Wendel and perhaps stolen the money from him—I was unable to find it because I had been able to explore only a limited amount of material. No doubt at least some further documentation would be in the FBI files.

And that brought up a very personal conflict. I had originally set out to find Anna Hauptmann because I wanted her authorization to examine and write about the material in the FBI files. We had talked about it during one of these visits and she had agreed to write the letter to FBI Director Kelley. "But I wouldn't like them coming to the house to see that I'm really Anna Hauptmann," she said. "My neighbors and friends know who I am, I've never hidden it except from reporters, but Manfred would get very upset."

I had then checked with a friend at FBI headquarters in Washington and he told me a couple of agents would probably be sent out from the field office nearest Mrs. Hauptmann's home to interview her, "to confirm she's who she says she is." And he added: "The bureau might give her a hard time, they might tip off the papers about her or even make some kind of official announcement, because everybody down here is pissed off about the Rosenberg kids and Alger Hiss suing for their files. If she writes that letter she's taking a chance her address will get out. That's not for attribution, you never talked to me."

And so I decided not to press the FBI matter. I had enough documentation, I was certain, to prove Richard had been innocent. Although there were many gaps—Fisch and Wendel, especially, and the Geisslers—although I would have loved to be able to prove which of them, or someone else, most logically could have been the kidnaper, I was satisfied for now that I had accomplished a great deal. Perhaps, when my book was published, Mrs. Hauptmann would want to press for further proof of Richard's innocence. She indicated as much in one of our talks. "When the world reads what you have written," she said at one point, "maybe I will face the reporters again and tell them what they did to us. I think that if I don't come out and fight everybody will say she's afraid to fight, so I think I must fight again after being silent for all these years. Now, I think, people will believe we were telling the truth."

I hoped the "fight" would include joint pressure on the FBI for the file on Richard Hauptmann. For now, Anna Hauptmann's serenity was most important; that, and her need to maintain her warm relationship with her son, who was still troubled by the disruption in their lives that publication of this book would no doubt cause.

After receiving the depositions from Mrs. McGrady, I asked Anna Hauptmann to tell me everything she remembered about Isidor Fisch. "Richard would sometimes say, 'Well, Isidor sold some furs, I got a few hundred dollars for my profit.' He would give Richard a little money now and then, saying he made a profit, he

464

did good business. The same thing with Mrs. Hile—he paid some profits and that way kept them all happy and on his side."

"How did Richard react when he learned Isidor died in Germany?" I asked.

"Richard just said, over and over, 'Dead? How can it be?' And I remember I also said, 'How can it be? Richard, he wrote us that he was making a fur coat for his sister, à la American, he said he was going out and having a good time, drinking good German beer and we have Prohibition. How can he be dead?' That's what he wrote us, in one of those letters Foley took, that he was going to a lot of parties and having a good time. But when Henry Uhlig came back after the funeral, he said there were no parties. Isidor was so sick he could hardly carry his bags off the boat.

"And then everybody on Hunter's Island talk and talk. Mrs. Hile said, 'My God, he has my money.' and Richard says, 'He has my money, too.' And we find out he has money from a lot of people. It was like an explosion, everyone coming together and learning Isidor was a liar and a cheat.

"But before Richard began to look for where Isidor kept the furs, when we got the letter from Pinkus Fisch saying he was dead, Richard and I wondered what Pinkus meant when he said Isidor tried to tell him something for Richard. I always thought maybe Isidor wanted to tell Richard it was Lindbergh money. But we didn't understand it when we got the letter. Richard was just wondering what it meant. 'Must be something very important,' Richard said. 'To call for me when he is dying, must be something important he wanted to tell me.' At first we thought it was about the furs in storage. But then when Richard was running around, he learned Isidor was a crook.

"Richard went to the place where Isidor's bill showed he bought a lot of furs. One day he went there, down in the fur center in Manhattan, and he came home and said, 'There's no such thing, it's an empty lot. Isidor lied.' I said how could it be, we have the bill with the furrier's address, but Richard said it was an empty lot. He said, 'Now I know, it was all lies, lies.' And then one day Louise Helfert was at Hunter's Island, on a Sunday, and she told Richard, 'Come to my place tomorrow, I have something important to show you.' Richard went there, he had the fur bills with him because he was still searching. And when he got there, Mrs. Helfert showed him blank bills with the name of the furrier whose address was an empty lot. Richard took out the bills that had the purchases typed in and Mrs. Helfert said, 'I did that typing, he asked me to do him a favor. I typed those bills on my machine.' And Richard came home so discouraged. 'It's all lies.'

"I remember one night when he was very discouraged, after a whole day of searching for the furs and for the pie company that didn't exist. He was dejected. He said, 'The money we invested with Isidor is forever lost.' And all this time there was a box in our closet with thousands of dollars. I've always thought it wasn't possible for Richard to be such a good actor in front of me, his wife who knew him so well, to pretend he was so worried about Isidor robbing him if he knew that in the shoe box there was more money than Isidor stole from us. Richard did not know the money was there at that time, in the spring of 1935, otherwise he would not be so discouraged. And if he knew it was there, if he knew it was Lindbergh money like the police claim, wouldn't he get rid of it?''

"What do you remember about the shoe box?" Stevie asked.

"You know, the things I already told you about how Richard found it when he was transplanting my snake plant," she said. "And what was testified at the trial by Hans Kloeppenburg, you know about that?" I nodded. "Well, Hans told me that, just the same way he told it in Flemington, right after Richard was arrested. That he saw Fisch bring the shoe box the night of his going-away party.

"But there was something else about the shoe box I could never explain at Flemington, at that awful trial. Remember, Manfred was born in early November that year, about a month before Fisch brought the shoe box to our home. I was thirty-five years old and the doctor said I had to be careful. In the summer, I was getting very big with Manfred and Mrs. Schussler from downstairs offered to clean my house. She cleaned everything, even that closet where the shoe box was, she got up on a chair and cleaned that top shelf. And there was no shoe box there. It wasn't there, because we didn't have it. And then later, when I was in the hospital with Manfred in November, they cleaned my house again—Mrs. Schussler, my niece, and I think another friend. And there was no shoe box there."

"I'd like to ask you something about this letter from Richard," I

466

said. "He wrote that justice didn't matter, 'to climb higher on the political ladder was more important as justice.' He means Wilentz, obviously . . ."

"Of course he does," she said, a flash of anger in her eyes. "That Wilentz, do you know what he did? Right after the jury said Richard was guilty, no more than a half hour later, a policeman went to visit Richard. He said to Richard, 'Tell us where the rest of the money is and you can probably save your life.' Richard said he didn't know anything about Lindbergh money and the police officer said, 'Come on now, you know where the money is. We know you have it. Where is it?' And he said again that Richard could save his life and he said that Wilentz promised it, because Wilentz sent him to talk to Richard. When Richard told me about it later he said, 'Annie, you could almost laugh. Wilentz proved with his witnesses' lies that I spent all the money and now he sends a man to ask me where the money is.' That's what Richard meant about the political ladder, that Wilentz was using Richard to climb higher.

"There was something else that happened. I don't want to say it was Wilentz who did this because I have no proof and I will not accuse someone without proof. But Richard was certain it had to be Wilentz.

"After the trial, when I was in a new apartment in the Bronx, a well-dressed young man came to see me. He didn't identify himself, he just said he had a plan to help Richard. I was looking for all the help anybody would give me to save Richard and I asked him to come in. And he told me his plan. He said I should go to Trenton and tell Richard to announce to the warden that he was ready to talk, but he wouldn't talk in Trenton. Only in Flemington, they had to take him back to Flemington and he would tell everything. I said to this man, 'But Richard doesn't know anything. Why should he say this?'

"And the man said, 'Just have him tell the warden he wants to talk, in Flemington. And on the way to Flemington we will kidnap him.' I said, 'What!' I was so surprised. And he said they would kidnap Richard with guns and they would take him to a hideout up the Hudson. 'We have a plastic surgeon there and he'll change Richard's face and you and Richard can go to another country.' And I said, 'Get out! Get out of my house.' I threw him out. If it was Wilentz that sent him, can you imagine something like that?"

"By now I can imagine anything," Stevie said.

"If that was an official visit and not just a nut," I said, "it happened because people were beginning to ask questions about whether Richard really did it. Lawyers and magazine writers."

"Yes," Anna Hauptmann agreed. "Too many questions were being asked. We had private investigators, we hired them with some of the money that came in when Fisher and I asked the public for help with money for Richard's appeals. We raised about thirty-five thousand dollars, and some of it went to private investigators. They were beginning to find things to prove a frame-up."

"I can't imagine even Wilentz would have gone so far, to kidnap Richard. The state police, yes."

"Why not Wilentz?"

"Well, a plot like that would have one of two purposes. Either Richard escapes and is later recaptured, and all the headlines will convince everyone that he really was guilty, or they will shoot Richard to death while he's trying to escape and end forever all chances of appeals or of finding evidence that he was innocent. Escape and recapture would have benefited Wilentz only *before* the trial. The idea would be to kill him. And even being so cynical, I just can't conceive of Wilentz's being involved in something like that."

"Maybe you're right," Mrs. Hauptmann said. "But it was Wilentz who did to Richard what was done."

Anna Hauptmann went on to say that Richard would never have gone along with an escape plot, even had it been offered him. "He was so certain of his innocence," she said, "that he would never even consider a pardon. It was never offered him, but that time I went to see Richard because Governor Hoffman asked me to get him to tell any kind of story and save his life, there was talk about a pardon. I think it was about his going before the Pardons Board. And Richard said, 'I will refuse a pardon because I'm not guilty.' " Mrs. Hauptmann added: "He would refuse a pardon because a pardon is for when you're guilty. Like President Nixon. Richard wanted justice, not a pardon."

There was something else about the closet where the shoe box was stored, Mrs. Hauptmann said, that she'd forgotten to mention. "After the trial, the police gave up my old apartment and I guess the reporters went in there to investigate. Some reporters came to me and said, 'Mrs. Hauptmann, we want to take you to your apartment. We're interested in that closet.' I said, 'All right, I'll go with you.' You know both of you, from what I said to police the first day they questioned me and from what I said at the trial, about that closet. That I saved coupons from Kirkman soap and put them in a draw in the kitchen table. Then when I had so many, I had a Prince Albert tobacco box on the top shelf of that closet, near the edge of the shelf because I could barely reach the top shelf. I would stretch up and tip the can down and put the coupons in and then stretch up again and put the box on the shelf.

"But in Flemington, at the trial, Wilentz was asking me questions about that closet and he showed me a picture of it. I said it looked like I remembered it. Then he said, 'See your apron on the hook, you reached your apron all the time, didn't you?' And I told him of course I always used the apron. And when I looked at the picture I could see the hook where I put the apron was higher than the top shelf. I was so surprised, I didn't remember it that way. But I thought maybe I was mistaken, a picture is a picture.

"So we went in the old apartment, me and the reporters. I opened the closet door and reached up to the top shelf and I said, 'Oh, my God!' The reporters said, 'What is it?' I said, 'It's not the same. I can reach so easily now.' I took off my high-heeled shoes, I thought maybe that was it, but still I could reach to the top shelf very easily.

"And then the reporters took a flashlight and showed me what they had found. They said, 'See the paint marks on the wall?' I looked and I saw, the police had moved the shelves. The reporters told me, 'Everything has been painted new,' and I could see there was new paint. And they said, 'There's layers and layers of paint on the wall, but here, where the shelves used to be, there's only one or two layers. You can see the thick paint and then only the new paint where the shelves used to be.' And I could see it. The police lowered the shelves by many inches, by a foot, to take that picture showing my apron was higher than the top shelf. That's another thing they did to murder Richard."

I asked her about the trial, asked her when she first began to understand that the prosecution was distorting evidence and calling on perjurers to convict Richard.

"I think I began to be afraid in the Bronx court," she said. "We always thought that whatever happens we are not afraid because we didn't do anything. I didn't realize it would be so bad to take

Richard over to New Jersey for the trial. But in the Bronx, with the witness Whited lying that he saw Richard, and that Osborn, the handwriting man, I began to worry.

"But my feeling all along I think was still, we will be acquitted in the New Jersey trial. Until I saw everyone lying. 'My God,' I said, 'what can we do if they lie?' But despite the lies, inside I felt Richard would come out all right because he didn't do anything wrong."

She rose to get a newspaper clipping. "You see, we didn't know what was happening until after it happened to us. See what Schwarzkopf said, after the trial." The clipping, from the *New York Journal* of February 15, 1935, had a statement by Colonel Schwarzkopf. He had said:

I have made a friend. There is nothing I would not do for Colonel Lindbergh. There is no oath I would not break if it would materially help his well-being. There is not a single man in my outfit who would not lay down his life for Colonel Lindbergh.

"See what we had to face," Mrs. Hauptmann said after I had read it aloud. "This man admits he would break an oath, he would lie, for Colonel Lindbergh. That's why Richard was convicted, why they faked the evidence against him once they found he had Lindbergh money. Lindbergh was a prominent man, a hero to everybody. Richard was an alien, a workingman. His character was as good as Lindbergh's—Richard was not a liar—but his social standing was nothing. And the jury was taken in because the man who accused my husband had a high social standing, rich and powerful and a hero, like a god. I remember reading after, what the jurors said in stories they wrote, that Lindbergh convinced them. But Lindbergh lied. The way Schwarzkopf said he would lie for Lindbergh, the way Schwarzkopf did lie for him and got his police to lie and to fake evidence.

"Even the people who did not lie, they just stood by and let all the others lie. Like Mr. Foley, the Bronx district attorney, and his assistant, that Mr. Breslin. They were at the trial in Flemington almost every day, maybe every day. I don't remember for sure now. But they were there. Foley and Breslin knew about the letters from Fisch's brother, that Wilentz said didn't exist. They knew about

470

Richard's ledger book. They knew Dr. Condon was a liar. They knew all these things, and more, and they never said anything. I always wondered why men like Foley and Breslin, when they heard these lies and read about them, didn't come forward and tell the truth."

"The FBI knew, J. Edgar Hoover knew," Stevie said. "It wasn't their case. They weren't involved. If New Jersey wanted to take a chance on manufactured evidence, it wasn't the problem of the FBI or the Bronx prosecutor. They just closed their eyes."

"And how do they sleep at night?" Mrs. Hauptmann asked. "How do they face their God when they die? This I want to know.

"I just couldn't believe the lies at the trial," she went on. "But even so, I thought our witnesses showed that Richard was in the bakery with me that night of the kidnaping, I thought we had won. That afternoon, when the jury was given the case, I did all the washing that had piled up, mine and Manfred's. I was so certain Richard would be with us that evening as soon as the jury found him not guilty, that I was the least nervous of those around me. A reporter asked me if I was nervous and I said, 'Certainly not, I know Richard will be free and Richard knows it, too. That's why I'm washing my clothes and the baby's clothes, so they'll be nice-looking when the three of us we get home together.' Never for a moment did I think Richard would be found guilty.

"The police came for me when the jury was ready to report and drove me to the courthouse where I knew I would hear a verdict of acquittal. But as I got out of the car I think I had a little premonition. There was a terrific mob there, thousands of people with the bright lights turned on them for the newsreel cameras. People in the crowd wished me good luck, said nice things, but I was almost overcome by the amount of people. I thought, 'It is like the crucifixion. Like the sacrifice of human life.' And when I got inside and saw Richard handcuffed between two guards, I thought, 'Well, it must be the worst or they would not take such precautions.'"

"Then you weren't surprised at the verdict?" I asked.

"Oh, yes, I was shocked. I don't have words to tell how I felt. What I remember most, it is so clear I can still see it—the jury would not look at me. I stared at them, at everyone of them, trying to get them to look in my eyes while we were waiting for the judge to come in and hear their verdict. But not one of them dared to look at me or at Richard. Even when they answered, when they said

471

guilty, they stared down at the floor. I think they knew they were doing something dreadful, many of them knew they were killing my Richard because of the lies of witnesses.

"I know that when I heard the verdict I wanted to cry out, but I couldn't. I don't remember too much after that because I was like in a dream, with shock. One thing I remember is when I returned to Manfred, I threw myself on the bed beside him and cried, 'My baby, what have they done to your father?' "

Mrs. Hauptmann went into the kitchen for a glass of water. When she returned a few moments later, she was smiling. "All of my life I have prayed that the truth will come out. I feel when the truth is finally written I can die and be with Richard."

She had one other letter to give us, she said. "This is his last letter to me. He couldn't finish it, he couldn't even sign it. I like to know what they did to him in those last days to make him write like this. Could they have beaten him to make him confess to something he didn't do or to make him tell them where the money was that Wilentz proved he spent every penny of? Here, look at it, look what they did to him."

The letter was written in German and I did not understand it. But it was plain that something had happened to Richard in the days just before he was electrocuted. The script is small and tight and written in a palsied hand, unlike all the other letters I've seen written by Hauptmann. It was the writing of an elderly man, a man who had deteriorated almost overnight.

"I want the world to see that," Anna Hauptmann said. "To see what they did to Richard."

We had the letter translated. Dated April second, the day before his death, it says:

My dear Anny,

I received your letter just at the moment when I started to doubt God. Forgive me, my dear Anny, but my entire inner life had collapsed. This was a result of the treatment I was given during the past ten hours. Oh, how little faith I had, why do I let myself be misled by the people of this world. I should know better from my past life. They only want my death in order to solve a case in the wrong manner; however, dear Anny, again and again I still expected that they would come to their senses and shy back from committing a murder. I myself can

472

hardly understand that they could make me doubt my own faith. How weak we are, we human beings; God has shamed me in my weakness. However, He had put it into my heart that I should live and that I should see you and Manfred again. God forgive me and help me in my lack of faith. From now on I shall leave everything in His hands because He will do the right thing: because He will stay with me whatever may come. I am praying, dear Anny, that He may also be with you and our baby and with mother and with the whole world.

"Please publish that for the world to see," Mrs. Hauptmann asked again.

She is a woman of remarkable strength and faith, this Anna Hauptmann. While Stevie and I had grown angry at what was done to Richard Hauptmann, she spoke of her faith in God.

"Can you imagine?" Anna Hauptmann said at one point. "I'm not talking for myself, I mean any person who would go through what I went through, sitting in a courtroom day after day and hearing people telling lies, looking at Richard and telling lies. And I knew it, that he was innocent and he was killed by lies, I knew it day after day and year after year. Sometimes I wonder how I lived through it. Sometimes I thought I could almost go insane. Thinking, saying, 'God, You let it happen. You know the truth. Why did you let it happen?'

"I talked to my pastor. I told him, 'God knows Richard is innocent, He above all knows it. Why did He let Richard die?' And he said, 'Mrs. Hauptmann, we must not ask questions about what God does. He must do it for some reason. I sometimes ask why He let me get sick, so that I can't complete the work I want to do, and then I understand He does it for some reason.'

"That helped me. But still, I always wanted the truth to come out, I did not want to leave it that just God knew the truth. Maybe in a certain time the truth will come out and people will say, 'Oh, how wrong we were in our judgment. We must never do this again.' And I used to think, 'What will all those people say then, the jury, the prosecutor Wilentz, all those witnesses who lied. What will their excuses be when the truth comes out?' "

"I wonder what Wilentz will say?" Stevie asked. "He'll never admit he had any knowledge of it."

"I believe in his heart he knows Richard was innocent," Mrs. Hauptmann said.

"He knew some of it, he had to," I said. "He must have seen the evidence . . ."

"I am not a religious fanatic," Mrs. Hauptmann continued. "But I believe God was with me through the trial. Wouldn't those people who lied think that some day there will be a higher Judge they must face? Those people who perjure themselves, some of them must believe in God."

Stevie was close to tears. "I'm not very religious," she said. "I don't know if I believe in heaven and hell, but sometimes I hope there is a hell for those people who do something terrible like this, I hope there is a punishment so they . . ."

"I believe in a God in heaven," Mrs. Hauptmann interrupted. "I find out so many times, I get strength from that belief. If I didn't have this, I have nothing. It helped me survive. You know, there's a thing about right and wrong, lies and conscience, it means to me more than all the riches in the world, to tell the truth. I don't complain. God has been with me all the time, all these years, that's all I need. To the last breath I have I know Richard was innocent and I'm not afraid to die, I'm not afraid of anything."

"You have more than Wilentz and the others have," Stevie said.

"I wouldn't want to change with Wilentz or any of them. You know, I had the strength of my faith, I could take it. But I feel so bad about Richard's mother and my parents. Just think what those people went through. Richard wrote to them many times and told them the truth of what happened, what was done to him. But they didn't know he was innocent, the way I knew, and they must have suffered terribly.

"You see, I never doubted that Richard was telling the truth. He was with me that night, when the baby was taken. Maybe if he hadn't been with me, I might have doubted him and wondered if he could have done it. But I was certain with the certainty that only a wife has—he was with me all night and we went to sleep together."

21

It was time to seek an interview with David Wilentz. Now eighty, reportedly ill for a time, Wilentz was still practicing in Perth Amboy, New Jersey, a partner in one of the largest, most politically oriented and influential law firms in the state. I telephoned him with some trepidation, not because of what I had written about Wilentz and the Lindbergh case but because the last time I had met Wilentz it had been under rather strained circumstances. That was back in 1969. Jonathan Kwitny, a young investigative reporter, had written a series of articles for our paper, the *New York Post*, about David Wilentz's relationship to one of the more powerful Mafia figures in his state.

The articles charged that the *mafioso*, Anthony Russo, had made many hundreds of thousands of dollars from land speculation, apparently without investing a penny of his own money, and had been represented by prominent lawyers and political leaders, among them David Wilentz, then the state Democratic national committeeman. Mafia man Russo had financed major land deals with more than $800,000 in mortgage loans from banks in which Wilentz and members of his law firm were directors or legal counsel. A large part of Russo's $500,000 profits were realized when the state transportation department condemned tracts of land Russo had purchased with the loans and paid Russo far more for the land than it had cost him. In one case, Russo had advance knowledge that the state was going to condemn a small portion of land he owned and, with the Wilentz firm representing him, he persuaded

475

the state to pay him three times what the tract had cost him only two years earlier. The implication drawn by the articles was that Wilentz had used his political influence to help Russo make an unconscionable profit at the expense of the taxpayers.

Before publishing the articles it was necessary, of course, to get Wilentz's reaction to the charges, his explanation or defense. Our editor assigned me to accompany Kwitny to Perth Amboy as a witness to the expected confrontation. It was an angry session, well over an hour long. Wilentz conceded that Kwitny's documentation was unassailable, insisted there had been no impropriety on his part, and accused us and the *Post* of being motivated solely by the desire to besmirch his reputation. He warned us that he might sue for libel. In a telephone call to the *Post*'s general counsel, a member of Wilentz's law firm said that a libel action was imminent. The articles were published. There was no libel suit. There was some talk of an official state investigation of the land deals, but nothing much ever came of it. The only real effect of the articles was that they were reprinted by the Republican party in Middlesex County, distributed to the voters by the thousands, and helped contribute to the first loss by Democrats in the county since 1928, when Wilentz became county leader.

Telephoning him now, in January 1976, I was worried that he might remember me and refuse to speak with me. When I got through to him I identified myself, told him I had left the newspaper to free-lance, and said I was writing a book about the Lindbergh case.

"It seems everybody's getting interested in that case again," he said. "You know there's going to be a big TV movie about it in a few weeks?"

I told him I was aware of the NBC dramatization scheduled for late February, that I had been reading a copy of the script and it pretty closely followed the published facts. But my book will be different, I went on. It would present strong documentation from police and FBI reports to show that Richard Hauptmann had been innocent, the victim of perjured testimony and evidence manufactured by police.

Wilentz's response was immediate and sharp: "Well, what do you want me to do?"

"I want to talk to you about it because there are indications you knew some evidence had been tampered with."

476

"That's utterly ridiculous," he said.

"Maybe it is, but I have to talk to you simply to be fair. You know I can't publish this book without making an attempt to interview you."

He agreed to see me. I drove down to Perth Amboy a week later and parked outside the large concrete building that houses the offices of Wilentz, two partners, and thirty or more attorneys who work for them. Wilentz seemed friendly as he showed me into his office. If he recognized me or my name from our previous painful meeting in this same office more than six years before, he did not give a sign. His office is a large chamber equipped only with the essentials of business—desk, chairs, a couch, bookcases filled with lawbooks. The few adornments were photographs of his grandchildren on the wall behind his desk and, on other walls, photographs of David Wilentz posing with Harry Truman, John F. Kennedy, and Lyndon B. Johnson. Each president had autographed his picture.

Wilentz was a small man, appearing even tinier because of his dark conservative suit, the trousers of which seemed to have been freshly pressed though this was late afternoon. His eyes were still bright and penetrating and—did I imagine it now as I may have imagined it with Jon Kwitny years before?—still appearing to be able to drill inside a man's mind. He waved me to a comfortable chair and settled behind his desk into a chair that seemed overlarge for him.

"I'll come right to the point," I began.

"Please do."

"I've been given copies of police and FBI documents that show Hauptmann was innocent." His eyes showed no reaction. "The attic board, the handwriting testimony, all the eyewitnesses—almost everything presented to the jury—was faked by the police. And you must have been aware of at least some of . . ."

He interrupted, his eyes staring at the center of my forehead, his right hand pointing toward me in anger: "If there was a frame-up as you *claim*," he said, "how could I have known about it? But I don't believe there was a frame-up, I cannot believe that no matter what evidence you *say* you've found—but if there was such a thing I could not have known what the police had done."

"I'll concede that. It isn't likely the police would have confessed their crimes to you," I said. "But I do have at least one piece of evidence that you knew some documents that would have helped Hauptmann were suppressed.''

"Show me your evidence.''

I began to explain about the "missing" employment book that I was certain would have shown Hauptmann had been working on the day of the kidnaping, as he'd originally claimed. I told Wilentz that he must have known about the book for he had told reporters that Hauptmann had worked a half day on the day of the kidnaping. In your own words to reporters in the Bronx, I went on, you said he had done some work on that date and yet at the trial you proved he didn't begin working until much later in the month.

"I don't remember talking to reporters about that," Wilentz said. "Show me the clipping where I said that.''

"I didn't bring it along. My material fills three cartons and I didn't carry any of it down here. But I've summarized what I found so I could discuss it . . .''

He broke in again, a warm tint of color touching his cheeks. How dare I come in to "cross-examine" him with evidence I "claimed" to possess? He was not, he said, going to permit me to pull that kind of cheap trick on him. I insisted that I was not being mischievous or deceitful, but that it was hardly possible for me to bring my files with me on such a visit.

That pretty much destroyed any possibility of a productive interview. Wilentz shouted that I'd better leave his office if my sole purpose in seeing him was to cross-examine him. I protested:

"Mr. Wilentz, you have a reputation as one of the best cross-examiners in history. Do you think I'd be that stupid, trying to cross-examine you?" I laughed. Wilentz didn't.

"I will not let you play that game, coming in and talking to me and then saying, 'David Wilentz denies . . .' ''

"I wouldn't dream of trying that on you," I said. "You've been dealing with journalists since long before I was born. I know damn well I'm not going to sucker you into any reporters' traps. But if we can't discuss the evidence, will you tell me what it was like back then, being at the center of the biggest trial in history?"

Wilentz soon relaxed and grew almost charming, in the way an elderly man can be charming when he reminisces about one of the notable moments in his life. He talked about the months between Hauptmann's arrest and the start of the trial, smiling as he recounted the difficulty he had in keeping reporters from learning prema-

478

turely the details of the evidence he would present against Hauptmann, his fears that when someone like Walter Winchell published an exclusive story obtained from the police, other reporters would believe Wilentz had fed him the information and would be angry about it. And he began to speak about how troubled he felt at the idea of prosecuting Hauptmann, troubled for very special reasons:

"I didn't even want that case," he said. "I remember going to the governor, the one before Hoffman, and telling him I didn't think it was right for me, a Jew, to prosecute Hauptmann and perhaps lose the case because of prejudice. You see, that whole area in south Jersey was heavily German, it still is, and I told the governor I had some worry about my ability to give the state its best. He told me to forget it, he insisted that I prosecute. I didn't really want it."

"I must tell you that's not what I've written," I said. "My book will say you took the Lindbergh case away from the local prosecutor because you were politically ambitious and wanted the national recognition."

"I don't care what you write in your book."

"I've read that accusation in several magazine articles . . ."

"Where? Tell me where? Not once in forty years has anyone accused me of that."

"I read it in Governor Hoffman's articles for *Liberty* and in . . ."

"That's not so. Not in forty years have I seen anything like that written about me. That's just not so." Wilentz went on to explain that under New Jersey law a county prosecutor may elect to request that the attorney general supersede him in a particular case. "Perhaps there's a conflict of interest, the prosecutor knows the defendant or is friendly with one party to a suit, it's not uncommon for him to ask the attorney general to handle the case. In this case I think the prosecutor, Tony Hauck, felt that if my office came into it then the state would pay all the expenses of the trial and the county wouldn't be burdened with it. Perhaps Hauck didn't realize the state would have paid all the expenses anyway. But no matter what, Hauck asked me to take it over and I never really wanted it." Wilentz ended by saying:

"If I had really been politically ambitious I would have run for governor. I didn't run for governor. And I did not prosecute Hauptmann because of political ambition."

Perhaps so. But Wilentz in the past had told reporters, including Jonathan Kwitny, that he had wanted his party's nomination for the governorship but was persuaded by other leaders of the party that a Jew could not be elected governor back then, thirty and forty years ago. I didn't want to get into another argument with him, however, and I most certainly couldn't quote Jon Kwitny without risking instant dismissal, so I turned the conversation to other areas. In a short while—it was about four o'clock—Wilentz summoned his secretary and asked whether his chauffeur was ready to drive him home. And that ended my interview. I had not really expected much more than I got out of it.

Throughout our conversation Wilentz occasionally touched upon one or another aspects of the evidence he had presented against Hauptmann. On each such occasion he maintained that he believed the prosecution's case had been overwhelming, and honest. But, he said again and again, even assuming for argument that the police had tampered with the evidence, the prosecutor would have been the last to know for the police would have kept it from him.

That is obviously so. However, I still believe Wilentz must have been aware that at least some of the evidence had been contrived and that some documents helpful to Hauptmann's defense had been suppressed. I believe it not only because of the conflict between the statement Wilentz made to reporters about Hauptmann's employment on the day of the crime and the proof he later presented to the jury that he hadn't begun working that day, but also because of other circumstantial evidence.

After Richard Hauptmann was executed, Governor Hoffman gained access to the files of his state police. He wrote about the documents he found in those files in his long series of magazine articles. Hoffman did not have access to Wilentz's files. Hoffman did not write about the most important evidence that had been suppressed—Hauptmann's ledger books, the letters from Fisch's brother, the employment book, the police laboratory reports. If the governor was not aware of this and other evidence, the fair inference is that those documents were not in police files but were in the files of Attorney General David Wilentz. And if Wilentz had physical possession of the documents, he and his aides undoubtedly examined them in preparing their courtroom strategy, their assault on Hauptmann's alibi. It is extremely unlikely that the prosecutor did not study those documents, if only out of a desire to counter Hauptmann's defense.

That Richard Hauptmann was the victim of men who distorted truth and manufactured evidence and rushed him into the electric chair—Wilentz's remark to Governor Hoffman still rings: "The hell with it"—is beyond question. That Hauptmann was made a scapegoat because of police frustrations, because of an obsession to punish someone, anyone, for committing such a foul act upon the child of the hero Lindbergh, upon Lindbergh himself, is evident. The proof is overwhelming.

Again, while there was no conspiracy per se to convict Hauptmann at all costs, to mold and shape the evidence to fit the man who possessed almost one third of the Lindbergh ransom money, Hauptmann was the victim of something more dreadful. He was the victim of individual perjurers who believed they were acting justly, morally—with God on their side—in twisting truth to make more perfect the case against the man they believed was guilty. It was a classic instance of the weakness of the adversary system of justice. These police officers and witnesses hid the evidence and truth of their own investigations and observations, lied and falsified and suppressed the knowledge they possessed. Had the evidence been revealed, it would most certainly have resulted in Hauptmann's acquittal, would, in fact, have made it impossible for Wilentz to bring the prisoner to trial.

Disturbing though it may seem, the sad fact is that from long experience I did not find it hard to believe that policemen and prosecutors were guilty of constructing a false case against Hauptmann and sending him to his death. I have seen enough such cases—though never one that led to an execution—to no longer be surprised at official misconduct as a distressingly common experience is our adversary system. Even judicial murder does not shock.

But I don't think I will ever be able to understand how Lindbergh could have become a part of all this. From all that I've read of him, Lindbergh was an independent man who could not easily have been swayed by the likes of Schwarzkopf and Captain Lamb, District Attorney Foley and David Wilentz. I am not so naive as to believe that our public heroes are gods; they are but men, behind the public image and adulation; and Lindbergh, in his flirtation with Nazi Germany before World War II, demonstrated his fallibility as a hero. But it is the acts of Lindbergh the man that I question.

Until the body of a child was found and identified by Lindbergh, his home was practically the headquarters of the investigation. Colonel Schwarzkopf, Lindbergh's sycophant, slept at Hopewell; the garage was turned into a police command post by Captain Lamb. Lindbergh must have known footprints were found leading from the spot where the ladder was dropped to a small road where a car had been parked. Lindbergh must have known fingerprints had been found on the ladder and in the nursery. Lindbergh must have known Dr. Condon was for a long time the chief suspect in the case, for Lindbergh himself had said he did not trust Condon. Lindbergh must have known Violet Sharpe, the maid in his mother-in-law's home, was believed to have been the "inside accomplice" who helped kidnap his child; he must have been told why police were so certain, after her suicide, that she had been part of the kidnap plot.

Charles A. Lindbergh was privy to all the details in these areas of the police investigation, and probably many others. And of his own experience and knowledge, he knew there had been a "lookout" at St. Raymond's Cemetery; he knew that he could not have identified any man's voice after more than two years, for he said as much himself.

Unfortunately, Lindbergh died while I was researching this book. Even had he lived until its publication, he would probably never have responded to questions about the evidence I've found. The only explanation I can offer for the ease with which Lindbergh cooperated in the vengeful prosecution of Hauptmann is that which I had framed as a question when I first discovered the documents concerning his role: Could he have done all this because he wanted to end the anguish his wife was going through and to restore some normality to their lives?

I am not an attorney or an expert on criminal jurisprudence. It is probably presumptuous of me to suggest a change in criminal procedure so that such a judicial murder as was inflicted upon Richard Hauptmann and has been inflicted upon many others can never happen again. But I will be presumptuous.

Hauptmann was wrongly convicted because the police files were considered inviolate, not to be gazed upon by the defense. There is a growing movement, especially in the federal courts, toward the right of "discovery"—that is, the right of the defense to examine evidence in the possession of the prosecutor, before trial. But discovery is not enough, in many instances. In a case like Hauptmann's, where a defendant is not arrested and indicted until many months and even years after the commission of the crime charged to him, the original police investigatory reports are of greater importance than the documents directly relating to the indicted prisoner. For Hauptmann's defense, all those hundreds of reports pointing to other suspects, including Condon and Violet Sharpe and the Geisslers; to the fact that Lindbergh's friend, Thayer, had said the first two ransom notes had been taken away by a bootlegger and stock swindler; to the fact that handwriting experts seemed doubtful in the beginning that Hauptmann had written the notes—all this evidence, and other evidence I've found, was more vital to Hauptmann's defense and his life than anything the prosecutor would have been required to turn over to the defense under the rule of discovery. Even if discovery were written into every state's criminal laws, a defendant like Hauptmann would still have been denied the right to learn the truth. For discovery only theoretically opens all investigatory files; in practice, only material pertaining to the defendant is given over to his lawyers. One can be certain that, had there been the right of discovery in 1935, the documents in police files pertaining to investigations *before* Hauptmann was arrested would never have been given to the prosecution by police, to fall into the hands of defense counsel. Those documents, proving that most of the evidence against Hauptmann was perjured, would remain hidden in police files.

There is, I believe, a way to guarantee that our ideal of criminal justice—better that a hundred guilty men escape than one innocent man be imprisoned—can come near to being attained.

My proposal is this: In every felony investigation, in every crime in which a man, if convicted, faces the loss of liberty for more than one year, a copy of every police report should be placed in a depository of evidence that is under the control of an appeals court of each state and of the federal courts. Each day, all the investigative reports in a particular felony should be microfilmed and sent to the court depository. Those reports would then, by law, be sealed so that neither police nor prosecutor could touch them; after all, the police would have their original copies. Finally, those reports would be turned over to defense counsel the moment someone was indicted for the particular crime. The defendant would then be given sufficient time to study those reports and to make motions for dismissal of the indictment based on any evidence of official illegalities contained in them. Should the motion be denied, the defendant would have the right to question police officers about their reports during the trial.

To be sure, some guilty men and women would go free. But guilty men and women are going free every day, through plea bargaining, bribes, perjury, influence—the thousand and one devices the knowledgeable guilty use to evade punishment.

But if one Richard Hauptmann can be saved, the expense would be worth it. And there are dozens of Hauptmanns serving long prison terms or waiting to be executed at this moment, victims of overzealous police and prosecutors. In spite of Supreme Court decisions of the past two decades, which police claim have hampered them, the legal process still fails to protect the innocent as it failed so terribly, forty years ago, to protect Hauptmann. The dismal truth, amply documented from as far back as the Salem witch trials and right up to Watergate and the investigation of CIA assassination plots, is that those arrayed on the "right" side of the law have consistently lied to us.

For month after month I had read and analyzed and interviewed and submerged myself in the life and death of Richard Hauptmann, until feeling had left and I worried about the coldness within me. But now, as my work came to an end, it was no longer just a slow soft sympathy of my mind reaching out to understand, but a torrent of blood rushing and pulsing; instinctive and physical, not cerebral; a hatred, at first, directed toward those majestic pillars of law who had once been men but were transformed into mindless avengers for a mindless society: the State, the People. So unprofessional, this emotion, but I could not remain professional and objective when I know what they had done to Hauptmann and what they could do to any one of us, for the show of justice, the show of national strength, for power and vanity and an excuse to compose orations.

And yet, as I thought about Hauptmann, that distortion of feeling soon left. In its place came a sadness as I recalled once more something that Hauptmann had said to Governor Hoffman:

"They think when I die, the case will die. They think it will be like a book I close. But the book, it will never close."

484

Notes

Whenever possible through the text of this book I have identified specific police and FBI documents and other source materials. Because of the gravity of my charges against those who helped convict Richard Hauptmann, and in the interests of finally setting the record straight after some forty years of distortion, I shall document the source notes that follow, all my evidence, as completely as possible. A few items of peripheral material that are, in effect, footnotes, are included in these notes.

I am indebted to a large number of people for their cooperation, their assistance in locating documents and survivors of the Lindbergh case, their willingness to spend hours with me and my tape recorder; to all of them I express my deepest thanks and I repeat in all sincerity the standard disclaimer: all errors, and all opinions, are my own responsibility.

I owe a special obligation and give special thanks to Stevie Trudeau, without whom my work would have been drudgery rather than joy, and to Mrs. Anna Hauptmann, whose spirit continues to amaze.

I'm also indebted to: Murray Bleefeld; Assistant U.S. Attorney John Wing; Jeannie Sakol, who read my manuscript and gave valued advice; Jonathan Kwitny, for his encouragement, enthusiasm, and contacts; Nigel Nicolson, who gave me permission to quote freely from his father's diaries and who graciously sent me copies of those portions of Harold Nicolson's letters that were not published previously; and Bronx District Attorney Mario Merola.

And for their assistance I wish to thank: Leonard Katz; Jack Arbitell; Harold Olson; Grace and Patrick McGrady; Bronx Chief Assistant District Attorney Seymour Rotker and his secretary, Frances Shulman; Hans Kloeppenburg; Martin Schlossman; Burlington County Chief of Detectives Harry McConnell; Stephanie Bennett; Russell Hopstatter; Frank Fitzpatrick; Eddie Parker; Mrs. Blair Rodman; Harry Green; J. Mortimer Woodcock; Robin Moore; Robert Whiteman and Marsha Strickland of Liberty Library Corp.; Patterson Smith; Andrew Dutch; Maurice Edelbaum; Ada Hoffman; Ronald Martinetti; New Jersey State Police Superintendent Major George Quinn; Deputy Attorney General Clinton Cronin of New Jersey; Bobbi McClellan, for the typing she did on the manuscript; and Frank Scaduto, for assistance in research.

Preface

The brief summary of the Lindbergh case is based primarily on the FBI synopsis dated April 19, 1935 and titled: "Bruno Richard Hauptmann, with alias—kidnaping and murder."

Chapter 1

My telephone conversation with Murray Bleefeld occurred in April 1973 and was tape-recorded.

The stories about the Brooklyn youth gang killings appeared in the *New York Post*, July 12–13, 1954.

Full details of the Nimer murders can be found in New York newspapers of the period, most especially in the *Post*, *World-Telegram*, and *Journal-American*, from September 2 through October 23, 1958.

Alan Hynd's article, "Everybody Wanted to Get Into the Act," was originally published in *True*, March 1949, and has been republished in several books, including Hynd's *Violence in the Night* (Fawcett, 1955), and in *A Treasury of True* (A. S. Barnes, 1956).

Chapter 2

My reconstruction of the official version of the kidnaping and early investigation is based on many dozens of sources. The most important of them are: Sidney Whipple, *The Lindbergh Crime* (Blue Ribbon Books, 1935), and his introduction to *The Trial of*

Bruno Richard Hauptmann (Doubleday, Doran, 1937); *The Crime and the Criminal—A Psychiatric Study of the Lindbergh Case* by Dr. Dudley D. Shoenfeld (Covici, Friede, 1936); *True Story of the Lindbergh Kidnapping* by John Brant and Edith Renaud (Kroy Wren, 1932); *Kidnap* by George Waller (Dial, 1961); *The Hero: Charles A. Lindbergh and the American Dream* by Kenneth S. Davis (Doubleday, 1959); *The Lindberghs* by P. J. O'Brien (International Press, 1935); "The Lindbergh Legends" by John Lardner, in *The Aspirin Age*, edited by Isabel Leighton (Simon & Schuster, 1949); the New York *Times*, *Daily News*, *Post*, and *American*, various dates in 1932, 1933, and 1934; and Alan Hynd's *True* article.

The quotation by Adela Rogers St. Johns is from *The Honeycomb* (Doubleday, 1969).

Material about Frank Costello is from conversations with Leonard Katz and from his book *Uncle Frank* (Drake, 1973).

Chapter 3

My sources for this chapter are all those noted for Chapter 2, with the addition of *Jafsie Tells All* by John F. Condon (Jonathan Lee, 1936). A photostat of Dr. Mitchell's autopsy report was supplied by Harold Olson.

Chapter 4

The tape-recorded interviews with Murray Bleefeld took place in Robin Moore's New York City apartment in the spring of 1973.

Chapter 5

The anecdote about Condon's treatment by Inspector Walsh is from *Jafsie Tells All*. The recapitulation of the police investigation after Violet Sharpe's death and through to the arrest of Hauptmann is derived from the same material noted in Chapter 2 sources.

Chapter 6

Once again, the recapitulation is from the same sources listed under Chapter 2.

The material about Hearst and St. Johns is from *The Honeycomb*, pp. 289–346.

The testimony at the trial was taken from Sidney Whipple's edited version, occasionally supplemented by consulting a copy of the complete transcript at the Yale University Law Library; Whipple, I found, frequently summarized defense aspects of the case in such a way that some crucial points in Hauptmann's favor were deleted from his record.

The New York Law Journal article was published January 7, 1936.

The article from which Hauptmann's quotations were taken was originally published in *Liberty*, May 2, 1936, and reprinted in the summer, 1971, issue of *Liberty: The Nostalgia Magazine.*

Chapter 7

The continued recreation of the trial is from Whipple, supplemented by consulting the actual trial transcript, when necessary, because of Whipple's editing.

The statements by Albert D. Osborn on the Hughes-Irving forgery and other statements on that case have been taken from *Hoax: The Inside Story of the Howard Hughes-Clifford Irving Affair*, by Stephen Fay, et al. (Viking, 1972).

The statements about Hauptmann's police station writings, and the length of time and number of pages Hauptmann was made to write, is derived from a book written after Hauptmann's execution by one of the several handwriting experts who were retained by the prosecution to bolster its case if needed, but who was never called to the stand: J. V. Haring, *The Hand of Hauptmann* (Hamer Publishers, 1937). In his book, Haring reproduces several of the sheets which Hauptmann wrote at police dictation; on some of those sheets is written the time and date.

Condon's statement that the writing on the trim board in Hauptmann's closet was probably not done by Hauptmann is from *Jafsie Tells All*.

Colonel Schwarzkopf's agreeing to suborn the perjury of Commodore Curtis is from *Kidnap*, p. 355.

Chapter 8

Again, the trial is based on Whipple's book and on Yale's copy of the original transcript.

Arthur Koehler's story of his detective work with the ladder is taken from his trial testimony and from articles he published in the *Saturday Evening Post*, April 20, 1935, *American Forests*, May, 1935, the *Journal of Criminal Law*, Vol. 27 (1937), pp. 712–724, and also from a chapter in *Twelve Against Crime* by Edward Radin (Putnam's, 1950), which was based on material supplied to the author by Koehler.

Chapter 9

Hauptmann's testimony is taken from the Yale copy of the original transcript, for Whipple heavily edited that testimony in his book.

The quotations from Adela Rogers St. Johns is from *The Honeycomb* and from her earlier book *Final Verdict* (Doubleday, 1962).

Chapter 10

Trial testimony is from the Yale transcript.

The anecdotes concerning David Wilentz outside the courtroom are from *The Honeycomb*.

All the material on Lindbergh's reaction to Judge Trenchard's bias and the Lindberghs at home listening to the verdict on the radio is from *Diaries and Letters of Harold Nicolson*, edited by Nigel Nicolson, Vol. I (Atheneum, 1966). The section of Harold Nicolson's letter concerning Lindbergh's summary for his wife of the evidence against Hauptmann, which was not used in the printed *Diaries*, was copied from the original for me by Nigel Nicolson. That section reads:

The main points were: (1) The handwriting. Five separate experts stated that there could be no doubt at all that the ransom notes were in Hauptmann's writing. The only expert who doubted this was one produced by the defence and he was proved to have been paid to say it. (2) The ladder. That was the most brilliant piece of detective work. They traced the wood from which it had been made to a lumberyard in which Hauptmann had worked. They also proved that one piece came from his own attic. The section cut from the attic roof fitted exactly into the timbers. (3) Condon's telephone number scribbled on the wall of Hauptmann's room. He was never able to explain that. (4) His possession of the notes, and the fact that he began investing money in April 1932. (5) Recognition of his voice by Condon, Lindbergh, and the taxi driver. L. says that Hauptmann had a very strange voice and that it was unmistakable. (6) The fact that his alibis were all proved fraudulent. Then we went to bed. . . .

Lindbergh's summation was either naive or pure deceit—probably a combination of the two. For example, Lindbergh certainly must have known that the prosecution's handwriting experts were also paid—receiving more for their testimony than the defense had available for its entire case—because the newspapers commented on it at the time, with some heat. As for the other four points in his summation, they have been sufficiently commented upon in the text of this book with the exception of point five: Condon and the taxi driver, Perrone, did not identify Hauptmann's voice, neither at the trial nor in any of their statements to police and prosecutor.

The reaction of the crowds, and of Hauptmann and his wife, when the verdict was delivered, is from *Kidnap*, *The Lindbergh Crime*, and from newspaper accounts.

Chapter 11

The article St. Johns wrote after the verdict came in is reprinted in *The Honeycomb*.

Chapter 12

The trip Murray Bleefeld and I made to Mt. Holly, to begin our search for documents about Ellis Parker and Paul Wendel, was in September 1973. All of Bleefeld's remarks are from a taped interview lasting several hours and conducted during that day.

Chapter 13

The interviews with Fitzpatrick, Chief McConnell, Russell Hopstatter, and Eddie Parker and the phone interview with Mrs. Blair Rodman took place during several days, on several trips to Mt. Holly; they have been condensed in time.

All the quotations from Jack Arbitell and Martin Schlossman are from tapes of my interviews with them.

The summary of Wilentz's testimony at the Parker trial is from a document in the files of the U.S. attorney's office, Newark, N.J., titled "Testimony: *U.S.* v. *Parker, et al.*" Parker's application for executive clemency can be found in this same file.

Chapter 14

The two weeks that I spent in the Bronx district attorney's office was the first important break in my investigation, and I must again give much credit to Mario Merola, Seymour Rotker, and Frances Shulman for their courtesy and assistance.

The testimony at Hauptmann's extradition hearing is from a typed transcript, "The people of the State of New York on the relation of Bruno Richard Hauptmann, against John Hawley, as Sheriff of Bronx County, and the Warden of the County Jail of Bronx County." It is dated October 15, 1934.

The newspaper articles cited about Hauptmann's employment on March 1, 1932, are both from the *New York Times*: the comments by Foley and Wilentz were published October 19, 1934 and the Furcht "retraction" on October 25, 1934.

Photographs of the time sheets introduced at the trial, I discovered later on in my research, were published in the *New York Times* and other newspapers during the trial period, January–February, 1935.

"Lieutenant Arthur Scanlon" has since retired from the New York City police department. At his request, he retains his pseudonym.

The letter to Assistant District Attorney Breslin, dated December 12, 1934, almost two months after Hauptmann's arrest, was from Albany County DA John T. Delaney. Delaney wrote that he was enclosing two photostatic letters from Albert H. Hamilton— one a request for copies of the ransom notes, dated August 29, 1933, and the other a report dated October 15, 1933, stating that "Manning Strawl" wrote all the ransom notes. This conclusion was reached almost a year before anyone ever heard of Hauptmann. As for "Manning Strawl," I have not been able to identify him. It appears likely that the name is a pseudonym or that "Strawl," though a suspect in the case, had no criminal record.

The New York City police files were searched for me as were the state police files; there is no arrest record or fingerprint record of such a man. A check of the files at the *New York Post* library and in the New York Times Index from 1928 through 1940 was fruitless. The Albany County DA's office has no record of the man.

Perrone's statement of May 12, 1932, is written by hand, apparently by the police officer who questioned him, and appears to be the rough draft of a more formal report. The statement is in the Bronx DA files.

Perrone's statement of May 20, 1932, is typed on the letterhead of the Justice Department and is titled: "Statement of John Joseph Perrone, taken at Hopewell, N.J., May 20, 1932." A carbon copy of this report is also in the Bronx DA files.

Perrone's statement of July 11, 1934, eight pages long, is typed on the letterhead of the Justice Department and is signed by agent Thomas Sisk. It is also in the Bronx DA files.

Agent Seery's report of his interview with Perrone is typed on a Justice Department letterhead and dated March 9, 1934. One detail in the report was put aside for the time because I could not fit it into my investigation immediately; only later, after I had received documents about the Geisslers as suspects in the case, did this part of Seery's report have meaning: Perrone told Seery that the first man who flagged him down for a half-block ride, apparently the accomplice of the man who gave Perrone the ransom note to be delivered to Condon, bore a "marked resemblance to Henry Liepold (deceased)." Liepold was the friend of the Geisslers who committed suicide after repeated questioning by police about his knowledge of the J. J. Faulkner exchange of ransom money. Liepold and the Geisslers are discussed more fully in Chapter 15.

Chapter 15

Robert Thayer's statement that Condon had described the ransom symbols before he could have seen them is contained in a report written by Lieutenant John Keaton on a New Jersey state police investigation form; a copy is in the New York City police files.

Thayer's statements about Mickey Rosner and the ransom notes in Rosner's possession were made to various New Jersey police officials in May 1932 and are quoted by Governor Hoffman, who had access to the files of the state police, in his series of articles published in *Liberty* through May and June, 1938. I have used a copy of Hoffman's original typescript, given me by Patterson Smith, a New Jersey specialist in books on crime and criminology, for this study of the case. The Thayer statements are reproduced in Part 8 of Hoffman's series. Hoffman's daughter, Ada, and the aide who helped him write the articles, Andrew Dutch, confirmed in telephone conversations that the governor had possession of these and other documents from which he quotes throughout his series. But when Hoffman died, state police "raided his office and confiscated his Hauptmann files," his daughter told me. The Thayer statement of May 16, cited above, a copy of which is in my possession, was fully and accurately quoted by Hoffman in his series, as are all other reports that I've been able to obtain official copies of. Thus, I have no doubt Hoffman accurately quoted all the reports he published; to have misquoted or fabricated police reports would have been stupid, for Hoffman knew he would have been sharply criticized by police had he done so. Further, Andy Dutch said he personally handled the reports and extracted material from them to be used in Hoffman's articles. "They are one hundred percent accurate," he told me. Certainly, state police chief Schwarzkopf would not have remained silent had Hoffman misquoted or invented documents to support his charges that the evidence against Hauptmann had been deliberately twisted by police, that Hauptmann had been "framed." But Schwarzkopf did remain silent about Hoffman's articles, no doubt because the charges could not be refuted.

Lindbergh's remarks about his suspicions of Condon and Reich are contained in a report by Justice Department agent Hugh Larimer, May 21, 1933.

The report of the investigation of the J. J. Faulkner gold bills and Condon's relationship with one member of the Geissler circle was written by Finn on January 23, 1934. Addressed to "Assistant Chief Inspector, 18th Division," it is titled: COOPERATION ACCORDED BY BANKS RE: LINDBERGH RANSOM MONEY. A part of this document was reproduced by Finn in his series in *Liberty*, in the issue of October 12, 1935.

The source of the Perrone statement may be found in the notes for Chapter 14, agent Seery's report of March 9, 1934.

The source of the statements by Dr. Condon on his meeting with John, the extortionist, are fully identified in the text of this book.

Those statements are in the files of the Bronx DA and the New York police.

Hauptmann's driver's license applications are reproduced in Finn, *Liberty*, and in Haring, *The Hand of Hauptmann*. Copies of Hauptmann's interrogation sessions are in the Bronx DA files, as is a copy of the transcript of the lineup at which Condon could not identify Hauptmann.

The quotations from agent Turrou are from his book, *Where My Shadow Falls* (Doubleday, 1949). Turrou's official report of his conversation with Condon is dated October 11, 1934; a carbon is in the Bronx DA files.

Condon's statement about his fear of being indicted in New Jersey is in a document headed: "Statement of John F. Condon taken on May 14, 1932, at the District Attorney's office . . ." His statement that he didn't show Cemetery John the child's safety pins is from his interrogation in the Bronx on May 20, 1932.

The comment by Schwarzkopf that the extortionist walked away from Condon in order to consult his "partners" standing at a distance is from Hoffman, Part 7.

A copy of the FBI document concerning Lindbergh's sighting of a "lookout" is in my possession and can also be found in New York police and Bronx DA files.

My study of Lindbergh's identification of Hauptmann's voice is based on the Nicolson *Diaries* and on articles in the *New York Times* and other New York and New Jersey newspapers, September 28 through October 10, 1934.

Chapter 16

Finn's report on his interview with Cecilia Barr is dated November 28, 1933, and is headed: INVESTIGATION RE: U.S. CURRENCY No. B35435796A. Finn reproduced that report in *Liberty*, November 2, 1935.

The statement by Rossiter may be found in the files of the Bronx DA. That statement was made on September 25, 1934, to Assistant DA Breslin. The description of the rear of Hauptmann's Dodge is from photographs of that car published in numerous newspapers and magazines after Hauptmann's arrest, including Finn, *Liberty*, November 9, 1935.

Hochmuth's health record was obtained from New York police

files and is also reproduced in Hoffman, Part 3. Hoffman's later questioning of Hochmuth is described in that series, Part 13.

The report on Whited is from a document signed by New Jersey state trooper Corporal Joseph Wolf; quoted in Hoffman, Parts 5 and 8.

Ben Lupica's statement was made on September 21, 1934, and may be found in the files of the Bronx DA's office.

Agent Sisk's perjury is commented upon in Turrou, *Where My Shadow Falls* and in Finn, *Liberty*, November 16, 1935.

The complete laboratory reports on the condition of the ransom money Hauptmann was known to have passed and on the bills found in his garage may be seen in Finn, *Liberty*, October 26, 1935; the published reports conform in every respect to copies I was given from the New York police files.

All the documents concerning Hauptmann's bank and brokerage house accounts, indicating that no gold certificates ever passed through those accounts, are reproduced in Justice Department agent J. A. Genau's report of October 18, 1934. The report, sixty-five pages long, is a summary of the major financial evidence gathered by federal agents after Hauptmann's arrest. It was suppressed by the authorities.

The quotation from Sidney Whipple is from *The Trial of Bruno Richard Hauptmann*.

The Wickersham Commission reports are more formally titled: *National Commission on Law Enforcement and Observance: Report on Lawlessness in Law Enforcement*. They were published by the U.S. Government Printing Office in 1931. Emanuel Lavine's book, *Third Degree* (Vanguard, 1930), was based on hearings of the commission.

All the material relating to Hauptmann's financial condition has been extracted from agent Genau's report of October 18, 1934, and from a New York City police memorandum called "Question Hauptmann," which reproduces entries in his smaller memo books.

Agent Seykora's interview with the Wollenbergs is dated October 12, 1934; a copy is in the Bronx DA's office.

The discussion of the fur transactions contained in Hauptmann's "missing" ledger is also from agent Genau's lengthy report.

The material on Isidor Fisch is based on several police and FBI documents copied from the Bronx DA and New York police files.

Those documents are: transcript of interview with Max Falek in the Bronx DA's office, October 4, 1934; similar interviews with Katie Fredericksen, October 4, 1934; Gerta Henkel, October 3, 1934, Hans Muller, October 11, 1934, and Mr. and Mrs. Otto Wollenberg, October 12, 1934; Justice Department reports of agent Francis X. O'Donnell, September 23 and 27 and October 1, 1934; of agent P. M. Breed, September 28, 1934; agent Genau, October 29, 1934; agent L. G. Turrou, September 22 and 24, 1934; Detective Max Leef, October 5 and 7, 1934. Copies of all of these transcripts and reports are in my possession; copies may also be found in the files of the Bronx DA and the New York police.

Copies of the letters from Pinkus Fisch to Hauptmann, translated into English, were found in the New York police files.

Chapter 17

The letters from the Osborns to Schwarzkopf and Breslin are in both the Bronx DA and New York police files.

The list of handwriting exhibits was compiled from the full transcript of the trial.

The further evidence that perhaps police did indeed force Hauptmann to copy the specimen handwriting paragraph and all its spelling errors can be found in Finn's *Liberty* article dated November 2, 1935, in which he wrote that the specimen was "handed" to Hauptmann in the police station.

The material on Samuel Small, the penmanship authority, is from the typescript of Governor Hoffman's articles, Part 5.

My interview with Theo Bernsen took place in September 1974.

These are the reports I examined concerning searches of Hauptmann's attic before Bornmann made his amazing discovery: report of Trooper Horn, September 19; report of Sergeant John Wallace, September 20; report of Justice Department agents J. S. Kavanaugh and P. M. Breed, of a search later in the day on September 20; report of state police Corporal Samuel Leon, September 20; report of agent Wright of search on morning of September 21; report of Sergeant Zapolsky, September 22; report of agent Breed, September 23; report of New York City detective Petrosino, September 24. These reports are in the files of the Bronx DA and in the New York police files. Governor Hoffman published those of the state police and again they conform with the reports of which I have copies.

Bornmann's reports are quoted by Hoffman, in Part 13 of his series.

Dr. Hudson's anecdote about Captain Lamb asking whether fingerprints can be counterfeited is from Hoffman, Part 6, from an interview with Grace and Patrick McGrady, who were personal friends of Hudson, and from a deposition made by Hudson on September 14, 1935, for C. Lloyd Fisher. The material on the Hall-Mills case and Lamb's role in it is derived primarily from *The Girl in Lover's Lane* by Charles Boswell and Lewis Thompson (Fawcett, 1953), one in a series of condensations of true murder trials, and from a study of newspaper articles on the case in the *New York Post* library.

The statements by Arch Loney and Roy Knabenshue, critical of Koehler's "evidence" of the wood grains, were published in the *New York Times*, March 27 and 30, 1936.

J. Mortimer Woodcock was interviewed on tape at his home in Ridgefield, Conn., in October 1975.

The statement on Hauptmann's use of his plane after the kidnaping is taken from several sources, including police interrogation of Hauptmann on September 19 and 20, 1934, and police interviews of Anna Hauptmann and Victor Schussler on September 20, 1934.

The three-quarter-inch chisels I personally viewed are at State Police Headquarters, North Trenton.

William J. Reilly, the foreman of the lumberyard that Koehler claimed Hauptmann had visited with a Lindbergh ransom bill, was questioned on October 1, 1934. The transcript is in the Bronx DA files.

The reports on footprints by Trooper Wolf, March 2, 1932, and by Trooper DeGaetano, March 3, 1932, are quoted in Governor Hoffman's articles, Parts 8 and 14.

The statement from Finn is from *Liberty*, October 12, 1935, and from a report he wrote September, 27, 1934, titled: LICENSE PLATES NOTED AT TUNNEL AND FERRIES RE: HAUPTMANN'S AUTOMOBILE. It is in the files of the New York police.

Chapter 18

Harold Olson's story of his search for his parentage was written after my discussions with him during 1974 and 1975.

The reconstruction of Hauptmann's last months of life, including his conversations with his attorney and ministers, is based primarily on the typescript of Hoffman's articles for *Liberty,* supplemented by an examination of newspaper articles of the period. All the conversations with Hauptmann and his wife, Anna, are quoted as they appear in Hoffman's typescript, as is the medical report on the injuries Hauptmann received while in police custody.

The recollections of Bleefeld and Schlossman are from our recorded conversations in 1974 and 1975.

Hauptmann's letter to Governor Hoffmann is published in full in Haring, *The Hand of Hauptmann.*

Hauptmann's last moments, before going to his death, have been reconstructed from the Hoffman articles and from a book later written by the executioner: *I Killed for the Law*, by Leo Sheridan (Stackpole Sons, 1938).

Chapter 19

The interviews with Mrs. Anna Hauptmann took place at her home and over the telephone on several dozen occasions beginning in the autumn of 1974 and continuing up to the present. Although we did not tape-record those conversations, at the end of each meeting, on the first several occasions we spent with her, Stevie Trudeau and I sat in the car and immediately reconstructed Mrs. Hauptmann's words. Later Mrs. Hauptmann permitted us to make notes of our talks; in order to be certain that our reconstruction of the earlier conversations was accurate, we deliberately took Mrs. Hauptmann over the same ground after we received permission to make notes. Those notes fill three stenographic books.

The interview with Hans Kloeppenburg was recorded at his home in south Jersey on April 17, 1975.

Chapter 20

Hauptmann's letters are published with the permission of Anna Hauptmann.

The depositions given me by Grace McGrady were made by the private investigator during and after Hauptmann's trial. At the completion of this book I finally learned the name of the investigator and telephoned him. He confirmed that Mrs. McGrady's copies of the affidavits were true copies and that he himself had interviewed Steinweg, Trost, and the Manckes and took their statements from them.

498

Mrs. Hauptmann's comments about the police tampering with the closet in which Hauptmann said he had placed Fisch's shoe box is at least partially corroborated by still another woman involved in the case. Arthur Hicks, once a lieutenant on the Washington, D.C., police force, went into private practice on his retirement. He was hired by Evalyn Walsh McLean, Washington socialite and owner of the Hope diamond, to help find evidence of Hauptmann's innocence. Mrs. McLean had become involved because she'd been swindled out of more than $100,000 by a noted con man who persuaded her that he could effect the return of the missing child. Still convinced at the time Hauptmann was arrested that the con man, Gaston Means, had actually been in contact with the true kidnap gang, she decided to "solve" the crime. She didn't, of course. But Hick's investigation did disclose that the closet shelves had been lowered by police before the trial, so that Mrs. Hauptmann would appear to be lying when she said she couldn't reach the top shelf. Hicks's evidence, including photographs, was published in Hynd's article in *True*, in a series that Hynd wrote with Mrs. McLean, published in *Liberty* in July, August, and September, 1938, and also in Governor Hoffman's articles.

Chapter 21

The articles on David Wilentz appeared in the *New York Post* on October 17, 18, 20, 21, and 23 and November 7, 1969.

My interview with Wilentz took place on January 26, 1976. He would not permit me to tape-record our session. Immediately after we concluded the interview I went out to my car and reconstructed the interview on tape.

Index

503

504

on evidence, 409–12; execution, 26–27, 53, 251, 253, 254, 422–24; and extortion, 45, 53; his finger- prints, 382–83; and Fisch, 192–94, 198, 201, 202–3, 207–10, 236, 292, 342–43, 346–52, 354, 355–57, 359–67, 398, 427–30, 456–57, 462, 463, 464–66; on Fisch's shoe box, 190–91, 193–96, 197–98, 209–10, 215; Pin- kus Fisch's correspondence with, 343, 360–66, 372, 435–36; handwriting analysis, 142–48, 156, 369–78; handwriting tested by police, 105–6, 145–46, 148, 198–200, 204–6, 371, 373–74, 446–47; Anna Hauptmann on, 434–40, 453–55, 472–74; on Hochmuth, 326; Hoffman, meet- ings with, 72, 73–75, 409–15, 421–22; innocence of, 15–16, 74–75, 83–84, 266, 274; on lad- der, 197; and lawyers, 121, 150, 218; letters to Anna, 453–55, 472–73; Lindbergh's voice iden- tification of, 124–27, 128, 318–22, 341–42; as "lone kidnaper," 53, 68, 69, 123, 137, 318; lumbermill clerk's identification of, 174, 395–96; medical report on, after beatings, 442; memo books, 204–6, 343–45, 350; motive, 229; Perrone's identification of, 292–97, 323; pistol, 206; police beatings, 198–200, 412–13, 442–43; police interrogation of, 99–104, 105, 107–8, 150–51, 153–54, 198–200, 241, 385; police suicide story, 174–75; psychia- trists on, 229; and ransom money, 96, 97, 106–7, 237–38, 332–39, 343, 345–47, 363–64, 396,

398–99, 427–28, 456–57, 462–63, 465; and ransom notes, 142–48, 156; sentenced, 223–24; on Sisk's testimony, 150–51; state confiscation of his money, 184; Wendel on, 246; Wilentz's por- trayal of, 225–30. *See also* Bronx extradition hearings; Hauptmann trial

Hauptmann, Manfred, 100, 403, 407, 419, 427, 428, 439–40, 453, 471, 472, 473

Hauptmann trial, 88–89, 117–39, 141–222, 235; Anna Hauptmann on, 471–72; Anna Hauptmann's testimony, 216–18; Anna Haupt- mann on, 431–32, 440–45, 466–67, 468–69, 470–71, 476–78, 479–83; Condon's testimony, 131–39, 299; his cross-examina- tion, 201–16; Curtis' offer to tes- tify, 156–57; defense's case, 184, 213, 214–18; evidence, falsified and suppressed, 84, 168, 174–75, 225–30, 263–64, 265, 276–87, 300, 312, 334, 339–42, 347, 350, 361, 366–67, 372, 374, 378–79, 384–85, 392–93, 395, 397–99, 442, 460, 468–69, 470–71, 476–78, 479–83; expert testimony, 180, 182; eye- witness testimony, 141–42; Frank on Hauptmann's ac- counts, 157–59, 345–47; guilty verdict, 220–23, 228; handwriting experts' testimony, 142, 143–48, 171, 183–84, 223, 276–77, 287; Hauptmann on, 409–12, 484; Hauptmann's examination, 183– 200, 216, 263–64; judge's instruc- tions to jury, 218–20; jury, 119–20, 124, 215, 220, 221–22, 323; ladder identified as Haupt-

505

509

Public Welfare Department of New York, 325

Quinn, George, 393, 394
Quinn, John, 257, 259

Rail 16, 160–62, 164, 175–79, 379–82, 384–91, 400, 411–12. *See also* Ladder
Ransom box, 101
Ransom money, 8, 27, 49, 60, 89–95, 96–99, 103, 171, 174, 219, 223, 237, 304–6, 324, 332–39, 356–57, 398–99, 405, 445; delivery of, 56–60, 304; Fisch and, 236–38, 456–61, 462, 463, 465; Hauptmann and, 96, 97, 106–8, 227, 238, 308–9, 332–33, 361, 371, 380–81, 385, 462–63, 465–66, 481; Hauptmann's accounts and, 345–47, 363–64; Hauptmann's first passing date, 334–39; Hauptmann's testimony on, 190–91, 193–96, 197–98; lab tests of, 334–36, 342, 339; police portrait of passer, 92–93, 96–97, 98; Wendel and, 236–38, 246, 267. *See also* Extortion plot; Fisch's shoe box; Geissler family
Ransom notes, 32–33, 43, 45, 105, 147, 219, 242, 270, 292, 296, 299–302, 370–71, 378, 483; Condon and, 49, 53, 58–59, 60, 131, 341; German language expert on, 377–38; handwriting analyzed, 142–48, 156, 276–77, 369–79, 386, 399–400, 429; signature symbol, 33, 49, 144, 243–44, 299, 300, 341; Wendel and, 242–44, 261, 270–71
Rauch, Mrs., 101
Reich, Al, 49, 54, 136, 304, 315–16, 317, 322, 342
Reilly, Edward J., 120–21, 123, 128–29, 130, 131, 134–35, 144, 158, 161, 201, 216–17, 218, 220, 263, 283, 287, 347, 387, 447; Anna Hauptmann on, 431, 434; concedes *corpus delicti*, 148–50; his examination of Hauptmann, 184–99, 201, 206; Hauptmann on, 409, 414
Reilly, William F., 396
Reles, Abe, 255
Reliance Employment Agency, 187–89
Reliance Property Management, 278, 284. *See also* Majestic apartments
Reward money, 37, 152
Ridgefield *Press*, 389
Riis, Jacob, 18
Rodel, Leo, 307
Rodman, Mrs. Blair, 266
Rogers, Earl, 124
Roosevelt, Franklin D., 17, 89, 237
Roosevelt, Theodore, 18
Rosenberg sons, 275, 464
Rosenheim, Maxie, 49
Rosner, Mickey, 43, 44, 45, 61, 147, 300–1, 341, 371
Rossiter, Charles B., 142, 324–25, 342
Rotker, Seymour, 275, 276, 278, 285
Ruby, Jack, 168
Runyon, Damon, 118, 119, 220
Russo, Anthony, 475–76

Sacco, Nicola, 8
Sackville-West, Victoria, 221
St. Johns, Adela Rogers, 43, 118, 199, 120–21, 124, 184–85, 202, 204, 228, 236–37
St. Raymond's Cemetery meeting, 58–60, 190, 246, 317–18, 334; "lookout" at, 317–18, 482
"Sam," 61–62